Third Edition

BEHAVIOR DISORDERS OF CHILDHOOD

Rita Wicks-Nelson
West Virginia University Institute of Technology
Montgomery, West Virginia

Allen C. Israel
University at Albany
State University of New York

PRENTICE HALL
Upper Saddle River, New Jersey 07458

Library of Congress Cataloging-in-Publication Data

Wicks-Nelson, Rita
    Behavior disorders of childhood / Rita Wicks-Nelson, Allen C.
  Israel. — 3rd ed.
      p.   cm.
    Includes bibliographical references and index.
    ISBN 0-13-396870-7
    1. Child psychopathology.   I. Israel, Allen C.   II. Title.
  RJ499.W45 1997   96-2174
  618.92'89-dc20   CIP

Editor in chief: Peter Janzow
Editorial/production supervision: Pine Tree Composition
Cover designer: Carol Ceralde
Buyer: Mary Ann Gloriande

This book was set in 10/12 Baskerville by Pine Tree
Composition, Inc. and was printed and bound by R. R.
Donnelley & Sons Company. The cover was printed by
Phoenix, Inc.

© 1997, 1991, 1984 by Prentice-Hall, Inc.
Simon & Schuster/A Viacom Company
Upper Saddle River, New Jersey 07458

Printed in the United States of America
10 9 8 7 6 5 4 3 2

ISBN: 0-13-396870-7

Prentice-Hall International (UK) Limited, *London*
Prentice-Hall of Australia Pty. Limited, *Sydney*
Prentice-Hall Canada, Inc., *Toronto*
Prentice-Hall Hispanoamericana, S.A., *Mexico*
Prentice-Hall of India Private Limited, *New Delhi*
Prentice-Hall of Japan, Inc., *Tokyo*
Simon & Schuster Asia Pte. Ltd., *Singapore*
Editora Prentice-Hall do Brasil, Ltda., *Rio de Janeiro*

To **Leonard C. Nelson,**
Mary Wicks,
the memory of **William Wicks**
RW-N

To **Daniel** and **Sara**
ACI

CONTENTS

4 RESEARCH: ITS ROLE AND METHODS

5 CLASSIFICATION AND ASSESSMENT 91

6 ANXIETY DISORDERS 111

7 DEPRESSION AND PROBLEMS IN PEER RELATIONS 142

8 CONDUCT DISORDERS

9 ATTENTION-DEFICIT HYPERACTIVITY DISORDER

10 MENTAL RETARDATION

11 DEVELOPMENTAL LANGUAGE AND LEARNING DISABILITIES   270

12 AUTISM AND SCHIZOPHRENIA **298**

PREFACE

The writing of this third edition of *Behavior Disorders of Childhood* has been achieved in an atmosphere of excitement and challenge. We are fortunate to be working in a field of expanding and rapid progress. In the few years since the last edition of this text, efforts to understand behavioral problems of the young have continued to evolve. Much has been learned, and much still remains to be fully understood. We have tried in this third edition to capture the excitement in the field, and to convey both what is known and what is yet to be known.

This text shares the fundamental characteristics of the first two editions. Designed as a relatively comprehensive introduction to the field of behavior disorders of childhood and adolescence, it includes central issues, theoretical and methodological underpinnings, descriptions and discussions of many disorders, clinical and research data, and treatment approaches. As is often the case, space limitation demands some selectivity of content.

Three major themes, or predilections, continue to be woven throughout the text. Their importance has become firmly established. The first is the assumption that the developmental context can contribute much to understanding childhood behavior problems. As normal developmental sequences and processes are increasingly elucidated, they are being brought to bear on identifying and explaining the growth of disordered development. The text reflects our interest in relating normal and disturbed growth.

Also obvious throughout the book is the view that behavioral problems are the result of interactions among variables. With few if any exceptions, behavior stems from multiple influences and their continuous interactions. Biological structure and function, inheritance, cognition, social and emotional factors, family, social class, and culture can be expected to come into play.

Our third bias is toward empirical approaches and the theoretical frameworks that rely heavily on the scientific method. We believe that the complexity of human behavior calls for systematic conceptualization and observation, data collection, and hypothesis testing. The methods and results of research thus are critical components of virtually all chapters.

Problems of the young are intricately tied to broad social, cultural, and ethical issues. Many of these are addressed, including the ethics of treatment, the use of medications in treating children, educational mainstreaming, and the impact of parental divorce and chronic disease. Discussions of such topics often make clear the importance of research in informing social and ethical choices.

The text is not formally broken into sections, but it will be apparent that the first five chapters present broad underpinnings of the field: historical context, developmental context, theoretical perspectives, research methodology, and classification/diagnosis. All of these chapters draw heavily on the psychological literature, but they also show the multidisciplinary nature of the study of childhood problems. We assume that most readers will have some background in psychology, but we have also made an effort to serve those who may have relatively limited background and experience.

Chapters 6 through 14 discuss specific behavior disorders: anxiety, depression, conduct problems, attention deficit-hyperactivity, learning disabilities, and autism, to name a few. Definition and description, prevalence, causal hypotheses, identification, and treatment are discussed in detail. The chapters are similar but not identical in organization. Chapter variations reflect what is currently of most interest and what is best established. Chapter 15, the closing chapter, focuses on concerns for youth, including the enormous need for prevention of behavior disorders.

We extend sincere thanks to several individuals who helped in various ways in this project: Michael O'Neill, George Tremblay, Steven Safren, Arthur Houts, Ph.D., and Aaron Sher, M.D. The staff of the Vining Library of West Virginia Institute of Technology lent a willing hand. And particular thanks to Sara and Daniel for their patience, cooperation, and delay of gratification.

Finally, we note that the order of authorship was originally decided by a flip of the coin to reflect our equal contributions. In all of our work we have shared equally.

Rita Wicks-Nelson   *Allen C. Israel*

1

INTRODUCTION

This book is written for all those concerned with behavioral or psychological problems displayed by the young. Disordered behavior attracts attention because it is often atypical, annoying, or strange. We may react to it with confusion, embarrassment, anger, fear, repulsion, or sadness. And we may be motivated to change it because it does not easily fit into the fabric of social life. For the most part, though, the desire to understand and treat problems is fueled by the belief that all youth should have the opportunity for ideal growth and fulfillment.

This is an exciting and promising time to study behavioral dysfunction. The need is great and is recognized in many parts of the world. Research into both normal and abnormal development has grown by leaps and bounds, with contributions by experts from many professional disciplines. As is usually true in science, new understandings have often led to new questions and paradoxes. But there is no doubt that progress is occurring.

Central to the concern about disordered behavior are questions about its origins, maintenance, and amelioration. Why is a child excessively shy, fearful, or aggressive? What processes underlie intellectual deficiencies, severe social isolation, and self-mutilation? How might maladaptive behavior be changed? When we ask these questions, we raise fundamental issues of how people develop and how normal development goes awry. Thus, one theme of this text is the recognition that normal and abnormal behavior go hand in hand, and that we must study one in order to understand the other.

A second theme has to do with the causes of behavior. With few if any exceptions, behavior stems from multiple influences—psychological, sociocultural, and biological—that interact with each other. They must ultimately all be reckoned with if we are to truly understand and be able to change problem behavior.

This leads to the third theme of the text. We believe that the complexity of human behavior calls for systematic conceptualization and observation, data collection, and hypothesis testing. Thus, the methods and results of scientific research are critical to discussions of abnormal behavior.

So let us begin at the beginning, by examining the idea of abnormality. It is a concept that might appear simple on the surface but in fact has many dimensions and is controversial (Wakefield, 1992).

DEFINING DISORDERED BEHAVIOR

There is no concise and simple way to define and identify disordered functioning. Behavioral repertoires come in endless varieties. Accent 1–1 provides actual examples of some kinds of problem behaviors observed in youngsters. We will examine many more throughout this book, and also see that behavioral disorders are evaluated and treated from several perspectives.

Frequently problem behavior is viewed as "abnormal". *Ab* means "away" or "from," while *normal* refers to the average or standard. Thus, *abnormal* simply means something that deviates from the average. However, common usage also assumes that the deviation is harmful in some way to the organism. Furthermore, an often-made assumption is that the deviation is pathological. Psychological or behavioral problems are therefore often referred to as *psychopathology*. Unfortunately, the terms abnormal and psychopathology are often associated with the idea that problem behavior is caused by disease or other biological factors.

ACCENT 1–1   The Faces of Problem Behavior

The boy, who was born with two extra chromosomes, was a happy baby who was somewhat slow in walking and did not speak until age four. In nursery school he was easily victimized by other children. Throughout childhood he was fearful, had a low attention span and tolerance for frustration, and did not want to attend school. By adolescence he was acting antisocial: he set fires and stole. He also displayed some bizarre behaviors, such as putting on many layers of clothing and smearing his mother's clothes with catsup and mayonnaise. (From Mansheim, 1979, pp. 366–367)

• • •

Karen was a nine-year-old girl with a history of refusal to eat solid foods. Six weeks previously, she had choked on a piece of popcorn, with coughing and gagging. From that time on, she had refused to eat any solid foods and had lost about fifteen pounds. She had also developed multiple fears concerning choking. She would not brush her teeth for fear a bristle would come out and she would choke. She slept propped on pillows for fear a loose tooth would come out while she was asleep and that she would choke and suffocate. She was afraid to go to sleep and requested to sleep with her mother because of her fears. She also had frequent nightmares and vivid dreams of choking. (From Chatoor, Conley, and Dickson, 1988, p. 106)

• • •

Joe, who is eight years old, has a history of multiple problems. They include chronic hyperactivity, destructive behavior, short attention span, difficulty following verbal directions, low frustration tolerance, impulsiveness, poor interpersonal relationships, fighting, lying, stealing, disobedience, running away from school, and setting fires. His parents had discounted the importance of these behaviors, preferring to believe that little boys should be allowed to express themselves. Joe had been recommended for special education placement in the first grade, but his parents had refused the recommendation. His behavior worsened in the second and third grades, and after Joe exposed himself to female peers, the school forced further evaluation. (From Rapport, 1993, pp. 284–285)

We make no such assumption in this book, since the causes of problem behavior are complex, include psychosocial factors, and most often cannot be traced directly to biological factors.

Judgments are always required to determine whether or not behavior is "abnormal." We must establish some behavioral standard and decide whether the behavior of interest does or does not meet the standard in quality or quantity. Of course, dramatic differences are easy to identify. Most of us would agree that individuals who cannot learn to speak or to feed and dress themselves are "abnormal." Less dramatic instances are harder to judge. Individuals may display behaviors that are quite common or only slightly deviant—and yet appear maladaptive. In these instances parents, teachers, other adults, and occasionally children themselves rely on numerous criteria to make the judgment that "something is wrong."

Sociocultural Norms

The role of sociocultural norms, perhaps the broadest criterion for judging behavior, was tellingly discussed many years ago by the anthropologist Ruth Benedict. After studying widely diverse cultures, Benedict (1934b) proposed that each society selects certain behaviors that are of value to it and socializes its members to act accordingly. Individuals who do not display these behaviors, for whatever reasons, are considered deviant by the society. Deviance is always related to cultural norms. Benedict noted, for example, that the suspiciousness typically exhibited in one Melanesian culture would be considered pathological in our society. The Melanesians would not leave their cooking pots for fear of the food being poisoned by others (Benedict, 1934a). Further, Melanesians who displayed the helpfulness, kindness, and cheerfulness that is viewed as positive in our society were considered abnormal in their culture.

Cultural norms are applied to children as well as to adults, and may broadly influence expectations, judgments, and beliefs about the behavior of youth. Youngsters in the United States, for example, are expected to show less self-control and deference to adults compared to children in some parts of the world (Weisz et al., 1995). We would be relatively more likely, then, to express concern about the over-controlled, passive child. Similarly, in technologically advanced societies that value certain intellectual skills special concern would be voiced about the child who does not measure up to these standards of intellectual development.

A study by Weisz et al. (1988) showed that culture might influence the degree to which childhood problems are considered serious. Parents and teachers in the U.S. and Thailand read descriptions of child problems and then answered questions about them. As Figure 1–1 shows, the Thai adults were less worried than the U.S. adults. This finding

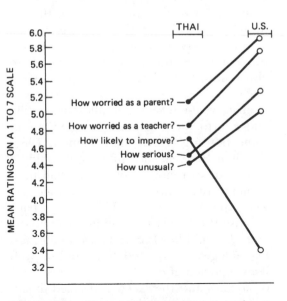

FIGURE 1–1 Thai and U.S. adults' rating of concern about childhood behavior problems.

Weisz et al., 1988. Copyright 1988 by the American Psychological Association.

appears consistent with the teachings of Thai Buddhism—for example, that every condition changes and that behavior does not reflect enduring personality.

In another study Weisz and his colleagues (1995) found that teachers in Thailand reported more conduct problems in students than teachers in the U.S., while trained observers reported just the opposite. The researchers suggested that Thai teachers may hold more demanding behavioral standards.

Culture can also influence how problem behaviors are explained. For example, forty North African and Middle Eastern mothers living in Israel were interviewed about their retarded children (Stahl, 1991). Almost half gave magic-religious causes for the condition. They believed in Fate, demons entering the body, an Evil Eye, prenatal fear in the mother, and punishment from God. They relied on treatments accordingly: burning the child's hand to drive out demons, burning a piece of cloth belonging to the person who cast the Evil Eye, prayer, or help from a rabbi. All of this is consistent with the cultural beliefs of their native countries.

In a society as heterogeneous as that of the United States, subcultural norms are also found. Consider, for example, a study that compared two groups of New York City families: well-educated, middle-class families and Puerto Rican families living in low income housing (Korn and Gannon, 1983). For their five-year-old children, the middle-class families reported two-and-a-half times as many problems as the low-income, less well educated families. This was probably because the families set different standards and the middle-class families were more psychologically oriented. The kind of problems reported also differed in the two kinds of families and they seemed related to subcultural values and child management. For example, many more middle-class than lower-class families set a standard bedtime and did not allow their children to take a bottle to bed with them. They also reported more sleep problems. Puerto Rican families placed high value on "good" behavior, disciplined their children more severely, and reported more discipline problems.

Sociocultural norms are tied to specific variables. One of these is the social setting. Energetic running may be quite acceptable on the playground, but would create havoc in the classroom or a dental office. And singing aloud might well be tolerated at home, but rarely allowed in the library. Individuals are expected to act in certain ways in certain situations—in short, to meet situational norms.

Sociocultural norms are also specified according to gender. In most societies males are expected to be relatively more aggressive, dominant, active, and adventurous; females to be more passive, dependent, quiet, and sensitive (Bem, 1985; Bergen and Williams, 1991). These sex stereotypes strongly guide judgments about normality. We would probably be less inclined to worry about the hypersensitive, shy girl and the excessively dominant boy than about their opposite-sex counterparts.

Finally, it must be noted that sociocultural norms may change over time, due to broad societal changes or changes in ideas about mental health. For example, in the 1800s childhood disturbances could be attributed to "masturbatory insanity," but that label no longer exists (Rie, 1971). And nail biting, once seen as a sign of degeneration, is considered quite harmless today (Kanner, 1960, cited by Anthony, 1970).

Developmental Criteria

Age is always of consideration in judging behavior, but it is especially crucial with youth because they change so rapidly. Assessment of behavior requires developmental norms. The typical rates and sequences of the growth of skills, knowledge, and social-emotional behavior serve as developmental stan-

The behavior that is expected of or considered appropriate for a child varies across cultures.

(Laimute Druskis) (Michael Heron)

dards to evaluate the possibility that "something is wrong." Adults would be mistaken to worry about the one-year-old who is not yet walking, because many children of this age do not walk. However, if the same child is unable to sit without support, concern would be appropriate, because virtually all babies can sit up before their first birthdays.

It is not only failure to initially display developmental age norms that identifies psychopathology. Children sometimes "act their age" but then fail to progress. Temper tantrums might not be labeled a problem in a three-year-old but would likely be seen as problematic if they persisted into the twelfth year. Children may also achieve age norms and then regress.

Several other normative factors may be considered. Behavior that meets age norms may still be judged disturbed if it occurs too frequently or infrequently, is too intense or insufficiently intense, or endures over too long or too short a period of time. It is not unusual for a child to display fear, for example, but fearfulness may be a problem if it occurs in an excessive number of situations, is extremely intense, and does not weaken over time. Concern might also be expressed for the child whose reactions change, such as when a friendly, outgoing girl turns shy and solitary. Adults are rightly concerned too when a child displays several questionable behaviors or seems troubled by several things.

More rarely, some youth exhibit behaviors that appear qualitatively different from the norm; that is, are not at all seen in normal youngsters. For example, most children become socially responsive to their caretakers soon after birth, but children diagnosed as autistic display atypical unresponsive behaviors.

The Role of Others

Finally, the feelings and beliefs of others in the immediate environment play a role in identifying problem behaviors. The labeling of a problem is likely to occur when others are disturbed, for example, when a sibling complains of being physically attacked or when a teacher is worried about a child's social withdrawal. Because childhood disorders are often identified by adults, adult attitudes, sensitivity, tolerance, and ability to cope are bound to influence how children are perceived and treated.

In fact, several research studies show the influence of various factors on parental identification of children's problems and referral to clinics (McMahon and Forehand, 1988). For example, there is limited evidence that first-born and only children are more readily identified as having problems than are other children (Jensen et al., 1990). Parental characteristics may also play a role. One study distinguished two groups of children referred to a clinic for acting-out problems (Rickard et al., 1981). Group 1 showed more actual acting-out behaviors than nonclinic children. Group 2 did not. What further differentiated the groups was parental depression. The parents of group 1 children were not depressed, while those of group 2 children exhibited depression. Thus, it appears that parental depression, rather than children's actual behavior, may have led to clinic referral for group 2 children. Yet another investigation indicated that parents who abused their children tended to overestimate problem behaviors emitted by the offspring (Reid, Kavanagh, and Baldwin, 1987).

In summary, then, we can see that defining, identifying, and conceptualizing behavioral or psychological disorders is a complex matter that depends on many factors. Disordered behavior is not simply an entity carried around in a person. It can be thought of as a judgment about behavior, based on society's values, beliefs about how youth develop, and the social context.

HOW COMMON ARE DISORDERS OF YOUTH?

An often-asked question about child and adolescent disorders is: How common are they? Determining the rate of disorders is important because it suggests the extent to which prevention, treatment, and research are needed. Rates are typically reported as prevalence or incidence. *Prevalence* refers to the number or percentage of cases of a disorder in a population at any specific time. *Incidence* refers to the number or percentage of new cases that have appeared within a specific time period.

It is not easy to establish rates of disorders. One method entails surveying youth who have been brought to the attention of mental health services, medical facilities, schools, the legal system, and so forth. The obvious problem with this method is that it excludes youth who have gone unnoticed or for whom help has not been sought due to such factors as denial, shame, fear, or high levels of tolerance by adults. Another method to determine rates of disorders entails surveying entire general populations, or representative samples of such populations. These *epidemiological* studies are extremely useful because they collect other information that can shed light on the disorders. Nevertheless, epidemiological studies often differ in the populations they study, the quality of sampling, how they define problem behavior, and how they measure behavior. Thus their results vary, and comparison is sometimes difficult. (Epidemiology is further discussed in Chapter 4.)

An interesting finding from population studies is that many children show specific behaviors that may or may not be considered signs of disturbance. In one of the earliest systematic investigations, almost five hundred mothers of a sample of all six- to twelve-year-olds in Buffalo, New York, evaluated their children's behavior in detail (Lapouse and Monk, 1958). They reported among other things that 49 percent of their offspring were overactive, 48 percent lost their tempers twice weekly, and 28 percent experienced nightmares. This study is of historical interest, and more recent studies from various countries confirm that such behavioral problems are commonly reported (Cotler, 1986). Problems that are isolated or only moderately disruptive, or those that spontaneously decrease or disappear, are viewed as transient developmental crises that may or may not require professional consultation. An important task for researchers is to better understand when behavior problems will be transient crises and when they will persist or predict later disturbance (Campbell, 1987).

Many recent epidemiologic studies employed standardized scales to establish the prevalence of problems and often employed criteria that would result in a clinical diagnosis. As shown in Figure 1–2, five such

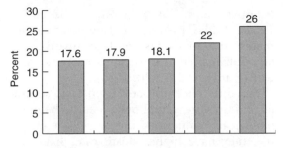

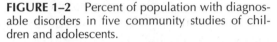

FIGURE 1–2 Percent of population with diagnosable disorders in five community studies of children and adolescents.

(Data from Verhulst and Koot, 1992.)

major studies from four different countries produced prevalence rates from 17.6 percent to 26 percent (Verhulst and Koot, 1992). Even these studies varied a good deal, so their relative agreement is interesting. Twenty percent prevalence for clinic-level disorder for children and adolescents is fairly widely reported today (Costello et al., 1993; Saunders et al., 1994). Perhaps 10 percent of youth has significantly impaired functioning. An additional point worth noting is that disorder may have increased over recent years. For example, small increases occurred in parental and teacher reports of various problems shown by youth in the United States from 1976 to 1989 (Achenbach and Howell, 1993). There were significant increases in children scoring in the clinical range. Thus, it appears that substantial needs on the part of young people exist. Moreover, it is estimated that most needy youth are not receiving support and treatment sufficient to overcome their behavioral problems (Costello et al., 1993).

Sex Differences

A common finding about the disorders of youth is that many occur more frequently in males than in females. These include autism, hyperactivity, antisocial behavior, language problems, and learning disabilities

(Cantwell and Rutter, 1994; Weisz et al., 1987). When prevalence is greater in females, the problems tend to involve the emotions, as in depression, shyness, and fear (Rutter and Gould, 1985).

Sex differences can be attributed to several factors. In some ways boys appear to be more biologically vulnerable than girls; for example, they have higher death rates from the moment of conception. Some vulnerabilities may stem from the Y chromosome carried by males and to the male child being relatively less physically mature (Rutter, 1986a).

Social factors undoubtedly play a role in creating sex differences in prevalence. More than girls, boys are adversely affected by family discord, divorce, mental illness, and job stress (Zaslow and Hayes, 1986). Parents are more likely to argue in front of boys; they also respond more negatively to boys' oppositional reactions to stress than to girls' emotional reactions to stress (Rutter, 1986a). Sex role socialization may encourage aggression in boys and anxiety and depression in girls. The picture is complex. Adults may be less tolerant of male hyperactivity, disruption, and lack of persistence (Huston, 1983; Serbin and O'Leary, 1975). Of course, adult tolerance may be lower because males are more difficult to handle from early life. It is possible, then, that biological endowment interacts with socialization and social expectation to create a vicious cycle for the male child (cf. Earls and Jung, 1987; Jensen et al., 1990).

Age of Onset

Research also provides data on when behavioral disorders are likely to arise. Age of onset may be important to understanding the causation, severity, and outcome of disorders (Giaconia et al., 1994). For instance, the earlier that drugs are used, the greater the chance of severe drug dependency in adulthood.

Behavioral disorders of youth can arise at most any age and increase and decrease in frequency across age (Kashani et al., 1989; Rutter and Gould, 1985). However, age of onset is related to specific disorders (Cantwell and Rutter, 1994). Developmental delays in language and speech are usually seen early in life, when children are first acquiring these skills. Autism, too, arises early. Deficiencies in attention are typically diagnosed prior to school or when children begin school, as are problems in intelligence and learning. Fears and anxieties can arise at any age, but specific fears are somewhat age related. Aggression, noncompliance, stealing, and the like can also arise at any age. Depression, anorexia, drug abuse, and schizophrenia often first occur with the approach of adolescence, although they may be seen earlier (Kazdin, 1993a).

The link between age of onset and certain dysfunctions is not coincidental, of course. Chronological age is correlated with children's developmental level. In turn, developmental level makes some behavioral problems more likely than others. For example, the cognitive and emotional levels of four-year-olds make it unlikely that preschoolers experience the thoughts and feelings that are labeled as depression at later ages.

The ages at which disorders seem to arise may sometimes actually be the ages at which disorders are first noticed or identified. Environmental demands play a role here. An example is mental retardation, which is defined as children's intellectual functioning being below that of their age-mates. More cases of retardation are identified during the school years than pre- or postschool years (Patton, Beirne-Smith, and Payne, 1990). The demands of the classroom—and school policy to evaluate intellectual performance—filter out children who previously appeared to function adequately in their home environments.

Despite the complexities of defining and identifying behavioral disorders, it is clear that progress is being made in understanding the needs of youth. This is a relatively recent circumstance, which is illuminated in the next section.

SOME HISTORICAL INFLUENCES

Humans have long speculated on behavioral dysfunction, but early interest focused primarily on adults. The first recordings of specific childhood problems appeared in the early 1800s (Rie, 1971). By the end of the century a few attempts had been made to classify childhood disorders, and causes had been proposed. Mental retardation received the most attention, but psychoses, aggression, hyperactivity, and "masturbatory insanity" had all been noted.

Several developments then radically altered views of children and adolescents, how their development might go awry, and how they might be treated (Table 1–1). We will now look at these major developments, many of which will be returned to in later chapters.

The Influence of Sigmund Freud

Prior to the twentieth century most theories of disordered behavior emphasized biological causes or etiologies. Freud's work helped change this (Chess, 1988).

As a young neurologist, Freud collaborated with others, especially Joseph Breuer, who believed that certain disorders could be caused by psychological events. Freud was particularly interested in the belief that psychological experiences in childhood appeared connected to later symptoms such as paralysis and blindness for which no physical cause was evident. These problems seemed to be alleviated when the patient was able to talk emotionally about earlier experiences. Such observations set Freud on a lifelong course to construct a grand theory of development and a treatment method for disordered behavior.

Based on his study of adults, Freud was convinced that psychological childhood conflicts were the key to understanding behavior. He also hypothesized that all children pass through the same developmental stages, and he related these stages to later behavior. In *Three Essays on the Theory of Sexuality,* published in 1905, and in his 1909 lectures at Clark University in Massachusetts, Freud introduced his radical ideas about the importance of childhood (Evans and Koelsch, 1985; Rie, 1971). His views were controversial from the start, but they came to provide a systematic framework for conceptualizing both childhood and adult behavior.

By the 1930s, Freud's ideas had been widely interpreted by Melanie Klein, Erik Erikson, Heinz Hartmann, and others. Freud's daughter, Anna, elaborated his ideas and especially applied them to children (Fine, 1985). These efforts helped to establish psychiatry as a major discipline in the study and treatment of childhood disorders. In 1935 Leo Kanner published the first child psychiatry text in the United States.

Behaviorism and Social Learning Theory

While Freud was stirring up the academic world with his innovative ideas, a school of psychology was being introduced in the United States that would rival Freud's ideas (Sears, 1975). Behaviorism was launched by John B. Watson's essay *Psychology As a Behaviorist Views It* (1913). Unlike Freud, Watson placed little value on describing developmental stages and on early psychological conflicts. Instead, he drew on theories of learning to emphasize that most behavior originates through learning processes. Wat-

TABLE 1–1 Some Early Historical Landmarks

1896	The first child clinic in the U.S. was established at the University of Pennsylvania by Lightner Witmer.
1905	Alfred Binet and Theophil Simon developed the first intelligence tests to identify feebleminded children.
1905	Sigmund Freud's *Three Essays on the Theory of Sexuality* described a startlingly different view of childhood development.
1908	In *A Mind That Found Itself,* Clifford Beers recounted his mental breakdown and advocated an enlightened view of mental disorders, initiating the mental hygiene and child guidance movements.
1909	G. Stanley Hall invited Sigmund Freud to Clark University to lecture on psychoanalysis.
1909	William Healy and Grace Fernald established the Juvenile Psychopathic Institute in Chicago, which would become the model for the child guidance clinics.
1911	The Yale Clinic of Child Development was established for child development research under the guidance of Arnold Gesell.
1913	John B. Watson introduced behaviorism in his essay *Psychology as a Behaviorist Views It.*
1917	William Healy and Augusta Bronner established the Judge Baker Guidance Center in Boston.
1922	The National Committee on Mental Hygiene and the Commonwealth Fund initiated a demonstration program of child guidance clinics.
1924	The American Orthopsychiatric Association was established.
1928–1929	Longitudinal studies of child development began at Berkeley and Fels Research Institute.
1935	Leo Kanner authored *Child Psychiatry,* the first child psychiatry text published in the U.S.

son thought that people's behavior, whether good or bad, could be explained by learning experiences. He stated enthusiastically:

Give me a dozen healthy infants, well-formed, and my own specified world to bring them up in and I'll guarantee to take any one at random and train him to become any type of specialist I might select—doctor, lawyer, merchant, chief and yes, even beggar-man and thief, regardless of his talents, penchants, tendencies, abilities, vocations, and race of his ancestors. (Watson, 1924/1970, p. 104)

In addition to a strong emphasis on learning and environment, Watson was committed to testing ideas by the experimental method (Horowitz, 1992).

E. L. Thorndike (1905) also made an early contribution to behaviorism by formu-

lating the *Law of Effect.* Simply put, this law states that behavior is shaped by its consequences. If the consequence is satisfying, the behavior will be strengthened in the future; if the consequence is discomforting, the behavior will be weakened. Thorndike considered the *Law of Effect* a fundamental principle of learning and teaching; later researchers substantiated his claim. Of special note is B. F. Skinner who became widely known for investigating and writing on the application of behavioral consequences to the shaping of behavior (Skinner, 1948, 1953, 1968). Skinner can be viewed as Watson's direct descendent in his emphasis on learning, the environment, and experimental methods (Horowitz, 1992).

Behaviorism thrived in the United States during the first half of this century. Its im-

Both Sigmund Freud (center) and his daughter Anna Freud (foreground) were influential in the development of the psychodynamic conceptualizations of childhood disorders.

(AP/Wide World Photos)

John B. Watson was a highly influential figure in the application of the behavioral perspective.

(The Bettman Archive)

pact on behavior disorders came gradually as Mowrer, Bijou, Baer, and others applied learning principles to children's behavior. In his focus on observational learning, Bandura emphasized cognition (Grusec, 1992). The work of these men focused on different aspects of learning, but it all emphasized the importance of the social context. The approach is thus often described as the social learning perspective. When applied explicitly to the assessment and treatment of behavior problems, it is often called behavior modification or behavior therapy.

The Mental Hygiene and Child Guidance Movements

Despite the interest in adult psychopathology by the early twentieth century, much remained to be learned, and treatment often consisted of custodial hospital care. The mental hygiene movement in the United States aimed to increase understanding, improve treatment, and prevent disorders from occurring at all.

In 1908 Clifford Beers wrote an autobiographical account, *A Mind That Found Itself,* telling of the insensitive and ineffective treatment he had received as a mental patient. Beers proposed reform and obtained support from renowned professionals, including Adolf Meyer. Recognizing both psychological and biological causes of behavior disorders, Meyer believed that they stemmed from failure to adapt, and he proposed a "commonsense" approach to studying the patient's environment and to counseling. He set the course for a new professional role—psychiatric social worker (Achenbach, 1974).

Beers's efforts also led to the establishment of the National Committee for Mental Hygiene to study mental dysfunctions, support treatment, and encourage prevention. Because childhood experiences were viewed as influencing adult mental health, children became the focus of study and guidance (Rie, 1971).

In 1896, at the University of Pennsylvania, Lightner Witmer had already set up the first child psychology clinic in the United Sates (McReynolds, 1987; Ross, 1972). This clinic primarily assessed and treated children who had learning difficulties. Witmer also founded the journal *Psychological Clinic* and began a hospital school for long-term observation of children. He related psychology to education, sociology, and other disciplines.

An interdisciplinary approach was also taken by psychiatrist William Healy and psychologist Grace Fernald in Chicago in 1909, when they founded the Juvenile Psychopathic Institute. The focus of the institute was delinquent children, and its approach became the model for child guidance. Healy was convinced that antisocial behavior could be treated by psychological means, by helping youngsters adjust to the circumstances in which they lived (Santostefano, 1978). This required understanding the whole personality and the multiple causes of behavior. Freudian theory provided the central ideas for dealing with psychological conflicts, and attempts were made to gather information about family and other important relationships (Santostefano, 1978; Strean, 1970). The psychiatrist, psychologist, and social worker formed a collaborative team toward this end, meeting to discuss cases.

Healy and his wife, psychologist Augusta Bronner, continued to use this approach when they opened the Judge Baker Guidance Center in Boston. The National Committee for Mental Hygiene subsequently established several other child clinics, adopting the same approach. The cases now also included personality and emotional problems. These clinics flourished in the 1920s and 1930s.

In 1924 the child guidance movement was formally represented by the formation of the American Orthopsychiatric Association, with Healy as its first president and Bronner as its second. To this day the association includes a variety of professionals concerned about children and adolescents.

The Scientific Study of Youth

It was also during the early twentieth century that systematic study of youth became widespread. A central figure in this endeavor was G. Stanley Hall. Like many others of this period, Hall knew little about the development of the young, and so he collected questionnaire data about fears, dreams, preferences, play, and the like (Grinder, 1967; Sears, 1975). Some questionnaires focused on dysfunctions of youth with the goal of understanding mental disorder, crime, social disorder, and the like (White, 1992). Hall wrote extensively on children and adolescents and trained students who later became leaders. As president of Clark University, Hall invited Freud to lecture in 1909. He also helped establish the American Psychological Association and was its first president.

At about the same time, an important event occurred in Europe: Alfred Binet and Theophil Simon were asked to design a test to identify children who were in need of special education (Siegler, 1992; Tuddenham, 1962). They presented children of various ages with different tasks and problems, thereby establishing age-norms by which intellectual performance could be evaluated. The 1905 Binet-Simon test became the basis for the development of intelligence tests. It also encouraged professionals to search for ways to measure other psychological attributes.

Another outstanding figure was Arnold Gesell, who meticulously recorded the physical, motor, and social behavior of young children in his laboratory at Yale University (Thelen and Adolph, 1992). He charted developmental norms, relying on structured observation, naturalistic observation, and parental report. Gesell was fascinated with the benefits of photography to record infant and child behavior and left a voluminous film archive. An organizing concept of his work was *maturation*, the intrinsic unfolding of development relatively independent of environmental influences. Gesell was also a strong advocate for children to have optimal rearing environments.

Commencing around 1920 child study began to benefit from several longitudinal research projects that evaluated youth as they developed over many years. Research centers existed at the universities of Michigan, California, Colorado, Minnesota, Ohio, and Washington; at the Fels Research Institute; Columbia Teachers College; the Johns Hopkins University; and the Iowa Child Welfare Station. A body of knowledge about normal development began to accumulate that eventually was applied to the study of child and adolescent disorders.

Today the study and treatment of disorders of young people consist of multidisciplinary and diverse efforts. The events described above remain influential, some more than others. Many new influences are also evident. Research into all areas of child and adolescent development has reached new heights of sophistication and complexity and is being brought to bear on the questions of abnormality. Of special influence are a renewed interest in human cognition, emphasis on the social context, advances in the biological sciences, and a joining of developmental psychology with the clinical and medical fields. These influences and others bring new excitement and innovation.

YOUTH AS SPECIAL CLIENTS

The Interdisciplinary Approach

Notable among professionals who work to ameliorate the behavioral problems of youth are psychologists, psychiatrists, social workers, and special education teachers.

Most psychologists working with child and adolescent problems have specialized in clinical psychology. Others may have specialized in developmental, school, or educational psychology. They usually hold the doctoral degree (Ph.D. or Psy.D.), which demands four to five years of university graduate study. Psychology has sturdy roots in the laboratory and an interest in both normal and abnormal behavior. Training in psychology thus includes psychological research as well as direct contact in assessing and treating troubled individuals. Many psychologists have a strong background in assessing behavior by psychological testing.

Psychiatrists, on the other hand, hold the doctorate in medicine (M.D.); they are physicians who have specialized in the care of the mentally disturbed. Psychiatrists function in ways that are similar to psychologists, but they tend to view problem behavior more as a medical dysfunction. They make a unique contribution to psychopathology by conducting medical evaluations and prescribing medication when appropriate.

Social workers generally hold the Master's degree (M.A.) in social work. Like psychologists and psychiatrists, they may counsel and conduct therapy, but historically their special focus has been working with the family and other social systems in which children are enmeshed.

Special education teachers, who usually have obtained the Master's degree, emphasize the importance of providing needy children with optimal educational experiences. They are able to plan and implement individualized educational programs, thus contributing to the treatment of many disorders.

Troubled youths also come to the attention of nurses, general physicians, teachers in regular classrooms, and workers in the legal system. Indeed, these professionals may be the first to hear about a problem. Thus, interdisciplinary consultation commonly occurs and often is ideal. A good amount of coordination is necessary if this approach is to be effective. Who functions as the coordinator may depend on the type of disorder, the developmental level of the client, the first point of professional contact, and the treatment setting.

Working with Parents

Dealing with disorders of youth frequently demands working closely with parents, who vary greatly in their motivation and capacity to participate.

Parents seek help for their offspring for many reasons. Of course, most are truly concerned about the welfare of their sons and daughters. Parents may also be driven to alleviate their worries and conflicts with their offspring. Or they may be referred by schools or the courts, sometimes against their own wishes. All these factors can influence motivation for treatment. So too may other variables, such as family stress and parental dysfunction (Armbruster and Kazdin, 1994). For example, Figure 1–3 shows that dropping out of treatment in one psychiatric center was affected by both the

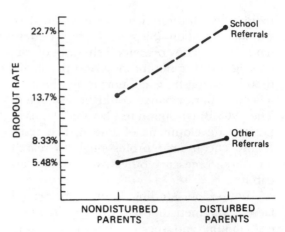

FIGURE 1–3 Dropout rate after initial screening at a child psychiatry clinic.

(From M. S. Gould, D. Shaffer, & D. Kaplan, The characteristics of dropouts from a child psychiatric clinic, Journal of the American Academy of Child Psychiatry, 24(3), 316–328, 1985, © by Am. Acad. of Child & Adolescent Psychiatry.)

referral source and parental dysfunction (Gould, Shaffer, and Kaplan, 1985). The drop-out rate was especially high for families that had both disturbed parents and school referrals.

Parents also vary in the ability to understand, support, and carry out recommendations. Some parents fear that they will be blamed for their offsprings' problems (Kraemer, 1987), which may lead to defensiveness. Some have inappropriate goals; for example, authoritarian parents may desire their child or adolescent to be excessively obedient. Parents can resent professional suggestions, be overly dependent, or expect therapists to "fix" the problem without their involvement. But parental involvement, including that of fathers, is often critical (Webster-Stratton, 1985b). Indeed, parents may provide a unique perspective that would otherwise be missed by the professional (e.g., Deaton, 1985). Thus, the competent and sensitive professional works toward optimizing the quality of parental participation.

Working with and for the Young Client

Direct interaction with youth is both rewarding and demanding. Young children may be especially incapable of identifying problems and seeking treatment, and they most often enter treatment at the suggestion or coercion of adults. Professionals must be sensitive to the child's perspective and create and maintain motivation.

They must also pay special attention to the client's developmental level. Chronological age is a rough indicator of developmental level, but actual measurement of functioning is desirable. Such knowledge can be helpful in judging the significance of problems. Understanding a child's developmental competencies and failures also provides guidelines for treatment. An example is training children to control their own behavior by giving themselves verbal directions. Impulsive children may be taught problem-solving steps and encouraged to say the steps to themselves (Kendall and Panichelli-Mindel, 1995). However, very young children would not be expected to do as well with this technique as older children.

Finally, clients have rights that must be recognized and protected. To the extent that they are able, youth have a right to assent to treatment, participate in decisions about the goals of treatment, and to understand how the goals will be attempted. Confidentiality standards must be maintained. Moreover, mental health workers often face tough questions concerning social values.

A well known demonstration of the complexities that can arise in working with children was described by Rekers and Lovaas (1974) when they treated five-year-old Kraig, who displayed feminine behaviors. The therapy plan involved social reinforcement for masculine mannerisms, activities, and interests. Rekers and Lovaas justified the intervention on the grounds that the parents had requested help, that Kraig was being socially rejected, and that without treatment Kraig was at risk for developing gender disorders later in life. Not all professionals agreed with this ethical position. Some argued that a diversity of behaviors is valuable and that sex stereotypes are questionable guides for behavior (Nordyke et al., 1977; Wolfe, 1979). Others felt that greater attention should have been given to Kraig's involvement in treatment decisions (Ollendick and Cerny, 1981).

Today's sensitivity to child abuse makes it of special concern with regard to legal rights (DeKraai and Sales, 1991). Therapists have increasingly been required by law to report abuse. Mental health workers may believe that reporting abuse may actually preclude beneficial intervention. Nevertheless, at the least it is their duty to know the laws and inform clients of the kinds of things that must be reported.

While ethical and legal dilemmas regarding behavioral disorders are common, they are of special concern when young people are involved. Judgments about social issues are often central to these dilemmas, and youth may be limited in speaking for themselves.

SUMMARY

Behavioral disturbance often elicits emotional reactions in others, as well as motivations to help youth reach their potential. Central to questions about psychopathology are basic issues of how people develop and how normal development goes awry. Thus, development is a central theme in this text. Development is viewed as arising from a multitude of factors. Since science can best answer questions about normal and abnormal behavior, empirical research is crucial.

The identification of behavior disorders rests on several criteria: sociocultural norms, age and other developmental norms, and the reactions of others. The attitudes, sensitivities, and tolerance of adults are important in determining whether or not a child or adolescent is viewed as having a problem.

The occurrence of disorders can be assessed by surveying mental health and other service settings, but this strategy underestimates prevalence and incidence. Epidemiologic studies survey entire populations or representative samples of the populations. Behaviors that are viewed as disturbed are actually quite prevalent in the general population of youth. These behaviors may be transient or persist or predict future problems. Recent epidemiologic studies report that about 20 percent of youth have diagnosable behavior disorders. Most are not receiving treatment.

Many disorders occur more frequently in boys than in girls, but girls show a higher occurrence of disorders such as depression and anorexia. Gender differences may be determined by biological or environmental factors or their interaction. Disorders can occur at any age, but many are age related. This association with age is related to developmental level and social variables.

Interest in childhood disorders evolved gradually. Several historical influences became important early in this century: Freud's work, the rise of behaviorism/social learning theories, the mental hygiene and child guidance movements, and a dramatic increase in the study of youth. These events brought new knowledge and conceptualizations of childhood and adolescent disorders. Today, many additional influences are evident.

Professional care of children and adolescents is interdisciplinary, involving psychologists, psychiatrists, social workers, education specialists, and several other professionals.

Working with young people requires special consideration of their motivation for treatment and level of development. Parental participation is important, and parents' needs, motivations, and abilities cannot be ignored. Professional care of the young client also raises special ethical and legal dilemmas. Because youth are often limited in their ability to advocate for themselves, mental health workers must assume some responsibility for this task.

2

THE DEVELOPMENTAL CONTEXT

We have already acknowledged the importance of the relationship between normal and abnormal development. This relationship is the focus of the present chapter. A few decades ago developmental psychology, which traditionally takes normal development as its subject matter, and clinical child/adolescent psychology and psychiatry began to recognize that each had something to offer and to gain from the other. By the 1970s their cooperative efforts became meaningful enough to warrant recognition and a new label—developmental psychopathology (Cicchetti, 1984, 1989). Developmental psychopathology is a general framework for understanding disordered behavior in relation to normal development (Achenbach, 1990; Rolf and Read, 1984). It is interested not only in the origins and developmental course of disordered behavior (Sroufe, 1986), but also in individual adaptation and success.

The developmental approach makes several specific contributions to the study of the problems of youth. Perhaps the most obvious is that descriptions of the usual course of growth provide a standard by which abnormality can be judged and conceptualized. The more we understand about normal achievements and sequences, the firmer is our foundation for identifying, understand-

ing, and treating disorder. Such knowledge comes from charting the course of typical development across the lifespan, in conjunction with theories and models of development.

Developmental research findings and developmental theories offer facts and hypotheses, too, as to how developmental change occurs, and thus how it might go awry. Since no one theory can explain all the numerous changes that take place during life, diverse accounts must be considered.

The developmental framework is also concerned with specific issues that are relevant to child and adolescent disorders. For example, developmentalists are interested in conceptualizing the variables that promote or hinder optimal development and in understanding the stability of behavior over time. Such issues are relevant to understanding disordered as well as normal development.

In this chapter we will examine the meaning of development, overview normal development, and then examine select issues relevant to behavioral dysfunction.

WHAT IS DEVELOPMENT?

If we were to ask strangers passing on the street to define the term development, many would surely offer "growth" as a synonym. And most would note that development requires time. These are sound ideas. Development does indeed include growth and it occurs over time. For example, children gradually become physically larger and display a larger number of social responses. However, development is much more complex and developmentalists themselves do not always agree on its characteristics and how it proceeds. Nevertheless, the following can serve as a guide for the developmental framework (e.g., Cicchetti and Schneider-Rosen, 1986; Santostefano, 1978; Sroufe and Rutter, 1984; Hodapp, Burack, and Zigler, 1990).

1. Development refers to change over the lifespan. Change may be quantitative; that is a change in size and number of elements. Development also involves change in quality or in features. Thus, the number of ways a child interacts with others may increase but so might the features of the behaviors.

2. Many developmentalists agree that there is a basic common general course of early development of the physical, cognitive, and social-emotional systems of all normal individuals. Within each system early, global structures and functions become more finely differentiated and then integrated. Integration occurs across systems as well.

3. Agreement does not exist with regard to developmental stages across the lifespan. Some theorists view development as occurring in distinct qualitative stages or steps that appear in the same order in all individuals. Other theorists describe development as gradual change that may or may not have a fixed ordering; they do not believe that distinct stages can be identified.

4. Development proceeds in a coherent pattern; that is, for each individual earlier development is systematically and logically linked to later development. Present functioning is thus connected to the past as well as to the future. However, different developmental pathways may lead to different or same outcomes and pathways may be linear or more complex.

5. Over the lifespan, developmental change may take many forms. New and higher modes of functioning and goals are attained but change may not always be positive.

6. Human beings are malleable but there are limitations on change.

7. Development is the result of interactions or transactions among biological, psychological, and sociocultural variables.

In the remainder of this chapter we will see how many of the above considerations are applied to both normal and atypical development. We will begin by overviewing normal development. For readers already possessing knowledge about development, the overview serves as a reminder of the developmental context; for others, the overview provides important concepts and facts about growth.

AN OVERVIEW OF NORMAL DEVELOPMENT

Normal development encompasses a wide array of complicated processes. Our purpose here is thus a modest one: to selectively survey aspects of early development as a broad framework within which we can consider behavioral problems of youth.

Genetic Influence

Genetic contributions to behavioral development operate in complex ways, at both the species and individual levels. Through evolutionary processes all humans are biologically programmed to develop in certain ways and have certain characteristics in common. However, there is room for much individual variation.

It was only during this century that we have come to understand basic genetic processes. All body cells contain chromosomes, segments of which are called genes. Chromosomes are composed of deoxyribonucleic acid (DNA), the hereditary material that directs development and cell activity. Most cells have twenty-three pairs of chromosomes. One pair, the sex chromosomes, differs in females and males: females have two X chromosomes and males have an X and a Y chromosome. The Y chromosome has fewer genes and is smaller and lighter.

In contrast to other cells, the ovum and sperm undergo a special maturational process, meiosis, that results in each having only twenty-three single chromosomes, one from each of the original pairs. Thus, at conception each prospective parent contributes half of the chromosome complement to the offspring. Prospective mothers contribute an X chromosome, whereas prospective fathers can contribute either an X or a Y.

The processes of meiosis and conception assure billions of possible chromosome combinations for any one individual. Other genetic mechanisms result in even greater variability. Chromosomes may exchange genes, break and reattach to each other, and change by mutation, which is spontaneous alteration of the DNA molecule. Environmental interactions contribute further to produce an infinite variety of humans.

Hereditary influences on behavioral characteristics are often misunderstood, even today. In general, the path between genetic endowment, the *genotype,* and observable characteristics of the individual, the *phenotype,* is much more indirect and flexible than what is often believed. Genes act indirectly by guiding the biochemistry of cells. They are best thought of as helping to set a range within which characteristics will develop. Characteristics for which genetic influence has been established can be altered to some degree by the environment. Many traits can be altered substantially; for example, height is genetically influenced but is affected by diet and disease. Furthermore, hereditary effects are often not set over time; in fact, genes program change as well as stability (Plomin and Thompson, 1988).

The Child as a Physical Being

Conception takes place in the Fallopian tube. Within a few days the zygote attaches itself to the wall of the uterus. The developing mass floats freely in the amniotic sac except for its attachment by the umbilical cord to the placenta of the prospective mother (Figure 2–1). If all goes uneventfully, birth occurs about thirty-eight weeks after conception. These weeks of prenatal growth are crucial in that the organism can be dramatically affected by biological and environmental factors.

From the moment of conception, growth occurs in a quite predictable manner, following general principles. Growth takes place from the head to the tail regions (the cephalocaudal direction). Thus the head develops earliest, and at birth it is about a quarter of the total body length; by later adolescence this has changed to an eighth (Jones, Garrison, and Morgan, 1985). Growth also occurs from the center of the body to the extremities (the proximodistal direction). This is illustrated in prenatal development by the growth of the chest and trunk prior to the limbs, fingers, and toes.

Throughout life, different body parts develop at different rates. For example, the skeleton, muscles, and internal organs grow rapidly during infancy and early childhood, slow down in middle childhood, and then accelerate in adolescence. In contrast, the reproductive system develops slowly until adolescence, when it grows rapidly (Tanner, 1970). The notable changes that occur at adolescence, resulting in adult-like body size and proportion, are known as the adolescent growth spurt. By age twenty or so most physical growth has occurred, although further change takes place in adulthood.

The nervous system. The nervous system begins to develop shortly after conception when a group of cells called the neural plate thickens, folds inward, and forms the neural tube. This tube differentiates into the nervous system, and most brain cells are produced prenatally (Nowakowski, 1987). At birth the brain is about 25 percent of its adult weight, making it proportionately larger than most organs (Tanner, 1978).

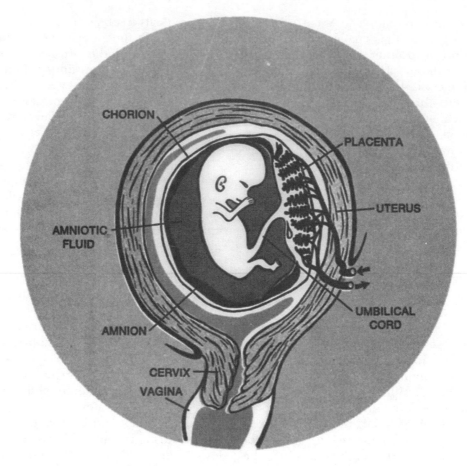

FIGURE 2–1   Schema of the developing child showing indirect contact with the mother's circulatory system.

Further growth occurs after birth. By age five the brain reaches about 95 percent of its adult weight. Neurons (nerve cells) grow in size and in number of synaptic connections to other neurons. Myelin, a fatty cover, continues to be laid down on the axons of some neurons; myelin speeds up nerve transmission. Different parts of the nervous system develop in spurts more rapidly than others, and the pattern is related to functioning (Greenough, Black, and Wallace, 1987; Prechtl, 1981; Wolfe, 1981). For example, nerves that control reflexes are well developed at birth, but areas that control voluntary movement grow substantially during the first year of life and later.

Brain development depends on biological programming, but also on experience (Bertenthal and Campos, 1987; Greenough et al., 1987). Rats and other animals, for example, which have had opportunity to explore object-filled, enriched environments develop more brain synapses than animals reared in simple environments. Moreover, experience may shape early nervous system growth not only by encouraging new cell connections but also by helping to eliminate redundant connections and neurons providing those connections (Casaer, 1993).

Movement.   Like physical growth, motor development is quite predictable. Infants display many involuntary reflexes. Some reflexes are related to vital bodily functioning, such as the blinking and sucking reflexes. Others seem of little importance, but perhaps played a role in human evolution. Whereas many reflexes persist into adulthood, others disappear early or perhaps are transformed into voluntary action (Thelen, 1986). The absence of reflexes at birth or the persistence of specific ones beyond certain times are signs of nervous system dysfunction. Abnormal reflexes may thus give early warnings of developmental problems.

Voluntary movement develops in a universal sequence. It generally follows the head-to-tail principle; for example, babies gain control of their arms more quickly than their legs. Children also control the center of the body before the extremities, and large areas before small muscle groups. Thus, when they begin to use crayons they first use the entire arm and only gradually acquire hand control. Once control is gained over specific muscle groups, children begin to integrate many operations into complex movements. Table 2–1 shows the average age at which some of the basic motor milestones are achieved. As with reflexes, deviations from the timing and patterning of these milestones may indicate nervous system dysfunctioning.

Between the ages of six and twelve there is a noticeable increase in children's ability to jump rope, skate, climb, ride bicycles, and the like. Indeed, such skills often peak in the teen years.

TABLE 2–1 Some Early Gross Motor Milestones

Rolls over	2–4 months
Sits without support	5–7
Stands holding on to furniture	8–9
Creeps on hands and knees	9–10
Stands without support	10–13
Walks alone	11–14
Walks upstairs alone, two feet per step	21–25

Physical and motor development depend on both biological and environmental influences. Biological programming is suggested by the facts that growth follows a standard sequence and is similar for most all children. Body shape, height, and weight are clearly influenced by inheritance. And voluntary movement is based on certain muscles being biologically coordinated to work together as a self-correcting unit (Goldfield, 1989; Thelen, Skala, and Kelso, 1987). In fact, it is likely that children would sit, stand, use their hands, and walk even if the environment failed to encourage such behaviors.

Still, environmental effects are obvious. Youth who consume excessive calories are likely to be overweight and those who are physically active are likely to develop muscle strength and coordination. Experience also plays a role in complex movements: Most people can readily hop and skip but gymnastic skill requires much learning. Observing others and practicing activities are important (Adams, 1984). So is feedback from others and one's own body. Since using a sewing machine is not identical to running an electric saw, specific skills must be practiced. Individuals learn "motor programs"—mental representations of what acts follow other acts—and try to match these programs. Motor development thus has cognitive components (Pick, 1989). In general, the degree to which complex skills are acquired depends on hereditary tendencies, maturation level, motivation, and opportunities to learn and practice (Jones et al., 1985).

When motor development goes awry, the individual may be considerably disadvantaged in manipulating and learning about the world. Physical handicaps can lessen motivation for mastering the environment (Jennings, Connors, and Stegman, 1988), and slow motor development may influence how the child is perceived by others and the self.

Other aspects of physical growth, such as the timing of maturation, can also affect psychosocial development (Carron and Bailey,

Practice plays an important role in the development of complex motor skills. Motor development can impact other areas of functioning and influence self-concept.

Spencer Grant, Monkmeyer

1974; Dubas, Graber, and Petersen, 1991; Siegel, 1982). Boys appear to benefit from early growth: They are rated as more popular, poised, and attractive than late maturers, who are seen as anxious and lacking in self-esteem. The picture is less clear for early maturing girls but for some is negative. These girls select older peers, tend to break social norms, become involved in adolescent dating and drug use, or drop out of school (Stattin and Magnusson, 1990).

Physically attractive people are viewed as smarter, more likeable, and good (Patzer and Burke, 1988; Stephan and Langlois, 1984). In contrast, physical abnormality is often avoided or reacted to with a mix of sympathy, contempt, and embarrassment. Individuals may be overly polite because they are unsure how to act when other people have noticeable physical abnormalities. In turn, those with physical difficulties may be further disadvantaged because they do not receive appropriate feedback about their behavior.

The Child as an Intellectual Being

The newborn may seem quite unaware of its surroundings and unable to profit from experience. This is far from true. Infants cannot report what they sense, but researchers can determine exactly what they are looking at, whether their heart rates and muscle activity change in response to different odors, and the like. Such measures confirm that infants come into the world with considerable capacity to sense their surroundings. Seeing, hearing, smelling, tasting, and touching—all of which develop rapidly during the first years of life—are the basis for experiencing the environment. When these are disturbed, children's abilities to function are interfered with. In the normal course of events, though, information is accurately perceived and processed through learning and cognition.

Three basic learning processes are widely recognized: classical conditioning, operant learning, and observational learning. These processes operate soon after birth and become complex as the higher mental processes develop. Memory, attention, mediation, imagery, and concept formation all enable children to better understand their environments. Learning and thinking will be discussed at various places in this text. Here, we overview Jean Piaget's theory and the growth of language.

Piaget's theory of cognition. Piaget was interested in both biology and epistemology, which is the philosophical study of how humans know the world. He worked with the young, including his own children, in hopes of better understanding cognition (Flavell, 1963; Petersen, 1982). Piaget eventually constructed a theory of cognition that became one of the most influential psychological theories of this century.

Piaget viewed the child as a biological organism that adapts to its environment by actively organizing and interpreting experiences. In so doing, the child's mind moves from quite simple mental structures, called *schemas,* to more sophisticated ones. Some experiences can be interpreted by already existing schemas; this is referred to as *assimilation.* But some new experiences also require *accommodation,* the modification and growth of schemas. Through these reciprocal functions the child develops increasingly advanced schemas of the world. Both biological maturation and experience are necessary for cognitive development.

Piaget hypothesized that cognitive growth occurs in four distinct periods or stages, roughly correlated with chronological age (Table 2–2). Consistent with all stage theories, it was assumed that the stages occur in a particular sequence and build on the preceding ones. At any one stage intelligence is qualitatively different than it is at any other stage. This has implications for how children might perceive the world at any particular stage, what they are prepared to learn, and how developmental problems might be interpreted.

Piaget's influence declined during the 1980s (Beilen, 1992). However, his theory has encouraged an enormous amount of research, has offered assumptions and concepts used by other theorists, and is still being fruitfully applied to understanding development.

Language and communication. The growth of communication skills, a dramatic process by any standard, is closely linked to learning and cognition. Among the skills required for language are the abilities to distinguish and produce sounds, string sounds into words and words into grammatical sentences, derive meaning from language, and grasp the social context in which a message is being sent. Table 2–3 presents some of the widely recognized steps in early language acquisition. By the time children begin ele-

---

TABLE 2–2 Piaget's Stages of Cognitive Growth

Sensorimotor birth to 2 yrs.	World is first known through innate sensorimotor reflexes. Behavior becomes voluntary, refined, integrated, planful. Ability develops to mentally represent the world in images and words.
Preoperational 2 to 7 yrs.	Broadened view of the world is achieved as concepts of space, number, color, etc. develop. World is re-created in play. Children can deal with varied situations.
Concrete operational 7 to 11 yrs.	Ability develops to see the world from others' viewpoints. Ability develops to understand that processes can reverse, and that objects can change in form without change in mass (conservation of mass). Ability develops to simultaneously hold in mind several dimensions of a problem. There is increased understanding of relationships.
Formal operational 12 yrs. onward	Truly logical thinking appears: Child can better abstract, think about possibilities, form and evaluate hypotheses, deduce and induce principles.

TABLE 2–3 Early Acquisition of Language and Communication

	Reception	*Expression*
Birth to 6 months	Reacts to sudden noise Is quieted by a voice Locates sound Recognizes name and words like "bye-bye."	Cries Babbles, laughs Initiates vocal play Vocalizes to self Experiments with voice
6 to 12 months	Stops activity to *no* Raises arms to *come up* Obeys simple instructions Understands simple statements	Makes sounds of the culture's language Combines vowel sounds Imitates adult sounds Says first words
12 to 18 months	Carries out two consecutive commands Understands new words Listens to nursery rhymes	Uses ten words Requests by naming objects Connects sounds so that they flow like a sentence
18 to 24 months	Recognizes many sounds Understands action words like *show me*	Uses short sentences Uses pronouns Echoes last words of a rhyme
24 to 36 months	Follows commands using *in, on, under* Follows three verbal commands given in one utterance	Uses possessive, noun-verb combinations Mother understands 90% of communications
36 to 48 months	Increases understanding of others' messages and social context of communication	Uses increasingly complex language forms, such as conjunctions and auxiliary verbs

Based on Bryant, 1977; Whitehurst, 1982.

mentary school, most have mastered basic skills (Baker and Cantwell, 1991), although communication continues to be perfected for many years, even throughout adulthood for some individuals.

How language is acquired has long fascinated philosophers and scientists. Perspectives range from an extreme focus on biological programming to a focus on environmental input (Whitehurst and Valdez-Menchaca, 1988). The biological system is obviously constructed so that language is achieved, but language development relies heavily on social input. Social stimulation facilitates early language acquisition, and the child's babbling and talking attract the attention of caretakers. Language is clearly related to intellectual functioning

and it is also a social activity. Thus, language difficulties can result in academic problems, social interactional problems, social isolation, and low self-esteem.

The Child as a Social and Emotional Being

Developmental theorists and researchers have much to say about the growth of the child as a social-emotional being. Our discussion only highlights three areas of continuing interest: temperament, emotional growth, and early social relationships.

Temperament. The word temperament refers to basic disposition, make-up, or personality. The concept of temperament is an old one, certainly going back to the classical

Greek era. The present surge of interest in temperament was begun by Chess and Thomas's longitudinal study of New York City children. Chess and Thomas (1977) were especially interested in explaining the development of problem behaviors. They recognized environmental influences on development, but they were struck by the individual differences in how infants behaved from the first days of life. Based on parental interviews and actual observations, they found that young babies showed distinct individual differences in temperament, defined by nine categories of behavior (Table 2–4). They also found some stability of temperament over time.

Although subsequent researchers have focused on somewhat different behaviors, temperament is generally viewed as individual differences in emotionality, activity, and sociability (Prior, 1992). Most researchers believe that temperament is based on the biological make-up of the person, is somewhat stable across time and situations, and provides a foundation for the developing personality (e.g., Caspi et al., 1995; Rothbart, 1986).

There is evidence for modest hereditary influence on temperament (Buss and Plomin, 1986; Wilson and Matheny, 1986). For example, identical twins, who have identical genes, are more similar in temperament

than fraternal twins and tend to follow a more similar developmental path. Nevertheless, environmental impact can also be seen. The stability of temperament over time is only modest to moderate (Bates, 1987; Persson-Blennow and McNeil, 1988), and some of the instability is undoubtedly due to environmental influences. The infant's way of behaving enters immediately into social interactions that, in turn, influence the general environment and the child's behavioral tendencies. Thus, temperament can be expected to be transformed, and the individual's changing characteristics continue to play a role in his or her development (Kagan, Arcus, and Snidman, 1993).

Emotional growth. Emotional expression is a part of temperament, and it is worthwhile to ask further about the nature and growth of the emotions (e.g., Izard, 1986). Even very young infants show emotional expression, and respond appropriately to the emotional expression of their caretakers (Harris, 1994). Of course, it is impossible to know exactly what they are experiencing. Perhaps specific facial expressions are interpreted by the brain so that infants have feelings akin to the pleasure, anger, and disgust felt by older people (Izard and Dougerty, 1986). But early emotions are unlikely to be identical to later emotions, because emotional "feelings" depend on experiences in the world and cognitive ability to interpret these experiences. Nevertheless, many emotions and their expression seem to be present in some form by the time children are two or three years of age.

The understanding of emotion also begins remarkably early (Harris, 1994). For example, infants appear to understand that emotion is directed at targets or objects. Thus, if a caretaker expresses fearfulness in the presence of an object, the young child is less likely to approach the object. The child seems to use the caretaker as a social reference. Two- and three-year-olds are able to

TABLE 2–4 The Chess and Thomas Categories of Temperament

1. Activity level
2. Regularity of biological functioning (e.g., eating, sleeping)
3. Approach/withdrawal to new stimuli. Approach is positive, such as smiling. Withdrawal is negative, such as crying.
4. Adaptability to changing situations
5. Level of stimulation necessary to evoke a response
6. Intensity of reaction
7. Mood (e.g., pleasantness, friendliness)
8. Distractibility to extraneous stimuli
9. Attention span and persistence in an activity

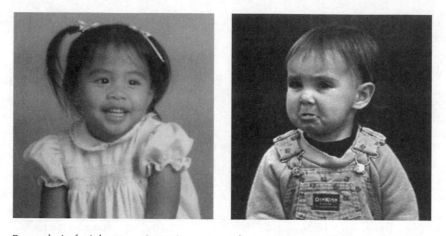

From their facial expressions, it appears that very young children experience basic emotions such as happiness and unhappiness.

(Courtesy of L. Wicks) (Jim Whitmer/Stock, Boston)

name and talk about basic emotions, and recognize that an emotional state depends on how the individual appraises the situation he or she is responding to. By age five or six, both the expression and understanding of emotions become quite refined (Bullock and Russell, 1986).

Humans are biologically prepared for such growth, and early developmental milestones may be universal. However, emotion is also shaped by the specific social environments encountered by infants and children (Harris, 1994; Malatesta et al., 1886). The emotions enter into virtually all human experience. Both the quality and intensity of the emotions play some role in most behavioral difficulties, either as a central factor (such as in extreme fears) or as a side effect (such as unhappiness resulting from academic failure).

Social relationships. Regardless of individual disposition, virtually all infants and their caretakers seem biologically prepared to interact in ways that foster their relationship. Most parents are remarkably adept in understanding their babies' signals and needs, and they optimize social interactions

(Papousek and Papousek, 1983). Infants, in turn, are sensitive to parental emotional-social signals. Early child-parent interactions thus flow like a dance, with each partner's behaviors coordinated with the other's (Elias, Hayes, and Broerse, 1988). Such interactions are the basis for the special social-emotional bond, called attachment, that becomes evident when the child is seven to nine months of age.

Early attachment is indicated by the child staying close to the adult but also venturing to explore the environment and by being upset when the adult leaves. The securely attached child appears to use the parent as a secure base and reacts positively to a parent who has returned after a brief departure. Secure attachment depends to some degree on parental sensitivity and responsiveness to the child (Ainsworth et al., 1978; Schneider-Rosen and Rothbaum, 1993). Infant temperament, and how it interacts with parental characteristics, also may play a role in determining attachment (Goldsmith, Bradshaw, and Reiser-Danner, 1986; Thompson, Connell, and Bridges, 1988). The child who meets parental expectations, is easy to care for, and readily smiles and vo-

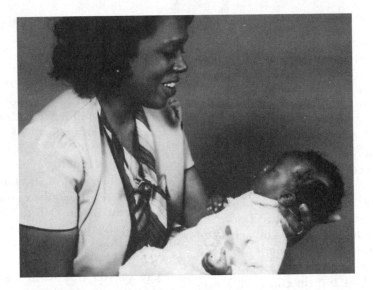

Infants and their caretakers are predisposed to interact in ways that foster attachment.

(Courtesy of A. Russell and R. Molla.)

calizes is likely to foster positive feelings and behaviors in the adult. The social context also matters; for example, attachment of stressed mothers and their temperamentally difficult babies is of higher quality when the mothers feel that they are receiving support from other adults (Crockenberg, 1988).

Early attachment is considered important partly because it is believed to help set a course for later social relationships and adaptation. Purportedly, attachment experiences are internalized, that is, become a basis for the child's constructing an internal working model for subsequent relationships and adaptation. Indeed, research shows that secure attachment is associated with adaptive behavior in childhood and adolescence, such as competence and positive peer interactions (Azar, 1995; Dunn and McGuire, 1992; Sroufe and Fleeson, 1986). This association does not prove that attachment directly causes later adaptive behavior, but it gives special importance to attachment. The concept of attachment has been fruitfully applied to behavior disorders, such as mental retardation and conduct disorder (e.g., Routh et al., 1995).

Most studies of attachment focus on the mother as the primary caretaker. However, children become attached to fathers, grandparents, siblings, and others early in life. With age, attachment manifests itself differently, and additional emotional bonds are established. Not surprisingly, when children of seven, ten, and fourteen years of age were asked to name those most important to them, all named close family members but more ten-year-olds mentioned extended family and more fourteen-year-olds added friends (Levitt, Guacci-Franco, and Levitt, 1993).

Many other aspects of social and emotional development have been studied. These include how individuals acquire gender role and become aggressive, kind, empathetic, moral, achievement oriented, self-disciplined, and impulsive. Such behavioral tendencies, or personality attributes, have been explored in depth, and many will turn up in various discussions throughout this text.

The Social-Cultural Context

Development occurs in a sociocultural context that can best be considered as domains of overlapping, interacting social influences. Although there is more than one way to depict this, Figure 2–2 serves as a general schema. Here we see the developing youngster embedded within the family, school, and neighborhood—with which interaction is ongoing, direct, and reciprocal. Note too that these realms overlap, that is, interact and affect each other. All of these contexts are embedded in a larger cultural domain, with which they also interact. The arrows in the schema indicate movement through time, and change over time is anticipated in both the individual and the contexts. Moreover, it is expected that the importance of any one domain will vary depending on the developmental level of the individual.

With this general depiction in mind, we will selectively examine the family, peers (who operate both in the neighborhood and school), the school, social class, and culture. Within such contexts the individ-

ual's social, intellectual, and physical attributes develop.

The family. In all societies, the family is considered a major, if not *the* major, arena for socialization of children (Maccoby, 1992). Family influence is dominant during childhood when malleability is high, it is especially pervasive and strong, and it may endure over the entire lifespan.

Important views of the family have been offered by psychoanalytic and social learning theories (Lynn, 1974; Rutter and Cox, 1985). Psychoanalytic theory views development as the result of the child's moving through psychosexual conflicts that are largely played out with the parents. The child is seen as identifying with the parents, especially the same-sex parent, thereby adopting parental values, standards, and sex role. Many of the specific hypotheses made by this theory have not been borne out (Rutter and Cox, 1985). Social learning theorists rely heavily on learning principles to conceptualize family influence. Parents are seen as shaping their children's development through reinforcement and punishment and by serving as behavioral models. The effects of these crucial processes depend at least in part on the child's cognitive level, expectations, and beliefs (Kagan, 1984).

Theories of the family have been useful in proposing hypotheses about family functioning, and in recent decades empirical investigations have provided a wealth of information about family interactions, roles, and structures.

FAMILY INTERACTIONS AND ROLES. Direct observations of nuclear families (that is, parents and offspring) indicate some differences in father and mother interactions with their children. Fathers spend less time with their offspring, provide less care, and engage in more active, physical activity and play (Biller, 1993; Collins and Russell, 1991;

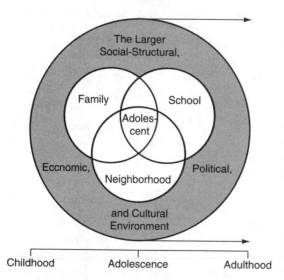

FIGURE 2–2 Social-Cultural Context and Development over Time.

Adapted from Jessor, 1993.

Ninio and Rinott, 1988). Fathers also tend to treat their children in gender stereotypic ways; for example, they encourage gender-related play and more readily accept dependency in girls. In contrast, mothers interact more around caregiving activities and tend to treat daughters and sons more alike (Lytton and Romney, 1991). These differences should not be over-emphasized, however, as father and mother interactions with their children are probably more alike than different. This might be particularly so when fathers assume a relatively strong role in caregiving. Moreover, it is clear that both parents have influence on their offspring. Historically, mother influence has received much more attention and only during the last two decades has extensive research been directed towards fathers. With regard to behavioral problems of youth, mothers have often been implicated whereas the role of fathers is comparatively uninvestigated (Phares, 1992).

Family interaction studies do indicate that the nuclear family is a complex, interacting system. For example, the presence of a third family member changes social interaction between two other members (Stewart et al., 1987). Patterson's (1986) work with families with an antisocial child describes how a hostile response by one family member elicits hostility in return, and other family members might also join in. Based on many similar research findings, the once popular view of family influence flowing only from parents to children is now rejected. It is currently well recognized that parents not only influence children and each other but that children also influence parents. This is not to say that the parent-child relationship is symmetrical, or even should be. Parents select the settings in which children develop, control access to material goods, exert physical control, and have greater knowledge than their children (Maccoby, 1992).

Such asymmetry suggests the importance of parenting styles (Dobow, Huesmann and Eron, 1987; Maccoby, 1992). Table 2–5 presents three parenting styles and the child characteristics thought to be associated with them. It is generally agreed that both excessive (authoritarian) and too little (indulgent/permissive) parental control have negative developmental consequences for children (Eccles et al., 1993). In contrast, the authoritative style is associated with positive child outcomes. A warm versus cold, distant style is also associated with positive child outcomes. An additional aspect is the

TABLE 2–5 Patterns of Parental Behavior and Related Child Characteristics

Authoritarian: Parents set rules with little input from children and forbid children to challenge them. Rule deviation results in fairly severe punishment, often physical.	Children tend to withdraw and show little social interaction. They have low self-esteem, and lack spontaneity and internal locus of control.
Indulgent/permissive: Parents tolerate childrens' impulses, make few demands for mature behavior, use little punishment, allow children to regulate their own lives.	Children tend to be impulsive, aggressive, and lack independence and ability to take responsibility.
Authoritative: Parents expect mature behavior, set standards and enforce them, encourage children to express ideas, recognize both parental and children's rights, encourage independence and individuality.	Children tend to be independent, socially responsible, able to control aggression, self-confident and of high self-esteem.

Based on Maccoby and Martin, 1983.

degree to which parents are involved with their children or committed to parenting. Parents low in involvement give little time, attention, or emotional commitment to their offspring. It is reasonable to assume that the optimal amount of involvement lessens as children become older, but some degree of involvement throughout life seems to have positive consequences.

FAMILY STRUCTURE. A relatively recent change in U.S. families is that most women, even mothers of young children, work outside of the home. This has created interest in the effects of parental employment, which could influence parents' investment in their children, perceptions of and expectations for children's behavior, and parenting styles (Greenberger and Goldberg, 1989; Greenberger, O'Neil, and Nagel, 1994). What does research tell us about the influence of maternal employment? Overall, effects depend on specific factors (Lerner and Galambos, 1986). These include maternal factors (e.g., mothers' attitudes), the work situation (e.g., prestige of the job), family factors (e.g., fathers' involvement), and child characteristics (e.g., temperament, age, gender). Variables can combine to foster or hinder optimal development. For example, positive outcomes are more likely when mothers are satisfied with their work and roles and less stressed (Gottfried and Gottfried, 1988).

When we consider family structure, we tend to think of the nuclear family of two parents and their offspring. But great numbers of youth in the United States experience divorce; one in four children are affected before age sixteen (Barnes, 1994). Many live in single-parent, step-families, or other family arrangements. These children are at some developmental risk (Emery, 1982; Wallerstein and Corbin, 1991). However, the families vary a great deal, as do children's needs and coping abilities. It is not the structure itself that matters, but the way in which the family is able to function (Emery, Hetherington, and DiLalla, 1984).

Finally, it is important to consider the general finding that children living in the same family grow up to be quite different from each other, partly because their experiences are different (Plomin and Rende, 1991). Many things make this so. Each child has a unique place in the family and experiences unique interactions. Particular events, whether a divorce or change of residence, occur at a different age for each child. And each child probably has a unique perspective of family events and functioning. In addition, of course, young people are shaped by forces outside the family.

Peers.   In all societies children are exposed to other young people, and peer relationships contribute to development. Much before preschool age, children begin to distinguish between what is "adult" and "child." Peer relationships change over time, growing in complexity and importance throughout childhood into adolescence (Brownell, 1986; Hartup, 1983; Corsaro and Eder, 1990).

Relationships with peers are qualitatively different than those with adults and they do not serve the exact same functions. This is an important area for further research because some children show a stronger preference for peers over adults than do others (Harper and Huie, 1987). Moreover, with so many parents working outside of the home, children spend much time with peers in day care and the neighborhood.

Peers can influence each other in many ways, and the functions of peer cultures differ somewhat with age. Overall, peers provide opportunities for the learning of social skills, help set social values, serve as standards against which children judge themselves, and give or withhold emotional support. Peers reinforce behavior, serve as behavioral models, and enter into friendships and other social relationships.

Some children are more accepted and popular with their peers than others. Some are actively disliked and rejected. Poor peer relationships, especially rejection, is linked to childhood and adolescent problems in complex ways (Boivin and Begin, 1989; Parker and Asher, 1987). Thus, it is important to understand the factors involved in peer status. The child's characteristics play some role. The accepted child is likely to be socially competent, friendly, helpful, and considerate (Dunn and McGuire, 1992). Rejection is related to aggression, noncompliance, hyperactivity, and disruptive action. But there are exceptions to this, and peer status is linked to other social domains. For example, teachers can play a role in shaping peer status (White and Kistner, 1992). Several studies also indicate that peer status is related to child-parent interaction and parental characteristics. For example, parents of popular children were found to be authoritative/democratic, whereas parents of rejected children tended to be authoritarian/restrictive (Dekovic and Janssens, 1992). Parental child-rearing style was also linked to the child's behavior, with the democratic style being associated with prosocial behavior. It seems reasonable to assume that what children experience in parent interaction shapes how they relate to peers. At the same time, we know that child characteristics affect parents' behavior. Thus, the causal connections among these factors seem complex.

School. The primary function of the school is to teach intellectual skills and knowledge accumulated by society. Formal education is also charged with broader tasks of socialization (Busch-Rossnagel and Vance, 1982). Schools in the U.S. are expected to transmit social, moral, and political values consonant with democratic ideals. The messages given about these values can act powerfully on development. Furthermore, schools operate as social systems in and of themselves. Classroom structure, pedogogy, rules, methods of discipline, standards, and expectations all play a role in shaping individual children. Indeed, a considerable amount of research now indicates that schools exert sizeable influences on academic achievement and social behavior such as delinquency and later employment (Sylva, 1994). Some of these influences appear to operate directly while others operate indirectly by affecting students' motivation to learn, their self-concepts with regard to learning, and their cognitions about learning (such as the belief that effort leads to achievement).

There is evidence that some schools are linked more strongly than others to student achievement, regardless of the characteristics of the students who attend them. That is, certain qualities of school climate and practice foster scholastic and positive social behaviors (Eccles et al., 1993; Howlin, 1994; Rutter, 1983a). Among these are:

1. Clear, agreed-on goals and values
2. Goals that foster positive attitudes toward education, prosocial group behavior, social cohesiveness, and opportunities for all students
3. Most class time given to individualized, structured curriculum with student feedback
4. Positive teacher-student relationships, and teachers who model positive behaviors
5. Opportunities for students to act responsibly and to participate in the running of the school
6. Good discipline, with appropriate praise and encouragement and little use of punishment
7. Good working conditions

School experiences may influence children's futures by setting into motion particular events that continue the shaping process (Rutter, 1983a). By helping the child achieve academically, schools may open career doors. By instilling values, work habits, and self-esteem, schools may continue to impact learning and social development.

Social class and culture. Social class, or socioeconomic status (SES), is determined by factors such as family income, educational achievement, and occupational level, which correlate with each other. Virtually all societies are stratified according to social class, and social class is marked by differences in many facets of life—environmental conditions, social interactions, values, attitudes, expectations, and opportunities.

For example, there is evidence that families that are economically insecure believe that they have little control over their lives. They thus may socialize their children in ways that ensure job security, acceptance by others, and sensitivity to being exploited by others (Kagan, 1984). Middle-class families seem to emphasize choice, intellectual challenges, and job status; they expect their children to have control over their lives and influence others. These differences may translate into how children are managed. In fact, child rearing practices do vary by social class (Rutter and Cox, 1985). In general, lower SES parents tend to be more restrictive, use more physical punishment, anticipate less independence, and rear children to be more compliant. Moreover, research suggests that higher social class is associated with parents' giving more time, effort, and verbal attention to their young children (Hart and Risley, 1992).

The adverse influence of social class is especially notable in lower-class families. Children of poor families are more likely to die and to suffer from disease and disability. Figure 2–3 shows the death rate of infants under one year for the total U.S. population and for the white and black populations. The disadvantage of black people is due at least in part to their disproportionate rate of poverty. Birth weight—a factor in infant death, deformity, and later developmental problems—is related to social class. Poor maternal and medical care probably underlies this unfortunate association. Poverty also works against family stability and in-

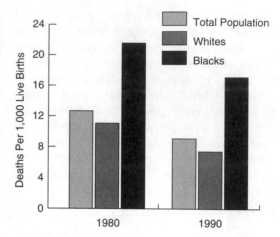

FIGURE 2–3 Death rate of infants under one year of age.

U.S. Bureau of the Census, Statistical Abstract of the United States: 1994 (114th Ed.). Washington, DC, 1994.

creases stress. Upon reaching school, children of poor families do less well, and as adults they acquire less desirable jobs and have higher rates of unemployment. This disadvantageous pattern often repeats itself over generations.

The influence of social class—and all of the other social influences we have examined—operates within some broader cultural context. A society's beliefs and values make their way into social structures, social roles, and ways of "doing business," all of which impact the socialization of children. So we see, for example, that mothers and teachers in Japan and the United States interact differently with children, and that this is linked to children's characteristics (McDermott, 1991). Culture not only affects the goals toward which youth are shaped but also influences how these goals are attained.

Our overview of the social-cultural context of development is necessarily selective. We have tried to capture important examples and issues, and show that influences are not independent of each other. Rather, they overlap and one social context impacts others (Bronfenbrenner, 1986). The social world is complex, dynamic, and challenging. As we will see in the following section, development itself is best described in this way.

HOW DEVELOPMENT OCCURS: MULTIFACTOR, INTEGRATIVE MODELS

Today most developmentalists view growth as the result of numerous variables: biological, psychological, and sociocultural. These multifactor, or integrative, models of development are variously known as interactional or transactional models. They assume that many factors interact to bring about developmental change, and that interaction is ongoing (transactional). Although this assumption may now seem commonsensical, there is a long history of trying to explain development in simpler ways. Perhaps the simpler approach was due partly to the difficulty of dealing with more complex explanations of behavior. Developmentalist who employ integrative models do so in somewhat different ways. Here, we will examine two examples (Compas, Hinden, and Gerhardt, 1995), both of which address behavior problems.

The Biopsychosocial Model

As its name implies, the biopsychosocial model presumes that development is a function of interacting biological and psychosocial variables. In past times, the dichotomy was made between biological and environmental (psychosocial) determinants of development. Some had argued that biological influences, especially genetic programming, primarily determined how children would "turn out." Others had argued that environmental experiences and learning played the critical role in development. Today this nature-nurture dichotomy is rejected on the basis of empirical evidence. For example, research with animals shows that optimal development of the brain and visual system

depends on both genetic programming and stimulation from the environment (e.g., Aoki and Siekevitz, 1988).

An especially telling example of the interplay of biology and environment in humans is provided by children born prematurely or suffering medical complications just before or after birth (Sameroff, 1990; Greenberg and Crnic, 1988). Overall, these individuals have more neurological and intellectual difficulties later in life than full-term infants. Still, it was discovered that many do well, and that it is difficult to predict developmental outcome based on the severity of birth complications. When children are severely biologically damaged, the outcome is likely to be poor. But for most cases, an important predictor of outcome is social class/home environment. When family and cultural factors enhance development, children with even severe birth complications can become indistinguishable from those who suffered no birth complications. It is now commonly acknowledged that the development of children born with adverse medical experiences requires a multifactor explanation that considers biological and psychosocial variables.

The "Goodness-of-Fit" Model

Earlier in this chapter, we referred to the research on temperament. Recall that Chess and Thomas identified individual differences in temperament early in life. These investigators also found that many children could be classified as temperamentally "difficult": They displayed negative mood, high-intensity reactions, irregularities of sleep, and the like. These children were more likely to have behavioral problems. However, Chess and Thomas recognized that final outcome depended partly on how the children "fit" or matched their environments. If the parents of a difficult child downplayed the difficulties and optimally managed them, behavior problems were less likely to develop. In other words, development depended on how well the person and environment fit each other.

This basic conceptualization is central in the work of Eccles and her colleagues (1993), which deals with early adolescence. In the United States, the adolescent years are widely viewed as a time of biological and psychosocial transition, which is successfully negotiated by most individuals. However, 15–30 percent of adolescents drop out of school, regularly consume alcohol and drugs, and get into legal trouble. Many of the problems begin in early adolescence. Eccles and her colleagues hypothesize that this situation results from a mismatch between the needs of developing adolescents and the opportunities provided by the school and family. We will look at one of their analyses.

The researchers found that teachers and adolescents agreed that there was less opportunity for students to participate in decision making in the seventh grade (junior high) than in the sixth. However, the adolescents also reported that they desired increased participation during this time of their lives. Thus, a mismatch between the social environment and adolescent needs was revealed—and would be expected to breed problems. Noteworthy is that the more physically mature females (who were reaching adolescence earlier) perceived the mismatch as greater than girls who were less physically mature. Eccles and her colleagues found this especially interesting because other studies had shown that early-maturing girls report engaging in more school truancy and misbehavior compared to less mature girls as they moved into junior high school. All these findings suggest that a mismatch between adolescent need for autonomy and the school environment might explain the development of problems. In this developmental analysis, pubertal status interacts with the social environment to bring about a poor person-environment fit. Such a multifactor, interactional analysis has much

to offer as we seek to better understand the development of behavior problems.

CONCEPTUALIZING DEVELOPMENTAL INFLUENCES

An enormous number of variables obviously can play a role in development. Conceptualizing them simply as biological, psychological, and sociocultural is only a first step in thinking about developmental influences. There are several other useful ways to view developmental factors or influences.

Normative and Nonnormative Influences

A distinction can be made between normative and nonnormative influences (Gerrity, Jones, and Self, 1983). *Normative age-graded* influences affect most all individuals at similar times of life. For example, puberty occurs for most people between the ages of eleven to fourteen, and entrance into elementary school between five to seven. *Normative history-graded* influences affect most all people of the same generation, or cohort. Examples are the experience of war or economic depression or a women's movement. In contrast, *nonnormative* influences, although not necessarily unusual in themselves, may occur only to certain persons, perhaps at unpredictable times and in atypical circumstances. Examples are severe illness, premature death of a parent, and being born into the upper social class. Nonnormative events are the chance events that affect development. We would expect the content of normative and nonnormative influences to vary somewhat across cultures, but in any case there is value in recognizing both types of influence when examining development.

The Timing of Influences

It is widely held that events and experiences may have different influences depending on the developmental status of the organism. There are several reasons for this (Rutter, 1989c). How the nervous system is affected by experience depends on its developmental status. The effects of experience also depend on the psychological processes that emerge at different times. Thus, separation from parents is probably less impactful for children at five months of age than at three years because attachment is less formed at five months. Timing may also be important in that events occurring at nonnormative times (for example, late physical maturation or teenage marriage) can result in heightened stress or opportunities.

Developmentalists have been especially interested in the influence of early experience on the origin of behavior problems. Research with animals indicates that early experiences can indeed impact brain and behavioral development. Theoretical propositions have also argued for the importance of early influence. Freud (1949) regarded the infant's love for its mother as the prototype for all later love relationships and thus crucial for social-personality development. We have seen how this idea has been applied to the research on early attachment. Social learning theorists have suggested that early learning might be especially important simply because it is the basis for later learning. The extreme position about early experience argues that the first few years of life are critical in that they set later development. Much research indicates that this extreme view is unfounded. The more moderate and popular view asserts that early life may be a sensitive but not critical period, that no experience sets an irretrievable path through life (e.g., Ramey and Campbell, 1987; Rutter and Garmezy, 1983). Humans are malleable, most developmental outcomes are determined by many variables, and later experience can often moderate what has gone before. This is not to say, of course, that effort should not be made to provide children with early optimal environments.

Permissive and Efficient Causes of Behavior Problems

In noting that behavior has multiple influences, Cicchetti and Schneider-Rosen (1986) have discussed causation as either permissive or efficient. *Permissive* causes are dispositions toward certain behaviors. *Efficient* causes bring these dispositions to realization. Take the example of Down's syndrome, in which the child has a particular chromosome abnormality. This abnormality is a strong permissive cause. Nevertheless, even in the face of a clearly biological cause, the specific developmental outcome will depend somewhat on factors that realize the condition (efficient causes), many of which are social and psychological, such as the quality of care the child receives.

The distinction between permissive and efficient causes is useful in that it recognizes that the many factors that may play a role in development do not necessarily play the same or equal roles. Moreover, there may be cases in which no factor is clearly permissive. Here, different influences may add or multiply and reach a threshold to produce an adverse outcome.

Direct and Indirect Influences

It is also fruitful to recognize that effects may be direct or indirect. When a direct effect operates, variable X leads straight to outcome Y. Indirect effects are operating when X influences one or more variables that, in turn, lead to Y. It is usually more difficult to establish indirect effects because a pathway of influence exists that may be complex.

RISK AND RESILIENCY

Still another way to conceptualize developmental influences falls under the rubric of risk and resiliency. There is enormous interest today in understanding the factors that make it more or less likely that a child will develop disordered behavior. Such information might increase knowledge about etiology and be valuable in preventing problems.

Risk factors, or risks, are variables that increase the chance of behavior deviations or difficulties. In the presence of risk, some individuals succumb (are vulnerable) whereas others maintain healthy functioning, that is, are resilient. Resilience implies protection from risk factors, or the ability to bounce back in the face of life's adversities (Smith and Prior, 1995).

Risk

Researchers have identified many risk factors. Table 2–6 shows one way to conceptualize risk. Some risk factors can be viewed as stemming from individual disposition to respond maladaptively to life experiences. Disposition may arise through biological mechanisms or life experiences, or the combination of these. Difficult temperament is an example of a dispositional risk factor. Risk is also based in life adversities or events that bring stress or strain (Garmezy, 1994; Garmezy and Masten, 1994). Stress factors can be acute, occurring suddenly and perhaps calamitously, or they can be chronic (e.g., poverty). Some life events, such as the early death of a parent, may appear on the surface to be acute and limited, but they hold the potential for chronic demands and strains.

Research has gone beyond the simple identification of risk factors. Current understanding of risk includes the following findings (Kopp, 1994; Lambert, 1988; Liaw and Brooks-Gunn, 1994; Rutter, 1987).

1. Some risk factors are strongly associated with developmental problems (e.g., specific chromosome abnormalities), whereas outcome is more variable for others.

2. There is some connection between risk factors and specific disorders. For example, risk factors may be somewhat different for intellectual deficits than for behavioral difficulties. The same may hold for levels of dysfunction within a disorder; for instance, genetic and prenatal factors are relatively strong risks for severe mental retardation compared to mild retardation.

3. It is likely that youth are more vulnerable to risk at certain times in development, for example, during early prenatal growth and during adolescence. Moreover, at any one time youth may be more affected by certain risk factors than others.

4. The number of risk factors present is important. A single factor may certainly have an impact, but multiple risk factors have been shown to be especially deleterious. As the number increases, so does negative outcome.

5. Risk may accumulate over time to set up pathways of risk. That is, the impact of a risk factor may increase the likelihood of future risks. Such pathways may be complex, and may well be different for specific disorders or even for different outcomes within a disorder.

TABLE 2–6   Some Developmental Risk Factors

Constitutional
   Hereditary influences; gene abnormalities
   Prenatal, birth complications
   Postnatal disease, damage
   Inadequate health care, nutrition
Family
   Poverty
   Abuse, neglect
   Conflict, disorganization, psychopathology, stress
   Large family size
Emotional and Interpersonal
   Psychological patterns such as low self-esteem, emotional immaturity, difficult temperament
   Social incompetence
   Peer rejection
Intellectual and Academic
   Below average intelligence, learning disability
   Academic failure
Ecological
   Neighborhood disorganization, crime
   Racial, ethnic, gender injustice
Nonnormative Stressful Life Events
   Early death of a parent
   Outbreak of war in immediate environment

Based in part on Coie et al., 1993.

Researchers are interested in examining the processes that underlie risk. The distinction may be made between distal and proximal variables. Take for instance, the risk factor of low social class. This is a distal factor, a description of the environment that can be considered as background, or some distance from the individual. But social class is associated with or mediated by variables that operate in the immediate context, such as lack of social support or parental rearing style associated with social class. It is such proximal variables that are likely to tell us more about the processes of risk (e.g., Bendersky and Lewis, 1994).

Resiliency

In the presence of risk factors, why do some individuals succumb while others appear to rise above threat, to be resilient? As with risk, protection has been viewed as residing in the individual or the environment.

One of the first studies of resiliency was conducted on the Hawaiian island of Kauai (Garmezy and Masten, 1994; Werner and Smith, 1982). The participants, who were studied into late adolescence, were at potential risk due to chronic adversities associated with poverty and family variables. Although most developed problems, one-third were successfully negotiating their lives. The investigators summarized the reasons for resiliency into three broad categories. One category concerned personal attributes; those who enjoyed success were, for example, intelligent, sociable, and socially competent. Second, family strengths existed in that families provided affection and support in times of stress. Third, support outside the family, from individuals and institutions such as the school and church, appeared to foster self-worth and self-efficacy in the children. The resilient children apparently had been exposed to less actual risk and more protection.

Resiliency is often conceptualized as arising from the child's competence and adaptability. Garmezy (1975) suggested that competence is indicated by self-esteem, self-discipline, belief that events can be controlled, regulation of impulsive behavior, and ability to think abstractly and flexibly. Research has identified intelligence and other personal attributes as minimizing the impact of risk. For example, self-understanding and the ability to independently think and act appear to protect adolescents from the negative effects of their parents' psychiatric disturbance (Beardslee and Podorefsky, 1988). Other personal attributes that may provide protection in specific situations include age, gender, and social skills (Luthar, 1993).

Nevertheless, as we have already recognized, protection is also afforded by certain environmental variables. Unsurprisingly, family factors can be crucial. For example, children facing the stress of parental divorce can be protected by a close relationship with one parent. Support from the wider social environment—from teachers, peers, and others—can also make a critical difference.

As with risk, there is a need to better understand the complexities of resiliency and the mechanisms that underlie it. For example, do personal attributes and factors in the social environment interact to produce protection? If so, how and when? The competent, self-assured girl may protect herself, for example, by rejecting self-blame or alternatively she may understand the need for social support and be especially effective in obtaining it. Perhaps several mechanisms are likely. Current research on resiliency is focusing on understanding such underlying processes.

Ultimately, of course, it is hoped that research into risk and protection will contribute strongly to prevention and amelioration of behavior disorder. While we are far from a comprehensive approach, it is not too early to offer suggestions. Table 2–7 is taken from Rutter's description of four gen-

TABLE 2–7   Rutter's Description of Four Protective Mechanisms

Reduction of Risk Impact
  The impact of risk can be reduced by:
    providing the child with practice in coping
    reducing demands of the risk factor
    preparing the child for the situation
    exposing the child when he/she can cognitively handle the situation
    decreasing exposure to the risk factor

Reduction of Negative Chain Reactions
  Exposure to risk often sets up a chain of reactions that perpetuates risk effects into the future. Interventions that prevent such chains are protective.

Development of Self-esteem and Self-efficacy
  People's concepts and feelings about their social environments, their worth, and their ability to deal with life's challenges are important. Positive development results from satisfying social relationships and success in accomplishing tasks.

Opening of Opportunities
  Many events, particularly at turning points in people's lives, reduce risk by providing opportunities for adaptive growth. Examples are changes in geographic location, chance to continue one's education, shifts in family roles.

Adapted from Rutter, 1987.

eral ways in which young people might be protected. Rutter sees these as operating at key turning points in people's lives, when risk can be redirected. For Rutter, protection resides in the ways in which people deal with life changes and in what they do about their stressful or disadvantageous circumstances. Continued research in this area is bound to lead to better knowledge of why and how vulnerable youth succumb to risk in varying degrees while resilient youth react in constructive ways—even in the face of seemingly overwhelming adversity.

CHANGE AND CONTINUITY

Developmentalists have an interest in understanding change and continuity over time. Here we will look at two related aspects of this issue that are relevant to disordered behavior: the relationship between early and late disorders and developmental pathways.

Is Early Disorder Linked to Later Disorder?

Development is defined in terms of change, and humans certainly are malleable. But there are limits to malleability and so some continuity over time might be expected (Lerner, 1987). This is exemplified in physical aging. When a man reaches old age, his face appears both similar to and different from how it looked at age ten, twenty, and forty. However, it may be quite difficult to specifically describe how the transformation occurred and to predict appearance at old age from appearance in youth. This example can be applied to psychological functioning. In a general way we can anticipate both change and continuity as individuals travel along life's pathways, although much is yet to be learned about transformation.

When the issue of continuity and change is applied to the study of behavior disorders, a central question is: Do behavior problems at earlier times in life carry over to, or predict, disorders in later life? This question is important for understanding the development of behavior problems, and it also has implications for treatment and prevention. Behavior problems are always of concern to the degree that they cause discomfort and unhappiness and close the door of opportunities for growth. When they continue into adulthood in some fashion, they have even graver implications.

It is important to note that it is often quite difficult to trace the course of a disorder over time. At different developmental levels behaviors that appear different from each other may actually express the same underlying disturbance. To take a simple example, a five-year-old may demonstrate aggression by slapping a playmate, while an adolescent is more likely to use subtle sarcasm. The term *heterotypic continuity* refers to the continuance of a behavior in which the form of the behavior changes with development or over time. Efforts to understand the link between early and later disorders must deal with this phenomenon.

What is known about the continuity of disorders? Unsurprisingly, we see both continuity and change. Some problems are quite transitory. For example, the frequency of enuresis (bed wetting past four or five years of age) drops considerably after childhood. Childhood aggression and antisocial behavior are relatively stable over time (McMahon and Forehand, 1988). Children who show hyperactivity tend to display academic and social deficits in adolescence, and about half display some continuation of maladaptive behaviors into adulthood (Weiss and Hechtman, 1986). Specific links between early and later emotional problems, such as depression, have become better established than they once were (Cantwell and Rutter, 1994). Moreover, some disorders are notably stable, such as severe mental retardation and autism.

Again, developmentalists seek to understand processes by which continuity may occur. As an example, we will look at the study conducted by Caspi, Elder, and Bem (1987), in which the continuity of behavior of eight- to ten-year-olds was traced across thirty years. The behavior examined was an ill-tempered interactional style, represented in childhood by temper tantrums (biting, kicking, striking) and verbal explosions (swearing, screaming, shouting). For boys, an association was found between this behavior and adult undercontrol, moodiness, irritability, and lower dependability, production, and ambition. The men experienced erratic work patterns and downward occupational mobility, and were likely to divorce. For girls, childhood tantrums were related to marriage to men of low occupational status, unhappy marriage and divorce, and ill temperedness as mothers. The researchers suggest two processes by which maladaptive behavior is maintained over time. *Cumulative continuity* stems from children's channeling themselves into environments that perpetuate the maladaptive style. The ill-tempered boy may limit opportunity by dropping out of school, thereby creating frustrating situations, to which he responds with more irritability, undercontrol, and the like. *Interactional continuity* originates in the transaction between the person and the environment. The person acts, others respond accordingly, and the person reacts to this. It is assumed that the coercive, ill-tempered style of the child pays off in the short-run so that through reinforcement it is maintained, only to eventually be destructive.

Caspi and his colleagues make no explicit assumption that ill-temperedness has genetic origins, but other research indicates that both experiential and biological variables may well play a role in linking early and later behaviors. This line of investigation increasingly describes developmental pathways by which early and later behaviors are linked.

Pathways of Development

From our discussion of the many variables that contribute to development, it is obvious that it is difficult to predict the developmental path of any one individual. Nevertheless, researchers have begun to describe a number of developmental pathways. Some indicate stability and others indicate change.

Figure 2–4 indicates five trajectories that map development across the adolescent years in terms of adaptation (Compas et al., 1995). Path 1 is characterized by stable adaptation, that is, positive self-worth and lack of problems. Path 2 indicates stable maladaptation. Path 3 shows maladaptation at the beginning of adolescence that turns into positive outcome. Path 4 shows adaptation at the beginning that turns into decline. Path 5 indicates a temporary decline in adolescence but a bouncing back to adaptive behavior. The figure notes risk and protective factors and provides examples of populations of youth who as a group show these various trajectories. Interesting in itself, the mapping of pathways also allows us to better envision the possibili-

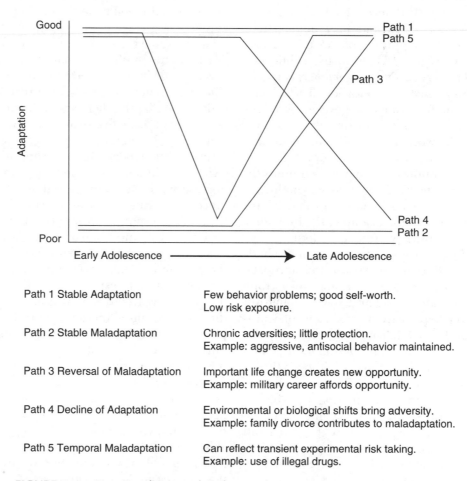

Path 1 Stable Adaptation	Few behavior problems; good self-worth. Low risk exposure.
Path 2 Stable Maladaptation	Chronic adversities; little protection. Example: aggressive, antisocial behavior maintained.
Path 3 Reversal of Maladaptation	Important life change creates new opportunity. Example: military career affords opportunity.
Path 4 Decline of Adaptation	Environmental or biological shifts bring adversity. Example: family divorce contributes to maladaptation.
Path 5 Temporal Maladaptation	Can reflect transient experimental risk taking. Example: use of illegal drugs.

FIGURE 2–4 Five Developmental Pathways during Adolescence. From Compas, Hinden, and Gerhardt, 1995.

ties of optimal development. This work, which is based on investigations that followed certain people over time, is another example of how the developmental approach can advance knowledge of behavioral dysfunction, and how normal and abnormal development go hand-in-hand.

DEVELOPMENTAL PSYCHOPATHOLOGY AND OTHER APPROACHES

We began this chapter by describing developmental psychopathology as a broad framework for relating normal and abnormal development and behavior. As Achenbach (1990) and others have made clear, the approach adopts general developmental principles and findings but does not impose specific theoretical explanations. Achenbach views the developmental approach as a way of integrating other approaches and theories around a core of developmental issues and questions. He thus labels it a "macroparadigm," a broad perspective that subsumes other perspectives, or "microparadigms." Figure 2–5 presents this idea in schematic form. Each microparadigm in this schema offers a specific view of behavior disorders. Each makes its own assumptions, offers theoretical concepts, asks specific questions, and adopts certain methods to answer

questions. It is to such perspectives that we turn in the next chapter of this text.

SUMMARY

The developmental approach to the study of behavior disorders offers developmental norms, hypotheses, and a framework within which to understand problems of youth. Development refers to change over the lifespan that proceeds in a coherent manner along various pathways. Change can take many forms, but has limits. Developmental change is a product of transactions among biological, psychological, and sociocultural variables.

The biological basis of development is the chromosomes, which direct the biochemistry of the body. Hereditary influence, which is complex and indirect, sets a range within which characteristics develop and programs change as well as stability.

Early physical and motor growth occur in universal, orderly sequences, which suggests biological programming. The nervous system, which grows from the neural plate, is relatively well developed at birth, and further development depends on both biological and environmental influences.

Motor capacity changes from simple, reflexive to voluntary, coordinated function-

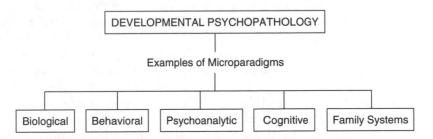

FIGURE 2–5 Developmental Psychopathology as a Macroparadigm.

Adapted from Achenbach, T. M. (1990). Conceptualizations of developmental psychopathology. In M. Lewis & S. M. Miller (Eds.), Handbook of developmental psychopathology, NY: Plenum Press. By permission.

ing. Complex motor skills depend on heredity, motivation, and opportunities to learn and practice. Motor development, the timing of maturation, and physical attractiveness can influence psychosocial growth.

From birth, children have the capacity to perceive the environment and to learn. Learning and thinking develop gradually. Piaget's theory of cognitive development proposes that through assimilation and accommodation children develop increasingly sophisticated schemas of the world. Such development is hypothesized to occur in four distinct stages.

By age five, basic language skills are acquired. The capacity for language clearly is programmed into the human species, but interaction with others shapes development. Language skill has implications both for intellectual and psychosocial functioning.

Among the many facets of socioemotional growth that researchers study are temperament and the emotions. Temperament refers to biologically based, modifiable individual differences in emotionality, activity, and sociability. The rudiments of emotion are present from early life, and by age five or six children show considerable ability to express emotion and to interpret the emotions of others. Both temperament and the emotions play a role in social interaction and behavior problems.

Attachment, the early socioemotional bond between infants and their caretakers, has been studied extensively. Parental sensitivity to the infant, infant temperament, and the social context influence attachment. From this first relationship, the child's social environment broadens to include an array of other relationships.

The social context of development consists of overlapping, interacting domains of structures and influences. Family interaction is complex, with each person impacting others. Fathers and mothers interact somewhat differently with their offspring, but both parents influence their children. Stud-ies of parenting styles suggest that an authoritative, warm style and appropriate involvement foster favorable development. Today's analyses of family life must consider the many changes in family structures and roles. And it is important to recognize that children growing up in the same family are quite different from each other.

Peers influence each other in many ways. Some children are readily accepted by their peers; others are rejected. Poor peer relationships are associated with childhood and later problem behavior.

Schools that promote positive academic and social behaviors appear to have certain characteristics. Development is influenced by knowledge and skills acquired in school and also by the values, work habits, and self-concepts that schools encourage.

The impact of social class operates in part through family socialization practices that vary with social class. Low SES disadvantages children due to poverty, less than optimal health care, higher family stress, and lower school achievement. Social class and other social influences operate within a larger cultural context of beliefs and values.

Today, multifactor, integrative models of development are popular. They assume that biological and psychosocial variables continuously interact to bring about development. The biopsychosocial and goodness-of-fit models are important examples.

There are several useful ways to conceptualize developmental factors or influences. Development is affected by normative age-related and history-related events, and non-normative factors. With regard to behavior problems, the concepts of permissive and efficient causation are useful. Permissive causes are dispositions toward certain behaviors; efficient causes realize the dispositions. In some instances, no factor appears permissive; rather, several causal factors add or otherwise combine to cause psychopathology. The timing of experience is also considered influential. Early experience is important but does not set an irretrievable pathway. When analyzing developmental effects, it is also useful to recognize that influence may be direct or indirect, with indirect effects often more difficult to establish.

There is increasing understanding of the factors that put children at risk for developing dysfunctional behavior or provide protection from risk. Both risk and resiliency reside in the individual and the environment. Researchers are examining the processes by which risk and resiliency operate.

The issue of change and continuity of behavior is a central concern of developmentalists. Both change and continuity are seen in disturbed as well as adaptive behavior. Among the processes by which maladaptive behavior is maintained are cumulative and interactional continuity. Several trajectories of adaptation-maladaptation through the adolescent years have been suggested by research studies. Stability characterizes two of these trajectories, while instability characterizes others.

The developmental approach contributes to understanding both normal and problem behaviors. Developmental principles and findings serve as a framework, or macroparadigm, for organizing other approaches or perspectives.

3

PERSPECTIVES AND MODES OF TREATMENT

In Chapter 2 we examined developmental processes and how the developmental perspective can help us understand behavior disorders of childhood and adolescence. Within this broad developmental paradigm one can identify a number of different views. Each emphasizes some of the influences that contribute to a developmental view of behavior disorders (Achenbach, 1990). We now examine several of these "microparadigms" or perspectives that have been applied to the study of behavior disorders. Before turning to particular viewpoints, however, let us look at the meaning of the terms *perspective* and *paradigm*.

TAKING DIFFERENT PERSPECTIVES

Much of what we now know about behavior problems comes from applying the objective methods of science. However, the writings of Thomas Kuhn (1962) and others have made us increasingly aware that science is not a completely objective endeavor. To understand this point it is best to remember that scientists, like all of us, must think about and deal with a complex world. To do this they make assumptions and form concepts. When a set of such assumptions is shared by a group of investigators,

Kuhn refers to them as a paradigm. Here we employ the terms *perspective, paradigm,* and *view* interchangeably to refer to this perceptual/cognitive "set" that the scientist takes in order to study and understand phenomena.

What are the implications of adopting a particular perspective? Perspectives help us make sense of a puzzling and complex universe. They enable us to view new information in the context of previous experience and to have a basis for reacting to it. Taking a perspective is thus adaptive and functional. At the same time, perspectives limit us as well. They guide us in "selecting" the issues chosen for investigation, but may preclude us from asking certain questions. Once a question is selected for investigation, a decision must be made: What will be observed in order to answer this question? All things are not observed, just some things. Perspectives influence this choice and also how observations are done. In turn, particular methods and instruments help in detecting certain phenomena but result in our missing others. Once information is collected, the adoption of a paradigm affects the interpretation we make of the "facts" we have collected. Overall then, perspective-taking strongly organizes how a problem is approached, investigated, and interpreted.

THE BIOLOGICAL PERSPECTIVE

In its most general form the biological perspective holds that biology plays a central role in the development of behavioral disorders in children and adolescents. The conjecture that psychopathology is due to a defective or malfunctioning biological system can be traced in the Western world to Greek culture. Hippocrates (460–370 B.C.), who is considered the father of medicine, was an advocate of somatogenesis (soma refers to body, genesis means origin). He postulated that proper mental functioning relied on a healthy brain and that deviant thinking or behavior was thus the result of brain pathology.

The biological paradigm initially assumed that biology directly causes abnormal behavior. The original psychiatric classification system developed by Kraeplin in the late 1800s, and the forerunner of current systems, was clearly based on this assumption. Early discoveries of biological causes for particular behavioral problems (for example, the revelation that a spirochete bacterium caused syphilis and the mental deterioration of syphilis's late stages) led to the hope that similar causes would be found for all abnormal behavior. With limited exception, this has not proven to be the case.

Today a widely employed conceptualization of the role of biology is the notion of diathesis-stress—that a biological predisposition toward a disorder (a diathesis) interacts with environmental or life events (stress) to produce a particular behavioral problem. This is a variant of the more broadly conceived notion that biological factors transact with psychological and sociocultural influences.

As we saw in Chapter 2, influence of biological factors on a child's behavior can occur through a variety of mechanisms. Here we will examine three: the structure of the brain, the nervous system and its biochemical functioning, and genetic influences.

The Structure of the Brain

The structural integrity of the nervous system, particularly the brain, is one of the biological influences that has been examined. A cross-section of the human brain is illustrated in Figure 3–1. The brain is typically described as being divided into three major subsections: the hindbrain, midbrain, and

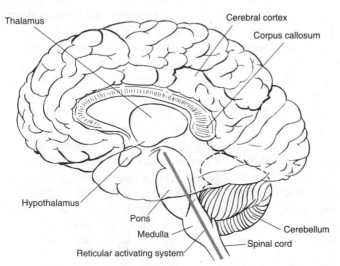

Thalamus

Cerebral cortex

Corpus callosum

Hypothalamus

Pons

Medulla

Reticular activating system

Cerebellum

Spinal cord

FIGURE 3–1 Cross-section of the human brain.

forebrain. The hindbrain, which regulates basic body functions such as sleeping, breathing, heart rate, and body movements, includes the cerebellum, pons, and medulla. The midbrain contains much of the reticular activating system, although this extends into the pons and medulla as well. The reticular activating system regulates sleep and waking. The midbrain also coordinates communication between the hindbrain and the forebrain. The forebrain consists of the two cerebral hemispheres connected by the corpus callosum. Each hemisphere has four regions or lobes. The frontal lobes are located near the front of the brain. The temporal lobes are located near the temples on the side of the brain. The parietal lobes are located near the top-rear of the brain and the occipital lobes are located at the rear of the head.

The cerebral hemispheres are involved in a wide variety of activities such a sensory processing, motor control, and higher mental functioning including information processing, learning, and memory. The thalamus and hypothalamus are structures that lie below the cerebral hemispheres, between the forebrain and midbrain. The thalamus is involved in processing and relaying information between the cerebral cortex and other parts of the central nervous system. The hypothalamus regulates basic urges such as hunger, thirst, and sexual activity. The limbic system, which is composed of parts of the cerebral hemispheres, the thalamus, and the hypothalamus, through its regulation of the endocrine glands and the autonomic nervous system (discussed below), plays a central role in the regulation of emotions and biological urges.

Actual damage to the structural or physiological integrity of the biological system may produce a variety of intellectual and behavioral difficulties. Such known or presumed influence on behavior may occur during pregnancy (prenatally), at about the time of birth (perinatally), or during later development (postnatally).

Prenatal influences.   Damage to the developing fetus by toxic substances is receiving a great deal of public and professional attention. At one time it was believed that the placenta protected the fetus from harmful substances that might enter the mother's blood stream. We now know that a variety of *teratogens* appear to be related to fetal death, disease, malformation, or functional/behavioral effects (Jacobson, Jacobson, and Fein, 1986). The effects of drugs such as thalidomide, alcohol, tobacco, cocaine, heroin, and methadone on prenatal development have received a great deal of study. The potential negative effects of radiation and environmental contaminants such as polychlorinated biphenyls (PCBs) are also well known. In addition many maternal diseases (e.g., rubella, syphilis, gonorrhea) are known to have harmful effects. Acquired Immune Deficiency Syndrome (AIDS) is a growing threat to newborn babies that is of particular current concern.

Clearly many of the findings produce much controversy because they are related to sensitive economic, social, and political issues. Indeed caution is appropriate since ethical considerations do not permit research that would provide clear conclusions, such as studies in which pregnant women would be intentionally exposed to any of these conditions. We thus must rely on animal studies, the results of which may not hold for humans, and on investigations of humans under natural (uncontrolled) conditions. Interpretation of the impact of particular teratogens in such instances is difficult since exposure to any one teratogen can be associated with exposure to others, as well as to other potentially harmful effects such as poor prenatal care, malnutrition, and other factors associated with substance abuse and poverty (cf. Gonzalez and Camp-

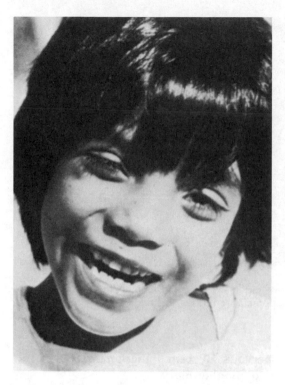

The girl pictured above is one of two daughters born to a, since deceased, alcoholic mother. On the basis of history, mental deficiency, and physical findings, both were diagnosed as having *fetal alcohol syndrome.* Several key features of the syndrome are visible in this girl, including narrow eye openings, underdeveloped-thin upper lip, flattening or absence of the usual indentation under the nose, and possible drooping of the upper eyelids. Behavioral deficits are also implicated in this syndrome.

(Courtesy of March of Dimes Birth Defects Foundation)

bell, 1994; Niccols, 1994). These other factors can influence outcome prenatally and during the child's subsequent development.

Since a wide variety of potential teratogens exist (Kopp and Kaler, 1989), it may not be entirely possible to avoid exposure. Indeed, as women increasingly enter the workplace they increase their risk of exposure to toxic agents. However, a pregnant woman does have some control over her environment; she can take special care not to expose herself to disease and to obtain treatment if a disease is contracted. In addition to teratogens, several other variables such as age of the mother and maternal stress have been associated with infant death and developmental difficulties (Kopp, 1994).

Perinatal and later influences. It is important to note that nervous system damage may also occur during or after birth. At birth, experiences such as excessive medication given to the mother, unusual delivery, and anoxia (lack of oxygen) may result in damage to the newborn. There is evidence to suggest that the frequency of some perinatal complications is greater in lower SES children. Furthermore, as noted in Chapter 2, perinatal complications and SES factors have an interactive effect on the infant's subsequent development (e.g., Liaw and Brooks-Gunn, 1994).

Postnatal damage may occur as a result of experiences such as accident, illness, malnutrition, or accidental poisoning. Exposure of children to lead, even at relatively low levels, is one example of accidental poisoning that has received considerable attention and would appear to have negative impact on processes such as attention and cognitive development (e.g., Fergusson, Horwood, and Lynskey, 1993; Tesman and Hills, 1994).

Regardless of when biological insult occurs, both the site and the severity of brain damage help determine the nature of the difficulties. A precise description of the relationship between damage and dysfunction cannot always be made, however. Thus, the link between brain damage and psychopathology is unclear and in many ways controversial (cf. Taylor and Fletcher, 1990).

One of the major concerns of those who work with children is whether problems arising from brain damage can be remediated. A controversial issue is whether the child's immature central nervous system is

Many head injuries are the result of accidents. The use of helmets for bicycling and other activities can appreciably reduce the number of head injuries.

highly "plastic," that is, more likely to recover after injury, than is the adult system. The issue is a complex one (Fletcher, 1988; Huttenlocher, 1994; Thatcher, 1994). Although there is sometimes remarkable recovery of function in children that is not achieved in adults, younger age is sometimes not associated with better outcomes and age or timing of injury is only one factor affecting recovery. Size, location, and progression of the lesion, severity of the insult, secondary complications such as infection, and type and degree of environmental stimulation are some others. An emphasis on plasticity encourages efforts to develop lost or unachieved functioning, but it may have some negative consequences. Frustration for the child, parent, and teacher may result when complete plasticity is assumed but is not realized. The assumption that the young brain is highly plastic may also lead to imprecise forms of intervention. On the other hand, identification of loss and realistic expectations for recovery can lead to advances in our understanding and to improved remediation.

Nervous System Functioning and Biochemistry

Much of both early and current thinking about the role of biological influences on disordered behavior implicates imbalances in body chemistry. Hippocrates speculated that adequate mental functioning relied on a proper balance of the four bodily humors: blood, phlegm, yellow bile, and black bile. Thus, for example, excessive black bile was thought to produce melancholia, or what we would today label depression.

While specific mechanisms for specific disorders are often questioned, there is fairly broad agreement that biochemistry in some form contributes to disturbed behavior. The biochemistry of neurotransmitters and central nervous system functioning have become important foci of biology's contribution to the study of behavior disorders.

The nervous system has billions of neurons, which conduct the electrochemical impulses by which communication occurs. Neurons have three major parts: a cell body, dendrites which branch out from the cell body and can receive messages from other cells, and axons which transmit messages to other cells. These messages must cross the gap between neurons (the synaptic gap or cleft). When an impulse reaches the end of the axon, neurotransmitters are released that cross the synaptic gap and communicate with another cell through receptor sites on that cell (Figure 3–2).

Neurotransmission can go awry in a number of ways. For example, too much or too little of a particular neurotransmitter can be released. Problems can also exist in reuptake—the process by which the neuron reabsorbs the neurotransmitter for subsequent transmissions. Also, the density and

sensitivity of receptors to a particular neurotransmitter or the presence or absence of other chemicals, known as blocking agents, at the receptor sites can affect neurotransmission. A number of different neurotransmitters have been identified as playing a role in various forms of abnormal behavior such as depression and attention-deficit hyperactivity disorder (cf. Emslie et al., 1994; Pliszka et al., 1994). Norepinephrine, serotonin, dopamine, acetylcholine, and gamma amibutyric acid (GABA) are some of the major neurotransmitters that have been studied. The role of neurotransmitters is described in later chapters on various disorders.

How the biochemistry of the body, not only the brain, reacts to situations an indi-

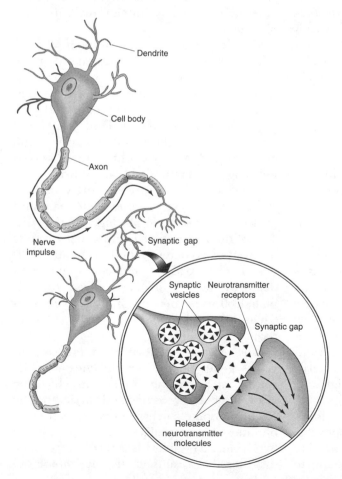

Dendrite

Cell body

Axon

Nerve impulse

Synaptic gap

Synaptic vesicles   Neurotransmitter receptors

Synaptic gap

Released neurotransmitter molecules

FIGURE 3–2 Impulses are transmitted from one neuron to another, across a synaptic cleft or gap, through the release of neurotransmitters.

vidual may encounter is also part of the biological perspective on behavior disorders. The autonomic nervous system helps to regulate one's emotional state. It consists of two branches. The sympathetic nervous system mediates increased arousal, preparing the body for action. The parasympathetic nervous system, on the other hand, works to slow arousal and conserve the body's resources. One of the ways the autonomic nervous system operates is through stimulation of the endocrine system, a collection of glands that release hormones into the bloodstream. Research on neuroendocrine functioning is an important part of the study of a variety of child and adolescent disorders. For example, differences in autonomic reactivity in panic disorder, neurohormonal dysregulation in obsessive-compulsive disorder, and the role of growth hormone regulation in depression have received attention (cf. Dummit and Klein, 1994; Emslie et al., 1994; Leonard et al., 1994). These and other biochemical influences will be discussed in later chapters.

Genetic Influences

The study of genetic influences on human behavior is extremely complex and currently expanding in several directions (Lombroso, Pauls, and Leckman, 1994; Plomin, 1994a; Rutter et al., 1990a). Application to child and adolescent disorders is comparatively under-researched, but this is changing. Genetic research can tell us subtle things about etiology, for example, whether all or only some cases of a disorder are likely to have a genetic component. Genetic research can even confirm the role of environment in causation and point to characteristics of the environment that might be especially important (Plomin, 1994b).

A complete discussion of genetic influence on childhood disorders is not possible here. The topics selected for examination are intended to introduce this area and to facilitate understanding of later discussions of the genetics of specific behavior disorders.

Inheritance through single genes. Beginning with the work of Gregor Mendel, scientists have sought to describe inheritance of certain characteristics controlled by one gene pair. Mendel correctly hypothesized that each parent carries two hereditary factors (later called genes), but passes on only one to the offspring. He also noted that one form of the factor is *dominant*, in that its transmission by either parent leads to the display of that form of the characteristic. The other form, the *recessive*, displays itself only when it is transmitted by both parents. Both of these patterns, and the sex-linked pattern described below, are involved in the inheritance of many human attributes and disorders.

Huntington's chorea is an example of a disease transmitted by a dominant gene. This disease causes death, but does not show up until adulthood, when limb spasms, and mental deterioration and perhaps dementia become evident. Many people know of this inherited disease due to the death by it of Woody Guthrie, a well-known folk singer and father of Arlo Guthrie.

Tay-Sachs disease provides an example of a disorder carried by one gene pair and transmitted *recessively*. A degenerative disease of the nervous system, it usually results in progressive deterioration of mental abilities, motor capacities, and vision, and then death by the age of one to three. An estimated 60 to 90 percent of all cases of Tay-Sachs is found among children of Ashkenazic Jewish heritage.

The *sex-linked* pattern of inheritance involves genes on the sex chromosomes. Of special interest is the situation in which the relevant gene is recessive and carried on the X chromosome, such as in red-green color blindness, hemophilia, and Lesch-Nyhan Syndrome. The latter is a rare, untreatable disorder that results in unusual motor development, mental retardation, and extreme self-mutilation in children. The disorder is found only in males, who die early and thus do not have offspring. The Lesch-Nyhan child has a normal father and a mother who carries the disorder, having one normal X chromosome and one affected X chromosome. Sons receive their only X chromosome from their mothers. Those who receive the recessive defective gene will develop the disorder, since the Y chromosome transmitted from the father carries no gene at all to offset the defective gene. Daughters receive one X chromosome from each parent. If a girl receives the defective recessive gene from her mother, it is usually offset by the dominant normal gene from her father; she has no affliction herself but could transmit Lesch-Nyhan to her son.

Researchers continue to explore the effects of single gene pairs or other relatively simple genetic etiology on specific behavior disorders. Such research has been facilitated by new genetic methods (cf. Lombroso et al., 1994). *Segregation analysis* uses statistical procedures to examine the pattern of disorder as well as genetic makeup within a family and compare it to a specific genetic model of inheritance, such as a dominant or recessive gene model. The results allow inferences about the pattern of genetic inheritance for a disorder. *Linkage analysis* explores whether the pattern in which a specific disorder appears among family members is the same as for genetic markers. The approximate chromosome location is known for the genetic markers. For example, inherited disorders, such as color blindness, that are known to be linked to a particular chromosome have been used as markers. If the behavior disorder and color blindness appear in family members in the same pattern then it can be presumed that the genes that control them are close neighbors on the same chromosome. Advances in molecular genetics have also identified a large group of DNA fragments (called restriction fragment length polymorphisms and variable tandem repeats) for which chromosomal location is known. These fragments can serve as genetic markers for linkage analysis in the same way as indicted for color blindness.

The efforts of Nancy Wexler and a team of research scientists in searching for the gene responsible for Huntington's disease is an example of recent advances. Through the use of linkage analysis techniques the disorder had been mapped to an area on chromosome 4 and recently Wexler's group was able to identify the gene responsible for Huntington's disease (Huntington's Disease Collaborative Research Group, 1993).

Investigating the effects of multiple genes. In contrast to the effects due to a single gene pair, most of the behaviors we are concerned with in studying child and adolescent behavior disorders are thought to involve many genes as well as environmental influences. Such multifactorial inheritance is much more difficult to trace than single gene effects. Accordingly, the study of genetic influences on human behavior relies on a combination of evidence from a variety of research methods. We will now look briefly at the major research methods of behavior genetics.

Youth with behavior disorders often have parents, siblings, and other family members with similar problems. However, such aggregation of behavior problems in families does not mean a genetic influence is operating. Family environment may also be operating. One of the goals of research is thus to determine the degree of genetic influence operating in specific behavior disorders.

The three major research strategies of behavior genetics that have been applied to behavior disorders are the twin, family, and adoption methodologies (Plomin, 1994b). These methods are employed to assess *heritability,* a statistic that indicates the degree to which genetic influence accounts for variance in behavior among individuals in the population studied. Importantly, the contribution of environmental influences is also obtained.

The essence of *twin designs* is a comparison of identical twin resemblance (concordance) to fraternal twin resemblance. Identical or monozygotic (MZ) twins have identical genes. Fraternal or dizygotic (DZ) twins are on average only 50 percent alike genetically; in fact, they are no more alike genetically than any two siblings. In its most basic form, the twin method points to genetic influence if there is greater concordance among identical twins than among fraternal twins. That is, genetic influence is suggested when a disorder occurs more frequently in both members of MZ twin pairs than it does in both members of DZ twin pairs (cf. Edelbrock et al., 1995).

Family studies expand upon the logic of twin studies. The relatives of an individual identified as exhibiting a certain behavior or disorder (the proband) can be examined to determine whether or not the relatives exhibit the same behavior or problem. Identical twins are 100 percent genetically related. First-degree relatives' (parents and their offspring and siblings) average genetic relatedness is 50 percent. Half-siblings and other second-degree relatives are 25 percent genetically related. Third-degree relatives, such as cousins, are only 12.5 percent genetically related. If there is a genetic influence on a disorder, family members who are genetically more similar to the proband should be more likely to exhibit the same or related difficulties. Statistical estimates of heritability are possible.

Adoption studies are designed to evaluate the relative contributions of genetics and environment by studying adopted and nonadopted individuals and their families. One strategy is to start with adopted children who display a particular behavior disorder and to examine rates of that disorder in members of the children's biological families compared to rates in their adoptive families. Another strategy is to start with biological parents who exhibit a particular disorder and examine the rate of disorder in offspring separated from the parent in early childhood and raised in another household. Rates of disorder in these children can then be compared to a number of comparison groups (e.g., siblings not given for adoption and raised by the biological parent). Also associations between risk factors, such as family conflict, and behavior problems can be compared in adopted and nonadopted youngsters. Adoption strategies can thus help reveal complex relations between genetic and environmental influences (cf. Braungart-Rieker et al., 1995).

All behavior genetic methods have limitations and potential confounds. For example, in adoption studies, prenatal as well as genetic factors are part of the biological parent's "contribution." Thus, greater rates of disorder among biological relatives than adoptive relatives could be due to prenatal influences. Combinations and refinement of methods, and more sophisticated quantitative analyses, seek to address many of the shortcomings of individual methods. These advances also permit evaluation of hypothetical models of genetic transmission and of the interaction of genetic and environmental influences (Plomin, 1995; Plomin, DeFries, and McClearn, 1990; Rutter et al., 1990a).

Results from behavior genetic research suggest that heritability estimates for behavioral dimensions or disorders rarely exceed 50 percent, and that heritability is often appreciably lower than this (Plomin, 1994b). This means that substantial variation in behavior is attributable to nongenetic influences. In this way behavior genetic research has provided evidence for the importance of environmental influence. Influences of family environment that are shared by siblings and that contribute to their development can be revealed. Behavior genetic research has also highlighted the importance of environmental influences that are not shared by children growing up in the same family. These influences, known as nonshared environment, make children in the same family different from one another. They are also important to the development of behavior disorders (Hetherington, Reiss, and Plomin, 1994; Plomin, Chipuer, and Neiderhiser, 1994).

Chromosome abnormalities. Approximately 40 percent of spontaneously aborted fetuses are known to have chromosomal abnormalities. Among live births it has been estimated that 3.52 infants per 1,000 are born with an abnormal number of chromosomes and 2.23 with structural abnormalities of the chromosomes (Gath, 1985).

Chromosomes that are aberrant in either number or structure are known to cause death or a variety of deficiencies. These "accidents" are often not inherited, so that they influence only the specific developing embryo. A large number of different chromosomal anomalies have been described. Mental retardation is commonly associated with many of them. Perhaps the most widely recognized disorder attributed to a chromosome aberration is Down's syndrome. Characterized by mental deficiency, it is usually caused by an extra #21 chromosome. A group of abnormalities that results from sex chromosome aberrations has also been discovered. These disorders are often characterized by below-average intelligence, atypical sexual development, and other difficulties.

Newer methods of chromosomal analysis, such as staining methods, allow detection of quite subtle abnormalities in size, shape, and other characteristics of portions of chromosomes. Also, the discovery of a group of structural features known as fragile sites has proven helpful in understanding the origins of certain disorders. For example, the fragile X anomaly is due to a fragile site on the X chromosome. This condition is thought to be responsible for many cases of severe mental retardation (Lombroso et al., 1994; Rutter et al., 1990a).

THE PSYCHODYNAMIC PERSPECTIVE

The psychoanalytic theory of Sigmund Freud was the first modern systematic attempt to understand mental disorders in psychological terms. Freud's theory also drew heavily on biology. Freud was a physician who had trained to be a neurologist. His thinking about how the psychic system operated was formulated to parallel the workings of biological systems and to reflect the then-current developments in the natural sciences. Freud's ideas went through a number of transitions during his lifetime. The evolution of his conceptualizations has come to be known as classical psychoanalytic theory. Only a brief description of this complex and highly systematized theory will be given here. More elaborate and detailed summaries have been provided by a number of writers (e.g., Kessler, 1988; Wolman, 1972).

Freud's theory is *deterministic*—there is a specific cause for all behavior, even the most trivial. The principles that describe how behavior is determined are universal, applying to both "normal" and "abnormal" behavior. Emphasis is given to intrapsychic factors rather than environmental or social influences. Equally important is the idea that mental processes are *unconscious*; that is, determined by forces that are inaccessible to rational awareness. The analogy of an iceberg, nine-tenths of which is below the surface, illustrates the importance placed on unconscious influences.

Although Freud based his theory on clinical observations of adults, he came to view personality and psychological difficulties in children as well as in adolescents and adults as the result of problems experienced during the first five to six years of life. Since the child is viewed as moving through a series of distinct stages of growth, Freud's theory is *developmental,* with an emphasis on early childhood. To move through early development and beyond, the individual is provided with a fixed amount of psychic energy. The theory describes a dynamic process of transfer of this energy among various aspects of the personality. To explain this ongoing transfer, psychoanalytic theory employs a *structural* and *conflict* model as a metaphor for this process.

In this brief discussion, we seek to provide an overview of the framework Freud used in talking about the structural-conflict model, stages of development, and the development of psychopathology. We first describe the structural system.

The Structures of the Mind

Freud hypothesized three parts of the mental apparatus: the *id,* the *ego,* and the *superego.* Each of these mental "structures" describes part of a system of psychic functioning. The id, present at birth, is the earliest structure and is the source of all psychic energy. Operating entirely at an unconscious level, the id seeks immediate and unconditional gratification of all instinctual urges (the *pleasure principle*). If this cannot be done directly, the id employs *primary process* thinking, obtaining what is desired through fantasy.

The other psychic structures, the ego and superego, both evolve from the id and must obtain their energy from it. The ego is primarily conscious, and its principle task is to mediate between instinctual urges and the outside world. The mature ego employs its cognitive and decision-making functions to test reality. The superego develops when the immature ego cannot handle all conflicts. In order to deal with some of these, the ego incorporates or introjects the parents' standards, and this is the beginning of a separate superego. The superego sets ideal standards for behavior and is the conscience,

or self-critical part, of the individual. In trying to satisfy the id's instinctual urges, the ego must consider not only reality but also the ideals of the superego. The *psychodynamics* of the Freudian perspective arise out of the attempts of these three systems to achieve their frequently conflicting goals.

Psychosexual Stages

The psychoanalytic perspective relies on a stage theory of development. As the child develops, the focus of psychic energy passes from one bodily zone to the next. The process leads the individual through stages of psychosexual development in a fixed order. Each stage derives its name from the bodily zone that is the primary source of gratification during the period.

The *oral stage* extends from birth through approximately the first year of life. The mouth is the center of pleasure and the infant is highly dependent on the mother for nurturance. Thus, the themes of this stage are not only oral pleasure but also dependency and taking in. The crucial conflict that ends this period is weaning, when the infant must give up some oral pleasures and dependencies.

During the second and third years of life the locus of satisfaction shifts to the anal zone. The retention and expulsion of feces are the major sources of stimulation and pleasure during this *anal stage,* and toilet training is the major task for this period. The period has several themes that derive from the source of stimulation and the developmental task. Primary among them are holding and giving, which may be reflected, for example, in an ungenerous and inward-directed personality. These psychological themes also have gender-related implications. Presumed sexual roles of masculine-active-expulsion and feminine-passive-reception begin to be distinguished during this stage (Wolman, 1972).

During the next period, the *phallic stage,* the genitals become the focus of pleasure, as indicated in the young child's masturbation, curiosity, and inspection of sexual organs. The chief conflict of this period is the desire to possess the opposite-sex parent and the fear of retaliation from the same-sex parent. For the boy this conflict is called the *Oedipus complex.* The parallel process for the girl is known as the *Electra complex.* The resolution of the Oedipal and Electra complexes is central to both sex-role and moral (superego) development.

The final two periods are the *latency and genital stages.* Following the resolution of the conflicts of the phallic stage, the child enters the latency stage. As the name suggests, this is a period of relative stability, in which the sexual and aggressive impulses of the child are subdued. With puberty, however, these impulses are revived, and the adolescent enters the genital stage, during which heterosexual interests predominate. This stage continues for the remainder of the individual's life. These final two stages are less important to the understanding of behavioral disorders, since Freud suggested that the basic personality structure is laid down by the end of the phallic stage.

According to Freud, each of the stages of development involves a developmental crisis, and the child is hindered in development by not more-or-less resolving the conflicts at any one stage. Failure to reach resolution results in the individual becoming psychologically fixated at the stage. Two situations are at the root of *fixation.* The child may not be able to meet the demands of the environment while also satisfying its own needs, and may thus be psychologically frustrated. Alternatively, needs may be met so well that the child is unwilling to leave the stage, and behaviors associated with the stage continue inappropriately. Thus either frustration or the results of overindulgence can fixate the child at a particular stage, ad-versely affecting development at all subsequent stages.

Anxiety and the Defense Mechanisms

From the psychoanalytic perspective, the concept of anxiety is crucial to the development of disordered behavior. Anxiety is the danger signal to the ego that some unacceptable id impulse is seeking to gain consciousness. As this signal begins to reach consciousness, the ego creates defense mechanisms such as repression, projection, displacement, and reaction formation to deal with the anxiety. For example, reaction formation is a defense in which the child develops a behavior that is the opposite of the original impulse. Symptoms arising from defense mechanisms are a compromise between impulses seeking expression and the demands of the ego. Thus, symptoms are disguised expressions of unacceptable impulses. One of Freud's most frequently cited cases illustrates the latent (disguised) meaning of a child's symptoms. These symptoms occurred when the child experienced the Oedipal conflict of the phallic stage.

The case of five-year-old Hans, who was afraid of horses, has served as a model for the psychoanalytic interpretation of childhood phobias (Freud, 1909–1953). Freud actually saw Hans only once, and the case is based on treatment by the boy's father under Freud's direction. Hans was very affectionate toward his mother and enjoyed spending time "cuddling" with her. When Hans was almost five, he returned from his daily walk with his nursemaid frightened, crying, and wanting to cuddle with his mother. The next day, when the mother took him for the walk herself, Hans expressed a fear of being bitten by a horse and that evening insisted upon cuddling with his mother. He cried about having to go out the next day and expressed considerable fear concerning the horse. These symptoms, which continued to get worse, were interpreted by Freud as reflecting the child's sexual impulses toward his mother and his fear of castration by the father. The ego began its defenses against these unacceptable impulses by repressing Hans's wish to attack his father, his rival for his mother's affection. This was an attempt to make the unacceptable impulse unconscious. The next step was *projection*: Hans believed that his father wished to attack him, rather than that he wished to attack his father. The final step was *displacement*. The horse was viewed as dangerous, not the father. According to Freud, the choice of the horse as a symbol of the father was due to numerous associations of horses with Hans's father. For example, the black muzzle and blinders on the horse were viewed as symbolic of the father's mustache and eyeglasses. The fear Hans displaced onto the horse permitted the child's ambivalent feelings toward the father to be resolved. He could now love his father. In addition, thinking of horses as the source of anxiety allowed Hans to avoid anxiety by simply avoiding horses (Kessler, 1966).

Criticisms and Modifications of Psychoanalytic Theory

Classical psychoanalytic theory has been modified by a number of workers. Probably the best known of these are the so-called neo-Freudians who minimized the importance of sexual forces and stressed the importance of social influences; they include Karen Horney, Erich Fromm, Harry Stack Sullivan, and Erik Erikson. Others, such as Freud's daughter Anna, remained more loyal to the orthodox tradition, but elaborated and emphasized the role of the ego in development.

Despite the many modifications of Freud's original theory, this general perspective has been severely criticized on both conceptual and methodological grounds.

For example, psychoanalytic formulations rest primarily on the impressions and recollections of clinical cases. They also involve large inferential leaps from what is observed to what is interpreted as existing. In addition, the mechanisms Freud postulated are intrapsychic and often unconscious and are therefore difficult, if not impossible, to investigate. Thus, much of the criticism of psychoanalytic theory has rested on its untestability. However, criticism has come on other grounds as well.

Those working within the psychoanalytic tradition today have attempted to expand their methodologies. For example, the use of systematic observation has been attempted. Some workers in this tradition have also attempted to incorporate recent research findings on infant and child development into their conceptualizations (Shapiro and Esman, 1992; Zeanah et al., 1989).

Psychoanalytic theory certainly has an important place in the history of childhood disorders and their treatment, and activity continues based on the conceptualizations and treatments derived from this viewpoint (Bemporad, 1991; Target and Fonagy, 1994). The strong influence of the psychoanalytic perspective in drawing attention to the importance and intensity of infant and early childhood experiences, the importance of relationships with parents, and the phases of child development have been noted.

THE BEHAVIORAL/SOCIAL LEARNING PERSPECTIVE

The central concept of the behavioral/social learning perspective is that childhood disorders are learned in the same way that other behaviors are learned. As indicated in Chapter 1, the publication of John B. Watson's essay *Psychology as a Behaviorist Views It* (1913) set into motion a perspective that would serve as the major rival to the psychoanalytic position. While this perspective was also deterministic, it differed from the psychoanalytic paradigm in a number of key ways. Unlike Freud, Watson emphasized observable events rather than unconscious intrapsychic conflicts. Developed in the psychological laboratory rather than in a clinical setting, the behavioral perspective heavily emphasized objective empirical verification. Learning and the influence of the environment were seen as the appropriate focus of study. Furthermore, development was viewed as a continuous process rather than a fixed sequence of stages. The assumption was made that learning continues throughout the life span, and therefore that "personality" is not set by a certain age. Finally, unlike classical psychoanalytic theory, the behavioral perspective did not develop as a single comprehensive theory aimed at explaining all behavior. Rather, a number of theories, often employing similar language but each describing a different aspect of the learning process, were suggested.

Classical Conditioning

Pavlov's demonstrations of dogs learning to salivate to previously neutral stimuli served to focus attention on the process of classical conditioning. Two early studies based on this model stand out because of the great impact they had on the application of classical conditioning to human problems. Watson and Rayner's (1920) now famous case of Little Albert was an early illustration of the conditioning of fear. Albert, an eleven-month-old child, initially showed no fear reactions to a variety of objects, including a white rat. He did, however, exhibit fear when a loud sound was produced by the striking of a steel bar. Watson and Rayner attempted to condition fear of the white rat by producing the loud clanging sound each time Albert reached for the animal. After several of these pairings, Albert reacted with crying and avoidance when the rat was presented without the noise (see Figure 3–3). Thus, it appeared that fear could be learned through classical conditioning. Needless to say, there are significant ethical difficulties with conducting studies such as Watson and Rayner's, and therefore behavioral researchers have tended to focus their attention on applying classical conditioning principles to the treatment of disorders.

The second landmark study was Mary Cover Jones's (1924) demonstration that the principles of classical conditioning could be applied to the removal of fearful responses. Peter, a boy of two years and ten months, exhibited a fear of furry objects. Jones first

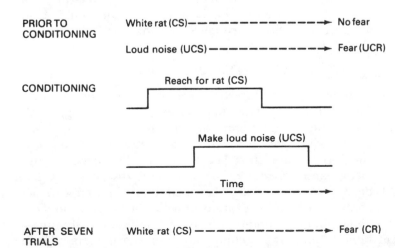

FIGURE 3–3 Watson and Rayner's case of Little Albert. The repeated pairing of an unconditioned stimulus (noise) that produced fear with a previously neutral stimulus (rat) resulted in the rat itself producing a conditioned response of fear.

attempted to treat Peter by placing him with a rabbit and children who liked the rabbit and petted it. The treatment appeared to be working but was interrupted when Peter became ill for nearly two months. Just prior to his return to treatment, he was also frightened by a large dog. With Peter's fear back at its original level, Jones decided to treat Peter with a counterconditioning procedure. This involved allowing Peter to eat some of his favorite foods while the animal was moved progressively closer, thus pairing the feared stimulus with pleasantness. The procedure was apparently successful in reducing the boy's fears, and he was ultimately able to hold the animal by himself.

This case demonstration lacks sufficient control, and we cannot draw conclusions regarding the effectiveness of the procedures derived from classical conditioning. Of additional concern is Jones's inclusion of nonfearful children in treatment sessions. Did the presence of the children, like the food, make the situation pleasant, or did they also serve as models for nonfearful behavior? Despite these limitations, Jones's contribution was important, and stimulated the development of numerous treatments based on the principles of classical conditioning.

Operant Conditioning

The approach to learning set forth in Thorndike's *Law of Effect* and in the work of B.F. Skinner and his followers is probably the behavioral perspective most extensively applied to children's disorders. Operant, or instrumental, conditioning emphasizes the consequences of behavior. Behavior is acquired or reduced, is emitted in some circumstances but not in others, through reinforcement, extinction, punishment, and other learning processes (see Table 3–1). As for classical conditioning, the majority of efforts derived from operant conditioning have focused on the treatment rather than the etiology of disordered behavior.

Williams's (1959) report on altering a twenty-one-month-old child's tantrums is an early, oft-cited example of the use of these principles for treatment of childhood disorders. Following a long illness the child had developed severe tantrums. It was assumed that the parents had been reinforcing this behavior by attending to it. For example, the child's screaming as the parents left his bedroom was reinforced by their remaining in the room. After determining that there were no medical problems, a program of removing the reinforcement for the tantrum behavior (extinction) was begun. After leisurely putting the child to bed, the parents left and did not reenter the room. Although the child cried for forty-five minutes the first night, by the tenth occasion he no longer fussed when left alone. No negative side effects occurred, and the child was reported to be well-adjusted at three years of age.

The principles of operant conditioning have increasingly been applied to a broad range of difficult and complex problems, and the treatment procedures themselves have become more varied and complex. The specific applications of these procedures will be discussed throughout the succeeding chapters of this book. They all share the assumption that problem behavior can be changed through a learning process, and that the focus of treatment should be on the consequences of behavior.

Observational Learning

The investigator most widely associated with observational learning, or modeling, is Albert Bandura, who, along with his associates, has conducted a large number of studies that bear upon the genesis and treatment of childhood disorders. It has been demonstrated that children can acquire a variety of behaviors—aggression, cooperation, delay of gratification, sharing—by watching others perform them. These studies suggest how observational learning

TABLE 3–1 Some Fundamental Operant Conditioning Processes

Term	Definition	Example
Positive reinforcement	A stimulus is presented following a response (*contingent* upon the response), increasing the frequency of that response.	Praise for good behavior increases the likelihood of good behavior.
Negative reinforcement	A stimulus is withdrawn contingent upon a response, and its removal increases the frequency of that response.	Removal of mother's demands following a child's tantrum increases the likelihood of tantrums.
Extinction	A weakening of a learned response is produced when the reinforcement that followed it no longer occurs.	Parents ignore bad behavior, and it decreases.
Punishment	A response is followed by either an unpleasant stimulus or the removal of a pleasant stimulus, thereby decreasing the frequency of the response.	A parent scolds a child for hitting, and the child stops hitting; food is removed from the table after a child spits, and the spitting stops.
Generalization	A response is made to a new stimulus that is different from, but similar to, the stimulus present during learning.	A child is fearful of all men with mustaches like that of a stern uncle.
Discrimination	The process by which a stimulus comes to signal that a certain response is likely to be followed by a particular consequence.	An adult's smile indicates that a child's request is likely to be granted.
Shaping	A desired behavior that is not in the child's repertoire is taught by rewarding responses that are increasingly similar to (*successive approximations* of) the desired response.	A mute child is taught to talk by initially reinforcing any sound, then something that sounds a little like the word, and so on.

can lead to both the acquisition and removal of problem behaviors.

Studies by Bandura and his colleagues on children's imitation of aggressive behavior illustrate how a problem behavior may be acquired through the observation of a model. In one well-known experiment, Bandura (1965) showed nursery school children a five-minute film in which an adult exhibited a number of unusual, aggressive behaviors toward a Bobo doll. The behaviors were also accompanied by distinctive verbalizations. One group of children saw a final scene in which the model was rewarded for aggression; another group saw a final scene in which the model was punished; and the remaining group did not see any final scene.

Later, each child was left alone to play in a room containing the Bobo doll and other toys. The child could engage in imitative aggressive behavior or in nonimitative behavior. As you might expect, the children who had seen the model punished exhibited fewer imitative aggressive responses in the playroom. The experimenter then reentered the room and told each child that for each aggressive behavior like the model's he or she could reproduce, a treat would be given. All three groups now showed the same high level of imitative aggression. The study demonstrated that acquisition of the aggressive behavior had occurred and, moreover, that its performance depended on certain environmental "payoffs."

While the phenomenon of observational learning seems straightforward and simple, it is actually quite complex. Numerous variables influence the imitative process. For example, multiple models, conflicting models, and attributes of the models themselves can affect whether imitation will occur. In addition to direct imitation of modeled behavior, observation can lead to generalized inhibition or disinhibition of behavior. For example, a child who observes another child being scolded for running about may become quieter in other ways (inhibition). Observing a great deal of shooting and fighting on television, in contrast, may lead a child to exhibit other forms of aggression, such as verbal abuse and physical roughness, with peers (disinhibition). In neither case is the exact behavior of the model imitated; rather, a class of behaviors becomes less or more likely to occur due to observation of a model.

Whether imitation is specific or generalized, complex processes are required for observational learning to occur (Bandura, 1977b). Such learning relies on the child's attending to the salient features of the model's behavior. The child must also organize and encode this information and remember it. The acquired behavior must then be performed when it is anticipated that it will meet with desired consequences. The process of learning by observation is viewed by Bandura and others as more than a simple mimicking of behavior. The social learning perspective that has developed from this and other research has placed increasing emphasis on cognitive processes such as attention, memory, and problem solving (Rosenthal, 1984).

THE COGNITIVE PERSPECTIVE

Cognitive processes are an important aspect of contemporary psychology and of conceptualizing the behavior problems of children and adolescents. A tendency to think negatively, misperceive social cues, make faulty attributions regarding the causes of events and behavior, and fail to enact adequate problem-solving are examples of cognitive processes hypothesized to be related to behavioral disorders. For example, thinking negatively about the self, the world, and the future (Beck, 1976) and viewing oneself as helpless (e.g., Abramson, Seligman, and Teasdale, 1978) are examples of cognitive views of depression that have influenced current thinking. Cognitive models of how disorders develop and are maintained, as well as interventions based on cognitive views, have continued to evolve (cf. Beck, 1993; Mahoney, 1993; Spence, 1994). One particular perspective influenced by the cognitive trend in psychology that has contributed to the understanding and treatment of child and adolescent problems is the cognitive-behavioral perspective.

As indicated above, behaviorally oriented clinicians such as Bandura began to suggest that increased attention be paid to the role of cognitive processes (cf. Kendall, 1993; Meichenbaum, 1993). This integrated model came to be known as the cognitive-behavioral perspective. From this perspective, behaviors are learned and maintained by interacting systems of external events and cognitions, and cognitive factors influence whether environmental events are attended to, how events are perceived, and whether these events affect future behavior. Bandura's (1977b) examination of imitative learning, Meichenbaum and Goodman's (1971) training program to teach hyperactive children to "think before they act," and Camp's "Think Aloud" program applying a mediational approach to decrease aggressive behavior and increase prosocial behavior in aggressive boys (Camp, Blom, Herbert, and van Doornick, 1977) are some early examples of these efforts.

Kendall (1991) suggests that the various cognitive functions hypothesized to contribute to the development, maintenance, and treatment of behavior disorders can be organized in terms of cognitive structure, cognitive content, cognitive processes (operations), and cognitive products. *Cognitive structures,* sometimes also referred to as schema, are the internal organization and representation of information. Anxious children and adolescents, for example, may have a dominant schema of threat, and be prone to see impending danger, loss, criticism and the like. *Cognitive content* refers to the information that is stored. *Cognitive processes* are the procedures by which the system operates, perceiving and interpreting experience. Models of how information processing contributes to aggressive children's social adjustment, for example, have been proposed that include steps such as (1) encoding of external and internal cues, (2) representation and interpretation of those cues, (3) clarification or selection of goals, (4) response construction, (5) evaluation and expectation of response, and (6) enactment of behavior (cf. Crick and Dodge, 1994). *Cognitive products* are the results of the cognitive system. Attributions, the way the child explains the causes of behavior, are examples of cognitive products. The tendency of aggressive children to attribute hostile intent to their peers is a specific example of a cognitive product.

Kendall (1991) also suggests that a further way of distinguishing cognitive functioning is to differentiate between cognitive deficiencies and cognitive distortions. *Cognitive deficiencies* refer to an absence of thinking. The lack of forethought and planning that was targeted in the self-instructional program for impulsive-hyperactive children by Meichenbaum and Goodman (1971), referred to above, is an example of how cognitive deficiencies might be implicated in childhood disorders. Table 3–2 presents the steps involved in this intervention as an illustration of how cognitive deficiencies might be remediated. *Cognitive distortions* refer to thought processes that are dysfunctional. Depressed children viewing themselves as less capable than their peers even though others do not is an example of cognitive distortion. Various illustrations of the ways in which the cognitive perspective has contributed to the understanding and treatment of child and adolescent behavior disorders are presented throughout the book.

THE FAMILY SYSTEMS PERSPECTIVE

The family systems perspective, like the psychodynamic perspective, was largely developed in the context of treatment. Virtually all approaches to behavior disorders acknowledge the family as having a major impact, and we shall see throughout the book how family factors contribute to behavior problems in children and adolescents. A variety of viewpoints might describe how a

TABLE 3–2 Sequence of Steps Employed in Meichenbaum and Goodman's Self-Instructural Training

1. While the child watches, an adult model self-instructs aloud while performing the desired task.
2. The child performs the task as the adult instructs aloud.
3. The child self-instructs aloud while performing the task.
4. The child whispers the instructions while doing the task.
5. The child uses private speech to guide performance.
6. The number of self-statements employed by the child is then enlarged over several training sessions.

Adapted from Meichenbaum and Goodman, 1971.

family factor (for example, parental conflict) contributes to a problem in a youngster (for example, acting out or aggressive behavior). The focus in the majority of these approaches, however, has remained on the designated child. The family's role is to assist the child in achieving change. In contrast, family systems theorists view the family unit, rather than the individual, as the appropriate "organism" to study and treat.

No one theory guides all family systems work and, indeed, a number of different approaches exist (cf. Combrinck-Graham, 1990; Nichols and Schwartz, 1991). There are, however, commonalities in many of these approaches. One central thesis is that families are more complicated than the sum of their parts (Bowen, 1980). The family is viewed as a complex social system that may have designated the child as the "identified patient." The child's symptoms play a role in maintaining this system. Therapy, from such a perspective, must address family themes and methods of communication rather than individual child behaviors and parental reactions. Therefore, there are two key concepts involved in this viewpoint: a nonlinear, systems theory of family influences and a focus on the family rather than the individual as the problem unit.

Most non-systems explanations of family influences are linear; that is, A is seen as causing B. For example, it might be reasoned that family stress operating on a child with a certain psychological and biological make-up may cause a particular psychosomatic disease. The systems perspective, in contrast, suggests a circular relationship of parts, with complex and interrelated feedback mechanisms. The central argument of the systems perspective is that the behavior of any child cannot be attributed to biology or merely to a *reaction* in the family system. It is the system's interactions that are problematic and that maintain the child's "symptomatic" behavior.

THE PSYCHOEDUCATIONAL PERSPECTIVE

What we refer to here as the psychoeducational perspective is a view that arises out of an approach to working with children in an educational context. Commitment to reeducation is what characterizes the variety of approaches that fall under this rubric.

The term *special education* has also been used to describe the efforts of educators to deal with the problems of atypical children. That the vast majority of children receive extended formal education as a right rather than as a privilege is a given in today's society. This has not always been the case, nor has education always been assigned an important role in dealing with children's problems (Fagan, 1992).

Lilly (1979c) has provided an overview of the history of special education. The initial view of the special education approach, particularly for the mentally retarded, was optimistic. Residential treatment centers were developed to prepare handicapped individuals to return to the community. Residential schools evolved, however, into permanent residences for more severely handicapped children. Moreover, little attention was given to persons whose problems were milder. Compulsory education laws then forced the educational systems to provide services for the less severely handicapped.

Another development—the construction of general tests of intelligence—had a long-lasting and far-reaching impact on special education. These tests defined a new group of mildly handicapping conditions. The presence of children with "milder" conditions in the school systems led to the development of special classes. With expansion of services, legislation for mandatory special education, and the development of university-based research and training programs, special educational services experienced rapid growth beginning in the 1950s.

Subsequent changes in special education occurred as a result of court cases and legislation. Many of these changes initially arose out of concern for the mentally retarded (cf. MacMillan, 1982). However, the principles evolved have been extended to other problems. In 1975 the delivery of special services was dramatically affected by P.L. 94–142, The Education for All Handicapped Children Act. This influential law and the application of the psychoeducational perspective will be discussed in more detail later in the book. However, it is appropriate to recognize here two matters that have been of particular importance (Lilly, 1979a; MacMillan and Kavale, 1986). One is that special educators have been prominent in questioning the need to employ traditional categories or special labels with children. They have often led the fight against the use of categorization and for recognition of the role of social and environmental factors in the etiology of childhood problems.

The second issue is whether children should be placed in special classes (cf. Sylva, 1994). Although special classes were origi-

nally developed to help children who were not succeeding in regular classrooms, a number of educators began to question their efficacy (e.g., Dunn, 1968). Whether children with problems should be placed in special classrooms or instead included or "mainstreamed" into the regular school system remains a complex and controversial question with far-reaching implications. Drawing attention to this concern is one of the continuing contributions of the psychoeducational approach.

MODES OF TREATMENT

As we indicated earlier, the perspective that a therapist adopts affects the style of the therapy offered. Thus, for example, a professional with a behavioral or social-learning perspective is likely to offer treatments that are action oriented, focus on present problems, and assume that therapy is a learning

Working with children in an educational context and a commitment to education as a means of intervention characterize the psychoeducational approach.

process governed by principles common to all learning situations.

Another dimension by which one can categorize treatments is by what we will term the *mode of treatment,* that is, how services are delivered. For example, as we indicated previously, therapists operating from a variety of theoretical perspectives advocate for the inclusion of the family in treatment. Thus, working with the family is a mode of treatment employed by therapists from a variety of perspectives. Treatment of children is delivered in a variety of other modes as well. Indeed, particularly as child and adolescent disorders come to be seen as arising out of a combination of influences, any one therapist is likely to employ several different modes of treatment and in treating a particular child may use a combination of these modes (e.g., Tuma and Pratt, 1982).

Therapists may see the young client in individual one-to-one sessions. These sessions may resemble the verbal interchanges of adult sessions, or particularly with young children, play may be the primary mode of interaction between the therapist and the child. But therapists may also spend relatively little time with the child and focus instead on training the parents to work with the child. Such parent training may have the added benefit of providing general parenting skills that will be useful in other situations or with other children. Sometimes various members of the family are seen in separate individual treatment. Alternatively, the therapist may choose to work with the family as a unit. Often consultation is given to significant other adults who work with the child—a teacher, for example. Various forms of treatment may also be delivered in a group rather than an individual format. Medications may also be employed in the treatment of children and adolescents.

The modes indicated above are only some of the forms of treatment employed in working with youth. In this section we will briefly present an overview of some of the most commonly used modes of treatment. In later chapters we will present specific examples of these modes as they are employed with particular problems.

Individual and Group Psychotherapy

The typical view of psychotherapy is that it is a one-to-one verbal experience. With adults this is the most common mode of treatment. However, treatment in groups has also been offered by therapists from a variety of theoretical perspectives. The same assumptions and methods that guide individual therapies may be used, but in a group format. While the group format may be selected for convenience or in order to provide services to larger numbers of children and adolescents, there are other rationales for this choice (Johnson, Rasbury, and Siegel, 1986). Groups offer the opportunity for socialization experiences not present in the individual mode. Also, group treatment may be more appealing to the child or adolescent because it is less threatening, demonstrates that peers have difficulties, and often includes opportunities for activities not likely to occur in one-to-one relationships with an adult therapist.

Whether in individual or group format, treatments that would be described as verbal forms of psychotherapy are a major form of intervention, particularly with older children and adolescents. However, the need to alter treatment procedures to fit the child's level of cognitive and emotional development is one factor that has produced nonverbal modes of working with children.

Play Therapy

A common mode is the use of play as a therapeutic vehicle. This is consistent with the importance of play in the development of young children (Rubin, Fein, and Vandenberg, 1983; Smith, 1988). Play as a mode of therapy is for many therapists a solution to the lesser verbal abilities of the child. Rather than relying exclusively on abstract verbal interactions, the therapist uses play to help concretize communications. As a means of communication, play is used in therapy by most practitioners. However, play therapy as a more structured and distinct approach to treatment also exists (Russ, 1995). The two most well known perspectives on play therapy are derived from the psychodynamic and client-centered perspectives.

Play therapy was the focus of a controversy between two of the principal and early developers of child treatment from a psychoanalytic perspective. Early analysts agreed that change was needed in analytic techniques in order to effectively treat children. This led to the use of play as a mechanism for children to express their thoughts and feelings. However, among the controversies that arose was whether to view children's play as the equivalent of verbal free association in adults. Also there was disagreement over the psychoanalytic interpretation of children's play.

Melanie Klein (1932) was one of the first therapists to emphasize play in the treatment of children, and her ideas gained wide popularity. She used the term play therapy to refer to the process whereby the child's play was used as the basis for psychoanalytic interpretation much as verbal free association was used in the psychoanalysis of adults. Anna Freud (1946) disagreed with the emphasis and significance given to play by Klein and others. She viewed play as only one potential mode of expression. Anna Freud also felt that although the child did express emotions and thoughts through play, these should not be cognitively equated with the purposeful production of free association by adults.

The two women also disagreed on the interpretation of the material derived from play. Klein placed a heavy emphasis on symbolic interpretation of play and gave it a prominent role throughout the psychoanalytic process. Anna Freud, in contrast, gave less emphasis to play interpretation and did not see it as always symbolizing conflict. She, for example, disagreed with Klein that a child opening a lady's handbag symbolically expresses curiosity regarding the contents of the mother's womb. Rather the child may

The use of play as a mode of therapy is common with younger children. Play allows for the establishment of rapport, but also provides a means of communication more age-appropriate than verbal forms of therapy.

(Judy Gelles/Stock, Boston)

be responding to an experience on the previous day when someone brought a present in a similar receptacle (A. Freud, 1946). The contemporary psychoanalytic position tends to favor Anna Freud's positions on play and other issues (Johnson, Rasbury, and Siegel, 1986). Indeed, the term "play therapy" as it is used today refers to child treatment in which play is the major mode of expression, regardless of the therapist's orientation, rather than Melanie Klein's more narrow definition.

Another major influence on the evolution of play therapy was the work of Virginia Axline. Axline developed her approach from the client-centered perspective associated with Carl Rogers. The basic principles outlined by Axline (1947) remain the guidelines for contemporary client-centered play therapy (Johnson, Rasbury, and Siegel, 1986). The principles of the client-centered approach are the same for adults and children of varying ages. The therapist makes adjustments in communication style to create the appropriate accepting, permissive, and nondirective therapeutic environment. The use of play with young children helps to create such an environment.

Parent Training

Many professionals have taken the position that change in the child's behavior may best be achieved by producing changes in the way that the parents manage the child. This viewpoint is consistent with the observation that it may often be the parent's perception, rather than actual child behavior, that results in children being referred for treatment.

Parent training procedures have been applied to a wide variety of childhood problems. A number of approaches have emerged and a number of popular books appear on the shelves of bookstores everywhere. However, in terms of systematic applications and research, most work has come from the social learning/behavioral approach.

Behavioral parent training has received a great deal of clinical and research attention and a number of reviews and discussions have appeared (e.g., Dangel and Polster, 1984; McBurnett, Hobbs, and Lahey, 1989; Twardosz and Nordquist, 1987). Original efforts focused on teaching parents to manage the consequences, or contingencies, they applied to children's behavior. More recent approaches include a wider variety of skills such as skills in verbal communication and expression of emotion (Twardosz and Nordquist, 1987). In addition, investigators have found that stressors such as socioeconomic disadvantage, single parent status, social isolation, and maternal depression are related to poorer outcome of parent training (e.g., Forehand, Furey, and McMahon, 1984; Israel, Silverman, and Solotar, 1986; Webster-Stratton, 1985a; Wahler and Dumas, 1984). This has led to the examination of a variety of modifications to existing programs (cf. Webster-Stratton, 1994). In addition, parent training is frequently employed as part of a multifaceted approach to treatment. Other components may include additional therapeutic work with the parent, direct work with the child, or work with the teacher and school.

Treatment in Residential Settings

Residential treatment is usually considered a mode of intervention for severe behavior problems. The problems may be so difficult to treat that working with the youths on an outpatient basis does not provide enough contact or control. Also, there may be a concern that children may harm themselves or others and, therefore, that closer supervision is necessary. The child may also be removed from the home because circumstances there are highly problematic, suggesting that successful interventions could not be achieved at home. Unfortunately, the lack of availability of alternative placements can result in children being institutionalized when interventions in less restrictive environments, like group or foster homes, might be successful. On the other hand, treatment in residential settings is often undertaken when other modes of intervention have not proven successful.

Residential treatment may occur in group homes, child psychiatry units in medical hospitals, units in nonmedical settings, and in juvenile facilities that are part of the legal/judicial system. Treatment in such settings usually involves a variety of services including therapeutic, educational, and vocational interventions. Because programs differ so much in what the actual content is, they have been difficult to evaluate, and therefore we know less than we would like about their effectiveness (cf. Kazdin, 1985).

Pharmacological Treatment

Pharmacological treatments (medications) are part of the interventions employed for a variety of childhood and adolescent behavior disorders (Buckstein, 1993; Gadow and Pomeroy, 1991). They differ from the modes of treatment discussed above in that the use of medications is most closely linked to a single perspective, the influence of biological factors. However, psychopharmacological agents are often employed in combination with other modes of treatment. Medications that affect mood, thought processes, or overt behavior are known as psychotropic or psychoactive and thus the term psychopharmacological treatment is often employed. Table 3–3 provides examples of some of the pharmacological agents employed in the treatment of children and adolescents.

Psychotropic drugs produce their therapeutic effects by their influence on the process of neurotransmission. Poling, Gadow, and Cleary (1991) describe some of the ways that these medications can affect neurotransmission:

1. By altering the body's production of a neurotransmitter.
2. By interfering with the storage of a neurotransmitter.
3. By altering the release of a neurotransmitter.
4. By interfering with the inactivation of a neurotransmitter or the reuptake of a neurotransmitter.
5. By interacting with receptors for a neurotransmitter.

For some psychoactive drugs there is a specific and clearly hypothesized mechanism for their action, while for others the specific reasons for their effectiveness are unknown. The action of certain drugs in producing antipsychotic effects is an example of a mechanism of action that has been specified. A lock-and-key analogy can be employed to describe how these drugs act by blocking receptors for the neurotransmitter dopamine (Poling et al., 1991). The molecules of the neuroleptic (antipsychotic) drug and dopamine are similar, but not identical, keys. The receptor is the lock. The dopamine key fits the receptor lock perfectly and can unlock it and affect transmission to the neuron on which the receptor is located. The neuroleptic key, in contrast, will enter the dopamine receptor lock, but will not unlock it. This imperfectly fitting key does, however, prevent dopamine from entering the receptor. Thus dopamine molecules are prevented from combining with receptors and affecting neurotransmission. Blocking dopamine's function is thus the mechanism by which certain antipsychotic agents are presumed to have their therapeutic action.

The use of psychoactive drugs, support for their effectiveness, and their presumed

4

RESEARCH: ITS ROLE AND METHODS

In preceding chapters we saw how the developmental approach and theoretical perspectives of psychopathology provide frameworks for the investigation of problem behaviors. An enormous amount of research is being conducted to test various hypotheses and otherwise study dysfunction in young people. This chapter discusses the role of research and major methods of investigation. Basic research designs and strategies are described, and examples of their applications are provided. Research methods vary along several dimensions, but all aim to go beyond common sense speculation to objective, reliable knowledge.

THE NATURE OF SCIENCE

The word science comes from the Latin word for knowledge, or to know, but refers to knowledge gained by a particular method of inquiry. The application of the scientific method to human behavior is a relatively recent historical event. Humans have long considered themselves special creatures, too complicated and mysterious for scientific study. Even today we hear that scientific inquiry might be inappropriate or perhaps even dangerous when applied to humans. For the most part, though, psychology and related disciplines are committed to the view that the scientific method can provide the most valid information about disordered behavior.

The overall purpose of science is to describe phenomena and to offer explanations for them. Investigators may wonder: How many parents use physical punishment as a means of disciplining their children? What will happen if a learning-disabled child is provided with an enriched school experience? Why are particular adolescents withdrawn socially? Sometimes it is necessary only to count or describe cases to answer such questions. At other times it is necessary to determine the exact conditions under which a phenomenon occurs or its relationship to other variables. Determining cause-and-effect relationships is especially helpful in understanding behavior.

Theoretical concepts and assumptions are likely to guide research goals, choice of variables, procedures, analyses, and conclusions. In the early stage of research, theoretical concepts may be little more than hunches or guesses based on informal observations. Later they may be more developed and specific. Some subjectivity and creativity are always involved in generating research questions and in deciding how to best seek answers.

Researchers often try to test specific hypotheses derived from theory. Hypothesis testing is valuable in that it tends to build knowledge systematically rather than haphazardly. Any one investigation rarely proves that a hypothesis is correct or incorrect; instead, it provides evidence for or against the hypothesis. In turn, a hypothesis that is supported serves as evidence for the accuracy and explanatory power of the underlying theory. A failed hypothesis, in contrast, serves to disprove, limit, or redirect the theory. Thus, observations and theories work together to advance scientific understanding.

Just as researchers ask a variety of questions, they employ a variety of subjects, settings, and methods. In all cases, however, observation and measurement, reliability, and validity are important considerations.

Observation and Measurement

At the heart of scientific endeavors are observation and measurement. The scientific method thus can be applied only to aspects of the world for which these processes can be used. Both observation and measurement are challenging for behavioral scientists. It is relatively simple to observe and measure overt action, but thought and emotion, which are intricately entwined with action, are more elusive. Typically the scientist must operationalize what is being measured. For example, aggression might be operationalized as the frequency of a person striking another person. To take another example, depression might be operationalized by the degree to which a person reports feelings of sadness and hopelessness.

In the attempt to tap all sources of information, behavioral scientists make many kinds of observations and measurements. They directly observe overt behavior with or without special apparatus; record physiological functioning of the heart, brain, or sense organs; ask people to report or rate their own behavior, feelings, and thoughts; and

collect the reports of others about the subject of investigation. Such endeavors may be conducted in the laboratory or in natural settings, and confidence in them and importance accorded them varies.

Reliability

In addition to assuming that knowledge can be gained by observation, the scientific method also assumes that events repeat themselves, given identical or similar conditions. Thus, they can be observed again by others. If the same events are not reported under similar conditions, the original finding is considered unreliable, or inconsistent, and remains questionable. The need for reliability of results places a burden on researchers to clearly and concisely conceptualize, observe, measure, and communicate their findings so that others may replicate and judge their work. Science must be open to the scrutiny and evaluations of others.

Validity

While reliability refers to the consistency or repeatability of results, validity refers to the correctness, soundness, or appropriateness of scientific findings. Validity is a complex matter and in general must be judged in terms of the purpose of the research and how the results are used. The concepts of internal and external validity are central to understanding validity.

Internal validity refers to the extent to which explanations for phenomena are judged to be correct or sound. Or to put it in another way, it refers to the degree to which alternative explanations can be ruled out (Campbell and Stanley, 1963). The more certain we are that alternative explanations can be ruled out, the more confidence we have in the offered explanation.

Internal validity is closely tied to the notion of control in research. It is maximized by research designs and procedures that build in control over the variables that could affect the findings of the investigation. By controlling the procedures, the researcher is able to speak confidently about the exact conditions experienced by the subjects. By controlling extraneous factors, the researcher optimizes the likelihood of being able to attribute the findings to specific factors. As we shall see, it is only the "true" experiment that approaches such control.

External validity asks the question of generalizability: To what populations and situations can the results of an investigation be generalized (Campbell and Stanley, 1963)? Researchers are virtually always interested in this question. Generalizability cannot be assumed, however. It cannot automatically be concluded, for example, that research findings based on a particular population of preschool girls hold for older girls or for boys. Similarly, the results of laboratory studies may or may not generalize to the world outside of the laboratory.

The question of generalizability is rarely if ever completely answered, although evidence increases as various populations and settings are tested. It is ironic that attempts to increase internal validity may decrease external validity because the former requires controls that may create artificial situations. This dilemma is one of several that must be taken into account in the selection of a research method.

BASIC METHODS OF RESEARCH

In the following discussion several basic research methods are described. As will be obvious, each has weaknesses and strengths and may be more suitable in some situations than others.

The Case Study

This method is commonly used in researching behavioral disorder. It focuses on an individual, describing the background, present and past life circumstances, and characteristics of the person. The usual aim is to gain knowledge of the nature, course, causes, correlates, and outcomes of behavior problems.

The following is an abbreviated version of a case report of a boy who was considered at risk for a serious disorder, childhood schizophrenia.

Max was a seven-year-old boy when he was first referred for psychiatric evaluation by his school principal. . . . Long standing problems such as severe rage outbursts, loss of control, aggressive behavior, and paranoid ideation had reached crisis proportions.

Max was the product of an uncomplicated pregnancy and delivery, the only child of a professional couple. There was a history of "mental illness" in the paternal grandmother and two great aunts. Max's early development was characterized by "passivity." . . . He used a bottle until age three. Verbal development was good; he spoke full sentences at one year. Toilet training was reportedly difficult. . . .

Max was clumsy and had difficulty manipulating toys, his tricycle, and his shoelaces. When he began nursery school, he was constantly in trouble with other children. . . . Max "developed a passion for animals" . . . At age five Max acquired an imaginary companion, "Casper—the man in the wall" who was ever present. Max insisted that he could see him, although no one else could. Casper's voice, he said, often told him he was a bad boy.

Max's behavior was so unmanageable during the first and second grade he was rarely able to remain in the classroom. . . . Max described animals fighting and killing people. . . . The psychologists noted a schizoid quality because of the numerous references to people from outer space, ghosts, and martians, as well as the total absence of human subjects. . . . Despite his high intelligence (IQ 130), Max was experiencing the world as hostile and dangerous. The psychologist considered Max to be at great risk for schizophrenia, paranoid type (Cantor and Kestenbaum, 1986, pp. 627–628).

The case study continues, telling of Max's enrollment in special schools and psychotherapy. A major focus of treatment was to reduce Max's anxiety, which was thought to cause his aggression and bizarre behaviors. Parental involvement, rewards for appropriate behavior, and medication were all employed. Despite some quite disturbed behaviors, improvement occurred, and Max eventually was able to attend a university engineering program.

The primary goal of this case report was to illustrate a therapeutic approach to treating seriously disturbed children and to emphasize that treatment must be tailored to each child's needs. The case study can well meet such a goal, for one of its strengths is its power to illustrate. Case studies can richly describe phenomena, even phenomena that are so rare that they would be difficult to study in other ways.

The weaknesses of the case study concern reliability and validity. The descriptions of life events often go back in time, and the accuracy and completeness of such retrospective data are often suspect. Thus, reliability of the data is at question. When case studies go beyond description to interpretations, there are few guidelines to judge the validity of the interpretations. External validity also is weak in the case study method: Since only one person is examined, the findings cannot be generalized confidently to others. There are ways to increase reliability and validity, however (Kazdin, 1981). For example, several case studies demonstrating the same principle can increase generalizability.

Despite weaknesses, case studies have played a critical role in the development of clinical psychology and psychiatry (Chess, 1988; Wells, 1987). Clinicians consider them "do-able" and relevant to their concerns (Morrow-Bradley and Elliot, 1986). Case reports can work hand-in-hand with other research methods, to provide hypotheses and clinically examine results produced by other methods.

Systematic Naturalistic Observation

Systematic naturalistic observation consists of directly observing individuals in their "real world" in order to describe behavior occurring in the situation, answer specific questions, or test hypotheses.

An example is an investigation by Dadds and colleagues, who were interested in the development or maintenance of childhood depression (Dadds et al., 1992). The researchers compared parent-child interaction in families that had a child, seven to fourteen years of age, who was clinic-referred for depression, conduct disorder, or depression/conduct disorder. Based on past research, it was hypothesized that parents in all the clinic families would display aversive behaviors toward the clinic-referred children and siblings, but that only the conduct disordered children (with or without depression) would reciprocate with aversive

Direct observation allows the researcher to systematically measure behavior as it is occurring.

behavior. The families, as well as a control group of non-clinic families, were video-taped during a typical evening meal. The tapes were then coded by independent observers who were trained to use the Family Observation Schedule, an observation instrument that provides twenty categories for parent and child behaviors. Table 4–1 shows some of the categories. Reliability of the coding was checked by a different observer, who coded one-third of the tapes. All observers were unaware of the family's group status and the hypotheses being tested.

For the sake of brevity, we will focus on the main findings, which partially supported the hypotheses. Parents with clinic-referred children did indeed show more aversive behaviors compared to control parents. And the conduct-disordered children who were not depressed acted in negative, coercive ways. However, children with depression and depression/conduct disorder did not display anger and did not show aversive behaviors. Siblings behaved much like their clinic-referred brothers and sisters. Thus, despite aversive parental behav-

iors, differences existed in the interactions of families with children referred for different kinds of child problems.

This research is a sophisticated study that utilized trained observers blind to the status of the families, a carefully constructed coding system, and a reliability check on the observations. It permitted many statistical comparisons and testing of hypotheses based on behavior in a natural setting. It demonstrates that naturalistic observation can surpass the clinical case study. On the other hand, direct observation is often confined to the particular behaviors selected for study, and so it may lack the richness of the case study. The degree to which naturalistic observations can be generalized depends on how subjects are selected and other factors.

Correlational Methods

Correlational methods determine whether a relationship exists between or among variables. The variables may be measured in the natural environment or the laboratory in a variety of ways. Researchers then calculate a

---

TABLE 4–1 Examples of Behavior Categories Used in the Dadds et al. Study

Parent-Child Categories
Smile: Facial movement conveying happiness
Frown: Facial movement conveying anger, sadness, disapproval
Praise: Specific praise offered the child by the parent
Question: Nonaversive request for information from the child
Aversive Question: Request for information deemed aversive due to content or tone of voice
Instruction: Nonaversive verbal command that specified a clear behavioral action
Aversive Instruction: Verbal command that specified a clear behavioral action, presented aversively

Child Behavior Categories
Smile: Facial movement conveying happiness
Frown: Facial movement conveying anger, sadness, disapproval
Noncompliance: Refusal to initiate compliance with specific instruction within 5 seconds
Complaint: Verbal complaint involving whining, screaming, protest, temper
Aversive Mand: Aversive or unpleasant directive by the child to another person (e.g., "Fix my dinner now!")
Physical Negative: Actual or threatened physical attack or damage to another person or destruction of an object

From Dadds, M. R., Sanders, M. R., Morrison, M., Rebetz, M. (1992). Childhood depression and conduct disorder: II. An analysis of family interaction patterns in the home. *J. Abnormal Child Psychology, 101,* 505–513. Reprinted by permission, Plenum Pub. Corp.

correlation coefficient, which is a quantitative measure of the existence, direction, and strength of the relationship.

Correlational research can be extremely helpful. It is useful when initial exploration is the goal of research. Here the investigator may first want to determine whether any relationships exist among variables before specific hypotheses are advanced.

Correlational studies also can be helpful when ethical considerations preclude manipulation. Suppose, for example, that an investigator seeks knowledge about the impact of child abuse, poor nutrition, or family conflict on children's behaviors. It would be ethically impossible to manipulate these factors by exposing children to them. However, unfortunate as it is, some children are exposed to these situations in the naturally occurring environment, and correlational research can determine whether these situations are related to children's behavior. Such knowledge can suggest hypotheses. Moreover, when a relationship is revealed, it is possible to predict one variable from the other.

In its simplest form the question asked in correlational research is: Are factors X and Y related, and, if so, in what direction are they related, and how strongly? The first step of the research is to select a sample that represents the population of interest. Next, two scores must be obtained from each participant, one a measure of variable X and the other a measure of variable Y. Statistical analysis of these data must then be performed. In this case the Pearson product-moment coefficient, r, could be computed.

The value of Pearson r,* which always ranges between +1.00 and −1.00, indicates the direction and the strength of the rela-

tionship. Direction is indicated by the sign of the coefficient. The positive sign (+) means that high scores on the X variable tend to be associated with high scores on the Y variable, and that low scores on X tend to be related to low scores on Y. This is referred to as a positive, or direct, correlation. For example, a positive relationship exists between children's age and body weight: Older children usually weigh more. The negative sign (−) indicates that high scores on X tend to be related to low scores on Y, and low scores on X tend to be related to high scores on Y. An example of a negative correlation (also called an indirect, or inverse, correlation) is adult age and lung capacity: As adults increase in age, their lung capacity tends to decrease.

The strength or magnitude of a correlation is reflected in the absolute value of the coefficient. Thus a correlation of +.55 is equally as strong as one of −.55. The strongest relationship is expressed by an r of +1.00 or −1.00, both of which are considered perfect correlations. As the coefficient value decreases in absolute value, the relationship becomes weaker. A coefficient of 0.00 indicates that no relationship exists at all. In this case the score on one variable tells us nothing about the score on the other variable.

Let us consider a hypothetical example of correlational research. Suppose that an investigator expected that children's self-concept and performance on a certain achievement test are positively related. After obtaining an appropriate sample of children, the researcher would obtain two scores for each child—one a measure of self-concept and one a measure of achievement. The hypothetical data might appear as in Table 4–2. Pearson r for these data would be calculated and its value found to equal +.82. How would this finding be interpreted? Obviously, a correlation exists, and the positive sign indicates that children who scored high on the measure of self-concept tend to score high on the achievement test. Moreover, the

*Pearson r is just one of several correlation coefficients that could be calculated, depending on the nature and complexity of the study. The general procedures and interpretations described above apply to other correlation coefficients.

TABLE 4–2   Self-Concept and Achievement Scores

Data from a Hypothetical Study of Children's Self-Concept and Performance on an Achievement Test. The Pearson *r* value is +0.82, which indicates a strong positive relationship between the variables.

Child	Variable X Self-concept Score	Variable Y Achievement Test Score
Daniel	2	5
Nicky	3	4
Sara	4	12
Beth	7	16
Jessica	9	10
Alia	11	22
Brent	13	18

magnitude of the coefficient indicates that the relationship is strong (since +1.00 is a perfect positive relationship). Thus, the researcher's hypothesis is supported by the correlational analysis.

The degree to which correlational research is reliable depends mainly on the reliability of the measures used. The degree to which the study gives valid information about the relationship of the variables depends on how well it was conducted. However, a common mistake is to automatically draw cause-and-effect conclusions from the results. Causal links cannot be validly assumed from correlational analyses; two problems of interpretation exist.

The problem of directionality and other variables.   One problem is that cause may flow in either direction. The other is that some other variable(s) may be responsible for the revealed correlation. In the above hypothetical example, it is possible that self-concept causes achievement scores or that achievement causes self-concept scores. Or perhaps other variables, such as general intelligence or family dynamics, produce the

correlation between self-concept and achievement.

There are, however, a few things that can be done to indicate what causal relationship might exist. For one, the nature of the variables can be examined for a suggestion of cause-and-effect. If a positive correlation were found between diet and school performance in children, for example, it would seem more likely that diet influenced schoolwork than vice versa.

Still, other variables could be responsible for the relationship between diet and school performance, perhaps social class factors. If there were good reason to suspect some role for social class, a partial correlation statistical procedure could be useful. This method partials out, or removes, the effects of other variables, allowing the investigator to determine whether the two original variables are still correlated. The trouble with partialing, however, is that one can never be sure that all possible causative variables have been examined.

Techniques such as structural equation modeling, too complex to discuss here, do permit researchers to have more confidence in their hypotheses about cause-and-effect. Our discussion of correlational research has focused on the basics of the method, but we shall have further opportunity throughout the text to see how the techniques are used in research.

The Experimental Method

The true experiment comes closest to meeting the rigorous standards of the scientific method. Regardless of its particular purpose, it is characterized by the following:

1. An implicitly stated hypothesis
2. Subjects appropriately selected and assigned to groups that are exposed to conditions or manipulations
3. Two or more conditions or manipulations selected by the investigator (the independent variable)

4. Observation and measurement (the dependent variable)
5. Control of the procedures by the investigator
6. Comparison of the effects of the manipulations

Control is of utmost importance. The experiences of the subjects are prearranged and meticulously presented, with the different groups being exposed to different conditions. This permits final judgment about the causes of the findings of the study.

To illustrate the experiment, we draw on a study by Ramey and Campbell (1984). These investigators tested the hypothesis that early education prevents intellectual retardation in at-risk children. Based on past research, they believed that such children would benefit from a child-centered, intellectually stimulating environment provided as part of a day-care service.

Potential participants were identified through prenatal clinics and the local social service department. Each family was then surveyed with the High Risk Index to determine parental education, income, presence or absence of fathers and relatives, children's intellectual performance, and the like. Families meeting a criterion score were considered at risk. Final selection was made after the mother was interviewed and given an intelligence test. Participants were chosen either before or soon after the birth of the subject child.

Families then were paired according to similarity on the High Risk Index, and the children from each pair were randomly assigned to either the treatment or control group. Such matching and random assignment were crucial to the experiment because these procedures aimed to create groups that were approximately equal in relevant characteristics.

The independent variable in this study was the provision of the educational program. All the children in the treatment group began day care by three months of age, and their development was tracked until they reached fifty-four months. The day-care center operated five full days a week, for fifty weeks of the year. The educational program included language, motor, social, and cognitive components, varying somewhat with the child's age. Special emphasis was given to the development of communication skills. Thus, a good deal of attention was paid to verbal exchanges, and children were read to each day. Reading, mathematics, and social skills programs were used.

Control-group children did not attend the day-care center and were not exposed to the educational program. Efforts were made to otherwise equate their experiences with those of the treatment group: They were given similar nutritional supplements, pediatric care, and supportive social services.

To assess the possible influence of the independent variable, all children were tested twice annually with standardized developmental or intelligence tests. These measures were the dependent variable. The examiners were randomly assigned to the testing sessions.

The test results revealed that beginning at eighteen months, children in the treatment group scored significantly higher than children in the control group, and the group difference was statistically significant.* Figure 4–1 shows one way of examining the findings. It indicates that at twenty-four, thirty-six, and forty-eight months the educationally treated children were much less likely to obtain intelligence scores at or below eight-five than were the control chil-

---

*Statistical significance refers to the statistical probability that a finding is a chance result. The accepted rule is that a significant finding would occur by chance five times or less were the study to be repeated one hundred times. (This level of probability, the .05 level, is indicated in research by the term $p < .05$.) Thus, we are reasonably sure that the result is not a chance finding.

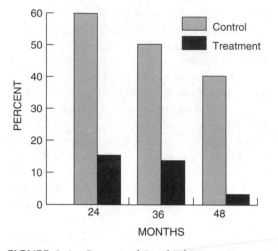

FIGURE 4–1   Percent of Stanford-Binet IQ scores at or below 85 at three ages for treatment and control subjects.

From Ramey and Campbell, 1984.

dren. The researchers thus concluded that the educational program resulted in intellectual benefits for the treated at-risk youngsters.

Is this conclusion justified; that is, does the study have internal validity? The method by which the subjects were selected and assigned makes it unlikely that the results simply reflect group differences that existed before the study was conducted. Moreover, efforts were made to treat the experimental and control groups similarly except for the independent variable. To the degree this was accomplished, it can be confidently concluded that the study is internally valid, and that the results are due to the treatment. With regard to this issue, caution is appropriate, however. When research is conducted in the laboratory, it is relatively easy to control the experiences of the groups. In field experiments such as Ramey and Campbell's the degree of control and thus internal validity is less clear. An additional issue concerns the actual collection of data. It appears that those who gave the standardized tests may have known

the group to which each child had been assigned, raising the question of bias in data collection. At the same time, possible bias of the individual testers was offset by their being randomly assigned to testing sessions.

What about external validity, or generalizability, of the findings? As mentioned earlier, this matter is rarely completely settled, but validity is enhanced in the Ramey and Campbell study by its being done in a setting in which such training might eventually occur. To the extent that other day-care settings would be similar to the original setting, external validity could be expected. External validity would also be anticipated the more similar new subjects would be to the original sample. The findings appear to apply to both sexes because no differences were found between girls' and boys' scores.

The Ramey and Campbell study is one variation on the experimental method. Other experiments might, for example, be conducted in the laboratory, select subjects in somewhat different ways, include more groups, or collect data at only one point in time. Although specific statistical analyses might vary, their purpose would be the same: to determine whether group differences go beyond what might be expected by chance. When a significant statistical difference is found, and the experiment is rigorously designed and conducted, a causal connection between the independent and dependent variables can be assumed. Thus, the experiment is a powerful tool for explanation.

Single-Subject Experiments

The typical experiment, described in the previous section, is conducted with groups of people, and with one or more control groups serving to help rule out alternative explanations of the findings. A strategy akin to this sort of experiment is to conduct an experiment with a single or a few individuals, provided that some control to rule out alternative explanations is employed. This approach is sometimes referred to as single-case designs (Kratochwill and Levin, 1992), or as time-series studies because measurements are taken across time periods. With careful control, internal validity is possible. External validity is not strong as generalization from single subjects cannot be made with confidence. However, external validity can be increased by repeating the study with different subjects.

Single-subject designs are frequently used to evaluate the influence of a clinical intervention. One way to control the possibility for alternative explanations is to use what is known as the ABA' design. The problem behavior is carefully defined and measured across time periods, during which the subject is exposed to different conditions. During the first period (A), measures are taken of the behavior prior to any intervention. This baseline measure serves as a standard against which change can be evaluated. In period B the intervention is carried out while the behavior is measured in the identical way. The intervention is then removed for a period of time known as the reversal period (A').

Figure 4–2 gives a hypothetical example of the ABA' design. Appropriate play behavior occurs at low frequency during the baseline, increases during the treatment phase B, and decreases when the intervention is removed in the A' phase.

In studies in which behavior improves during intervention, particularly if clinical treatment is the aim, a fourth period (B'), during which the successful intervention is reintroduced, must be added. Typically the relevant behaviors show improvement again.

Nevertheless, the ABA' design is limited in that the intervention may make reversal (A') unlikely. For example, when treatment results in increased academic skill, the child may not display decreases in the skill when intervention is removed. From a treatment standpoint this is a positive outcome; from a

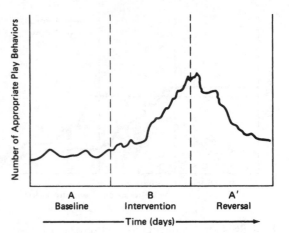

FIGURE 4–2 Hypothetical example of the ABA' design.

research standpoint, however, there is no way to demonstrate that the intervention caused the positive behavior. The ABA' design also has an ethical problem in that the researcher may hesitate to return to baseline conditions once a manipulation is associated with positive change. And again, although the manipulation may appear responsible for the change, without a return to baseline condition a definite demonstration of its effects is lacking.

In some instances in which the ABA' design is inappropriate, alternative designs with multiple baselines may be used. In one multiple baseline design, two behaviors are recorded across time. After baselines are established for both, the intervention is made for only one behavior. During the next phase, intervention is applied to the other behavior as well. For example, a clinician may hypothesize that a child's temper tantrums and throwing of objects are maintained by adult attention to these behaviors. Withdrawal of attention would thus be expected to reduce the behaviors. Support for the hypothesis can be seen in Figure 4–3, a hypothetical graph of the frequency of both behaviors across time periods. Because behavior change follows the pattern of the

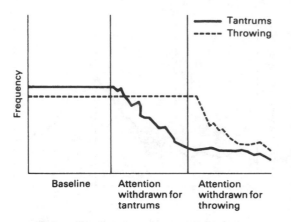

FIGURE 4–3 Frequency of tantrums and throwing across the phases of a hypothetical multiple baseline, single-subject experiment.

treatment procedure, it is likely that withdrawal of attention and not some other variable caused the change.

In another type of multiple baseline design, treatment is given to more than one person, following different time lines. For example, Koegel, O'Dell, and Koegel (1987) evaluated the effects of a new treatment to enhance language development in autistic children. As Figure 4–4 shows, two children began the old treatment (Teaching Method I) at the same time, and individual baselines were recorded. Child 1 was then put on the new treatment, and Child 2 followed several months later. Data were recorded in the clinic for two kinds of verbal imitation. The demonstration of similar patterns of change for both children that occurs only when the new treatment is introduced increases confidence that the treatment actually caused improvement (internal validity). Moreover, external validity is enhanced by the fact that the effect held across two persons.

In addition to reversal and multiple baseline procedures, other methods of control and statistical analyses have been developed for single-subject studies (Barlow and Hersen, 1984; Kratochwill and Levin, 1992). All these designs permit the re-

searcher-clinician to test hypotheses while working with one or a few subjects and, in the case of treatment, focus on the child of immediate concern.

Controlled Observations and Mixed Designs

In studying behavior disorders, researchers often use designs that involve what are referred to as *classificatory variables*. Subjects are selected who differ on some characteristic (classification) and are compared. For example, youth who are considered delinquent or nondelinquent are measured in some way under controlled conditions and compared. There may or may not be manipulations of other factors.

Consider, for example, the investigation of Goldberg and Konstantareas (1981), who were interested in exploring attentional processes in hyperactivity. Hyperactive and normal boys were the subjects of this controlled observation. The hyperactive boys had previously been so classified. Their behavior was compared to that of ten boys who were functioning in a typical manner in public school. There were no statistical differences between the groups in age range and intellectual levels.

Each boy was individually tested on a vigilance task. The apparatus consisted of a television-like box and a pair of keys that controlled, in part, the stimuli on the screen. It was hypothesized that due to attentional deficits the hyperactive boys would make more errors on the task. Statistical analysis of the group means supported the hypothesis. It was thus concluded that the hyperactive boys showed deficits in attending to stimuli.

This conclusion was warranted and extended previous similar findings. However, it is problematic to assume that hyperactivity itself caused the group differences. There is no clear way to rule out the possibility that factors merely associated with hyperactivity produced the results. Perhaps

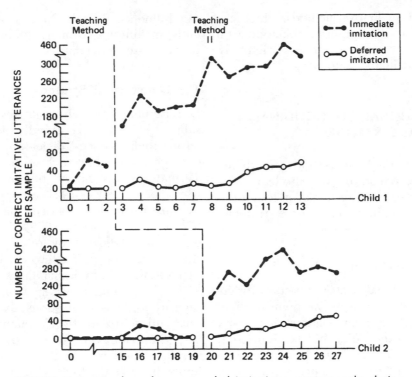

FIGURE 4–4 Number of correct verbal imitations across months during Teaching Methods I and II.

From Koegel, O'Dell, and Koegel, 1987. *J. Autism and Developmental Disorders, 17,* 187–200. Reprinted by permission, Plenum Pub. Corp.

the hyperactive children had lower self-expectations or were overly anxious in the situation due to a history of failure. Research designs that use classificatory variables can be confused with experimental designs. When classificatory factors are employed to select comparison groups, interpretation of causation must be made cautiously however.

Caution is also required in interpreting the results from mixed designs. In mixed designs, subject groups are chosen on the basis of classificatory factors and then a manipulation also occurs (Davison and Neale, 1996). Take the hypothetical case in which both hyperactive and normal boys (the classificatory factor) are given two kinds of vigilance tasks (a manipulation). Suppose the hyperactive group does well with one task but not the other while the normal group does well with both tasks. The problem of interpretation still exists despite the manipulation: It is not clear that hyperactivity itself rather than some associated feature caused the results.

To summarize, most of the research methods we have discussed in this section give central importance to quantitative measurement and statistical analysis. The variables of interest are operationalized and other variables are controlled as much as is feasible or practical. In this way, it is assumed, scientific knowledge is best acquired. Nevertheless, some researchers question the wisdom of relying too heavily on this quantitative approach, arguing among other things that it is too restrictive. They value more open-ended qualitative methods, which can be employed alone or in combination with quantitative methods. Accent 4–1 briefly discusses the qualitative approach.

CROSS-SECTIONAL, LONGITUDINAL, SEQUENTIAL STRATEGIES

In addition to the basic methods already described, research studies can also be categorized as either cross-sectional or longitudinal, or as a combination of these strategies known as sequential designs.

The Cross-Sectional Strategy

The cross-sectional strategy observes different groups of subjects at one point in time. For example, the peer relations of fourth-, sixth-, and ninth-graders can be compared. The strategy is relatively inexpensive and efficient and can provide much information (Verhulst and Koot, 1991). It is thus a popular approach.

However, tracing developmental change with cross-sectional research is problematic. For example, someone interested in whether the frequency of aggression changes with development may measure aggression in five, ten, and fifteen-year-olds. If the younger children displayed more aggression, it might be concluded that aggression decreases as children develop. However, this conclusion may not be warranted. Age *difference* is not necessarily age or developmental *change*. Perhaps specific experiences of the different age groups, due to societal changes over time, are responsible for the findings. Younger children might have watched more violent television or received more reinforcement for aggression during an era characterized by greater violence and aggression. Thus the finding may reflect societal change rather than the developmental course for aggression. To make matters more complex, the same societal changes can influence different age groups differently, making it extremely difficult to interpret cross-sectional data.

The Longitudinal Strategy

Longitudinal research evaluates the same subjects over time, repeatedly observing or testing them. It "sees" development as it occurs. One of the first such studies was Lewis Terman's investigation of the gifted in which, beginning in 1921, a population was examined several times over many decades (Cravens, 1992; Sears, 1975). Terman's research was followed by other now-classic studies that traced the growth of intellectual, social, and physical abilities.

The longitudinal strategy is unique in its capacity to answer questions about the nature and course of development. Does an early traumatic event, such as the death of a parent, play a role in the origin of childhood psychopathology? To what extent does adolescent aggression carry over into adulthood? Can early intervention prevent later problems in infants who experience prenatal difficulties? The longitudinal method can be extremely helpful in answering these kinds of questions (Verhulst and Koot, 1991).

Still, it has serious drawbacks. Longitudinal studies are extremely expensive and require the investigators to commit themselves to a project for many years. Also it is difficult to retain subjects over long periods of time and drop-outs may bias the subject sample. For example, drop-outs may be more transient, less psychologically oriented, or less healthy than the subjects who continue. So subject loss can bias the results. Repeated testing of subjects can also be a problem: They may become test-wise, and efforts to change or improve the testing instruments make it difficult to compare earlier and later findings. Finally, subjects are not the only ones who change over the years; so may society. Thus, for example, if

ACCENT 4–1   Qualitative Research Methods

Throughout this century, psychology has been largely committed to the belief that truth or scientific knowledge must be grounded in, or deduced from, direct observation (Krahn, Hohn, and Kime, 1995). What has been most valued in research is quantitative measurement done by objective investigators in controlled situations. Most all the methods discussed in this chapter fall under the rubric of quantitative research methods (the case study being the least quantitative).

In recent years interest has grown in diverse approaches referred to as qualitative methods. In these approaches, data are often collected by encouraging people to speak of their life experiences, attitudes, or beliefs. Diaries, letters, and other written records may be examined. Naturalistic observation is also important and the situation is more fully described in narration rather than according to a restrictive coding system. Moreover, the data may be viewed as more credible when the observer has become a participant in the situation or setting and so understands the dynamics of the situation (participant observation). A basic assumption of qualitative research is that human behavior and development are best understood from a personal frame of reference. Thus, for example, a person's narration of his or her experience may serve as the data in an investigation. Large amounts of data are often collected in the form of stories or incidents that tell much about the context of people's experiences. Once collected, the narrative data are then conceptualized, analyzed, and interpreted (Strauss and Corbin, 1990). This process entails coding or categorizing statements or

written observations. What gets coded, how the coding is accomplished, and how data are interpreted varies with the approach and aims of the study. Some researchers make relatively few interpretations, wishing to allow the speakers to speak for themselves. The research findings may be used to develop basic knowledge, illustrate and enrich quantitative findings, evaluate programs, and so forth.

Recent qualitative research in psychology has examined, among other topics, life satisfaction in the elderly, parent-child interaction in cancer clinics, stress related to loss of jobs, parents' perception of child psychotherapy, and parents' adjustment to the birth of a handicapped child (Krahn, Hohn, and Kime, 1995).

Qualitative methods have short-comings. Sample size is often small, huge amounts of data can be difficult and costly to analyze, and guidelines for analysis need to be better established and communicated. Also problematic is the subjective nature of the data. How is science to find "the truth" when it is assumed that the truth springs from and can be different for individuals? These issues raise serious questions about reliability and validity, and attempts are being made to address the questions. Some researchers are combining the qualitative and quantitative approaches. The qualitative procedures allow for flexible, broad-scope investigation while the quantitative procedures allow for more traditional data collection and hypothesis testing. The data sets, obtained in different ways, also serve as a check on each other. This strategy, known as *triangulation,* can extend the scope of the findings and increase confidence in them.

individuals were followed from birth to age twenty from 1930 to 1950, their development might be different from that of persons of the same age span followed from 1970 to 1990, due to historical variables. The 1930–1950 group might have had different experiences than the 1970–1990 group (e.g., in health care, educational environments). Thus, these possible *generational,* or *cohort,* effects must be considered in interpreting longitudinal studies.

Sequential Designs

To overcome some of the weaknesses of the cross-sectional and longitudinal strategies, researchers interested in developmental change can combine the two approaches in a variety of sequential designs (e.g., Farrington, 1991). Take, for example, a hypothetical study in which groups of children of different ages are studied over a relatively short time span. At Time I children at ages three, six, and nine years are examined in a cross-sectional study. Similar examination of the same groups of children occurs again three years later at Time II, and again another three years later at Time III. Figure 4–5 depicts the study. As can be seen by reading down the columns of the figure, cross-sectional comparisons can be made at three different times. In addition, as can be seen reading from left to right across the figure, the children (A, B, and C) are studied longitudinally over a six-year period (1994–2000). The age range in the investigation is thus twelve years (from three to fifteen years), although the study is completed in six years (1994 to 2000).

Various comparisons can provide a wealth of information from such a sequential design. To take a simple case, if aggression were found to decrease with age at Time I, and II, and III (cross-sectional analyses) and also across time for each group of children (the longitudinal analy-

ses), evidence would be strong for developmental change over the entire age range. Moreover, by comparing aggression at age six, or nine, or twelve (as shaded in the figure), the impact of societal conditions could also be evaluated. It might be found, for example, that aggression at age nine increased from 1994 to 1997 to 2000. Since only one age is involved, this increase is not developmental and likely indicates a change in societal conditions during the years under investigation. Thus, sequential designs can be powerful in separating age differences and developmental changes, while taking generational effects into consideration.

RISK RESEARCH

We have already seen that the concept of risk is important in understanding, predicting, and potentially reducing behavior problems. For this reason, we will explore risk research more extensively.

The cross-sectional strategy can help identify possible risk factors. We could, for example, study children with learning disabilities at one point in time to determine if parental discord is a strong correlate. If so, the hypothesis could be made that parental discords puts children at risk. However, it is more advantageous to "see" development over time. There are different ways to approach this task.

In *retrospective* designs, youth are identified, some of whom display the problem of interest and others of whom serve as comparison controls. Then information is collected about their earlier characteristics and life experiences. The purpose of this follow-back method is to seek hypotheses about the relationship of early variables and the later-observed characteristics. One obvious weakness of this method concerns the reliability of the data. Old records and memories of the past may be sketchy, biased, or mistaken. Another obvious limitation of the

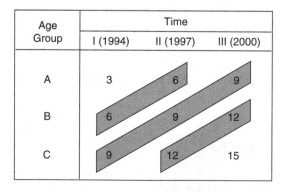

Age Group	Time		
	I (1994)	II (1997)	III (2000)
A	3	6	9
B	6	9	12
C	9	12	15

FIGURE 4–5 Schema of a sequential research design in which children of different ages are examined cross-sectionally and longitudinally.

method is that the discovery of a relationship between the past and present does not establish causation. Nevertheless, this kind of study is relatively easy to conduct and it can help form hypotheses about risk factors. When a control group is not used, the results are not as useful.

Prospective designs investigate risk longitudinally, observing subjects at certain time intervals. As time passes, some of the subjects may show problem behaviors. The researcher can then examine the data to determine what variables are linked to the occurrence of the disorder. Prospective studies have the drawback of all longitudinal research (e.g., expense, loss of subjects). In addition, when researchers begin these demanding investigations, they must select the variables that will be observed along the way. Selection is often based on educated guesses and relevant variables can be missed. Another serious drawback is that the number of youth who eventually develop a disorder of interest may be quite small so that data must be collected on large numbers of participants. Despite these difficulties, the prospective design is invaluable in identifying risk factors and is commonly employed (e.g., Kopp, 1994).

Furthermore, there is a way to enlarge the number of participants who may eventually display behavioral dysfunction. This entails selecting subjects who are known to be at risk because of a factor already associated with the disorder. Such prospective longitudinal research is called *high-risk research*.

A well known example of this approach involves children who are at high risk for developing schizophrenia due to having a parent with schizophrenia. Mednick and Schulsinger (1968) were among the first to use this strategy when they followed 207 adolescents and a low-risk, matched control group. None of the participants were schizophrenic when the study began. A major evaluation was conducted when the subjects averaged twenty-five years and again when

they averaged forty-two (Parnas et al., 1993). Several similar investigations are presently ongoing (Erlenmeyer-Kimling et al., 1990; Marcus et al., 1993). In addition to confirming that having a schizophrenic parent increases risk for the disorder, this research has shown several factors to be variously associated with the development of schizophrenia. These include prenatal and pregnancy complications, childhood and adolescence attention and cognitive deficits, neurological problems, psychosocial factors, and structural and functional brain abnormalities. It would be misleading not to point out that high-risk research is demanding and expensive. In the case of schizophrenia, it appears that it has been fruitful.

EPIDEMIOLOGIC RESEARCH

Epidemiologic research has its basis in medicine and initially focused on infectious diseases. It is assumed that disease or disorder can best be understood and dealt with by viewing individuals in the context of the physical and social environments in which disorder develops (Costello et al., 1993). As we saw in Chapter 1, the method entails the collection of data from large general populations or representative samples of the populations.

A main goal of epidemiology is to establish the prevalence or incidence of disorders in a population. However, the goals are much more extensive than this. Epidemiology also seeks to understand how a disorder is distributed in the population, what factors are correlated with the disorder, the causes and modes of transmission, what groups of people are at high risk, and how the disorder can be reduced. Thus, the quests for scientific knowledge and healthier populations are intricately linked.

Within this framework, researchers interested in behavioral disorders of youth have begun to apply the developmental perspective. For example, they are particularly interested in the continuity and discontinuity of disorders, in the processes that link early and later behaviors, in the risk factors that might operate at different ages, and the consequences of a child's failure to meet environmental demands.

Assessment of behavior to determine disorder is always an issue in epidemiology. In the highly respected Isle of Wight study, conducted in Britain in the 1960s, clinicians did extensive assessments of children (Verhult and Koot, 1992). But expense and time limitations can preclude that sort of procedure. More recently, standardized structured or semi-structured interviews have been increasingly employed and are more efficient. The use of such standard instruments to obtain information has additional benefits. They are designed with the goal of diagnosis in mind, and the findings from different studies can be readily compared. At the same time, these instruments can limit the questions that might otherwise be asked by sensitive clinicians. The development of assessment techniques for epidemiology is an ongoing effort.

Correlational methods are often used in epidemiological studies. The cross-sectional strategy can be useful. For example, data collected from a community sample of youth can indicate the prevalence of disorders and the correlates of the existing disorders. However, longitudinal data are needed to understand developmental patterns of disorders (Costello, 1990; Costello et al., 1993).

Even now, however, epidemiology provides valuable information. Numerous studies provide data on the rates of disorders and how the disorders are distributed in populations (e.g., by sex, social class, race). This knowledge is crucial for the delivery of optimal mental health services. Identification of correlates makes possible the formulation of hypotheses about risk and causation and

helps rule out other considerations (e.g., Offord and Fleming, 1991). For instance, population studies have failed to show a link between autism and social class, thus ruling out social class variables as risk or causal factors in this dysfunction. As epidemiological research becomes ever more advanced, increased benefits will be reaped. In the United States, this is an exciting time in epidemiology as the federal government has committed major funding for the study of youth (Costello et al., 1993).

ETHICAL ISSUES

Scientific research is enormously beneficial, but it brings concern about the welfare and rights of participants. Underlying such concern is sensitivity to individual rights, both legal and ethical, and to past documented abuse of research subjects. One well-known instance in which the problem of abuse was raised involves study, began in 1932, of the natural course of syphilis. The investigation was continued into the early 1970s, even though the development of antibiotics could have provided treatment for the subjects long before that (Kelty, 1981).

Abuse in social science research probably has not been as dramatic as in biomedical research, but ethical issues do exist. In the widely discussed Milgram (1963) study, for example, subjects were deceived into thinking that they were applying electric shocks to another human. The study was designed to evaluate whether subjects would obey a directive to harm others. Many of them did, but they suffered discomfort about their behavior. A post-experimental interview was included to alleviate this stress. Nevertheless, serious questions were raised about the ethics of researchers deceptively setting up a situation that brought guilt, anxiety, and embarrassment to the participants (e.g., Baumrind, 1964; Murray, 1988).

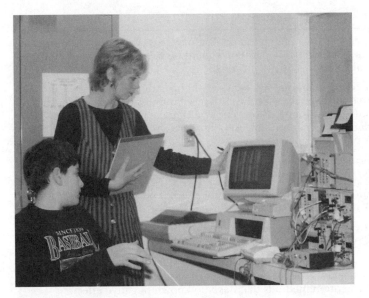

When a youngster participates in research, informed consent by a parent or guardian, and where possible the youth, should be obtained. What constitutes informed consent by a youngster is a complex issue.

Research with children has sometimes involved procedures in which the participants were made uncomfortable, for example, by waiting alone in a room (Cozby, Worden, and Kee, 1989). Studies investigating aggression have engaged children in aggressive acts, or have exposed them to aggressive live or filmed models. And children have served as subjects in research on the effects of medications. Clearly, there is potential for harm that must be guarded against.

In general, ethical concerns primarily address the issues of deception, informed consent, possible harm and discomfort to subjects, and confidentiality. For many years the American Psychological Association has published a manual of ethical guidelines for research. The Society for Research in Child Development publishes similar guidelines, which specifically address research with children. Table 4–3 summarizes these guidelines. Psychological research also falls under the guidelines of the National Commission for the Protection of Human Subjects of Biomedical and Behavioral Research. The commission has mandated that institutions involved in research set up boards to judge the ethics of proposed research before the research is begun. Institutional Review Boards consider such things as the scientific soundness of the research, the risk/benefits ratio, and privacy (Langer, 1985). Special consideration is given to cases involving young subjects, particularly concerning informed consent.

Since the issue of informed consent is especially complex with young people, we will look at it further. Informed consent requires that subjects consent to participate, reasonably understand the risks and benefits of the research, and be provided appropriate information (Frankel, 1978; Levine, 1991; Weithorn, 1987). This includes understanding the purpose of the research, the role of the subjects, procedures, and possible alternatives to participation. Clearly, young children often cannot understand these nuances. Given adequate information, most parents are competent to give informed consent, and they are required to do so because children are not of legal age.

TABLE 4–3 Ethical Standards for Research with Children

Principle 1: Non-harmful Procedures. No research operation that may physically or psychologically harm the child should be used. The least stressful operation should be used. Doubts about harmfulness should be discussed with consultants.

Principle 2: Informed Consent. The child's consent or assent should be obtained. The child should be informed of features of the research that may affect his or her willingness to participate. In working with infants, parents should be informed. If consent would make the research impossible, it may be ethically conducted under certain circumstances; judgments should be made with institutional review boards.

Principle 3: Parental Consent. Informed consent of parents, guardians, and those acting in loci parentis (e.g., school superintendents) similarly should be obtained, preferably in writing.

Principle 4: Additional Consent. Informed consent should be obtained of persons, such as teachers, whose interaction with the child is the subject of the research.

Principle 5: Incentives. Incentives to participate in the research must be fair and not unduly exceed incentives the child normally experiences.

Principle 6: Deception. If deception or withholding information is considered essential, colleagues must agree with this judgment. Participants should be told later of the reason for the deception. Effort should be made to employ deception methods that have no known negative effects.

Principle 7: Anonymity. Permission should be gained for access to institutional records, and anonymity of information should be preserved.

Principle 8: Mutual Responsibilities. There should be clear agreement as to the responsibilities of all parties in the research. The investigator must honor all promises and commitments.

Principle 9: Jeopardy. When, in the research, information comes to the investigator's attention that may jeopardize the child's welfare, the information must be discussed with parents or guardians and experts who can arrange for assistance to the child.

Principle 10: Unforeseen Consequences. When research procedures result in unforeseen, undesirable consequences for the participant, the consequences should be corrected and the procedures redesigned.

Principle 11: Confidentiality. The identity of subjects and all information about them should be kept confidential. When confidentiality might be threatened, this possibility and methods to prevent it should be explained as part of the procedures of obtaining informed consent.

Principle 12: Informing Participants. Immediately after data collection, any misconceptions that might have arisen should be clarified. General findings should be given the participants, appropriate to their understanding. When scientific or humane reasons justify withholding information, efforts should be made so that withholding has no damaging consequences.

Principle 13: Reporting Results. Investigators' words may carry unintended weight; thus, caution should be used in reporting results, giving advice, making evaluative statements.

Principle 14: Implications of Findings. Investigators should be mindful of the social, political, and human implications of the research, and especially careful in the presentations of findings.

Summarized from the Report from the Committee for Ethical Conduct in Child Development Research, *SRCD Newsletter* (Winter 1990). Society for Research in Child Development, Inc.

However, unlike in past times, children are now considered under the law as "persons" whose decisions must be considered (Gaylin, 1982). Thus, the question: What constitutes informed consent for children? It is suggested that adolescents be given the same information as adults and be asked to sign consent forms (e.g., Ferguson, 1978; Langer, 1985). The same procedure can be used for the school-age child, but researchers need to convey information in more concrete terms, with personal consequences spelled out. At the very least, children as young as seven years should be asked whether they assent to participate. With infants and toddlers, informed consent is not a reasonable expectation, and parental or guardian consent may be sufficient for a child's participation.

Such proxy consent has problems, however, because parent and child needs are not always identical. Furthermore, parents may feel coerced by social and economic pressures into permitting their child's participation. For example, if research participation is desired by an agency that offers therapeutic care, the parents of a child needing care may be afraid to refuse permission. These considerations raise doubts about parental consent. In some cases that were brought to the attention of the courts, guardians were appointed to oversee decisions about the children.

Parental legal rights, the child's competence to understand and make decisions, and the significance of the decision to the child all play a part in guiding ethical standards for informed consent. An important distinction is made between the child's participation in a therapeutic or nontherapeutic procedure (Levine, 1991). In some situations, the child's decision may not be binding and parental consent may be sufficient. For instance, the child's refusal to participate may be disregarded when the research risk is minimal and the child may benefit. With nontherapeutic research, the child's consent may be considered of utmost importance—for example, when risk is greater than minimal and the research is unlikely to directly benefit the child.

In the final analysis, the ethics of research, like other ethical concerns, can never be a completely settled matter. Ongoing discussion and tension are appropriate. The prevailing emphasis on human rights and recognition of past abuse has led to quite stringent surveillance and guidelines. It is important that reasonable balance be maintained, however, so that beneficial research goes forward (e.g., Arnold et al., 1995).

SUMMARY

Knowledge of human behavior is gained by scientific methods that vary with regard to settings, procedures, methods, and purpose. The aim of science is to describe phenomena and offer explanations for them. Theoretical concepts guide all aspects of research, including the hypotheses advanced. Hypothesis testing builds knowledge systematically and is tied to the advancement of theory.

Observation and measurement are at the heart of science. The assumption that events repeat themselves, given the same or similar conditions, places importance on the reliability, or consistency, of research findings. Also crucial is the issue of validity, the soundness or correctness of findings. Internal validity refers to the degree to which alternative explanations for results can be confidently ruled out. External validity refers to generalizability of findings to other populations and settings.

Basic research methods include the case study, systematic naturalistic observation, correlational studies, the experiment, single-subject experiments, and controlled observations and mixed designs. Each of these has weaknesses and strengths. Interest in qualitative methods has increased.

In addition to these research methods, cross-sectional and longitudinal strategies may be adopted. Cross-sectional studies examine groups of people at one time. They are efficient and economical and can establish age differences. The longitudinal strategy is much better for tracing development, but it is expensive, requires lengthy commitment from researchers, and may suffer bias from subject loss and repeated measurement. In addition, longitudinal data may reflect generational, or cohort, effects. Sequential designs combine the longitudinal and cross-sectional strategies to permit examination of developmental change, age differences, and the influence of generational (historical) variables.

Retrospective (follow-back) studies and prospective longitudinal research of individuals with behavior disorders are useful in identifying risk and possible causal factors. High-risk research follows the development of persons believed to be at risk for a disorder. High-risk studies have been fruitful in investigating schizophrenia.

Epidemiological research aims to establish the rates and distribution of disorders in a population, the factors correlated with disorders, and risk and causal variables. It has been most successful in providing information about prevalence, correlates, and risks.

Ethical issues in research focus on deception, informed consent, possible harm and discomfort to subjects, and confidentiality. Youth's participation in research raises concerns over and above those expressed for adults. Informed consent is especially complex when research subjects are children. Several professional and government groups provide ethical and legal guidelines. Concern for research participants must be weighed with the potential benefits derived from studying human behavior.

5

CLASSIFICATION
AND ASSESSMENT

This chapter is concerned with how childhood and adolescent behavior disorders are defined, grouped, and evaluated. The terms classification or taxonomy and diagnosis are used to refer to the process of description and grouping. By *classification* and *taxonomy* we mean delineating major categories or dimensions of behavior disorders for either scientific or clinical purposes. *Diagnosis* usually refers to the process of assigning an individual to a category of the classification system. *Assessment* refers to an ongoing process of evaluating youngsters, in part to assist to processes of classification and diagnosis. These entwined processes thus are intricately related to the scientific and clinical aspects of child and adolescent disorders.

CLASSIFICATION AND DIAGNOSIS

A classification system is a way to systematically describe a phenomenon. Biologists have classification systems for living organisms, and physicians classify physical dysfunction. Similarly, systems exist to classify behavioral disorders. These systems describe categories or dimensions of problem behaviors. A category is a discrete grouping, for example, a category of anxiety disorder

or conduct disorder. In contrast, the term dimension implies that a behavior is continuous and can occur to various degrees. Thus, for example, a child may exhibit high, moderate, or low levels of anxiety.

Some systems work better than others, and we may ask: What makes a good system of classification? Before we examine current systems for classifying child and adolescent disordered behavior, we need to examine the criteria by which any system is judged.

First and foremost, the categories or dimensions of the system must be clearly defined. This means that the criteria for defining a category must be explicitly stated. Next, it must be demonstrated that the category or dimension exists. This means that features used to describe a category or dimension tend to occur together regularly—in one or more situations or as measured by one or more methods. A classification system composed of categories or dimensions that are either poorly defined or that do not exist is doomed to failure.

Classification systems must also be reliable and valid. These terms were applied to research methods in Chapter 4. When applied to classification or diagnosis they retain the general meanings of consistency and correctness but are used in somewhat different ways.

With regard to reliability, *interrater reliability* refers to the consistency with which diagnosticians use the same category to describe a person's behavior. It addresses the question, for example: Is Billy's behavior called separation anxiety by two or more professionals who observe it? *Test-retest reliability* asks if the use of a category is stable over some reasonable period of time. For example, is Mary's problem diagnosed as learning disability again when she returns for a second evaluation?

A system must also be *valid*. To have validity, diagnostic categories, for example, must be clearly discriminable from one another. Also, a diagnosis must provide us with more information than we had when we originally defined the category. Thus, diagnoses should give us information about the etiology of a disorder, the course of development that the disorder is expected to take, response to treatment, or some additional clinical features of the problem. Does the diagnosis of conduct disorder, for example, tell us something about this disorder that is different from other disorders? Does the diagnosis tell us something about what causes this problem? Does it tell us what is likely to happen to youngsters having this disorder and what treatments are likely to help? Does it tell us additional things about these young people or their backgrounds? The question of validity is thus largely one of whether we know anything we did not already know when we defined the category.

Finally, a classification system is judged by its *clinical utility;* that is, by how complete and useful it is. A diagnostic system that describes all the behavioral disorders that come to the attention of clinicians in a manner that is useful to them is more likely to be employed.

Clinically Derived Classification Systems

Clinically derived classification systems are based on the consensus of clinicians that certain characteristics occur together. Historically the classification of abnormal behavior focused primarily on adult disorders. Until recently there was no extensive classification scheme for child and adolescent behavior disorders.

DSM.   The most widely used classification system in the United States is the American Psychiatric Association's Diagnostic and Statistical Manual of Mental Disorders (DSM). The Tenth Revision of the International Classification of Diseases (ICD) developed by the World Health Organization (WHO, 1992) is an alternative system which is widely employed and Diagnostic Classification: 0–3 is a system developed to classify mental disorders of very young children (Zero to Three, 1995). Since the DSM system is the dominant system in the United States, we will focus our discussion on it.

The DSM is a categorical classification system that is an outgrowth of the original psychiatric taxonomy developed by Kraeplin in 1883, and from which children's disorders were omitted. DSM-I contained only two categories of childhood disorders: Adjustment Reaction and Childhood Schizophrenia (American Psychiatric Association, 1952). By the 1960s it had become obvious that a more extensive system was needed. DSM-II added the category of Behavior Disorders of Childhood and Adolescence, which was subdivided into six kinds of disorders (American Psychiatric Association, 1968). The next two revisions, DSM-III and III-R, expanded appreciably the number of categories specific to children and adolescents. As in the past, some adult diagnoses could also be used for youth. These two revisions and the most recent revision, DSM-IV, also involved some changes in the organization of particular categories (American Psychiatric Association, 1980; 1987; 1994).

In DSM-IV all disorders are classified in one of two major groups called axes. On Axis I the clinician indicates any existing clinical disorder (e.g., Conduct Disorder) or other condition that may be a focus of treatment (for example, an academic problem). On Axis II Mental Retardation or a Personality Disorder, if present, is indicated. These two axes represent the diagnostic categories that are the core of the DSM system. In addition to these two axes, it is recommended that each individual be evaluated in three other arenas, so that a fuller picture is created. Any current medical conditions that are relevant to understanding or treating the youngster are indicated on Axis III. Axis IV is used to indicate any psychosocial or environmental problems that may affect diagnosis, treatment, or prognosis (e.g., death of a family member, housing problems). Axis V is for reporting the clinician's judgment of the child or adolescent's overall level of functioning.

Table 5–1 presents the major DSM-IV diagnostic categories described as "usually first diagnosed in infancy, childhood, or adolescence." Each category is further divided into subcategories. A clinician may give a youngster any of these diagnoses or a diagnosis from elsewhere in the DSM-IV can also be employed. Some of the other diagnostic categories that might be employed for youngsters are: psychoactive substance use disorders, schizophrenia, mood disorders, anxiety disorders, eating disorders, and psychological factors affecting medical condition.

The current DSM handling of child and adolescent disorders is considerably more complex and provides more specific subcategories than did earlier versions. While this was intended to correct the limited attention to childhood problems in earlier versions, the outcome has been controversial. One issue is whether the existence of specific subcategories is justified by empirical evidence. Another is that the more specific subcategories may threaten the reliability of a system. In earlier attempts at diagnosing adult disorders, agreement among diagnosticians

TABLE 5–1 DSM-IV Disorders Usually First Diagnosed in Infancy, Childhood, or Adolescence

Mental Retardation
Learning Disorders
Motor Skills Disorder
Communication Disorders
Pervasive Developmental Disorders (e.g., Autistic Disorder)
Attention Deficit and Disruptive Behavior Disorders
Feeding and Eating Disorders of Infancy or Early Childhood
Tic Disorder
Elimination Disorders
Other Disorders of Infancy, Childhood, or Adolescence (e.g., Separation Anxiety Disorder, Selective Mutism)

Adapted and reprinted with permission from the *Diagnostic and Statistical Manual of Mental Disorders, Fourth Edition*. Copyright 1994, American Psychiatric Association.

was considerably lower for subgroups than for larger categories (e.g., Beck et al., 1962). Two-thirds of these disagreements between diagnosticians resulted from inadequate criteria for making a diagnosis. Thus efforts were made in DSM-III, DSM-III-R, and DSM-IV to improve reliability by replacing general descriptions of disorders with clear and more delineated diagnostic criteria. The diagnosis of Separation Anxiety Disorder, for example, requires that the child 1) exhibit three or more of eight specific symptoms for at least four weeks, 2) have an onset of these symptoms before the age of eighteen (an inclusion criterion), and 3) that the disturbance does not occur exclusively during the course of Pervasive Development Disorder, Schizophrenia, or other psychotic disorder (an exclusion criterion).

This strategy for improving reliability has been somewhat successful, but it is still the case, as would be expected, that reliability is good for some disorders and poorer for others. The reliability of diagnoses of childhood anxiety disorders is consistent with this general description (Werry, 1994). Under certain circumstances moderate to strong reliability can be achieved. Even here, however, reliability varies depending on the specific anxiety disorder, the source of information (parent, child), and the child's age and sex (Rapee et al., 1994). Furthermore, these higher levels of reliability are reported under research conditions in which the diagnostic/information gathering procedures employed are different than those likely to be used in clinical practice.

There have also been efforts to examine the validity of the DSM approach to classification. For example, during the development of DSM-IV, the validity of describing three subtypes of Attention Deficit Hyperactivity Disorder was examined (Lahey et al., 1994). Several differences were found among children who met the criteria for the three subcategories. Not only did they display different behaviors; the groups also differed in age, sex ratio, academic impairment, and peer acceptance. Therefore, knowing whether a child meets the diagnostic criteria for one and not another subcategory also imparts additional information that did not enter into the diagnostic process. These findings thus support the validity of the three diagnostic subcategories. Nevertheless, despite evidence for the validity of some diagnostic categories, there is still considerable concern regarding the validity of many of the DSM child and adolescent categories, even among those who are in large part sympathetic to the system's approach to classification.

There is broad agreement that starting with DSM-III and DSM-III-R, and continuing with DSM-IV, positive directions were taken: the increased use of a structured set of rules for diagnosis, and greater comprehensiveness. Also, in developing DSM-IV, work groups attempted to draw on empirical data in a more consistent fashion (Widiger et al., 1991). The system, however, is not without its critics and substantial conceptual and political issues remain unresolved

(Nathan, 1994). In addition to questions concerning reliability and validity, concern has been expressed about the very comprehensiveness of this system. The motivation for and wisdom of making such a wide variety of youngsters' behaviors classifiable as mental disorders has been questioned (e.g., Harris, 1979; Schacht and Nathan, 1977). Designating problems in academic skill areas such as reading and mathematics as mental disorders is an example of this concern. Also, although DSM-IV was probably more open to diverse views than earlier versions, there were still relatively few nonpsychiatrists, members of racial and other minority groups, or women participating in its development (Nathan, 1994).

Some observers accept that the DSM system is a dominant reality in the present zeitgeist. Indeed, a classification system, like anything else, is viewed as being influenced by the general social atmosphere within which it exists. Despite its acceptance and use, however, the system is in some ways fundamentally inconsistent with some approaches to children's problems (e.g., Kendall, 1987; Valla et al., 1994). For example, DSM does not employ situational variability to moderate diagnostic labels. This may be problematic for a behavioral perspective in which situational factors are presumed to influence behavior. Furthermore, some have argued that the DSM promotes a disease model which emphasizes biological etiology and treatment and deemphasizes environmental factors and the cultural context (e.g., Resnick, 1993).

Also, despite many improvements, it is still the case that decisions regarding DSM often rest on political or professional issues or the need to compromise. This is the case since the choice and definitions of categories ultimately rests on a decision by a select group of professionals. Thus, other criticisms of the DSM system are based on the fundamental question of whether the foundation of the whole approach (i.e., consensus among clinicians) is sound (e.g., Eysenck, 1986; Tsuang, 1993).

Empirical Approaches to Classification

The empirical approach to classifying child and adolescent behavior problems is an alternative to the clinical approach. This approach employs statistical techniques to identify patterns of behavior that are interrelated. The general procedure is for the respondent to indicate the presence or absence of specific behaviors in the youngster. The information from these responses is quantified in some way. For example, a "0" is marked if the child does not exhibit a certain characteristic, a "1" is given if a moderate degree of the characteristic is displayed, and a "2" is indicated if the characteristic is clearly present. Such information is obtained for a large number of youngsters. Statistical techniques are then employed to indicate which behaviors tend to occur together. Factor analysis and cluster analysis are the primary statistical techniques employed in these studies. These procedures are based on correlations among items. The correlation of every item with the others is calculated, and groups of items that tend to occur together are thus identified. These are referred to as factors or clusters. The term "syndrome" is also often employed to describe behaviors that tend to occur together, whether identified by empirical or clinical judgment procedures. Thus, rather than relying on clinicians' views as to which behaviors tend to occur together, empirical and statistical procedures are employed as the basis for developing a classification scheme.

There have been multiple efforts to develop empirically defined syndromes. This research has involved different instruments, responded to by different kinds of adult caregivers, evaluating different populations of youth, seen in different settings. The results are quite consistent (Achenbach, 1985; Quay, 1986a).

Substantial evidence exists for two *broadband*, or general, clusters of behaviors or characteristics. One of these clusters has been given the various labels of externalizing, undercontrolled, or conduct disorder. Fighting, temper tantrums, disobedience, and destructiveness are some of the characteristics frequently associated with this pattern. The second grouping has been variously labeled internalizing, overcontrolled, or anxiety-withdrawal. Descriptions such as anxious, shy, withdrawn, and depressed are some of the characteristics associated with this grouping.

Among the instruments used to derive the two broad-band clusters just described is the Child Behavior Checklist (CBCL), which can be completed by the parents of children 4–18 years of age (Achenbach, 1991b). The Teacher Report Form (TRF) is a parallel instrument completed by teachers of children 5–18 years old (Achenbach, 1991c) and the Youth Self-Report is designed to be completed by youths 11–18 (Achenbach, 1991d). Research with these instruments has identified eight empirically defined less general, or "narrow-band" syndromes common to the three instruments. Three of these syndromes fall within the broader category of Internalizing, two within the Externalizing grouping, and three are neither clearly Internalizing or Externalizing (Achenbach, 1991a). These syndromes are described in Table 5–2. Every child who is evaluated receives a score on each of the syndromes and a profile of syndrome scores for a particular child can be described (see Figure 5–1). Thus this approach to classification evaluates youngsters on several dimensions rather than designating a category of disorder.

There are two sets of norms available against which to compare an individual child's or adolescent's scores. A youngster's scores can be compared to norms for nonreferred children or adolescents or norms based on young people referred for mental health services. There are separate norms

TABLE 5–2   Eight Syndromes Common to the CBCL, TRF, and YSR

Internalizing
   Withdrawn
   Somatic Complaints
   Anxious/Depressed
Neither Clearly Internalizing nor Externalizing
   Social Problems
   Thought Problems
   Attention Problems
Externalizing
   Delinquent Behavior
   Aggressive Behavior

Adapted from Achenbach, 1991a.

for each sex in particular age ranges, as rated by each type of informant. Thus, there are separate CBCL norms for boys 4–11, boys 12–18, girls 4–11, and girls 12–18 and, separate norms for parent, teacher, and youth informants (Achenbach, 1991b, c, d).

The availability of the CBCL, TRF, and YSR makes it possible to compare multiple informants' reports about the child with respect to a common set of problem items and dimensions. So, for example, when two or more respondents using these instruments describe a child, a statistic can be computed indicating the degree of agreement. This degree of agreement for a particular child can then be compared to the degree of agreement between comparable informants for a large representative sample. Thus, it is possible to know if the degree of agreement between Tommy's mother and teacher is less than, similar to, or greater than the average mother-teacher agreement about boys in Tommy's age range.

Achenbach (1993) suggests that in addition to describing the multiple characteristics of a single youngster, the Child Behavior Checklist (and TRF or YSR) can also be employed to identify groups of youngsters who have similar patterns of syndrome scores. A profile of scores on the eight syndromes is prepared for each youth. By statistically analyzing large samples of profiles of youngsters referred for clinical services and putting them into groups of similar profiles, a typology of profiles can be

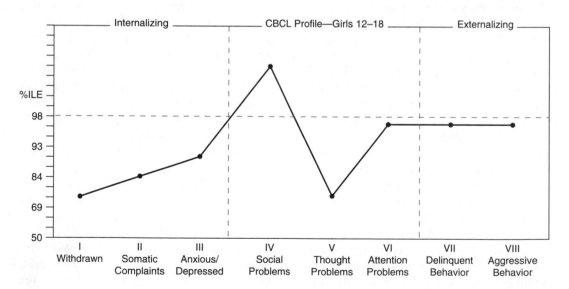

FIGURE 5–1   A profile of a 15 year-old girl based on a Child Behavior Checklist completed by her mother.

Adapted from Achenbach, 1993.

formed (Achenbach, 1993). An individual youngster's profile can be examined for the degree to which it is similar to one of these profile types.

Reliability and validity. Reliability studies of empirically derived systems generally indicate that problem scores are quite reliable. The pattern of reliability is both interesting and informative (Achenbach, 1991a).

Test-retest correlations from two ratings by the same informant are often in the .80 and .90 range. So, for example, correlations for mothers' ratings on the CBCL taken one week apart ranged from .82 to .95 for different syndrome scores. Agreement between different raters observing the child in the same situation is also quite good, although lower than for two evaluations by the same person. Agreement of mothers and fathers on the CBCL, for example, varied depending on syndrome and ranged between .48 (Thought Problems) and .79 (Attention Problems). If one averages parent agreement across syndromes, the interparent correlation also varied by the age and gender of the child and ranged from .65 to .75. Level of agreement, however, is notably lower between raters who observe youngsters in distinctly different situations. The average correlation between parents and teachers for the CBCL and TRF Total Problem Score, for example, was .44. Degree of agreement varied as a function of youngster's age and sex. Finally, children's self-ratings on the YSR were significantly, but modestly, related to parents' ratings (.36 for boys, .40 for girls) and teachers' ratings (.27 for boys, .25 for girls). These lower correlations may reveal something about young people's behavior, rather than just about the reliability of the approach to classification (Achenbach and Edelbrock, 1989). At the very least, they suggest that a youngster's behavior may vary considerably with different individuals and in different situations. Also, certain attributes may be more or less evident to individuals other than the youngsters themselves (e.g., aggression versus feelings of loneliness). Such findings alert us to the possible limitations and bias of any one rater's perspective (Achenbach, McConaughy and Howell, 1987; Orvaschel, Ambrosini, and Rabinovich, 1993).

The validity of empirically derived classification systems is indicated by a variety of studies. The findings described above indicating that the same broad-band syndromes have emerged in a variety of studies employing different instruments, different types of raters, and different samples suggest that the categories reflect valid distinctions. Also, Achenbach (1991b) reports on comparisons of the Child Behavior Checklist and other commonly employed checklists, completed by the same sample of parents. Correlations were significant for total problem scores, the broad-band syndromes (internalizing-externalizing), and almost all of the comparable narrow-band syndromes. It is important to remember that these significant correlations emerged even though the instruments and their categories often consist of different items. The findings show that the syndromes are valid ones because they emerge under a variety of conditions.

Another way of examining validity is to investigate whether differences in scores relate to other criteria. Comparison of youngsters referred for outpatient mental health services to a sample of nonreferred young people matched for SES, age, and gender indicated that the clinical sample differed significantly from the nonreferred sample on all scores and that this was true for all sex/age groups (Achenbach, 1991b). Scores on these empirical syndromes have also been shown to predict outcomes such as academic problems, use of mental health services, and police contacts six years later (Achenbach et al., 1995b). Findings such as these support the validity of the empirical and dimensional approach to classification.

The Dangers of Labeling

As we have already noted, classification and diagnosis are intended to facilitate understanding and treatment of behavior disorders. As scientists, we can study groups of young people to seek common etiologies. As clinicians, we can benefit from previous knowledge in our approach to new cases. However, categories, like perspectives, may also limit the information we seek or the interpretations we make of events. This is one reason why applying a category to an individual young person and transforming it into a label can be dangerous.

Although classification is intended as a scientific and clinical enterprise, it can be seen as a social process (Rothblum, Solomon, and Albee, 1986). The diagnostic label becomes a social status, which carries implications for how people are thought of and treated. If this impact is negative, the label actually detracts from the original purpose of categorizing—that of helping young people.

From the start, formal classification has had the categorization of disorders, not persons, as its stated intent (Rutter and Gould, 1985). Indeed, Cantwell, one of the creators of the current DSM approach, notes: "Any classification system classifies psychiatric *disorders* of childhood; it does *not* classify *children*. Thus it is correct to say, 'Tommy Jones has infantile autism.' It is incorrect to say 'Tommy Jones, the autistic' . . ." (Cantwell, 1980, p. 350). Often ease of communication is the reason for a particular phrasing. For example, the term autistic children may be employed rather than repeating the phrase "children receiving the diagnosis of autism." Thus it is realistic to expect the use of terms such as "autistic children" or "depressed children," here and elsewhere, despite the intent to avoid misplacement of labels. In light of such practices, it is important to be aware of the potential negative effects of the labeling process.

One of the dangers inherent in classification, that of only "noticing" information consistent with a label, is illustrated in a study by Foster and Salvia (1977). Teachers were asked to view a videotape of a boy and rate his academic work and social behavior. The tape displayed age- and grade-appropriate behavior in all cases, but some teachers were told that the boy was learning disabled, while others were told that he was normal. Teachers watching the "learning disabled" boy rated him as less academically able and his behavior as more socially undesirable than did teachers watching the "normal" child.

The use of labels also invites other difficulties. The danger of overgeneralization is one concern: It may be assumed that all youngsters labeled with Attention Deficit Hyperactivity Disorder, for example, are more alike than they actually are. Such an assumption readily leads to neglect of the *individual* child or adolescent. It is also possible that if people react to the youngster as a member of a category, then the youngster may behave in a manner consistent with the expectations of the label. Critics also point to the logical fallacy that often results from the use of labels. A label originally used to *describe* a behavioral pattern may then be stated as the *cause* of the same behavior. For example, a clinician who observes a pattern of restlessness, high levels of active behavior, and poor attention may describe this behavior as hyperactivity. In a subsequent conference with the child's parents, the clinician may then state that the child's problem behavior is caused by hyperactivity. Clearly, this mistake can interfere with the search for better understanding.

Lilly (1979b) and others also suggest that traditional diagnostic categories ignore the fact that a youngster's problems "belong" to at least one other person—the one identifying or reporting them. As Algozzinne (1977) has noted, the young person may not be inherently "disturbed," but is labeled deviant because of the reactions of others to his or her behavior. Algozzine modified the instructions for the Behavior Problem Checklist. Adults were asked "how disturbing" particular items would be in working with children. The responses of adults to this "Disturbing Behavior Checklist" were submitted to a factor analysis. Interestingly, behavior rated as to degree of *disturbingness* seemed to cluster in much the same way as in previous studies of *disturbed* behavior. As we shall see throughout this book, there is much evidence that supports the notion that how a youngster is described and viewed may reflect as much on who is doing the describing as it does on the behavior of the child or adolescent.

Many experts involved in the study and treatment of children or adolescents are concerned about the problems of categorical labels, and advocate to reduce the possible harmful effects. Some recommend that services be provided without inflexible references to categories. It is acknowledged, however, that categorization is embedded in our thinking and problem solving. Completely discarding categorization, even if it were desirable, is probably impossible. Thus, it is both valuable and necessary to be sensitive to social factors inherent in the use of categories, the social status imparted by a label, and the impact of labels on the young person and others (Hobbs, 1975; Rutter and Gould, 1985).

ASSESSMENT

Evaluating child and adolescent problems is a complex process that most often involves assessing multiple aspects of functioning. Thus, a broad range of behavioral, affective, cognitive, and physical components must be considered. Knowledge of age-related changes in and base-rates of problems is also required. The young person must also be understood in the context of family, peer,

and school systems and, therefore, aspects of these systems must often be addressed, as well. In addition, information must be obtained from a variety of sources (e.g., the youngster, parents, teachers). Assessment thus requires the use of multiple and varied methods and familiarity with assessment instruments for individuals of many different ages. The process requires considerable skill and sensitivity.

Assessment is best accomplished by a team of clinicians carefully trained in the administration and interpretation of specific procedures and instruments. Because it is usually conducted immediately upon contact with the young person or family, it demands special sensitivity to anxiety, fear, shyness, manipulativeness, and the like. If treatment ensues, assessment should be a continuous process, so that new information can be gleaned, and the ongoing effects of treatment can be ascertained. In this way the clinician remains open to nuances and can avoid rigid judgments about a multifaceted and complex phenomenon.

The Interview

The general clinical interview is clearly the most common form of assessment. Information on all areas of functioning is obtained by interviewing the youngster and various others in the child or adolescent's social environment. The fact that behavior is likely to vary according to the situation or be viewed differently by various observers argues for interviewing a variety of individuals who have contact with the youngster (for example, parents, siblings, teachers).

Whether the youngster will be interviewed alone probably varies with age. The older child generally is more capable and is more likely to provide valuable information than is a younger child. Nevertheless, clinicians often elect to interview even the very young child in order to obtain their own impressions. Preschool and grade school children can provide valuable information if appropriate developmental considerations are involved in tailoring the interview to the individual child (Bierman and Schwartz, 1986). For example, an adultlike face-to-face interview may be intimidating for a young child. This difficulty may be reduced if the interview is modeled after a more familiar play or school task.

Most clinicians seek information concerning the nature of the problem, past and recent history, present conditions, feelings and perceptions, attempts to solve the problem, and expectations concerning treatment. The general clinical interview is used not only to determine the nature of the presenting problem and perhaps formulate a diagnosis. It is employed to also gather information that allows the clinician to conceptualize the case and to plan an appropriate therapeutic intervention.

A recent development in the interviewing of children and adolescents is the use of structured interviews (Gutterman, O'Brien, and Young, 1987; Hodges and Zeman, 1993). The general clinical interview, discussed above, is usually described as open-ended or unstructured. Such interviews are

most often conducted in the context of a therapeutic interaction and are employed along with a variety of other assessment instruments. Thus, it has been difficult to evaluate the reliability and validity of the interview itself. Structured interviews have arisen in part to create interviews that are likely to be more reliable. They also have been developed for the more limited purpose of deriving a diagnosis based upon a particular classification scheme such as the DSM or for use in screening large populations for the prevalence of disorders. Table 5–3 lists several of the structured interviews used with children and adolescents.

In the unstructured general clinical interview there are no particular questions that the clinician must ask, no designated format, and no stipulated method to record information. That is not to say that there are no guidelines or agreed upon procedures for conducting an effective interview. Indeed, there is an extensive literature on effective interviewing (cf. Cox and Rutter, 1985). However, unstructured interviews are intended to give the clinician great latitude. In contrast, structured interviews are essentially a list of problem behaviors and

---

TABLE 5–3   Some Structured Interviews Used in Diagnosing Childhood Disorders

Anxiety Disorders Interview for Children (ADIS-C)
  Developed for differential diagnosis of anxiety disorders in children. (Silverman and Eisen, 1992)

Child Assessment Schedule (CAS)
  A conversational format modeled after traditional child clinical interview—relatively low in structure. (Hodges et al., 1982)

Diagnostic Interview for Children and Adolescents (DICA)
  A highly structured interview with separate versions for younger and older children. (Welner et al., 1987)

Diagnostic Interview Schedule for Children-Revised (DISC-R)
  A highly structured interview with questions organized diagnostically. (Shaffer et al., 1993)

Interview Schedule for Children (ISC)
  Low in structure—primary aim is assessment of affective symptoms and associated problems. (Kovacs, 1985)

Schedule for Affective Disorders and Schizophrenia in School-Aged Children (K-SADS)
  Intermediate in structure and, despite title, it assesses a wide range of childhood disorders. (Puig-Antich and Chambers, 1978)

events that the interviewer must cover. In addition, rules are provided for how the interview is to be conducted and how the data are to be recorded.

It is useful to distinguish two kinds of structured interviews: highly structured and semistructured (Edelbrock and Costello, 1988b; Hodges and Zeman, 1993). Highly structured interviews seek to minimize the role of clinical judgment and thereby produce higher levels of interrater reliability. This is achieved by specifying the exact wording and sequence of questions and by providing well-defined rules for recording and rating the respondent's answers. These interviews are thus likely to yield more objective and quantifiable data. In the semistructured interview, the interviewer is allowed some flexibility in what is asked, how questions are phrased, and how responses are recorded. This allows interviews to appear less stilted and more spontaneous since the clinician can adjust them to the individual client. However, since the interview may be conducted in a slightly different manner by each clinician, the results are more likely to differ as well. At present it is not clear which degree of structure yields better data. What degree of structure is most desirable should probably be determined by the purposes and circumstances of the interview.

The investigation of the reliability of interviews must take into account many variables. This necessity is illustrated in a study by Edelbrock and his colleagues (Edelbrock, et al., 1985). The Diagnostic Interview for Children, a structured interview that covers a broad range of symptoms and behaviors, was administered to 242 children and their parents. The children had been referred for inpatient or outpatient mental health services. Interviews were conducted twice, with both children and parents, approximately nine days apart. Interestingly, the reliability based on the child reports was lower for younger than for older children, whereas the reliability based on parent reports was higher for the younger children. The authors suggest that these findings are related to the cognitive development of the children on the one hand, and to shifts in parents' perceptions and awareness of their child's behavior on the other.

The validity of interviews, like any other assessment instrument, needs to be evaluated as well (Hodges and Zeman, 1993; Silverman, 1994). This is particularly difficult for structured interviews designed to achieve a diagnosis, since the validation of the interview is inevitably affected by the validity of the diagnostic system on which it is based. As we have seen, diagnostic systems like the DSM are still evolving, and knowledge of their validity is still being studied. An additional complication in investigating validity is that there is no "gold standard" or ultimate criterion to serve as the basis of comparison. Is the comparison to clinician judgment, parent report, the Child Behavior Checklist?

Beyond questions of how to improve structured interviews for diagnostic and research uses is the question of their potential for more general clinical practice. It is probably too early in the development of such instruments to determine what impact they will have on the practice of the typical clinician.

Projective Tests

At one time the most common form of psychological test employed to assess children was the projective test. These tests are less commonly used today due, in large part, to the continuing lack of empirical evidence for their reliability and validity.

Projective tests were derived from the psychoanalytic notion of projection as a defense mechanism: One of the ways the ego deals with unacceptable impulses is to project them onto some external object. It is assumed that the impulses cannot be expressed directly. Therefore, an ambiguous stimulus is presented, allowing the youngster to project "unacceptable" thoughts and impulses, as well as other defenses against them onto the stimulus. Projective tests are also used by some clinicians in a manner that involves less psychodynamic inference. This type of analysis examines formal aspects of the test response, for example, whether the child describes the entire stimulus or just part of it. Interpretations are then made based on this response style rather than on the content of the response.

In the Rorschach test the youngster is asked what he or she sees in each of ten ink blots (Figure 5–2). Scoring is based on characteristics of the response such as the portion of the blot responded to (location), factors such as color and shading (determinants), and the nature of what is seen in the blot (content). The Human Figure Drawing or Draw-a-Person test (Machover, 1949) requires the youngster to draw a picture of a person and then a second person of the opposite sex. Typically the clinician then asks questions about the drawings. Murray's (1943) Thematic Apperception Test (TAT) and the Children's Apperception Test (CAT; Bellak and Bellak, 1949; Bellak, 1993) pro-

vide the youngster with pictures for which he or she is asked to make up a story. Figure 5–3 presents pictures similar to those used in the CAT.

Observational Assessment

Early attempts to observe children's behavior made use of diaries or continuous observations and narrations that were deliberately nonselective (Wright, 1960). From this tradition evolved observations of a more limited, pinpointed set of behaviors that could be reliably coded by observers (Bijou, et al., 1969). Such observations are similar or even identical to those done in research studies.

Recent observational methods have come largely from workers with a behavioral/social learning perspective. The observations are frequently made in the child's natural environment, although sometimes planned situations are created in clinic or laboratory settings. Observations range from single, relatively simple, and discrete behaviors of the child, such as the occurrence of toileting, to observations of the child and peers, to complex systems of interactions of family members (e.g., Kolko, 1987; Israel, Pravder, and Knights, 1980; Patterson, 1977). Clearly, ongoing interactions are more difficult to observe and code than are the behaviors of a single individual; however, they are likely to be theoretically and clinically relevant.

The first step in any behavioral observation system involves explicitly pinpointing and defining behaviors. Observers who are trained to use the system then note whether a particular behavior or sequence of behaviors occurs. Most coding systems have been inspected for reliability. Indeed, behavioral/social learning studies commonly report on the reliability of the observations employed, even if a reliability check is not the major purpose of the research.

The aspect of reliability most frequently reported is interrater reliability. Two or

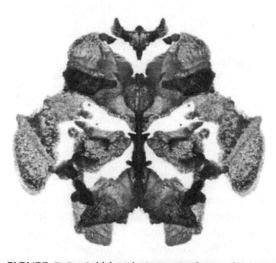

FIGURE 5–2   Inkblot designs, similar to the one pictured above, are employed in the Rorschach.

FIGURE 5–3 Drawings similar to those employed in the CAT.

more observers independently observe the same behavior, and the degree of agreement is calculated. Research indicates that a number of factors affect reliability as well as validity and clinical utility (cf. Hops, Davis, and Longoria, 1995). For example, the complexity of the observational system and changes over time in the observers' use of the system (observer drift) are two factors known to affect observation. Careful training and periodic monitoring of observers' use of the system are recommended for reducing distortions in the information obtained from direct observation (Hartmann and Wood, 1990; Mash and Lee, 1993).

The issue of reactivity is often cited as the greatest impediment to the utility of direct observation. *Reactivity* refers to whether the knowledge that one is being observed changes one's behavior. Thus, introducing a trained observer or videotaping equipment into a situation may cause those in the situation to react to this novel stimulus and behave in a different manner than usual. A number of strategies are recommended to help reduce reactivity. One is to use persons already in the situation (e.g., teachers) as observers. This is likely to reduce the artificial and novel aspects of observation. A second approach is to arrange for observers to be present for some period of time prior to data collection, so that their presence is less artificial and no longer novel.

Behavioral observations are the most direct method of assessment and require the least inference. The difficulty and expense involved in training and maintaining reliable observers is probably the primary obstacle to their common use in nonresearch contexts. Since direct observation has long been considered the hallmark of assessment from a behavioral perspective, attempts have been made to create systems that are more amenable to widespread use. Direct observation is, however, just one aspect of a multimethod approach to behavioral assessment that can include self-monitoring of behavior, interviews, ratings and checklists, and self-report instruments (cf. Mash and Lee, 1993; Ollendick and Greene, 1990).

Problem Checklists and Self-Report Instruments

Problem checklists and rating scales were described in our discussion of classification (pp. 95–97). There are a wide variety of these instruments (Barkley, 1988b; McMahon, 1984). Some are for general use (for example, the Revised Behavior Problem Checklist, Quay and Peterson, 1983; and the Child Behavior Checklist, Achenbach, 1991b) and others are used with restricted populations (for example, Conners's Rating Scales, 1990). The considerable empirical

literature suggests that these instruments may be valuable tools for clinicians holding a variety of perspectives.

For example, the parent-reported problems and competencies of 2,600 youth (fourteen to sixteen-years-old) assessed at intake into mental health services and 2,600 demographically matched nonreferred youngsters were compared (Achenbach et al., 1991). Checklist scores clearly discriminated between the clinic and nonreferred children regarding both behavior problems and social competencies. Furthermore, referral status accounted for greater differences in behavior than did factors such as age, SES, and gender. Figure 5–4 illustrates the differences between clinic and nonreferred children.

A general rating scale may thus help a clinician judge the parent's view of the child's adjustment against norms for referred and nonreferred populations. This can help in evaluating the appropriateness of the referral. Furthermore, rating scales completed by different informants may help the clinician gain a fuller appreciation of the clinical picture and of potential situational aspects of the child's problem (Achenbach, 1991a). Once a particular presenting problem is identified, the use of a more specific rating scale might also be part of the clinician's assessment strategy.

In addition to reports by parents, teachers, or other informants, the clinician or researcher may also draw on a wide variety of instruments to assess the youth's own report (cf. Reynolds, 1993). Here, too, there are general measures (e.g., the Youth Self-Report, Achenbach, 1990) and more specific measures. There are self-report measures specific to problems such as anxiety and depression and also instruments to assess constructs related to adjustment such as control beliefs and self-concept (Connell, 1985; Harter, 1985; Kovacs, 1992; Reynolds and Richmond, 1985). Many of these measures will be described in later chapters

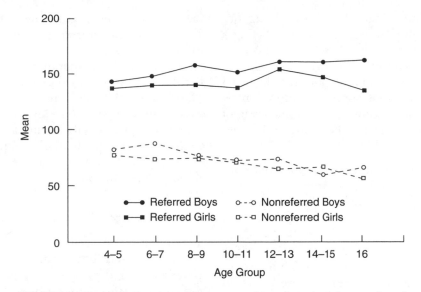

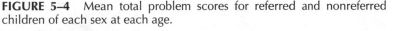

FIGURE 5–4 Mean total problem scores for referred and nonreferred children of each sex at each age.

From Achenbach et al., 1991.

that focus on particular child and adolescent problems.

Intellectual-Educational Assessment

The evaluation of intellectual-academic functioning is an important part of almost all clinical assessments. Intellectual functioning is a central defining feature for disorders such as mental retardation and learning disabilities, but it may also contribute to and be affected by a wide variety of behavioral problems. In contrast to most other assessment instruments, tests of intellectual functioning tend to have better established normative data, reliability, and validity. While our present discussion of these instruments is brief, additional information will be presented in later chapters.

Intelligence tests. By far the most commonly employed assessment devices for evaluating intellectual functioning are tests of general intelligence. In fact, they probably constitute the most frequently employed assessment device other than the inter-

view. The Stanford-Binet-Fourth Edition (Thorndike, Hagen, and Sattler, 1986), the Wechsler tests—the Wechsler Preschool and Primary Scale of Intelligence–Revised (Wechsler, 1989); the Wechsler Intelligence Scale for Children–Third Edition (Wechsler, 1991)—and the Kaufman Assessment Battery for Children (Kaufman and Kaufman, 1983) are some of the intelligence tests widely used in clinical settings. All are individually administered and yield an intelligence (IQ) score. The average score is 100, and an individual score reflects how far above or below the average person of his or her age an individual has scored.

Intelligence tests have long been the subject of heated controversy. Critics have argued that the use of IQ scores has resulted in intelligence being viewed as a real thing, rather than a concept. Furthermore it has led to intelligence being viewed as a rigid and fixed attribute, rather than as something complex and subtle. Critics also claim that intelligence tests are culturally biased and have led to social injustice (cf. Kamin,

1974; Kaplan, 1985). Although intelligence tests are popular and useful in predicting a variety of outcomes, these criticisms and continued concern with legal, ethical, and practical issues demand that they be used cautiously and that continued attention be paid to test improvement and monitoring of appropriate usage (cf. Perlman and Kaufman, 1990; Kamphaus, 1993).

Developmental scales. Assessment of intellectual functioning in very young children, and particularly in infants, requires a special kind of assessment instrument. A popular measure is the Bayley Scales of Infant Development (Bayley, 1969; 1993). The original scales extended from two to thirty months of age. The revised version expanded that range from one to forty-two months. Performance on developmental tests yields a developmental index rather than an intelligence score (IQ). Unlike intelligence tests which evaluate language and abstract reasoning abilities, developmental scales emphasize sensorimotor skills and simple social skills. For example, the Bayley examines the ability to sit, walk, place objects, attend to visual and auditory stimuli, smile, and imitate adults. The Bayley Scales include a Motor Scale, Mental Scale, and a Behavior Rating Scale that assesses aspects of the child's behavioral style (e.g., attitude, interest). Perhaps because intelligence tests and developmental scales tap different abilities, there is only a low correlation between performance on them (Sattler, 1988).

Ability and achievement tests. In addition to assessing general intellectual functioning, it is often necessary or helpful to assess functioning in a particular area. A variety of tests has been developed for this purpose (Katz and Slomka, 1990; Sattler, 1988). The Wide Range Achievement Test (Jastak and Wilkinson, 1984) and the Woodcock Mastery Tests (Woodcock, Mather, and Barnes, 1987), for example,

are two measures of academic achievement that are administered to an individual youngster. Tests such as the Iowa Test of Basic Skills (Hieronymous and Hoover, 1985) and the Stanford Achievement Test (Gardner et al., 1982) are group-administered achievement tests employed in many school settings. Specific ability and achievement tests are particularly important in working with children with learning and school-related problems.

Assessment of Physical Functioning

Assessment of physical functioning can provide several kinds of information valuable to understanding disordered behavior. Family and child histories and physical examinations may reveal genetic problems that are treatable by environmental manipulation. For example, phenylketonuria (PKU) is a recessive gene condition that is affected by dietary treatment. Avoidance of phenylalanine in the child's diet prevents most of the cognitive problems usually associated with the condition. In addition, diseases and defects may be diagnosed that affect important areas of functioning either directly (for example, urinary tract infection causing problems in toilet training) or indirectly (for example, a sickly child being overprotected by parents). Also, signs of atypical or lagging physical development may be an early indication of developmental disorders that eventually influence many aspects of behavior.

The assessment of the nervous system is considered particularly important to understanding a variety of problem behaviors, but especially mental retardation, autism, learning disabilities, and attention deficit disorders. Brain and other neurological dysfunction, measurable in various ways, is thought to be associated with abnormal physical reflexes, motor coordination problems, and sensory and perceptual deficits.

Currently, assessment of presumed neurological dysfunction in children usually consists of a combination of direct neurological approaches and indirect neuropsychological assessment. Such assessment requires the coordinated efforts of neurologists, psychologists, and other professional workers.

Neurological assessment. There are a number of procedures that directly assess the integrity of the nervous system (Solomon, 1985; Teodori, 1993). The computer has revolutionized neurological assessment, and new techniques have become the primary mode of evaluation. The electroencephalograph (EEG) is a procedure with a long history that has been improved by the availability of computers (Kuperman et al., 1990). The EEG requires placing electrodes on the scalp that record activity of the brain cortex, in general, or while the individual is engaged in information processing.

New technologies such as brain imaging techniques and diagnostic nuclear medicine have vastly improved our ability to assess and localize damage or abnormalities in brain structure (Fletcher, 1988; Solomon, 1985). For example, computerized tomography or the CT scan (also referred to as computerized axial tomography–CAT scan) allows tens of thousands of readings of minute variations in the density of brain tissue, measured from an X-ray source, to be computer processed so that a photographic image of a portion of the brain can be obtained. The resulting image can reveal abnormalities of the brain, such as blood clots or tumors. Other imaging techniques provide information about brain activity. Positron emission tomography (PET) scans determine the rate of activity of different parts of the brain by assessing the use of oxygen and glucose, which fuel brain activity. The more active a particular part of the brain is, the more blood carrying glucose flows to this area. A small amount of radioactive substance is injected into the blood stream, amounts of radiation appearing in different areas of the brain are measured,

many images are taken of the brain, and a computer-produced color coded picture is produced indicating different levels of activity. Magnetic resonance imaging (MRI) produces sharp images by placing the person inside a circular magnet that alters the electromagnetic field of the body. When the field is stopped the movement of the nuclei moving toward their original positions is computer synthesized, producing good images of the brain or other parts of the body. These new assessment tools are becoming increasingly important in individual assessment and research.

Neuropsychological assessment. Neuropsychological assessment employs tests that contain learning, sensorimotor, perceptual, verbal, and memory tasks. From the individual's performance on these tasks inferences are made about central nervous system functioning. Neuropsychological assessment is thus an *indirect* means of assessing brain function.

Neuropsychological assessments originally were employed in the hope that they could detect the presence or absence of brain damage. The development of direct methods of assessing the integrity of the central nervous system and the failure to find evidence of brain damage in suspected populations have resulted in a shift of focus. The emphasis is currently more likely to be on distinguishing groups of behavioral and learning disorders that are presumed to have a neurodevelopmental etiology. For example, any test that discriminates learning disabled from normal learners might be considered neuropsychological in this sense (Taylor, 1988b). Interest also exists in assessing changes arising out of alterations in the central nervous system, for example, evaluating recovery from head injury.

The current interest in neuropsychological assessment is, at least in part, attributable to increased sensitivity to the needs and legal requirements of providing services to children with handicapping conditions—some of whom exhibit problems presumed to have a neurological etiology. Also, advances in medicine have resulted in increasing numbers of children who survive known or suspected neurological trauma. The increase in survival rates of infants born prematurely is one example. Children with acute lymphocytic leukemia who receive treatment that includes methotrexate injected directly into the spinal column and radiation to the head are yet another example (Hooper and Hynd, 1993).

Neuropsychological assessment appreciates the need for broadly based assessment. Two of the most widely used collections of instruments are the Halstead-Reitan and Luria-Nebraska batteries (Hynd, Snow, and Becker, 1986; Slomka and Tarter, 1993). The early work of Halstead, begun in the 1930s, and its elaboration by his student Reitan, begun in the 1950s, resulted in two test batteries. The Halstead Neuropsychological Test Battery for Children is used for children between the ages of nine and fourteen. The Reitan-Indiana Neuropsychological Test Battery is used for children five to eight years of age. The Luria-Nebraska Neuropsychological Battery–Children's Revision is used for children eight to twelve years of age.

As the term battery implies, these instruments consist of several subtests or scales, each intended to assess one or more abilities. The use of a broad spectrum of tests, whether it be designated or fixed batteries, like the above, or flexible batteries based on combinations of other existing tests (e.g., the Wechsler Intelligence Scales, achievement tests, the Bender Visual-Motor Gestalt Test-see Figure 5–5) or, indeed, some combination of these approaches, is the usual strategy employed in neuropsychological approaches to assessment (Hamsher, 1990; Taylor and Fletcher, 1990).

Neuropsychological assessment in children is still a relatively young field, and continued development of instruments that derive from evolving research on cognitive development, neurological development, and brain-behavior relationships is needed.

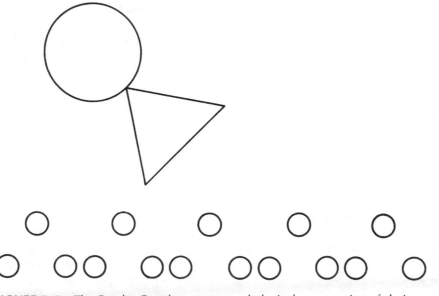

FIGURE 5–5   The Bender-Gestalt, a neuropsychological test, consists of designs, similar to those above, which the child is asked to copy.

Research to develop strategies that more clearly specify impairment and guide rehabilitation is ongoing.

One other issue that needs to be addressed is the often subtle assumption that the behaviors that are assessed and the neuropsychological assessments themselves are free from social and environmental influences. There is little empirical justification for this assumption (Taylor and Fletcher, 1990). For example, brain damage is correlated with social class and family variables that are disadvantageous to social adjustment and physical health (Rutter, Graham, and Yule, 1970; Sameroff and Chandler, 1975). These sociofamilial variables may themselves underlie *both* the brain damage and the observed behavioral or learning problems.

A Comprehensive Assessment

As we indicated in starting our discussion of assessment, evaluating child and adolescent problems is a complex process. By the time a youngster comes to the attention of a clinician, the presenting problem is usually, if not always, multifaceted. Also, since assessment is the first part of any contact, the professional's knowledge of the problem will be limited. Both of these factors, as well as common sense and caution, argue for a broad and comprehensive assessment process. Thus, whatever the clinician's perspective, the best interests of the young person are most likely served by a comprehensive assessment of multiple facets of the youngster and his or her environment.

SUMMARY

Clinically derived classification relies on consensus among clinicians regarding disorders and their definition. The DSM approach is the clinically derived system most likely to be employed in the United States. The recent versions of DSM include an increased number of categories of child and adolescent disorders, provide more highly structured rules for diagnosis, and use a multiaxial system to assess various aspects of functioning. While reliability has been improved by more structured diagnostic rules, there is still considerable variation across categories. The validity of some of the diagnostic categories has received considerable attention, but the validity of others is still questioned. Despite improvements, DSM is still criticized by some on clinical, scientific, ethical, and social-political grounds.

Empirical approaches to classification rely on behavior checklists and statistical analyses. There is good support for two broad syndromes—an undercontrolled, externalizing, conduct disorder syndrome and an overcontrolled, internalizing, anxiety-withdrawal syndrome—and support for subcategories within each general syndrome. Information from multiple informants suggests sensitivity to the possible influence of situational differences on behavior and to differences due to the respondent's perspective.

Critics of diagnostic systems remind us of the possible dangers of labeling children and adolescents. To the extent that such labels reduce our effectiveness as scientists and clinicians, they do not serve the young person's best interest.

Conducting a comprehensive assessment is necessary, not only for classification and diagnosis, but also to plan and execute appropriate interventions. The complex process of assessment requires a multifaceted approach.

The interview is the most common form of assessment. Structured interviews are a relatively recent development. Many of these interviews are organized so as to provide information for a DSM diagnosis. Projective tests are probably less widely used than was once the case due to questions concerning their reliability and validity. Observation of behavior is central to a behavioral/social learning approach and is a direct method of assessment. The practicality of implementing current observation systems in general clinical practice is an impediment to their widespread use.

Intellectual-educational assessments are conducted for a wide variety of presenting problems. General intelligence and developmental levels are evaluated, as well as specific abilities and achievement. Intelligence tests are popular, but in many ways controversial. Given a variety of concerns they should be used cautiously.

Assessment of physical functioning, especially of the nervous system, is important for many behavior problems. Methods include case histories, medical examinations, the EEG, and several newer techniques such as the CT scan, PET scans, and MRIs. Much attention has also been given to neuropsychological testing of youngsters with known or suspected problems in central nervous system functioning.

6

ANXIETY DISORDERS

With this chapter we begin an examination of specific behavior disorders. The children and adolescents discussed in this and the next chapter are variously described as anxious, fearful, withdrawn, timid, depressed, and the like. They seem to be very unhappy and to lack self-confidence. These youngsters are often said to have emotional problems that they take out on themselves; thus, the term *internalizing disorders* is often employed to describe such problems.

AN INTRODUCTION
TO INTERNALIZING DISORDERS

A variety of evidence supports the existence of an empirically defined broad-band internalizing syndrome (see Chapter 5). While there is widespread acceptance of this broad syndrome, the existence of reliable and valid subcategories is far less clear (cf. Daugherty and Shapiro, 1994). So, for example, rather than separate problems of anxiety and depression, a single subcategory designated as anxious/depressed has been found within the larger internalizing syndrome of empirical taxonomies (Achenbach, 1991a).

For clinically-defined classifications, the problems now under discussion were broadly referred to as *neuroses*, a term that is now employed less frequently. More specific terms such as phobias, obsessions and compulsions, anxiety disorders, and depression are employed in much of the current literature and in current clinical practice. The next two chapters of this text are organized around these frequently employed terms.

However, the use of these more specific clinical diagnostic categories, such as the various anxiety and depressive disorders described in the DSM system, are also often questioned (cf. Quay and La Greca, 1986). This is based, in part, on the difficulty often encountered in achieving adequate interrater reliability. Even with the use of structured diagnostic interviews, that were developed to improve reliability, results are best described as uneven (Silverman, 1994).

In addition to the issue of reliability, considerable evidence indicates that a given child or adolescent often meets the criteria for more than one of the different subcategories or disorders (Cohen et al, 1993; Brady and Kendall, 1992; Russo and Beidel, 1994; Verhulst and van der Ende, 1993). In Chapter 3 it was suggested that one of the criteria for a good classification system is that categories be distinct and not overlap. Thus, one issue that needs to be addressed for these subcategories is overlapping attributes and diagnostic criteria (Clark and Watson, 1991; Malcarne and Ingram, 1994; Shaffer et al., 1989).

The phenomenon of an individual meeting the criteria for more than one disorder is often termed *"comorbidity"*. The use of this term is controversial and has been questioned (cf. Lillienfeld, Waldman, and Israel, 1994). The term implies the simultaneous existence of two or more distinct disorders in the same individual. While the issues involved are complex, clearly one alternative view is that it is a mistake to conceptualize these disorders in distinct categorical terms. However, even if one accepts the value of retaining distinct categories, there are multiple ways to conceptualize a child's or adolescent's meeting the diagnostic criteria for more than one disorder (Carson and Rutter, 1991). It may be, instead, that many disorders have mixed patterns of symptoms. For example, mood disorders may be characterized by a mixture of depression and anxiety. Another alternative is that there are shared risk factors: Some of the same risk factors lead to the problems used to define both disorders. Or perhaps the presence of one disorder (or set of problems) creates an increased risk for developing the other disorder. A related idea is that the second set of problems is a later stage in a developmental progression where earlier problems may or may not be retained, even as additional difficulties develop. For example, it has been suggested that for some children and adolescents anxiety and depression are related in this kind of developmental sequence (Brady and Kendall, 1992). These are only some of the possible hypotheses to explain "comorbidity". At present the solution to this issue remains unclear.

It is important, however, to stress that the dilemma is an appreciable one. Children who receive an anxiety disorder diagnosis frequently also meet the criteria for one or more other diagnoses. Keller et al. (1992), for example, found that thirty-eight (14 per-

cent) of the 275 youngsters they studied received an anxiety disorder diagnosis. Many of the children receiving an anxiety disorder diagnosis also met the criteria for other disorders. For example, 37 percent of the youngsters receiving an anxiety disorder diagnosis also received a diagnosis for a depressive disorder. Similarly, Cohen et al. (1993) assessed for the presence of three different internalizing disorders (depression, separation anxiety, and overanxious disorder) and found that 20 percent of the youngsters with an internalizing disorder met the criteria for more than one of these disorders. The problem becomes even more complex when one also considers other noninternalizing disorders such as disruptive behavior disorders. In the Keller et al. study, for example, of the children receiving an anxiety disorder diagnosis, 16 percent also met the diagnostic criteria for attention deficit disorder and 16 percent were diagnosed with conduct disorder. In the Cohen and colleagues study, 36 percent of the youngsters with an anxiety disorder also met the criteria for one of these disruptive behavior disorders.

With these considerations in mind, let us turn to an examination of internalizing disorders. In this chapter we examine anxiety disorders, and in Chapter 7 we discuss the problems of depression and social withdrawal.

A DESCRIPTION OF ANXIETY DISORDERS

In examining anxiety disorders we will begin by exploring some general issues regarding these problems. We will then turn to an examination of the specific types of anxiety disorders and, in doing so, further elaborate on some general issues such as etiology and treatment.

Much like the situation for the larger category of internalizing disorders, there is considerable disagreement as to whether and how anxiety disorders should be subcategorized. It is argued that there is, at present, insufficient information to make any particular classification scheme clearly the most valid or useful (e.g., Barrios and Hartmann, 1988; Silverman, 1993). Despite differences in preference for terminology and classification, there is consensus on a general definition of the phenomenon of anxiety or fear (e.g., Barrios and O'Dell, 1989; Lang, 1984). Anxiety or fear is defined as a complex pattern of three types of reactions to a perceived threat: motor responses (e.g., running away, trembling voice, closing eyes), physiological responses (e.g., changes in heart rate, muscle tension, stomach upset), and subjective responses (e.g., thoughts of danger, thoughts of inadequacy, images of bodily harm).

Assessment of Anxiety Disorders

Assessment of anxiety disorders focuses on one or more of the response systems noted above. Various methods of measurement exist (Barrios and Hartmann, 1988).

Nearly all methods for assessing the motor aspects of children's and adolescents' fears and anxieties make use of direct observation (Dadds, Rapee, and Barrett, 1994). Behavioral avoidance tests require the youngster to perform a series of tasks involving the feared object or situation. The child or adolescent is directed to approach the feared stimulus situation in planned graduated steps. Thus, the youngster might be asked to move closer and closer to a feared dog and then increasingly interact with the dog.

Alternatively, rather than exposing the youngster to a planned graduated series of steps, observations can be made in the natural environment where the fear or anxiety occurs. Trained observers may use a specific observational system to record the youngster's behavior, in predefined categories, as it is happening. Checklists may also be employed wherein the observer checks off the

Observations of the child's behavior in the natural environment can be made as the child takes gradual steps in encountering the feared situation.

(Joel Gordon)

specific behaviors that are exhibited. Recording is usually done a short time after the behavior has occurred. Finally, global ratings of the youngster's fearful behavior are often obtained. For example, someone rates on a five-point scale the degree to which the child or adolescent approached a feared object or situation.

Assessing the subjective component of anxiety relies heavily on judgments of emotional discomfort. It may be difficult for adults to reliably identify the existence of such discomfort in children. In addition, children may have difficulty in labeling and communicating their subjective feelings. This creates a considerable assessment challenge.

The subjective component of the youngster's anxiety can be evaluated by a variety of self-report measures (James, Reynolds, and Dunbar, 1994). Global self-ratings of degree of anxiety or fear are often obtained. Youngsters may report how anxious they are by choosing from a series of facial expressions, by indicating a number on a drawing of a fear thermometer, or by selecting a number on a rating scale. The choice of instrument depends, in part, on the child's developmental level.

There are also questionnaires for a variety of specific fears such as darkness, medical procedures, and test taking. Such questionnaires ask a variety of questions about a single fear or anxiety. A number of general questionnaires also exist. They assess youngsters' reactions to a wide variety of situations, or assess a wide range of subjective reactions to the overall situation. An example of the first general category would be the Fear Survey Schedule for Children (Ollendick, 1983). Youngsters respond to each of eighty items by indicating their level of fear ("none," "some," or "a lot"). The Children's Manifest Anxiety Scale (Reynolds and Richmond, 1978) is an example of a questionnaire that assesses overall subjective anxiety.

It contains items such as, "I have trouble making up my mind" and "I am afraid of a lot of things."

The physiological component of anxiety is assessed by measuring parameters such as heart rate, skin conductance, and palmar sweat. Practical difficulties often inhibit obtaining these measures. The development of portable and inexpensive recording devices has greatly facilitated such recording. However, the physiological aspects of anxiety in children and adolescents are less frequently assessed than the other two response systems (King, 1994).

In addition to the various approaches to evaluating the three components of anxiety, a comprehensive assessment of a youngster presenting with anxiety will likely involve a variety of other assessment needs. As is usually the case, a general clinical interview is likely to yield information that is valuable to the clinician in formulating an understanding of the case and in planning an intervention. Structured diagnostic interviews (both general and more specific to anxiety disorders) are available and may be employed to derive a clinical diagnoses (Silverman, 1994). Given that youngsters with anxiety disorders often present with a variety of other problems as well, more general instruments such as the Achenbach behavior checklists may also be employed. Finally, it is likely that aspects of the youngster's environment may contribute to the anxiety difficulties and this will need to be assessed as well. For example, it may be desirable to assess the specific environmental events that are associated with heightened anxiety, to evaluate patterns of family communication, or to assess the reactions of adults or peers to the youngster's behavior. The assessment of multiple aspects of the problem and the use of multiple informants, including the child or adolescent, is likely to yield valuable information.

Classification of Anxiety Disorders

The DSM approach. DSM-IV describes one type of anxiety disorder that is "usually first diagnosed in infancy, childhood, or adolescence." Separation Anxiety Disorder is characterized by the child's excessive distress when separated from persons to whom there is a strong attachment and by the avoidance of situations that require separation. In addition to this disorder, a child or adolescent can be diagnosed with many of the other anxiety disorders. Phobic disorders are characterized by fear or avoidance of specific objects or situations other than separation or involvement with strangers. Panic Disorder is characterized by sudden attacks of intense anxiety. These attacks do not occur only in response to a particular phobic stimulus or threatening situation. Generalized Anxiety Disorder is characterized by frequent and excessive anxiety or worry about a number of activities or events rather than being focused on particular objects or situations. Obsessive-Compulsive Disorder is characterized by recurrent unreasonable thoughts or urges and repetitive and irrational behaviors. Appreciable anxiety occurs when these obsessive-compulsive rituals are resisted. Posttraumatic Stress Disorder involves anxiety that is linked to a catastrophic event (e.g., rape, assault, earthquake, airplane crash). The youngster persistently reexperiences the event, avoids stimuli associated with the event, and experiences persistent symptoms of increased arousal.

The empirical approach. Empirical systems that are based on statistical procedures have also yielded subcategorizations that are related to anxiety disorders. Within the broad category of internalizing disorders, for example, Achenbach (1991a) describes an anxious/depressed syndrome and other syndromes, such as "somatic complaints" and "withdrawn", that are likely to be related to anxiety problems. In addition, a number of the profile types (pp. 96–97) suggest combinations of problem behaviors that coincide with conceptions of anxiety disorders in children and adolescents (Achenbach, 1993).

Although some overlap can be seen in the clinical (DSM) and empirical approaches, they clearly represent different ways of organizing the anxiety disorders (e.g., Edelbrock and Costello, 1988a). Indeed, some large-scale empirical data suggests that this approach yields some rather different groupings and categories than are provided for in the DSM approach (Achenbach et al., 1989).

Determinants of Anxiety Disorders

The causes of anxiety disorders in children and adolescents are by no means clear, and much of the information that is available represents a downward extension from the adult literature. However, various data suggest important influences and directions for continued investigation. In this section we will briefly overview some of the suggested determinants or risk factors. Later in the chapter the role of various determinants will be further explored as we discuss particular anxiety disorders.

Multiple sources indicate that anxiety disorders occur in families (Last et al., 1991; Rutter et al., 1990b). The degree to which such familial aggregation results from genetic or environmental influences remains unclear, however (Thapar and McGuffin, 1995). It is likely that anxiety disorders are influenced by multiple determinants. Furthermore, different disorders may result from different combinations of influences. There may also be multiple paths and different combinations of risk factors for youngsters meeting the criteria for a particular disorder. An additional issue regarding family transmission of anxiety disorders is the specificity of transmission. For example, are children of parents with panic disorder at risk for panic disorder or for anxiety disorders in general?

Genetic influences do seem to be suggested for anxiety disorders (Kendler et al., 1992b; Torgersen, 1993). There is evidence, for example, for particular disorders such as obsessive-compulsive disorder (Leonard et al., 1994). In general, however, it appears likely that inheritance is determined by a number of genes (rather than a single gene) and is not specific to a particular disorder. Rather, what is inherited may be a general tendency, such as emotional reactivity and behavioral responsivity to stimuli (Gray, 1985).

Families may also influence the development of anxiety through environmental paths. Children may, for example, "learn" to be anxious from their parents, and families may "create" environments that place youngsters at risk for the development of anxiety problems (Ollendick and King, 1991). Exposure to frequent and/or highly stressful events and observation of anxious adults' styles of coping with such experiences seem likely to contribute to similar patterns of difficulty in the children of such families. In addition, youngsters may also be influenced to develop certain cognitive/attributional styles through exposure to these experiences. Thus, family experiences may influence a youngster's general sense of controllability or self-appraisal and these cognitions may, in turn, contribute to anxiety (King, Mietz, and Ollendick, 1995). Also specific cognitions that may develop, for example the perception of situations as hostile or threatening, may place the youngster at risk for developing or maintaining anxiety problems (Bell-Dolan, 1995).

Treatment of Anxiety Disorders

The treatment of anxiety disorders in children and adolescents has a long history. However, research regarding effective treatments is less extensive than for adults. The research literature is most extensive for interventions deriving from a behavioral or cognitive-behavioral perspective.

Pharmacological treatments for anxiety disorders in children and adolescents have made use of a variety of medications. Anxiolytics, particularly the benzodiazepines, have been most frequently suggested, and for some disorders the use of tricyclic antidepressants is recommended. However, in general, there are limited studies of the effectiveness of medication in treating anxiety disorders in children and adolescents, and many of these have methodological shortcomings. Systematic study is needed to establish safety and efficacy (Allen, Leonard, and Swedo, 1995). Thus, in practice, the use of pharmacological treatment for anxiety in youth is not common, or if medication is employed, it is likely to be as an adjunct to psychological interventions (Bernstein, 1994; Gislason and Neri, 1993).

FEARS AND PHOBIAS

Developmental Characteristics of Children's Fears

Knowing about normal fears is important to understanding fears that require clinical attention. Many investigators have explored the development of fears, and a number of trends are suggested.

General prevalence. Several classic studies of general populations indicate that children exhibit a surprisingly large number of fears. Jersild and Holmes (1935) reported that children aged two to six years averaged between four and five fears and exhibited fearful reactions once every four and a half days. MacFarlane, Allen, and Honzik (1954), in their longitudinal study of children from age two through fourteen, found that specific fears were reported in 90 percent of their sample. Forty-three percent of the six- to twelve-year-olds studied by Lapouse and Monk (1959) had seven or more fears. An interesting aspect of the latter study is the suggestion that mothers may underestimate the prevalence of fears in their children. Mothers reported 41 percent fewer fears than indicated by the children's own reports.

Although it appears that fears are quite common among children, the prevalence of intense fears is less clear. In one investigation in the United States, less than 5 percent of mothers indicated that their children exhibited extreme fear, as opposed to normal (5 to 15 percent) or no (84 percent) fear reactions (Miller, Barrett, and Hampe, 1974). This is consistent with Rutter, Tizard, and Whitmore's (1970) Isle of Wight study, in which serious fears were reported in only seven per thousand of the ten- and eleven-year-olds studied. In contrast, however, Ollendick's (1983) sample of children between the ages of three and eleven averaged between nine and thirteen extreme fears and Kirkpatrick's (1984) sample of adolescents ages fifteen through seventeen averaged between two and three intense fears. Other recent epidemiological data also suggest that extreme fears may be more prevalent (Rutter, 1989a). The prevalence of intense fears in youngsters remains uncertain.

Sex and age differences. Most research suggests that girls exhibit a greater number of fears than boys (e.g., King et al., 1989; Kirkpatrick, 1984; Ollendick, 1983). Some studies suggest a greater fear intensity in girls as well (Graziano, DeGiovanni, and Garcia, 1979). Findings of sex differences probably should be interpreted with caution since it is quite possible that gender-role expectations are responsible for differences between boys and girls in displaying and admitting to fears.

It is most commonly reported that both the number and intensity of fears experienced by children decline with age (e.g.,

MacFarlane et al., 1954; King et al., 1989; Lapouse and Monk, 1959). Figure 6–1, in general, illustrates this pattern. It is also usually reported that certain fears appear to be more common at particular ages: for example, fear of strangers at six to nine months, imaginary creatures during the second year, fear of the dark among four-year-olds, and social fears and fear of failure in older children (Miller et al., 1974). Bauer (1976) found similar trends and suggested that Piagetian notions of developmental changes in children's perception can inform our understanding of their fears. For example, increasing differentiation of internal reality from objective reality may help explain why younger children fear ghosts and monsters, while older children have more realistic fears of physical danger or injury. Social expectations and the acceptability of expressing certain fears at a particular age must also be considered. Older children, for instance, may be

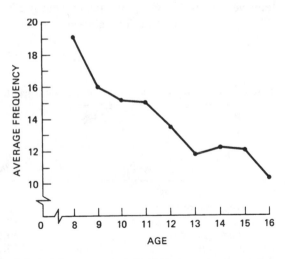

FIGURE 6–1 Frequency of fears across age.

Reprinted from *Journal of Child Psychology and Psychiatry, 30*, King, N.J., Ollier, K., Iacuone, R., Schuster, S., Bays, K., Gullone, E., & Ollendick, T. H., Fears of children and adolescents: A cross-sectional Australian study using the Revised-Fear Survey Schedule for Children, 775–784. Copyright 1989, with kind permission from Elsevier Science Ltd., The Boulevard, Langford Lane, Kilington OX5 1GB, UK.

socialized to believe that bedtime fears are inappropriate, and they therefore may not express them. Age combined with gender-role expectations may produce similar effects. For example, while equal proportions of younger boys and girls indicated that they had frightening dreams, 10 percent of sixth-grade boys as opposed to 70 percent of same-age girls reported this experience (Bauer, 1976).

Ollendick, King, and Frary (1989), in a study of American and Australian children and adolescents, also found that the number and intensity of fears decreased with age. However, when the kinds of fears reported were examined, eight of the ten most feared objects or situations were the same regardless of age (Table 6–1). Additional fears were, however, consistent with age differences in the content of fears. Among seven-to ten-year olds, "getting lost in a strange place" (43.6 percent) and "being sent to the principal" (42.9 percent) were among the ten most endorsed fears. For eleven- to thirteen-year-olds "having my parents argue" (36.7 percent) and for fourteen- to sixteen-

year olds "failing a test" (29.9 percent) were among the ten most common fears.

Should youngsters' fears receive clinical attention? Mild fear reactions and those specific to a developmental period might be expected to dissipate quickly. However, if the fear, even though short-lived, creates sufficient discomfort or interferes with functioning, intervention may be justified. Most authorities would not usually view age-appropriate fears as requiring clinical attention unless they were quite intense or continued longer than expected. *Phobia* is the term usually employed to describe fears that are exaggerated in these ways.

Clinical Description and Classification

Youngsters with phobias try to avoid the situation or object they fear. For example, children who have an extreme fear of dogs may refuse to go outside. When confronted with a large dog, they may "freeze" or run to their parent for protection. In crying out for help, the youngster may describe feel-

TABLE 6–1 The Ten Most Common Fears Reported by Age

| | | Percent of Youth Reporting Fear | | |
| | | | Age | |
Item	Total	7–10	11–13	14–16
Being hit by car/truck	54.7	62.2	52.8	48.4
Not being able to breathe	52.7	56.9	50.6	50.4
Bombing attack/being invaded	48.5	51.6	47.2	46.6
Fire—getting burned	45.4	52.1	43.0	40.8
Falling from high place	43.1	48.9	39.4	41.0
Burglar breaking into house	41.0	46.1	39.9	36.7
Earthquake	40.5	48.6	40.3	31.4
Death—dead people	36.6	41.1	36.7	31.1
Getting poor grades	33.8	33.6*	33.9	34.0
Snakes	33.1	35.3*	33.4*	29.7*

*Indicates that this fear was not one of the top 10 for this particular subsample.

Reprinted from *Behaviour Research and Therapy, 27,* Ollendick, T.H., King, N.J., & Frary, R.B., Fears in children and adolescents: Reliability and generalizability across gender, age and nationality, 19–26. Copyright 1989, with kind permission from Elsevier Science Ltd., The Boulevard, Langford Lane, Kilington OX5 1GB, UK.

ings of tension, panic, or even fear of death. Nausea, palpitations, and difficulty in breathing may also occur. These reactions may even occur when contact with the feared situation is merely anticipated. Thus, not only is the youngster restricted in his or her activities, but fears of encountering dogs are likely to change the lifestyle and activities of the family as a whole.

There is no well-established system of classification for fears. At one time it was fashionable to enumerate long lists of phobias including pyrophobia (fear of causing fire), taphephobia (fear of being buried alive), ergasiophobia (fear of activity), and even phobophobia (the fear of phobias) (Berecz, 1968). The possibilities were endless, as, indeed, were the lists generated. This method of classification did not prove useful, and subsequent attempts have tended to group phobias into broader categories.

Miller and his colleagues (1974) proposed a classification system that divided phobic reactions into fears of physical injury, natural events, social anxiety, and miscellaneous. Similar classifications have also been suggested by more recent factor analyses of fear questionnaires (e.g., Ollendick et al., 1989). These efforts suggest that fears can be reliably grouped into categories based on the specific object or situation (Table 6–2).

Among the DSM-IV categories that describe excessive fears of objects or situations are two that are often applied to children and adolescents: Specific Phobia and Social Phobia.

Specific Phobias

The essential feature of the DSM-IV diagnosis of Specific Phobia (formerly referred to as Simple Phobia) is a marked and persistent fear of a specific object or situation that is excessive or unreasonable. In addition, the diagnosis requires that exposure to the

TABLE 6–2 Factors and Sample Items from the Revised Fear Survey Schedule for Children

Factor 1—Failure and Criticism
My parents criticizing me
Failing a test
Being criticized by others
Having to stay after school

Factor 2—The Unknown
Ghosts or spooky things
Dark rooms or closets
Nightmares
Being alone

Factor 3—Minor Injury and Small Animals
Snakes
Guns
The sight of blood
Rats or mice

Factor 4—Danger and Death
Fire, getting burned
Being hit by a car or truck
Falling from high places
Earthquakes

Factor 5—Medical Fears
Having to go to the hospital
Getting a shot from the nurse or doctor
Going to the dentist
Going to the doctor

Adapted from Ollendick, King, and Frary, 1989.

phobic stimulus almost invariably provokes an immediate anxiety response, and it is noted that in children this anxiety may be expressed by crying, tantrums, freezing, or clinging. Also, for adults and adolescents, the person must recognize that his or her fear is excessive or unreasonable. It is recognized that this feature may be absent in children. The child or adolescent must avoid the phobic situation(s) or endure exposure with intense anxiety and distress. Finally, the fear must produce marked distress or interfere significantly with the youth's normal routine, academic functioning, or social relationships.

DSM-IV suggests that specific phobias be further subcategorized into five types: animal, natural environment (e.g., heights, storms, water), blood-injection-injury, situational (e.g., airplanes, enclosed places), and other (e.g., in children, avoidance of loud sounds or costumed characters).

Prevalence, course and etiology. It is difficult to accurately estimate the prevalence of specific phobias in children and adolescents due to the differing definitions and samples employed in the studies that are available. A rate of 7–8 percent is, however, fairly consistently reported in studies of the prevalence of "excessive worries or fears" or phobias. In a limited number of studies employing DSM-III or III-R criteria, rates of about 2.5–3.0 percent are reported (Silverman and Rabian, 1994). These studies generally report that phobias are more prevalent in girls than in boys.

There is not a great deal of research information on the natural course of specific phobias, but the general impression is that children's phobias are relatively benign and that improvement will occur over time with or without treatment (e.g., Agras, Chapin, and Oliveau, 1972). There is some reason, however, to question this perception and to think in terms of continuity over time (King, 1993). Reports of phobic adults, although limited by their retrospective nature, suggest that specific phobias are likely to begin in childhood and may for some individuals persist into adulthood (e.g.,

Kendler et al., 1992b). Furthermore, the age of onset reported by adults with phobias can give us some suggestion of the course of different phobias. Öst (1987), for example, found variations in reported age of onset among adults referred for treatment who received six different DSM-III diagnoses: agoraphobia (anxiety about being in a situation where escape might be difficult or embarrassing), social phobia, and four subgroups of specific phobias. The results shown in Figure 6–2 illustrate that, with the exception of claustrophobia, specific phobias appear to have the earliest age of onset and to occur during childhood. A reasonable suggestion, therefore, is that specific phobias are likely to begin during childhood, and that for at least some individuals they may persist over time.

A number of factors are likely to play a role in whether a child or adolescent develops a specific phobia. Phobias or phobic-like symptoms probably run in families (Silverman and Rabian, 1994). Indeed, there is even some suggestion that this pattern of family aggregation may exist by type of phobia (e.g., first-degree relatives of persons with animal phobias being likely to also have animal phobias, first-degree relatives of persons with situational phobias being likely to have phobias of particular situations; American Psychiatric Association, 1994). One question asked is whether this family aggregation is due to genetic factors. While there

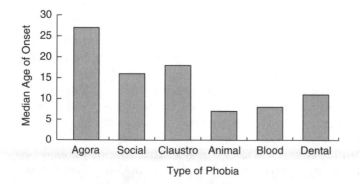

FIGURE 6–2 Median age of onset for various phobias.

Adapted from Öst, 1987.

is some suggestion that genetic factors play a role in the etiology of phobias, there is also some indication that the influence of heritability is lower for specific phobias than for other phobias (e.g., Kendler et al., 1992b), thus suggesting the importance of environmental influences.

Rachman (1977) postulated three different environmental paths by which, alone or in combination, phobias might be acquired: (1) direct experience (conditioning), (2) indirect experience (vicarious exposure), and (3) transmission of information. Although there is little research investigating the contributions of these various pathways to the development of phobias in youngsters, there is some suggestion of the importance of indirect experiences. Ollendick, King, and Hamilton (1991) asked a large sample of Australian and American youngsters (nine to fourteen years of age) to retrospectively report on the sources of their fears. They found that the development of ten highly prevalent fears were most frequently attributed to instructional and vicarious factors. However, it is likely the case that youngsters' fears are multiply determined. Indeed, these indirect sources of fears were often combined with direct conditioning experiences.

Treatment of specific phobias.

Research on the treatment of phobias in children and adolescents has received considerable attention. However, these investigations suffer from a number of limitations (King, 1993; Morris and Kratochwill, 1983). The vast majority, for example, deal with the treatment of fears and anxieties of mild to moderate intensity, leaving the effectiveness of treatment of severe problems less well explored. In addition, most treatment programs involve multiple strategies, and the relative importance of these components remains to be determined. It does seem clear, however, that exposure to feared stimuli is an essential element of successful fear-reduction programs. Thus it seems reasonable to conceptualize the multiple components of treatments as various ways of facilitating exposure to the feared object or situation.

SYSTEMATIC DESENSITIZATION. One of the most widely used behavioral treatments is systematic desensitization and its variants. A hierarchy of fear-provoking situations is constructed, and the youngster is asked to visualize scenes of increasing fearfulness. Actual representations of the feared object or situation, such as a picture or toys, are sometimes used in place of visualization. These visualizations or stimuli are paired with relaxation or some other response that is incompatible with fear. This is done until the most anxiety-provoking scene can be comfortably visualized. In some cases the actual feared object or situation is employed; treatment is then referred to as "in vivo desensitization." Systematic desensitization has been shown to be effective in reducing adults' fears, but support for its use with children, while encouraging, is not overwhelming. The evidence may be best for older children or adolescents and it can be argued that, even here, few methodologically adequate studies exist (Barrios and O'Dell, 1989).

MODELING. A commonly employed behavioral procedure is modeling. Jones's (1924) treatment of Peter's fear of furry objects is probably the earliest report of the therapeutic use of modeling. The work of Bandura and his colleagues (e.g., Bandura and Menlove, 1968) was the impetus for more recent controlled research. In all modeling therapies the child observes another person interacting adaptively with the feared situation. The model can be live or symbolic (e.g., film or slides). Modeling procedures have been demonstrated in numerous experimental studies to be superior to control conditions and to be effective over a fairly wide age range. Observation of a model who is similar to the child (e.g., age and fear levels) appears to result in better outcomes. Participant modeling, in which observation is followed by the fearful child joining the model in making gradual approaches to the feared object, is one of the most potent treatments (Barrios and O'Dell, 1989).

Lewis's (1974) often cited treatment of fear of the water illustrates the use of modeling, and participant modeling in particular. Forty boys between the ages of five and twelve were assigned to one of four treatment conditions. Children in a modeling-plus-participation condition observed a film of three boys of similar age performing tasks such as those in a swimming test. These coping models initially exhibited fear but gradually increased their competency in dealing with the tasks; eventually they were shown playing together happily in the water. Immediately following observation of the film, the children were taken by a second experimenter to the pool for a ten-minute participation phase. They were encouraged to engage in the activities involved in the swimming test and were given social reinforcements for attempting these activities. When the behavioral swimming test was repeated the next day, a control group showed no change. Boys in modeling-only and participation-only conditions exhibited significant improvement, but the most effective treatment was the combination of modeling and participation. A follow-up evaluation of twenty-five of the boys five days later suggested that the gains had been maintained and had generalized to a different pool and different swimming instructor. Once again the modeling-plus-participation boys seem to have fared the best.

These findings and others indicate that modeling treatments can be highly effective. However, it is not clear what is responsible for the success. Treatments such as Lewis's (1974) often involve other components, such as the social reinforcement given to the boys for swimming activities. The mechanism for change is also unclear. Is the child's fear actually being reduced? Alternatively, are coping skills being improved? Bandura (1977a; 1982), for example, suggests that the child's expectations of personal efficacy may be increased by the modeling and other procedures.

COGNITIVE SELF-MANAGEMENT STRATEGIES. Some investigators have examined the self-management of children's beliefs or cognitions as a treatment strategy. Kanfer's cognitive self-control approach to fear of the dark is an early example of the successful application of this coping strategy (Kanfer, Karoly, and Newman, 1975). However, it is difficult to generalize from these findings to clinical phobias, since the original intensity of the fear was not great; indeed, intensely fearful children were specifically excluded.

Subsequent studies, employing similar cognitive strategies, have explored the treatment of fears of a clinical magnitude. Graziano's homebased program for nighttime fears is one example (Graziano and Mooney, 1982). Graziano and his associates combined self-talk with various other elements (relaxation training, pleasant imagery, and contingency management) to successfully treat long-standing fear of the dark. Two to three years after treatment improvement was maintained in almost all of the cases.

Like Graziano's approach, many treatments actually combine multiple procedures. Combining one or more treatment procedures with contingency management—ensuring that positive consequences follow exposure to the feared stimulus, that positive consequences do not follow avoidance of the feared stimulus, and that the child is rewarded for improvement—is common. It is, therefore, difficult to know which elements are important for which children or for which fears (Barrios and O'Dell, 1989; King, 1993).

Social Phobias

The second category of phobia specified by DSM-IV is Social Phobia (or Social Anxiety Disorder). The diagnosis, compared to specific phobias, is a relatively new one and the disorder has received little systematic attention in children and adolescents (Beidel and Randall, 1994).

Description and diagnosis. Social phobia is a marked and persistent fear of acting in an embarrassing or humiliating way in social or performance situations. The fear occurs in situations in which the person is exposed to unfamiliar people or to scrutiny by others. In applying this criterion to children, it must be demonstrated that they have the capacity to engage in age-appropriate social relationships with familiar people—that the difficulties are not merely due to absence of appropriate social skills. Furthermore, the social anxiety must occur in peer settings, not just in interactions with adults. Similar to the criteria for specific phobias, exposure to the feared situation must almost invariably provoke anxiety. In children this may be expressed by crying, tantrums, freezing, or shrinking from social situations with unfamiliar people. The remaining criteria also parallel those for specific phobias: a recognition by adolescents that the fear is excessive or unreasonable (this may be absent in children); the feared situations are avoided or endured with intense distress; and an interference with academic functioning, or social relationships, or marked distress about the phobia.

Since there are only limited empirical data regarding social phobia in children and adolescents, the exact nature of the disorder is unclear. Also, a large proportion of youngsters diagnosed with social phobia meet the criteria for other anxiety disorders and for depression (e.g., Last et al., 1992). The task of clarifying distinctions between social phobia, anxiety disorders such as generalized anxiety disorder (overanxious disorder), and social relational constructs such as behavioral inhibition and shyness must, therefore, also be addressed. (These other anxiety disorders and related social relations constructs are discussed below and in Chapter 7.)

Children and adolescents with social phobias are described as experiencing distress in a variety of social situations (Beidel and Randall, 1994). For youngsters in the eight to twelve age range, the most commonly identified situations involve public speaking (reading aloud, giving a book report, giving a speech). Distress in these situations was reported by 88 percent of socially phobic children. Other situations identified included eating in public, writing in public, going to parties, using public restrooms, speaking to authority figures, and informal speaking with peers, parents, and friends. Although public speaking was the distressful situation encountered by the largest number of youngsters, it was not the stressful situation that occurred most often in a youngster's day. Diaries kept over a two-week period suggest that informal peer interactions occur most frequently, accounting for 42.9 percent of distressful situations encountered by a youngster. Other distressing situations were encountered less frequently: taking tests, performing in front of others, reading aloud, having a test returned, reading a report, writing on the board, and being called on in class.

Distressing social encounters are accompanied by a variety of somatic complaints (e.g., heart palpitations, shakiness, flushes/chills, sweating, nausea). It is unclear, however, whether or how children experience the negative cognitions that are characteristic of social phobia in adults (negative thoughts about their social performance and about others' evaluations of them). The reported low rates of such cognitions among youngsters may reflect real age-related differences, or may be due to difficulty in assessing these thoughts in children (Beidel and Randall, 1994).

The development of the Social Anxiety Scale for Children-Revised (La Greca and Stone, 1993) suggests that social anxiety in this age group of children can be grouped into three factors: fear of negative evaluation from peers, social avoidance and distress in new situations, and generalized social avoidance and distress (Table 6–3). This research also suggests that social anxiety is associated with less social acceptance by peers and lesser feelings of self-worth.

The characteristics of social phobia in adolescents, although described as being similar to children and adults, are not clear. Since adolescence is a developmental period during which social anxieties are quite common, the distinction between normal and abnormal social anxiety may be particularly difficult. As Clark et al. (1994) suggest, interpretation of severity, as defined in the DSM diagnostic criteria by phrases, such as "almost invariably," "marked distress," "intense anxiety," and "interferes significantly," becomes particularly important.

Prevalence. Social phobia is estimated to occur in approximately 1 percent of children and adolescents (e.g., Kashani and Orvaschel, 1990; Lewinsohn et al., 1993; McGee et al., 1990.) In terms of the prevalence in clinic populations, 14.9 percent of youngsters assessed at an anxiety disorders clinic were given a primary diagnosis of social phobia and 32.4 percent had a lifetime history of the disorder (Last et al., 1992). Based on retrospective reports, the age of onset is typically described as middle to late adolescence (e.g., Öst, 1987). The disorder can, however, occur earlier (Biedel and Randall, 1994). It is probably the case that prevalence increases with age and, based on discrepancies with adult rates, the disorder may be underrecognized, particularly in adolescents (Albano and Barlow, 1996; Clark et al., 1994).

SCHOOL REFUSAL AND SEPARATION ANXIETY

Historically, the term "school phobic" was employed to describe children who exhibited anxiety regarding school attendance. Severe anxiety and somatic symptoms such as dizziness, stomachaches, and nausea that "keep" the child at home were described. The parents, concerned with the child's health and anxiety, were often reluctant to force attendance. It was not clear, however, that in all cases the child actually feared the school situation. Thus, some workers questioned the use of the term school phobia to describe the disorder. Indeed, many cases of school phobia appeared instead to be due to a fear of separation from the mother and home. This theme, that avoidance of school may be just one manifestation of the larger fear of separation, has long been popular. Thus, some workers suggested the more comprehensive term "school refusal" (e.g., Hersov, 1960) and this term has become common. However, this term may be taken to imply a conscious decision by the child to refuse to go to school, a perspective that does not seem applicable to all cases. Thus, there is still much conceptual disagreement and terminological confusion in the litera-

TABLE 6–3 Examples of Items from the Three Factors of the Social Anxiety Scale for Children—Revised

Fear of Negative Evaluation From Peers
I worry about what other kids think of me.
I'm afraid that other kids will not like me.
I feel that kids are making fun of me.

Social Avoidance and Distress—New Situations
I feel shy around kids I don't know.
I feel nervous when I'm around certain kids.

Social Avoidance and Distress—General
I feel shy even with kids I know very well.
It's hard for me to ask other kids to play with me.

By permission of author Annette M. LaGreca.

Refusing to go to school and/or to be separated from parents is a common reason for referral for psychological services.

(Ed Lettau/Photo Researchers, Inc.)

ture (Blagg and Yule, 1994; Kearney, Eisen, and Silverman, 1995).

Classification

The DSM-IV category of separation anxiety disorder is intended to describe children with excessive anxiety regarding separation from a major attachment figure and/or home. Diagnostic criteria include eight symptoms involving worry or distress and related sleep and physical problems. These symptoms are associated with concerns of separation from or worry of harm befalling major attachment figures. Reluctance or re-

fusal to go to school is one of these eight symptoms; however, a child need not exhibit this behavior to receive the diagnosis since only three of the eight symptoms need be present to receive the diagnosis. Thus, not all children with separation anxiety disorder exhibit school refusal. In addition, as suggested by the term "school phobic," not all school refusers need show separation anxiety. Some children, for example, may fear some aspect of the school experience. The latter group might be diagnosed under the specific phobia or social phobia categories. Studies of clinic-referred children support a distinction between separation-anxious and phobic school refusers (e.g., Last and Strauss, 1990). Also, youngsters who refuse school often meet the diagnostic criteria for multiple disorders (Kearney et al., 1995).

School refusal is often also differentiated from truancy. Truants are usually described as absent on an intermittent basis, often without parental knowledge. The school refuser, in contrast, is usually absent for continuous extended periods, during which time the parents are aware of the child's being at home. Also, truants are often described as poor students who exhibit other conduct problems such as stealing and lying. However, the considerable co-occurrence of anxiety and conduct disordered problems in children has led some to suggest that the refuser/truant distinction may not be a useful one (Russo and Biedel, 1994).

We have chosen to describe school refusal and separation anxiety together since much of what has been written about the problem of school refusal and its etiology has derived from a separation anxiety perspective. In addition, given that compulsory education laws require all children to attend school, it seems likely that many children with separation anxiety would also have problems with school attendance. To the extent that school refusal is related to a phobic reaction to some aspect of the school situation, the considerations regarding specific and social phobias would apply.

Prevalence

School refusal is usually estimated to occur in .4 percent to 1.5 percent of the general population (e.g., Grannel de Aldaz et al., 1984; Ollendick and Mayer, 1984). Interestingly, however, some reports suggest that as many as 69 percent of referrals for any kind of child phobia are for school refusal, and the problem is seen in approximately 3 percent to 8 percent of clinic-referred children (Last and Strauss, 1990; Miller et al., 1972; Smith, 1970). Miller and others have suggested that this may be due to the fact that the problem creates considerable difficulty for parents and school personnel.

The prevalence of separation anxiety disorder is uncertain, but it is described in DSM-IV as "not uncommon" and it is probably one of the most common anxiety disorders in children with an estimated prevalence of about 4 percent (Anderson, Lytton, and Romney, 1987). The prevalence declines after early childhood and the disorder is probably uncommon in adolescence (Clark et al., 1994).

School refusal, on the other hand, can be found in children of all ages. There is the suggestion that in younger children the problem is likely to be related to separation anxiety, but children in middle age groups and early adolescence are likely to have complex and mixed presentations of anxiety and depressive disorders. Prognosis seems best for children under the age of ten years and successful treatment seems to be particularly difficult with older children (Berg and Jackson, 1985; Blagg and Yule, 1994; Miller et al., 1974). If left untreated, serious long-term consequences seem possible. In older adolescents separation anxiety may be the precursor of more serious problems (Blagg and Yule, 1994; Tonge, 1994). As adults such individuals may be at risk for a number of problems. Large-scale longitudinal studies are clearly needed to clarify hypothesized relationships to adult disorders such as agoraphobia and panic disorder (Burke and Silverman, 1987; Tonge, 1994).

Etiology

As suggested above, it is best not to view all cases of school refusal as being similar or as having a unitary cause. The most common conceptualization of school refusal in children does, however, attribute the problem to separation anxiety. Psychodynamic explanations describe the child's insistence on remaining at home as satisfying both the child's and mother's needs and conflicts concerning separation. The basic notion is that strong attachment leads the child to fear that something may happen either to the self or to the mother during separation. In the latter instance, the child may have aggressive wishes toward the parent that the child fears will be fulfilled (e.g., Kessler, 1988). There is little information about the father's role in this process.

Behavioral explanations of school refusal as separation anxiety presume that the child has learned an avoidance response because of some association of school with an existing intense fear of losing the mother. Once avoidance behavior occurs, it may be reinforced by attention and other rewards, such as toys and special foods, that the child receives while at home.

Clinical reports suggest that onset of the disorder often follows some life stress (death, illness, change of school, move to new neighborhood) but, to date, there is limited empirical support for such a connection.

A number of influences have been hypothesized to be related to the development of separation anxiety. However, while many of these influences are related to child and adolescent anxiety disorders in general, an association with separation anxiety disorder, in particular, is less clear. As indicated earlier, there is evidence that suggests a familial pattern for anxiety disorders. However, a pattern specific to separation anxiety is not evident. Family influences are certainly thought to be important, but the exact nature of these influences is not clear. Similarly, while a relationship to the development of secure attachments early in life (Ainsworth et al., 1978; Bowlby, 1977) seems logical, there is at present no support for a direct link between early insecure attachment and the development of separation anxiety disorder. Similarly, parents exhibiting high anxiety levels or panic and an overprotective style would seem likely to contribute to separation anxiety in the child. Again, while there are reports of such parenting patterns being associated with anxiety disorders in children, a specific link to separation anxiety is less clear (Tonge, 1994). Also, early and persistent temperamental patterns of social withdrawal and behavioral inhibition (see Chapter 7 for a more extended discussion) might logically be thought to be related to separation anxiety. A link to childhood anxiety disorders seems likely, but again a specific link to separation anxiety is not, at present, supported (Hirshfeld et al., 1992).

Treatment

In working with school refusers, the majority of clinicians of all orientations stress the importance of getting the youngster back to school (King, Ollendick, and Gullone, 1990). However, there may be disagreement among clinicians as to whether treatment should precede attempts to return to school or whether treatment and return should be concurrent, and also whether return should be gradual or immediate (Blagg and Yule, 1994). Whatever the choice on these issues, successful strategies take an active approach to the problem—finding a way of getting the youngster back to school even if this is difficult or requires the threat of legal intervention.

Most workers suggest that the prognosis is quite good when onset of school refusal is sudden and for younger children. Indeed, a frequently cited method used by Kennedy (1965) suggests that treatment can be rapid and successful. At an initial meeting the parent is instructed to take the child to school the following Monday, and school personnel are instructed to keep the child in school all day. No excuse is to be accepted for altering this plan, and physical complaints are dealt with by afterschool visits to the pediatrician. School attendance is praised, even when involuntary. The child is seen briefly by the therapist after school hours. Stories illustrating the transitory nature of fears and the "need to get back on the horse after a fall" are relayed to the child. On Wednesday a party is held to celebrate the child's having overcome the difficulty. Kennedy reported success in 100 percent of the fifty cases treated in this manner. Follow-ups of the subjects of no less than two years and up to eight years later indicate no recurrence of the problem. The absence of controlled comparison studies using these procedures, however, suggests caution in drawing firm conclusions.

Indeed, the treatment literature on school refusal consists primarily of case studies, and the adequacy or generality of studies with experimental designs is questionable (Burke and Silverman, 1987). Early treatment approaches focused almost entirely on the child. More recent interventions address the entire family, and perhaps aspects of the school situation itself. In addition, a single treatment strategy is not expected to work in all cases. Clinicians acknowledge variations among school refusers and thus most treatments contain multiple components, are formulated to match the particular aspects of the case at hand, and to address the complex interplay of individual, family, and school factors (Blagg and Yule, 1994).

THE OVERANXIOUS CHILD

Phobias, school refusal, and separation anxiety represent relatively focused anxiety disorders. However, anxiety is sometimes experienced in a less focused manner. Children and adolescents with more extensive anxiety are often described as overanxious.

Description and Diagnosis

Clinicians frequently describe children and adolescents who worry excessively and exhibit extensive fearful behavior. These disturbances are not focused on any particular object or situation and are not due to a specific recent stress. Such youngsters seem excessively concerned with their competence and performance, and they exhibit nervous habits (e.g., nail biting), sleep disturbances, and physical complaints such as stomachaches. Prior versions of the DSM employed the diagnosis of Overanxious Disorder of Childhood and Adolescence (OAD) to recognize this clinical entity. With DSM-IV, however, this separate diagnosis was eliminated. Instead, these children and adolescents would now be considered, along with adults, under the category of Generalized Anxiety Disorder (GAD). The DSM-IV criteria are presented in Table 6–4. We will use both terms here since much of the literature has employed the term overanxious disorder.

The case of a nine-year-old boy described by Anthony (1981) illustrates the features of an overanxious child:

Like his mother, John had a very low opinion of himself and his abilities . . . and found it difficult to cope with the "scary things" inside himself. His main problem had to do with the numerous fears that he had and the panic attacks that overtook him from time to time. He was afraid of the dark, of ghosts, of monsters, of being abandoned, of being alone, of strangers, of war, of guns, of knives, of loud noises, and of snakes. . . . Like his mother again, he had many psychosomatic complaints involving his bladder, his bowels, his kidneys, his intestines and his blood. . . . He also suffered from insomnia and would not or could not go to sleep until his mother did. . . . He was also afraid to sleep alone or to sleep without a light, and regularly wet and soiled himself. He was often afraid but could not say why and was also fearful of contact with others. (pp. 163–164)

TABLE 6–4 DSM-IV Criteria for Generalized Anxiety Disorder

A. Excessive anxiety and worry (apprehensive expectation), occurring more days than not for at least 6 months, about a number of events or activities (such as work or school performance).
B. The person finds it difficult to control the worry.
C. The anxiety and worry are associated with three (or more) of the following six symptoms (with at least some symptoms present for more days than not for the past 6 months). **Note:** Only one item is required in children.
    (1) restlessness or feeling keyed up or on edge
    (2) being easily fatigued
    (3) difficulty concentrating or mind going blank
    (4) irritability
    (5) muscle tension
    (6) sleep disturbance (difficulty falling or staying asleep, or restless unsatisfying sleep)
D. The focus of the anxiety and worry is not confined to features of another Axis I disorder, e.g., the anxiety or worry is not about having a Panic Attack (as in Panic Disorder), or being embarrassed in public (as in Social Phobia).
E. The anxiety, worry, or physical symptoms cause clinically significant distress or impairment in social, occupational, or other important areas of functioning.

Adapted and reprinted with permission from the *Diagnostic and Statistical Manual of Mental Disorders, Fourth Edition.* Copyright 1994, American Psychiatric Association.

Prevalence and Developmental Characteristics

Epidemiological studies of nonclinic samples suggest that overanxious disorder is a relatively common problem in younger children, although exact estimates vary. Costello (1989) reported a prevalence rate of 4.6 percent in a pediatric sample of seven- to eleven-year-olds, Anderson et al. (1987) reported a rate of 2.9 percent in a general population sample of New Zealand eleven-year-olds, and Cohen and colleagues (1993) reported a rate of about 14 percent in a general population sample of ten- to thirteen-year-olds. The disorder is usually reported to be more common in girls, and the median age of onset is estimated to be about ten years of age (e.g., Keller et al., 1992). The rates of the disorder are generally stable across the period from childhood to adolescence (Strauss, 1994). However there are exceptions to this finding. Cohen et al. (1993), for example, found a strong linear decline in rates of overanxious disorder for boys between the ages of ten and twenty, but very little decline for girls during this same age period.

Overanxious disorder or generalized anxiety disorder is probably the most common anxiety disorder among adolescents (Clark et al., 1994). However, estimates of rates in the general population of adolescents vary considerably. For example, Kashani and Orvaschel (1990) report a rate of overanxious disorder of 7.3 percent among fourteen- to sixteen-year-olds, and McGee and colleagues (1990) report a rate of 5.9 percent among fifteen-year-olds. Whitaker and colleagues (1990) report a rate for generalized anxiety disorder of 3.7 percent among a sample of ninth through twelfth graders. The somewhat stricter criteria for GAD as compared to OAD may account for this somewhat lower estimate. Finally, the findings of Cohen et al. (1993) indicate a rate of about 14 percent for girls in both the fourteen to sixteen and seventeen to twenty age ranges, but a prevalence of about 5 percent for boys in both of these age groups.

Whatever its prevalence in the general population of children and adolescents, it is clear that overanxious disorder is a common presentation among youngsters seen in clinical settings. Keller and colleagues (1992), for example, report that 85 percent of the youngsters with an anxiety disorder were diagnosed with overanxious disorder. Similarly, in a sample of young people presenting at a clinic for anxiety disorders, 52 percent met the criteria for overanxious disorder (Last, 1989). Furthermore, the disorder does not seem transitory. For example, Keller and colleagues (1992) report a mean duration of four and a half years for episodes of overanxious disorder. Persistence may be particularly likely for those with more severe symptoms. Cohen, Cohen, and Brook (1993) found that 47 percent of youngsters with the most severe symptoms continued to meet diagnostic criteria for overanxious disorder two and a half years later.

In addition youngsters who meet the diagnostic criteria for OAD or GAD are likely to show other indications of significant impairment (e.g., Whitaker et al., 1990). Greater impairment seems associated with more severe overanxious symptomatology and increased impairment is seen among adolescents (Clark et al., 1994; Strauss, 1994).

Indeed, an examination of developmental differences in children and adolescents meeting the DSM diagnostic criteria for overanxious disorder does provide some interesting information (Strauss et al., 1988). The criteria for OAD were met by 55 of the 106 cases of anxiety disorders examined in this investigation. In order to examine developmental differences, two groups were formed by dividing children under and over twelve years of age. Strauss and her colleagues found that the two groups did not differ in terms of the prevalence of the OAD diagnosis or sociodemographic characteristics. Both groups also showed similar rates of specific OAD symptoms. Older children, however, presented with a greater number of symptoms than did younger children and also reported higher levels of anxiety and depression. Furthermore Table 6–5 illustrates the percentage of children in each age group who also met the diagnostic criteria for other disorders. Within the anxiety disorders, young children were significantly more likely to receive a concurrent diagnosis of separation anxiety disorder, and older children a concurrent diagnosis of simple phobia. Older children were also significantly more likely to receive a concurrent diagnosis of major depression and younger children a concurrent diagnosis of attention deficit disorder. These findings suggest a

TABLE 6–5   Concurrent DSM-III Diagnoses for Younger versus Older Children with Overanxious Disorder

	Age Groups	
DSM-III Diagnoses	*<12 years* (%)	*≥12 years* (%)
Anxiety disorders		
Separation anxiety disorder	69.6	21.9*
Avoidant disorder	13.0	25.0
Simple phobia	8.7	40.6*
Social phobia	8.7	9.4
Agoraphobia	0	6.3
Panic disorder	0	15.6
Obsessive-compulsive disorder	4.3	9.4
Major depression	17.4	46.9*
Oppositional disorder	17.4	6.3
Conduct disorder	8.7	0
Attention deficit disorder	34.8	9.4*

*Statistically significant difference.

Adapted from Strauss, C. C., Lease, C. A., Last, C. G., & Francis, G. (1988). Overanxious disorder: An examination of developmental differences. *Journal of Abnormal Child Psychology, 16,* 433–443. Reprinted by permission from Plenum Publishing Corporation.

developmental difference in how OAD is experienced. However, it should also be noted that many other diagnostic categories were represented in one or both age groups. This finding that youngsters who meet the diagnostic criteria for OAD or GAD also are likely to meet the diagnostic criteria for other disorders is frequently reported (cf. Cohen et al., 1993; Strauss, 1994).

PANIC ATTACKS AND PANIC DISORDER

Definition and Diagnosis

A distinction is made between panic attacks and panic disorder. A *panic attack* is a discrete period of intense fear or terror that has a sudden onset and reaches a peak quickly. DSM-IV describes thirteen somatic or cognitive symptoms; four or more of which must be present during an episode (see Table 6–6). Three different categories of panic attacks, defined by the presence or absence of triggers, are described. *Unexpected (uncued)* panic attacks occur spontaneously or "out of the blue" with no apparent situational trigger. In contrast, *situationally bound* (cued) panic attacks occur, almost invariably, when the person is exposed to or anticipates a feared object or situation (e.g., a dog). *Situationally predisposed* panic attacks occur on exposure to a situational cue, but not all of the time; that is, they do not occur invariably and they may occur following exposure rather than immediately.

Panic attacks are not themselves a diagnosis within the DSM system, but rather may occur in the context of several different anxiety disorders. One of these disorders is Panic Disorder. To meet the diagnostic criteria for a panic disorder, the youngster must experience recurrent *unexpected* panic attacks. In addition, at least one of these attacks must be followed by at least a month of one or more of the following consequences: (a) persistent concern about additional at-

TABLE 6–6   DSM-IV Criteria for Panic Attack

A discrete period of intense fear or discomfort, in which four (or more) of the following symptoms developed abruptly and reached a peak within 10 minutes:

(1) palpitations, pounding heart, or accelerated heart rate
(2) sweating
(3) trembling or shaking
(4) sensations of shortness of breath or smothering
(5) feeling of choking
(6) chest pain or discomfort
(7) nausea or abdominal distress
(8) feeling dizzy, unsteady, lightheaded, or faint
(9) derealization (feelings of unreality) or depersonalization (being detached from oneself)
(10) fear of losing control or going crazy
(11) fear of dying
(12) paresthesias (numbness or tingling sensations)
(13) chills or hot flushes

Adapted and reprinted with permission from the *Diagnostic and Statistical Manual of Mental Disorders, Fourth Edition.* Copyright 1994, American Psychiatric Association.

tacks, and/or (b) worry about the meaning of the attacks (e.g., a heart attack, "going crazy"), and/or (c) an appreciable change in behavior related to the attacks.

Description of Panic in Children and Adolescents

While there is an established literature regarding panic attacks and panic disorder in adults, it is only recently that the occurrence of panic in children and adolescents has received attention. This was, in part, due to controversy as to whether there was sufficient evidence of the existence of panic attacks and panic disorder in youngsters (cf. Kearney and Silverman, 1992; Klein, et al., 1992). Much of the controversy revolved around whether children experienced both the physiological and cognitive symptoms of panic, and if so, whether these were experienced as spontaneous (uncued).

While methodological criticisms suggest caution (Kearney and Silverman, 1992), recent reviews of research indicate the presence of panic attacks and panic disorder in adolescents, and to a lesser degree in prepubertal children (e.g., Ollendick, Mattis,

and King, 1994). Many adults who experience panic attacks or panic disorder, for example, report that onset had occurred during adolescence or earlier. However, reports of the occurrence of *spontaneous* prepubertal panic may be rare (e.g., Klein et al., 1992).

An additional source of information regarding panic comes from studies of youngsters seen in hospitals or clinics and from normative studies. Reviews of this literature suggest that panic disorder occurs in adolescence, but is rare. For example, Whitaker and colleagues (1990) report a lifetime prevalence for panic disorder of 0.6 percent in a general adolescent sample of fourteen- to seventeen-year-olds. The prevalence reported in clinical samples of adolescents is higher—about 10–15 percent (e.g., Alessi, Robbins, and Dilsaver, 1987; Last and Strauss, 1989). Estimates of the exact prevalence vary depending on how information is gathered (Clark et al., 1994). Both panic attacks and panic disorder are reported more frequently in girls than in boys.

With regard to how panic is experienced, studies of adolescents seen in clinics indicate that these youths evidence both the physiological and cognitive symptoms of panic. For example, Bradley and Hood (1993) found that seven of the physiological symptoms were reported by more than 50 percent of their sample. Cognitive symptoms were reported less frequently: "going crazy" was reported by 32 percent and fear of dying by 25 percent. Whether panic attacks are cued or spontaneous is less clear. Psychosocial stressors (e.g., family conflict, peer problems) were reported by twenty-six of the twenty-eight adolescents in this study, and four youths reported other precipitants. Some studies, however, report that among youngsters who meet the diagnostic criteria for panic disorder, the panic attacks are judged to be spontaneous. There is a problem in judging the spontaneous nature of panic attacks in youngsters, who are probably less insightful than adults and therefore may report an attack as spontaneous if not specifically and carefully questioned about cues. This problem is particularly true in relation to younger children. In comparison to adolescence, not much normative information is available regarding panic in children. While both panic attacks and panic disorder are reported in clinical samples of children, they are less frequent than in adolescent samples (Ollendick et al., 1994).

Youngsters who present at clinics with panic attacks or panic disorder are likely to have a family history of panic attacks or other severe anxiety symptoms. These youngsters are also likely to present with a variety of other symptoms, and many meet the criteria for additional diagnoses (Ollendick et al., 1994). In addition to meeting the criteria for anxiety disorders, youngsters frequently also meet criteria for a diagnosis of depression. The high proportion of youngsters who report a history of separation anxiety has led to the suggestion that separation anxiety disorder is a precursor to panic disorder. This hypothesis requires further investigation; it seems likely that

separation anxiety disorder would be only one of many possible paths to the development of panic disorder.

REACTIONS TO TRAUMATIC EVENTS

How do youngsters react to natural disasters such as hurricanes, to experiencing the violence of a sniper attack, to kidnapping, or to other disasters such as fires or ship sinkings? Until recently there had been relatively little systematic study of children's reactions to such traumatic events.

Trauma is usually defined as an event outside of everyday experience that would be distressing to almost anyone. Early descriptions suggested that children's reactions to such trauma would be relatively mild and transient and thus they were not given a great deal of attention. However, reports emerged of more severe and long-lasting reactions. These reports became more salient with the introduction of a specific diagnosis of Posttraumatic Stress Disorder (PTSD). In addition, a shift from reliance on primarily parent report to direct examination of youngsters occurred. The value of obtaining information from the youngsters themselves was supported by comparisons of adult versus child reports of the child's reactions. Parents were found to report significantly lower levels of anxiety and other PTSD symptoms in their children than were reported by the youngsters themselves (Udwin, 1993; Vogel and Vernberg, 1993).

Terr's (1979; 1983) description of the reactions of twenty-six children kidnapped from their Chowchilla, California school bus in 1976 is one study that influenced how children's posttraumatic responses were understood. The children and their bus driver were held for twenty-seven hours. At first they were driven around in darkened vans and then moved to a buried tractor-trailer, where they remained until some of the victims dug themselves out. Terr interviewed the child victims and at least one parent of each child within five to thirteen months of the kidnapping. She found all of the children to be symptomatic, with 73 percent showing moderately severe or severe reactions. Assessments two to five years after the kidnapping also revealed that many symptoms persisted, including fears among all the children.

Diagnosis of Posttraumatic Stress Disorder

The diagnostic category of PTSD was introduced in the third version of the DSM, and in DSM-III-R some symptoms specific to children were added. The diagnosis of PTSD according to DSM-IV requires that the person be exposed to a traumatic event that includes a threat of death, serious injury or physical integrity to the self or others, and where the person's response involves fear, helplessness, or horror. In children this reaction may be expressed instead as disorganized or agitated behavior. Three categories of symptoms must be experienced for more than one month: reexperiencing of the traumatic event (e.g., repetitive play, dreams, intense distress on exposure to cues related to the event), persistent avoidance of stimuli associated with the trauma, and persistent symptoms of increased arousal (e.g., difficulty sleeping, irritability, difficulty concentrating). In order to meet the criteria for a diagnosis of PTSD, the disturbance must also cause significant interference in important areas of functioning.

Much of the research regarding youngsters' reactions to traumatic events has been concerned with the presence of these symptoms, whether or not full diagnostic criteria are met. Also, in examining youngsters' responses to traumatic events it is useful to consider a broader definition of post-traumatic stress and to evaluate symptoms such as anxiety and depression (Vogel and Vernberg, 1993).

Description of Youngsters' Reactions

Most youngsters become upset at reminders of the trauma and experience repetitive, intrusive thoughts about the event. This is true of children experiencing even mild levels of exposure to life-threatening disasters. Among preschool and school-age children, reenactment in play of aspects of the disaster is frequently reported. Initially such play may be part of the reexperiencing symptoms, but if play progresses it may be a useful part of the recovery process as well. Saylor, Powell, and Swenson (1992), for example, report that after Hurricane Hugo, children's play progressed from blowing houses down to acting out the role of roofers during rebuilding.

Youngsters may also exhibit increased frequency and intensity of specific fears. These occur to stimuli directly related to or associated with the experience, but not to unrelated stimuli. Thus, adolescent girls on a school trip who experienced the sinking of their cruise ship "Jupiter" developed fears of swimming, the dark, or boats and other forms of transportation, but did not show elevated levels of unrelated fears when compared to schoolmates who did not go on the trip or to girls from a comparable school (Yule, Udwin, and Murdoch, 1990).

Separation difficulties and clingy, dependent behaviors are also commonly reported. This may be exhibited in reluctance to go to school or a desire to sleep with parents. Other sleep problems such as difficulty in getting to sleep, nightmares, and repeated dreams related to the traumatic event are also common. A sense of vulnerability and loss of faith in the future have also been reported. In adolescents this may interfere with planning for future education and careers. Relatedly, school performance is reported to suffer. Other commonly reported symptoms include depressed mood, loss of interest in previously enjoyed activities, irritability, and angry or aggressive outbursts. Guilt about surviving when others have died can also occur.

Determinants and Intervention

Not all children and adolescents experience the same pattern or intensity of symptoms, and reactions may vary in how long they persist and may fluctuate over time. A number of factors seem to influence reactions. Individual differences in vulnerability that existed prior to the traumatic event are likely to influence the youngster's reaction. Degree of exposure to the traumatic event is another important influence. Pynoos and his colleagues (1987), for example, studied 159 California school children who were exposed to a sniper attack on their school in which one child and a passerby were killed and thirteen other children injured. Among these children, who averaged 9.2 years of age at the time of the attack, children who were trapped on the playground showed much greater later effects than those who had left the immediate vicinity of the shooting or were not in school that day. At a fourteen-month follow-up, for example, among the most severely exposed children, 74 percent still reported moderate to severe PTSD symptoms whereas 81 percent of the nonexposed children reported no PTSD (Nader et al., 1991). While level of exposure to this life-threatening trauma was an important factor, reactions did occur among children who did not experience a high degree of exposure. Subjective experience of threat and greater knowledge of the child who was killed were associated with increased reactions among less exposed children.

The reactions of children and adolescents to traumatic events are also related to the reactions of their parents. If the parents themselves suffer severe post-traumatic stress or for some other reason are unable to provide an atmosphere of support and communication, their children's reactions are likely to be more severe. This finding naturally leads to the question of how best to intervene when children and adolescents are exposed to traumatic events. There has been relatively little evaluation of interventions, and thus clear recommendations are difficult to make (Udwin, 1993; Vernberg and Vogel, 1993; Yule, 1994). Debriefing groups within a short time of the disaster are usually employed to encourage youngsters and their families to share their feelings and open channels of communication, to prepare them for possible reactions in the future, and to help them realize that such reactions are normal reactions to abnormal events. Additional group work or individual cognitive-behavioral interventions may help in coping or alleviating symptoms and may help to enhance a sense of coping and mastery.

OBSESSIVE-COMPULSIVE DISORDER

Obsessions are unwanted, repetitive, intrusive thoughts, while compulsions involve repetitive, stereotyped behaviors the child or adolescent feels compelled to perform. The disorder involves either obsessions or compulsions or a combination of the two. The DSM-IV criteria for Obsessive-Compulsive Disorder (OCD) are illustrated in Table 6–7. Beyond defining the nature of obsessions and compulsions, the criteria indicate that the person realizes the thoughts and behaviors are unreasonable. This particular feature is not required for the diagnosis of OCD in children, but may become part of the clinical picture in older children and adolescents. The disorder is known to occur in children under the age of seven (Swedo et al., 1989c). Among these very young children, odd repetitive acts may be seen as

TABLE 6–7 DSM-IV Criteria for Obsessive-Compulsive Disorder

A. Either obsessions or compulsions:

Obsessions as defined by (1), (2), (3), and (4):

(1) recurrent and persistent thoughts, impulses, or images that are experienced, at some time during the disturbance, as intrusive and inappropriate and that cause marked anxiety or distress

(2) the thoughts, impulses, or images are not simply excessive worries about real-life problems

(3) the person attempts to ignore or suppress such thoughts, impulses, or images, or to neutralize them with some other thought or action

(4) the person recognizes that the obsessional thoughts, impulses, or images are a product of his or her own mind (not imposed from without as in thought insertion)

Compulsions as defined by (1) and (2):

(1) repetitive behaviors (e.g., hand washing, ordering, checking) or mental acts (e.g., praying, counting, repeating words silently) that the person feels driven to perform in response to an obsession, or according to rules that must be applied rigidly

(2) the behaviors or mental acts are aimed at preventing or reducing distress or preventing some dreaded event or situation; however, these behaviors or mental acts either are not connected in a realistic way with what they are designed to neutralize or prevent or are clearly excessive

B. At some point during the course of the disorder, the person has recognized that the obsessions or compulsions are excessive or unreasonable. **Note:** This does not apply to children.

C. The obsessions or compulsions cause marked distress, are time consuming (take more than 1 hour a day), or significantly interfere with the person's normal routine, occupational (or academic) functioning, or usual social activities or relationships.

D. If another Axis I disorder is present, the content of the obsessions or compulsions is not restricted to it (e.g., preoccupation with food in the presence of an Eating Disorder).

Adapted and reprinted with permission from the *Diagnostic and Statistical Manual of Mental Disorders, Fourth Edition.* Copyright 1994, American Psychiatric Association.

strange even by the child. However, children may initially have their own explanations. For example, seven-year-old Stanley indicated that he had seen a show in which Martians contacted humans by putting strange thoughts in their heads. Stanley explained his compulsion to do everything in sequences of four as a sign that he had been picked as the martians' contact on earth. After two years of no contact Stanley gave up this explanation, but not his ritual (Rapoport, 1989). The child may thus come to recognize that the ideas or behaviors involved are unreasonable but still feel the need to repeat them.

Another part of the criteria for the diagnosis of OCD is that the obsessions or compulsions are highly time consuming and that they result in considerable interference with normal routines, academic functioning, and social relationships. Rapoport's (1989) description of Sergi illustrates the nature and consequences of the disorder.

Sergei is a 17-year-old former high school student. Only a year or so ago Sergei seemed to be a normal adolescent with many talents and interests. Then, almost overnight he was transformed into a lonely outsider, excluded from social life by his psychological disabilities. Specifically, he was unable to stop washing. Haunted by the notion that he was dirty—in spite of the contrary evidence of his senses—he began to spend more and more of his time cleansing himself of imaginary dirt. At first his ritual ablutions were confined to weekends and evenings and he was able to stay in school while keeping them up, but soon they began to consume all his time, forcing him to drop out of school, a victim of his inability to feel clean enough (p. 83).

Prevalence

Behavior with obsessive-compulsive qualities occurs in various stages of normal development (Leonard et al., 1990). The feeding and bedtime rituals of very young children are examples; disruption of these routines often leads to distress. Also, young children are often observed to engage in repetitive play and to show a distinct preference for sameness. Benjamin Spock (Spock and Rothenberg, 1992), in his widely read book for parents, notes that mild compulsions—such as stepping over cracks in the sidewalk or touching every third picket in a fence—are quite common in eight, nine, and ten-year-olds. Such behaviors, common to the child's peer group, are probably best viewed as games. Only when they dominate the child's life and interfere with normal functioning is there cause for concern. The specific content of OCD rituals generally does not resemble these common developmental rituals and the OCD rituals have a later stage of onset. It is not clear at present whether developmental rituals represent early manifestations of obsessive-compulsive disorder in some children (Leonard et al., 1990).

Obsessive-compulsive disorder is probably not as rare as was once believed. A prevalence of up to 0.3 percent (depending on how cases were classified) was reported for an unselected general child population (Rutter, Tizard, and Whitmore, 1970). Previous estimates based on records of child clinical agencies reported incidence rates from 0.2 percent to 1 percent (Judd, 1965; Hollingsworth et al., 1980). Due to several considerations, including attempts by the persons to hide their difficulties, lack of public awareness, and limited availability of treatment, these figures may have been underestimates. An epidemiological study of nonreferred adolescents suggests a current prevalence rate of 1 percent and a lifetime prevalence rate of 1.9 percent in the general

Keeping things in certain specific locations and order are common among children. It is only when these kinds of behaviors interfere with normal functioning that they should cause concern for clinicians and other adults.

adolescent population (Flament et al., 1988). Most estimates also suggest that at younger ages boys outnumber girls, but that by adolescence the genders are equally represented (Leonard et al., 1994). Among a sample of seventy consecutive child and adolescent cases seen at the National Institute for Mental Health (NIMH) seven had an onset prior to the age of seven years and the mean age of onset was ten years of age. The onset of obsessive-compulsive symptoms in boys tended to be prepubertal (mean age nine), while in girls the average onset (mean of eleven years) was around puberty (Swedo et al., 1989c).

Description and Developmental Course

Judith Rapoport and her colleagues at NIMH conducted a series of studies that increased the attention given to obsessive-compulsive behavior in youngsters. Initially, like most clinicians, Rapoport saw few cases of childhood obsessive-compulsive disorder. Indeed, when she began her work she did not know whether or not she would find enough cases to complete the initial research. However, even at this early point,

Rapoport was struck by the similarity between child and adult cases of the disorder. From the initial series of cases, the NIMH group also began to get a sense of the obsessions and compulsions that were common in this population (e.g., Swedo et al., 1989c). Table 6–8 indicates the most common obsessions and compulsions among the children and adolescents.

OCD is described as following a waxing and waning course over time, with psychosocial stressors often thought to be responsible for exacerbation of symptoms (Leonard et al., 1994). Also, multiple obsessions and compulsions are usually present at any one time, and usually the symptoms change over time, although no clear progression is identified (Rettew et al., 1992). In addition, most of the youngsters also meet the diagnostic criteria for at least one other disorder (e.g., Hanna, 1995). For example, in the seventy consecutive cases at NIMH described above, only twenty-six percent had no other diagnosis (Swedo et al., 1989c).

Research also suggests that the disorder is likely to follow a chronic course (Leonard et al., 1994). Even recent research, conducted during a period when recommended treatments were available, suggests that the problems persist. Leonard and her colleagues (1993) followed fifty-four youngsters who had received pharmacological treatment and were reevaluated two to seven years later. The group as a whole had improved, in that only 19 percent were unchanged or worse. However, 70 percent were still taking medication, 43 percent still met the diagnostic criteria for OCD, and only 11 percent exhibited no obsessive-compulsive symptoms.

Etiology

As a function of their work with these youngsters, including successful drug treatment trials, Rapoport and her colleagues came to believe in a biological basis for ob-

TABLE 6–8 Obsessions and Compulsions Among Children and Adolescents Receiving the Diagnosis of Obsessive-Compulsive Disorder

Obsessions	*Percent Reporting Symptom*
Concern with dirt germs or environmental toxins	40
Something terrible happening (fire, death or illness of self or loved one)	24
Symmetry, order, or exactness	17
Scrupulosity (religious obsessions)	13
Concern or disgust with bodily wastes or secretions (urine, stool, saliva)	8
Lucky or unlucky numbers	8
Forbidden, aggressive, or perverse sexual thoughts, images, or impulses	4
Fear might harm others or oneself	4
Concern with household items	3
Intrusive nonsense sounds, words, or music	1
Compulsions	
Excessive or ritualized handwashing, showering, bathing, toothbrushing, or grooming	85
Repeating rituals (going in or out of a door, up or down from a chair)	51
Checking (doors, locks, appliances, emergency brake on car, paper route, homework)	46
Rituals to remove contact with contaminants	23
Touching	20
Measures to prevent harm to self or others	16
Ordering or arranging	17
Counting	18
Hoarding or collecting rituals	11
Rituals of cleaning household or inanimate objects	6
Miscellaneous rituals (such as writing, moving, speaking)	26

Note: Percentages total more than 100 percent because many youths had more than one symptom.

Adapted from The biology of obsessions and compulsions, Rapoport, J. L. Copyright © (1989) by Scientific American, Inc. All rights reserved.

sessive-compulsive disorder. The disorder was found to be more prevalent among youngsters with a first-degree relative with obsessive-compulsive behavior than among the general population, and many parents of youngsters with the disorder met diagnostic criteria for OCD or exhibited obsessive-compulsive symptoms (Lenane et al., 1990; Riddle et al., 1992; Swedo et al., 1989c). In addition, a number of studies have reported that both OCD and Tourette's syndrome (or less severe tic disorders) occur in the same persons and have also found a familial association between the two disorders (Leonard et al, 1994). These findings were viewed as suggesting a possible genetic cause for OCD.

Further support for a biological basis for OCD came from findings of an association between obsessive-compulsive symptoms and certain known neurological disorders and from brain imaging studies suggesting that OCD was linked to the anatomy of the basal ganglia, a group of brain structures lying under the cerebral cortex (e.g., Luxenberg et al., 1988; Swedo et al., 1989a; Swedo et al., 1989b). There has also been the suggestion that some cases of sudden-onset obsessions and tics in children may be triggered by infection (Allen, Leonard, and Swedo, 1995).

Treatment

There are relatively few published reports on the treatment of obsessive-compulsive disorder in children. Two kinds of intervention, alone or in combination, seem to be the current treatments of choice (Leonard et al., 1994; van Balkom et al., 1994). The behavioral procedure that has been most successful is exposure with response prevention (March, 1995). The youngster is exposed to the situation that causes anxiety and the compulsive ritual is prevented by helping the youngster resist the urge to perform it. Stanley's (1980) clinical report de-

scribes an early use of response prevention in the treatment of an eight-year-old girl and her family.

Amanda was referred by her G.P. because of her excessive checking behaviour. Three months prior to this referral Amanda's parents became increasingly worried as more and more of her time was involved in carrying out her rituals, e.g., she was taking at least 20 minutes to dress in the morning instead of the 5 minutes which had been more than ample previously. The symptoms had first become noticeable 6 months before.

The rituals had begun slowly following the family's move to their present home. This had been the second major move made by the family in three years involving a change of house, school, geographic area and father's job. . . . both Amanda and her younger sister had coped reasonably well with the moves, and the parents did not think these had any connection with Amanda's symptomatology. No satisfactory reason for the development of the symptoms was identified. . . .

At interview Amanda presented as an alert, bright eight-year-old whose face fell at the mention of her "fussiness." . . . There was no evidence of obsessional symptoms in her school work and the teacher had not noticed anything unusual in her affect or behaviour.

Amanda was able to talk about her symptomatology as though it were a thing apart from herself. She saw it as an intrusion on her previously happy life and felt depressed by the restrictive elements of her ritual. She found her peer relationships were affected by no longer being able to invite friends home in case they disturbed her ornaments, toys, etc. . . . The family appeared to be functioning very cohesively, which may explain how each person had become involved in Amanda's symptomatology.

At the time of referral Amanda's symptoms included the following. . . .

(1) Every night she closed the curtains, turned down the bed and fluffed up her pillow three times before beginning to undress. Any disruption of this routine caused great distress.

(2) The top bedcover had to be placed with the fringes only just touching the floor all around.

(3) At night Amanda removed her slippers slowly and carefully, she then banged them

on the floor upside-down, then the right-way-up, three times and nudged them gently and in parallel under the bed.

(4) Before going to sleep Amanda had to go to the toilet three times. She often woke up in the middle of the night and carried out the same performance.

(5) Before carrying out a ritual Amanda sang:

> "One, two, three,
> Come dance with me
> Tra la la, Tra la la."

(6) All dressing and undressing had to be done three times. This included pulling up her pants three times after every visit to the toilet.

(7) All Amanda's toys had special places which had to be checked and rechecked before leaving the bedroom.

(8) The ornaments on top of the piano had special places. These positions were so precise that Amanda's mother found dusting and polishing almost impossible (p. 86–87).

The family was instructed not to give Amanda special attention and to treat her as a girl who did not have compulsive urges. The parents were also trained to initiate response prevention procedures. Starting with the least upsetting situation, the parents prevented Amanda from engaging in her rituals. Once she coped with a situation, the next step up the hierarchy was taken. After the first two days in which Amanda experienced considerable anxiety, she gradually began to relax. After two weeks all her symptoms had disappeared. No new or additional problems arose, and Amanda was still symptom free at the one-year follow-up.

Rapoport has also indicated the effectiveness of behavioral procedures. In addition, the NIMH group and others have reported evidence for the effectiveness of certain pharmacological agents (e.g., chlomipramine, fluoxetine, and fluvoxamine). These medications are thought to inhibit the reuptake of the neurotransmitter serotonin. Clomipramine is the medication that has been most extensively studied in the treatment of youngsters with OCD. It and the other serotonin uptake-inhibitors have been shown to be effective in treating obsessive and compulsive symptoms (Deveaugh-Geiss et al., 1992; Geller et al., 1995; Leonard et al., 1989).

SUMMARY

A variety of evidence supports the existence of a broadly defined category of child and adolescent internalizing problems. The existence and definition of valid subcategories are, however, far more controversial, due in part to findings that youngsters often meet the criteria for more than one of the subcategories or diagnoses. This issue, often termed "comorbidity", is a challenge inconceptualizing internalizing problems.

Anxiety or fear is generally defined as a complex pattern of three response systems: motor, physiological, and subjective responses.

In the context of a general and comprehensive assessment, various methods exist for assessing anxiety in children and adolescents. Direct observation and behavioral approach tests are employed to assess the motor aspects of fears and anxieties. The subjective aspects of anxiety are assessed through a variety of self-report measures. Physiological aspects of anxiety such as heart rate are less frequently assessed than the other two response systems.

DSM-IV describes one anxiety disorder within the "usually first evident in infancy, childhood, or adolescence" grouping: Separation Anxiety Disorder. A child or adolescent can also receive other anxiety disorder diagnoses which include Phobic Disorders, Panic Disorder, Generalized Anxiety Disorder, Obsessive-Compulsive Disorder, and Posttraumatic Stress Disorder.

The empirical approach to classification describes subcategories of internalizing disorders and profile types that are related to anxiety problems. Although some overlap can be seen with the clinical categories of the DSM system, the two approaches clearly represent different ways of organizing the anxiety disorders.

It seems likely that the development of anxiety disorders is influenced by multiple determinants. There is considerable evidence for family aggregation of anxiety disorders with likely contributions of both genetic and environmental influences.

In general, the most support exists for psychological treatments for anxiety problems in children and adolescents. Pharmacotherapy, if employed, is usually an adjunct to such treatment.

Fears are quite common in children. However, it is unclear how prevalent intense fears are. There also seem to be age- and gender-related variations in numbers and content of fears. Phobias, as distinguished from normal fears, are judged to be excessive, persistent or nonadaptive. Fears and phobias can be reliably grouped into categories based on the specific object or situation. In DSM-IV, the categories Specific Phobia and Social Phobia describe excessive fears of objects or situations.

Specific phobias are likely to begin in childhood, and for some individuals they may persist over time. The importance of familial environmental influences on the development of specific phobias is suggested. Treatments based on exposure to the feared stimulus have proven effective with children and adolescents.

Social phobias in children and adolescents have received less attention than specific phobias, and the exact nature of the disorder is unclear. Prevalence probably increases with age, but the fact that social anxieties are quite common during adolescence makes interpretations of prevalence and degree of disturbance difficult.

School refusal is the term commonly used to describe children whose anxieties keep them from school. This term accommodates cases of both separation anxiety and phobias related to aspects of the actual school situation. Separation anxiety is a common problem among children but becomes less common by adolescence. School refusal in adolescence is likely to be complex. School refusal is a common reason for referral for treatment. Treatment would appear to be most successful if it is begun early and it probably needs to be tailored to the specific kinds of school refusal exhibited.

Children and adolescents diagnosed as exhibiting Generalized Anxiety Disorder exhibit excessive worry and anxiety that is not focused on any particular object or situation. These youngsters are often described as overanxious. Such youngsters exhibit a variety of anxious behaviors, and the disorder may persist and be associated with significant impairment. Youngsters meeting the criteria for this diagnosis may be common in clinic samples and the question of overlap with other diagnoses is of concern.

Panic attacks may be cued or uncued and may occur in the context of several anxiety disorders. Panic disorder is associated with recurrent unexpected panic attacks. It is only recently that the occurrence of panic in children and adolescents has received attention. The presence of panic in adolescents seems suggested, but the existence, particularly of uncued panic, in younger children is less clear. Family histories of panic and severe anxiety are commonly reported, as are the presence of other anxiety symptoms and depression.

Until recently there has been little systematic study of youngsters' reactions to traumatic events. The diagnosis of Posttraumatic Stress Disorder requires reexperiencing of the traumatic event, avoidance of stimuli associated with the trauma, and symptoms of increased arousal. Much of the research regarding youngsters' reactions to traumatic events has been concerned with the presence of these symptoms. Not all youngsters experience the same pattern, intensity, or persistence of symptoms, and reactions may fluctuate over time. Degree of exposure to the trauma and reactions of parents are among the influences that may determine a youngster's reaction to a traumatic event.

Obsessive-Compulsive Disorder is characterized by repetitive and intrusive thoughts and/or behaviors. The problem is probably more common than once thought and often appears to follow a chronic course. Many researchers have begun to see a number of child cases. They have come to believe that there is a biological basis for the disorder. Treatment combining behavioral procedures and pharmacotherapy is being explored and seems promising.

7

DEPRESSION AND PROBLEMS IN PEER RELATIONS

In this chapter we will examine the problems of depression and peer relations. In isolating these as separate categories we confront many of the same problems that we found in examining anxiety disorders. For example, children and adolescents who meet the criteria for a diagnosis of depression are often also given other diagnoses. Similarly, the social withdrawal that one might associate with internalizing problems is part of a more general concern with deficits in peer relations and social skills. Such social deficits are characteristic of youngsters with a number of different disorders. Thus, the designation of these problems as distinct entities is not without controversy. Nonetheless, examining depression and peer relations makes sense in terms of how the research and treatment literature are organized.

CHILD AND ADOLESCENT DEPRESSION

Until recently depression in children and adolescents had not received a great deal of attention. However, interest has clearly increased. This can probably be traced to a number of influences. Promising developments in the identification and treatment of mood disorders in adults have played a role.

In addition, improvements in diagnostic practices have facilitated the application of diagnostic criteria to children and adolescents. The emergence of a number of measures of depression has also allowed researchers to examine the phenomenon in clinic and normal populations of youngsters. Furthermore, the new perspective of developmental psychopathology focused additional attention on depression in young people.

In everyday usage the term *depression* refers to the experience of a pervasive unhappy mood. This subjective experience of sadness, or dysphoria, is also a central feature of the clinical definition of depression. Descriptions of youngsters viewed as depressed suggest that they exhibit a number of other problems as well. Loss of the experience of pleasure, social withdrawal, lowered self-esteem, inability to concentrate, poor schoolwork, alterations of biological functions (sleeping, eating, elimination), and somatic complaints are often noted.

Prevalence

In community surveys, prevalence rates for major depression in youngsters vary between 2 and 5 percent, (e.g., Anderson et al., 1987; Kashani et al., 1987). In clinical populations estimates typically fall between

Sad affect or dysphoria is the central characteristic of most definitions of depression.

(Charles Harbutt/Actuality)

10 and 20 percent (e.g., Alessi and Magen, 1988; Puig-Antich and Gittelman, 1982). Gender and age are clearly relevant to estimates of the prevalence of depression in young people.

The picture regarding gender ratios in young children is somewhat unclear. Usually no gender differences are reported for children ages six to twelve (e.g., Angold and Rutter, 1992; Fleming, Offord, and Boyle, 1989). When differences are reported, depression is more prevalent in boys than in girls during this age period (e.g., Anderson et al., 1987). Yet among adolescents depression is far more common among girls and begins to approach the 2:1 female to male ratio usually reported for adults.

The data for adolescents also suggest a greater prevalence of depression than exists for younger children (e.g., Angold and Rutter, 1992; Cohen, Cohen, Kasen et al., 1993; Lewinsohn et al., 1993; Whitaker et al., 1990). The magnitude of the problem in adolescent populations is indicated by findings of lifetime prevalence rates among the general population as high as 20 to 30 percent for diagnosable depressive disorders (e.g., Compas, Ey, and Grant, 1993; Lewinsohn et al., 1993). This would mean that about 1 out of 4 youngsters in the general population experiences a depressive disorder sometime during childhood or adolescence.

Estimates of the prevalence of depression vary considerably (Kazdin, 1990; Reynolds and Johnston, 1994). In addition to variations related to gender and age, there are other developmental considerations which complicate getting accurate estimates. The difficulty of administering similar tests to youngsters of different ages is one consideration. Also, widely employed assessment tools, such as interviews, require that the youngster think in terms of psychological constructs and effectively communicate what is remembered. Such processes clearly depend on developmental level.

Defining Depression

Also important to variations in reported rates of depression are the different criteria that are employed to define depression.

A study by Carlson and Cantwell (1980) illustrates this point. A sample of 210 children was selected at random from over 1,000 children between the ages of seven and seventeen seen at the UCLA-Neuropsychiatric Institute. Three different criteria were employed to define depression. At intake the presence of depressive symptoms among the presenting problems was noted and this served as one criterion. The youngsters were also administered a version of the Children's Depression Inventory, a second criterion. Finally, separate interviews with 102 of the youngsters and their parents were conducted to assess the presence of affective disorder, according to DSM criteria. The use of the presence of depressive symptoms at intake as a criterion for diagnosing a depressive disorder led to the largest number of children being diagnosed; the depression inventory led to fewer, and DSM diagnosis led to the least. However, it is also clear that the results were not simply a matter of using more or less stringent criteria. Rather, there appear to be some differences in definition. For example, not all children designated as depressed by the depression inventory were so designated using the depressive symptom criterion as would be expected if the former were just a less stringent definition. Similarly, not all DSM Affective Disorder children were designated as depressed using the criterion of depression inventory score.

These and other findings indicate that different groups of youngsters may or may not be designated as depressed according to what methods were employed for testing (Kaslow and Racusin, 1990). Such variations may be due to differences in method employed (e.g. depression inventory vs. DSM diagnostic criteria) or use of different informants. As we have mentioned previously, different informants are likely to give quite different views of children's emotional and behavioral problems (Kazdin, 1994; Tarullo et al., 1995b).

This is illustrated in a study by Kazdin (1989b). DSM diagnoses of 231 consecutive child admissions to an inpatient psychiatric facility were made based on direct interviews with the children and their parents. This method of diagnosing depression was compared to criteria based on exceeding a cutoff scores on the Children's Depression Inventory (CDI). Both the children and parents completed the CDI. In addition, children and/or their parents completed a number of other measures to assess attributes reported to be associated with depression. Consistent with the findings of Carlson and Cantwell described above, different groups of children appeared to be designated as depressed depending on the criteria employed. In addition, characteristics associated with depression varied depending on the method used to designate the presence of depression. Some of these results are illustrated in Table 7–1. Defining depression as a high self-report score on the CDI indicated that depressed children were more hopeless; had lower self-esteem, made more internal (as opposed to external) attributions regarding negative events; and, based on a locus of control (IE) scale, were more likely to believe that control was due to external factors rather than themselves. Depressed and nondepressed children defined by the other two criteria (parent CDI and DSM) did not differ from each other on these characteristics. Employing the parent CDI criterion, children with high depression scores appear to be more problematic across a wide range of symptoms (as measured by the Child Behavior Checklist–CBCL) than those with very low depression scores. Depression as designated by the other two criteria did not appear to be associated with this wide range of problems. Thus, conclusions regarding correlates of depression may be affected by the criterion and informant employed to designate youngsters as depressed.

TABLE 7–1 Mean Characteristic Scores of Depressed and Nondepressed Children as Designated by Different Criteria for Depression

	CRITERIA					
	Children's Depression Inventory (by Child)		Children's Depression Inventory (by Parent)		DSM Diagnosis	
Measures	High	Low	High	Low	Depressed	Nondepressed
Hopelessness	7.3	3.3	5.3	5.0	5.4	4.8
Self-esteem	22.7	38.9	28.2	30.8	29.2	30.9
Attributions	5.4	6.5	5.8	5.8	6.0	6.0
Locus of Control (IE)	9.8	6.8	8.2	8.7	7.9	8.4
Total behavior problems (CBCL)	75.8	75.3	81.6	69.0	76.5	75.0

Adapted from Kazdin, A. E. (1989). Identifying depression in children: A comparison of alternative selection criteria. *Journal of Abnormal Child Psychology, 17*, 437–454. Reprinted by permission from Plenum Publishing Corporation.

Description and Classification

While there has always been a broad consensus that children can experience sad affect, there has been considerable variation of opinion as to whether or not youngsters experience the full range of affective, somatic, cognitive, and behavioral attributes characteristic of major depression in adults. How then is depression in children and adolescents to be described and classified for scientific purposes?

It has been suggested that it is important to make a distinction between the phenomenon (or symptom) of depression and the syndrome (or disorder) called depression (e.g., Rutter, 1986b). The symptom of depression refers to the experience of sadness, the loss of interest or pleasure, the lack of responsiveness, and the like, that are used to describe this negative mood state. The term "symptom" here is used in its colloquial sense (equivalent to terms such as "problem" or "experience of") and does not imply any illness. In contrast, it has been suggested that the concept of a depressive *disorder* be reserved for the notion of depression as a syndrome. As a syndrome, "depression" refers to a group of attributes that reliably go together. The syndrome consists of the symptom of negative mood state accompanied by certain somatic, cognitive, and behavioral problems. It is sometimes suggested that a further distinction should also be made between a syndrome and a disorder (e.g., Kovacs, 1989). The latter has all the characteristics of a syndrome, but there is also a persistence of the syndrome, and social impairment is observed in the youngster. In addition, for a disorder it is presumed that more is known about the problem (e.g., a characteristic family history). Hopefully, careful use of these distinctions in future work will help to clarify some of the confusion regarding childhood depression.

Recent history. A brief look at the recent history of thinking on childhood depression may also help clarify differing viewpoints. As we noted earlier (Chapter 3), the dominant view in child clinical work for many years was the orthodox psychoanalytic perspective. From this perspective depression was viewed as a phenomenon of the super-ego and of mature ego functioning (Kessler, 1988). It was argued, for example, that in depression the superego acts as a punisher of the ego. Since the child's superego is not sufficiently developed to play this role, it is impossible, within this perspective, for a depressive disorder to occur in children. It is not surprising, therefore, that depression in children received little attention.

A second major perspective on childhood depression added to the controversy regarding the existence of a distinct disorder. The concept of masked depression represented an interesting view. This view held that there is a disorder of childhood depression. However, it proposed that there are numerous instances when the dysphoric mood and other features usually considered essential to the diagnosis of depression are not present. It was held that an underlying depressive disorder does exist, but the youngster's depression is "masked" by other problems (depressive equivalents) such as hyperactivity or delinquency. The "underlying" depression itself is not directly displayed, but is inferred by the clinician. Some workers, indeed, suggested that masked depressions were quite common and may have resulted in childhood depression being underdiagnosed (Cytryn and McKnew, 1974; Malmquist, 1977).

The notion of masked depression is clearly problematic. There is no operational way to decide whether a particular symptom is or is not a sign of depression. Indeed, the symptoms that have been suggested as masking depression have included virtually the full gamut of problem behaviors evident in youngsters. The concept of masked depression is, thus, quite controversial. Even some of its early advocates came to view it as less important than once thought (Cytryn, McKnew, and Bunney, 1980).

The concept of masked depression was, however, important. It clearly recognized depression as an important and prevalent childhood problem. The central notions of masked depression—that depression in children does exist and that youngsters may display depression in a variety of age-related forms and in ways that may be different from adult depression—are still widely held. The concept that depression is manifested differently in children and adults contributed, in part, to the evolution of a broader developmental perspective.

A developmental perspective. Childhood depression strongly illustrates the value of normative data and the possible implications of a developmental viewpoint. For example, some workers suggested that behaviors which led to the diagnosis of depression were only transitory developmental phenomena—common among children in certain age groups (e.g., Lefkowitz and Burton, 1978). The classic Berkeley survey, for instance, found that 37 percent of girls and 29 percent of boys at age six exhibited insufficient appetite (a problem often thought to be associated with depression). By age nine these figures had dropped to 9 percent and 6 percent, respectively, and 14 percent of both sexes at age fourteen had insufficient appetites (MacFarlane, Allen, and Honzik, 1954). Thus, insufficient appetite should probably not be considered a deviant behavior among six-year-olds. However, if it is present at age nine, especially in boys, it might be considered atypical. Other behaviors, such as "excessive reserve," occur too often in children of all ages to be considered abnormal. Other investigators (e.g., Lefkowitz, 1977) suggested that substantial proportions of the children in the normal population may possess symptoms judged characteristic of depressive disorder in clinical samples.

Thus, it could be held that depression in childhood may not exist as a clinical entity different from common and transient developmental phenomena. Lefkowitz and Burton (1978) suggested that perhaps one of the reasons why clinicians gave the diagnosis of childhood depression was the mistaken belief that behaviors (symptoms) such as insufficient appetite or excessive reserve are rare and, therefore, important when manifested.

The distinction between depression as a symptom and depression as a syndrome is important to consider here. One or two "depressive" behaviors of a child may be viewed as typical of that developmental stage. However, it is different to suggest that a cluster of such behaviors is also likely to occur in a large number of children at the same developmental level (Kovacs, 1989). Awareness of normative and developmental patterns, in any case, is clearly important and might change clinical impressions, leading to changes in diagnostic practices. The developmental perspective has become an important element in the study of depression (Cicchetti, Rogosch, and Toth, 1994; Compas, Hinden, and Gerhardt, 1995; Hammen, 1992).

The DSM perspective. It is not possible at this point to make definitive statements about the "correct" description or classification of childhood depression. A wide range of conceptualizations exist, from those that question the existence of a distinct disorder in childhood, to those that perceive childhood depression in terms of the adult classification, to those that subsume most of the important aspects of child psychopathology under the umbrella of this disorder (Petti, 1989). There are potential liabilities in making a priori judgments about what childhood depression *is*. However, it is probably fair to state that the dominant view is that childhood depression is a syndrome or disorder in which the essential features are the same as those manifested in adults.

Several factors have probably contributed to the dominance of this viewpoint. However, the principle influence appears to be the DSM, that beginning with DSM-III, applied adult criteria for mood disorders including depression, to children. Table 7–2 presents the DSM-IV criteria for the diagnosis of Major Depression. There are no separate diagnostic categories for mood disorders in children or adolescents. However,

---

TABLE 7–2 DSMV-IV Criteria for Major Depressive Episode

A. Five (or more) of the following symptoms have been present during the same 2-week period and represent a change from previous functioning; at least one of the symptoms is either (1) depressed mood or (2) loss of interest or pleasure.

   (1) depressed mood most of the day, nearly every day. Note: In children and adolescents, can be irritable mood.

   (2) markedly diminished interest or pleasure in all, or almost all, activities most of the day, nearly every day.

   (3) significant weight loss when not dieting or weight gain or decrease or increase in appetite nearly every day. Note: In children, consider failure to make expected weight gains.

   (4) insomnia or hypersomnia nearly every day.

   (5) psychomotor agitation or retardation nearly every day (observable by others, not merely subjective feelings of restlessness or being slowed down).

   (6) fatigue or loss of energy nearly every day.

   (7) feelings of worthlessness or excessive or inappropriate guilt nearly every day (not merely self-reproach or guilt about being sick).

   (8) diminished ability to think or concentrate, or indecisiveness, nearly every day.

   (9) recurrent thoughts of death (not just fear of dying), recurrent suicidal ideation without a specific plan, or a suicide attempt or a specific plan for committing suicide.

---

the possibility of different symptoms being evident as a function of age is given some acknowledgment. For example, in prepubertal children symptoms such as somatic complaints and social withdrawal may be particularly common, whereas symptoms such as psychomotor retardation and delusions are less common. Also, as indicated in Table 7–2, irritable mood may substitute for depressed mood in both children and adolescents.

In addition to depression, DSM describes mood disorders that include mania. *Mania* refers to abnormally elevated, expansive, or irritable mood and excessive activity. Diagnoses may include mania or mania combined with depression (as in bipolar disorders). Manic disorders are thought to be rare in children, diagnosis is thought to be difficult in this age group, and in comparison to depression little information is available (Nottelmann and Jensen, 1995). There is, however, some indication that disorders including manic episodes may begin to occur in adolescence (Carlson, 1994; Poznanski and Mokros, 1994).

The dominance of the DSM system and the findings by several researchers that they could apply adult criteria in unmodified form to diagnose mood disorders in children and adolescents have contributed to the popularity of this perspective (e.g., Carlson and Kashani, 1988; Ryan et al., 1987). The view inherent in the DSM approach, that mood disorders found in youngsters are the same as those found in adults, is also supported by some research. Many of the cognitive attributes, biological correlates, and behaviors found in depressed adults are also reported in children and adolescents (e.g., Kaslow, Rehm, and Siegel, 1984; Kazdin et al., 1985; Puig-Antich, 1983). However, differences have also been found, and this has led many workers to conclude that it is premature to accept the use of the same criteria for depressive disorders across all age groups (Nurcombe, 1994; Poznanski

and Mokros, 1994). They suggest that research is not sufficient, and that certain findings require explanation. The gender ratio in prevalence is one example (Compas, Hinden, and Gerhardt, 1995; Nolen-Hoeksema and Girgus, 1994). There is a greater prevalence of depression among adult females than adult males, whereas in youngsters prevalence differences between the genders are not usually reported until sometime during adolescence. In addition, some of the serious concomitants of adult depression are less evident in children, and some biological correlates appear to differ as well (Kazdin, 1986b). Also, antidepressant medications have not been demonstrated to have the same effectiveness in children and adolescents as they have in adults (Johnston and Fruehling, 1994). Finally, the high rates of additional disorders found in youngsters diagnosed as depressed also suggest continued attention to developmental differences in the expression of depression. The association of depression with other difficulties may hold important information regarding both the development of depression and its treatment (e.g., Anderson and McGee, 1994; Kovacs et al., 1984; Lewinsohn et al., 1993).

Overall, then, caution would argue against premature closure regarding our conceptualization of childhood depression. Much developmental information still needs to be obtained, and existing information requires explanation.

Assessment of Depression

The development of assessment instruments has contributed considerably to the increased attention to child and adolescent depression. Assessment is likely to involve a number of strategies and to sample a broad spectrum of attributes. A general clinical interview and use of a general dimensional scale like the Child Behavior Checklist are common. Interviews intended to yield a

DSM diagnosis and a variety of measures that focus more specifically on depression have been developed (cf. Hodges, 1994; Curry and Craighead, 1993). These interviews and assessment devices have greatly facilitated research on depression in children and adolescents.

Among the measures of depression that have been developed, self-report instruments are the most common. They are particularly important given that many of the key problems that characterize depression, such as sadness and feelings of worthlessness, are subjective. The Children's Depression Inventory (CDI; Kovacs, 1992) is probably the most commonly employed measure of this type. It is an offspring of the Beck Depression Inventory, the most commonly employed inventory for adults. The CDI asks youngsters to choose which of three alternatives best characterizes them during the past two weeks. Twenty-seven items sample affective, behavioral, and cognitive aspects of depression. Research on gender and age differences, reliability, validity, and clinically meaningful cutoff scores has been conducted for the CDI (Kazdin, 1988; Reynolds, 1994). Reynolds has also developed two self-report measures to assess depressive symptomatology that are frequently employed and that have been reported to have good psychometric properties (Reynolds, 1994): Reynolds Child Depression Scale for use with children eight to thirteen (Reynolds, 1989) and Reynolds Adolescent Depression Scale for use with youngsters twelve to eighteen (Reynolds, 1987).

Many self-report measures are also rephrased so that they can be completed by significant others such as the child's parents (Clarizio, 1994). Measures completed by both the child and parent often show only low levels of correlation, and agreement may vary with the age of the youngster (Kazdin, 1994; Renouf and Kovacs, 1994). These results suggest that information pro-

vided by different sources may tap different aspects of the child's behavior. For example, children's self-report of depression, but not parents' reports, correlate with hopelessness and suicidal thoughts (Kazdin, Rodgers, and Colbus, 1986). Parents reports of depression in their child, on the other hand, correlate with the child's mood-related expression and social behavior (Kazdin et al., 1985).

Instruments may also be completed by other adults such as teachers and clinicians (Clarizio, 1994). Ratings by peers can also provide a unique perspective. The Peer Nomination Inventory of Depression (Lefkowitz and Tesiny, 1980) asks children to nominate peers who fit certain descriptions. Table 7–3 presents questions regarding depression, happiness, and popularity to which the peers are asked to respond. A

TABLE 7–3 Peer Nomination Inventory for Depression Items

Who often plays alone? (D)
Who thinks they are bad? (D)
Who doesn't try again when they lose? (D)
Who often sleeps in class? (D)
Who often looks lonely? (D)
Who often says they don't feel well? (D)
Who says they can't do things? (D)
Who often cries? (D)
Who often looks happy? (H)
Who likes to do a lot of things? (H)
Who worries a lot? (D)
Who doesn't play? (D)
Who often smiles? (H)
Who doesn't take part in things? (D)
Who doesn't have much fun? (D)
Who is often cheerful? (H)
Who thinks others don't like them? (D)
Who often looks sad? (D)
Who would you like to sit next to in class? (P)
Who are the children you would like to have for your best friends? (P)

Note: D = items that are included in depressed score
          H = items in happiness score
          P = items in popularity score
Adapted from Lefkowitz and Tesiny, 1980. Copyright (1980) by American Psychological Association.

child's score is the sum of the nominations received for all the depression items.

Measures of constructs that are related to depression have also been developed. Measures of attributes such as hopelessness (Kazdin et al., 1986) and self-esteem (e.g., Harter, 1985) have been and are likely to be helpful for both clinical and research purposes.

Influences on the Development of Depression

Biological influences. Biological views of depression in children and adolescents focus on genetic and biochemical influences. They derive largely from the adult literature since there are relatively little data available on children (Emslie et al., 1994; Rutter et al., 1990b).

GENETIC INFLUENCES. Genetic influences are generally thought to play a role in depression in children and adolescents. This view derives, in part, from findings regarding adult depression. For example, the data based on twin, family, and adoptive studies of mood disorders in adults suggest a heritability component in adult depressive disorders (Kendler et al., 1992; Weissman, Kidd, and Prusoff, 1982; Wender et al., 1986). Since there is little empirical evidence regarding a genetic component to depression before adulthood, findings regarding the aggregation of depression in families constitute the primary basis for implicating genetic influences in the etiology of child and adolescent depression. Findings that children of parents with major depressive disorder are at increased risk for major depression, that an increase in depression in family members is associated with the onset of depression before twenty years of age, and that increased rates of depression are found in adult relatives of children diagnosed with major depression are all viewed as being consistent with a genetic influence on depression in young people (Puig-Antich

et al., 1989; Weissman et al., 1984; Weissman et al., 1988).

Family studies, however, do not disentangle genetic and environmental influences. While a genetic contribution seems possible, even research that suggests a heritability component in adult depression also indicates the importance of environmental influences. Further investigation is needed to clarify the exact influence of genetics.

The complexity of these issues is illustrated in a study by Rende and his colleagues (1993). These investigators examined depressive symptomatology in a general (unselected) sample of 707 pairs of adolescent siblings. By comparing MZ twins, DZ same-sex twins, and same-sex full siblings from nondivorced families, as well as full, half, and unrelated same-sex siblings from step families, the authors were able to make use of twin and adoption study methodologies to examine genetic and environmental influences on depression. A significant genetic influence was found when the full range of depressive symptomatology was considered. However, a significant genetic influence was not found when only youngsters with high levels of depression were considered. Instead there was a significant influence of shared environment, that is, nongenetic influences shared by both siblings in a family. The authors suggest that one possible explanation for these findings is that genetic influence operates on personality and temperamental factors such as emotionality and sociability that affect the full range of depressive symptomatology. The expression of extreme depressive symptomatology, however, may result, against this background of moderate genetic influence, from environmental experiences that are shared by siblings in a family. Several psychological variables have been implicated in the development of depression that may operate in this manner. For example, being raised in a family where the mother is depressed has received considerable attention. The influence of maternal depression is discussed below.

BIOCHEMISTRY OF DEPRESSION. The study of the biochemistry of depression in adults has highlighted the role of neurotransmitters such as norepinephrine, serotonin, and acetylcholine. The impetus to study these neurotransmitters came largely from findings that the effectiveness of certain antidepressants with adults was related to levels of these chemicals or receptivity to them. For example, an early suggestion, the catecholamine hypothesis, proposed that low levels of norepinephrine were created by too much reabsorption by the neuron releasing it or by too efficient a breakdown by enzymes. This was thought to result in too low a level of norepinephrine at the synapse to fire the next neuron. Current research continues to explore the role of neurotransmitters; however, the mechanisms of action are clearly very complex, involving not only the amounts of neurotransmitters available, but the complex interaction among neurotransmitter systems and receptors.

Studies of the neuroendocrine systems (connections between the brain, hormones, and various organs) add complexity to this picture. Neuroendocrine systems involving the hypothalamus, pituitary gland, and the adrenal and thyroid glands are thought to play an important role in depression (Emslie et al., 1994). These systems are also regulated by neurotransmitters. Thus, the picture is likely to be a complex one. While there is significant promise for this line of research regarding child and adolescent depression, the rapid biological changes during this period (e.g., hormonal activity during puberty) offer a particular challenge.

Research on the biological aspects of depression suggests that during the earlier developmental periods of childhood and adolescence, the neuroregulatory system is not equivalent to that in adulthood. Thus, while many workers still find evidence for a bio-logical dysfunction in childhood depression, a simple translation of the adult findings is not sufficient (Puig-Antich, 1986). For example, disturbances of sleep are associated with clinical levels of depression. Research has indicated that EEG patterns during sleep are strong biological markers of major depressive disorders in adults (Gillin et al., 1979; Kupfer and Reynolds, 1992). But, many of the findings reported in adults are not characteristic of children diagnosed with major depressive disorders (Puig-Antich, 1986). However, some research does suggest that some abnormalities related to the rapid eye movement (REM) stage of sleep (e.g., a shortened period of time before REM sleep begins) may be present in depressed children and adolescents as well as in adults (e.g., Emslie et al., 1990; Kutcher et al., 1991).

In addition to limited and sometimes contradictory research, the understanding of findings regarding biological correlates of depression in children and adolescents requires comparison to normative data on these functions. Such normative data is not readily available (Emslie et al., 1994). In general, differences in biological markers of depression might suggest that the child and adult disorders are different. Alternatively, it might be concluded that these biological markers represent age-related differences in the same disorder.

Social-psychological influences. Despite increased interest in recent years, much of the thinking regarding social and psychological influences on child and adolescent depression is still based on theories derived from work with depressed adults. We examine several of these influences below and provide illustrations of work based on children and adolescents.

SEPARATION LOSS. Probably the most common psychological explanation of depression is separation or loss. Psychoanalytic explanations of depression, following from

The theme of separation-loss is a central concept in many theories of depression. The loss may be real or imagined.

Freud, emphasize the notion of object loss. The loss may be real (parental death, divorce) or symbolic.

Identification with and ambivalent feelings toward the lost love object are thought to result in the person directing hostile feelings concerning the love object toward the self. Some psychodynamic writers emphasize loss of self-esteem and feelings of helplessness that result from object loss, and minimize the importance of aggression turned inward toward the self (Kessler, 1988).

Some behaviorally oriented explanations also involve separation and loss. Both Ferster (1974) and Lewinsohn (1974) emphasized the role of inadequate positive reinforcement in the development of depression. Loss of or separation from a loved one is likely to result in a decrease in the child's sources of positive reinforcement. However, inadequate reinforcement may also result from factors such as not having adequate skills to obtain desired rewards.

Past support for the theory that separation played a role in the genesis of depression came from several different sources. For example, a fairly typical sequence of re-

actions of young children to prolonged separation from their parents was described by a number of investigators (e.g., Bowlby, 1960; Spitz, 1946). In this so-called anaclitic depression, the child initially goes through a period of "protest" characterized by crying, asking for the parents, and restlessness. This is followed shortly by a period of depression and withdrawal. Most children begin to recover after several weeks.

High rates of early parental loss or separation among children referred for treatment of a variety of psychological problems has also been cited. Seligman et al. (1974), for example, reported that among one hundred consecutive adolescent referrals, 36.4 percent had experienced loss of one or both parents. In contrast, in public school and medical clinic control samples, only 11.7 percent and 16.6 percent, respectively, had experienced such loss. Differences between the treatment and control samples were particularly high for parental loss between three to six years of age and twelve to fifteen years of age. Another comparison involving depressed and nondepressed children between the ages of five and sixteen indicated that 50 percent of the depressed group but only 23 percent of the nondepressed group experienced parental separation prior to the age of eight (Caplan and Douglas, 1969).

The connection between loss and depression has been examined primarily in regard to adult depression. For a long time the widely held view has been that such early loss puts one at high risk for later depression—especially women. More recent examinations of this issue question this view, in part, because most studies were plagued with methodological problems (Finkelstein, 1988; Tennant, 1988). The current view is that early loss is not in and of itself pathogenic. The link between such loss and later depression is not direct. Rather, it is hypothesized that such loss, as well as other circumstances, can set in motion a chain of adverse circumstances such as lack of care, changes in family structure, and socioeconomic difficulties that put the individual at risk for later disorder (cf. Bifulco, Harris, and Brown, 1992; Saler and Skolnick, 1992).

Much of the research on the association between loss and depression has relied on the retrospective reports of adults. Recently, investigations of the impact of loss on children has received attention. For example, Sandler and his colleagues found support for a model consistent with the indirect effects of loss suggested above (West et al., 1991). Among a sample of ninety-two families who had lost a parent within the previous two years, depression in youngsters (ages eight to fifteen) was not directly linked to the loss. Rather, the level of parental demoralization, family warmth, and stable positive events following the loss mediated the effects of parental death on depression in these youngsters.

COGNITIVE-BEHAVIORAL PERSPECTIVES. Many of the conceptualizations derived from behavioral, cognitive, and cognitive-behavioral perspectives contain related and overlapping concepts (Hammen, 1992; Kaslow, Brown, and Mee, 1994). Influences such as interpersonal skills, cognitive distortions, views of self, control beliefs, self-regulation, and stress are the focus of these perspectives on child and adolescent depression.

As indicated above, writers such as Ferster (1974) and Lewinsohn (1974) suggested that a combination of lowered activity level and inadequate interpersonal skills plays a role in the development and maintenance of depression. Thus, it is suggested that depressed individuals do not elicit positive interpersonal responses from others. While evidence supporting differences in activity levels is not available, there is evidence that depressed youths display deficits in social functioning and that they are viewed as less likable by others (Kaslow, Brown and Mee, 1994). For example, Bell-Dolan, Reaven, and Peterson (1993) obtained self, peer, and teacher reports of both depression and social functioning for 112 fourth to sixth graders. Negative social behavior (aggression and negative support seeking), social withdrawal, and low social competence were all related to higher ratings of depression.

A learned helplessness explanation of depression (cf. Seligman and Peterson, 1986) suggests that some individuals, due to their learning histories, come to perceive themselves as having little control of their environment. This learned helplessness is in turn associated with the mood and behaviors characteristic of depression. Separation may be a special case of learned helplessness: The child's attempts to bring the parent back may result in the child's thinking that personal action and positive outcome are independent of each other. As indicated above, the concept of helplessness as an element in depression is held by some psychodynamic workers as well.

Helplessness conceptualizations emphasize how the person thinks about activity and outcome—a person's attributional or explanatory style. An explanatory style in which one blames oneself for *negative* events (internal), views the causes of the event as being stable over time (stable) and generalizable across situations (global), is thought to be characteristic of depressed individuals. The opposite style, external-unstable-specific attributions for *positive* events, is also viewed as part of this depressed style. In recent revisions of this perspective—the hopelessness theory of depression—the interaction of stressful life events with cognitive style is given greater emphasis (Abramson, Metalsky, and Alloy, 1989). Attributional style is viewed as the diathesis that acts as a mediator between life events and depression. A number of studies have reported maladaptive attributional styles in depressed youngsters (e.g., Kaslow et al., 1988; McCauley et al., 1988). However, additional attention needs to be given to inconsistencies in findings, investigation of developmental patterns, and a clearer articulation of the relationship of attributional style and life events (cf. Kaslow, Brown and Mee, 1994).

The role of cognitive factors in depression is also the major emphasis of other theorists. Beck (1967; 1976), for example, assumes that depression results from negative views of the self, the world, and the future. Depressed individuals, Beck hypothesizes, have developed certain errors in thinking that result in their distorting even mildly annoying events into opportunities for self-blame and failure. Research studies have found evidence in depressed youngsters of the cognitive distortions suggested by Beck's theory (Kendall, Stark, and Adams, 1990; Leitenberg, Yost, and Carroll-Wilson, 1986). The nature of the cognitive distortion-depression link, however, requires further clarification (cf. Hammen, 1992). For example, cognitive distortion may not be general, but may be limited to certain kinds of situations, such as those that are interpersonal and emotional. It is also not clear whether these cognitions play a causal role in depression as an underlying vulnerability or are associated with depression in some other way, perhaps co-occurring with depression or being a consequence of depression.

The dimension of control, part of a helplessness perspective discussed above, has also been the focus of additional consideration. Deficits in one or more specific self-control behaviors (self-monitoring, self-evaluation and self-reinforcement) are hypothesized to contribute to the development of depression. According to this self-control model (Rehm, 1977), depressed individuals selectively focus on negative rather than positive events and immediate rather than delayed consequences of behavior, set overly stringent self-evaluative criteria, and provide themselves with little positive reinforcement and excessive punishment. Depressed children have been found to differ, for example, in how they evaluate their performance (e.g., Meyer, Dyck, and Petrinack, 1989). There is a growing body of literature suggesting self-control deficits in depressed youngsters. Thus, there is potential value in exploring the self-regulatory behavior that is modeled or encouraged by caretakers of depressed youngsters (Kaslow, Brown, and Mee, 1994). With this in mind, we turn to the influences on youngsters of maternal depression.

The impact of maternal depression. A major area of research on childhood depression has been an examination of children of depressed parents (cf. Zahn-Waxler, 1995). There are several reasons for the proliferation of such research. Because family aggregation of mood disorders in adults was known to exist, it was presumed that examining children of parents with mood disorders would reveal a population likely to experience childhood depression. Such a high-risk research strategy has the potential to be a more efficient means of investigating a problem than would random sampling of the population. In addition, such research might provide information on the continuity between child, adolescent, and adult mood disorders.

Depressive mood states in parents might be associated with dysfunction in their children via a variety of mechanisms. As suggested above, shared heredity may play a role. However, parental depression may have an impact through a variety of nonbiological pathways. For example, parents can influence their child through parent-child interactions, through coaching and teaching practices, and by arranging their child's social environment (Dodge, 1990).

Much of the research on the link between parental depression and child adjustment has focused on depression in mothers and relatively little is known regarding the impact of depression in fathers (Cummings and Davies, 1994; Kaslow, Deering, and Racusin, 1994). It is clear, however, that parental depression is a major risk factor for childhood depression. Research also suggests that it is necessary to examine the specificity of such links. For example, is the association with child adjustment specific to or unique for parental depression or do other forms of parental disorder and distress produce similar outcomes? Is parental depression only associated with childhood depression or is it linked to childhood disorder in general? What are the mechanisms underlying the association between parental depression and child disorder?

Research that examines parents diagnosed as having different disorders helps to answer the question of the specificity of the link between parent and child depression. For example, Weintraub, Winters, and Neale (1986) found that children with a parent with an affective disorders did exhibit difficulties in a number of different dimensions, as judged by both teachers and peers. However, although children of adult patients differed from normal controls, there were few differences between children of parents with mood disorders and children

with a parent diagnosed as schizophrenic. Furthermore, children of parents diagnosed as having different mood disorders did not differ from each other. These findings suggest that the child's vulnerability may be related to factors other than the parent's *specific* diagnosis. Children's difficulties may have more to do with the disruption caused by having a dysfunctional parent. Still, it is possible that there are disruptions to effective parenting that are common to parents with varying disorders and also difficulties that are more likely to occur among parents with a particular disorder.

The children of depressed parents are not only at specific risk for depression. The negative impact of depressed parents appears to emerge in multiple areas of children's functioning. Indeed, these youngsters appear to be at risk for a range of adjustment difficulties including conduct disorders, attention-deficit hyperactivity disorder, anxiety disorders, academic difficulties, and impaired social competence. A study by Orvaschel, Walsh-Allis, and Ye (1988) illustrates this point. A high-risk group of sixty-one children was identified from families in which at least one parent was in treatment for recurrent major depression. A low-risk control group consisted of children for whom neither parent met the DSM criteria for any psychiatric disorder. The youngsters ranged in age from six to seventeen, and there were no significant differences between the groups regarding age, gender, or verbal IQ. The families were also matched for social class and income levels.

Childhood disorders were assessed using the Schedule of Affective Disorders and Schizophrenia for School-Age Children. The semi-structured interview was administered first to mothers and then to their children. The same interviewer conducted both mother and child interviews, and interviewers were not blind as to the group membership of families. The authors indicated that

ACCENT 7–1   Suicide among Children and Adolescents: Reason for Concern

There is increasing public concern about suicide in young people. This is of course in part due to sadness at the death of any young person and the sense of lost potential. However, there is another basis for the concern. The Centers for Disease Control and Prevention (1995) has reported statistics that are quite dramatic regarding the rates of suicide among young people.

In 1992, over five thousand children, teens, and young adults committed suicide. This rate of about 5.5 suicides per l00,000 for people under twenty-five was about the same as in 1980. Children's suicide remained a rare event. However, the rate for fifteen- to nineteen-year-olds had risen from 8.5 to 10.9 per 100,000, an increase of about 28 percent. Even more alarming is the 120 percent increase among ten- to fourteen-year-olds, from .8 to about 1.7 per 100,000. As can be seen in the table below, risk is greatest for white males. However, from 1980 to 1992 suicide rates for black males rose from 0.5 to 2.0 per 100,000, an increase of 300 percent!

An increased use of guns appears to be one of the factors contributing to this grim situation. Among people under twenty-five, 64.9 percent of the suicides in 1992 were firearm-related. And among fifteen to nineteen-year-olds, firearm-related suicides accounted for 81 percent of the increase between 1980 and 1992 in the overall rate of suicide. Since suicide *attempts* among younger persons have not increased, the rise in *completed* suicides may be due, in part, to the use of more lethal means.

The Centers for Disease Control and Prevention (1995) has identified the following strategies to improve the prevention of suicide among young persons: 1) training school personnel and community leaders to identify youngsters at highest risk; 2) educating youngsters about suicide; 3) implementing screening and referral services; 4) developing peer-support programs; 5) establishing suicide crisis centers and hotlines; 6) restricting access to highly lethal methods; 7) intervening after a suicide to prevent other youngsters from attempting suicide.

RATE[a] OF SUICIDE AMONG YOUNGSTERS BY AGE GROUP: 1980 TO 1992

	Male			Female		
Race/Age Group	1980	1992	% Change	1980	1992	% Change
White						
10–14	1.4	2.6	+86	0.3	1.1	+233
15–19	15.1	18.4	+22	3.3	3.7	+12
Black						
10–14	0.5	2.0	+300	0.2	0.4	+100
15–19	5.6	14.8	+164	1.6	1.9	+19
Other[b]						
10–14	0.0	1.1	Undefined	0.0	0.2	Undefined
15–19	18.6	17.5	−6	3.0	5.0	+67

[a]Per 100,000 persons
[b]Data for other racial groups were limited and therefore combined.

ing the ready availability of firearms, are also likely to contribute to increased risk. Young people would seem to be particularly vulnerable since their problem solving and self-regulatory skills and their abilities to cope with stressful circumstances may be limited. Some youngsters may be faced with circumstances that cause considerable stress which they may view as beyond their control. These youngsters may also have limited understanding that undesirable situations can and often do change.

Treatment of Depression

Relatively little is known regarding the treatment of depression in youth compared to interventions for adults. That little systematic research exists is not surprising given the recency of attention to the problem of child and adolescent depression. Treatments attempted with depressed youngsters have been adaptations of interventions that seem to be successful in treating depression in adults. Pharmacotherapy and cognitive-behavioral treatments will be examined briefly.

Pharmacotherapy. The practice of prescribing antidepressant medication for children and adolescents is still controversial since the effectiveness and safety of pharmacotherapy with depressed youngsters remains unclear (Johnston and Fruehling, 1994). Tricyclic antidepressants such as imipramine, amitriptyline, nortriptyline, and desipramine have been the most widely studied medications. Selective serotonin reuptake inhibitors such as fluoxetine (Prozac) and other compounds such as bupropion have also been employed with depressed children and adolescents (Johnston and Fruehling, 1994; Kazdin, 1990a). The use of such medications is for the most part based on clinical reports or a small number of controlled trials. This research does not clearly support the superiority of these drugs over

placebo in either prepubertal children or adolescents (Geller et al., 1992; Kutcher et al., 1994; Puig-Antich et al., 1987) At present it is difficult to know whether these medications, many of which are reported effective in treating adult depression, are ineffective for youth, or whether adequately designed research is lacking. These medications are widely employed, however, and these, or other pharmacological agents, may ultimately prove to be effective, alone or in combination with other treatments. However, since antidepressant medications are principally developed and marketed for adults, there are less well established guidelines for their administration and little systematic data on their safety. Issues of safety and side effects are particularly of concern since little is known regarding the long-term impact on development, particularly in young children (Johnston and Freuhling, 1994).

Cognitive-behavioral treatments. There is little established information about the psychological treatment of depression in children and adolescents, particularly cases of clinical levels of depression (Kendall and Panichelli-Mindel, 1995). Much of the literature involves case reports. In addition, interventions suggested for youngsters have been based on downward extensions of interventions employed with adults. While this was a reasonable way to begin to explore effective treatment, there are limitations to such an approach that need to be addressed. Many of the early interventions emphasized a particular perspective on the etiology of depression and thus emphasized single or limited aspects of depression. As we have seen, it is likely that multiple influences contribute to the development of depression in youngsters and therefore treatments will need to address multiple concerns. In addition, whether or not the symptoms of depression are the same in prepubertal children, adolescents, and adults, the lives of depressed youngsters differ from those of adults (Stark, Rouse, and Kurowski, 1994). For example, children and adolescents will likely have ongoing daily contact with parental influences that may contribute to the problem of depression. Also, youngsters are exposed on a daily basis to the potential negative consequences of social skill difficulties and the impact of peer relation difficulties. Adults, on the other hand, may arrange their lives to avoid familial and social contacts. As we develop a better understanding of the social-psychological factors that contribute to depression in children and adolescents, treatments that differ from those employed with adults and that address relevant developmental experiences of depressed children and adolescents are likely to be the most effective.

Control-group outcome studies illustrate the evaluation of interventions deriving from a cognitive-behavioral perspective.

Butler and her colleagues evaluated the relative effectiveness of role-play, cognitive restructuring, an attention-placebo condition, or no treatment (Butler et al., 1980). Fifth and sixth-grade children were identified as depressed through self-report measures and teacher referral. Role-play consisted of teaching interpersonal skills as well as problem-solving techniques. Cognitive restructuring focused on altering maladaptive cognitions. The results favored the role-play intervention; however, the differences between groups were not clear-cut.

Stark, Reynolds, and Kaslow (1987) compared self-control, behavioral problem-solving, and a waiting list (no treatment) control in treating nine to twelve year-olds defined as moderately to severely depressed using the Children's Depression Inventory. The self-control treatment focused on teaching children self-management skills such as self-monitoring, self-evaluation, and self-reinforcement. Behavioral problem-solving emphasized education, self-monitoring of pleasant events, and group problem solving

directed toward improving social behavior. Both treatments resulted in improvements and were superior to the control group. The two treatments, however, did not differ from each other.

A study by Lewinsohn and his colleagues (1990) suggests the effectiveness of cognitive-behavioral treatment for depressed adolescents. Youngsters aged fourteen to eighteen who met diagnostic criteria for depression were randomly assigned to one of three conditions: adolescent-and-parent, adolescent-only, and wait-list control. Treatment was a cognitive-behavioral group intervention known as the Coping with Depression Course for Adolescents (a skills-training, multicomponent intervention meant to address areas thought to be problematic for depressed adolescents). Adolescents attended fourteen two-hour sessions, twice a week, that focused on teaching methods of relaxation, increasing pleasant events, controlling irrational and negative thoughts, increasing social skills, and conflict resolution (communication and problem solving) skills. In the parent involvement condition, parents met for seven two-hour weekly sessions and were provided with an overview of the skills being taught to their teenagers.

As compared to the wait-list control, treatment groups improved on depression measures. For example, at the end of treatment, only 52.4 percent of the adolescent-and-parent youngsters and 57.1 percent of the adolescent-only youngsters, as compared to 94.7 percent of control youngsters still met diagnostic criteria. The teenagers in the treatment conditions were followed for two years after the end of treatment, and their treatment gains were maintained. Control participants were not available for follow-up since they were offered treatment at the end of the treatment period. Figure 7–2 illustrates the findings of this study at pre-treatment, post-treatment and at the twenty-four-month follow-up for one of the

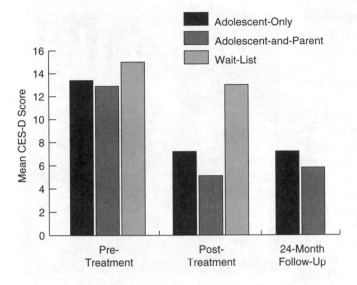

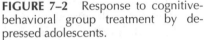

FIGURE 7–2   Response to cognitive-behavioral group treatment by depressed adolescents.

Adapted from Lewinsohn et al., 1990.

measures employed (the adolescents' report on the Center for Epidemiological Studies Depression Scale—CES-D).

Treatments derived from behavioral and cognitive-behavioral perspectives and treatments that address interpersonal and family aspects of depression in children and adolescents are promising (Kaslow and Racusin, 1994; Lewinsohn, Clarke, and Rohde, 1994; Mufson et al., 1994; Stark, 1994). However, it is clear that additional large-scale treatment studies are needed. Successful treatment strategies will need to include components capable of addressing multiple aspects of depression and of the social and family environments of depressed youngsters.

PROBLEMS IN PEER RELATIONSHIPS

There are several reasons why peer relations have become the focus of increasing attention (Putallaz and Dunn, 1990). Seminal papers, such as those by Hartup (1970, 1989), highlighted the unique developmental context provided by a youngster's peer group and the influence of peers on immediate and long-term social and cognitive growth. At the same time there was a de-

cline in the prevalence of Freudian theory, that had heavily emphasized parent-child relationships. This allowed for the recognition of the importance of other socialization influences. Finally, a variety of social and economic conditions increased the opportunities for youngsters to interact with their peers. For example, the increase in working parents has resulted in a rise in the number of children in day care and in the amount of time youngsters spend with peers. Such changes provided both an impetus and an opportunity to study children's social relations.

Peer Relations and Development

The literature on development indicates the importance of peer relationships. Such relationships provide the opportunity for learning specific skills that may not be available in other social relationships. Hartup (1989) suggests that two major kinds of relationships seem necessary to the child's development. *Vertical relationships* to individuals who have greater knowledge and social power, usually adults, provide the child with protection and security and are the contexts within which basic social skills emerge. Children must also experience *horizontal relationships*. These are relationships with individuals, such as peers and siblings, who have the same amount of social power as the children themselves. Some of the ways in which peer interactions may play a unique and essential role include the development of sociability and intimacy, the elaboration of cooperation and reciprocity, the negotiation of conflict and competition, the control of aggression, socialization of sexuality and gender roles, moral development, and the development of empathy. Of course, this does not mean that peer social development is independent of child-adult interactions. Indeed, early parent-child socialization seems related to later peer interactions (e.g., Park and Waters, 1989; Parke and Ladd, 1991; Rubin, 1994; Youngblade and Belsky, 1992) and both relationships with peers and adults are necessary for optimum growth (Hartup, 1989).

Peer interactions provide a unique and essential opportunity to develop certain skills.

Studying Peer Relationships

The study of peer relationships has relied heavily on the use of two forms of sociometric measures. The *nomination* format requires children to name, for example, classmates liked most or liked least. The *rating* format requires that children rate each of their classmates along some dimension(s) such as how much they like to play with each child.

Early research made use of sociometric measures to evaluate a youngster's peer status as popular or unpopular. More recently, a number of different peer status groups (popular, rejected, neglected, controversial, and average) have been articulated within a two dimensional approach to classifying peer status. The dimension of *social preference* reflects the extent to which children are liked or disliked by their peers. *Social impact*, on the other hand, refers to the degree to which children are noticed by their peers, or their social salience. Table 7–5 illustrates

TABLE 7–5   Peer Classifications

Social Preference (SP)	The difference between number of liked most (LM) and liked least (LL) nominations
Social Impact (SI)	The sum of number of liked most (LM) and liked least (LL) nominations
Popular	High SP score with higher than average LM and lower than average LL
Rejected	Low SP score with lower than average LM and higher than averge LL
Neglected	Low SI score with no LM votes from peers
Controversial	High SI score with both LL and LM scores higher than average
Sociometrically Average	All other children

Adapted from Kupersmidt and Patterson, 1991.

how the preference and impact dimensions are defined and employed to derive peer classifications. Such assignments are often employed in research on the relationship between adjustment and peer relations.

It should be mentioned, however, before proceeding that the study of peer relations and adjustment is quite complex. For one, there are important aspects of peer relations other than overall peer status (Dunn and McGuire, 1992; Newcomb, Bukowski, and Pattee, 1993). For example, although popularity and having a close friend are related, the concept of friendship is different than that of peer status or popularity (Newcomb and Bagwell, 1995). If youngsters have a close friend that can affect how they feel regardless of their peer status. Also, having a close friend may buffer some of the effects of being rejected or neglected by peers (La Greca, 1993).

What we know is limited in a number of ways. Much of the literature addresses the issues of peer rejection and of aggressive behavior. However, peer rejection is not only associated with aggression. Rejection can also be associated with social withdrawal. One must also be aware of developmental changes. For example, social withdrawal becomes more clearly related to rejection and also associated with internalizing problems as children get older (Dunn and McGuire, 1992; Rubin et al., 1995). Most research on peer relations has focused on the childhood period. Greater attention is needed to adolescence (Inderbitzen, 1994). Furthermore, the results of several studies suggests that gender differences deserve greater attention (e.g., French, 1990; Kupersmidt and Patterson, 1991).

Peer Relations and Adjustment

Peer relations and later adjustment. One of the most commonly cited reasons for interest in children's peer relationships is their association with later adjustment. Early reports cited an association between poor peer relations and with high rates of juvenile delinquency (Roff, Sells, and Golden, 1972), dropping out of school (Ullmann, 1957), and bad conduct discharges from the army (Roff, 1961). Cowen and his colleagues found an association with later psychiatric referrals (Cowen et al., 1973). In a series of studies they screened large numbers of children for signs of disturbance. Low peer status in the third grade was a better predictor of later psychiatric problems than traditional adjustment indices including IQ, academic achievement, and ratings by teachers and other school personnel.

Reviews of available literature generally support the notion that children with poor peer relations are at risk for later difficulties. The evidence is clearest for children with low peer acceptance and those who exhibit aggressiveness towards peers. The link between early shyness/withdrawal and later maladjustment is less clear since this relationship has been less studied (Parker and Asher, 1987). However, recent data suggests that some rejected children experience social withdrawal (e.g., French, 1988; 1990). This group of rejected children and children who are more withdrawn and socially isolated may also be at risk for later adjustment difficulties (e.g., Biederman et al., 1993; Asendorpf, 1993; Newcomb et al., 1993; Rubin, Stewart and Coplan, 1995).

An examination of archival data from the original Berkley Guidance Study (MacFarlane, Allen, and Honzik, 1954) illustrates the developmental stability of a shy-withdrawn style and its long-term impact (Caspi, Elder, and Bem, 1988). Ratings of shyness and excessive reserve when the children were eight to ten years old were significantly correlated with teacher ratings of withdrawal and related behaviors when the youngsters were preadolescents. Also, significant positive correlations were obtained between childhood shyness and adult shyness, evaluated when the participants were about forty. Furthermore, shy boys were more likely to delay entry into marriage, parenthood, and stable careers and they also exhibited less occupational achievement and stability. In contrast, shy girls from this cohort, born in the late 1920s, were more likely than their peers to follow what the authors term a conventional pattern of marriage, childbearing, and homemaking. These results do not relate early shyness to "pathological" outcomes. However, they do show a pattern of stability regarding how the individual approaches key life transitions requiring social initiation and interaction. The participants did not exhibit an extreme of shyness and were drawn from a relatively homogeneous sample. In a differently defined sample more adverse consequences might have occurred.

Peer relations and childhood problems. Problems with peers are frequently reported for both children and adolescents in the general population. Even though such problems are quite common, reports of difficulties with peers discriminate youngsters referred for psychological services from nonreferred youngsters (cf. Achenbach, 1991b). Indeed, problems with peers are one of the most frequently mentioned problems in referrals to mental health centers. Problems in social relationships are also part of the diagnostic criteria for a wide variety of disorders (e.g., autistic disorder, attention-deficit hyperactivity disorder, conduct disorder, social phobia). In addition, social relationship problems are associated with both externalizing and internalizing disorders in children (Baum, 1989; Strauss, 1988). Successful peer relations, on the other hand, may help insure the development of social competence in the face of multiple adverse factors. They may thereby serve a preventive function and reduce the likelihood of disorder (Cicchetti, Toth, and Bush, 1988).

A study by Kupersmidt and Patterson (1991) illustrates the relationship between peer status and adjustment. The sociometric status of a sample of second, third, and fourth graders was assessed through nominations for being liked most and liked least. Social preference and social impact and peer status group were determined for each child following the guidelines described in Table 7–5. Children designated as popular, rejected, neglected, controversial, or sociometrically average. Two years later when the children were in fourth through sixth grade a number of assessment instruments were completed including a modified version of the Achenbach Youth Self-Report (YSR). As an index of a negative outcome, the authors examined whether a child had scores in the clinical range in one or more specific problem areas (the narrow-band syndromes of the YSR). Figure 7–3 illustrates the relationship between sociometric status and this index of adjustment difficulties. Rejected boys and girls exhibited higher than expected rates of clinical-range difficulties. In addition, girls, with neglected peer status had even higher levels of clinical-range difficulties.

In addition to this nonspecific indicator of adjustment, the authors examined the relationship between peer status and each of the more specific problem areas defined by the various narrow-band behavior problem scores. There was no relationship between peer status and any specific behavior problem for boys. However, a finding of particular interest to us in this chapter emerged for girls. For the girls, the base rate for depression scores in the clinical range was 6.1 percent. Sociometrically average (5.1 percent), popular (3.3 percent), and controversial girls (4.0 percent) were below this base rate. Rejected girls (11.9 percent), however, were more than twice as likely to report high levels of depression than these other three groups. Also, neglected girls (27.3 percent) were more than twice as likely as rejected

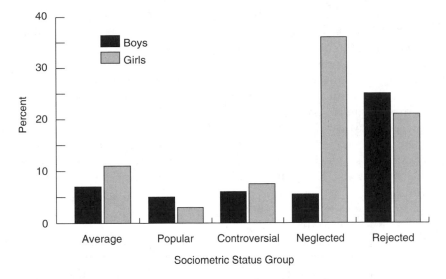

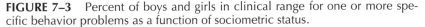

FIGURE 7–3 Percent of boys and girls in clinical range for one or more specific behavior problems as a function of sociometric status.

Adapted from Kupersmidt, J. B. & Patterson, C. J. (1991). Childhood peer rejection, aggression, withdrawal, and perceived competence as predictors of self-reported behavior problems in preadolescence. *Journal of Abnormal Child Psychology, 19,* 427–449. Reprinted by permission from Plenum Publishing Corporation.

girls and more than five times as likely as the other groups of girls to report depression problems.

While most of the peer literature has focused on aggression, there is also increasing evidence that a shy/withdrawn style may be more stable than was once thought (cf. Kagan, Reznick, and Snidman, 1990; Kerr et al., 1994). The complexity of this style is indicated by the variety of terms that have been used (e.g., shyness, social withdrawal, social isolation, social avoidance, social inhibition) to refer to an unusual lack of social interaction with peers. What is known suggests the value of distinctions within this general category (cf. Asendorpf, 1993; Coplan et al., 1994). We turn now to a brief description of an interesting body of recent research that has addressed the stability of one possible form of a socially withdrawn style.

Behavioral inhibition to the unfamiliar. Jerome Kagan and his colleagues (cf. Kagan

et al., 1990; Kagan, Snidman, and Arcus, 1993) have identified a temperamental quality that they describe as "behavioral inhibition to the unfamiliar." This style is, in general, characterized as withdrawn with a tendency not to approach unfamiliar objects or situations. This disposition, present at a very young age, is viewed as a persistent attribute in some portion of children. The quality may, however, be displayed in different forms at different ages. In young children, one to two years of age, "these dispositions appear most often to unfamiliar persons, contexts, and objects, and the withdrawal is often accompanied by crying and/or seeking a target of attachment." By the time the child is three the "feature of withdrawal is considerably more subtle. When an unfamiliar person enters a room, the temperamentally inhibited child, who would have retreated to the mother at one year of age, will cease playing and talking and show a prolonged latency to approach the adult. A year later, when in an unfamiliar room with an unfamiliar child, the inhibited child will fail to initiate play for the first ten to twenty minutes, remaining quiet and close to the mother." Children who remain behaviorally inhibited until age seven "will be quiet with an unfamiliar adult, will play apart from peers in a group context like school, will display a serious facial expression, and will become stressed by mild challenge or occasional failure." (Kagan et al., 1990, p. 220)

Kagan's findings are based on longitudinal research of children who are identified as extreme with respect to the probability of their withdrawal or approach to unfamiliar people or events. The children are assessed at several points in their development, and the stability and correlates of behavioral inhibition are examined.

Of particular interest is the development of internalizing problems in these inhibited children. At five and a half years of age, children who were originally classified as inhibited had developed more fears than uninhibited children. Furthermore, fears in the uninhibited children were usually associated with a prior trauma; this was not true for the inhibited children (Kagan et al., 1990). Other research suggests that inhibited children are at risk for the development of clinical disorders and anxiety disorders in particular. A collaborative effort between Kagan and his colleagues and Joseph Biederman and his colleagues, for example, examined two samples: Kagan's original sample and a sample of high-risk offspring of parents with panic disorder/agoraphobia and other disorders (Biederman et al., 1993). Significant differences between inhibited and not inhibited children were observed. Inhibited children were more likely to meet the criteria for four or more disorders, for two or more anxiety disorders, and for specific anxiety disorders (avoidant disorder, separation anxiety disorder, and agoraphobia). Furthermore, the rates of anxiety disorders for inhibited children increased over the three-year period that they were followed.

Thus, in terms of our discussion of peer relations, it may be that some portion of shy withdrawn children have the temperamental style that Kagan has described as behaviorally inhibited. These children may be at risk for the development of multiple disorders and would seem to be at particular risk for the development of anxiety disorders.

Treatment of the Withdrawn Child

Given the present chapter's focus on internalizing disorders, we emphasize the withdrawn or shy child rather than the aggressive child in our discussion of treatments. Many programs have been designed to improve the social skills of children. A thorough review of this material is beyond the scope of this section. Several reviews provide a good summary and critique of this literature (cf. Beelmann, Pfingsten, and Losel, 1994; Bierman, 1989; Dodge, 1989; La Greca, 1993; Schneider, 1992). These reviews suggest that interventions to improve children's social competencies have focused on the development of specific social skills and/or the cognitive processes presumed to underlie the peer difficulties. Social skills approaches can be grouped as either molecular or molar in focus (La Greca, 1993). Molecular approaches emphasize training discrete skills such as eye contact, responding positively to peers, initiating interactions. A molar focus might train skills such as participation in group activities, cooperation, and sharing. Social cognitive approaches stress training in social problem solving, taking another's perspective, self-control, and the like. Increasingly interventions have stressed more complex, multimodal approaches (Beelmann et al., 1994). Interventions seem reasonably successful in producing changes; however, the long-term effects and generalization outside of the in-

A withdrawn or socially isolated child may need assistance in developing appropriate social skills and increasing peer interactions.

tervention setting are less clear. Below, we describe examples of these successful interventions and also suggest avenues for improving generalization across time and setting.

Reinforcing increased peer interaction. Some workers have focused on the antecedents and consequences of low rates of peer interactions. Indeed, the effectiveness of reinforcement in increasing peer contact was the focus of some of the early work on social skills interventions (Allen et al., 1964; Walker et al., 1979). It was soon realized, however, that reinforcement of high rates of interaction may not always produce positive outcomes. It may also lead to unacceptable rates of aggressive behavior (Kirby and Toler, 1970) and thereby to being unpopular (Conger and Keane, 1981). In addition, there is some disagreement regarding whether rate of interaction is an appropriate treatment target for socially withdrawn children. It has, for example, been argued that little support exists for the notion that overall rate of peer interaction is an indicator of current social incompetence or of risk for later difficulties (cf. Dodge, 1989). However, others point to evidence that if children with very low rates of interaction are

selected for study, important and valid differences are found (cf. Hops and Greenwood, 1988).

Imitation, coaching, and instruction. Exposure to filmed models has been demonstrated to positively affect the behavior of preschool isolates (e.g., O'Connor, 1969, 1972). However, a number of methodological concerns with this research have been raised, and it is unclear whether effectiveness is due to observation of a model or to other variables, such as coaching and instruction (Conger and Keane, 1981).

Several investigators have explicitly employed coaching-instructional techniques. These interventions use a variety of procedures, including instruction in social skills knowledge and concepts, modeling and rehearsal with classmates, and reinforcement and encouragement of generalization (e.g., Bornstein, Bellack, and Hersen, 1977; Gottman, Gonso, and Schuler, 1976; LaGreca and Santogrossi, 1980; Oden and Asher, 1977). For example, Ladd (1981) selected third grade children low on peer acceptance who were also observed to be deficient in the three areas to be targeted. The latter criterion is important since it matches specific interventions to pretreatment deficiencies—something that is often lacking in treatment studies. Children were assigned to either a skill training treatment, attention control, or nontreatment control condition. Training consisted of instructions, guided and self-directed rehearsal, and feedback plus training in self-evaluation. Three verbal skills were targeted: asking questions, leading (offering useful suggestions and directions), and offering support to peers. Differences in both behavioral observations and sociometric ratings in favor of the treatment condition were obtained. It seems likely that the finding of both improvement in targeted behavior and actual social acceptance is due to the selection of intervention targets. In this study, behaviors that the children were deficient in, rather than general skills, were targeted. Thus, it is likely that these behaviors were related to the children's original unpopular status.

The use of peers in treatment. While most interventions for improving children's social abilities are implemented by adults, an interesting approach is the use of peers as helping agents. Peers can provide appropriate models for desired behavior. They are also already present in the setting where the relevant behavior occurs and can provide natural consequences that continue to maintain behavior over time. Indeed, a variety of peer-mediated interventions have been demonstrated to improve the social behavior of withdrawn children (Odom and Strain, 1984).

Furman, Rahe, and Hartup's (1979) program employing peers to assist socially withdrawn children is particularly intriguing. Furman and colleagues identified preschool children who engaged in peer interactions during less than 33 percent of observations and who were at least 10 percentage points below their class means. Twenty-four such social isolates were assigned to unstructured play sessions with a "therapist" twelve to eighteen months younger, to play sessions

with a same-age "therapist," or to no treatment. As Figure 7–4 illustrates, exposure to a younger peer was highly effective in increasing the social activity of withdrawn children. Both groups of children exposed to "therapists" showed improvement, while the control group did not. However, seven of the eight isolates exposed to a younger partner increased their social behavior at least 50 percent, while only three of the eight withdrawn youngsters exposed to a same-age partner exhibited comparable increases. The principal effect of the treatments was to increase rates of positive behaviors but not of neutral and punishing acts. The authors hypothesize that the effectiveness of the peer play sessions, particularly with younger children, was due to an increased opportunity to successfully practice initiating and directing social activity.

Additional evidence for the importance of employing peers as part of the process of intervention is provided in a treatment that

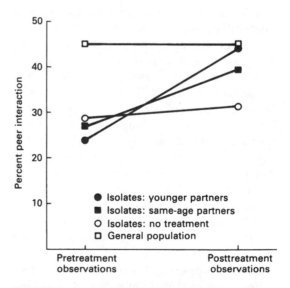

FIGURE 7–4 Pre- and posttreatment rates of peer interaction in the classroom.

From Furman, Rahe, and Hartup (1979) *Child Development, 50,* 915–922. Copyright © The Society for Research in Child Development, Inc. By permission.

employed the more common adult-directed training. Bierman and Furman (1984) assigned children who were identified as unaccepted by their peers and deficient in conversational skills to one of four treatment conditions. In the individual condition the child received coaching in conversational skills in the context of making a film. In the group experience condition, the child, along with two nontargeted peers, was involved in making the same film, but without any coaching in conversational skills. In a combined coaching and group condition, the child, along with the two peers, received coaching in the context of making the film. The remainder of the children were assigned to a no-treatment control condition. The children were evaluated on their conversational skills and peer acceptance prior to treatment, after ten sessions of thirty minutes each, and again six weeks later. The results in general show a specificity of the impact of interventions. At the end of treatment targeted children who had received skills training, compared to those who had not, had superior conversational skills. Whether training was received in an individual or group context did not significantly affect this outcome. This difference persisted at the follow-up assessment. Thus, skills training, whether done in an individual or group context, produced sustained improvements in conversational skills.

The results regarding peer acceptance are also quite interesting. Ratings of peer acceptance were obtained by averaging the ratings given by all the child's same-sex classmates. Children who were involved in group conditions had higher post-treatment acceptance scores than those not involved in group conditions. This difference, however, did not persist at follow-up. Specificity is again suggested in that the presence or absence of skills training did not affect these findings. That is, peer acceptance was affected only by the group experience variable.

For the children involved in the two group conditions an additional partner sociometric measure was available—a rating of acceptance of the target child by peers actually involved in the training with them. Children who received group skills coaching were more liked than those who received only the group experience. This was true at both the end of treatment and at follow-up. Thus, it would appear that group involvement can improve peer status, but this effect may be short lived. The partner sociometric results suggest that sustained peer acceptance may require more than a structured group experience, and that skills training incorporating the involvement of relevant peers may be an essential component of long-term success.

Inclusion of peers is probably only part of developing effective interventions that are sensitive to the multiple aspects of the social world of the child. It is probably important to not only include peers in training, but perhaps also more directly address the perceptions of peers regarding the rejected or ignored child. Bias in such perceptions may make peer reputation slow to change even when there are real changes in the targeted youngster's social behavior. Also, much of the attention to date has been on enhancing overall peer acceptance, while there has been little effort to develop interventions that promote peer friendship. Both are likely to be important, and as a youngster progresses from preschool to adolescent years, close friendships are likely to take on increasingly significant roles.

Much of the research on interventions has occurred in a school context. Inclusion of teachers in intervention planning is important because of their potential role in monitoring peer behaviors and providing appropriate consequences. Teachers can also provide interventions such as peer-pairing or cooperative group assignments that have the potential to foster the social integration of a child (La Greca, 1993; Malik and Furman, 1993). It is important to also remember that parents play an important role in a youngster's peer relations. Parents, for example, arrange opportunities for peer interactions and monitor and supervise peer contacts. The role that parents can play is illustrated in a study by Vernberg et al., (1993). Strategies employed by parents to help adolescents establish new friendships after relocation to a new community were found to cluster into four groups: met other parents, enabled proximity to peers, talked to adolescent, and encouraged activity. Based on three home interviews with each of 138 mother-adolescent pairs, the authors found that more frequent use of these strategies predicted greater companionship and intimacy with new friends among these adolescents. Interventions that include attention to improving and directing parent involvement in ways that encourage and enhance their children's social skills can be part of a multicomponent intervention. This seems particularly important for a clinician working with a youngster outside of a school setting.

SUMMARY

Childhood depression has only recently received concentrated attention. Estimates of the prevalence of childhood depression vary considerably. This is due to a number of considerations, most importantly the use of differing criteria and measures.

The psychoanalytic theory of depression suggested that the problem would not exist in children. The concept of masked depression, although problematic, resulted in greater attention to the problem and highlighted developmental issues. Data supporting the importance of a developmental perspective in understanding issues such as prevalence and symptom patterns are reemerging.

The view that childhood depression is a disorder with the same essential features as its adult counterpart is probably the dominant view at present. This is the approach taken by the DSM system. Research findings suggest both similarities and differences with the adult disorder.

Assessment of depression is likely to sample a broad spectrum of attributes and involve a number of strategies. This process has been facilitated by the development of interviews that are designed to yield specific DSM diagnoses, including depression. In addition, a number of self-report measures such as the Children's Depression Inventory are frequently employed and have received considerable research attention. Information from various informants does not always agree. It may be that different aspects of the child's behavior are being assessed. Thus, obtaining information from a variety of informants and with a variety of measures seems important. Instruments available to assess attributes associated with depression (e.g., hopelessness) add to our ability to conduct a thorough assessment.

Much of the thinking about the determinants of child and adolescent depression is based on theories or information derived from adults. Biological hypotheses such as those regarding genetics and the role of neurotransmitters are, for example, largely based on adult findings. The role of genetics and biochemistry in depression is recognized, but much remains to be clarified. Differences between children and adults regarding biological markers of depression leaves the issue of the similarity of the two disorders unresolved.

Separation/loss has been a major theme in many theories of depression. Cognitive and behavioral theories also suggest other contributions to the development of depression. A learned helplessness perspective suggests that a learned perception of lack of control leads to a cognitive style and behaviors characteristic of depression. Recent revisions of this perspective—hopelessness theory—emphasize the interaction of stressful life events and cognitive style. Cognitive theories such as Beck's and self-control models of depression have also received attention. The applicability of adult theories to childhood depression, while promising in many cases, is still unclear.

The impact of maternal depression and its relationship to childhood depression have received considerable attention. Maternal depression does appear to be related to childhood dysfunctions, but this relationship does not seem to be specific to childhood depression or inevitable. Various mechanisms may link maternal depression and child dysfunction.

Most contemporary views of depression in children and adolescents suggest a model that integrates multiple determinants.

Although completed suicide among youngsters is relatively rare, increased prevalence has caused considerable concern. Suicidal behavior is related to depression, but is also related to other problems as well and may occur in youngsters without a diagnosable disorder. The causes of suicidal behavior are often multiple and complex.

Relatively little is known regarding the treatment of depression in youth, and most treatments are largely adaptations of interventions for adults. The prescription of antidepressant medications for children and adolescents is widespread and may be an important component of treatment for some youngsters. However, the use of medications remains controversial since effectiveness and safety remain unclear. Treatments derived from behavioral and cognitive-behavioral perspectives and treatments that address

interpersonal and family aspects of depression in youngsters seem promising. However, continued development of treatments that are sensitive to multiple aspects of the psychological, social, and family influences on depressed youngsters and additional large scale treatment studies are needed.

Peer relationships provide the opportunity for learning certain skills that may not be available in other social relationships. The definition and measurement of peer relations and social competence requires continued attention. Problems with peers are one of the most frequently mentioned reasons for referrals for psychological services. Successful peer relations, on the other hand, may protect the child from the impact of adverse factors and thereby decrease the likelihood of disorder.

Poor peer relations have been of interest because of their association with current and later adjustment difficulties. While the link between shyness/withdrawal and later adjustment is less clear than it is for aggression, emerging evidence suggests a potential link to adjustment. The work of Kagan and his colleagues is an example of one variation of a shy/withdrawn style, its stability, and its relationship to adjustment.

Many programs have been designed to improve the social skills of children. Reinforcing increased rates of peer interactions, interventions combining imitation, coaching and instruction, and the use of peers in treatment have all been demonstrated to contribute to successful interventions. Continued development of and research on multifaceted treatments, particularly those addressing the complexity of peer relations and the potential contribution of parents and teachers is suggested.

8

CONDUCT DISORDERS

Clinicians commonly hear complaints of a youngster's noncompliant, aggressive, and antisocial behavior. Such concerns are voiced by parents, teachers, other adults, and peers. These behaviors are also problematic for parents and teachers of youngsters who have not had contact with clinical or legal systems. Most parents at some time or another have problems with their child fighting, lying, destroying property, or repeatedly failing to follow directions.

The fact that these problems are common and disruptive make them a topic of concern for parents and those who work with children. However, extreme and persistent forms of these behaviors cause a degree of disturbance and destruction well beyond the common experience. Thus they are of serious concern not only for the family, but for institutions such as the school, and society at large. The seeming persistence of these behaviors over time for some individuals—perhaps from early childhood through adult life—also contributes to their importance.

The following case description of Doug illustrates many of the features that characterize youth who exhibit persistent aggressive and antisocial behavior. This chapter deals with young people to whom labels such as conduct disorder, oppositional-defi-

ant disorder, and juvenile delinquency are often applied.

Doug is an eight-year-old white male who was brought for treatment by his mother because of his unmanageable behavior at home. The specific concern was with Doug's aggressive behavior, especially aggression toward his eighteen-month-old brother. When Doug is angry he chokes and hits his younger brother and constantly makes verbal threats of physical aggression. In the months immediately before his referral to treatment, Doug's behavior became more out of control, and his mother felt she was unable to cope. Apart from his aggression in the home, Doug has played with matches and set fires over the last three years. These episodes have included igniting fireworks in the kitchen of his home, setting fires in trash dumpsters in the neighborhood, and starting a fire in his bedroom, which the local fire department had to extinguish.

At school his behavior has been disruptive over the last few years. His intellectual performance is within the normal range (WISC-R full scale IQ = 96) and his academic performance is barely passing. His aggressive behavior against peers and disruption of class activities have led to his placement in a special class for emotionally disturbed children. Even so, his behavior is not well controlled. The school has threatened expulsion if treatment is not initiated.

Doug currently lives with his mother and two brothers. He is second born. For the first few years of Doug's life, there was considerable disruption in the home. Doug's father frequently abused alcohol. When drunk, he would beat his wife and children. The mother and father separated on a number of occasions and eventually were divorced when Doug was five years old. After the divorce, the mother and children moved in with the maternal grandfather who also drank excessively and physically abused the children. Less than two years ago, the mother had another child by her former husband. With the stress of the new child, the death of her father with whom she was living, and Doug's continuing problems, the mother became depressed and began to drink. Although she is not employed, she spends much of her time away from the home. She leaves the children unsupervised for extended periods with a phone number of a neighbor for the children to call if any problems arise with the baby. (Kazdin, 1985, pp. 3–4).

PREVALENCE

The exact prevalence of conduct disorders is difficult to establish. Differences in definition as well as socioeconomic and familial factors influence the number and kinds of problems reported. Nonetheless, aggression, as well as antisocial, oppositional, and similar behaviors, certainly are among the most common childhood problems. In their review of prevalence studies, Wells and Forehand (1985) note that 33 to 75 percent of clinic referrals were for conduct-disordered behavior. Studies of prevalence in the general population often report rates of around 4 to 6 percent for diagnosed conduct disorders (Earls, 1994). Estimates of the prevalence for specific antisocial behaviors are much higher, often about 60 percent. Disobedience, tantrums, demanding, and whining are also among the most common concerns expressed by parents in primary health care settings (Schroeder and Gordon, 1991). Many of these behaviors are also reported by parents of children not referred for problems (cf. Achenbach, 1991a). Boys show more of the behaviors associated with conduct disorders than do girls. In most cases the reported ratio is 4:1 (Earls, 1994).

DESCRIPTION AND CLASSIFICATION

The complexity and heterogeneity of the disruptive, negative, antisocial behaviors exhibited by children and adolescents is increasingly appreciated (Hinshaw, Lahey, and Hart, 1993). The various terms employed to describe such behavior (e.g., acting out, disruptive, externalizing, undercontrolled, oppositional, antisocial, conduct disorder, or delinquent) reflect the variety of ways that this behavior is described. While there is a general understanding of this broad category, attempts to refine and subcategorize the description of such behavior is a continuing goal. A distinction has often been made between inattention, hyperactivity, and impulsivity on the one hand, and aggression, oppositional behaviors, and more serious conduct problems on the other (Waldman, Lillienfeld, and Lahey, 1995). The behaviors in the first grouping are discussed in greater detail in the next chapter on Attention-Deficit Hyperactivity Disorder (ADHD). While keeping in mind that ADHD and these other problems often occur together, the oppositional and conduct disordered behaviors of the second grouping are considered here. In our discussion, the term conduct disorder is used to describe severe levels of this general group of aggressive-antisocial behaviors, whereas the proper noun Conduct Disorder specifically refers to a diagnostic category such as that defined by DSM-IV.

Empirically Derived Syndromes

Empirically derived syndromes involving aggressive, oppositional, destructive, and antisocial behavior have been identified in a wide variety of studies (cf. Achenbach and Edelbrock, 1989; Quay, 1986b). This syndrome has been given a variety of names including undercontrolled, externalizing, or conduct disorder. It would appear that this syndrome is a robust one in that it emerges employing a variety of measures, reporting agents, and settings.

Within this broad externalizing/conduct disorder syndrome there is also the suggestion that two narrower syndromes exist. These have been designated as undersocialized aggressive and socialized aggressive (e.g., Quay, 1986b), or aggressive behavior and delinquent behavior (Achenbach, 1993). The behaviors characteristic of these two narrow syndromes based on the Achenbach instruments (Child Behavior Checklist-CBCL; Teacher Report Form-TRF; Youth Self-Report-YSR) are listed in Table 8–1.

Empirical approaches to classifying conduct disorders have also suggested other ways of grouping problem behaviors within this broad category. These approaches are not mutually exclusive and indeed do overlap with the aggressive/delinquent distinction and with each other. Some approaches suggest a distinction based upon age of onset (cf. Hinshaw, Lahey, and Hart, 1993): a later- or adolescent-onset category consisting principally of nonaggressive and delinquent behaviors, and an early-onset category that includes these behaviors as well as aggressive behaviors. Two other approaches to subcategorizing that have been described are the salient symptom approach and the overt-covert dimension (Kazdin, 1989a). The salient symptom approach is based on the primary behavior problem being displayed. Distinguishing

TABLE 8–1 Behaviors from the Aggressive and Delinquent Syndromes[a]

Aggressive Behavior	Delinquent Behavior
Argues	Lacks guilt
Brags	Bad companions
Mean to others	Lies
Demands attention	Prefers older kids
Destroys own things	Runs away from home
Destroys others' things	Sets fires
Disobedient at school	Steals at home
Jealous	Steals outside home
Fights	Swearing, obscenity
Attacks people	Truancy
Screams	Alcohol, drugs
Shows off	Thinks about sex too much
Stubborn, irritable	Vandalism
Sudden mood changes	Tardy
Talks too much	
Teases	
Temper tantrums	
Threatens	
Loud	
Disobedient at home	
Defiant	
Disturbs others	
Talks out of turn	
Disrupts class	
Explosive	
Easily frustrated	

[a]Items listed are summaries of the actual content (wording) of items on the instruments. Some items are included in the CBCL, TRF, and YSR versions of these syndromes, while others are specific to one or two of these instruments. Adapted from Achenbach (1993).

ACCENT 8–1　Fire Setting

Much of the information that we describe addresses what can be termed overt conduct-disordered behavior (e.g., oppositional-defiant behavior, aggression). Fire setting represents a behavior that would be described as covert.

Ample documentation exists that juvenile fire setting produces serious damage in terms of loss of life, injury, and property damage. It is also associated with serious difficulties for the child, family, and community (Barnett and Spitzer, 1994; Kolko, 1985). Although fire setting by young people has come to the attention of clinicians and fire officials for a considerable period of time, it is only recently that this problem has received systematic attention.

Humphreys, Kopet, and Lajoy (1994) describe four basic categories of fire setters: curiosity fire setters, crisis (response to stress) fire setters, delinquent fire setters, and severely disturbed fire setters. Kolko and Kazdin (1986) have proposed a tentative model of fire-setting behavior that is somewhat different, although not incompatible. Their conceptualization is one of risk factors—influences that, if present, make fire setting more likely.

Fire play probably emerges as a part of normal development for many children as well as those that become fire setters (Kolko, 1985). Fire play occurs in a very large proportion of preschool children. However, this early interest along with the early presence of models to imitate may then be followed by additional later models and/or easy access to materials. This provides a possible context and the beginnings for the fire-setting problem.

What other factors may distinguish those children who actually set fires? One factor that is frequently cited based on clinical experience is the lack of social competence and difficulties in interpersonal situations. Indeed, a comparison of inpatient fire setters and other children hospitalized for a psychological disorder indicates that the fire setters possess less social skills (Kolko, Kazdin, and Meyer, 1985). Some workers view this deficiency as resulting in an inability to express anger effectively. This also relates to the issue of the motivation for fire setting. Here a distinction is often made between those who set fires as a form of aggression and those who set fires without an awareness of the consequences (e.g., curiosity, retardation).

It has also been suggested that fire setting is part of a cluster of covert antisocial behaviors that include destruction of property, stealing, lying, and truancy. Among inpatients, it was found that fire setters engaged in more of these kinds of behaviors than did non-setters. In contrast, the two groups were not different in aggressive behaviors (Kuhnley, Hendren, and Quinlan, 1982).

Family difficulties suggested as being related to fire setting resemble those that have been suggested for conduct disorders in general (Barnett and Spitzer, 1994; Kolko, 1989). For example, Kazdin and Kolko (1986) found differences in parental psychological adjustment and marital satisfaction associated with the presence of fire setting. In this sample twenty of the twenty-seven fire setters received a primary or secondary diagnosis of conduct disorder, compared to only eleven of twenty-seven nonfiresetters. The authors also found significantly higher scores of overall psychological difficulties, and depression in particular, among the mothers of fire setters than among the mothers of non-setters. No such difference existed based on the presence or absence of a conduct disorder diagnosis. Similarly, it was only the presence or absence of fire setting which appeared to be associated with poor marital adjustment. Thus, even in a sample of families all of whom have a severely disturbed child, families of fire setters appear to differ from those of non-setters.

These and similar findings have led some workers to suggest a particular conceptualization of many fire-setting children. In this conceptualization, fire setting represents a later stage of progression of antisocial symptoms to those that are more extreme (cf. Forehand et al., 1991; Kolko and Kazdin, 1986).

antisocial children whose primary problem is aggression from those whose primary problem is stealing is an example. The validity of this distinction is supported by findings that these two groups differ in other characteristics of the child, parental behavior, and response to treatment (e.g., Patterson, 1982). Expansion of this distinction suggests a broader distinction between overt confrontational antisocial behaviors (e.g., arguing, fighting, temper tantrums) and covert or concealed antisocial behaviors (e.g., fire setting, lying, stealing, truancy). In this approach subcategorization is based on a group of related behaviors rather than on a single problem. The reliability and validity of the overt-covert distinction is supported by evidence that problem behaviors do tend to cluster together in these groupings and that different outcomes are associated with such clusters (Loeber and Schmaling, 1985). These kinds of distinctions continue to be explored in the context of an empirical and developmental approach to understanding conduct-disordered behavior. The developmental approach is discussed further below.

The DSM Approach

Within the category of Attention-Deficit and Disruptive Behavior Disorders, DSM-IV includes the diagnostic categories of Attention-Deficit/Hyperactivity Disorder (discussed in Chapter 9) and two other diagnoses: Oppositional-Defiant Disorder and Conduct Disorder.

Oppositional-Defiant Disorder is dscribed as a pattern of negativistic, hostile, and defiant behavior lasting at least six months. At least four of the following behaviors must be present during that period:

1. loses temper
2. argues with adults
3. actively defies or refuses to comply with adult requests or rules
4. deliberately annoys others
5. blames others for own mistakes or misbehavior
6. touchy or easily annoyed
7. angry and resentful
8. spiteful or vindictive

In order to meet diagnostic criteria, a behavior must be judged to occur more frequently than is typical for a child of comparable age.

Oppositional and noncompliant behavior is clearly a common problem. It is prevalent among nonclinic children, and one of the most frequently reported problems of children referred to clinics (Achenbach, 1991a; Johnson et al., 1973; Rey, 1993). Perhaps not surprising, clinic referred children are more noncompliant than nonreferred children (e.g., Achenbach et al., 1991; Griest et al., 1980).

Noncompliance seems to be part of the problematic behavior shown by children exhibiting other conduct problems and antisocial behavior. It is unclear whether DSM-IV's approach of having a separate category of Oppositional-Defiant Disorder, is the best way to group these problem behaviors (cf. Frick et al., 1993; Russo et al., 1994). Whatever the issues of classification/diagnosis, it is clear that noncompliance represents a practical problem for parents, teachers, and clinicians. Also, noncompliant, stubborn, and oppositional behavior may represent for some youngsters the earliest steps on a developmental path of persistent antisocial behavior (Hinshaw et al., 1993; Loeber et al., 1993).

The essential feature of the diagnosis of Conduct Disorder is a repetitive and persistent pattern of behavior that violates the basic rights of others and major age appropriate societal norms. The list of symptoms describing the various manifestations of Conduct Disorder are presented in

Table 8–2. The diagnosis of Conduct Disorder requires that three or more of these behaviors were present during the past twelve months, with at least one present in the past six months. Two subtypes, Childhood-Onset and Adolescent-Onset, are specified based upon whether one or more of the criterion behaviors had an onset prior to age ten years.

TABLE 8–2 DSM-IV Diagnostic Criteria for Conduct Disorder

Aggression to people and animals
(1) often bullies, threatens, or intimidates
(2) often initiates physical fights
(3) used a weapon that can cause serious physical harm
(4) physically cruel to people
(5) physically cruel to animals
(6) stolen while confronting a victim (e.g., mugging, purse snatching, extortion, armed robbery)
(7) forced someone into sexual activity

Destruction of property
(8) deliberately engaged in fire setting with the intention of causing serious damage
(9) deliberately destroyed others' property (other than by fire setting)

Deceitfulness or theft
(10) broken into someone else's house, building, or car
(11) often lies to obtain goods or favors or to avoid obligations (i.e., "cons" others)
(12) stolen items of nontrivial value without confronting a victim (e.g., shoplifting, but without breaking and entering; forgery)

Serious violations of rules
(13) often stays out at night despite parental prohibitions, beginning before age 13 years
(14) has run away from home overnight at least twice while living in parental or parental surrogate home (or once without returning for a lengthy period)
(15) is often truant from school, beginning before age 13 years

Adapted and reprinted with permission from the *Diagnostic and Statistical Manual of Mental Disorders, Fourth Edition.* Copyright 1994, American Psychiatric Association.

DEVELOPMENTAL COURSE

Developmental Paths

Much attention has been given to the developmental aspects of conduct disorders and the conceptualization of developmental progressions (e.g., Farrington, 1986; Loeber et al., 1993; Patterson, DeBaryshe, and Ramsey, 1989; Robins, 1978). Loeber (1988) proposed a model that can serve to illustrate some of the attributes that might characterize the developmental course of conduct disorders. The model suggests that individuals pass through different stages of increasingly serious antisocial acts, but only a few individuals progress through all the stages. Thus, less serious behaviors precede more serious ones, but only some individuals progress to the next step at each stage. Progression is characterized by increasing diversification of antisocial behaviors, and previous behaviors may also be retained rather than replaced. Individuals may differ in their rate of progression, or innovation rate, defined as the number of novel categories of antisocial behavior during a time period.

Age of onset is probably the most mentioned aspect of the development of conduct disordered behavior. Many studies have found that early age of onset is related to more serious and persistent antisocial behavior (Earls, 1994; Tolan and Thomas, 1995). A number of authors have proposed two distinct developmental pathways leading toward antisocial behavior, one with a childhood onset and the other with an adolescent onset (cf. Hinshaw et al., 1993; Loeber, 1988; Moffitt, 1993a).

The adolescent onset pattern is the more common developmental pathway. There is little oppositional or antisocial behavior exhibited during childhood. During adolescence many youngsters begin to engage in illegal activities, and although most exhibit only isolated antisocial acts, some engage in enough antisocial behavior to qualify for a diagnosis of Conduct Disorder. Youngsters following this pathway tend to exhibit less severe behaviors and be less aggressive. They are also less likely to persist in their antisocial behaviors beyond adolescence—leading Moffitt (1993a) to suggest the term *adolescence-limited antisocial behavior.*

An example of the support for this adolescent-onset pathway comes from the Dunedin Multidisciplinary Health and Development Study (McGee et al., 1992). Prospective examination of a birth cohort of New Zealand youngsters revealed a large increase in the·prevalence of nonaggressive conduct disorder, but no increase in aggressive conduct disorder at fifteen compared to age eleven. These youngsters were clearly exhibiting problem behavior. For example, they were as likely to be arrested for their delinquent offenses as childhood-onset delinquents. However, their offenses were less aggressive, and the adolescent-onset cases included slightly more females than males in contrast to the predominance of males among conduct disorder cases at age eleven. This rather common emergence during adolescence of nonaggressive antisocial behavior that is not likely to persist beyond adolescence is contrasted to early-onset antisocial behavior.

The childhood-onset developmental pathway is better known and is the pathway that fits with the notions of the stability of conduct-disordered behavior. Indeed, Moffitt (1993a) terms this pattern *life-course persistent antisocial behavior.* Retrospective studies of antisocial adults are consistent with this picture of stable conduct-disordered behavior. It must be remembered, however, that a substantial number of children with an early onset of antisocial behavior do not persist on this pathway. The early-onset pathway is less common than the adolescent-onset pattern, with estimates of about 3 to 5 percent of the general population (cf. Hinshaw et al.,

1993; Moffitt, 1993a). Youngsters following this pattern are also more likely to exhibit other difficulties such as Attention-Deficit Hyperactivity Disorder, learning disabilities, and academic difficulties.

While there is stability of problematic behavior for some portion of children entering this pathway, even among these individuals behaviors change in the course of development. Hinshaw and colleagues (1993) describe the features of this heterotypic continuity of antisocial behavior.

. . . the preschooler who throws temper tantrums and stubbornly refuses to follow adult instructions becomes the child who also initiates fights with other children and lies to the teacher. Later, the same youth begins to vandalize the school, torture animals, break into homes, steal costly items, and abuse alcohol. As a young adult, he or she forces sex on acquaintances, writes bad checks, and has a chaotic employment and marital history. (p. 36)

Studies employing DSM diagnostic categories also suggest this developmental pattern. The first problem behaviors to emerge in the childhood-onset path may be the oppositional and defiant behaviors characteristic of Oppositional-Defiant Disorder (ODD). Later behaviors characteristic of the Conduct Disorder (CD) diagnosis may emerge, but the vast majority of these CD youngsters still meet the criteria for ODD. They have "retained" the early antisocial behaviors. However, it is also important to note that most youngsters with an ODD diagnosis do not progress to CD (Hinshaw et al., 1993).

Figure 8–1 is a hypothetical illustration of the changing prevalence of antisocial behavior with age and the prevalence and duration of the two different developmental pathways.

Investigators continue their efforts to describe the developmental pathways of antisocial behavior. At the same time they also seek to identify the influences that first put youngsters on those pathways and that de-

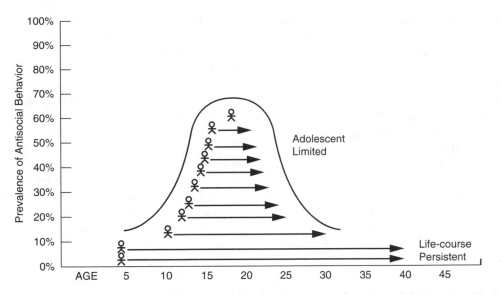

FIGURE 8–1   Hypothetical illustration of the changing prevalence of participation in antisocial behavior across the life course. (The solid line represents the known curve of crime over age. The arrows represent the duration of participation in antisocial behavior by individuals.)

From Moffitt, 1993. Copyright 1993 by the American Psychological Association.

termine whether the antisocial behavior will continue or desist.

Stability of Conduct Disorders

Perhaps the most disturbing aspect of conduct problems is their reported stability over time (Fergusson, Horwood, and Lynskey, 1995; Loeber, 1991; Olweus, 1979; Rutter et al., 1976; Tolan and Thomas, 1995). Early presence of conduct disordered behavior appears to be related to later aggressive and antisocial behavior and to a range of psychological and social-emotional difficulties later in life (Caspi, Elder, and Bem, 1987; Hafner, Quast, and Shea, 1975; Parker and Asher, 1987; Robins et al., 1971).

Persistence of aggressive and antisocial behavior has been noted repeatedly by both clinicians and researchers. To help understand how the continuity of behavior can be approached from a research perspective, let

us examine one study in detail. Roff and Wirt (1984) were interested in a causal model for delinquency. They selected aggressive behavior in childhood, peer status, socioeconomic status, degree of family disturbance, predelinquent behavior and school achievement as variables for investigation. In the early 1960s they began by gathering peer status information for approximately 17,000 third through sixth-grade children. Based on the ratings of same-sex classmates, a child's peer status was determined by the difference between the number of liked-most and liked-least choices the child received. The investigators then interviewed all teachers regarding five children in their classroom—the least and most popular boy and girl and a child of middle popularity. Through the use of available records, the investigators were able to follow into the young adult period 2,453 of the children for whom they had interviews. They found that the rates of delinquent behavior were much higher for the low peer status group than for children who were of middle or high popularity.

The authors decided to undertake further analyses for the low peer status group alone (1,127 children). Socioeconomic status was examined. Analysis of the teacher interviews for the types of problem behaviors exhibited by these children at the time of the interview was also undertaken. Coding and factor analyses of this information indicated four areas of problems. These were aggressiveness-rebelliousness, anxiety expressed as excitability and restlessness, poor school achievement, and a motivational deficit primarily involving apathy and indifference toward classroom activities. A measure of predelinquent behavior was also derived from the teacher interview. This measure was based on six variables—stealing in school, stealing in the community, trouble with the law, running away from home, lying, and truancy. A global rating of severity of family disturbance was also abstracted from the teacher interview.

Thus SES, the four behavior problem scores, the predelinquent measure, and family disturbance were the variables assessed for these eight to eleven-year-old children. By searching later juvenile records, each of the children was rated as either delinquent or nondelinquent as an adolescent. Delinquency was defined as the opening of a formal juvenile record indicating juvenile court referral. State Bureau of Investigation records indicated which of the subjects had committed adult criminal offenses between the ages of eighteen and twenty-four to twenty-seven. The statistical procedure of path analysis was employed to define the joint effects of all the measures taken when the children were eight to eleven years old and to suggest a causal model for later delinquent and adult criminal behavior.

Figure 8–2 illustrates the model as it applies to boys. Separate models were derived for each gender since the rate of delinquent and criminal behavior was much lower for females. Aggression and predelinquent be-

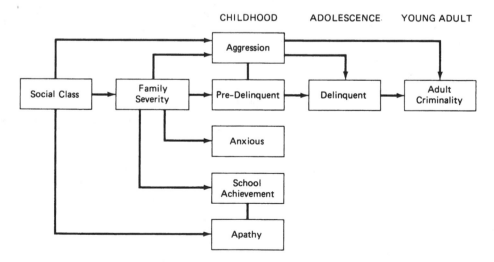

FIGURE 8–2 A model of antecedents of delinquency and criminal behavior for low peer-status boys.

Adapted from Roff, J. D., & Wirt, R. D. (1984). Childhood aggression and social adjustment as antecedents of delinquency. *Journal of Abnormal Child Psychology, 12,* 111–126. Reprinted by permission from Plenum Publishing Corporation.

havior appeared to be directly related to later delinquency for these low peer status males. Social class and severity of family disturbance contributed to these two childhood problem behaviors as well as to the other problems during childhood. However, they did not appear to be directly linked to delinquent outcome. In addition to there being a significant path from delinquency in adolescence to young adult criminal behavior, aggressiveness during childhood appeared to have a direct link to this adult behavior, as well. These results suggest a stable pattern of behavior over time for boys of low peer status, linking early aggression with later delinquency and criminal behavior.

The model for girls was different. There did not appear to be a direct path between early aggression and later antisocial behavior. Indeed, for girls, severity of family disturbance during childhood emerged as the best predictor of delinquency in adolescence. The frequency of adult criminal behavior among females was too low to permit an analysis into adulthood. These findings regarding girls are consistent with the interesting suggestion by others that early conduct problems in girls may be associated with a range of social-emotional difficulties later in life rather than primarily criminal outcome (Caspi et al., 1987; Rutter, 1989b).

CONDUCT DISORDERED BEHAVIOR: CAUSES AND CORRELATES

Aggression as a Learned Behavior

Aggression is a central part of the definition of conduct disordered behavior and is often suggested as a basis for differentiating among conduct disordered youth. Aggression is also a common difficulty among non-referred children. Children clearly may learn to be aggressive by being rewarded for such behavior (Patterson, 1976b). For example, Patterson, Littman, and Bricker (1967) found that among nursery school children aggressive acts that were followed by "positive" consequences (e.g., passivity or crying by the victim) were likely to be repeated, while "negative" consequences (e.g., retaliation or telling the teacher) resulted in the aggressor switching either behaviors or victims. Another interesting finding emerged from this study. Children who were initially passive and unassertive were frequently victimized. Some, however, eventually exhibited aggressive behaviors, were reinforced by positive consequences, and increased their frequency of such behavior. While illustrating the importance of reinforcement for aggression, this study also suggests another source of learning—imitation of aggressive models.

A great deal of attention has focused on how children learn through imitation of aggressive models. Bandura's (1965) study with nursery school children, described earlier (pp. 58–60), demonstrated that children imitated an aggressive, filmed model and that the consequences experienced by the model affected the performance, but not the learning of aggression. It has also been demonstrated that children may not only learn new and novel responses following observation of an aggressive model, but that aggressive responses already in the child's repertoire are more likely to occur—disinhibition of aggression.

Children certainly have ample opportunity to observe aggressive models. Parents who physically punish their children serve as models for aggressive behavior. In fact, children exhibiting excessive aggressive or antisocial behaviors are likely to have siblings, fathers, and even grandparents with records of aggressive and criminal behavior (Farrington, 1987; Huesmann et al., 1984; West, 1982) and to have observed especially high rates of aggressive behavior in their homes (Kashani et al., 1992; Patterson, De-Baryshe, and Ramsey, 1989). Aggression is

ACCENT 8–2   Bullies and Their Victims

Many people are familiar with the problem of bullying either through personal experience or through literature, television or movies. The most extensive research on this topic has been conducted in Scandinavia by Olweus (1993; 1994) who reports that approximately 15 percent of youngsters between the ages of 7 and 16 are involved in bullying either as bullies or victims (approximately 9 percent as victims, 7 percent as bullies, and 1.6 percent as both victim and bully) and that similar or larger percentages are reported in other countries. The percentage of youngsters who report being bullied decreases with age during the elementary years, while bullying itself is more stable. A larger percentage of boys than girls engage in bullying and are victims of bullying.

A youngster is being bullied when he or she is repeatedly exposed to the intentional negative actions of another youngster who is either physically or psychologically more powerful than the victim. Boys are exposed to more direct open attacks then are girls. Less visible, indirect bullying can occur in the form of spreading of rumors, manipulation of friendship relationships, and social isolation. Girls are more exposed to this more subtle form of bullying than to open attacks. Boys, however, are exposed to indirect bullying at rates comparable to girls.

The typical bully is described by Olweus (1994) as highly aggressive to both peers and adults, having a more positive attitude toward violence than students in general, impulsive, having a strong need to dominate others, having little empathy towards victims, and, if a boy, as physically stronger than boys in general. Not all highly aggressive youngsters are bullies and differences between bullies and other aggressive youngsters remain to be clarified.

The typical victim is described as more anxious and insecure than other students, cautious, sensitive, quiet, nonaggressive and suffering from low self-esteem. If they are boys, victims are likely to be physically weaker. In general victims do not have a single good friend in their class. These, so-called, passive or submissive victims are most common and this submissive, nonassertive style seems to precede being selected as a victim (Schwartz, Dodge, and Coie, 1993).

It is clearly important to address the bully/victim problem. Bullying can be viewed as part of a more general antisocial, conduct-disordered behavior pattern and thus these youngsters are at risk. Indeed, Olweus (1994) reports that 60 percent of boys classified as bullies in grades 6–9 were convicted of at least one officially registered crime by age 24 and 35–40 percent of former bullies had three or more convictions by this age as compared to only 10 percent of control boys.

The consequences for the victims of bullying also suggest the importance of intervening early. The victims of bullying form a large group of youngsters who are to a great extent ignored by the school and whose parents may be relatively unaware of the problem. One can imagine the effects of going through years of school in a state of fear, anxiety and insecurity. Some portion of these youngsters self-esteem is so poor and their hope for change so low that they view suicide as the only possible option (Olweus, 1994). A case described by Olweus illustrate the pain youngsters may suffer.

"Henry was a quiet and sensitive 13 year-old boy in grade 7. For several years he had been harassed and attacked occasionally by some of his classmates. . . . During the past couple of months, their attacks had become more frequent and severe, for one reason or another.

Henry's daily life was filled with unpleasant and humiliating events. His books were pushed from his desk all over the floor, his tormentors broke this pencils and threw things at him, they laughed loudly and scornfully when he occasionally responded to the teacher's questions. Even in class, he was often called by his nickname, the "Worm."

As a rule, Henry did not respond, he just sat there expressionless at his desk, passively waiting for the next attack. The teacher usually looked in another direction when the ha-

ACCENT 8–2 Bullies and Their Victims

rassment went on. Several of Henry's classmates felt sorry for him but none of them made a serious attempt to defend him.

A month earlier, Henry had been coerced, with his clothes on, into a shower which had been turned on. His two tormentors had also threatened him several times to give them money and steal cigarettes for them at the supermarket. One afternoon, after having been forced to lie down in the drain of the school

urinal, Henry quietly went home, found a box of sleeping pills in the bathroom and swallowed a handful of pills. Later on the same afternoon Henry's parents found him unconcious but alive on the sofa in the living room. A note on his desk told them that he couldn't stand the bullying any more, he felt completely worthless, and believed the world would be a better place without him. (Olweus, 1993; pgs. 49–50)

also ubiquitous in television programs and in other media.

Family Influences

The family environment can be a principal arena for the learning of aggressive behavior. However, family influences are not limited to the acquisition of aggression or to the mechanisms of family influence described

above. Indeed, family influences play an important role in the genesis of various conduct disordered behaviors. A high incidence of deviant or criminal behavior has been reported in families of delinquents and young children with conduct problems (Kazdin, 1985; Rutter and Giller, 1984; West, 1982). Longitudinal studies, in fact, suggest that such behavior is stable across generations (Glueck and Glueck, 1968; Huesmann et al.,

The viewing of aggression on TV and in movies contributes to the development of aggression and antisocial behavior.

1984). It seems, then, that conduct disordered children may be part of a deviant family system. Numerous family variables have been implicated including family socioeconomic status, family size, marital disruption, poor quality parenting and parental neglect, and parental psychopathology (Frick, 1994; Hetherington and Martin, 1986; Patterson, Reid, and Dishion, 1992). We will highlight a few of these influences.

Parent-child interactions. The manner in which parents interact with their children contributes to the genesis of conduct disordered behavior. So for example, parental involvement and supervision and parental discipline practices are related to conduct problems.

Defiant, stubborn, and noncompliant behaviors are often among the first problems to develop in children. Given that noncompliance occurs in both clinic and nonclinic families, what factors might account for the greater rate of noncompliance in some families? One possible factor is suggested by evidence that parents of clinic and nonclinic children differ in both the number and types of commands they give. Parents of clinic-referred children issue more commands, questions, and criticisms and also issue commands that are presented in an angry, humiliating, or nagging manner (Delfini, Bernal, and Rosen, 1976; Forehand et al., 1975; Lobitz and Johnson, 1975). Such parental behavior has been shown to be associated with deviant child behavior (Griest et al., 1980).

Two types of commands have been distinguished. *Alpha commands* are those to which a motoric response is appropriate and feasible. *Beta commands* are vague, interrupted, or carried out by the parent, and thus the child has no opportunity to learn to demonstrate compliance. Consequences that parents deliver also affect the child's noncompliant behavior. A combination of negative consequences (ig-

noring and verbal reprimands) for noncompliant behavior and rewards and attention for appropriate behavior seems to be related to increased levels of compliance (Forehand and McMahon, 1981).

The work of Patterson and his colleagues. Gerald Patterson and his colleagues have developed an intervention program for families with aggressive children based on a social learning perspective (Patterson et al., 1975; Patterson et al., 1992). Patterson developed what he refers to as *coercion theory* to explain how a problematic pattern of behavior develops in children labeled aggressive. Observations of referred families suggested that acts of physical aggression were not isolated behaviors. On the contrary, they tended to occur along with a wide range of noxious behaviors which were used to control family members in a process labeled coercion. How and why does this process of coercion develop?

One factor is parents who lack adequate family management skills. According to Patterson (1976b; Patterson et al., 1992), parental deficits in child management lead to an increasingly coercive interaction within the family. Central to this process are the notions of *negative reinforcement* and the *reinforcement trap*. For example, a mother gives into her child's tantrums in the supermarket and buys him a candy bar. The short-term consequence is that things are more pleasant for both parties. The child has used an aversive event (tantrum) to achieve the desired goal (candy bar), and the mother's giving in has terminated an aversive event (tantrum and embarrassment) for her. Short-term gains, however, are paid for in long-term consequences. The mother, although receiving some immediate relief, has increased the probability that her child will employ tantrums in the future. She has also been provided with negative reinforcement that increases the likelihood that she will give in to future tantrums.

In addition to this negative reinforcement trap, coercive behavior may also be increased by direct positive reinforcement. Aggressive behavior, especially in boys, may meet with social approval. However, escape-conditioning is even more important. The child uses aversive behaviors to terminate aversive intrusions by other family members (Patterson, 1982).

The concept of *reciprocity* adds to our understanding of how aggression may be learned and sustained. As indicated earlier, children as young as nursery school age can learn in a short time that attacking another in response to some intrusion can terminate that intrusion. In addition, the victim of the attack may learn from the experience and is more likely to initiate attacks in the future. The eventual victim of escalating coercion also provides a negative reinforcer by giving in. This also increases the likelihood that the "winner" will start future coercions at higher levels of intensity and thereby get the victim to give in more quickly.

This process is exacerbated by the ineffectiveness of punishment. The finding that in problem families punishment does not suppress coercive behavior but may serve to increase it has been referred to as *punishment acceleration*. The ineffectiveness of punishment may be due to the strong reinforcement history for coercive behavior and to inconsistent use of punishment in these families (Patterson, 1982).

The description of a coercive process and ineffective parenting has served as the basis for Patterson's intervention project and an evolving developmental model (Patterson et al., 1989; Patterson et al., 1992). In addition to describing the "training" of antisocial behavior in the home, Patterson has described a relationship between antisocial behavior in boys and poor peer relationships, academic incompetence, and poor self-esteem. It is thought that the coercive, noncompliant core of antisocial behavior, produced by ineffective parenting, produces these other disruptions. Furthermore, it is hypothesized that each of these outcomes serves as a precursor to subsequent drift into deviant peer groups. Patterson himself is cautious about statements of causation based on correlational data. Ongoing longitudinal research and experimental studies are expected to clarify these relationships.

Patterson and his coworkers have continued to evolve a methodologically and conceptually sophisticated developmental model of antisocial behavior. Their perspective has expanded to include a wide array of variables that impact on the family process. Their efforts have also attended to problems such as poor peer relations, school failure, low self-esteem, and depression, which are associated with antisocial behavior. However, at the core of this complex theoretical model is the parent training model (see Figure 8–3) that has proven to be so robust that Patterson and his colleagues call it *basic black;* "it is simple, elegant and seems appro-

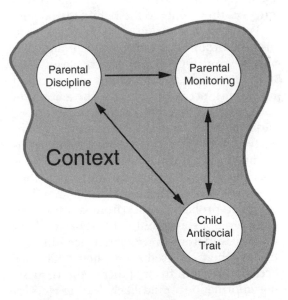

FIGURE 8–3 The Parent Training Model.

From Patterson, G. R., Reid, J. B. & Dishion, T. J. (1992). Reprinted by permission from Castalia Publishing Co.

priate for more than one setting." (Patterson et al., 1992, pg. 62).

The constructs of parental discipline and parental monitoring are described as contributing to and being influenced by the child's antisocial behavior. Parental discipline is defined by an interrelated set of skills: accurately tracking and classifying problem behaviors, ignoring trivial coercive events, and using effective consequences when necessary to back up demands and requests. Parents of problem children as compared to other parents have been found to be overinclusive in the behaviors that they classify as deviant. Thus these parents differ in how they track and classify problem behavior. These parents also "natter" (nag, scold irritably) in response to low levels of coercive behavior or behavior that other parents see as neutral. Other parents are able to ignore these behaviors in their children. Parents of antisocial children fail to back up their commands when the child fails to comply and they also fail to reward compliance when it does occur. These parents, therefore, also differ in the consequences they apply to their child's behavior.

Parental monitoring of child behavior is also important to the development and persistence over time of antisocial behavior. The amount of time a child spends unsupervised by parents increases with age. The amount of unsupervised time has also been found to be positively correlated with antisocial behavior. Patterson describes his treatment families as having little information as to where their children are, who they are with, what they are doing, or when they will be home. This situation probably arises from a variety of considerations including the repeated failures these parents have experienced in controlling their children even when difficulties occurred right in front of them. Also requesting information would likely lead to a series of confrontations which the parents prefer to avoid. These parents have low expectations regarding the likelihood of positive responses to their involvement either from their own children or social agencies such as schools (Patterson et al., 1992).

Extrafamilial influences and parental psychopathology. The question of why some families and not others exhibit inept management practices has received some attention. Patterson (Patterson et al., 1992) posits that any number of variables may account for changes over time in family management skills. Patterson's own findings and those of other investigators (e.g., Wahler and Dumas, 1989) support the relationship between extrafamilial stressors (e.g., daily hassles, negative life events, financial problems, family health problems) and parenting practices. In addition, handing down of faulty parenting practices from one generation to the next seems to help explain the problematic parenting characteristics of antisocial families. Social disadvantage and living in neighborhoods that require a very high degree of parenting skills also place some families at risk. Finally, various forms of parental psychopathology are associated with poor parenting practices. Parents with antisocial difficulties have been particularly implicated in the parenting practices associated with the development of conduct disordered behavior such as low levels of parental involvement (e.g., Capaldi and Patterson, 1991). Also, heavy drinking by parents may be associated with inept monitoring of the child and less parental involvement (West and Prinz, 1987). Figure 8–4 illustrates a model of how a variety of influences may lead to disruption of effective parenting and child antisocial behavior.

One of the influences in Patterson's model is parental divorce. Disruption of parenting practices in response to separation, divorce, single parenting and remarriage is widely acknowledged (e.g., Hetherington, Stanley-Hagan, and Anderson, 1989).

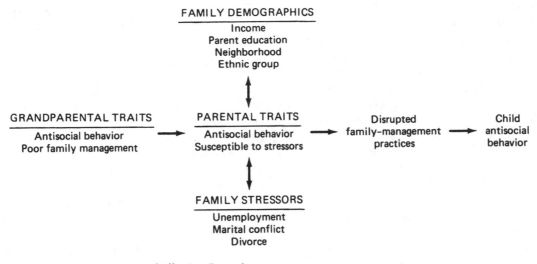

FIGURE 8–4   Disruptors of Effective Parenting.

From Patterson, DeBaryshe, and Ramsey, 1989. Copyright (1989) by American Psychological Association.

Marital discord.   There appears to be a clear association between marital discord and parental perceptions of behavior problems in their children (O'Leary and Emery, 1985). Indeed, the combination of marital dissatisfaction and high levels of child disruptive behavior is more likely than either factor alone to produce perceptions of behavior problems (Forehand, Brody, and Smith, 1986).

Parental conflict and divorce have frequently been cited in homes of delinquents and children with conduct disorders (Kazdin, 1985; Rutter and Giller, 1984). It would appear that the conflict leading to and surrounding the divorce are principle influences in this relationship (Amato and Keith, 1991). Less conflict and greater cooperation are associated with fewer problems in children (Hetherington et al., 1989). The relationship between family conflict and conduct disorders is found more often for boys than for girls (Emery, 1982; Reid and Crisafulli, 1990). If aggression between the parents is also present, childhood disorder seems even more likely than would be ex-

pected based on marital discord alone (Jouriles, Murphy, and O'Leary, 1989).

The relationship between marital conflict and conduct disorders can be explained in a number of ways. Parents who engage in a great deal of marital conflict or aggression may serve as models for their children. Perhaps such parents direct high rates of conflictual and aggressive behavior at others as well, including the child. The stress of marital discord and the adjustment of the single parent to divorce may also interfere with parenting practices and the ability of the parent to monitor the child's behavior. The relationship between discord and conduct problems may also operate in the opposite causal direction. That is, the child's disruptive behavior may contribute to marital discord. Alternatively, conduct problems and marital discord may not be causally related. Rather a "third variable," such as the presence of parental antisocial disorder, may explain this relationship (cf. Lahey et al., 1988). Indeed, there are high rates of antisocial personality disorder (APD) among conduct-disordered youngsters and APD is associated with high rates of marital instability (Frick, 1994).

It is appropriate to emphasize that much of this research only describes group differences and is correlational in nature. It is often assumed that parental behavior causes childhood conduct disorders. The relationship, however, may be at least reciprocal. Anderson, Lytton, and Romney (1986) found that mothers of conduct problem boys and mothers of normal boys both interacted more negatively with conduct problem boys than with normal boys. They suggested that the child's behavior is the influence in these interactions, not the mother's. In addition, we have also suggested that it may be inappropriate to assume that fundamental deficiencies in parenting skills account for conduct problems in children. It may be that a high level of environmental stress (related to family and community/neighborhood factors) experienced by the parents, and not the level of parenting skills alone, contribute to parent-

Children's observations of parental interactions clearly influence behavior. If these interactions are hostile, they may contribute to the development of aggression and other aversive behaviors in the child.

(Mimi Forsyth/Monkmeyer Press)

ing difficulties (McLoyd, 1990; Patterson et al., 1992; Wahler and Dumas, 1989).

Social-Cognitive Influences

Moral development. Since many of the behaviors characteristic of conduct disorders violate societal rules or norms, some workers have related the process of moral development to conduct problems. Research over several decades has documented the role of parents, schools, peers, sex-role socialization, television, guilt, empathy, and cognitive development in moral development, but much remains to be understood (Earls, 1994; Ellis, 1982; Hoffman, 1979; Rest, 1983).

The development of morality, like most developmental tasks, is a complex process. It is clear, however, that the kinds of action, feeling, and thought one can expect from a youngster is related to the youth's level of development. For example, a five-year-old is likely to act and judge others' behavior by objective standards. Breaking five dishes is worse than breaking one. Accident versus intention is not considered. Also, the source of moral rules is some authority—"My father said . . ."—and consequences are assumed to be imminent. Both the rules and the consequences are outside the child. As youngsters get older they can consider relative factors such as an individual's intention and the "social contract" nature of rules. Also, self-direction and self-imposed consequences presumably shape their actions and reasoning.

One line of research on moral development has focused on reasoning capacity and has centered on Kohlberg's (1964, 1976) extension and revision of Piaget's original account. His stage theory, like Piaget's, is based on the assumption that at each stage hierarchically more complex and abstract levels of reasoning are present. Children are assumed to pass through the stages in a fixed order. Movement to the next stage occurs only after the reasoning of the earlier stage is mastered. It is also assumed that an individual's level of moral development may stop at any point. Thus, a person may be below the level characteristic of most same-age individuals. Indeed, findings of low levels of moral reasoning among delinquent youth have been the basis of much of the speculation in this area (Nelson, Smith, and Dodd, 1990). It cannot, however, clearly be said that all conduct disordered youth have lower levels of moral reasoning. Considerable individual variability in moral reasoning may exist among samples of such youth (Blasi, 1980; Jurkovic, 1980; Nelson et al., 1990).

Kohlberg's conceptualization has generated a great deal of research and commentary, and also a great deal of controversy. The method for assessing moral reasoning (Table 8–3) has been criticized. Also some research suggests that children may possess age-appropriate moral concepts, but not reveal that understanding in every situation (e.g., Shultz, Wright, and Schleifer, 1986). Issues of sex-role influences and of cultural relativity have also been raised (Baumrind, 1986; Gilligan, 1982; Snarey, 1985; Walker, 1984, 1986).

The contribution of moral thought to the development of conduct-disordered behavior has been examined by other approaches as well. For example, it may be that parents of children with conduct problems are less likely to provide reasoned explanation along with their disciplinary actions. If explanations are provided, they may be based on the parents' power rather than concepts such as fairness. The developmental literature suggests that such strategies are less likely to result in the child's developing internalized standards (e.g., Hoffman, 1979). In this and other ways these children may not have the experiences required to create cognitive schemes necessary for appropriate social behavior.

In addition, numerous other attributes may be involved in what we call moral judgment. These may include empathy and the ability to take another's perspective, both of which have been found to be deficient in delinquent groups (e.g., Ellis, 1982; Jurkovic and Prentice, 1977). Lee and Prentice (1988) studied several of these variables. Adolescent delinquent boys in a state juvenile correctional facility and matched nondelinquents were given two individually administered measures of empathy. They also completed tasks to assess the stage of their role-taking development, that is, the ability to take another's perspective. Two measures to assess Piagetian level of cognitive development and two of Kolberg's moral dilemmas were also administered. Delinquents displayed more immature modes of role-taking and less formal operational thinking than did nondelinquents. Delinquents also displayed lower levels of moral reasoning than nondelinquents.

The question of if and how deficits in moral development contribute to conduct disorders and delinquency remains controversial and in need of continued investigation. Some investigators have, however,

TABLE 8–3 Kohlberg's Method of Assessing Moral Reasoning

An individual child's level of moral reasoning is assessed through administration of hypothetical dilemmas such as the following:

Bill saved up $10 for a catcher's mitt. When he arrives at the store, he sees the sales clerk going down the stairs to the cellar. The clerk doesn't see Bill. Bill looks at the gloves, and just as he sees one he likes, he reaches for his money. It's gone, he realizes he has lost it. He feels awful. It occurs to Bill that the mitt would just fit under his jacket. He hides the mitt and walks out of the store. Now you finish the story. (Kohlberg, 1964, p. 410)

The child's verbal response to this and other dilemmas are scored to provide an index of moral stage and moral maturity.

---

demonstrated that sociomoral training programs for conduct disordered and delinquent youths can produce changes in the levels of moral development exhibited. Furthermore, such changes are associated with changes in relevant conduct and academic measures (e.g., Arbuthnot and Gordon, 1986; Chandler, 1973).

Interpersonal relations and social cognition. Difficulties in interpersonal relations have repeatedly been found among conduct disordered youth (Baum, 1989). Research indicates that aggressive children are frequently rejected by their peers (Coie, Belding, and Underwood, 1988). These rejected children not only suffer immediate social consequences, but are also at risk for negative long-term outcomes such as delinquency, adult criminality, educational failure, and a variety of indices of adult psychological maladjustment (Parker and Asher, 1987). Although identification of the specific attributes that differentiate rejected children from their peers is a topic of continuing investigation, a number of interesting attributes have been identified (Baum, 1989; Dodge, 1989).

For example, aggressive children and adolescents who are rejected by their peers exhibit deficits in social information processing and interpersonal problem-solving skills. These children may generate fewer alternative solutions to social problems, seek less information, define problems in hostile ways, and anticipate fewer negative consequences for aggression (e.g., Spivack and Shure, 1974; Slaby and Guerra, 1988). Aggression also seems to be related to a belief system that supports its use. Thus, aggression may be held as a legitimate response— "It's O.K. to hit someone if you don't like him or her." Aggression may also be supported by its expected outcomes: reduced aversive behavior by others, tangible rewards, increased self-esteem, and avoidance of negative judgments by others (Bandura, 1986; Perry, Perry, and Rasmussen, 1986; Slaby and Guerra, 1988).

Cognitive aspects of the acquisition and persistence of aggression have been addressed by the social learning approach. For example, Perry, Perry, and Rasmussen (1986) explored two types of cognitions: children's perceptions of their ability to behave aggressively (perceptions of self-efficacy) and their beliefs about expected outcomes of aggressive behavior. Aggressive and nonaggressive boys and girls from fourth through seventh grades completed questionnaires designed to measure the two classes of cognitions. Aggressive children reported greater confidence in their ability to be aggressive, more difficulty in inhibiting aggression, and greater expectation that aggression would produce tangible rewards and reduce aversive treatment by others. While there were negligible sex differences in perceptions of self-efficacy, there were differences in expected consequences. Girls were more likely than boys to expect aggression to cause more suffering for others and to expect more disapproval from peers and themselves. This gender difference is of importance in light of recent findings regarding gender differences in aggression. Most research reports greater rates of aggression in boys than in girls. This research has focused primarily on overt physical aggression such as hitting. However, relational aggression, that is, harm to others through damage to their peer relations (such as excluding another from one's play group) is more characteristic of girls and significantly more distressing to girls (e.g., Crick, 1995).

Other research has confirmed that the gender of both the aggressor and the target of aggression affects the consequences that children anticipate for aggression (Perry, Perry, and Weiss, 1989). These and other findings highlight the role of children's perceptions and expectations regarding aggression.

Research suggests that social information processing mechanisms such as hypervigilance to hostile cues, hostile attributional bias, accessing aggressive responses from memory, and positive expectations of outcomes for aggression are related to the development and enactment of conduct disordered behavior (Dodge, 1993). Dodge and Somberg's (1987) examination of attributional biases among aggressive boys is an example of how such social-cognitive influences may operate. Previous research established that following provocation by a peer, the interpretation of the peer's intent affected the child's subsequent response. If the peer's intent was perceived to be hostile, retaliating aggressively was viewed as justified. In contrast, if the peer's intent was perceived as benign, the child was likely to refrain from aggression. Children who were themselves both aggressive and socially rejected were more likely to attribute hostile intent to peer's behavior in ambiguous circumstances. Dodge and Somberg were interested in investigating whether this hostile attributional bias was exacerbated by the child's emotions under conditions of threat.

Aggressive-rejected and nonaggressive-adjusted boys, eight to ten years old, viewed videorecorded scenes involving different pairs of boys in play activity. In each vignette one boy engaged in a behavior that led to a negative outcome for the second boy. The intention of the child varied across the scenes (either hostile, accidental, prosocial, or ambiguous). Subjects were asked two questions about each vignette: Which of the four intents did the boy have and how would they respond if the provocation happened to them (get mad, tell the teacher, ask the peer why it happened, forget it and keep playing). Each subject saw scenes and responded under two circumstances, relaxed and threat conditions. The threat condition was created when they "accidentally" overhead a conversation in the next room between the experimenter and another boy.

This prepared conversation led the subject to believe he would soon have to do a task with this other boy who disliked both him and the experimenter and that this boy would likely get into a conflict with the subject. As expected, aggressive subjects were more likely to attribute hostile intent to the boys in the vignettes and to indicate more aggressive responses to perceived hostility. The hypothesis that hostile attributions would be exaggerated under conditions of threat was also supported. These findings are illustrated in Figure 8–5.

Biological Influences

The idea that antisocial and criminal behavior has strong biological roots has a long history. As early as the late-nineteenth century, the Italian physician Lombroso wrote of the "stigmata of degeneration." Law violators were described as a distinct physical type at birth with distinct physical features such as long ear lobes, fleshy and protruding lips,

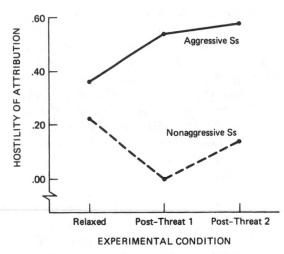

FIGURE 8–5 Attributions of hostility to ambiguous provocations by aggressive and nonaggressive boys under relaxed and threatening conditions.

From Dodge and Somberg (1987), *Child Development*, *58*, 213–224. Copyright „ The Society for Research in Child Development, Inc. By Permission.

and abundant wrinkles. Females were said to commit fewer crimes because their lesser intelligence and sexual coldness overcame their naturally jealous and vengeful nature (cited in Empey, 1978). This conceptualization had extensive impact on criminology and social policy for over a third of a century, but current-day scientists have accumulated sufficient evidence to reject it.

Genetics.   Contemporary versions of genetic contributions to antisocial behavior do, however, exist. Research findings are based primarily on adult samples. For example, by examining the extensive social records available in Denmark, Mednick and his colleagues evaluated rates of criminal behavior in the biological and adoptive relatives of adopted individuals with criminal records (Mednick, Gabrielli, and Hutchings, 1984). Higher rates of criminal behavior were found in biological relatives. Contemporary research recognizes, however, that linkages between biology and conduct disorders or criminality will be nowhere as direct as implied in earlier theories (cf. Susman, 1993).

There is little or no direct evidence regarding genetic contributions to childhood conduct problems and limited evidence regarding the role of genetics in adolescent delinquency. The findings suggest a lesser genetic component for adolescent delinquency than for adult criminal behavior. How might this difference be explained? The childhood-onset versus adolescent-limited distinction discussed earlier may be germane. Conduct disordered and delinquent behavior are quite common during adolescence, and in many cases do not persist into adulthood. It might, therefore, be reasonable to hypothesize an increased genetic component in antisocial behavior that persists from childhood into adult life (Rutter et al., 1990b).

However, even conclusions regarding the nature of genetic contributions to adult antisocial behavior need to be made with cau-

tion. Rosenthal's (1975) hypothesis that what is inherited are certain characteristics (for example, body build, sensitivity to alcohol) that make an individual prone to criminal behavior in response to environmental pressures seems reasonable. Most reviewers seem to agree that while biological influences may play some role, they inevitably interact in complex ways with environmental influences such as social conditions, family variables, and certain social learning experiences which are the major factors in determining etiology (e.g., Rutter et al., 1990b).

Psychophysiology.   Psychophysiological variables have also frequently been hypothesized to be related to antisocial behavior. A physiological need for stimulation has been hypothesized to account, in part, for antisocial personality and criminality. On the basis of the hypothesis that there is an optimal level of arousal for all human beings, it is reasoned that a person will seek to adjust his or her arousal level when it is either too high or too low. The antisocial personality is viewed as an individual with chronic underarousal who is thus motivated to provide additional arousal. Some support for this notions came from studies that found that the performances of delinquents and younger conduct disordered children were affected by the novelty and complexity of tasks (e.g., DeMyer-Gapin and Scott, 1977; Orris, 1969; Skrzypek, 1969; Whitehill, DeMyer-Gapin, and Scott, 1976). However, interpretation of these results as stimulation seeking is controversial (e.g., Rutter and Giller, 1984).

Findings of differences in heart rate and electrodermal responding (SCRs: skin conductance responses) also seem consistent with the hypothesis of low arousability. Raine and Venables's (1984) review of the literature found support for the existence of lower resting heart rate among antisocial youths. These findings are difficult to interpret, however, because of the relationship of resting heart rate with other variables such as SES, physical fitness, and larger body size. Differences between antisocial/conduct disordered youths and nonantisocial controls in SCRs to stimulation have also been reported (e.g., Borkovec, 1970; Delamater and Lahey, 1983; Schmidt, Solanto, and Bridger, 1985).

Quay (1993) hypothesizes a biological foundation for undersocialized aggressive conduct disorders (those characterized by poor peer and adult relations and aggression) that are severe and persistent. He suggests that a combination of heart rate and SCR findings, such as those described above, can provide a more specific hypothesis than general arousability. Based on Gray's (1987) theory of brain systems, he suggests that an overactive reward system (reflected in heart rate) combined with an underactive behavioral inhibition system (reflected in skin conductance) may be implicated in the genesis of undersocialized aggressive conduct disorders.

Neuropsychological deficits. The idea that brain dysfunction is among the causes of antisocial behavior is not new, but the scientific investigation of these influences is relatively recent. Moffitt's (1993b) review suggests that neuropsychological tests reveal deficits particularly in verbal and executive functions (e.g., sustaining attention, abstract reasoning, goal formation, planning, self-awareness). Neuropsychological measures were related to indications of poor outcomes such as early onset of conduct disorder, stability over time, aggressiveness, and the presence of attention-deficit hyperactivity disorder symptoms. Moffitt argues for further study of neuropsychological variables as causal factors for conduct disorder, and proposes a developmental model.

This model hypothesizes early differences in the infant nervous system that may be due to factors such as pre- or postnatal exposure to toxic agents. Compromised neurological functioning affects a variety of areas including temperament. This in turn *may* set in motion a chain of problematic parent-child interactions, particularly under conditions of family adversity. Conduct disorder is thus viewed as evolving from early individual differences in neuropsychological functioning that may be perpetuated and exacerbated by transactions with the social environment. It is also possible that early neurological damage may directly produce conduct disordered behavior rather than through the transaction mechanisms described by Moffitt (cf. Pennington and Bennetto, 1993). Neuropsychological conceptualizations of conduct disorder development may apply to only some conduct disordered youngsters. Refinements of theoretical concepts are needed, as is additional research that expands the populations studied and makes use of other methods of assessing neurological functioning such as electroencephalographic recording and brain imaging techniques.

Causes and Correlates of Delinquency

The term *delinquency* is primarily a legal rather than a psychological one. As a legal term it refers to a juvenile (usually under eighteen) who has committed an index crime or a status offense. An index crime is an act that would be illegal for adults as well as juveniles (e.g., theft, aggravated assault, rape, or murder). A status offense is an act that is illegal only for juveniles (e.g., truancy, association with "immoral" persons, violation of curfews, or incorrigibility). As Table 8–4 illustrates, there is little doubt that juvenile crime is a serious problem (U.S. Bureau of the Census, 1994). It is important, however, to make a distinction between delinquent behavior and what might be called official delinquency.

This distinction is important because some behaviors described as delinquent are quite common. Surveys based on adolescent

TABLE 8–4   Cases Disposed by Juvenile Courts for Youths Ages 10 to 17

Reasons for Referral	Year		
	1983	1987	1991
Violent offenses	55,000	67,000	103,000
Property offenses	451,000	498,000	577,000
Delinquency offenses (e.g., vandalism, drug law violations)	524,000	590,000	658,000

Source: U.S. Bureau of the Census, *Statistical Abstract of the United States: 1994* (114th edition). Washington, DC, 1994.

self-reports show that as many as 80 to 90 percent of youths report involvement in delinquent activity before reaching the age of eighteen. In contrast, if one examines official records (e.g., police, courts) a much lower rate of delinquency is suggested—15 to 35 percent for males and 2 to 14 percent for females. The estimate of rate varies with the stringency of the definition of "official record" (Moore and Arthur, 1989).

Thus, it would appear that delinquent behavior that is not as serious and does not persist over time is common (e.g., White, Moffitt, and Silva, 1989). Such behavior is not usually considered by professionals as an indication of persistent psychological or social difficulties, but is more likely to be thought of as within the normal range of adolescent experimentation. It is persistent or chronic delinquent behavior that is of greater concern. Indeed, it would appear that approximately half of official delinquents commit only one offense. The probability of future delinquent acts rises dramatically, however, with each additional offense, continuing into adulthood, and these recidivists account for a vast majority of juvenile offenses (Moore and Arthur, 1989). Chronic delinquency appears to start early. For example, Tolan (1987) reported that committing a first juvenile offense before the age of twelve was the single best predictor of the seriousness, number, and variety of future offenses.

It is important to recognize that whether an act by a juvenile gets classified as official delinquency may depend as much on the actions of others as it does on the youth's behavior. The norm violation must, of course, be noticed by someone and be reported to a law-enforcement official. A police officer can then arrest the youth or merely issue a warning. If the youth is arrested, he or she may or may not be brought to court. Once in juvenile court, only some individuals receive the legal designation of delinquent; others may be warned or released in the custody of their parents. Various definitions of delinquency can be used anywhere in this process. And then, of course, many individuals apparently commit offenses but don't get caught.

Subtypes of delinquency. Distinctions have been made between subtypes of delinquency. One that has received a great deal of attention is that between the socialized and unsocialized delinquent. This distinction is based on the results of factor analytic studies and other kinds of research, and on clinical observations (Quay, 1986b; Rutter and Giller, 1984). The *socialized*, or subcultural, subgroup describes youths who associate with a delinquent subgroup and accept the values of that subculture. This category is defined by characteristics such as (1) has bad companions, (2) steals in company with others, (3) belongs to a gang, or (4) stays away from home and school. These individuals are also described as experiencing little distress or psychopathology, and little difficulty in relating to peers.

The second category, *unsocialized,* or psychopathic, applies to delinquents who do not seem to be part of a delinquent subgroup. Furthermore, this subcategory is often thought to distinguish a form of delinquency in which emotional disturbance is present. Delinquent behavior in this unsocialized category is thought to develop from disturbances characterized by the conduct disorder—externalizing dimension described earlier.

Another subgroup of emotionally disturbed delinquents has also been described by some workers. Delinquency in this *disturbed-neurotic* group is thought to be related to the anxiety-withdrawal, internalizing dimension of behavior problems.

Although many of the causes and correlates described above for conduct-disordered behavior are also relevant to delinquency, other considerations such as the community and the larger social environment are particularly salient to juvenile delinquency.

Issues of definition and methodology can readily be seen when one examines the research on correlates of delinquency. Official records often indicate greater delinquency among lower-class and minority youths and boys. However, confidential reports of behavior by the youths themselves are less likely to show these differences (Moore and Arthur, 1989). This finding led some to conclude that reported differences in rates of delinquency based on social class, race, and gender were due to selection of certain groups for prosecution. Subsequent reviews, however, suggest that such bias is not as strong as originally proposed (e.g., Moore and Arthur, 1989; Rutter and Giller, 1984; West, 1985). Self-report studies may have given too much weight to minor and occasional misbehavior, which may be quite widespread. If one compares youths who admit to more serious and frequent misconduct to those who are convicted delinquents, the populations emerge as alike on the variables studied.

These findings suggest that while it is likely that certain advantaged youngsters probably do avoid the legal designation of delinquent, this in and of itself is probably not sufficient to explain differences in delinquency among certain social groups. Real associations between delinquency and social class, for example, probably do exist. They are, however, probably more moderate than was once contended.

What else do we know about the correlates of serious delinquency? They are much the same as those described earlier in the chapter as related to conduct disorders in younger children. Indeed, as we have already seen, early evidence of antisocial and aggressive behavior is one of the best predictors of later delinquency. This continuity of antisocial behavior, at least as defined by convictions for legal offenses, seems to reach its peak in adolescence and early adulthood and then to rapidly decrease between the ages of twenty to twenty-five. However, for a minority of delinquents, a criminal pattern does continue into adulthood. Indeed, individuals with adult criminal records, but no history of juvenile offenses, are rare. The identification of this persistent antisocial subgroup is of obvious importance. A number of studies suggest that the earlier existence of the cluster of aggressive and antisocial behaviors described for conduct disordered children coupled with parental criminality, ineffective supervision, and living in a "delinquent" neighborhood are predictive of belonging to this subgroup.

While the majority of efforts have focused on identifying influences associated with later delinquency and criminality, another perspective is possible. Not all individuals high on these risk factors become delinquents. This has led to a search for protective factors. Rutter and Giller's (1984) review suggested a number of potential protective influences—peer groups, employment, marriage, changed environmental circumstances, one good relationship, compensatory good experiences, and the existence of coping mechanisms. Furthermore, interactive effects may be important. One can conceive of risk factors as stressors. It may take a number of stressors to achieve a negative outcome or the impact of a particular stressor may be greater if others are present. Perhaps, then, the absence of certain combinations of stressors serves as a protective factor.

THE USE OF ALCOHOL AND OTHER DRUGS

The use of illicit substances, once considered an adult problem, is now common among adolescents and preadolescents. In addition to concern regarding illegal drugs such as marijuana, cocaine/"crack", hallucinogens (e.g., LSD), and heroine, there is concern regarding abuse of "legal" substances. Alcohol, nicotine, psychoactive medications (e.g., stimulants, sedatives), over-the-counter medications (e.g., sleep and weight reduction aids), and inhalants (e.g., glue, paint thinner) are accessible and potentially harmful. They may also play a roll in starting a young person on a course of long-term and increased substance abuse (Bailey, 1989).

Alcohol is the most commonly used drug among all age groups, including the young (National Institute of Drug Abuse, 1992). Reports suggest that the use of other drugs occurs together with the use of alcohol. Thus, much of the information that we have addresses both alcohol and other drugs.

What constitutes misuse or abuse? One extreme definition views any use of alcohol by a minor as abuse since such use is illegal. Less extreme and more prevalent are definitions that address drinking pattern and related negative consequences (e.g., difficulties with school, legal authorities, peers or family).

A variety of theories have been offered to explain the origins and maintenance of alcohol abuse (Holden, Moncher, and Schinke, 1990; Maisto and Carey, 1985). No single explanation has received clear acceptance, however.

One variety of explanation views adolescence as a period of transition (e.g., Jessor and Jessor, 1977). Certain behaviors mark this transition. Use of alcohol is an example of such a behavior since it is deemed appropriate for adults but not for adolescents. Individual differences and environmental variables are assumed to affect the rate at which an individual makes the transition to adulthood and thereby the age of onset of these behaviors. This transitional notion is consistent with findings that not all adolescents who are problem drinkers abuse alcohol as adults.

Social learning explanations of alcohol or other substance abuse emphasize exposure and consequences. Exposure to others who drink or abstain is assumed to not only provide an impetus toward certain behaviors, but to influence attitudes toward drinking. At greatest risk is the child of an alcoholic or other substance abuser (Bailey, 1989). The anticipation of positive or negative consequences for drinking is also a central aspect of such explanations.

The importance of teenagers' expectancy regarding the effects of alcohol is illustrated in a study of the development of drinking behavior (Smith and Goldman, 1994; Smith et al., 1995). Over a two-year period during which many of the youngsters first began to drink, expectations that drinking would facilitate social interactions predicted initiation into drinking. Those who expected social facilitation also drank more over the two-year period, and future expectations re-

Association with a peer group that supports the use of alcohol and other drugs is clearly a contributing influence to the development of substance use and abuse.

garding the effects of drinking were not reduced, but rather became more positive.

Kandel (1982), who also emphasizes socialization influences, draws on longitudinal studies to posit a developmental sequence. The use of legal drugs such as alcohol and tobacco precede the use of illicit drugs. It is virtually never the case that a nonuser goes directly to the use of illegal drugs. At least four distinct developmental stages in adolescent drug use have been identified: (1) beer or wine; (2) cigarettes or hard liquor, (3) marijuana, and (4) other illicit drugs. It has been suggested that problem drinking may be another stage that occurs between marijuana use and the use of other illicit drugs.

Participation in one stage does not necessarily mean that the young person will progress to the next stage. Only a subgroup at each stage progresses to the next level of use. However, it does appear that the earlier the youngster begins one stage, the greater is the likelihood of other drug use (Windle,

1990). Thus, the earlier that legal drugs are used, the greater the likelihood of illicit drug use (Kandel and Yamaguchi, 1993). Findings that alcohol and drug use are beginning early, even before the teenage years (e.g., Huizinga, Loeber, and Thornberry, 1993), are thus particularly disturbing. Also, heavier use at any stage seems to be associated with "progress" to the next stage.

There is no single factor that can easily explain which youths start or stay on this path. Explanations must include a variety of variables—biological, psychological, and social—that affect development over time (Morrison and Smith, 1987; Newcomb, Maddahian, and Bentler, 1986). However, early conduct problems are associated with later substance use, regardless of other variables (Lynskey and Fergusson, 1995). In addition, high rates of delinquency, sexual intercourse, and pregnancy are found to occur with substance use (Huizinga et al., 1993). Thus, prevention and treatment programs for substance use need to address multiple influences, be aware of developmental issues, and be comprehensive in scope.

TREATMENT OF CONDUCT DISORDERED BEHAVIOR

Parent Training

A variety of parent training programs have been implemented, and studies evaluating these interventions indicate that parent training is among the most successful approaches to reducing antisocial and aggressive behaviors in youth (Dumas, 1989; Kazdin, 1993c). One example comes from work on noncompliant behavior.

Forehand and his colleagues developed a treatment program for noncompliant children (four to seven years old) and their families (Forehand and McMahon, 1981). Parents are taught to give direct, concise commands (alpha commands), allow the child sufficient time to comply, reward compliance with contingent attention, and apply negative contingencies to noncompliance. The effectiveness of this program has been investigated in a number of studies and behavioral improvement has been shown to occur (McMahon and Wells, 1989). Forehand and his colleagues have also demonstrated that following treatment, parents of clinic children perceived their offspring to be as well adjusted as did parents of nonclinic children (Forehand, Wells, and Griest, 1980). Successful treatment of noncompliance also seems to reduce other problem behaviors such as tantrums, aggression, and crying (Wells, Forehand, and Griest, 1980). In addition, untreated siblings increase their compliance, and it seems likely that this is due, at least in part, to the mother's use of her improved skills with the untreated child (Humphreys et al., 1978). Finally, research demonstrates that training in a variety of tasks enhances generalization across a range of situations and from clinic to home (Powers and Roberts, 1995).

There are ethical issues involved in reducing noncompliance in children. Compliance is not always a positive trait, and the child's ability to say "no" to certain requests is something that seems desirable to either train or retain. In this regard it is important to assure that parents do not expect 100 percent compliance. This is neither the norm nor desirable in our society. A quiet, docile child should not be the treatment goal.

As we have seen, Patterson's conceptualization of the development of antisocial behavior evolved in the context of treating these children and their families. The importance of parenting skills in Patterson's formulation led to the development of a treatment program that focused on improving these skills (cf., Patterson et al., 1975; Patterson et al., 1992). Patterson's program is another illustration of the social-learning approach. The program teaches parents to pinpoint problems, to observe and record behavior, to more effectively use social and nonsocial reinforcers for appropriate or prosocial behavior, and to more effectively withdraw reinforcers for undesirable behavior. Families can be introduced to these procedures by studying a programmed text (Patterson, 1975, 1976a). Each family also attends clinic and home sessions and has regular phone contact with a therapist, who helps develop interventions for particular targeted behaviors and who models desired parenting skills. Problematic behaviors in the school setting are also targeted, and interventions involve both the parents and school personnel. Active treatment is terminated when both the therapist and family believe that a sufficient number of problematic behaviors have ceased, appropriate behavior has stabilized, overall family functioning has become more positive, and the parents have become able to handle additional problems with little, if any, assistance (Patterson, Chamberlain, and Reid, 1982).

Other programs that involve training of parenting skills have also been successful in working with families of conduct-disordered children. However, treatment is not always effective (Dumas, 1989; Kazdin, 1993c). Families who are socioeconomically disadvantaged and isolated appear to do less well. Parents who show significant improvement in parenting skills may have difficulty in maintaining them in the face of multiple problems and stresses. Parental personal (e.g., depression) and marital difficulties may also interfere with the successful completion of treatment. It would appear that the effectiveness of parent training can be enhanced by providing parents with help for their personal or marital difficulties (Dadds, Schwartz, and Sanders, 1987; Griest et al., 1982).

It does, indeed, seem that modification of problematic parenting skills can serve as the primary mechanism for change. It should be noted, however, that even those who acknowledge the success of such interventions do not necessarily agree on the processes that account for dysfunctional family interactions (cf. Robinson, 1985; Wahler and Dumas, 1989). The success of a particular treatment does not prove the theory that served to generate it.

Social Problem-Solving Skills Training

Parent training approaches focus on family aspects of conduct disordered behavior. Other treatments focus more specifically on aspects of the child's functioning. Among these interventions are those that derive from the interpersonal and social-cognitive aspects of conduct disordered behavior described above. They address the processes involved in the social-cognitive deficiencies and distortions among conduct-disordered youngsters (Kazdin, 1993c; Kendall and Panichelli-Mindel, 1995). In a step-by-step approach, these treatments, through games, academic activities, and stories, make use of structured tasks to teach cognitive problem-solving skills and increasingly apply these skills to real-life situations. Treatment usually combines several different procedures

including modeling and practice, role playing, and consequences for the skills displayed. These treatments are effective, but there are questions regarding the factors that contribute to obtained changes. The effectiveness for youngsters of different ages is also unclear. Also, even when improvement occurs, do those who are treated fall within the range of age appropriate normative functioning by the end of treatment (Kazdin, 1993c; Kendall and Panichelli-Mindel, 1995)?

Kazdin, Siegel, and Bass (1992) compared three different interventions applied to youngsters ages seven through thirteen referred for severe antisocial behavior: a cognitive problem-solving skills treatment (PSST), like those described above, a parent management training (PMT) modeled after Patterson's work, and a combined PSST plus PMT condition. Both the PSST and PMT conditions lead to significant improvements in functioning at home, at school, and in the community both immediately after treatment and at a one-year follow-up. The combined treatments, however, had significantly greater therapeutic effect than either treatment alone on the youngsters' functioning and on parental stress and functioning. In addition, the combined treatments resulted in a greater proportion of the youngsters falling within normative levels of functioning. These findings suggest the value of interventions that address the multiple influences operating in conduct disordered youth and their families. Knowing which treatments or combinations of treatments will be effective for which youngsters and families, however, remains a considerable challenge (cf. Kazdin, 1995).

Treatment of Delinquency

As some observers have noted, interventions for youthful offenders probably depend as much or more on prevailing social and political attitudes as they do on research evidence. Sheldrick (1985) has illustrated the history of approaches to the problem in Britain. Until the middle 1800s child and adult offenders were treated equivalently under British law. Children were hanged for theft in the eighteenth century. Those who were not dealt with in this manner served sentences in harsh and brutal prisons or were sentenced to be sent to Australia. It was not until the 1900s that children were treated distinctly from adults, and the concept of punishment was supplemented with the notion of reform. Parallel developments can be seen in the United States.

Beginning in the 1970s changes in attitudes seem to have occurred again with the questioning of the value of a treatment orientation. The relative value of punishment versus a therapeutic orientation remains an issue of much debate. The current ambiguity as to whether delinquency is a homogeneous phenomenon, or how to classify it into different types, along with the recognition that only a small proportion of offenders will continue on with a delinquent/criminal career, make the issues even more complex.

Conclusions regarding optimal treatment are difficult to draw due to methodological issues and a lack of consistent findings (e.g., Kazdin, 1987; Mulvey, Arthur, and Reppucci, 1993; Tolan and Guerra, 1994). However, several approaches are promising, and certain directions are suggested as potentially fruitful. Reducing juvenile delinquency includes many facets. Alterations in the operation of the legal and policing system are certainly part of such efforts. Here we will concentrate on interventions that are likely to involve psychologists, psychiatrists, teachers, and similar professionals.

Family interventions. In general, the kinds of interventions that have been described as successful with younger conduct-disordered children, such as parent training, have been far less successful with adolescents and chronic juvenile delin-

quents (Kazdin, 1993c; McMahon and Wells, 1989). In part it may be that these interventions call for families who are willing and able to participate in a demanding and time-consuming change process. Many of the antisocial youths who have reached this point in the process may not have such families.

A treatment program for delinquents and their families, called functional family therapy, has been developed by Alexander and his colleagues (Alexander and Parsons, 1982; Morris, Alexander, and Waldron, 1988). This program integrates behavioral-social learning, cognitive-behavioral and family systems perspectives. The problem behavior of the child is assumed to serve a function—it is the only way that some of the interpersonal functions of the family can be met. Treatment focuses on the interpersonal processes of the family system. The goals of therapy are to improve the communication skills of families; modify cognitive sets, expectations, attitudes, and affective reactions; and establish new interpretations and meanings of behavior. Evidence supporting this approach has been reported (Alexander, 1973; Alexander and Parsons, 1973; Alexander et al., 1976; Alexander et al., 1989).

Therapists employ a variety of techniques: modeling, prompting, shaping and rehearsing effective communication skills, and feedback and reinforcement for positive changes. In addition, contracts are created to establish reciprocal patterns of positive reinforcement that may have broken down or that rarely existed in these families. For example, a contract regarding a privilege for a certain family member also specifies that person's responsibilities for securing those privileges and provides bonuses for all parties for compliance with the contract.

The program has been demonstrated to significantly improve the interactions of families of status offenders who were arrested for running away or possessing alcohol. In addition to improved interactions, significantly lower rates of recidivism were also obtained six to eighteen months following treatment (Alexander and Parsons, 1973; Parsons and Alexander, 1973). Klein, Alexander, and Parsons (1977) also demonstrated a preventive impact for the treatment program. Examination of juvenile court records for siblings of initially referred delinquents indicated that siblings from this behavioral-family systems treatment had significantly lower rates of court referrals than siblings from control groups. Although this treatment has been primarily applied to families of status offenders, one report has replicated positive outcomes with families of youths who have committed more serious and repeated offenses (Barton et al., 1985).

The rationale for this approach and the treatment results described suggest that functional family therapy holds some promise. However, as reviewers have indicated, there is considerably less evidence available than for other approaches, such as the parent training/family approaches described above, and replications of these findings by other groups would be desirable (Dumas, 1989; Kazdin, 1990c). In addition, for more seriously delinquent youths, the question of the availability and ability of families to engage in this process of change can again be questioned.

Multisystemic therapy (MST; Henggeler and Borduin, 1990) uses treatment strategies derived from family systems therapy and from behavior therapy to treat serious juvenile offenders and their families. The approach seeks to preserve the family and to maintain the youths in their homes. MST addresses not only the family system, but skills of the offender and extrafamilial influences such as peers, school, and neighborhood. Family sessions are conducted in the home and community settings and are flexible and individualized for each family.

Henggeler, Melton, and Smith (1992) report on a comparison of MST to the usual services offered by a Department of Youth Services to serious juvenile offenders and their families. These youths were viewed as at imminent risk for out-of-home placement. They averaged 3.5 previous arrests, 54 percent had at least one arrest for a violent crime, and 71 percent had been incarcerated previously for at least three weeks. The findings of this study (illustrated in Figure 8–6) indicate that MSI was significantly more effective than the usual services in terms of arrests and weeks in incarceration assessed at fifty-nine weeks postreferral as well as in terms of self-reported delinquency scores at post-treatment. In addition, families receiving the MST intervention reported increased family cohesion, whereas reported cohesion decreased in the other families. Also a composite measure showed that aggression with peers decreased for MST youths, but remained the same for the youths receiving usual services. Several other reports by Henggeler and his colleagues suggest the usefulness of MST with a variety of populations and suggest the long-term effectiveness of this approach (Borduin, 1994).

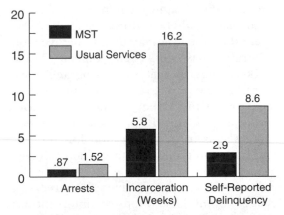

FIGURE 8–6 A Comparison of Multisystematic Therapy (MST) to Usual Services for Serious Juvenile Offenders.

Adapted from Henggeler, Melton, and Smith, 1992.

Institutional and community-based programs. Institutionalization might be considered a traditional and perhaps obvious approach to intervention with delinquents. Reform schools, training schools, and detention centers may include some therapeutic, educational, or rehabilitative programming or may only provide custodial care. Evidence that incarceration reduces recidivism has not been encouraging (Griffin and Griffin, 1978; Mulvey et al., 1993). It is likely that persistence of appropriate behavior upon release has as much or more to do with the environment to which the youth returns as it does with the nature of institutional programming. Furthermore, placing youths in such institutions may expose them to a pervasive and sophisticated delinquent subculture in which deviant behaviors may be learned and reinforced. These concerns and the success of some community-based programs have led to attempts to deal with delinquency outside of institutional programs.

One approach has been labeled "diversion" (Lemert, 1971). The goal is to divert youthful offenders away from the juvenile justice system and to provide services for them through a variety of different agencies (for example, educational, job training). It was hoped that by providing adequate skills and avoiding stigmatization and labeling, recidivism would be reduced. Some have argued that the original intent of diversion programs has not been fulfilled. Some workers suggest that such programs have increased the numbers of youths involved in legal processing. Others, however, see more promise in such an approach and indeed there seems to be justification for minimal and community-based intervention (Mulvey et al., 1993). Given that a large number of delinquents are not destined for careers of crime, even less intensive interventions would appear to be the best strategy for first or minor offenses. However, it must be recognized that some portion of youthful offenders will require additional intervention.

In such cases, community-based programs that remove the youth from the juvenile justice system seem recommended.

Davidson and his colleagues examination of treatment alternatives is an example of findings that support such a conclusion (Davidson and Basta, 1989). In one investigation several different forms of intervention were provided to 213 male juvenile offenders averaging 14.2 years of age. Youths were randomly assigned to treatments that differed in content; however, all had a college student volunteer who worked with them six to eight hours per week in the community. The various treatment conditions that took place *entirely* outside the juvenile justice system did not differ in terms of their effectiveness and resulted in lower rates of recidivism than a control group of youths not give treatment but routinely processed by the court. Treatment with a juvenile justice system component, however, did not result in lower recidivism than this nontreated control group. The results of this intervention program have been replicated in other locations and using other kinds of volunteers and paid staff (Davidson and Basta, 1989). For example, Figure 8–7 illustrates the lower rates of recidivism achieved by youths working with paid project staff in the Adolescent Diversion Project as compared to those processed through juvenile court and those who were simply released to their parents.

The search for effective alternatives to institutionalization has led to several other approaches. Three of the most popular community-based services are intensive probation supervision, restitution, and wilderness programs. *Intensive probation supervision* involves more frequent contact (several times per week versus the usual once or twice per month) between the probation officer and the delinquent youth and more intensive involvement with the youth's family and other services (e.g., job training). *Restitution* requires the youth to pay money or to

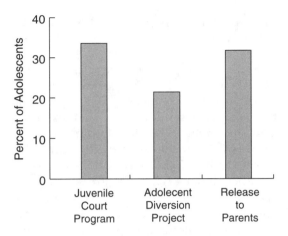

FIGURE 8–7 Percentage of adolescents having one or more new juvenile court appearances during the treatment period and one-year follow-up for each intervention.

Adapted from Davidson and Basta, 1989.

perform some service for the victim or the community. *Wilderness* approaches (e.g., Outward Bound and Homeward Bound) utilize the challenges presented by a wilderness setting to promote individual development and group cooperation. The effectiveness of these various programs has not been clearly established (Borduin, 1994).

The Teaching Family Model (TFM) developed at Achievement Place is an oft-cited example of a community-based program for delinquent youth and an example of many behaviorally based (largely operant) interventions. Achievement Place is a homestyle residential treatment program begun in 1967 by the faculty and students of the Department of Human Development at the University of Kansas (Fixsen, Wolf, and Phillips, 1973; Phillips, 1968). Adolescents who have legally been declared delinquent or are dependent neglect cases live in a house with two trained teaching parents. The youths attend school during the day and also have regular work responsibilities. The academic problems, aggression, and other norm-violating behaviors exhibited by these adolescents are viewed as an expression of failures of past environments to teach appropriate behaviors. Accordingly, these deficits are corrected through modeling, practice, instruction, and feedback. The program centers on a token economy in which points and praise are gained for appropriate behaviors and lost for inappropriate behaviors. Points can be used to purchase a variety of privileges that are otherwise unavailable. If a resident meets a certain level of performance, the right to go on a merit system and thus avoid the point system may be purchased. This is seen as providing a transition to usual sources of natural reinforcement and feedback, such as praise, status, and satisfaction. The goal is to gradually transfer a youngster who is able to perform adequately on merit to his or her natural home. Teaching-parents help the natural parents or guardians structure a program to maintain gains made at Achievement Place.

One of the outstanding features of the TFM approach is the large quantity of research the program has produced (cf. Willner et al., 1978). Numerous single-subject design experiments have evaluated the components of the program, thereby suggesting cause-and-effect relationships. The effectiveness of TFM has been evaluated by both its developers and independent investigators (Kirigin et al., 1982; Weinrott, Jones, and Howard, 1982). These evaluations suggest that the TFM approach is more effective than comparison programs while the adolescents are involved in the group home setting. However, once they leave this setting differences disappear.

Difficulties in transitions back to the youths' own families and long-term effectiveness are common in all interventions with delinquent populations. Given this consideration, the developers of TFM have suggested a "long-term supportive family model" in which specially trained foster parents would provide care for a single adolescent into early adulthood (Wolf, Braukmann, and Ramp, 1987).

There seems to be general consensus that current services are limited in their effectiveness (cf. Borduin, 1994; Henggeler, 1994). Interventions with antisocial youth are likely to require the cooperation of multiple human service agencies. Often the coordination of such services is difficult to achieve and individualizing such efforts to fit the needs of youngsters and their families is even more challenging. Recent approaches known as *individualized care* or *wraparound services* employ interdisciplinary teams to develop a plan that is both individualized and comprehensive (Burchard and Clark, 1990; Borduin, 1994). Also the logic of early intervention and prevention is compelling, and here too programs that include multiple components that address the child, family, and school are most likely to be effective (Conduct Problems Prevention Research Group, 1992).

The difficulties and lack of success achieved in treating conduct disordered adolescents has also led some to suggest a change in the way in which conduct disorders are conceputalized. The suggestion is that the disorder be viewed as "social disability" (Wolf et al., 1987) or as analogous to a chronic physical disease such as diabetes (Kazdin, 1987; Mulvey et al., 1993). These kinds of models suggest not single and short-term treatments, but multiple interventions throughout the child's life—perhaps into early adulthood.

The multidetermined nature of antisocial behavior and the potential stability of conduct-disordered behavior, certainly suggest early, multifaceted, flexible, and ongoing interventions.

SUMMARY

Aggression, oppositional, and other antisocial behaviors are among the most common problems among referred youngsters as well as in the general population. Boys typically exhibit these behaviors more often than do girls.

Empirical approaches have consistently identified a syndrome of aggressive, oppositional, antisocial behaviors. This syndrome has been labeled undercontrolled, externalizing, or conduct disorder. Two narrow syndromes have been described within this broad syndrome and have been designated as either undersocialized aggressive and socialized aggressive or as aggressive behavior and delinquent behavior. Other ways of distinguishing among groupings of conduct-disordered behavior, such as overt versus covert, have also been suggested.

DSM-IV contains a grouping of disorders that includes Oppositional Defiant Disorder (ODD) and Conduct Disorder (CD) along with Attention-Deficit Hyperactivity Disorder. ODD is described as a pattern of negativistic, hostile, and defiant behavior. CD is described as a repetitive and persistent pattern of behavior that violates the basic rights of others and societal norms. Two subtypes, childhood onset and adolescent onset, are indicated.

Conduct disordered behavior has been conceptualized in terms of developmental progressions or paths. There are a number of attributes that describe an individual's progression along a developmental path. Age of onset is probably the most mentioned aspect. An adolescent onset path is the most common and antisocial behavior among such youngsters is less likely to persist beyond adolescence.

Pathways characterized by childhood onset are likely to involve more stability of conduct-disordered behavior and such youngsters are more likely to exhibit additional difficulties as well. Persistence of aggressive and antisocial behavior is noted by both clinicians and researchers.

Conduct-disordered behavior likely develops through a complex interaction of influences. A variety of influences have received attention including the learning of such behavior through imitation and the consequences such behavior receives. Family influences also occur through degree of parental involvement and parenting practices. The work of Patterson and his colleagues has contributed to our knowledge in this area. The parents' own psychological difficulties, marital discord, and extrafamilial/community influences are also noted. Characteristics of the youngster such as moral development, social information processing skills, and interpersonal problem-solving skills are also thought to contribute to the development of conduct-disordered behavior. Biological influences, such as genetics, psychophysiology, and neuropsychological deficits may also play a role.

As a legal term, delinquency refers to juveniles who have committed a crime. Delinquent behavior that is not serious and does not persist over time is common. Persistent, chronic, delinquency is of greater concern. The use of alcohol and illegal drugs by youngsters is a particularly widespread concern.

A variety of interventions have been attempted with conduct-disordered youngsters. Parent training is among the most successful approaches. Family interventions and institutional and community-based programs are among the approaches to working with youthful offenders. Current services are probably of limited effectiveness. The development of long-term, individualized, and multifaceted interventions are recommended.

9

ATTENTION-DEFICIT HYPERACTIVITY DISORDER

He never sits still; he's always into something.
She won't pay attention to what I say.
He doesn't think before he acts.
In school, she's up and out of her seat in a flash.
He's not doing well in school, and is behind his
  peers.

These kinds of concerns, voiced by parents and teachers, are the main presenting problems for children who receive the diagnosis of Attention-Deficit Hyperactivity Disorder (ADHD).

Only a few disorders of youth garner as much public interest and are so surrounded by controversy as ADHD. Most of the general public has at least passing knowledge of the disorder, which is widely referred to as attention-deficit disorder or hyperactivity. These terms reflect the changing conceptualizing of the disorder. Controversy about ADHD has focused on both its nature and the pharmacological treatment that was widely introduced in the late 1960s. The issues of how best to view and treat the disorder still exist.

DIAGNOSTIC CRITERIA

What we now refer to as ADHD was first described in the mid-1800s. Early conceptualizations of ADHD emphasized overactivity or motor restlessness, and the terms *hyperkinesis, hyperkinetic reaction,* and *hyperkinetic syndrome* were variously applied (Barkley, 1989). However, several other behavioral problems were recognized as being associated with hyperactivity, especially attention deficits and impulsivity. In time, attention deficits took center stage and hyperactivity was downgraded.

This shift in conceptualization was so important that the disorder was referred to in DSM-III (1980) as attention deficit disorder with hyperactivity (ADDH), or without hyperactivity. Clearly, attention problems had become the core for diagnosis. In DSM-III-R (1987), the disorder was relabeled Attention-Deficit Hyperactivity Disorder (ADHD), and the category of attention deficit without hyperactivity was effectively dropped. ADHD echoed the past by again giving greater recognition to hyperactivity. Children were diagnosed on the basis of displaying eight of fourteen behaviors, which could be different mixes of inattention, hyperactivity, and impulsivity.

DSM-IV (1994) brought further change and a slightly different label: Attention-Deficit/Hyperactivity Disorder. The DSM-IV criteria are shown in Table 9–1. Notably new is that people can be placed into three categories based on displaying predominantly at-

208

TABLE 9–1 DSM-IV Criteria for Attention-Deficit/Hyperactivity Disorder

A. Either (1) or (2):

    (1) six or more symptoms of **inattention** for at least 6 months, maladaptive and inconsistent with developmental level:

        (a) fails to attend to details or makes careless mistakes in schoolwork or other activities
        (b) difficulty in sustaining attention
        (c) does not seem to listen when spoken to
        (d) does not follow through on instructions or duties
        (e) difficulty organizing tasks and activities
        (f) avoids, dislikes tasks requiring sustained mental effort
        (g) often loses things necessary for tasks or activities
        (h) distracted by extraneous stimuli
        (i) forgetful in daily activities

    (2) six or more symptoms of **hyperactivity-impulsivity** for at least 6 months, maladaptive and inconsistent with developmental level:

        hyperactivity
        (a) fidgets with hands or feet or squirms
        (b) leaves seat inappropriately
        (c) runs about or climbs inappropriately (in adolescents or adults, may only be feelings of restlessness)
        (d) difficulty playing quietly or in quiet activities
        (e) often "on the go" as if "driven by a motor"
        (f) talks incessantly
        impulsivity
        (a) blurts out answers before questions completed
        (b) difficulty awaiting turn
        (c) interrupts or intrudes on others

B. Symptoms present before age 7

C. Impairment present in 2 or more settings

D. Clear evidence of significant impairment in social, academic, or occupational functioning

ADHD Combined Type: Criteria A1 and A2 are met
ADHD Predominantly Inattentive Type: Criteria A1 met
ADHD Predominantly Hyperactive-Impulsive Type: Criteria A2 met

Adapted and reprinted with permission from the *Diagnostic and Statistical Manual of Mental Disorders, Fourth Edition.* Copyright 1994, American Psychiatric Association.

tention deficits, predominantly hyperactivity-impulsivity, or both attention deficits and hyperactivity-impulsivity. There is research support for the validity and usefulness of this subgrouping (Bauermeister et al., 1995; Lahey and Carlson, 1991; Lahey et al., 1994).

The diagnosis demands onset before age seven and the display of symptoms for at least six months. Because the criterion behaviors appear to some degree in normal children and may vary with developmental level, a diagnosis is given only when symptoms are at odds with developmental level.

In addition, the youngster's functioning must be judged as somewhat maladaptive in at least two settings (e.g., home and school); that is, ADHD must be at least somewhat pervasive over settings. The requirement of pervasiveness is also new in DSM-IV and merits further comment.

Behavioral manifestations of ADHD depend somewhat on the settings in which they are observed. Some children appear pervasively inattentive, hyperactive, and impulsive with parents, teachers, or peers. Others appear to show disturbed behavior in only one setting and are said to show situational ADHD. Evidence exists that pervasiveness is linked to severity of the disorder and other correlates. The ICD diagnostic system has long required that symptoms be displayed pervasively; thus, DSM and ICD are now in agreement on this point. Nevertheless, concern is expressed that the requirement of pervasiveness may fail to identify cases with relatively mild symptoms (August and Garfinkel, 1993).

Despite the modifications of labels and diagnostic criteria over the last few decades, there has been wide agreement that attention deficits, hyperactivity, and impulsivity are primary in ADHD. In the following sections we will discuss these primary difficulties and then examine other problems often associated with the syndrome. In general, we will use the labels attention-deficit hyperactivity disorder (ADHD) or hyperactivity to refer to youth displaying these problems.

PRIMARY MANIFESTATIONS

Attention Deficits

The attention problems of ADHD show up in various ways. Parents report that the children, compared to most of their peers, skip rapidly from one activity to another and do not pay attention to what is said to them. Teachers complain of lack of concentration, "off-task" behavior, and inattention to directions. A puzzling aspect of these reports is that children who are described in some situations as unable to concentrate or pay attention are reported in other situations as sitting for hours playing a game, drawing, or building with blocks (Weiss, 1991). This suggests that attention can be focused and sustained when the child is interested or otherwise motivated. Inattention seems to be a problem mostly in repetitive, boring, routine situations.

Although the reports of adults provide reasonably good global descriptions of ADHD, only controlled research can elucidate the nature of inattention. In the laboratory, comparisons of children with ADHD and control subjects reveal that the former do less well on many tasks that demand attention. Such poor cognitive performance could be due to other variables, however, such as motivation or comprehension. To isolate attention itself, researchers have manipulated attention and then examined the specific effects. It is recognized that attention has several dimensions, and measurement has been problematic.

One dimension is selective attention, that is, the ability to attend to relevant environmental stimuli or ignore irrelevant stimuli. Some studies indicate that the introduction of irrelevant stimuli does distract children with ADHD, especially if the irrelevant stimuli are novel or salient and the tasks boring, distasteful, or difficult (Douglas, 1983). Other studies indicate little distractibility or no more than shown by normal children. On balance, the research does not strongly indicate a deficit in selective attention (Taylor, 1994; Whalen, 1989). Moreover, attempts to alleviate ADHD by placing children in environments that restrict irrelevant stimuli do not appear effective. In some cases, irrelevant stimuli even enhance performance (van der Meere and Sergeant, 1988).

Sustained attention has also been extensively studied. Sustained attention refers to paying attention to a task over a period of time. Off-task behavior in school and at home could reflect problems in sustaining attention. In the laboratory, sustained attention often has been tested with a continuous performance test (CPT). Although several versions exist, the fundamental task is for the person to push a button to identify a target stimulus, such as a letter when it appears in a series of letters consecutively projected on a screen. Errors can be made by not reacting to the target (which shows inattention or lack of vigilance) and by reacting to nontarget stimuli (which may show inattention or impulsivity). Children with ADHD often make more of both errors and are slower than normal children and children with other diagnoses (Douglas, 1983; Barkley, 1990). However, a true deficit in sustained attention would lead to a worsening of performance as the length of the task increases. Research does not consistently show this and thus does not provide strong evidence for a sustained attention deficit (Corkum and Siegel, 1993; van der Meere, Wekking, and Sergeant, 1991).

In fact, researchers have not been able to identify a specific attention deficit in ADHD. This partly accounts for a growing doubt that inattention is the best way to describe the problems of ADHD. We will return to this issue later.

Activity Problems

The motor problems of ADHD involve both excess and inappropriate activity. Children with ADHD often are described as always on the run, restless, fidgety, and unable to sit still. These children squirm, wiggle, tap their fingers, and elbow their classmates (Greenhill, 1991; Whalen, 1989). All too often they have minor mishaps, such as spilling drinks and knocking over objects, as well as more serious accidents that result in bodily harm. The quality of the motion often seems different from ordinary activity by being excessively energetic, haphazard, disorganized, and lacking in goals. Hyperactive children appear to have difficulty in regulating their actions according to the wishes of others or the demands of the particular situation.

Much of the information about activity problems comes from parent and teacher reports. More objective assessment can be made with direct observations and with small devices worn by the child (actometers, pedometers) that measure movement. These objective devices demonstrate the excessive movement of children with ADHD. However, when multiple measures of activity are taken, they correlate with each other only modestly. In addition, considerable individual variation exists in activity problems, and hyperactivity also depends on the situation at hand.

Situational specificity was shown in a study that used a recording device to monitor motor activity continuously for one week (Porrino et al., 1983). Hyperactive boys were more active than controls overall, but especially during reading and mathematics in school, playing on the weekends, and sleeping. Figure 9–1 shows some of the results. Another investigation found that control children were less active in regular as compared to open-structure classrooms, but hyperactive children did not modulate their actions according to room structure (Jacob, O'Leary, and Rosenblad, 1978). In general, motor excess and restlessness are more likely in sedentary or highly structured situations, such as sitting in school and church, than in relaxed settings with fewer external demands (Greenhill, 1991).

Impulsivity

The third component of ADHD is impulsivity. The essence of impulsivity is a deficiency in inhibiting behavior, which appears as "acting without thinking." The child may jump in and try to solve a problem before figuring out the first step, heedlessly engage in dangerous behaviors, interrupt others, cut in line in front of others, or take short cuts when performing a task. The child seems unable to hold back, control behavior, and delay gratification. This kind of behavior, reported by parents and teachers and seen in objective observations, often

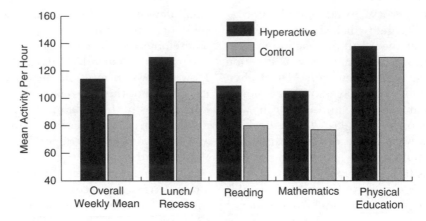

FIGURE 9–1   Activity scores over four days for twelve hyperactive and twelve control children. There were significant group differences in overall activity and during reading and mathematics.

Adapted from Porrino, L. J., Rapoport, J. L., Behar, D., Sceery, W., Ismond, D. R., & Bunney, W. E. (1983). A naturalistic assessment of the motor activity of hyperactive boys: I. Comparison with normal controls. *Archives of General Psychiatry, 40,* 681–687. Copyright 1983, American Medical Association. Reprinted by permission.

leads others to judge the child as careless, lazy, and rude (Barkley, 1990).

In the laboratory, the most common task for assessing impulsivity has been the Matching Familiar Figures Test (MFFT). Children are presented with pictures that vary slightly and are asked to select the one that best matches a standard picture. Relatively fast selection and errors in matching across sets of such pictures are taken as indicators of impulsivity. These indicators can discriminate ADHD, although not unfailingly (Whalen, 1989). Impulsivity has been tested in other ways. For example, Schachar and Logan (1990) used a stop-signal procedure. Upon hearing a signal, the individual is supposed to inhibit responding to a task. The investigators found that normal children achieve inhibition by second grade, and that pervasively hyperactive children do less well than normal and other diagnosed groups.

There are problems in measuring and conceptualizing impulsivity. It has been suggested that the MMFT may tap more gen-

eral cognitive functioning, and MFFT performance does correlate with intelligence. In addition, impulsivity correlates with activity level and appears not be an independent factor (Barkley, 1990).

How Best to Conceptualize ADHD

Despite an enormous amount of interest and investigation, ADHD is still somewhat of an enigma. While there is fundamental agreement about the primary difficulties of the disorder, there is less consensus about how to conceptualize them.

As we have already mentioned, there is evidence that attention deficits cluster together as one factor that can occur independently of a second factor comprised of both hyperactive and impulsive behaviors. Three types of disorders can be identified, that with predominant attention deficits, predominant hyperactive-impulsive behaviors, or both attention deficits and hyperactive-impulsive problems. These types differ in sex ratios, age, and impairment (Lahey et al., 1994). For example, a group of children with predominant attention deficits has been found to have a greater proportion of girls, be the oldest, and have more academic impairment. In contrast, a group with the combination of factors has been described as having more boys and more general impairment. It is findings such as these that support DSM-IV's new conceptualization of AD/HD. It should be noted, however, that children displaying the combination type or predominantly hyperactive-impulsive behavior have historically been considered "hyperactive" and by far most studied. It is thus these youth who are addressed in this chapter.

Even so, there are differing and changing opinions on how to best conceptualize the difficulties displayed by these children and adolescents. For example, the attention deficits of ADHD are increasingly viewed as involving higher-level cognitive processing rather than elementary attention deficits (Taylor, 1994). In one study, White and Sprague (1993) found that children with ADHD did less planning and less systematic comparison and analysis of stimuli on a matching task. Their behavior appears to have more to do with the regulation and allocating of attention, that is, with high-level cognition. Researchers continue to inquire into the processing difficulties manifested in ADHD (e.g., Leung and Connolly, 1994; Sonuga-Barke, Houlberg, and Hall, 1994).

ADHD is also increasingly described as a deficit in motivation and behavioral regulation. Sonuga-Barke (1994), for example, suggests that the motivation to minimize delay might explain many ADHD behaviors. That is, children with ADHD might have an aversion for delay and thus adopt an impulsive style that minimizes delay. Barkley (1990) and his colleagues have for some time viewed ADHD as a problem in motivation and behavioral regulation. They note that in typical development, behavior comes under the control of socially important stimuli such as the consequences of behavior, the requests and commands of other people, learned rules, the environmental setting, and the like. Thus, humans come to behave in socially expected and appropriate ways. According to Barkley, such control is inadequate in ADHD, especially when there is a need to inhibit behavior. An important aspect might be limited sensitivity to the consequences of behavior, as children with ADHD appear to need extraordinarily strong and salient reinforcers. Furthermore, as some have hypothesized, abnormally high brain thresholds for reinforcement or arousal may be involved. High reinforcement thresholds might explain why children with ADHD fail to pay attention, persist at tasks, or comply to others' directives, particularly when consequences are inconsistent or weak. High brain thresholds for arousal could result in the child seeking stimulation through heightened activity and inattention. Barkley's analysis emphasizes biologically based motivation deficits rather than attention or other cognitive deficits.

Although no specific consistently supported view of ADHD exists at this time, the ongoing research to understand the primary manifestations of ADHD is intensive.

The behaviors we have just discussed are central in ADHD, but persons with ADHD are reported to experience several additional difficulties, including more than their share of motor incoordination, language problems, somewhat lowered intelligence, learning problems, disruptive and disorderly conduct, lack of conscience, social problems, chronic health problems, depression, anxiety, and low self-esteem (Dulcan, 1989; DuPaul, Guevremont, and Barkley, 1991). These secondary difficulties are not unique to ADHD, of course, but they are of considerable clinical interest. Perhaps of greatest interest are the academic and social/conduct problems linked to ADHD. Since these secondary problems are widely reported, we will examine them more closely.

ASSOCIATED ACADEMIC AND LEARNING PROBLEMS

As a group, children with ADHD perform slightly lower on general intelligence tests than normal control subjects (Anastopoulos and Barkley, 1992). Many fall into the normal range, so perhaps deficits occur especially when hyperactivity is pervasive and there is nervous system dysfunction or specific learning problems (August and Garfinkel, 1989; Schachar, 1991). Intellectual impairment has been linked to hyperactivity in children as young as three years of age (Sonuga-Barke et al., 1994). However, the entire range of intelligence is found with ADHD, including giftedness (Barkley, 1990).

Academic failure is more striking than deficient intelligence, and is evidenced by achievement test scores, school grades, failure to get promoted in school, and placement in special education classes (Anastopoulos and Barkley, 1992; Dulcan, 1989). Children with ADHD often do not appear to achieve what they seem capable of learning. In one sample of boys in the United States, about 75 percent was underachieving in reading, spelling, and mathematics (Cantwell, 1986). More than one-third was performing a full grade level below their expected level in at least two academic subjects. In another sample, at least three times as many adolescents with ADHD had failed a grade compared to a normal group (Barkley, 1990). A large study of New Zealand children similarly indicated that 80 percent had various learning problems, with about one-half having difficulties in at least two areas (McGee and Share, 1988).

Due to academic failure and poorer performance than would be predicted from general intelligence, many children with ADHD are considered to have learning disabilities (LD). In fact, co-occurrence of ADHD and LD is widely reported in both clinic and epidemiologic studies (Flicek,

1992; Pennington, Groisser, and Welsh, 1993). Estimates of the percentage of ADHD children who have learning disabilities vary greatly depending on sampling, criteria for the two disorders, and other factors. In epidemiological studies a range of 9 to 11 percent has been reported; in clinic populations the range is much higher, perhaps 20 to 50 percent (Anastopoulos and Barkley, 1992; Robins, 1992). Children with both ADHD and LD show greater symptomatology and are at greater developmental risk.

Investigators are examining the cognitive functions that distinguish ADHD and LD. They are also trying to establish causal links between the two disorders. Several links are possible (McGee and Share, 1988; Pennington et al., 1993; Stevenson et al., 1993). As shown in Figure 9–2, the primary deficits of ADHD may interfere with learning to the degree that warrants diagnosis of LD. Or learning difficulties may create an inattentive, impulsive behavioral style that is diag-

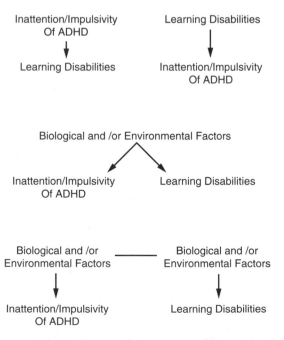

FIGURE 9–2 Possible links between ADHD and Learning Disabilities

nosed as ADHD. Alternatively, perhaps some common biological and/or environmental factors simultaneously but independently cause ADHD and LD. Still another explanation is that ADHD and learning disabilities have distinct causes that are correlated with each other. The relationship between these disorders could also be reciprocal in that they build on each other.

ASSOCIATED SOCIAL AND CONDUCT PROBLEMS

Misconduct and social problems are reported in high percentages of cases of ADHD. Such troublesome behavior may lead adults to seek professional help even more than the primary problems of the disorder.

How do children with ADHD actually behave that so upsets others? Whalen and Henker and their colleagues (1985; Buhrmester et al., 1992) recognize variation across these children but also suggest that as a group their behavior can be described as falling into four categories.

First, the children are bothersome, intractable, socially awkward, disruptive, noncompliant, and disagreeable. The annoying and inappropriate quality of their actions may seem unintentional, and the negative reactions of others sometimes take the child by surprise. Indeed, the child's intent may be altruistic, as in the case of a ten-year-old who, in trying to help a man in a wheelchair while balancing a carton of milk, succeeded in dribbling more and more milk on the man. Such an isolated incident would not in itself be disastrous, but children with ADHD all too often get in "trouble" in situations that they ought to be able to handle.

Second, these children have high social impact. They are talkative and socially busy; they often initiate social exchanges. Some interactions are clearly prosocial, as ADHD is not linked to diminished prosocial behav-

ior. However, high social activity may increase risk for negative interpersonal experiences. And it is likely that the social behavior of children with ADHD falls short in subtle ways with regard to style, content, and appropriateness.

Third, children with ADHD tend to be louder, faster, and more forceful than peers. Their vigor and intensity frequently is out of keeping with the social situation, social expectations, and the needs of others.

Fourth, many of the youngsters are highly aggressive, both verbally and physically. This puts them at risk for being disliked and being excluded from opportunities for social learning.

The social problems of children with ADHD appear related to how others judge them and interact with them. Other youngsters may view these children as troublesome, noisy, and unhappy; they tend to dislike and reject them (Flicek, 1992; Pope, Bierman, and Mumma, 1987). Parents and teachers tend to be more directive, controlling, and intrusive with ADHD children compared to normal children (Barkley, 1988a, 1990; Hechtman, 1991).

Given all these considerations, it is unsurprising that children with ADHD are often reported as oppositional and conduct disordered. Perhaps 65 percent of them qualify for the diagnosis of Oppositional Defiant Disorder (Barkley, Anastopoulos et al., 1992). Perhaps 20 to 30 percent qualify for the diagnosis of Conduct Disorder, and this figure rises for adolescents (August and Garfinkel, 1993; Barkley, 1990). These figures must be taken as rough indicators, however, as different rates of co-occurrence are reported depending on age and other factors. Nevertheless, we know that the rates are substantial. The similarity of ADHD, Oppositional Defiant Disorder, and Conduct Disorder is reflected in their being listed together in DSM-IV.

The overlap of these disorders is of notable interest. If the disorders are strongly associated, should they be considered distinct? Probably not, as epidemiologic and clinic research indicates that the disorders are distinct although highly correlated (e.g., Fergusson, Horwood, and Lloyd, 1991; Weiss, 1991). Despite some inconsistent findings, ADHD appears to be more strongly associated with cognitive impairment and neurodevelopmental abnormalities. Conduct problems appear more strongly related to adverse family factors and psychosocial disadvantage.

It is increasingly recognized that it is critical to examine subgroups of ADHD based on the presence or absence of conduct/oppositional behaviors. Important differences are emerging between the subgroups. Compared to ADHD alone, the combination of ADHD with other disruptive behaviors is generally more strongly related to parental antisocial behavior, marital conflict, maternal stress, and negative adolescent-parent communication and conflict (e.g., Barkley, Anastopoulos, et al., 1992). Moreover, children who display both sets of problems appear more disturbed, are more likely to be pervasively hyperactive, and are more likely to have continuing problems (McArdle, O'Brien, and Kolvin, 1995).

Questions have been raised about the causal link between ADHD and conduct problems, but further research is needed on this issue (Schachar and Tannock, 1995). There is some evidence that the hyperactivity and impulsivity of ADHD forecast conduct disorder (Loeber et al., 1995). Indeed, this might be expected because a criterion for ADHD demands impairment before age seven, whereas some manifestations of conduct problems are unlikely at an early age (e.g., breaking into someone's house, forcing someone into sexual activity). However, as we have already seen with ADHD and learning disabilities, overlapping problems might be linked in several ways. Furthermore, once an array of problems exist, they may interact with each other and other variables in complex ways.

PREVALENCE

The prevalence of attention-deficit hyperactivity disorder is frequently estimated at about 3 to 5 percent of the school-age population (APA, 1994). This figure is based on clinic cases. When parents and teachers provide data in population studies, prevalence is variable and reaches as high as 20 percent (August and Garfinkel, 1989; Taylor, 1994). The variation in the data can be accounted for by differences in populations, criteria, and measuring instruments. For example, when the criteria demand only situational ADHD, prevalence is higher than when pervasiveness is demanded. Data on the overall prevalence in adolescence is limited. However, a decline from childhood rates is apparent, especially for boys (Schaughency et al., 1994).

More boys than girls consistently receive the diagnosis of ADHD, with the ratio of perhaps four to nine boys to one girl (APA, 1994). The reason for the gender difference is unknown (James and Taylor, 1990; Taylor, 1994). It is possible that girls are underidentified, since adults appear more tolerant of hyperactivity in girls. Still, identified girls are actually less hyperactive than affected boys. ADHD in girls is at times described as somewhat different than in boys, for example, as more likely to involve neurodevelopmental delays in cognitive, language, and motor skills, which suggests brain damage. However, whether ADHD is different in boys and girls is not agreed on, and this is a topic that warrants research (Achenbach et al., 1995a; Schaughency et al., 1994).

There is evidence that ADHD is associated with low social class or psychosocial adversity (Rutter, 1989b). Moreover, cross-cultural variation can be striking. Differing clinical practices may partly account for this finding (Taylor, 1994). For example, the diagnosis of hyperactivity has been made more frequently in the United States than in the United Kingdom, probably due to differences in clinical criteria. When standard questionnaire ratings of behavior are employed, however, a difference is not found. Nevertheless, ratings in the United Kingdom and China showed that almost three times as many Chinese boys were identified. Upon closer examination it was revealed that the Chinese boys were actually more attentive and less active than the U.K. boys. Consider further a study in which clinicians from China, Indonesia, Japan, and the United States were asked to rate the behaviors of boys presented in video vignettes. Ratings of hyperactivity and disruptive behaviors were higher for the Chinese and Indonesian than for the Japanese and U.S. mental health workers (Tao, 1992). These findings strongly suggest that cultural expectations and values play a role in interpreting what is "abnormal".

ETIOLOGY

The search for causes of ADHD implicates several variables, many of which are biological or thought to affect biological functioning. However, no single factor completely explains ADHD (DuPaul et al., 1991). Most children with ADHD are normal with respect to any specific factor that has been implicated, and, conversely, many children who are positive for a factor do not display ADHD (Whalen, 1989).

Biological Functioning

Brain damage or injury was once considered the primary cause of hyperactivity. An association between brain damage in adults and various behavioral deficits had long been recognized (Bryan and Bryan, 1975). Research with children who had suffered from an epidemic of encephalitis after World War I linked this brain disease with behavioral problems, including inattention and hyperactivity (Kessler, 1980). Other causes of potential brain injury, such as birth trauma and head injury, were also linked to these problems (Barkley, 1990).

Soon investigators attributed behavioral disturbances such as these to brain damage without evidence that damage actually existed. For example, Kahn and Cohen (1934) attributed school problems (hyperactivity, distractibility, impulsivity, poor attention) to brain stem lesions (Satz and Fletcher, 1980). Strauss and Lehtinen (1947) suggested that distractibility or hyperactivity was a fundamental sign of brain injury (Barkley, 1990).

When it became evident that brain damage could not be identified in most children who showed these difficulties, it was assumed that some undetectable "minimal brain dysfunction" existed. By the late 1950s and early 1960s, this approach was criticized on the basis of being circular: Brain dysfunction can lead to certain problems, so the presence of these problems means the existence of brain dysfunction (Satz and Fletcher, 1980). Such circularity was viewed as misleading and inadequate, and the need for better empirical evidence was recognized. Theories of brain dysfunction subsequently became more closely tied to empirical evidence.

Over the years, several hypotheses about brain dysfunction have been proposed. One focuses on abnormalities of arousal-inhibitory processes, which might go hand in hand with hyperactivity and inattention (Ferguson and Pappas, 1979). Another proposes that immaturity of the nervous system underlies ADHD (Anastopoulos and Barkley, 1988). Although each hypothesis has some support, neither is sufficiently supported.

Brain structures and functioning. Various parts of the brain have been proposed as the site of dysfunction in ADHD. These include the hypothalamus, reticular activating system, limbic system, corpus callosum, and frontal lobes (Semrud-Clikeman et al., 1994; Zametkin and Rapoport, 1987). It is difficult to pinpoint particular brain areas that might be involved (Hechtman, 1991). The attention system itself involves several areas, and areas responsible for activity and motor response could well be involved. Imaging techniques now available to study the brain are expected to provide new understandings.

Of all brain structures, the frontal and frontal-limbic areas have been of special interest. Children with ADHD have been found to have decreased blood flow, glucose utilization, and EEG activation in the frontal lobes. Parents of ADHD children who themselves displayed symptoms of hyperactivity showed lowered metabolism in the frontal area (Hechtman, 1991; Taylor, 1994; Zametkin and Rapoport, 1986). In addition to these findings from direct brain measures, some neuropsychological tests indicate frontal lobe involvement (Barkley, Grodzinsky, and DuPaul, 1992). These tests indicate deficits in inhibiting motor responses, a function attributed to the frontal lobes and their connections to underlying areas.

Neurotransmitters. Investigators have tried to identify abnormalities in central nervous system neurotransmitters. Most emphasis has been given to norepinephrine, dopamine, and serotonin (Hechtman, 1991; Taylor, 1994).

One approach has been to examine levels of neurotransmitters or their metabolites in plasma, cerebrospinal fluid, and other body parts (Zametkin and Rapoport, 1987). Consistent differences between ADHD children and controls have not been found for these measures. Another approach has examined the behavioral effects of certain drugs known to influence the relevant neurotransmitters (Murphy, Greenstein, and Pelham, 1993). The best evidence implicates norepinephrine and dopamine. These neurotransmitters are considered important in the functioning of the frontal/limbic areas of the brain (Anastopoulos and Barkley, 1992).

Nevertheless, the research findings are not definitive. Many difficulties are inherent in biochemical research, not the least of which is the intricacies of the neurotransmitter systems. More than one neurotransmitter may be involved (Hechtman, 1991). Furthermore, establishing a link between ADHD and neurotransmitter abnormalities still would leave the question of cause and effect unanswered (Whalen, 1989). Neurotransmitters must somehow affect behavior, but the opposite also may occur.

Electrophysiological aspects. There is evidence that children with hyperactivity show abnormal electrophysiological responding (Hechtman, 1991; Taylor, 1994). A substantial minority have abnormal EEGs, which has sometimes been interpreted as delayed maturation of the nervous system. Measures of heart rate, skin conductance, and brain reaction to stimulation indicate diminished reactions. Thus, underarousal appears to characterize ADHD. If this is true, children with ADHD may be excessively active in order to obtain stimulation (Zentall and Meyer, 1987). However, the overall findings do not appear unique to ADHD, and they also characterized learning disabilities, which are so often comorbid with ADHD. Furthermore, the findings are far from consistent.

Pregnancy and Birth Complications

The idea that ADHD is traceable to pregnancy and birth complications has only inconsistently been upheld (Sprich-Buckminister et al., 1993). The notion that most ADHD is caused by prenatal or perinatal brain damage certainly is not supported. At

Several variables are implicated in the etiology of ADHD, which is characterized, in part, by restless hyperactivity that goes beyond age-appropriate motor behavior.

(Monkmeyer/Kopstein)

the same time, investigations continue to turn up interesting correlations.

Prenatal maternal alcohol consumption is of particular importance (Streissguth et al., 1989; Streissguth et al., 1984). In an extensive study that followed fifteen hundred women from pregnancy to the time their offspring were seven years old, prenatal alcohol use was linked to activity level, attention deficits, and difficulties in organizing tasks. Research conducted in Germany indicates that hyperactivity associated with prenatal alcohol exposure persists over time into childhood and to a lesser extent into adolescence (Steinhausen, Willms, and Spohr, 1993).

Other pregnancy and delivery correlates of ADHD continue to be inconsistently reported (Sprich-Buckminster et al., 1993). We might anticipate that prenatal variables would be only weakly linked to ADHD because of the well known modifying effects of the social environment. Indeed, Chandola et al. (1992), who found a link between ADHD and length of labor and hemorrhage,

reported that the predictive value of their findings was "disappointingly low." Still, they recognized the possibility that prenatal insult may predispose some infants to ADHD.

The fact that children with ADHD show a higher than usual incidence of minor physical abnormalities (MPAs) has suggested prenatal causation. These abnormalities develop during the first three months of pregnancy (Anastopoulos and Barkley, 1988). Over thirty-five have been identified; examples are asymmetrical or low-seated ears and a wide gap between the first and second toes (Whalen, 1989). Most of the abnormalities are found frequently in the general population, with perhaps two to four occurring in persons with no known physiological or psychological disorders. MPAs also occur in higher numbers in a variety of disturbances, such as autism and Down's syndrome, so they are certainly not unique to ADHD. Moreover, MPAs appear disproportionately in the first degree relatives of children with ADHD, and so genetic transmission is suspect (Deutsch et al., 1990). In addition, it has been found that ADHD independent of conduct or oppositional disorder was not associated with MPAs (Weiss, 1991). These various findings do not lead to any clear conclusions about if and how MPAs are connected to the etiology of ADHD.

Genetics

Not infrequently parents with high-activity children come into clinics expressing the belief that such disturbance runs in families and is inherited. Is this impression accurate? There is growing support for the idea.

To begin with, activity level appears to have a genetic basis in the general child population. This suggests that inheritance may at least partly account for the high level of activity observed in ADHD. Nevertheless, it is important to study clinically defined ADHD.

In fact, parents and siblings of children with ADHD are often reported to show more psychopathology, including hyperactivity, than would be expected. Many of the studies are considered methodologically weak, however, and they do not differentiate between social and genetic transmission (Deutsch and Kinsbourne, 1990). Nevertheless, limited data from adoption studies also point to inheritance.

So does research with twins. Although earlier studies had indicated greater concordance in identical twins than in fraternal twins, these studies were viewed as methodologically weak (Rutter et al., 1990b). More recent twin studies continue to support the genetic hypothesis, however (Gillis et al., 1992; Goodman and Stevenson, 1989; Stevenson et al., 1993). It has also been found that inheritance plays a role in producing co-occurrence of ADHD and learning disabilities. Overall, then, it seems likely that genetic transmission plays a role in ADHD, but continuing research is needed to further confirm and understand such influence.

Diet

The belief that diet causes hyperactivity is commonly held by the general public but is not strongly accepted by the professional community (Taylor, 1994; Anastopoulos and Barkley, 1992). The topic is thus worthy of detailed discussion.

In 1975, Feingold, a physician researcher interested in allergies, published a book, *Why Your Child is Hyperactive,* which inspired both controversy and investigation into dietary effects on hyperactivity. Feingold asserted that food containing artificial dyes and flavors, certain preservatives, and naturally occurring salicylates (for example, in apricots, prunes, tomatoes, cucumbers) was related to hyperactivity. He claimed that 25 to 50 percent of hyperactive-learning disabled children responded favorably to diets that eliminated these substances (Harley and Matthews, 1980; Tryphonas, 1979). On the other hand, it was claimed that when children on the diet ingested a prohibited food, hyperactivity occurred dramatically and persisted for two to three days. This position received pervasive media coverage and was rapidly espoused by many parents, who reported impressive anecdotes about behavioral improvement in their children on Feingold's diet. Some of the fanfare undoubtedly was due to the fact that Feingold advocated the diet for mental retardation, delinquency, learning problems, and autism as well as for hyperactivity. Evaluation by skeptical committees called for well-designed research to examine the efficacy of the Feingold diet.

Conners and his colleagues were among the first to examine hyperactive children while they were on a special diet and while they were on a control diet. Teachers, but not parents, found the diet more effective. Subsequently, three "challenge" studies were run in which children who were on the Feingold diet and had shown improvement were "challenged" by a cookie with food dyes or a cookie with no dyes. The results were ambiguous but for the most part did not support Feingold's claims (Conners, 1980). Other research is consistent with this finding (Gross et al., 1987; Harley and Matthews, 1980; Spring, Chiodo, and Bowen, 1987).

Nevertheless, some researchers point to evidence that a small number of hyperactive children benefit from special diets (Marshall, 1980; Weiss, 1982). Furthermore, some data indicate that these children have higher than usual rates of allergies and that other than food allergies could be involved (e.g., pollen, mold). Marshall (1989) suggests that severe allergies combined with stressors might play a role in causing ADHD in a subgroup of children. This is consistent with the more general conclusion that some foods (such as wheat, cow's milk, and food dyes) may worsen behavior in children who are intolerant of them (Taylor, 1994).

Anecdotal reports of the effects of sugar on ADHD are common. Parents of hyperactive and normal children often believe that sugar intake causes their offspring to become hyperactive and disorganized. A limited number of correlational studies show a link between sugar consumption and behaviors that characterize ADHD (Prinz and Riddle, 1986). Most experimental studies suggest that sugar has no effect. In two experiments, for example, hyperactive boys on a sucrose-free diet received a challenge beverage either with sucrose or the sugar substitute, aspartane (Wolraich et al., 1985). No significant differences were found for the groups on measures of physical activity, attention, impulsivity, and learning. The effects of sugar on performance of clinic and nonclinic samples have been looked at in other studies, with mixed results (Kaplan et al., 1989; Roshon and Hagen, 1989; Spring et al., 1987).

It should be noted that research into dietary influence is not easy to do. Correlational studies can be difficult to interpret, and well-controlled experiments are difficult to conduct. It is hard to manage what people eat and to select appropriate control diets. Given these considerations, the evidence suggests that diet does not play a strong role in the etiology, nor the treatment, of ADHD but may affect a small number of children (Richters et al., 1995).

Environmental Lead

It is widely recognized that exposure to lead is dangerous to humans. High levels of lead have been associated with serious deficits in biological functioning, cognition, and behavior (Tesman and Hills, 1994). Low levels of exposure over long periods of time also adversely affect children.

A number of correlational studies have examined lead levels and attention and activity levels. Lead levels of the blood typically have been examined and occasionally the amount of lead in the dentine of children's deciduous ("baby") teeth. Some studies have not shown a relationship to behavior. However, major studies sensitive to methodological issues have found small links (Fergusson, Horwood, and Lynskey, 1993; Silva et al., 1988; Thomson et al., 1989). The Fergusson and colleagues research found that dentine lead levels at ages six to eight correlated with inattention at ages twelve to thirteen. The possible effects of other variables (such as SES, family social environment, the child's prenatal history, and school experience) were controlled in this and some of the other studies. The relationships, although statistically significant, were small.

Given the weak correlations found in these studies, decreases in environmental lead would probably not substantially impact the prevalence of ADHD. Nevertheless, high technology societies concerned about children's development recognize the importance of eliminating lead poisoning (See Accent 9–1).

ACCENT 9–1   Protecting Children from Lead Poisoning

Australia was among the first countries to recognize lead poisoning, and by 1904 physicians argued that children were damaged by leaded water tanks and leaded paints that covered porches and railings (Tesman and Hills, 1994). In the United States, reports of lead poisoning had become more prevalent by the 1920s and concern gradually increased. Lead in gasoline was reduced, and in the late 1970s the inclusion of lead in residential paints was prohibited. Nevertheless, soil and dust in many parts of the country are believed to be contaminated by lead, and the Department of Health and Human Services warns that lead poisoning is still a threat to children. Thus, although controversy exists over the exact level of blood lead that is dangerous and over some of the research findings, parents are being called upon to protect their children.

According to Dr. Sue Binder of the Centers for Disease Control and Prevention (CDC), the following practices can reduce the risk of lead poisoning (Weber, 1992).

1. Ask your physician to test your children's blood lead levels if you suspect exposure to the metal from house paint, auto emissions from nearby major highways, contamination from water supplies, and the like. The CDC recommends testing for all children by twelve to fifteen months.

2. If you live in an old house, have the painted surfaces tested prior to renovations. Use do-it-yourself kits or laboratories that can test paint chips and other household samples. If paint is contaminated, do not remove it without consulting local health agencies about safety procedures. Be sure that children do not have contact with lead surfaces.

3. To prevent exposure from soils contaminated from nearby highways or house paint, plant grasses and shrubs on bare patches of lawn and around the outside walls of the house.

4. Water can be contaminated from solder used on copper pipes in the past (it is now banned). Flush water pipes by running cold water before drinking or cooking with the water. Avoid using hot tap water for these purposes.

5. Lead exposure can also come from leaded crystal and some ceramic vessels; avoid these.

6. Wash children's hands and faces before they eat; wash toys frequently.

Information about preventing lead poisoning is widely available, including from the CDC and the U.S. Environmental Protection Agency. The old adage "better safe than sorry" seems appropriate in this matter.

Psychosocial Factors

Although psychosocial variables are not considered critical in the etiology of ADHD, they do appear to play a role. The family has been the focus of study, with context factors (such as stress, marital discord, parental psychopathology) and parent-child interaction being examined.

Goodman and Stevenson's (1989) study of twins found an association of ADHD behaviors with seven adverse family variables, including parental malaise, marital discord, coldness to the child, and criticism of the child. Importantly, assessment of ADHD behaviors was accomplished by objective measures and teacher ratings, as well as parental ratings. The link with family adversity—such as family dysfunction, single parenting, and urban status—has been found in other studies as well (e.g., McGee et al., 1991; Stormont-Spurgin and Zentall, 1995).

Campbell (1987) studied parental ratings of their three-year-olds when the children were referred for help. When the children were age six, those who had received the more negative ratings of ADHD behaviors had families that had experienced more stress and were lower in social status. Interestingly, an unfavorable mother-child relationship also predicted stability of the problems. Stormont-Spurgin and Zentall (1995) found that families of preschoolers with ADHD + aggression were more restrictive and aggressive than families whose preschoolers displayed ADHD.

Studies of hyperactive school-age children indicate that their mothers are less consistent and more impatient and power assertive (Campbell, 1995). Similarly, families with adolescents with ADHD report more conflicts and show more negative interactions, which are worse when the adolescents also are oppositional (Barkley, Anastopoulos et al., 1992). Thus, family variables are implicated no matter what the age of the offspring. It should be noted, however, that the direction of causality, if any, between family variables and child behavior is unclear.

It is not unreasonable to speculate that at least for some children ADHD results from being born with a predisposition for the relevant behaviors that then interacts with psychosocial variables. A burdened or chaotic home, regardless of social status, may fail to foster attentive and reflective behavior. Organized and regular routines, rules authoritatively enforced, quiet activities, and the like may be especially crucial for children vulnerable to ADHD. The controlling, intrusive parental style that is associated with ADHD may cause or worsen the child's behavior (Hechtman, 1991). Also, teacher behaviors might well play a role in shaping a child's attentiveness and reflectivity. How a classroom is organized and how activities are structured can influence academic achievement, perhaps especially for children predisposed to ADHD behaviors (Whalen, 1989). As with parents, teacher perception and tolerance of student behavior may influence daily social interactions.

Psychosocial correlates of ADHD must be cautiously interpreted, of course. Few researchers and clinicians believe that parents or teachers solely cause ADHD. However, psychosocial variables, particularly family factors, provide the critical context within which the disorder develops. Family relationships may be especially significant (Taylor, 1994).

Overall, it is quite striking that after much research, the etiology of ADHD remains uncertain. Several factors may underlie the difficulty in establishing causation. Different criteria have been used in clinics to identify ADHD, which means that research has been conducted with different samples. In addition, samples chosen from the general population are likely different than clinic samples. There may also be subgroups of ADHD based on behavioral symptoms, and whether the symptoms are displayed situationally or pervasively. Investigations of etiology undoubtedly have been confounded by this heterogeneity. In the final analysis, ADHD is probably caused by several different factors, or the combination of several factors, and causation may vary with subgroups. Whereas biological etiology is believed to be central to ADHD, psychosocial variables cannot be precluded and are involved in shaping the problem behaviors and maintaining them over time.

DEVELOPMENTAL COURSE AND PROGNOSIS

Until quite recently clinical description and research of hyperactivity focused on school-age children, mostly boys. Undoubtedly this was because ADHD is especially notable when children enter school and must conform to the requirements of attentive, "good" deportment. Nevertheless, the importance of studying attention-deficit hyperactivity disorder across developmental levels has become evident. Since ADHD is believed to emerge by age seven, examination of the earlier years of life can be critical to understanding the development of the disorder. At the same time, we now know that hyperactivity does not simply fade after childhood, as was once believed. Follow-up studies of ADHD are thus important to describe the developmental course of the disorder, help predict outcome, and suggest intervention and prevention.

It is believed that at least some cases of ADHD begin in infancy, but this is not easily established. How would ADHD manifest itself so early in life? It seems reasonable that the temperamental traits of high activity level and inattention might indicate the disorder. On the other hand, these early attributes are not very stable and not strong predictors of later difficulties. Nevertheless, Sanson et al. (1993) reported early difficult temperament for a group of children who were hyperactive and aggressive at eight years of age. By three to four years of age, these children, as well as a group that later displayed only hyperactivity, were identified as being more active and less cooperative and manageable. Other investigations also show that by preschool age inattention and restless behavior can be identified, and language deficits are reported for some of the children (Campbell, 1990, 1995; McGee et al., 1991). Parents complain of difficulty in managing the noncompliance of their offspring, which appears worse than normal. Inadequate caregiving and family adversity are noted (Carlson, Jacobvitz, and Sroufe, 1995). Thus, in some children destined to be diagnosed as ADHD, the primary manifestations of the syndrome as well as some secondary problems are evident very early. It is not known whether ADHD is different for these children than for those who are only identified later.

Once children exhibit ADHD behaviors, difficulties often remain stable and may increase throughout childhood. These are the years that have been best documented. As we have seen, in addition to the primary behaviors of ADHD, for many children social relationships are far from satisfactory, conduct is disturbing, and academic achievement falls. Negative feedback about school performance and other behaviors can accu-mulate to adversely affect self-concept and motivation.

About 50 to 80 percent of children with ADHD continue to display problems in adolescence (Fischer et al., 1993). The primary deficits of ADHD, especially hyperactivity itself, may lessen in a substantial number of cases. Even for these individuals, however, other difficulties exist: poor school performance, conduct problems, antisocial behavior, substance use and abuse, social problems, low self-esteem, and emotional problems (Fischer et al., 1993; Slomkowski, Klein, and Mannuzza, 1995).

Studies that follow ADHD children into adulthood indicate that a substantial proportion—perhaps 50 to 65 percent—still variously demonstrate the primary deficits and/or impaired social relationships, depression, low self-concept, antisocial behavior, drug use, and educational and occupational disadvantage (Barkley, 1990; Mannuzza et al., 1993; Weiss and Hechtman, 1986). Perhaps one-quarter are more-or-less chronically antisocial. Most are employed and economically independent, but work history is somewhat unstable and job status is on the low end.

It is important to emphasize that not all children with ADHD experience maladaptations in later years. Indeed, most are reasonably adjusted in adulthood. Thus the question: What predicts stability or negative outcome? It does appear that family interaction, adversity, and social status play a role in the maintenance of ADHD, probably through complex pathways. These variables seem especially critical when noncompliance and aggression are also present (Campbell, 1995). Negative outcomes in adolescence and adulthood are related to several other earlier-occurring variables including intelligence, aggression and conduct problems, poor peer relationships, and severity of childhood ADHD (Fischer et al., 1993; Mannuzza et al., 1993; Weiss and Hechtman, 1986).

Two general conclusions can be noted regarding the prediction of later problems. One is that no one single factor well predicts the outcome of childhood ADHD. Many factors are involved. Given this, the second general conclusion is that to some degree different outcomes appear linked to specific early factors (Fischer et al., 1993; Lambert, 1988). Educational outcome appears especially associated with earlier academic skill and intelligence, as well as family factors such as social class and child-rearing practices. In contrast, adolescent and adult antisocial behavior are linked to several early factors but are unlikely without the occurrence of early aggression and conduct problems. As is usual, behavior develops from complex transactions between the child's characteristics and the psychological and social context.

ASSESSING ADHD

As with all assessment, the major task of assessment of ADHD is to describe an individual's functioning within a social context so that judgments can be made about normality and possible treatments. Several aspects of ADHD are useful in guiding assessment (Barkley, 1990; Hinshaw and Erhardt (1993).

To begin with, since ADHD is best conceptualized as a biopsychosocial disorder, assessment must be *broad based and include various procedures* to evaluate the primary and secondary manifestations of the disorder, family functioning, and biological functioning. Second, because ADHD may be situationally specific, it usually demands assessment of *different settings*. Third, since ADHD is increasingly viewed as developmental—that is, beginning early and continuing over time—sound assessment deals with a changing *developmental context*. Thus what is assessed and how assessment is conducted will vary to some extent with developmental level.

The following discussion will focus, although not exclusively, on the psychological and social factors most important in childhood ADHD. The approach of Barkley (1990) and his colleagues is heavily drawn on. Interviews, rating scales, and direct observation are the major components discussed.

Interviews

Parents are the chief source of information in many cases of attention-deficit hyperactivity disorder. It is often helpful if parents complete detailed assessment forms prior to the first meeting. In any event, standard structured or semistructured interviews can be used. It is important that information be obtained about specific parent-child interactions, not only for diagnosis but also for treatment planning. Barkley thus asks parents to identify particular situations that are problematic. Table 9–2 shows some of the situations that are presented to parents. Details about the troublesome situations are asked, for example, what the child does, how the parents respond, and how often problems occur in the situation. Table 9–3 illustrates this question format for one situation: when visitors are in the home. Note that noncompliance is quite evident and that interaction becomes increasingly aversive. This is a common pattern in child-parent exchanges.

Teacher interviews are important because next to parents teachers probably spend most time with youth and can directly address difficulties in the school setting. The focus is on learning and academic problems and on peer interaction. In addition, information can be obtained about parent-school interaction and cooperation and school services. Under Public Law 94-142, some youth with ADHD have rights to special evaluation and educational services (see p. 266).

TABLE 9–2   Interview Format Suggested by Barkley

Questions	*Situations*
1. Is this a problem area?	Overall interactions
2. What does the child do in this situation?	Play alone
3. What is your response?	Play with others
4. What will the child do next?	Mealtimes
5. If the problem continues, what will you do next?	Dressing in morning
6. What is usually the outcome of this interaction?	Washing and bathing
7. How often do these problems occur in this situation?	Parent on telephone
8. How do you feel about these problems?	During television
9. On a scale of 0 to 10 (0 = no problem, 10 = severe problem), how severe is this problem to you?	Visitors at home
	Visiting others' homes
	In public places
	While mother is occupied
	Father at home
	Chores
	Bedtime
	Other situations

Copyright by Guilford Press, 1981. Reprinted with permission from R. Barkley, Hyperactivity. In E. Mash & L. Terdal (Eds.) *Behavioral Assessment of Childhood Disorders.* New York: Guilford Press, 1981.

The individual being assessed should also be interviewed. The nature and length of this interview depend on the age and ability of the youth. Barkley has reservations about the reliability of information obtained from young children. Older children and adolescents are more able to report on their functioning, family dynamics, school performance, peer relationships, and the like. With younger children the interview may simply be a time for getting acquainted, establishing rapport, and observing the child's appearance and behavior. Observations of behavior must be interpreted cautiously, however, as children with ADHD are known to act more appropriately during office visits than what is reported in other settings.

Rating Scales

Over the years, parent and teacher rating scales and checklists have been popular tools for assessing ADHD. Some are broad band and thus not only identify ADHD but also its co-occurrence with other disorders. In general, these scales can help determine whether behavior is deviant from the norm and different from behaviors displayed by other diagnostic groups. Several of them suggest cutoff scores to identify ADHD. Narrow-band scales are useful in assessing specific aspects of ADHD, such as school behavior. Parent and teacher rating scales may be less useful for adolescents; self-report scales are considered more appropriate. The many rating scales that exist vary in reliability and validity and, as always, their soundness must be examined.

The Child Behavior Checklist is now the most widely used broad-band instrument (Rapport, 1993). The Teacher Report Form and the Youth Self Report versions of this instrument can be employed as well.

The Conners scales are also widely used instruments. They are easy to use, and there is good evidence for their validity (Edelbrock and Rancurello, 1985). The Conners Parent Rating Scale consists of forty-eight items that yield scores on five factors: impulsive-hyperactive, learning problems (attention), conduct problems, psychosomatic problems, anxiety (Goyette, Conners, and

TABLE 9–3 Illustration of Interview Format Suggested by Barkley

Examiner: How does your child generally behave when there are visitors at your home?

Mother: Terrible! He embarrasses me tremendously.

E: Can you give me some idea of what he does specifically that is bothersome in this situation?

M: Well, he won't let me talk with the visitors without interrupting our conversation, tugging on me for attention, or annoying the guests by running back and forth in front of us as we talk.

E: Yes? And what else is he likely to do?

M: Many times, he will fight with his sister or get into something he shouldn't in the kitchen.

E: How will you usually respond to him when these things happen?

M: At first I usually try to ignore him. When this doesn't work, I try to reason with him, promise I'll spend time with him after the visitors leave, or try to distract him with something he usually likes to do just to calm him down so I can talk to my guests.

E: How successfully does that work for you?

M: Not very well. He may slow down for a few moments, but then he's right back pestering us or his sister, or getting into mischief in the kitchen. I get so frustrated with him by this time. I know what my visitors must be thinking of me not being able to handle my own child.

E: Yes, I can imagine it's quite distressing. What will you do at this point to handle the situation?

M: I usually find myself telling him over and over again to stop what he is doing, until I get very angry with him and threaten him with punishment. By now, my visitors are making excuses to leave and I'm trying to talk with them while yelling at my son.

E: And then what happens?

M: Well, I know I shouldn't, but I'll usually grab him and hold him just to slow him down. More often, though, I may threaten to spank him or spend him to his room. He usually doesn't listen to me though until I make a move to grab him.

E: How often does this usually happen when visitors are at your home?

M: Practically every time; it's frustrating.

E: I see. How do you feel about your child creating such problems in front of visitors?

M: I find myself really hating him at times (*cries*); I know I'm his mother and I shouldn't feel that way, but I'm so angry with him, and nothing seems to work for me. Many of our friends have stopped coming to visit us, and we can't find a babysitter who will stay with him so we can go out. I resent having to sacrifice what little social life we have. I'm likely to be angry with him the rest of the day.

Ulrich, 1978). Different versions of a Conners Teacher Rating Scale exist, the longer ones tapping factors similar to the parent scale factors (Conners, 1969; Goyette et al., 1978). Table 9–4 shows a few of the items. In addition, there is also an abbreviated 10 item teacher scale that is very popular. On all the Conners scales, children are rated on whether they display each behavior (0) not at all, (1) just a little, (2) pretty much, or (3) very much.

The Werry-Weiss-Peters Activity Rating Scale consists of items rated by parents across situations: mealtime, television, homework, play, sleep, public places, school. For each setting the child is rated on a few items

characteristics, parent characteristics, situational consequences, and stressful family events. The situational variables and feedback conditions relevant to ADHD are described (e.g., need for especially salient reinforcers).

3. Parents are trained to attend to their children's behavior, and are advised to increase attention to appropriate behavior and ignore inappropriate behavior. Underlying this step is the belief that positive interaction must be strengthened if the parent is to be a more effective manager of child behavior.

4. Positive parental attention is extended to independent play situations and to child compliance with simple requests. Parents are then trained in methods of giving commands so as to optimize compliance in their children. For example, they are taught to reduce question-like commands (such as "Why don't you pick up your toys now?") and to reduce task complexity. They are asked to use brief commands at home and to reinforce compliance.

5. Parents are asked to set up a home token economy for reinforcing the child's completing home responsibilities. This involves the child's earning tokens or points that can be exchanged for a variety of reinforcers.

6. The home economy system is monitored, and in addition parents are trained to use time-out and response cost for noncompliance with rules or requests.

7. The techniques that parents are using in child management are reviewed, especially punishment techniques. Parents are also en-couraged to extend time-out to other home situations if needed.

8. Management procedures are now extended to misbehavior in public places such as stores and restaurants.

9. Parents have by now acquired effective management techniques. A general review is provided, and discussion is held about how parents might use their skills in the future.

10. About four to six weeks later a "booster" session is typically held to evaluate progress and review and refine the intervention procedures. Additional sessions can be scheduled if desired.

The parent counseling/training program is often an integral part of a broader clinical approach to ADHD. Whether it is recommended depends on its appropriateness to the individual case. For example, parents may resist the program or may require marital counseling first, or the child's difficulties may center primarily on the school setting.

Classroom management. Much research has been devoted to the classroom management of ADHD. Improvement has been found with regard to attention, disruptive behavior, and academic performance. The techniques employed include token reinforcement, punishment, and contingency contracting. In the latter technique, the child and the teacher sign a written agreement

---

TABLE 9–5 Hypothetical Child-Teacher Contingency Contract

I agree to do the following:
 1. Take my seat by 8:10 every morning.
 2. Remain in my seat unless Ms. Duffin gives permission to me or the class to leave seats.
 3. Not interrupt other students when they are speaking to class.
 4. Complete morning written work as assigned before lunch break.
 5. Complete afternoon written work as assigned before gym or recess in the afternoon.

I agree that when I do the above, I will:
 . . . earn extra time in the computer corner
 . . . earn extra time to do artwork
 . . . earn checkmarks that I can trade for art supplies

I agree that if I do not do 1–5 above each day, I will:
 . . . not be able to participate in recess activities

Based in part on DuPaul, Guevrement, and Barkley, 1991.

specifying how the child will behave and the contingencies that will accrue (Table 9–5). Teachers typically receive training and consultation to conduct these programs. In addition, parents and teachers can work together in home-based programs. In one early study, for example, ten-year-olds were reinforced for meeting academic and social goals in the classroom (O'Leary et al., 1976). The specific goals and reinforcers were individually set for each child. Teachers completed a daily checklist, which the child carried home in order to earn an array of enticing items: special dessert, play time with parents, dinner at a fast-food restaurant, and the like. Compared to a no-treatment control group, children treated for ten weeks showed improvement on two rating scales.

Empirical investigations show that on-task, attentive, appropriate behaviors can be shaped, but that they do not necessarily improve academic performance. On the other hand, when academic improvement is targeted, attention and appropriate behavior may also increase (DuPaul et al., 1991). Thus, academic products—such as math problems and reading performance—are often the favored targets.

Research suggests that stimulus control techniques might benefit learning in ADHD children (Barkley, 1990). Increasing stimulation within the task—for example, by the use of color, shape, or tape recordings—might increase attention to the task. Keeping the length of the task within the child's attention span and using timers to pace performance might be of benefit. Rules that are written and clearly displayed also may help guide the child. Placing the child's desk away from others and near the teacher can reduce peer reinforcement of inappropriate behavior and also facilitate teacher monitoring and feedback.

Teacher variables have mostly been neglected with regard to the success of classroom management of ADHD (Greene, 1995). Yet, teachers have considerable control in setting up the learning environment. Research suggests that they also have preferences for time-efficient behavioral techniques and for positive techniques (e.g., praise, tokens) rather than procedures such as time-out and response cost. They may also perceive treatment that combines behavioral methods and medication as most effective and appropriate. Differences among teachers is expected, however, and some teachers are especially effective in working with difficult students. It thus seems important to better understand which teachers would be most accepting of and effective in implementing behavioral programs. Moreover, as Greene notes, teacher-student compatibility might be important. Variables such as the teacher's flexibility, tolerance for the disruptions common in ADHD, and interactional style are worthy of investigation.

There seems little doubt that behavioral methods can help many ADHD children in the short run. However, questions remain about whether training in one situation carries over to others. Moreover, children benefitting from behavior modification have not been sufficiently followed over time to determine the durability of effects. Extensive programs that are gradually faded are more likely to be effective. Generalization of behavioral treatment over situations and time certainly cannot be automatically assumed. In addition, behavioral programs often require much effort and time, sometimes beyond what is feasible for teachers and parents. Finally, benefits may be smaller than what is found for treatment with medication.

Self-Regulation and Cognitive-Behavioral Intervention

Self-regulation would seem a natural target in treating ADHD, as self-control is often viewed as a central deficit in the disorder. Moreover, self-control can increase generalization and maintenance of appropriate behavior, as the behavior would not solely depend on external cues and contingencies in new situations.

Several techniques have been employed to enhance self-regulation. Self-monitoring involves individuals learning to observe and record their own behaviors. For example, they may record the frequency of on-task behavior. This is often followed by self-reinforcement for the desired behavior. Typically children award themselves points which can be exchanged for reinforcers. As an example of this approach, Bowers et al., (1985) compared teacher-reinforcement and self-reinforcement in the classroom. While performing in a reading workbook, eight- to eleven-year-olds were assigned points either by the teacher or by themselves for being on-task. The points could be exchanged weekly for money. Both conditions improved attention to and accuracy of the work, but self-reinforcement was the more effective for attention. Other studies also demonstrate that self-monitoring and self-reinforcement can be effective (Barkley, 1990).

Another technique, self-instruction, involves children being trained to make statements to themselves to help focus and guide their behaviors on a task. The self-statements may include questions that help clarify the task, answers to the questions, and self-guidance (e.g., "slow down," "the next step is . . ."). The verbalizations usually are combined with modeling, reinforcement, and other procedures, making it difficult to evaluate the effectiveness of the self-statements. It appears that self-instruction reduces the primary deficits of ADHD, but only modestly and inconsistently (Dush, Hirt, and Schroeder, 1989; Anastopoulos and Barkley, 1992).

Overall, cognitive-behavioral interventions have had mixed results at best. If anything, impulsivity but not other problems may be alleviated (Kendall and Panichelli-Mindel, 1995). Self-instruction usually requires reinforcement, so the child is not free of external control. In addition, there is little evidence for generalization to other settings or tasks or over time. Nevertheless, a measure of interest still exists in these efforts, as some children might benefit depending on age, task, and specific techniques. For example, cognitive techniques combined with other methods might facilitate control of aggression and anger in children with ADHD (Hinshaw and Erhardt, 1993).

Combining Treatments

As we have seen, different treatment approaches show some success but each also has limitations. Stimulant medication, which demands relatively little of caretakers, can help many but not all children and has other drawbacks. The behavioral approach has its successes but is not sufficiently effective and is demanding of caretakers. Overall, the difficulty is not so much to effect improvement as it is to maintain improvement. Since no one approach "cures" ADHD, treatment often involves various combinations of approaches.

Are combined treatments effective? Several studies fail to show more positive outcome for combinations of treatments than for single treatments, particularly when medication is combined with behavioral or cognitive-behavioral methods (Anastopoulos and Barkley, 1992). That is, medication alone was as effective as when it was combined with other approaches. Still, there is some evidence that the combination of medication and behavioral intervention may have greater benefits and that each approach may effect improvement in different behaviors (Hinshaw and Erhardt, 1993). A study by Ialongo and colleagues (1993) indicated that a combined approach was important in improvement being maintained over time. Favorable outcome has also been reported for multimodal treatment employed for serious antisocial behavior in boys with ADHD (Satterfield, 1994; Satterfield et al., 1987). Thus, the call has gone out for further research on the long-term efficacy of treatments and their combinations. The National Institutes of Mental Health has initiated a six-center investigation of multimodal treatment (Richters et al., 1995).

Overall, it appears that many variables may influence the outcome of the different interventions, including the behaviors targeted, the specific techniques used, medication type and dosage, severity of the disorder, comorbidity, and the age of the youth (e.g., DuPaul and Barkley, 1993). It is difficult to predict what intervention might best serve any one child at any particular time. Some clinicians prefer trying behavioral techniques initially, to see whether medications might be avoided. Others believe that a combination of treatments might be the best approach for many children, since different treatments might address different deficits. In addition, parent management of their youngsters with ADHD is important when children need to "vacation" from medications to control possible side effects. Moreover, training in self-regulation might be appropriate for adolescents with ADHD, but relatively little is known about psychological intervention with this population. What is apparent is that treatment is best tailored to suit the individual's needs, even as these change over time.

SUMMARY

The conceptualization of attention-deficit hyperactivity disorder has changed somewhat over the years. Hyperactivity itself was initially the focus of concern but attention deficit subsequently was considered the central difficulty. Both problems, in conjunction with impulsivity, are presently recognized as the primary manifestations of ADHD. DSM-IV criteria necessitate the presence of disturbance by age seven and impairment in at least two settings.

Attention deficits are reported by parents and teachers, who complain that the children have poor concentration, do not follow directions, and do not stay on task. Research does not consistently implicate selective or sustained attention and it appears more likely that higher-order attention mechanisms are involved. Activity problems are defined in terms of restless, excessive, disorganized, and inappropriate motor behaviors. These problems are more likely to show up in structured environments. Impulsivity—acting without thinking—is widely reported. The primary manifestations of ADHD are multidimensional, and measurement has been problematic.

More recently, ADHD has been viewed as a deficit in motivation or behavioral regulation, which might be caused by inadequate control of behavior by consequences or high need for arousal. Barkley, a major proponent of this view, emphasizes that impairment is tied to biologically-based motivation.

Although ADHD children show intelligence that is typically in the normal range, many experience academic failure and are learning disabled. The link between ADHD and academic/learning failure is not well understood. ADHD children also display an array of conduct disordered and otherwise socially disturbing behaviors. The overlap of ADHD with other problems has caused diagnostic uncertainty and has confounded research findings. It is important to study ADHD that co-occurs with other problems since this is associated with more severe problems, less favorable outcome, and perhaps different developmental pathways.

About 3 to 5 percent of the school population is estimated to show ADHD, although there is much variation in the data. Boys are diagnosed more frequently than girls.

Many biological factors are implicated in etiology. Some brain dysfunction is considered likely. There is special interest in the frontal/limbic area of the brain, and in the neurotransmitters norepinephrine and dopamine. Abnormal EEGs and diminished physiological reactions suggest under-arousal. However, inconsistent findings preclude drawing firm conclusions about brain malfunctioning.

This inconclusive picture applies to other possible etiologies as well. Pregnancy and birth complications are only weakly tied to ADHD. Diet and lead poisoning appear only to have small influence. In contrast, evidence is growing for genetic influence.

Associations have been revealed between ADHD and family factors, including poverty, stress, and negative family interactions. Presently there is high interest in the psychosocial environment, as specific home and school environments might elicit, shape, and maintain ADHD behaviors. Overall, the etiology of attention-deficit hyperactivity disorder remains elusive, and it is likely that ADHD can result from various factors or their combinations.

ADHD is commonly reported by age three or four, and more commonly referred for professional consultation during the early school years. It often remains stable or increases during childhood; perhaps 50 to 80 percent of cases continue into adolescence, and 50 percent into adulthood. The primary symptoms decrease, but academic, social, and antisocial difficulties exist. Continuity of ADHD is linked to several variables, and there appears to be specific pathways to specific outcomes.

The identification of ADHD requires broad-based assessment that takes into account developmental level and more than one setting. Barkley's (1981, 1990) comprehensive model includes interviews with the children, parents, and teachers; standardized rating scales; direct observation; medical examinations; intelligence testing; and other procedures.

Stimulant medication is a common treatment for ADHD; it relieves the primary and many secondary manifestations in about 70 percent of the cases. Several concerns are expressed about such pharmacologic treatment, and a major shortcoming is the lack of long-term relief.

Behavior modification, also popular, emphasizes consequences for attention, rule adherence, academic effort, socially appropriate behaviors, and the like. Parent and teacher training are widely employed. Lack of generalization and maintenance of treatment gains led to an interest in training ADHD children to regulate their own behavior. Cognitive-behavioral training may be beneficial in some instances, but has not fulfilled expectations.

There is no evidence that any treatment shows long-term efficacy or cures ADHD. Nor is there much evidence that combinations of treatments are more powerful than a single treatment, at least when that single treatment is medication. Nevertheless, treatment outcome appears to depend on many factors, and research is underway to further study the effects of single and multimodal treatments.

10

MENTAL RETARDATION

From the beginning of history, even in simple societies, some individuals have been considered intellectually disabled and socially deficient (Clarke and Clarke, 1985). However, until about 1700 mental retardation (MR) was little understood and scarcely recognized as different from other disorders (Reschly, 1992). In the early 1800s the concept of mental retardation more firmly took root as involving deficient mental functioning and handicaps in the daily tasks of living. Beliefs and concepts continued to evolve and are evolving even today.

The labels applied to the condition also changed over time. The terms *idiot*, from the Greek meaning "ignorant person," *imbecile*, from the Latin meaning "weakness," and *moron*, meaning foolish or having deficient judgment were all once employed (Potter, 1972; Scheerenberger, 1983). These terms gradually took on negative connotations, and changes in terminology were in part an attempt to substitute more positive labels. The current trend to use *mental handicap* continues this effort. However, as long as we denigrate and are insensitive to mental retardation, any label applied to it might eventually carry negative meaning.

Perhaps more strongly than most other behavioral disorders, mental retardation has been viewed as a trait of the individual. Or-

ganismic etiology has often been assumed. Nevertheless, formal definitions of retardation have for some time avoided etiological assumptions. Even more important, the many ways in which the environment causes and impacts mental development are now being given more than passing attention. This approach is reflected in the new conceptualization of MR offered in 1992 by the American Association on Mental Retardation (AAMR).

DEFINING MENTAL RETARDATION: AAMR'S PARADIGM SHIFT

Mental retardation is recognized by all major classification systems. However, AAMR has led efforts to understand and ameliorate MR. Once known as the American Association on Mental Deficiency, this influential organization was founded in 1876. Over the decades it has offered leading definitions of mental retardation. Its 1992 publication *Mental Retardation: Definition, Classification, and Systems of Supports* provides the following definition:

Mental retardation refers to substantial limitations in present functioning. It is characterized by significantly subaverage intellectual functioning, existing concurrently with related limitations in two or more of the following applicable adaptive skill areas: communication, self-care, home living, social skills, community use, self-direction, health and safety, functional academics, leisure, and work. Mental retardation manifests before age 18. (p. 5)

In this definition, subaverage intellectual functioning refers to a score of approximately 70–75 or below on a general test of intelligence, such as the Stanford-Binet and the Wechsler scales. Concurrent limitations in adaptive skills are tied to intellectual limitations rather than to some other circumstance such as cultural or language diversity. Assessment of adaptive skill must consider standards set by age-mates of the same social group. The age criterion signifies that mental retardation is viewed as a developmental disorder. Age eighteen is adopted because it approximates when individuals in our society usually assume adult roles. By this age crucial psychosocial and brain development has typically occurred.

AAMR's definition is fundamentally accepted by DSM-IV and ICD-10. All three systems recognized that retardation may occur with other psychological disorders.

AAMR's definition of mental retardation reflects the history of how the condition has been viewed and identified. At first primarily considered a medical disorder, diagnosis of MR had been based on physical examinations and global, ill-defined judgments of everyday competence. The construction of more objective general tests of intelligence, along with greater recognition of nonmedical factors, then resulted in an emphasis on intelligence test performance. Perceived limitations and abuse of these tests, in turn, resulted in greater attention to adaptive behavior. Thus, individuals who fall into the retarded range on intelligence tests but otherwise get along adequately at home, school, or work are not now judged as mentally retarded. Deficits in adaptive behavior without poor performance on intelligence tests also do not warrant the diagnosis of retardation.

In fact, the major aspects of the current definition are not a dramatic departure from definitions going back to 1959. Why then does the 1992 AAMR manual claim a "paradigm shift" in the understanding of mental retardation? Briefly put, it has to do with a stronger rejection of mental retardation as an absolute trait of the individual, and a greater emphasis on interaction between the individual with limited intellectual functioning and his or her environment. These ideas now stand at the center of how mental retardation is viewed.

Figure 10–1 indicates that the paradigm takes a broad view of the individual functioning in complex ways in a sociocultural context. The diagnosis of MR depends on how the individual is actually functioning; if functioning changes, so might the diagnosis. Functioning is related to capabilities (shown on the left side), which interact with the environments in which individuals live, learn, play, work, and socialize (shown on the right side). This model also indicates that functioning potentially influences the supports provided to the individual, and supports in turn influence functioning.

AAMR notes four assumptions that are essential for applying the model. First, valid assessment must consider cultural, linguistic, and behavioral diversity. Second, adaptive skills must be judged according to typical community environments, and limitations in these skills should be a basis for treatment and support. Third, possible strengths in adaptive skills and personal capabilities should be recognized. And finally, it is assumed that functioning will usually improve with appropriate, sustained support. Thus, the model implicates assessment not only of the individual but also of the environment and available supports. As this text is being written, training sessions on the new paradigm are being offered. It can be

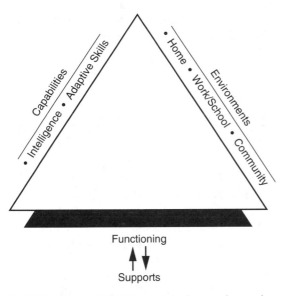

Functioning

Supports

FIGURE 10–1 AAMR's model of mental retardation.

From *Mental Retardation: Definition, Classification, and Systems of Support,* 9th Ed. AAMR, 1992, p. 10.

expected that the model will have far-reaching implications.

THE NATURE AND MEASUREMENT OF INTELLIGENCE

Performance on intelligence tests is critical for diagnosing mental retardation, so understanding these tests is essential. As with all psychological tests, reliability and validity must be considered. Both of these are related to how intelligence is conceptualized.

Most of us have an intuitive idea about the general nature of intelligence and would willingly identify individuals we believe are "very smart" or "not so smart." We might agree, as have theorists, that intelligence involves the knowledge possessed by a person, the ability to learn or think, or the capacity to adapt to new situations. Beyond these general definitions, however, we might run into disagreements. Indeed, theorists them-

selves argue about the precise nature of intelligence, are constructing new theories about the nature of intelligence, and are investigating new ways to measure intelligence (Matarazzo, 1992). Nevertheless, the history of intelligence testing sheds light on what the current tests are actually measuring. These tests consist of various tasks that tap different abilities, but also a general ability that is referred to as *g*.

The Binet Scales

Credit for the first successful intelligence tests is given to Alfred Binet, who was asked by the Minister of Public Instruction in Paris to find a way to better identify children who needed special educational experiences (Tuddenham, 1962). Binet and his colleague T. Simon approached their task in a practical way, by testing children on brief tasks that were relevant to the classroom. Their original 1905 scale consisted of thirty tasks of diverse content that gradually became more difficult. In the 1908 revision the scale was ordered according to age, that is, all the tasks passed by normal five-year-olds were placed together, as were those passed by normal six-year-olds, and so on. Such age-ordering reflected the belief that mental development increases with age throughout childhood. On the basis of their performance, children were assigned a mental age (MA), the age corresponding to the chronological age (CA) of children whose performance they equaled. Thus, a seven-year-old who passed the tests that the average seven-year-old passed was assigned a MA of seven; a seven-year-old who passed the tests that the average six-year-old passed obtained a MA of six.

In 1911, just prior to Binet's death, another revision of the scale was published, adding and refining specific tasks. All of this work reflected concern for scientific integrity. Reliability was checked by testing groups of children and then retesting them

Alfred Binet (1856–1911), a French psychologist, helped develop the first intelligence tests.

(New York Public Library collection)

later. Validity was established by comparing children's test scores with other judgments of their ability, such as teachers' ratings of actual school performance.

Binet was interested in theories of intelligence and the early scales reflected several assumptions about intelligence (Siegler, 1992). He believed that intelligence encompassed many complex processes. He also believed that atypical performance was best understood by comparisons to average performance. Binet viewed intelligence as malleable within limits, rather than fixed, and influenced by the social environment. In addition to his scientific interests, Binet was an advocate for children. He feared that children could be inaccurately evaluated and argued that carefully constructed standardized tests were necessary to minimize this possibility. Furthermore, Binet and his colleagues devised methods to improve intel-

lectual functioning, and they recommended that educational programs be fitted to each child's special needs and be conducted in small-sized classes (Tuddenham, 1962).

The Stanford-Binet. The testing movement in the United States began when Henry Goddard translated and used the Binet scales with residents of the Vineland Training School in New Jersey (Cushna, 1980). Goddard widely distributed the scales and directed early research on mental retardation (Achenbach, 1982). Then, in 1916, Lewis Terman—working at Stanford University—revised the early scales into the Stanford-Binet test (S-B). He adapted the items to the U.S. population and tested a relatively large number of children with them. Terman and his associates also adopted the idea of the intelligence quotient (IQ) as the ratio of an individual's mental age to chronological age, multiplied by one hundred to avoid decimals. This ratio IQ enabled direct comparison of the performance of children of different ages. Today, this comparison is done through statistical comparisons so that what is still often called IQ is no longer a quotient but a score that nevertheless denotes age comparisons.

Goddard and Terman made several assumptions about intelligence testing that were markedly different than those of Binet's. Both assumed that standardized tests measured inherited intelligence that would remain stable over the life of the individual (e.g., Cravens, 1992). They also saw the need for *eugenics*, the improvement of the human species by control of inheritance (Gould, 1981). These assumptions eventually caused serious conflicts about the meaning of "intelligence" and the use of intelligence tests.

Not all who used the Stanford-Binet adhered to hereditary beliefs, of course, and the test has been further revised and updated, independent of this issue. In the current S-B (the fourth revision) items are no longer grouped into age levels. Instead, similar items are grouped into fifteen subtests (e.g., vocabulary, copying, memory for objects), most of which are taken by each examinee. The subtests assess four cognitive areas for ages two to twenty three years: verbal reasoning, abstract/visual reasoning, quantitative reasoning, and short-term memory (Anastasi, 1988; Thorndike, Hagen, and Sattler, 1986). Each person achieves a Standard Age Score (SAS) for each of the four cognitive areas and for the entire scale. The SASs are compared with the performance of the standard norm group of the same chronological age. The average SAS is set at one hundred by statistical procedures. Thus, an obtained SAS higher than one hundred means that the person has performed better than average for his or her age; an obtained SAS less than one hundred means a less-than-average performance. These SASs are what most people call IQ, or more correctly "deviation IQ." (See Table 10–1 for a summary of various measures of intelligence.)

The Wechsler Scales

The Wechsler intelligence tests are widely employed. Based on the work of David Wechsler, they originated in 1939 with the Wechsler-Bellevue test. Three instruments now exist: the Wechsler Adult Intelligence Scale (WAIS-R), the Wechsler Intelligence Scale for Children (WISC-III) for six to sixteen-year-olds, and the Wechsler Preschool and Primary Scale of Intelligence (WPPSI) for the age range of four to six.

All the Wechsler scales follow the same format. They consist of different kinds of subtests—such as vocabulary, puzzles, and arithmetic problems—each of which contains items that become gradually more difficult. The examinee completes as many items as possible on each subtest. The subtests are designated as either verbal or performance tasks. The former emphasize verbal skills, knowledge of the environment, and social understanding. Performance subtests emphasize perceptual-motor skills, speed, and nonverbal abstraction. The Wechsler scales permit the calculation of three deviation IQs: a verbal IQ, a performance IQ, and a full scale IQ that combines verbal and performance scores. As with the S-B, performance is compared with the norm group of similar age, and the average performance is one hundred.

Infant Tests of Intelligence

Because it is believed that early identification of mental deficiency is beneficial, efforts have been made to evaluate very young children. Several individually administered tests exist. An example is the Bayley Scales of Infant Development-II, which covers ages one to forty-two months. Performance on this test is usually termed developmental quotient (DQ), since it assesses somewhat different abilities than tests for older children. Infant tests give greater emphasis to sensorimotor functioning and less emphasis to language and abstraction. This may partly account for the fact that performance on infant tests is not highly correlated with later IQ.

TABLE 10–1   Measures Relevant to Tests of Intelligence

CA	Chronological Age.
MA	Mental Age. The age score corresponding to the chronological age of children whose performance the examinee equals. For the average child, MA = CA.
IQ (ratio)	The ratio of mental age to chronological age multiplied by 100. IQ = MA/CA × 100.
IQ (deviation)	A standard score derived from statistical procedures that reflects the direction and degree to which an individual's performance deviates from the average score of the age group.

Whatever the reason, standardized developmental tests administered during the first few years of life cannot be solely relied on to predict later intellectual performance for most children. However, they may be better predictors of mental deficiency than of average and superior intelligence. They may also be especially useful when used in conjunction with histories and neurodevelopmental assessments (e.g., Bregman and Hodapp, 1991). Thus, if an infant's performance is substantially behind that of its age-mates, the infant has a history of perinatal damage, and there are other signs of nervous system dysfunction, a diagnostician might strongly suspect mental retardation. Efforts are underway to develop more useful measures of early intelligence, for example, of attending to and processing of visual stimuli (Laucht, Esser, and Schmidt, 1994; Slater, 1995). These newer measures are promising but are not highly predictive of later intellectual deficits either, so the most reasonable course of action is to provide infants who have below average performance with regular follow-up examinations and enriched environments.

Interpretation of IQ Tests

The use of intelligence tests raises a host of important questions. What do these tests actually measure? Do tests produce reliable measures? Do early IQ scores predict later intellectual performance? These concerns are both theoretical and practical.

Validity: What IQ tests measure. Perhaps the most central issue is the question of what an IQ score tells us about a person. Recall that Binet and Simon sought to measure academic ability and produced some evidence for the validity of their scale. Indeed, if intelligence is defined as ability that relates to school performance, evidence exists for validity. Most intelligence tests emphasize verbal abilities, which are important

in academics. After age five, the correlations of IQ with school grades and reading, spelling, and mathematic achievement scores are moderately high, generally in the range of .40 to .75 (Berger and Yule, 1985; Matarazzo, 1992). Moreover, the relationship between IQ and academic performance appears even stronger for individuals whose IQ scores fall into the below average range.

However, correlations with out-of-school achievements are relatively low (Baumeister, 1987). The limitations of intelligence tests are widely noted. Binet himself believed that factors other than intelligence could affect test performance (Siegler, 1992). Wechsler (1991) noted that the tests do not assess attitudes, persistence, enthusiasm, and the like, which may contribute to general intelligence. Cooperation, social responsiveness, and motivational variables such as expectancy for success and failure may influence test scores and everyday intelligence, but their influence is not well discriminated on intelligence tests (Scarr, 1982; Zigler and Balla, 1982). In addition, intelligence tests are given in highly controlled situations and the questions are highly structured. Thus, IQ performance may not adequately reflect the everyday world, where individuals are called on to adopt various strategies to solve problems in various situations (Fredericksen, 1986). IQ scores thus can be expected to be more valid in some situations than in others. Furthermore, validity can be different for groups of people to the extent that these groups function in different situations (Garcia, 1981).

Are IQ scores stable or changing? The stability of IQ scores over time has long been argued. The issue can be examined by studying a group of people longitudinally, comparing their earlier IQ scores to later IQ scores. When such test-retest measurements are made after preschool age, IQ scores are quite stable for groups of normal functioning individuals (e.g., Matarazzo, 1990). And, in general, correlations between sets of scores become stronger as the time between testings decreases. Such stability indicates that tests of intelligence are reasonably reliable over time.

It is important to note that correlational analyses examine groups of people. However, individual scores can also be examined over time. Earlier in this century it was widely held that individual IQ scores could not change. But information gradually emerged to challenge this view. McCall, Applebaum, and Hogarty (1973), for example, concluded from their own and other data that IQ changes of thirty and forty points occur fairly often. Conditions such as illness, fatigue, the family situation, educational opportunity, social adjustment, and mental health have all been associated with change in individual IQ (Robinson and Robinson, 1976).

Do these findings apply to mentally retarded individuals? In general, the IQs of the mentally handicapped are more stable than those of persons with average and superior scores, and the lower the scores the greater the stability (Berger and Yule, 1985). But, again, change can occur. For example, Silverstein (1982) tested mildly retarded children for four consecutive years, starting when they averaged about eleven years of age. Almost 12 percent of the children showed ten to twelve points change in either direction. More dramatic change has been documented when the social environment has been deliberately improved (Clarke and Clarke, 1984).

Caution is necessary, then, in interpreting measured intelligence and using scores to categorize people as mentally retarded. IQ scores are relatively stable, but they are not cast in stone. Indeed, their use as a primary tool for identifying retardation and making decisions about education and placement is discouraged (Weinberg, 1989). Scores should be interpreted within the context of the person's life, including how the person functions in different environments and the available supports.

THE NATURE AND MEASUREMENT OF ADAPTIVE BEHAVIOR

The concept of adaptive behavior is quite old and is presently enjoying renewed interest. It was in 1959 that AAMR first included deficits in adaptive functioning as a criterion for mental retardation. Over the years, various definitions of adaptive behavior have been offered. A review of these definitions suggests several commonalities (DeStefano and Thompson, 1990).

1. Adaptive behavior is viewed as developmental; that is, it differs for age groups and can be expected to grow. During infancy and early childhood, sensorimotor, communication, self-help, and primary socialization skills increase. During later childhood and adolescence, reasoning and judgments about the environment and social relationships increase in importance. Still later in life, vocational performance and the assumption of social responsibility become more central.

2. Most definitions of adaptive behavior recognize several domains of functioning. These include taking care of one's physical needs, getting along with others, accepting and being responsible to the social group in which one is interacting, and being able to apply cognitive competencies to everyday living (e.g., telling time, handling money).

3. Agreement exists that judgments about adaptive behavior need to take culture into account. Different expectations might exist in different cultural settings.

4. It is also widely agreed that judgments about adaptive behavior are best made with regard to specific situations as adaptiveness varies. For example, so-called "six-hour retardation" has been recognized. Here, the child appears retarded in functioning while at school, but functions adequately at home and in the neighborhood.

Numerous standardized instruments exist to measure adaptive behavior (Patton, Beirne-Smith, and Payne, 1990). All these tests focus on the domain of everyday life—on current ability to meet environmental demands. They vary greatly in quality and in their intended use (DeStefano and Thompson, 1990). Some tests are designed to evaluate broad populations while others are restricted, for example, to assess only young children, severely retarded behaviors, or functioning in a specific area. Most depend heavily on interviews with parents and other caregivers. Here, we look at two widely employed scales that aim at broad assessment.

Vineland Adaptive Behavior Scales

Working for many years at the Vineland Training School, Edgar Doll emphasized the importance of social adequacy and the ability of retarded persons to manage their lives. He was among the first to take seriously the task of assessing adaptive behavior. In 1935 he published a scale to measure social competence, which he assumed grew with chronological age (Myers, Nihira, and Zetlin, 1979). Doll believed that social competence could be quantified by summing performance across eight domains of behavior (Doll, 1965). A social age (SA) and a social quotient (SQ) were calculated, similar to MA and IQ, to reflect the examinee's standing as compared to nonhandicapped individuals.

Doll's test was revised and expanded in 1984 by Sparrow, Balla, and Cicchetti, and is now called the Vineland Adaptive Behavior Scales. Three versions exist. Two versions are semistructured interviews for parents and other caretakers, which can be used from birth to eighteen years of age and with low-functioning adults. The third version consists of items for teachers of three-to twelve-year-olds. All versions cover four major behavioral domains: communication, daily living skills, socialization, and motor skills. Additionally, with the exception of the teacher's version, there is an optional do-

The ability to perform everyday adaptive behaviors has become an important criterion in evaluating mental retardation.

(New York State Office of Mental Retardation)

main of maladaptive behavior. Scores from the separate domains and an overall score can be compared to scores earned by a large, normal standardization group and also to the performance of smaller special groups such as mentally retarded, emotionally disturbed, and hearing-impaired persons.

AAMR's Adaptive Behavior Scales

For several years AAMR has published adaptive behavior scales to be employed in the community and in the schools (Myers et al., 1979). The recent revisions are called the Adaptive Behavior Scales–Residential and Community (ABS–RC) and the Adaptive Behavior Scales–School Edition (ABS–SE). An adaptive behavior scale now also exists for infants and young children to age six (Shaw, Hammer, and Leland, 1991).

The ABS–RC is based on the performance of persons with development disabilities living in U.S. communities or institutions (Nihira, Leland, and Lambert, 1993). It examines a wide range of behaviors in persons from age three into adulthood, in several domains of functioning. Statistical analyses show that five factors are tapped: personal self-sufficiency, community self-sufficiency, personal-social responsibility, social adjustment, and personal adjustment.

The ABS–SE is similar to the ABS–RC scale in behavioral domains and the information it provides (Lambert, Leland, and Nihira, 1993). It is designed for children ages three through sixteen, primarily for students with mild and moderate levels of retardation (DeStefano and Thompson, 1990). Its norm group consists of persons with developmental disabilities attending public schools in the United States, and nondisabled students.

Strengths and Weaknesses of Adaptive Behavior Scales

Although the construction of adaptive behavior scales has lagged behind that of intelligence tests, these scales are being improved and extended. Increased attention is being given to reliability and validity. In reply to the federal government's mandate to better meet the needs of developmentally disabled infants, researchers are extending the tests to this young population.

If adaptive behavior scales are to be useful at all, they must accurately reflect current functioning. Whether they do or not depends partly on the accuracy of reports from parents and caregivers. Ratings of specific questions are more likely to be accurate than ratings of general and vague questions (e.g., Can the child count to ten? versus Can the child count?). At the least, caretakers must be sensitive and have opportunities for observing behavior.

One way to examine the validity of adaptive behavior scales is to determine their relationship to IQ scores. We would expect measures of intellectual development to correlate with how individuals can care for themselves, act independently, and relate to others in daily living. In fact, several studies show a moderately strong correlation (.40–.60) between IQ and adaptive behavior (DeStefano and Thompson, 1990). In general then, adaptive behavior overlaps with intelligence but taps factors other than the mental processes tapped by IQ tests. This is, of course, what these tests are intended to do.

Other validity studies show a relationship between daily living behaviors and important nonacademic variables. For example, high scores in the maladaptive domain (e.g., has temper tantrums, is destructive) relate to being institutionalized. And importantly, research is gradually establishing the connection between adaptive behavior scores and later adjustment in the community (McGrew, Bruininks, and Thurlow, 1992).

Still, it is recognized that adaptive skills can vary in different environments, at different times, and within different social classes. They are not fixed and can depend on the match between the individual and the immediate situation (Scott, 1994). It has thus been argued that adaptive behavior should not be used to classify individuals as mentally retarded. Zigler and his colleagues (1984), for example, give a hypothetical example of a child with an IQ of 65 who fails in school. This child might easily be classified as mentally retarded. Yet with added resources, perhaps just special help from a caring teacher, the child might perform adequately in school (that is, adapt) and no longer meet the criteria for retardation. In this case, the child might be declassifed by the school—and lose special supports. Yet the child's intellectual processes would not have changed; what changed was the social environment.

But even these investigators do not suggest that adaptive behavior is unimportant in understanding retardation. Evaluating adaptive behavior makes it possible to better understand factors that might influence and predict the ability to succeed in life. Further, the scales are used not only to diagnose but also to plan and assess intervention and to select subjects for research.

LEVELS OF RETARDATION AND SUPPORTS

It has been long recognized that great variability exists in the capabilities and behaviors of people with mental retardation. Thus, levels of retardation have been set, usually according to IQ scores. Degree of severity of retardation has been considered helpful in placement, intervention, and research.

Table 10–2 shows the levels of retardation set by DSM-IV and behavioral descriptions for each level. Educators have used similar levels to assist them in making judgments of learning capacity. *Educable* is equivalent to mild retardation; *trainable* to

moderate/severe retardation; *custodial* to profound retardation.

It is notable that AAMR's new model completely eliminates classifying people by IQ levels. Instead, for each person descriptions are given of four dimensions:

1. The individual's strengths and weaknesses in intellectual functioning and adaptive skills
2. The individual's strengths and weaknesses with regard to psychological/emotional functioning
3. The individual's strengths and weaknesses with regard to physical functioning and health
4. The current environment and the optimal environment that would facilitate continued growth

A profile is then developed of needed supports across the four dimensions. The profile stipulates, for each dimension, the level of support required: intermittent, limited, extensive, or pervasive. The past practice of assigning a level of IQ is thus replaced with an analysis of levels of environmental supports. A diagnosis might thus be "a person with mental retardation with extensive supports needed in the areas of social skills and self-direction" (American Association on MR, 1992, p. 34). This approach emphasizes the goal of growth in multiple areas of functioning and reflects AAMR's concept of mental retardation as intricately linked to the environment. AAMR believes, and we agree, that categorizing people according to level of retardation encourages the view that mental retardation is a static quality of the individual, whereas the new approach focuses the potential of the environment to provide supports and services that will enhance opportunities for personal life satisfaction.

PREVALENCE

The prevalence of mental retardation is estimated at about 2 to 3 percent of the general

TABLE 10–2 Levels of Mental Retardation According to DSM-IV

Level	IQ Range	% of MR Population	Functioning
Mild	50–55 to about 70	85	Social and communication skills usually develop in preschool years Minimal sensorimotor deficits Can acquire about sixth-grade academic skills by late teens Usually achieve adult vocational and social skills for self-support May need guidance, assistance, supervised living, but often live successfully in the community
Moderate	35–40 to 50–55	10	Communication skills usually develop in early childhood Personal care, with support Unlikely to progress beyond second-grade academic skills Can benefit from social and occupation skills training and do supervised unskilled or semiskilled work Adapt well to supervised community living
Severe	20–25 to 35–40	3–4	May learn to talk and minimally care for self at school age Limited ability to profit from pre-academic training In adulthood, may perform simple tasks with supervision Most adapt well to community living with family or in group homes
Profound	below 20/25	1–2	Most have a neurological condition Sensorimotor impairments in childhood Motor, self-care, communication skills may improve with training Optimal development requires structure, constant supervision with individual caretaker May do simple supervised tasks

population when IQ is taken as the criterion (Scott, 1994). This figure coincides with what would be expected from the theoretical distribution of IQ scores. Intelligence, it is assumed, is normally distributed. Figure 10–2 depicts the theoretical normal curve, and also shows how performance on intelligence tests is fitted to this theoretical curve. In this example, the Wechsler Intelligence Scale for Children is used. The mean IQ score is 100 and as scores increasingly differ from the mean, they decrease in frequency. This relationship is measured by statistical units called standard deviations, which relate to the percentage of scores under the curve and to specific scores. IQs of seventy or less fall two or more standard deviations below the mean, and they make up about 2.27 percent of all the scores.

So far we have said nothing about prevalence when mental retardation is defined by both IQ and adaptive behavior. In fact, prevalence had mostly been estimated by IQ alone. However, there are sufficient data now to indicate that when the dual criteria are used prevalence drops to under 1 per-

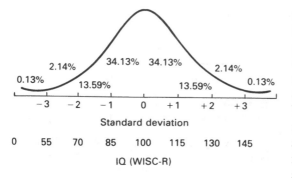

FIGURE 10–2   Theoretical normal distribution of IQ scores.

cent (Scott, 1994). This is thought to reflect the fact that about half of those with mild retardation do not require services and are thus not identified in prevalence studies.

Prevalence data for MR is especially interesting when age of the population and severity of retardation are inspected. Figure 10–3 demonstrates the general finding that the greatest number of cases is found at school-age and adolescence. Preschool youngsters are only rarely identified, and with advancing age in adulthood fewer and fewer individuals are identified.

Figure 10–3 also shows that extremely low IQ is rare and mild retardation is most commonly seen. When preschoolers are identified, they most often have IQs below fifty, apparently because the more severe cases are obvious and elicit attention. But a dramatic shift occurs when children enter school. Now even mild retardation is identified, probably because the children are unable to meet the new demands in this situation. The decline in adulthood in moderate and mild retardation is probably due to several factors. Death may account for some decline, as well as unavailability for assessment. Also, with the intellectual demands of school gone, essentially unchanged individuals may successfully undertake unskilled jobs and function adequately in society (Clarke and Clarke, 1985). Still other individuals may continue to learn and mature into adulthood, so that they are increasingly able to meet various demands.

Other variables are important when prevalence is examined (Crnic, 1988; Scott, 1994). Low socioeconomic groups account for a disproportionate number of cases, especially of mild retardation. MR is also more prevalent in some minority groups. And it appears more among males than females. Males may be at greater biological risk, but if there are higher social expectations for males, cultural standards may play a role.

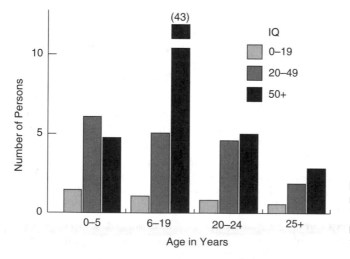

FIGURE 10–3   Estimated number of retarded persons in a community of 100,000.

From Tarjan, Wright, Eyman, and Keeran, 1973.

The epidemiology of mental retardation clearly suggests that different environments vary in sensitivity to retardation (Baumeister, 1987). We are thus reminded that behavior deficits are interpreted within the social context.

ETIOLOGY

There are many etiologies associated with mental retardation, but in most cases no clear cause is established. Historically there has been a tendency to view MR as falling into two categories: that caused by biological factors and that caused by psychosocial factors (American Association on MR, 1992). This account has been replaced by multifactor explanations, which recognize, however, that in any single case, one factor may contribute more than others. It is still useful to categorize causation or risk in some way, and we follow Scott (1994) in recognizing three major kinds of influences: organic, polygenic, and psychosocial/cultural.

Organic Causation

Attributing MR to organic factors implies that some condition or circumstance is causally associated with disordered brain function and intellectual deficits. Empirical evidence exists to support this idea. Major organic causes are known and believed to be the primary cause in about 25 percent of cases of mental retardation (Scott and Carran, 1987).

Zigler and his colleagues have emphasized that although IQ scores are said to be normally distributed in the general population, they actually fall into a distribution that resembles the normal curve except for a "bump" at the low end (Burack, 1990; Zigler et al., 1984). The excess of low scores, they suggested, is accounted for by individuals who have suffered major biological impairment. Indeed, although organic factors are associated with all levels of mental deficiency, they are especially associated with the more severe levels. For example, known organic cause exists in an estimated 55 to 75 percent of children with severe retardation and only 10 to 25 percent with mild retardation (Scott, 1994). Brain impairment may be due to abnormal genetic mechanisms, prenatal and birth variables, or postnatal circumstances.

Chromosome abnormalities. Aberrations in the number and structure of the chromosomes are associated with specific syndromes of mental retardation. For the most part, the exact way in which these abnormalities cause lowered intelligence and other problems is not understood. We will discuss Down's syndrome, the most common genetic disorder of mental retardation, which occurs in approximately one in a thousand births (Thapar et al., 1994).

Down's syndrome was described in 1866 by Langdon Down, a British physician. For several years it was noted that concordance in monozygotic twins approached 100 percent, which implicated a genetic process (Rainer, 1980). In 1959, only three years after human chromosomes were fully described, Lejeune and others discovered trisomy 21 in persons with Down's syndrome. As shown in Figure 10–4, the #21 chromosome appears in a triplet instead of a pair. Ninety-five percent of all cases are attributed to this abnormality, with the remainder caused by related aberrations (Thapar et al., 1994).

The occurrence of Down's syndrome increases with maternal age. It is believed that advancing maternal age is related to failure of the chromosome pairs to divide in meiosis, with trisomy 21 being a result. However, the extra chromosome has been traced to fathers in a minority of cases (Evans and Hammerton, 1985; Holmes, 1978). Whatever the mechanism, a woman who has had a baby with Down's syndrome has a 1 percent risk of having another such child.

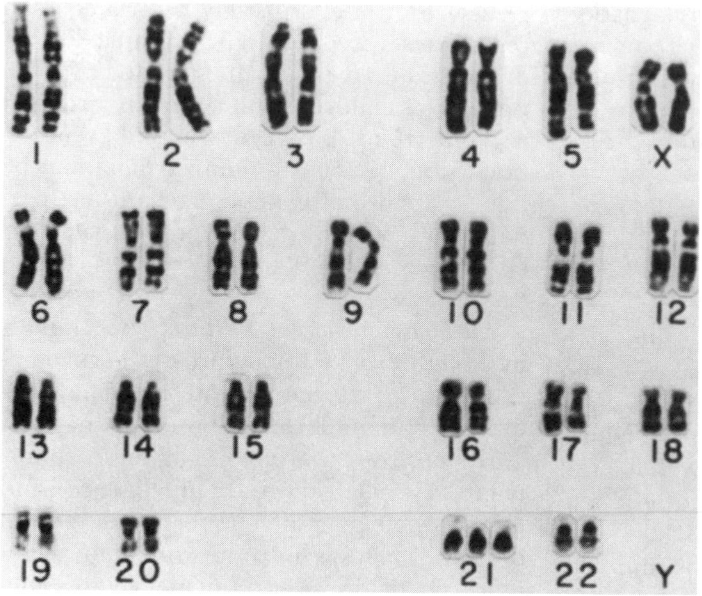

FIGURE 10–4 The chromosome complement of a female with #21 trisomy.

Courtesy of the March of Dimes Birth Defects Foundation.

Down's syndrome children are born with a variety of physical abnormalities that make them look strikingly alike. Most characteristic is the epicanthal folds at the corners of the eyes and the upward slant of the eyes, which gave rise to the now outdated name "mongolism." Other frequently seen attributes include facial flatness, fissured and thick tongues, broad hands and feet, and poor muscle tone (Aman, Hammer, and Rojahn, 1993). Children with Down's syndrome are at risk for serious health problems, such as heart defects and hearing impairment. Life expectancy is below normal, but has climbed substantially in recent years (Carr, 1994).

Tested intelligence typically ranges in the moderate to profound levels of retardation and is occasionally higher (Szymanski and Kaplan, 1991). Developmental deficits are usually evident during the first few years of life, and the rate of development progressively slows throughout childhood and adolescence (Bregman and Hodapp, 1991; Carr, 1994). The relative impairments and strengths associated with Down's syndrome are becoming better understood. Language functioning is relatively weak; this is particularly so for grammar while pragmatic language skill is better. There is also weakness in scanning the environment to extract information. Social skills are relatively high; these children cooperate with others and respect social rules. At the same time, their emotions seem muted.

As with all children, the home environment is important to development. Mother-child interaction may be subtly different than normal by the first or second year (Berger, 1990; Landry and Chapieski, 1989). A disproportionately high percentage of infants and toddlers with Down's syndrome are insecurely attached to their caretakers (Atkinson et al., 1995). One study found that mothers used more physical stimulation than mothers of nonretarded infants, who used speech to a greater extent (Smith and Hagen, 1984). The development of the infants with Down's syndrome declined the least when their mothers frequently spoke to them with reference to the environment. Other research indicates that parents may demand too much from their infants (Berger, 1990). At the same time, many parents do appropriately judge and encourage their child's competence.

Single-gene inheritance. A number of specific syndromes associated with mental retardation are inherited in Mendelian single-gene patterns. Many of the syndromes involve defective metabolism in which handicaps gradually worsen. Recessive genes are often implicated, although sex-linked and dominant gene patterns are found. Treatment, when it exists, often involves a diet to reduce the biochemical substance that is inadequately metabolized or to add a missing biochemical. Table 10–3 lists some of these known metabolic disorders. Such conditions account for only a small proportion of mental deficiency; nevertheless, it is encouraging that advances in genetics hold promise for prevention and specific treatments.

The fragile X syndrome is among the inherited disorders associated with MR. It is of particular interest because, although discovered relatively recently, it is second to Down's syndrome as a genetic cause of retardation (Bregman and Hodapp, 1991). This condition derives its name from an abnormal "fragile" site on the X chromosome. The syndrome is inherited in an unusual X-linked pattern (Thapar et al., 1994). Some males who inherit the defective gene appear normal but can pass the gene to female offspring. It is the female carriers who produce fragile X offspring. Many of these women carriers are developmentally unaffected; others (perhaps one-third) have an IQ of less than eighty-five and may display learning, attentional, emotional, and other problems (Hagerman, 1992). Carrier mothers pass the condition to half their sons. When the mothers themselves have been affected, these sons also show symptoms. When the mothers have not been affected, only about 80 percent of their sons are affected. The males tend to have long faces, large ears, and oversized testicles.

Studies of affected persons (mostly males have been studied), indicate that mental retardation can be severe, but the range of moderate to mild is more common. The rate of development progressively slows during childhood and especially during puberty, from about ten to fifteen years of age. There is evidence for specific language and information processing deficits and strengths in daily living skills. Some affected males have near normal IQs but have learning difficulties and various other problems such as attention deficits, hyperactivity, and social impairments.

Prenatal and birth complications. Prenatal exposure to disease, chemicals, drugs, radiation, poor nutrition, and Rh incompatibility may jeopardize the intellectual development of the child. Low birth weight and prematurity are associated with neurological and intellectual deficits (Bregman and Hodapp, 1991). Preterm infants who show neurological insults on ultrasound assessments (e.g., hemorrhage in the brain) are more likely to show later disability than preterm babies without such neurological indicators.

Birth complications, such as anoxia and injury, can also take a toll. Anoxia occurs in about five of a thousand births, about 20 percent of the infants are adversely affected, and cerebral palsy with mental retardation can follow (Scott, 1994). It is now thought that birth complications often reflect pre-existing conditions, and that these conditions may underlie both difficult birth and retardation. In such cases, birth complications in themselves may contribute relatively little to the etiology of MR.

Postnatal factors. Mental retardation may also be caused postnatally by a variety of variables including seizures, malnutrition, diseases such as encephalitis and meningitis, head injuries from accidents, and lead poisoning. All these factors can interfere with nervous system functioning and develop-

TABLE 10–3 Some Inherited Metabolic Disorders Associated with Mental Retardation

Disorder and Mechanism	Metabolic Disturbance	Manifestation	Treatment
Phenylketonia recessive inheritance	Inability to convert the amino acid phenylalanine due to deficient liver enzyme	Retardation, hyperactivity, unpredictable behavior, convulsions, eczema.	Diet low in phenylalanine, if begun early, can prevent or reduce retardation.
Maple Syrup Urine Disease recessive inheritance	Abnormal metabolism of amino acids—leucine, isoleucine, valine	Infants develop rigidity, seizures, respiratory irregularities, hypoglycemia. Most die in few months if untreated or are severely retarded.	Diet low in leucine, isoleucine, valine.
Hartnup Disease recessive inheritance	Defective transport of amino acid, tryptophan	Symptoms vary. Mental deficiency; photosensitive skin rash; coordination problems. Personality change and psychoses may be only symptoms. Mild cases not detected until late childhood or adolescence.	Nicotinic acid and antibodies may relieve rash, but retardation is not relieved.
Neimann-Pick Disease recessive inheritance	Abnormal metabolism and storage of fats in neurons, liver, spleen	Early mental regression and developmental arrest. Abdominal enlargement; anemia; emancidation; occasionally a red spot in retina.	No known treatment; death usually occurs before age 4.
Schilder's Disease sex-linked inheritance	Decrease in fats in CNS resulting in demyelination of cerebral white matter	Onset more common in older children and adults. Personality and behavioral changes. Paresis; cortical blindness and deafness; convulsions; dementia.	No established treatment; may respond to steroids.
Galactosemia recessive inheritance	Inability to convert galactose (carbohydrate) to glucose	After few days of milk intake, jaundice; vomiting; diarrhea; failure to thrive. Leads to rapid death or mental retardation; cataracts; liver insufficiency; occasional hypoglycemia; convulsions.	Early galactose-free diet permits normality.

Based on Cytryn and Lourie, 1980.

ment. Sometimes causation appears relatively clear, as when intellectual decrements are traced to disease of the brain. However, it is not always easy to establish clear causation; for example, malnutrition that affects the brain may be confounded with other variables. Nevertheless, many postnatal circumstances can be thought of as factors that put the child or adolescent at organic risk.

Polygenic Influences

The organic influences just discussed are assumed to cause retardation through abnormal brain development or brain damage. In contrast, polygenic influences derive from multiple genes whose effects combine to produce variation in intelligence in normal populations. Mental retardation is viewed as representing the lower scores in this variation.

The argument that inheritance influences intelligence and mental deficiency is an old one that in past times was often based on flimsy or flawed "proof." For example, in his influential study of the Kallikak family, Goddard (1912) traced the quite distinct genealogical lines of Martin Kallikak. One line originated from Kallikak's liaison with a barmaid; the second from later marriage to a woman of "better stock." From information on several hundred of Kallikak's descendants, Goddard found a pronounced difference in the two families; namely, that the first liaison had resulted in more mental deficiency, criminality, alcoholism, and immorality. Obvious weaknesses existed in this study, most notably the questionable accuracy of the data. Moreover, the results were taken as evidence that mental deficiency was inherited, although family environment could just as well have played a role.

Current understanding of hereditary influence on tested intelligence has a firm base in research with twins, adopted children, and families. Intelligence test performance of identical twins is overall more similar than for fraternal twins (McGue et al., 1993). This holds even on specific intellectual tasks. When identical twins are reared apart, similarity is somewhat less but is still quite high. Studies of families and adopted children lend support to these findings. In general, it is estimated that about 50 percent of the variation in tested intelligence in populations is due to genetic transmission of multiple genes (Plomin, DeFries, and McClearn, 1990).

Earlier we pointed to evidence that organic factors are more strongly associated with the more severe levels of retardation. The opposite is thought to hold for polygenic influences. Thus, one investigation revealed that the IQ of siblings of children with severe retardation averaged 103, hinting that severe retardation did not "run in families" and that some specific organic factor caused the retardation in the affected children. In contrast, the IQ of siblings of children with mild retardation averaged 85, suggesting a family factor that could be polygenic inheritance (Broman et al., 1987; Scott, 1994).

Psychosocial/Cultural Influences

Despite the evidence that some cases of retardation, especially mild deficiency, might be linked to polygenes, environmental influences might also be causal. Interest in psychosocial and cultural factors is historically tied to what was once called cultural-familial retardation (Crnic, 1988). The terms "garden variety" and "undifferentiated" also were used, reflecting the large number of cases of MR that were not readily distinguished from one another. Individuals assigned such labels had no identifiable organic etiology and usually appeared normal. Their IQ scores fell into the 50–70 range, and they possessed relatively good adaptive skills. They were often first identified upon entering school, and as adults often blended into the general population.

Other family members were frequently described in similar ways. A typical example is the description of six-year-old Johnny, who achieved a Stanford-Binet score of 67 (Robinson and Robinson, 1976). The family had eight children, several of whom were recognized as slow in school, and lived in a crowded, run-down, untidy, and disorganized house. The parents worked at unskilled jobs. Johnny's mother reported that he was a good child and she was surprised that his teacher perceived any problem. In school, Johnny could not master kindergarten reading readiness tasks and had problems in handling a pencil, folding paper, coloring within lines, and differentiating one symbol from another. He seemed to have a short attention span. He liked the other children but they tended to ignore him and exclude him from their recess play.

It has been observed for many years that mild retardation that "runs in families" occurs disproportionately in the lower socioeconomic classes—and some minority groups—and could be caused by psychosocial/cultural disadvantage. Severe social isolation can result in serious retardation, but even a milder lack of stimulation might lead to intellectual deficits. Educationally and economically deprived parents may lack skills and knowledge to stimulate children's language and cognitive development. Parents of any social class who are stressed and lacking social support undoubtedly find it difficult to provide their offspring with continuous sustenance and achievement motivation. This problem is likely to be more prevalent among parents of lower social class.

In fact, specific associations have been demonstrated between home environment variables, social class, and children's intellectual development. A recent study found, for instance, that lower social class, parental practices (interacting with the child, talking to the child, and being actively interested in what the child does), and IQ at age three were related (Hart and Risley, 1992). Investigations of disadvantaged children show that many psychosocial variables correlated with social class put the child at risk, such as parental education, parental attitudes, social support, and stressful life events (Sameroff, 1990). The more risk factors present, the higher the risk. The adverse effects of psychosocial variables may operate through inadequate stimulation for early brain growth, or inadequate enhancement of learning and attitudes favorable to achievement. Thus, while many of those reared in poverty do well, a disproportionate number display intellectual deficits (Patton, Beirne-Smith, and Payne, 1990).

Nevertheless, it is difficult to pinpoint any one cause of MR in disadvantaged children. This population is also at risk for major inherited abnormalities, prenatal and birth adversities, postnatal malnutrition, disease, and other adversities that can affect the developing brain. Polygenic inheritance also cannot be ruled out. Furthermore, given what is known about the intricacies of development, a multifactor explanation appears reasonable for much retardation as it takes into account organic, polygene, and psychosocial influences, and their possible interactions.

LEARNING AND COGNITION

One of the ways to better understand mental retardation is to search for the learning and cognitive processes that underlie deficient intellect. Historically, investigators motivated by a variety of theoretical and practical concerns have been interested in establishing the degree to which learning might occur, the kinds of deficits that exist, and whether training might overcome intellectual and adaptive deficits.

Studies of Conditioning

Early investigations of classical and operant conditioning aimed at showing that learning

ACCENT 10–1   Mild Retardation: Are Intelligence Tests Biased?

The issue of bias in intelligence testing is almost invariably raised with regard to mild retardation and psychosocial/cultural influences. Are intelligence tests constructed and administered in such ways that they handicap those of low SES and certain racial/ethnic background? In fact, children of poor families and of some minority families (e.g., African-American, Hispanic, and Native American) perform relatively poorly on these tests, on average. In interpreting this fact it should be recognized that social class is often confounded with racial/ethnic background, and that their independent effects have not been adequately examined (e.g., Helms, 1992).

The group differences just cited have resulted in serious concerns about intelligence testing (Cronbach, 1975). One concern has been that minority students have been disproportionately labeled mildly or educably retarded and placed into special education classes in the public schools. Many people believed that group differences on test performance (and subsequent school placements) reflected test bias rather than true differences in intelligence. Confrontations with the educational system, some of which reached the courts, ensued over a variety of testing practices and test fairness issues (MacMillan, Keogh, and Jones, 1986). Questions were raised about bilingual students being assessed with standard English tests, about the content of tests not relating well to the subcultures in which students were being reared, and about the qualities of the tests being used.

Legal outcomes often, but not always, favored plaintiffs for the minority groups. The influential *Larry P. v. Riles* case, a class action suit in which the plaintiffs were black people, resulted in severe restrictions on the use of intelligence tests for identifying and placing black children into special education programs in California. On the other hand, the California ruling in *PASE v. Hamilton* judged that Wechsler and Stanford-Binet items were not biased against black children when these tests were used with other criteria for placement. In a more recent turn of events in California, black parents claimed discrimination in a legal suit on the basis that their children were denied the opportunity to take the tests, which could aid in assessment (Turkington, 1992). Some accommodation was made to these parents. Overall, educational systems have been forced to stringently monitor the use and administration of intelligence tests.

School placement is only one area of controversy in a long line of concerns about bias in intelligence testing. Historical accounts describe how IQ tests played an important role in establishing immigration quotas for people of southern European background and laws for the sterilization of mentally deficient individuals (Patton et al., 1990; Gould, 1981). Inherent in such uses and abuses of tests was the assumption that measured intelligence is a stable, inherent, biologically programmed characteristic of individuals. The more accepted view today is that intelligence tests assess important, circumscribed behaviors that result from the interaction of heredity and environment and that at least to some degree can be changed throughout life by environmental factors.

---

is indeed possible in those with mental retardation (Haywood, Meyers, and Switsky, 1982). Both kinds of learning were demonstrated at even the severe and profound levels of retardation.

Over the years, operant conditioning has been of special interest. Conditioning can be difficult to achieve in severely and pro-

foundly retarded individuals. When behavioral repertoires are limited and response rates are low, extensive shaping is required. Also, reinforcement effects can be inconsistent and extinction can easily occur. In general, though, operant conditioning principles apply well to the retarded (Matson and Coe, 1991). New behaviors can be shaped by successive approximations; desirable behaviors can be maintained and undesirable behaviors weakened by consistent application of appropriate contingencies. Thus, behavior modification is an effective approach to intervention.

Piagetian Theory

According to Piaget's theory, the mind of the child qualitatively changes through assimilation and accommodation as adaptation to the environment occurs (p. 22). The capacity of the mind to integrate information and think in more complex ways indicates that growth is occurring. This developmental framework suggests ways in which the mental apparatus might go awry.

Piagetians proposed that retarded children follow the same universal sequence of stages as other children, but that they advance more slowly and stop short of full mental growth. Piaget's colleague, Inhelder, was the first to study retardation from this perspective (Woodward, 1979). She found evidence that in profound retardation development reaches only the sensorimotor stage; in moderate retardation only the beginning of preoperations; in mild retardation no more than concrete operations.

Subsequent research indicated that those with retardation do progress through the same sequences as nonretarded children, although they do so more slowly and ultimately do not progress as far (Hodapp and Zigler, 1990). The subjects of this research were children with retardation for which there was no clear organic cause and children with Down's syndrome. It was also shown that the nonorganic group exhibited the same basic reasoning processes as nonretarded children of the same mental (developmental) age. However, those with Down's syndrome displayed specific deficits in certain areas compared to nonretarded children of the same mental age (for example, problems in attention).

Information Processing

Information processing is a complex concept. One relatively simple and general way of viewing information processing is shown in Figure 10–5. According to this model, the sensory register receives information through the senses and rapidly passes it to short-term memory, with some possible loss of information. Short-term memory can deal with a limited amount of information for a limited time; some information might be lost and some appears to rapidly and automatically move on to long-term memory. However, short-term memory is also referred to as working memory, because it can keep information somewhat longer to actively process it to prepare it for long-term memory. It is long-term memory that permanently stores information, which can be retrieved with varying degrees of ease. Information can be retrieved directly from long-term memory or it can be routed back to short-term memory, where it might be used with other information in problem solving or other thinking.

Theorists also acknowledge what they call the executive functions of the information processing system, or metacognition. Executive functions involve the abilities to select, monitor, evaluate, and revise information processing strategies depending on the situation. Part of executive functions is metamemory, the understanding of one's own memory system and how it works with specific information processing tasks (Haywood et al., 1982).

The information processing system is commonly conceptualized in terms of a structural component and a control component. The structural component is the hardware of the system, the brain, which is not easily modified. The control component is the mental processes that at least in principle can be modified. Applying this model to retardation, it is assumed that cognition may go awry due to structural defects and/or

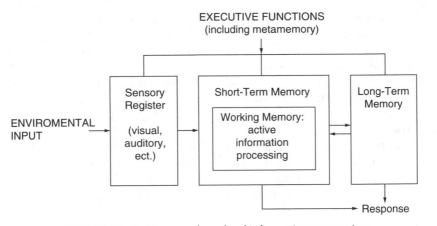

FIGURE 10–5 A general mode of information processing.
Adapted from Atkinson and Shiffrin, 1968, and Swanson, 1987.

control problems. Unmodifiable structural (brain) defects might exist especially in the presence of organic syndromes, and could result, for example, in abnormally slow processing in working memory (e.g., Nettelback, 1985). Alternatively, more modifiable deficits might exist in the mental processes employed by those with mental retardation.

Attention, believed to be crucial in all effortful information processing, is one process that has been studied in various ways. The study of discrimination learning has contributed to knowledge about attention. Typically the individual is presented with sets of stimulus figures over several trials and must learn to discriminate between stimuli that have been preselected as "correct" or "incorrect." It is possible to do so on the basis of information given in each trial. Zeaman and House (1979) found that children with retardation performed more poorly than average children, that higher IQ was related to better performance, and that performance depended on attention to stimuli. Those with retardation had a low probability of attending. Once they attended, they rapidly solved the problems.

Vigilance tasks requiring sustained attention also have been used to study attention.

There is some evidence that sustained attention in retarded children increases with age, just as in average children, but at a slower rate (Warm and Berch, 1985). The studies involved relatively simple monitoring tasks, and most were conducted with youth with mild and moderate deficiency. It appears that feedback can help retarded adolescents; in this case the difference between those with retardation and their chronological-age peers on simple vigilance tasks is small.

Much research is being conducted on the information processing strategies that prepare information for long-term memory. Successful strategies include rehearsing, organizing and clustering material, and elaborating and transforming material so that it fits with what is already stored. Some of these strategies obviously demand complex thinking.

With retardation, there is a failure to employ effective strategies or use them effectively (Borkowski and Cavanaugh, 1979; Borkowski, Johnston, and Reid, 1987; MacMillan et al., 1986). In some cases, performance improves when the children are taught effective strategies and/or instructed to use them. For example, in paired associate learning, a pair of stimuli (usually words or pictures) is first presented, and then the subject is given one of the stimuli and asked to give the other. By age five or six most normal children are able to produce and employ mediators that help them associate the paired stimuli. They may, for instance, connect the stimuli "snow" and "ice cream" by thinking the word "cold" or imagining mounds of a white substance. This strategy of elaboration improves throughout childhood in normal children. However, children with retardation do not easily generate and use mediators in paired associate learning. When they are provided mediators by experimenters or instructed to use mediators, their performance often improves (Borkowski and Cavanaugh, 1979).

To some extent the children can even continue to use acquired strategies later on with tasks identical to the training tasks. However, they do not generalize strategies to new tasks, thus seriously curtail potential training effects (Borkowski et al., 1987; Glidden, 1985). Such failure appears related to deficits in executive functions and metamemory. That is, children with retardation inadequately select and monitor strategies, and they develop metamemory more slowly than nonretarded children (MacMillan et al., 1986). Training in generalization might be helpful. With nonretarded children, adults teach generalization by pointing to task similarities, monitoring errors and showing how to correct them, and otherwise coordinating cognitive strategies (Turnure, 1985). The best way to teach, and the degree to which teaching is effective at the different levels of retardation, remain to be established. However, "functional cognition," thinking about and understanding real-life tasks, is considered important.

Overall, research on information processing suggests that on some tasks those with retardation (especially less severe) simply appear delayed, but on other tasks there may be specific intellectual or motivational deficits (Bregman and Hodapp, 1991).

In concluding this discussion on learning and cognition, we should mention two overriding issues. First, the research is especially vulnerable to confounding factors. Those with retardation frequently have language difficulties, atypical motivation, and different learning experiences with regard to research tasks. These differences can confound the interpretations of investigations aimed at identifying intellectual deficits. Second, there is immense variability across persons diagnosed with mental retardation. Learning ability varies with levels of retardation, and underlying cognitive processes also might differ. Moreover, variation might be anticipated across etiological groups. For example, it appears that information processing deficits are at least somewhat different for fragile X and Down's syndromes (Bregman and Hodapp, 1991). Thus, the task of understanding learning and cognition in retarded individuals is enormous.

INTERPERSONAL DEFICITS AND BEHAVIOR PROBLEMS

A considerable amount of interest exists in the social and behavioral dysfunctions displayed by those with retardation, especially at the moderate and mild levels. Intellectual deficits may directly interfere with the development of interpersonal skills. Alternatively, having mental retardation can increase the likelihood that children will have experiences that hinder social growth or lead to problem behaviors.

Interpersonal Skills

As we have seen, the concept of adaptive skills encompasses several aspects of behavior, including how well one gets along with others and functions in the social environment. People with mental retardation often show deficits in social skills crucial to personal relationships. These include:

1. Motor skills, such as facial expressions and body contact
2. Verbal behaviors, such as asking questions, greeting, and making "small talk"
3. Affective behaviors, such as responding with empathy
4. Social cognitive skills, such as role-taking and understanding social cues and norms (cited in Davies and Rogers, 1985).

For those with mental retardation, social competence may be even more important than it is for normal children. Nonretarded children often hold negative attitudes about their retarded peers and reject them. However, negative attitudes are less likely when those with retardation exhibit social competence (Siperstein and Bak, 1985). In general, social skills are essential to making friends and important for success in school, the workplace, and the community (Bradley and Meredith, 1991).

A limited amount of research indicates a developmental lag in children exhibiting MR, but also gradual progress in the attainment of such skills as role taking, interpersonal conflict resolution, and understanding the perspectives of others. In recent years, social skills training has been provided in various settings for individuals of various ages. Most training programs are behaviorally based and include instruction, modeling, role playing, and reinforcement (Marchetti and Campbell, 1990). Acquisition of social skills has been demonstrated, although further research is required to examine the extent to which behavioral improvement is maintained and displayed in everyday environments.

Behavior Problems

Children and older people with mental retardation exhibit various behavior problems that meet criteria for clinical diagnoses. Studies of community, clinic, and institutionalized samples indicate that prevalence is relatively high. From epidemiologic research, Bregman (1991) concluded that between one-third and two-thirds of those with mental retardation show significant psychopathology, a rate much higher than found for control groups. Scott (1994) notes that the retarded population shows three to four times more problems than the general population. Although disordered behavior occurs at all levels of MR, prevalence increases as intelligence decreases.

In mild and moderate retardation, the kinds of disturbances exhibited are similar to those shown in the general population. Conduct disturbances, aggression, anxiety, depression, attention problems, hyperactivity, obsessive-compulsive disorder, schizophrenia, autism, stereotypies, and self-injury have all been reported. In severe retardation, self-injury and stereotypies such as purposeless hand flapping and bodily rocking seem particularly high (Corbett, 1985; Bregman, 1991). The connection between specific syndromes and specific problems is being examined. Recall, for example, that children with fragile X syndrome have high rates of attention deficits and hyperactivity.

What accounts for high rates of psychopathology in mental retardation? Several causes are suggested. Neurological factors no doubt explain some disturbed behavior, as seizures and head trauma are associated with behavioral problems (Bregman, 1991). Genetic disorders are also related to psychopathology, although the mechanisms are unknown. Biological factors perhaps explain the higher rates of behavior problems in severe retardation. But psychosocial factors also come into play. Social isolation can curtail exposure to appropriate behavioral models; educational failure and the stigma of labeling can lead to feelings of incompetence. Certain kinds of institutional care and even the use of medication may also be associated with behavior problems. And unsurprisingly, the home environment is important. For example, instability in families and caregiving was found to be related to behavior disturbance in mildly retarded young adults (Richardson, Koller, and Katz, 1985).

Such environmental experiences can be linked to anxiety, depression, dependency, anger, and other signs of disturbance.

In earlier times social and behavioral problems were simply considered a part of mental retardation. Since they were taken for granted, they were not adequately described, counted, and studied. This situation has changed. There is greater recognition that social and behavioral disorders may or may not be an inherent part of mental retardation, and that in either case, they warrant attention. Such dysfunctions lower the quality of life for persons with retardation, interfere with community adjustment, and correlate with institutionalization (Aman et al., 1993; Scott, 1994).

FAMILY REACTIONS AND INFLUENCES

The birth of a handicapped child is likely to be a traumatic event. Most parents expect that their children will be attractive, smart, and socially successful. Parents of a handicapped child thus grieve for unfulfilled expectations, as well as face psychological and economic strain (e.g., Gunn and Berry, 1990).

Parental reactions to having a handicapped child have been studied by questioning and observing parents. Many common themes emerge from the data. Some researchers suggest that family reaction/adjustment occurs in three stages (Blacher, 1984). Upon first being informed of their child's condition, parents often experience shock and denial. Some "shop around" for other professional opinions, perhaps in denial or in search of the best medical judgment. When abnormalities are not obvious, families are more apt to deny the diagnosis. Looking back on the event, parents with handicapped children believe that families benefit by being told the truth as early as possible, receiving information about the disorder, and being treated sympathetically

(Quine and Rutter, 1994). When the diagnosis is better accepted and the child's special needs become recognized, a second stage occurs. Chronic sadness, low self-esteem, hopelessness, guilt, disappointment, and anger are reported. Parent-child attachment may be delayed, but some parents become especially attached to their handicapped child. Eventually a third stage is usually reached, characterized by emotional reorganization, adjustment, and further acceptance. Parents reconstruct the needs of the entire family and become more comfortable with their situation. They actively seek services and may become advocates for the handicapped.

Although families do report the experiences described above and some may follow the stages, a stage model may be too simple. Rather, families may continually adjust and readjust in more complex patterns. In addition, some family members may be affected more than others or in different ways. For example, mothers often bear a disproportionate burden of care (Scott, 1994). Siblings, especially sisters, similarly engage in more caretaking, but research only inconsistently shows adverse effects on siblings (Boyce and Barnett, 1993; Cuskelly and Dadds, 1992). At the same time, many siblings appear more considerate and kind to the handicapped child, which could be a forerunner of altruism and humanistic concerns in adulthood (Dunn, 1988).

Families vary in their capacity to adjust, and many factors can be influential. The severity of the retardation is one factor. Moderate and severe levels demand much immediate care and planning for lifetime care and supervision; mild retardation can mean a long period of uncertainty about the existence of deficits. Other influential factors are parental beliefs and coping skills, marital interaction, parental intellectual functioning, social class variables, professional services, and social support (e.g., Atkinson et al., 1995; Flynt, Wood, and

Scott, 1994; Sloper et al., 1991). Because so many factors—child characteristics, family characteristics, and social variables—can play a role in determining how well families do, researchers are trying to better understand them. It is a complex picture. For example, one study showed that mothers are more affected by the child's behavior and fathers by variables external to the child, such as unemployment and financial strain (Sloper et al., 1991). Such findings argue for the importance of both psychosocial and economic support for families.

Family adjustment is, of course, critical to the child's development. As with all children, the growth of intelligence is tied to opportunity for learning that is mediated by significant adults. The social and medical needs of retarded children also demand special parent involvement. Adequate intervention requires that parents be both knowledgeable and motivated to work with their child.

Fortunately, greater recognition is now being given to family needs. Efforts are being made to provide economic assistance, medical care, child and family therapy, training in child management, and training of parents as teachers for their handicapped children. Nevertheless, in his 1992 presidential address to AAMR, Jack Stark noted that families were experiencing high levels of burnout, financial struggles, and insecurity about future services. Support for families has always been important, but perhaps is especially crucial now that the philosophy of treatment for retardation strongly encourages family involvement and home care.

PLACEMENT, TREATMENT, AND EDUCATION

Attitudes about mental deficiency have reflected the general beliefs of the times and have prescribed how those with mental retardation would be treated by the societies in which they lived (Cytryn and Lourie, 1980). Roman laws permitted extermination of those with retardation; medieval Europe looked upon them as jesters or creatures of the devil. The last century is marked by distinct periods of more or less favorable attitudes toward MR (Table 10–4).

We can trace modern attitudes to the late 1700s, to the case of the "Wild Boy of Aveyron," otherwise known as Victor. The boy was first seen running naked through the woods in France, searching for roots

TABLE 10–4 Attitudes toward Mental Retardation

Period	*Society's attitudes*
Mid to late 1800s	Optimism, belief in education, "moral training" in special schools to return the person to society.
Late 1800s–Early 1900s	Focus on neuropathology; retardation seen as incurable defect; therapeutic nihilism; protecting retarded persons from society.
Early to mid 1900s	Introduction of intelligence tests, which discover mild retardation; assumption of link with antisocial behavior; custodial institutionalization; sterilization. "Tragic Interlude."
Mid 1900s–Present	Recognition of rights of retarded persons to public education, treatment, and life in community; the concept of normalization. Implementation of right of all handicapped children to education; deinstitutionalization and community living.

Adapted from Szymanski, L.S., and Kaplan, L.C. (1991). Mental retardation. In J.M. Weiner (Ed.), *Textbook of child and adolescent psychiatry*. American Psychiatric Association, Copyright, 1991.

and acorns to eat. He escaped more than once before his final capture and assignment to a medical officer, Jean M. Itard, at the National Institute for the Deaf and Dumb in Paris. Expectations were rampant: The wild boy would be astonished at the sights of Paris; he would soon be educated; he would describe his fascinating existence in the forest. When he arrived in Paris, however, Victor was a dirty child who suffered from convulsions, swayed back and forth, bit and scratched, and showed no affection for those who attended him (Itard, as cited in Harrison and McDermott, 1972). Victor's senses were underdeveloped; his memory, attention, judgment, and reasoning deficient; and his ability to communicate almost nil. Some people drew a parallel between Victor and children considered incurably afflicted with "idiocy." Itard believed that Victor had existed alone in the woods from at least age four or five, and he attributed the boy's deficiencies to lack of contact with civilized people. But Itard's attempt to treat the Wild Boy of Aveyron was largely unsuccessful, and Victor lived in custodial care until his death.

Nevertheless, the efforts to treat Victor did much to stimulate interest in the "feebleminded" or "retarded" (Rie, 1971). By the mid to late 1800s, a favorable climate existed toward mental retardation and special education. Itard's student, Sequin, was a leader in this optimistic era, and promising ideas spread rapidly across the United States. Residential schools opened to educate retarded children and then return them to the community (Szymanski and Crocker, 1985). This enlightened view, marked in 1876 by the formation of the forerunner of AAMR, was gradually overwhelmed, however, by several events. Increased interest in biology as a cause of MR, developments in genetics and eugenics, the rise of psychoanalysis, and misuse or misunderstanding of IQ tests all strengthened the view that mental deficiency was incurable and that those with retardation were a detriment if not a danger to society. This led to widespread institutionalization, with institutions growing in number and size throughout the first half of this century. Custodial care rather than actual treatment became commonplace.

Soon after the mid 1900s, the climate again became favorable. Improved medical care had led to longer lifespans for retarded individuals and better diagnosis and treatment for certain conditions. Follow-up studies of retarded persons who had been released to the community showed that many had done quite well. In addition, the 1960s brought a renewed widespread interest in the rights of poor, handicapped, and minority populations. The concept of *normalization,* first popularized in Scandanavia, became a framework for how people with mental deficiency would be treated. The central idea of normalization is that treatment should aim at producing behaviors that are as normal as possible and should accomplish this goal by methods as culturally normal as possible (Mesibov, 1992; Thompson and McEvoy, 1992; Wolfensberger, 1980). The emphasis is on giving persons with handicaps experiences that are as normal as possible, which may require living arrangements to be adapted to the needs of handicapped persons. Each person is seen as having the right to living arrangements, treatment, education, and work that are most suitable, most normal, and least restrictive as possible.

Deinstitutionalization and Alternative Living Arrangements

The idea of normalization played a role in the movement to deinstitutionalize persons with retardation. Convincing arguments were made against public institutions, many of which were large and poorly staffed. It was argued that the residents did not receive individualized training and medical care, much less human interaction. In fact, it was believed that residents often learned damaging behaviors, such as excessive dependency. These arguments—along with concern over the costs of institutions, the creation of funding for alternatives, and other considerations—led to change.

In the United States, the number of persons in public institutions for retardation declined in the late 1960s, as did the number of institutions (Braddock and Heller, 1985a; Craig and McCarver, 19840). From 1964 to 1985 the rate of institutionalization in state mental retardation facilities declined by about a half (Mechanic and Rochefort, 1990). Moreover, individuals were placed in institutions at older chronological age, and fewer people with mild to moderate retardation were placed (Epple, Jacobson, and Janicki, 1985; Scheerenberger, 1982).

Along with these changes came the rise of community settings which served as alternatives for traditional institutional living (Bruininks, Hauber, and Kudla, 1980; Emerson, 1985). These included small regional centers, small group homes, and foster homes, which interface with the larger community and provide a more homelike atmosphere and greater opportunity for privacy and independence. Such placements can fall short of ideal, of course. When relocation from a traditional to a community setting occurs, it can be traumatic to the individual relocating and to their families, who worry that the new setting will not be protective (Braddock and Heller, 1985b). Alternative settings can also have the negative qualities observed in traditional institutions, such as social isolation, regimentation, the fostering of dependency, and lack of power of the residents (Landesman, 1990; Lord and Pedlar, 1991). Moreover, developmental outcome can be expected to depend on the match between the individual and the living arrangement. Nevertheless, there is consensus that alternative living arrangements can provide more normal, and likely more positive, experiences.

Regardless of the increase in alternative residential settings, most persons with retar-

Special Olympics is an example of community programs that attempt to normalize the lives of retarded persons and to provide them with success experiences and a sense of self-worth.

(Joel Gordon)

dation remain with their families through-out childhood. What influences families to keep their child at home or out-of-home? Several factors enter into the decision. Table 10–5 shows some of the reasons that families in one study gave for placing their child with severe handicaps (Bromley and Blacher, 1991). Daily stress, the child's functioning, and social support have been cited in other research. Thus, it appears that help in reducing the child's problems and daily stress could impact placement. Family members need breaks from the daily burden of caregiving, freedom to pursue their own interests, and relief from times of increased stress (Botuck and Winsberg, 1991; Hagamen, 1980; Joyce, Singer, and Isralowitz, 1983). Such assistance can be provided by in-home or out-of-home respite care for disabled children or adolescents. In-home care involves trained caregivers coming to the home on a part-time schedule to care for the handicapped youngsters. Out-of-home programs entail the handicapped child traveling to some other place for care; for example, the child may live at home during the week and stay at a hospital or foster home on week-ends. Mothers receiving respite

care report that they feel relief and greater well being, experience less depression, have more time for personal care and other family members, enjoy leisure activities, and relate in a more positive way to their disabled children.

Treatment

No matter where children and adolescents with retardation reside, the need for treatment must be addressed. Such treatment must take into account not only intellectual/adaptive functioning, but also social and behavioral problems. In a substantial number of cases, particularly involving severe retardation, medical conditions must be attended. In the following discussion, we focus on treatment of behavioral problems.

Medication. Medications are not known to strengthen intellectual functioning in cases of retardation but are employed widely for medical and behavioral symptoms (Aman et al., 1995; Gadow, 1992). Psychotrophic medications can alleviate the numerous behavioral problems that coexist with retardation, including anxiety, affective disorders, overactivity, aggression, self-abuse, stereotypies, eating disorders, and psychotic behavior. Indeed, there is some evidence for the efficacy of psychopharmacology in cases of retardation (Bregman, 1991). However, controlled research is much needed.

The management of medication requires special consideration. For example, there could be some differences in how nonretarded and retarded individuals respond to medication (Gadow, 1992). Furthermore, people with retardation are a heterogeneous group and thus each individual requires thorough assessment. Inappropriate use of drugs and overdosing have been documented, resulting in close government monitoring (e.g., Bregman, 1991). Good practice requires especially careful supervision, which includes determining drug effi-

TABLE 10–5 Factors Reported by At Least Forty Percent of Parents as Strongly or Very Strongly Influencing the Decision for Out-of-Home Placement

	Percent
Day to day stress	81
My child's level of functioning and potential for future learning	75
My child's behavior	60
Feelings of my nonhandicapped children	55
My spouse's attitude toward placement	48
Medical or physical problems of my handicapped child	48
Availability of respite care	46
Availability of babysitters	43
Advice from professionals	41

Adapted from Bromley and Blacher, 1991

cacy and possible side effects, as some clients are unable to provide a clear picture of how they are being affected by medication.

Individual, group, and family psychotherapies. Children and adolescents with retardation can benefit from psychotherapies that aim to reduce behavioral/psychological problems (Szymanski and Kaplan, 1991). Intellectual deficits do not preclude individual "talking" therapies, although modifications may be required (Bregman, 1991; Szymanski, 1980). Certainly, psychotherapeutic techniques must be adapted to the developmental level of the client. It is probably best that therapists be directive, and set specific goals. Language must be concrete and clear, and nonverbal techniques need to be used in the face of communication difficulties (e.g., play or other activities). Short, frequent sessions may be necessary.

In group therapy the focus may be on activities or family interactions (Szymanski and Rosefsky, 1980). Contact with parents may be important in helping them adjust to the condition of their offspring. Multiple family groups can provide opportunities for families to learn from each other, improve communication, share feelings, and encourage independence in those with retardation. Evaluation of such therapy indicates that it can be helpful.

Behavior modification. The single most important innovation in treating retardation has been the application of behavioral techniques. In the 1960s advocates of behavior modification began to work in institutions that provided custodial care but little training or education (Whitman, Hantula, and Spence, 1990). Over the next decades, behavior modification became dominant, and an enormous amount of research was conducted. A wide range of behaviors at all levels of handicap was targeted. On the one hand was a thrust to eliminate maladaptive behaviors such as aggression, self-injury, tantrums, and rigid stereotypes. On the other hand was a focus on enhancing skills in language, self-help, imitation, academic study, and work. The acquisition of daily living skills was recognized as crucial (Danforth and Drabman, 1990; Taras and Matese, 1990). Children and adolescents who cannot dress and feed themselves and otherwise take care of their basic needs are often limited from participating in educational and social activities. Those who are unable to shop, order food in restaurants, swim, or bowl can hardly enjoy independence in community living. Thus, self-help programs have targeted the gamut of behaviors. In more recent years training in social skills and self-control have been common, especially for mild and moderate retardation (e.g., Matson and Coe, 1991). Such training often includes cognitive components.

Consistent with the behavioral approach, efforts have been made to train caregivers, whether the setting is the home, community programs, or residential institutions (e.g., Whitman et al., 1990). Teaching packages and courses have been developed to disseminate information to caretakers. Evaluation of outcomes has been conducted, with attempts to establish the value of programs to the everyday activities of the child (Kiernan, 1985). Overall, behavior modification has had considerable success in serving young people with retardation, who so often in past times had been viewed as unable to learn. This is not to say that the application of behavioral techniques is simple; it requires skill, effort, and perseverance. But enormous gains have been made, and more is yet to be accomplished.

Education

If Itard's efforts to train the Wild Boy of Aveyon marked the beginning of endeavors to educate the retarded, only in the present century did improved methods of individualized education come into their own. In the

United States, there was a dramatic expansion of special education for the mildly retarded person from around 1925 to 1960 (Lilly, 1979c). But the public schools were not compelled to admit more severely retarded children, nor were parents given public assistance for the education of these youngsters.

In the late 1950s, lack of education for handicapped children and possible abuse of intelligence tests were closely scrutinized. Growing commitment to the idea that all handicapped children have a right to appropriate education eventually resulted in a sweeping legal reform: Public Law 94-142, the Education for All Handicapped Children Act of 1975. Several other federal regulations strengthened the thrust of this law by extending opportunity and rights to all handicapped people. P.L. 99-457 amended The Education for All Handicapped Children Act, ensuring programs for developmentally delayed infants. The Vocational Rehabilitation Act of 1973 and the Americans with Disabilities Act of 1990 ensured access to education and jobs and broad opportunities. In the early 1990s the Education for All Handicapped Children Act was expanded under the title the Individuals with Disabilities Education Act (IDEA). These regulations did not, of course, spring from a social vacuum; rather, they reflected general attitudes, which advocates diligently worked to implement.

The purpose of P.L. 94-142 was to assure that all students with handicaps obtain an appropriate free public education; to guarantee the rights of these students and their parents; to assist states and localities in providing education; and to assess and assure the effectiveness of educational efforts. These purposes and mandates were refined in several legal cases (e.g., Osborne, 1992). Appropriate education essentially means educational experiences tailored to the child's needs. An individualized education plan (IEP) is constructed for each student receiving special education. IEPs must consider the child's present functioning, educational objectives, long-term goals, educational services to be provided, expected duration of services, and procedures for evaluations. The programs must be reviewed annually by a committee and the child's parents. Furthermore, students with disabilities must be educated with nonhandicapped children, to the maximum extent that is appropriate; that is, they must be placed in the least restrictive environment possible. They also must be placed in programs as close to home as possible.

P.L. 94-142 and IDEA have resulted in dramatic changes in education. In particular they have strengthened individualized programming, increased parental participation in the education of their handicapped youngsters, and encouraged maintenance of handicapped youth in the community and in regular classrooms.

Historically, special education for the mentally handicapped typically had meant assigning them to special classes or schools, thus drastically limiting contact with normal children. This policy, especially as it applied to mildly retarded children, had been attacked in several ways (MacMillan et al., 1986). First, it had been argued that minority group students were disproportionately labeled as mentally handicapped largely on the basis of biased IQ tests. Second, it had been claimed that special education did not seem to benefit the children. Third, it had been asserted that individualized programming could be accomplished within the regular classroom, so there was no need to segregate handicapped students. P.L. 94-142 partly answered these criticisms. While this law did not require the mainstreaming or inclusion of all children in regular classrooms, it did mandate placement into the least restrictive environment that can meet the child's needs. As Table 10–6 shows, many placements are available and can be categorized along a continuum of integration: regular class-based, special class-based, special school-based, and nonschool-based

TABLE 10–6   Alternative Educational Placements for Students with Retardation, According to Needs for Support and Program Integration

Children with intermittent or limited support needs	*Regular class-based programs* Special materials and equipment Special consultation Itinerant services Resource room with special education teacher Diagnostic-prescriptive teaching center
Children with limited or extensive support needs	*Special class-based programs* Special education class Part-time in regular class Full-time in special class
Children with extensive or pervasive support needs	*Special school-based programs* Special day school Special residential school
Unless temporary, children with pervasive support needs	*Nonschool-based programs* Hospital instruction Homebound instruction

From Patton, Beirne-Smith, and Payne, 1993. By permission.

programs. These four major categories provide increasing levels of support, and proper placement requires matching the child with appropriate support. The overall impact of federal education mandates has been to integrate many handicapped students into local school systems.

A variety of opinions are expressed about the success of inclusion, and a variety of issues are raised. The most fundamental questions are whether inclusion is beneficial to those with retardation and how it affects other youngsters in the setting. As might be expected, it is not easy to arrive at definitive answers to these questions. Research must address all levels of retardation and the many alternative programs that children and adolescents experience. Even within a type of placement, activities, quality of teaching, and support services vary a good deal. Thus, a child in one classroom, whether special education or not, may have very different experiences from a child in another classroom.

There is evidence that students with mild mental handicap can be disadvantaged by being placed exclusively into contained special classrooms or resource rooms rather than spending time in regular classrooms (Ysseldyke et al., 1991). Both quality of instruction and time spent on academic tasks can be somewhat substandard. There is also evidence that students with severe retardation are better served by being in regular rather than separate schools (McDonnell et al., 1991). Improvements have been noted in social skills, communication, and interactions with nonhandicapped children. Claims are also made that nondisabled students have improved attitudes and perceptions about persons with disabilities. Patton (1990) and his colleagues suggest that, in general, success is highest when families are involved with the educational system, because family understanding of the child's abilities, deficits, and needs are combined with the educators' expertise.

Despite findings that support integration of the handicapped into regular educational settings, a considerable amount of research has not clearly supported the anticipated academic and social benefits (Howlin, 1994; Patton et al., 1990). Methodological problems in the research does not allow an unambiguous conclusion about the benefits of integration versus segregation of mentally handicapped students. However, Howlin (1994) notes several strong arguments for integration of students with mild or moderate difficulties. Inclusion in regular classrooms can avoid stigmatization, at least in principle, and also encourage the modeling of academic and social skills. Most importantly, integration in regular school settings can put the child on a path to playing a full role in society in adulthood.

Howlin's implied concern about what happens to children with retardation when they reach adulthood is shared by most professionals and advocates of the handicapped. Indeed, there is considerable emphasis today on the goals of life-long community integration and productive adulthood, particularly for those with mild to moderate retardation. The Hawaii Transition Project is an example of a program designed to achieve these goals. It is a multi-year project that prepares adolescents for post-high school roles (Patton et al., 1990). Initially, the student, parents, and school personnel identify potential postsecondary opportunities and services, seek to match the student with community resources, and begin communication with these resources. During a second active planning stage, student assessment is conducted, specific community referrals are investigated, and school programming is adapted to support the student's transition to a new role and setting. Finally, the transition is facilitated with the help of adult service providers, resulting in the student being enrolled in an appropriate postsecondary educational or work setting.

Unfortunately, only an insufficient number of programs are designed to actively and systematically promote productive adulthood in the community for the mentally handicapped. Indeed, Polloway and his colleagues (1991) argue that educational curriculum from elementary school onward should be geared toward long-range planning for adult integration into the community. Although present efforts are far from ideal, it is promising that retardation is increasingly viewed in terms of supports required for optimal development rather than inherent deficiencies of the individual.

SUMMARY

Mental retardation is characterized by subaverage intellectual functioning with deficits in adaptive skills manifested before age eighteen. Subaverage intellectual functioning refers to performance of 70 to 75 or less on individual standardized tests of intelligence. Adaptive behavior is judged in comparison to age norms, and is often measured by standardized scales. Although this definition is consistent with past definitions, AAMR has recently proposed a paradigm shift, with greater emphasis being placed on the interaction of the individual and the environment.

Modern intelligence testing began with Binet's test, which identified children in need of special education. The Stanford-Binet and Wechsler tests are widely used today to identify MR. They consist of a variety of intellectual tasks, and performance is judged in comparison to age norms. These tests correlate reasonably well with academic performance, but less so with other achievements. They also are reasonably reliable over time for groups of people, but change in individual scores are often observed. Many psychologists have noted several limitations of IQ tests.

Infant tests of intelligence, which yield a DQ, do not correlate highly with later IQ test performance. However, they can be helpful in screening infants for MR when used with clinical information.

Adaptive behavior scales assess domains of everyday behavior and rely on reports of adults who come into contact with the client.

They correlate moderately well with intelligence test scores. The Vineland Adaptive Behavior Scales and AAMD's Adaptive Behavior Scales are two of the most widely used.

Levels of MR, from mild to profound, have been widely recognized and are based on IQ scores. Mild retardation makes up about 85 percent of all identified cases. In a break with the past, AAMR no longer categorizes people according to levels of functioning. Instead, AAMR advocates categorizing environments based on the level of support they might provide.

Retardation is most prevalent in persons of school age, low SES, and male gender. Social expectations play some role in creating this epidemiologic profile.

The causes of mental retardation can be categorized as organic, polygenic, and psychosocial. Known biological factors include genetic abnormalities and inherited single-gene conditions. Biological etiology is particularly closely associated with moderate and severe levels of retardation. Polygenic and psychosocial etiology are more closely associated with mild MR and what was once called cultural-familial retardation. In these cases, a biological factor is not obvious but low intelligence characterizes the family and could reflect polygenic inheritance. Social disadvantage is also common in such cases of retardation, implicating psychosocial variables.

Mild retardation especially has been discussed with regard to the cultural bias of IQ tests. Legal decisions have forced the stringent monitoring of intelligence testing in the public schools.

Research into learning and cognition has shown that operant learning principles generally apply to those with retardation. Cognitive development occurs in Piagetian stages, but development is slow, and the most advanced stages are not achieved. Analyses of information processing implicate both structural and processing control components (e.g., some attention processes, strategy use, generalization, executive functions). Some intellectual problems are developmental lags but others appear to be true differences from normal processes.

Retarded persons show interpersonal deficits and a high rate of behavior problems. In mild retardation the types of behavior problems displayed are similar to problems found in the general population. In severe retardation the problems are of somewhat different type and prevalence is higher. Biological impairments undoubtedly partly account for psychopathology, but psychosocial factors play a role as well.

Family adjustment to having a retarded child has been described as occurring in three stages, but is probably more complex. Child characteristics, family characteristics, and social variables affect family adjustment. Greater recognition is now being given to the importance of the family and to family needs.

Attitudes toward retardation have varied over time and have been associated with favorable or unfavorable treatment of retarded persons. Since the mid 1900s, the concept of normalization and concern for the rights of disabled people have served as a framework for placement, therapy, and education of the mentally handicapped. Deinstitutionalization went hand-in-hand with an increase in community living arrangements. Treatment of psychological/behavioral problems includes medication, psychotherapy, and especially behavior modification. The latter is also employed to increase adaptive behaviors and intellectual skills. P.L. 94-142, the Individuals with Disabilities Education Act (IDEA), and related laws have brought dramatic changes to the educational system, including the mandate to provide the most appropriate free public education in the least restrictive environment. Children and adolescents with retardation are now more integrated in schools and communities, although many questions remain about how to enhance their life experiences and development over the lifespan.

11

DEVELOPMENTAL LANGUAGE AND LEARNING DISABILITIES

In Chapter 10 we discussed mental retardation, a developmental disorder that broadly affects intellectual functioning. This chapter is about youth who display near average general intelligence but also *specific* developmental impairments that are discrepant with their general intellectual ability. It is assumed that something goes awry with normal developmental processes, so that the child is affected relatively early in life. Language and communication abilities are impaired in some of the children, and/or there are specific difficulties in learning. Developmental language disorders and learning disabilities are reflected in academic failure.

Successful negotiation through the educational system is increasingly important to occupational and social success in most of the world. Thus, specific developmental problems that interfere with academic success are of increasing concern. In addition, difficulties in communicating and learning affect everyday functioning, social interaction, and daily enjoyment of life.

Our discussion of specific developmental disorders includes language problems and what is commonly referred to as learning disabilities—that is, difficulties in basic reading, writing, spelling, and arithmetic skills. Unsurprisingly, language and learning disabilities often go hand in hand, as is recog-

nized in the major guidelines for defining difficulties in learning.

DEFINITION: THE CREATION OF THE LD CATEGORY

Specific developmental disorders have been recognized for over a hundred years. It was noted that brain injury or damage in adults led to a variety of behavioral symptoms, such as speech problems, inattention, and learning difficulties (Hammill, 1993). Similar problems in children were thus hypothesized to be caused by brain dysfunction of some sort, perhaps too subtle to be identified. Thus, as for attention-deficit hyperactivity disorder, the label minimal brain damage or dysfunction was applied. At the same time, until the 1960s children whose school performance was below their general ability were often referred to as "underachievers" (Kessler, 1988). Much attention was given to their psychosocial behavior, motivation, anxiety, and family functioning. It was also recognized that some of these children had specific learning problems, such as in reading and arithmetic, and some were said to have "minimal brain damage." Many parents and professionals believed that the needs of these children were not being met.

In 1963 representatives from several organizations met at a symposium sponsored by the Fund for Perceptually Handicapped Children. In his address to the conferees, Samuel Kirk (1963) noted that the children of their concern exhibited a variety of deficiencies that were assumed to be related to neurological dysfunction, especially learning difficulties, perceptual problems, and hyperactivity. Kirk suggested that the term *learning disabilities* would be suitable for all of these children, and also would avoid the need to establish nervous system dysfunction in identifying the youngsters. Importantly, he thought that the term could encourage and guide the assessment and educational remediation so needed by the children. That evening the conferees organized into the Association for Children with Learning Disabilities (Hammill, 1993).

Learning disabilities (LD) was not a new term, but Kirk's presentation marked the creation of a new field (Hallahan and Kauffman, 1978; Taylor, 1988a). The term gradually became widely accepted by professional groups and parents, and a field of study grew around it. Educators and parents henceforth played an important role in an area previously dominated by physicians and psychologists. Parents whose children might otherwise have been labeled mentally retarded were given hope that the problem was limited and could be treated. Teachers were relieved of the suspicion that they were to blame for the failure of certain students. School administrators and other concerned professionals were provided with a label that could make children eligible for special services. Thus, from the beginning, those labeled with learning disabilities were not only a heterogeneous group of children, but the social context for labeling these youngsters was a complex one (Senf, 1986).

The definition of learning disability given by Kirk's group became extremely important because it was adapted by the federal government in mandating special education for learning disabled children. It was incorporated into P.L. 94-142, The Education for All Handicapped Children Act of 1975, and has had continuing impact on how state departments of Education define and identify learning disabled students (Mercer, King-Sears, and Mercer, 1990). The definition used by the federal government states:

"Specific learning disability" means a disorder in one or more of the basic psychological processes involved in understanding or in using language, spoken or written, which may manifest itself in imperfect ability to listen, think, speak, read, write, spell, or to do mathematical calculations. The term includes such conditions as perceptual handicaps, brain injury, minimal brain dysfunction, dyslexia, developmental aphasia. The term does not include children who have learning problems which are primarily the result of visual, hearing, or motor handicaps, or mental retardation, or emotional disturbance, or of environmental, cultural, or economic disadvantage (U.S. Office of Education, 1977, p. 65083)

This is not to say, however, that there was complete satisfaction with this definition. To the contrary, ongoing dissatisfaction is still expressed about several issues, especially about operationalizing the definition, the exclusionary criteria, and neurological etiology.

Specific Criteria for LD

As is obvious, the above definition of LD is conceptual and lacks specific guidelines to identify a learning disability. Is it necessary to establish dysfunction in basic psychological processes? If so, how is this to be done, and what criteria should be used, especially since these basic processes are not well established? What criteria are to be used to decide that language, reading, writing, arithmetic, and other skills are below expectations for the child? These questions have not been easy to answer. Nevertheless, methods have been generated to identify developmental learning disabilites (Morris, 1988; Stanovich, 1991). These methods grew out of criteria set by the Office of Education and, interestingly, they most often do not directly target the psychological processes assumed to be deficient.

One method identifies children with learning disabilities as performing below expected grade or age level in at least one academic area. Variations occur in the specific criterion, although it is often set as from two years to one-half year below expected level. Thus, with the two-year criterion, a sixth grader who is achieving at the fourth-grade level in arithmetic can be labeled as learning disabled, providing that certain other factors do not account for the performance. One obvious problem in this approach is that a large discrepancy would seem more serious for a younger child than for an older child. For example, being two years behind is more serious for a third grader than for a sixth grader. This problem can be reduced by setting the criterion, for example, at one year deficiency for younger children and two for older children. Of course, judgments still must be made as to what the criterion should be at each grade level.

The other more common way to identify LD is by a discrepancy between general intellectual ability and achievement level. It is assumed that performance on measures of general ability will exceed performance on measures of the domain-specific impairment. Comparisons are typically made between IQ and achievement tests that tap the suspected domain, be it language, reading, spelling, arithmetic, so forth. However, there is no absolute agreement on how large a discrepancy between intelligence and achievement scores should define a learning disability. In practice, the size of any found discrepancy is statistically compared to the discrepancy between intelligence and achievement that would be expected in the general population to which the child can be reasonably compared. If the found discrepancy is significantly larger than what would be expected, a learning disability is said to exist. However, state education departments, which usually determine the standards, set different standards about the size of the discrepancy that is considered significantly large (Mercer et al., 1990). This has obvious implications for the number of children who will be identified as learning disabled and receive special education.

Still other problems exist with the IQ-achievement discrepancy approach. The strategy assumes that IQ and achievement are independent and that a learning disability will not affect IQ (Siegel, 1989). Nonetheless, intelligence tests measure most of the abilities considered deficient in LD, and learning disabilities may cause a decrease in IQ (Stanovich, 1986, 1991). As it is, for most LD groups, the average IQ is about 90 (Taylor, 1988a).

Exclusionary Criteria

Another widely expressed concern about the definition of LD has to do with the exclusion of children whose learning problems are primarily due to certain sensory and motor handicaps, emotional disturbances, or disadvantaged environmental background. The degree of handicap required for exclusion is arguable. Also, it is not always easy to determine what is primary. Emotional disturbance can be primary or secondary to learning problems. The exclusion of children who are environmentally disadvantaged has been of special concern. Of course, these children can be classified as learning disabled as long as deficits in psychological processes are primary. However, it is difficult to make this distinction, and for that matter to distinguish some cases of learning disabilities from underachievement due to other causes, for example, to lack of motivation (Stanovich, 1986).

Other Dissatisfactions

Other dissatisfactions with the definition have been expressed. For example, The National Joint Committee for Learning Disabilites recommended a definition that deletes any reference to "basic psychological processes" (Hammill, 1993). Federal guidelines have, in fact, never spelled out criteria for such processes. The NJCLD definition does, however, state that learning disabilities are presumed to be due to central nervous system dysfunction.

Many of the disagreements over the definition of LD clearly reflect basic controversy about how to conceptualize learning problems. Others reflect concern about how the definition is operationalized as this affects the number of children receiving special education and who will be excluded from special education. Over the years, different definitions and criteria have led to difficulties in establishing prevalence rates, inconsistency in assigning children to special education, and incomparability of groups chosen for research purposes. Still, to put the issue in broad perspective, it can be argued that despite the shortcomings of defining learning disabilites, the creation of the category has called attention to a real problem (Taylor, 1988a). Considerable effort is being made to describe and identify learning disabled children, to understand their functioning, and to maximize their achievements.

LANGUAGE DISORDERS

Language disorders have historically been referred to as *aphasia,* a term that meant loss of language in adults due to brain damage or dysfunction. Since this meaning does not accurately fit developmentally impaired children, the terms *developmental aphasia* and *developmental dysphasia* are often used instead. Even more commonly employed in the United States are the terms *specific language disorders* (SLD) or *specific language impairments.*

As we saw in Chapter 2, basic language skills develop rapidly in sequence so that most six-year-old children are amazingly

TABLE 11–1 Basic Components of Language

Phonology	Sounds of a language and rules for combining them
Articulation	Actual production of speech sounds
Morphology	Formation of words, including the use of prefixes and suffixes (e.g., un, ed, s) to give meaning
Syntax	Organization of words into phrases and sentences
Semantics	Meanings in language
Pragmatics	Use of language in social contexts

adept in language use. Table 11–1 defines the basic components of language that must be mastered. As complex as language is, there are many ways in which development can go awry. It has been useful to conceptualize language functioning in terms of phonological (articulation), expressive, and receptive language. These categories are employed by DSM and ICD to categorize developmental language disorders. Table 11–2 provides descriptions of problems for each of the categories.

Phonological disorder has to do with the misproduction of speech sounds. The child makes errors, distortions, substitutions, and omissions in producing speech. For example, incorrect sounds (phonemes) may be used in the place of more difficult ones, as in the use of *wabbit* for *rabbit.* Or difficult phonemes may be omitted, as when *bu* is used instead of *blue.* Most children display some misarticulation as they acquire speech, so developmental norms are important in diagnosis.

Expressive language disorder involves the production of speech with regard to vocabulary, sentence structure, and other aspects of language production. Thus, for example, the child may have a limited vocabulary and speak in extremely short, simple sentences. However, the child understands speech and age-appropriate concepts, thus correctly obeys simple commands or points to objects and uses them in response to others' communications.

TABLE 11–2 Descriptions of Phonological, Expressive, and Receptive Language Difficulties

Phonological	Severe cases apparent by 3 years; others by age 6	Speech sounds incorrectly made at developmentally appropriate age; some sounds omitted or some substituted by other sounds
Expressive Language	Severe cases apparent before 3 years; less severe may become apparent as late as adolescence	Impairment in expressed language: small vocabulary, vocabulary errors, short sentences, simplified grammar, unusual word order, slow rate of language development, etc.
Receptive Language	Typically apparent before age 4; less severe cases not until 7 or older	Impaired language comprehension; in mild cases, difficulty with meaning of particular kinds of words (e.g., spatial) or statements (e.g., if-then); in severe cases, inability to understand basic vocabulary and simple sentences

Receptive language disorder involves difficulties in comprehending another's communication. The child may fail to respond to speech, seem deaf, respond inappropriately or not at all, or be uninterested in television. Single words, phrases, the multiple meanings of a word, past tense, or word order may all be problematic. Children with receptive difficulties usually also show deficits in expression and less often in articulation. Thus, receptive language disorder is generally the most severe language impairment (Feinstein and Aldershof, 1991).

Table 11–3 gives DSM-IV's diagnostic criteria for these developmental language disorders, which DSM calls Communication Disorders. The category of Mixed Receptive–Expressive Disorder reflects the fact that receptive problems do not typically occur alone. To warrant a diagnosis, language impairments must be severe enough to interfere with daily functioning. Further-

TABLE 11–3 DSM-IV Criteria for Communication Disorders

Phonological	*Expressive*	*Receptive-Expressive*
A. Failure to use age-appropriate speech sounds (e.g., use of substitutions and omissions)	A. Scores from standardized measures of expressive language are substantially below scores for nonverbal intelligence and receptive language	A. Scores from standardized measures of both receptive and expressive language are substantially below those for nonverbal intellectual capacity

B. The difficulties interfere with academic or occupational achievement or with social communication

C. If mental retardation, a speech-motor or sensory deficit, or environmental deprivation is present, the language difficulties are in excess of those usually associated with these problems

more, the impairments cannot be accounted for by general intellectual or sensorimotor deficits, nor by insufficient environmental stimulation.

Prevalence

The prevalence of SLD is not well established. Usual estimates fall into the range of 2 to 5 percent of the general population, but prevalence varies with severity and type of disorder and the age of the individuals (APA, 1994). The expressive type is probably more common than the receptive type. Phonological problems decrease throughout childhood and are uncommon in adolescence. In clinic populations, prevalence of SLD is strikingly higher, ranging from 25 to 97 percent in children, who are primarily referred for other problems (Cohen et al., 1993). For example, one study of children referred to mental health centers in Canada for a variety of reasons found that 53 percent had a language impairment, and that the impairment had not previously been suspected in 34 percent of these cases. Higher prevalence in boys than girls is widely noted both in the general population and in referred samples.

Since language use develops rapidly in early life, disorders are often evident prior to the child's going to school. However, milder impairments may not be evident until school work places greater cognitive demands on the child. Many of the problems seem to be delays in the use of normal language. Still, abnormal features, such as the use of jargon, may be present, especially in the case of a receptive disorder. Thus, there is evidence for both delay of normal development and deviant or qualitatively different development. The weight of the evidence suggests, however, that for most children the difficulties are best viewed as late development that will not necessarily "catch up" (Bashir and Scavuzzo, 1992).

Low social class has been correlated with SLD (Whitehurst and Fischel, 1994), and the disorders have also been noted in many different cultures.

Underlying Psychological Deficits

We would certainly expect language to be related to many perceptual, learning, and cognitive abilities. As Johnston (1992) puts it:

. . . language is normally a well-integrated part of mental life. We apply the organising forces of non-verbal intellect to learn language in the first place, and we rely on language symbols for complex reasoning. . . . If language is late and slow to develop, there should be a cognitive reason. If language symbols are poorly controlled, there should be a cognitive consequence (pp. 106–107).

Indeed, Johnston presents data that children with SLD do show a variety of cognitive deficits, some of which could be the basic psychological processes assumed to underlie language and learning disabilities.

According to Bishop (1992b), six hypotheses have been proposed to explain developmental language disorders. These hypotheses target various psychological impairments. Each is briefly summarized with Bishop's evaluation.

1. Impairments are due to defects in the *output* of speech; that is, in converting competent linguistic skills into speech. Bishop notes that this hypothesis cannot readily explain receptive language problems, which are evident even when speech is not required of the person.

2. Impairments are due to *auditory perception,* especially to deficiency in processing rapid or brief sounds. It has been established that auditory limitations can hinder language development, especially phonology. What is still at questions is whether these limitations can explain the full range of language problems.

3. Impairments are due to a *lack of a specific brain module* that is necessary for grammar acquisition—the so-called "language acquisition device." Despite the apparent appeal of

the idea of an underlying brain module, evidence is still required.

4. Impairments are due to a more general higher level conceptual deficit. Based on Piaget's theory, it is proposed that children with SLD lack the ability to *use symbols to represent* the world. There is evidence that such a deficit sometimes correlates with SLD, but evidence is lacking that the deficit causes SLD.

5. Impairments are due more to a deficit in *learning processes,* particularly in hypothesis testing and concept formation. In fact, hypothesis testing does not seem deficient in children with SLD, although there are difficulties in learning rules when the task requires that information be encoded and remembered over time.

6. Impairments are due to a *limited capacity to process* information, so that large amounts of information cannot be rapidly handled. This hypothesis is so general that it might explain almost any pattern of results. At the same time, it is challenged by the fact that children with SLD can perform well on some tasks, such as nonverbal tasks.

From her review, Bishop suggested that the combination of auditory deficits (2 above) and limited processing capacity (6 above) might explain some cases of SLD. If information processing is slow, auditory information would be especially affected because sound signals are very brief. In turn, language would be affected because it depends on rapid processing of sound.

Bishop also noted that the research on the deficits that might underlie SLD is confusing. Different investigators present evidence to support their various hypotheses but much of the evidence is correlational, that is, based on comparisons of children with SLD with other groups. It is obviously very difficult to establish causation in this way. Bishop suggested that other methods, including longitudinal follow-ups, must be given more weight. She also noted that given the heterogeneity of language disorders, perhaps it is unreasonable to expect to find a single underlying cognitive deficit.

LEARNING DISABILITIES

As we have seen, the term learning disabilities, or disorders, usually refers to problems in reading, arithmetic, writing, and spelling—skills that are learned in the classroom and essential to further learning as well as everyday functioning. Such specific developmental disabilities are recognized not only by the educational system but also by both DSM and ICD. DSM previously referred to them as academic disorders and now calls them learning disorders.

DSM diagnostic criteria are provided for disabilities in reading, mathematics, and written expression. As Table 11–4 indicates, diagnosis is based on a substantial discrepancy between measures of the skill (achievement) and the individual's intelligence, age, or education. The disturbance must interfere significantly with academic achievement

---

TABLE 11–4 DSM-IV Criteria for Disorders of Reading, Mathematics, and Written Expression

A. Achievement, measured by standardized tests, is substantially below that expected given the person's age, measured intelligence, and age-appropriate education

B. The disturbance significantly interferes with academic achievement or activities of daily living that require the ability

C. If a sensory deficit is present, the difficulties are in excess of those usually associated with the sensory deficit

Adapted and reprinted with permission from the *Diagnostic and Statistical Manual of Mental Disorders, Fourth Edition.* Copyright 1994, American Psychiatric Association.

or daily living. It cannot be accounted for by a sensory deficit. These criteria are in keeping with the definition of learning disabilities used in P.L. 94-142.

The vast majority of children with LD are reading disabled (Taylor, 1989). As a group, however, children with learning disorders are heterogeneous. In the classroom, teachers report that these children confuse one word with another, fail in simple arithmetic computations, rapidly forget too much of what they have learned, or struggle to write neatly (Figures 11–1 and 11–2). Deficits may exist in only one or two areas, so that the child shows an uneven profile of skills. However, deficits often occur in several areas. Also, although some children show quite isolated deficiencies within an area, the deficits tend to be pervasive. In arithmetic, for example, deficits may exist in only some or all of the needed computational, visual-spatial, memory, and mathematical reasoning skills. In spelling, deficits may exist in only some or all of the required skills for associating sound with symbols and recognizing and remembering written words. Thus, academic failure is best viewed in terms of the components of reading, writing, spelling, and arithmetic.

Older children and adolescents with learning disabilities often are unable to meet the increasing academic demands made upon them. These demands entail using complex language and performing in areas such as science and social studies (Lerner, 1989; Schumaker, Deshler, and Ellis, 1986). Knowing how to learn and study seems problematic. In addition, there are deficits in knowledge, as the handicapped youngsters have not learned as many facts and concepts as nondisabled children (Taylor, 1989). This becomes more obvious as they proceed through grade levels. In turn, the lack of a knowledge base makes new learning more difficult. Individuals with learning disorders thus may be increasingly handicapped by what they have failed to learn in the past. Deficits in basic cognitive processes may certainly underlie ineffective study, but lack of motivation and interest also may be involved.

Prevalence

A widely accepted estimate of the prevalence of learning disabilities among U.S. school-age children is 5 to 10 or 15 percent (Silver, 1991; Taylor, 1989). However, this is indeed an estimate. Boys are more often identified than girls, perhaps three to five times as often. The sex difference may be partly explained by referral bias. Males may be more easily referred because they are less able to tolerate reading and other deficits and thus act out.

Prevalence rates are difficult to establish not only because of differences in definitions and criteria, but also because prevalence is related to demands on the school system for special education. Thus, for example, between 1977 and 1987, the number of learning disabled children served by special edu-

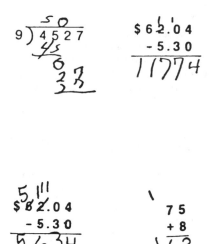

FIGURE 11–1 Arithmetic computation errors made by (top) a 12-year-old boy and (bottom) a 10-year-old girl.

From Taylor, 1988a. Permission to reprint by Guilford Press. Copyright 1988 by Guilford Press.

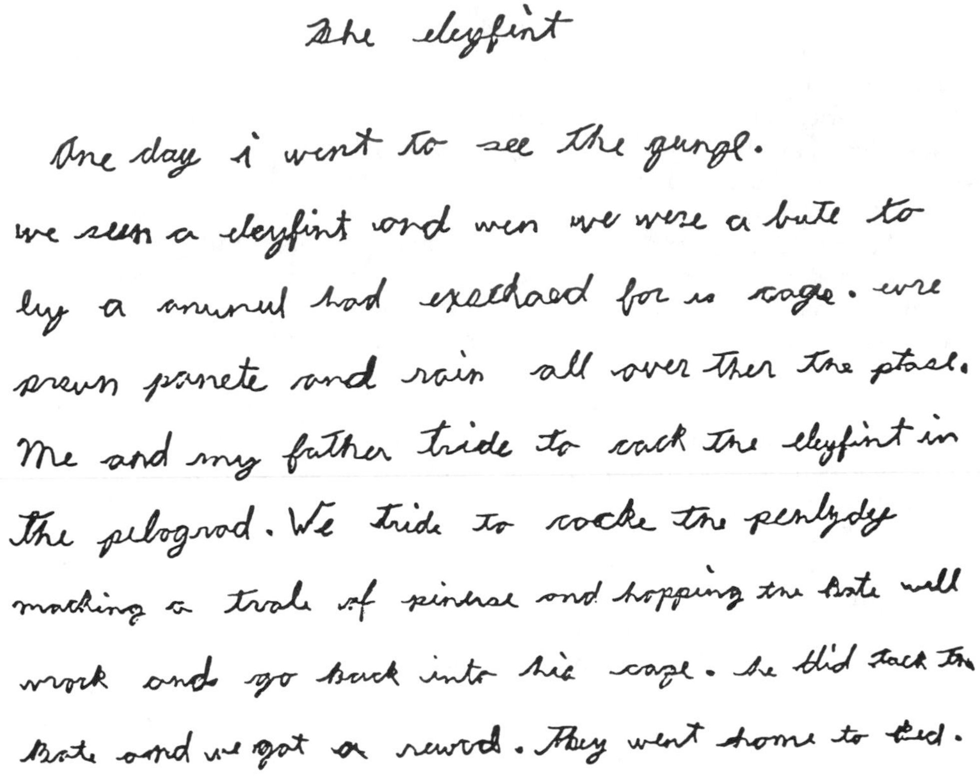

> the eleyfint
>
> One day i went to see the gungl.
> we seen a eleyfint ond wen we were a bute to
> ly a amunul had exelhaed for is cage. were
> preun panete and rain all over ther the ptasl.
> Me and my father tride to cach the eleyfint in
> the pelograd. We tride to rocke the penlydy
> maching a trale of pinerse ond hopping tru bate will
> work and go back into hie cage. he thid tack tm
> Bate ond we got a rewrd. They went home to bed.

The Elephant

One day I went to see the jungle. We seen a elephant and when we were about to leave an animal escaped from his cage. Every person panicked and ran all over the place. Me and my father tried to catch the elephant in the playground. We tried to catch the elephant by making a trail of peanuts and hoping the bait would work and he would go back into his cage. He did take the bait and we got a reward. Then we went home to bed.

FIGURE 11–2   The writing of an 11-year-old boy and the probable translation. The writing shows imagination, a rich vocabulary, and a basic grasp of story telling. There also are misspellings of common and uncommon words, added and missing words in sentences, poorly formed letters, and retracing of letters that suggests difficulty in the mechanics of writing.

From Taylor, 1988a. Permission to reprint by Guilford Press. Copyright 1988 by Guilford Press.

cation just about doubled (Kirk and Gallagher, 1989). It is debatable whether actual prevalence increased or whether more children were being placed into the LD category.

Prevalence rates regarding social class and cultural groups also are related to school placement and to sociopolitical issues (Kessler, 1988). Initially, white middle-class children compared to black children were disproportionately placed in learning disabilities classes, and black children disproportionately placed in classes for the educably mentally retarded. Indeed, learning disabilities were said to be middle-class disorders (Senf, 1986). However, by the early 1980s group differences had been substantially reduced in learning disabilities classrooms (Chinn and Hughes, 1987). This change probably reflected pressure to recognize standardized tests as discriminatory towards certain groups, to avoid the stigma of mental retardation, and to obtain school placements that would optimize learning.

Underlying Cognitive Deficits

Children with learning disorders show a wide variety of cognitive deficits, and much individual variation exists in the deficiencies displayed. The following discussion highlights some of the general findings.

Attention deficits. An association between learning problems and attention deficits has long been recognized. Learning disabled children are among those who have impairments in sustained attention (Krupski, 1986). For example, non-ADHD learning disabled youngsters (as well as ADHD children) appear to show deficits on vigilance tasks, which require sustained attention. Selective attention deficits frequently are also mentioned as part of learning disabilities: LD children are said to be overly sensitive to a variety of environmental stimuli and thus respond to stimulation that is irrelevant to the task at hand. However, these children are not distracted by all irrelevant stimuli. Distal distractors, which occur at some distance and are easily distinguished from the task, have no adverse affect. Examples are background classroom noise and intermittent flashing of lights on the ceiling. On the other hand, task performance can be impaired by distractors that are embedded in the task. An example of such a task would be asking the child to sort cards on the basis of the cards having or not having a drawing of a flower. When some of the cards also have a distractor (e.g., the

drawing of a square) the task is more difficult.

Some of the attention deficits of LD appear similar to those for Attention-Deficit Hyperactivity Disorder. Indeed, research samples have contained an unknown mix of LD, ADHD, and LD-ADHD subjects, making it difficult to draw firm conclusions about LD. Thus, although attention is implicated, a complete picture is lacking (e.g., Ackerman et al., 1986; Felton and Wood, 1989).

Perceptual problems. Perceptual and perceptual-motor deficits also have long been recognized as part of LD. In general, perceptual problems are associated with brain dysfunction and motor coordination problems, which are seen in some learning disabled children. Then too, it appears quite reasonable that perceptual processing deficits might interfere with learning, for example, by limiting the ability to distinguish the sound of one word from another or perceive differences between written letters such as *b* and *d*.

By far, hearing and vision are the perceptual modes most studied. Auditory information processing consists of numerous tasks such as discrimination, sequencing, and comprehending sounds, assigning meaning to sounds and remembering them (Bryan and Bryan, 1986). Visual processing encompasses the same functions with regard to visual material. It is assumed that difficulties with even one of these basic processes may interfere with the others and affect academic performance.

Perceptual processing is usually evaluated by standardized tests or laboratory tasks. When compared to nonhandicapped subjects, children with learning disorders show a variety of deficits in both the auditory and visual modalities (Bryan and Bryan, 1986). For example, they may more slowly respond to visual stimuli and show deficits in short-term memory for auditorily presented letters, words, and named objects (Mann, 1986).

However, interpreting the findings as perceptual impairments has become suspect. The results could be due to other factors, such as differences in attention, language skills, learning strategies, following instructions, or motivation. Moreover, even when perception is implicated, the direction of causation can be questioned: Perhaps learning disabilities cause perceptual problems rather than the other way around.

In recent years there has been a tendency to downplay the importance of perception in learning disabilities (Bryan, 1991; Hammill, 1993). However, at least some learning disabilities involve perceptual deficits (Rourke, 1994), and it is important that research continue in this area.

Memory and cognitive strategies. There is evidence for memory deficits in learning disabilities, especially in short-term working memory (Hulme and Roodenrys, 1995; Silver, 1991). For example, arithmetic problems make heavy demands on working memory, and a specific deficit for numbers exists for at least some children with arithmetic disorders. Memory impairment is also correlated with reading disability (Stanovich, 1986). Poor readers typically recall fewer items from lists of linguistic material than do good readers (Mann and Brady, 1988). This finding holds for lists of letters, words, nonsense syllables, sentences, digits, and namable objects—and whether the lists are heard or seen. Different explanations are offered for the memory deficits displayed by poor readers. One is that disabled readers fail to remember the sounds connected to words (Mann, 1986). Another popular explanation concerns failure in using memory strategies.

In fact, poor readers do use fewer strategies that promote memory, such as rehearsal, clustering, and elaboration (Bauer, 1987; Bauer and Newman, 1991). They also use them less often and less efficiently. For example, in learning lists of words, rehearsal is used less and so is organization of the words by meaning (Pressley and Levin, 1987). In more complex tasks, such as the learning of prose, poor readers do not elaborate, or add context to help learning, and do not as efficiently select cues from the text that would aid the retrieval of information from memory. At least in some cases, the readers are capable of using the strategies but do not do so.

Executive function skills, or metacognition, also show deficits (Torgesen, 1986). LD children fail to adapt to learning tasks. They lack knowledge about when, why, and how to use the strategies they possess (Pressley and Levin, 1987). They fail to notice what a specific task requires, and to monitor how well they are doing. Moreover, when they realize that they are having difficulty, they give up instead of switching strategies and trying harder, as efficient learners do. Whereas giving up has to do with motivation, it is clear that metacognition is inadequate in some cases.

READING DISABILITIES

An enormous amount of research is being conducted on reading impairment. This is partly because most children with learning disabilities are reading disabled. It is also in recognition that reading disabilities not only limit academic and occupational success, but also hinder everyday activities like reading a newspaper, vicariously traveling the world with *National Geographic* magazine, and delighting in poetry.

For these reasons, we will further discuss reading disabilities, specifically the question of how reading disabilities can be explained. It is important to remember that reading disability is being defined as a specific developmental disorder, not as a more general reading problem that might arise from an array of causes such as lack of interest or opportunity. As such, the term *dyslexia* is often used.

In his influential theory of reading, Orton (1937) put visual deficits at the heart of the problem and this hypothesis remained central for some years to come. Orton noted that among other difficulties, visual deficits caused dyslexic children to reverse letters (*d* for *b*; *saw* for *was*) and even write in mirror images (Vellutino, 1979). Other theorists suggested that dyslexia was caused by eye defects that led to impairments in scanning or tracking visual stimuli or by deficits in the processing of form, pattern, and spatial organization in visual stimuli. These theories implied defects at the early sensory stage of visual processing, which distorted visual stimuli. Such deficits were inferred from the accuracy and speed with which children matched stimuli, drew figures, and the like. They were thought to be caused by brain abnormalities or dysfunctions.

Despite the popularity of the visual-perceptual hypothesis, it was gradually challenged by contrary evidence. In fact, it is presently believed that although visual processing may cause reading problems for some children, it is not central in most cases (Silver, 1991; Snowling, 1991). The prevalent view emphasizes that dyslexia is a complex language deficiency.

In one demonstration of this, Vellutino (1987) asked poor readers in the second through sixth grades to copy words and other stimuli after a brief visual presentation. They then were requested to name the words. Poor readers had difficulties in naming words they had correctly copied. For instance, they copied *was* correctly, and even correctly named the letters as *w, a, s*. However, they named the word *saw*. The incorrect naming thus appeared to be a language problem rather than a visual defect.

The relationship between reading deficits and language deficits is variously demonstrated. Reading deficits are more common in children who have language delays (Bashir and Scavuzzo, 1992; Mann and Brady, 1988). Also, poor readers do worse than excellent readers on many language tasks but not on nonverbal tasks. Since reading involves the recoding of language, the child who is weak in phonology, syntax, and semantics could be expected to be at risk for reading disabilities (Vellutino, 1979).

Considerable research now argues that central to specific reading disability is a deficit in phonological awareness and coding. Lack of phonological skills predict reading problems. What do these skills consist of? Phonological awareness involves the recognition that words can be segmented into sounds. (For example, the word *but* has three sounds: *b, u, t*.) Young children who are aware of the sounds of their native language and can map sounds to letters and words become the better readers. Children with phonological deficits have difficulty in naming actual words and artificial "words." Short-term memory deficits for verbal material may involve deficits in using or retrieving sounds to represent the verbal items, and so phonological deficits may underlie these memory problem (Hulme and Roodenrys, 1995). At the same time, training in phonological awareness and coding can improve reading.

Phonological skills are especially important in the early stages of learning to read, and other abilities—for example, comprehension and syntax—are surely critical in the enormously complex skill of reading. Much less is known about deficits in these latter areas. It is possible to identify children who have comprehension problems without phonological difficulties. In at least some cases, the comprehension deficits appear not to be confined to reading but reflect a more global deficit in language comprehension (Stothard and Hulme, 1995). Be that as it may, much evidence indicates that most specific reading disabilities stem from deficits in phonological processing (Stanovich, 1994).

Thus, there has been a notable shift in hypotheses about the underlying psychological causes of dyslexia. As we will see later, the shift away from perceptual hypotheses has had implication for treatment.

SOCIAL AND MOTIVATIONAL FACTORS

Although intellectual functioning clearly is the main concern of learning disabilites research, the role of social and motivational variables is recognized (Bryan and Bryan, 1990). Current ideas and interest in children's social and emotional life are being applied, even though socioemotional functioning is hardly mentioned in the major definitions of language and learning disorders.

Social Status

Numerous studies provide evidence that peers, teachers, and parents hold negative attitudes about at least some portion of learning disabled children and tend to reject them (Gresham and Elliott, 1989; Margalit, 1989; Rourke, 1988).

Several investigators requested children to rate classmates or to nominate classmates who, for example, would make a good president or would not be welcomed at their birthday party (Pearl, Donahue, and Bryan, 1986). Children with learning disorders were often rated less popular than nondisabled peers, and they were more rejected or neglected. Figure 11–3 represents this general finding.

Similar negative attitudes have been shown by teachers, who associate learning disabilities with a variety of annoying and otherwise problematic characteristics. Among these characteristics are conduct and personal problems, anxiety, immaturity, disruptiveness, and hyperactivity (e.g., Heavey et al., 1989). Learning disabled children have received lower ratings than nondisabled youngsters on cooperation, organization, coping, tactfulness, responsibility, and other such attributes. Parents not only recognize their handicapped children's academic problems, they also note anxiety and deficiencies in impulse control.

In reviewing the research, Pearl et al. (1986) noted that youngsters with learning disabilities seem not particularly appealing

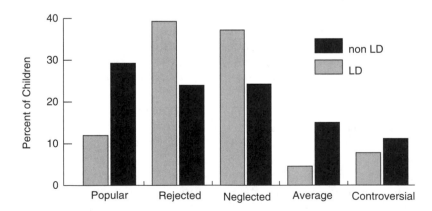

FIGURE 11–3   Percentage of disabled learners and nondisabled learners selected by classmates into each social category. All children were in regular fourth- through sixth-grade classrooms.
Data from Stone and LaGreca, 1990.

as playmates or students, and they are not seen as easy to live with. They may even make less favorable impression on strangers than other children (Taylor, 1988a).

Social Competence and Behavior Problems

Research suggests that children with learning disorders are less socially competent than non-LD peers, as measured by inventories and laboratory tasks (Pearl et al., 1986; Ritter, 1989; Toro et al., 1990). This is manifested in a variety of ways: difficulty in identifying the emotional expression of others, misreading of social situations, errors in guessing how other children feel in particular situations, and deficits in social problem solving. In addition, learning-disabled children may display atypical conversational behavior with peers, at times more passive and deferential and at times more hostile (Pearl et al., 1986). They may also be less skillful in maintaining conversations.

It is important to note that not all of the children show social deficits (Gresham and Elliott, 1989). Moreover, situational influences may be quite strong in determining whether a child behaves competently or not.

Many hypotheses have been put forth to explain how social skill deficits are linked to LD. The proposals tend to focus on some cognitive or perceptual deficit. For example, linguistic disability is said to lead to poor interpersonal communication, and perceptual disability to failure to accurately interpret the emotional expressions of others (Rourke, 1988). It has even been suggested that a specific deficit in social skills be included in the definition of learning disabilities (Swanson, 1991). This suggestion is based on the assumption that social skill deficits result from neurological dysfunction, just as learning difficulties do. Another hypothesis emphasizes that social skill deficits indirectly stem from academic deficiencies, probably acting through peer rejection. In this case, perhaps there is a lack of opportu-

The study of social interaction has become increasingly important as psychologists appreciate its role in the development of learning and learning difficulties.

nity to acquire social skills, perform them, and be reinforced for them. No one hypothesis satisfactorily explains the social skills deficits associated with learning disabilities.

Research into the behavior problems of children with language and learning disabilities is still quite limited. There is some evidence for higher than average risk for a variety of disturbances, including internalizing problems (Rourke, Young, and Leenaars, 1989; Rutter, Mayhood, and Howlin, 1992; Thompson and Kronenberger, 1990).

A link has been noted between learning disabilities and juvenile delinquency. One investigation found that 36 percent of incarcerated juveniles had a learning disability and that learning disabled youth were more than twice as likely as nondisabled youth to commit a delinquent act (Dunviant, 1982, cited by Brier, 1989). Drawing on research findings, Brier proposed that a child with LD is more likely to become delinquent if he or she shows, among other factors, ADHD/aggressive behaviors, relatively low IQ, social problems, language problems, and frustration over school achievement. Research is needed to test this proposal, which suggests that the risk of a learning disabled child becoming delinquent increases with the number of these factors and the degree to which they are present.

It should be pointed out that most children with learning disabilites are not viewed by others as having social or behavioral problems, and considerable individual differences exist in socioemotional behavior (Rourke, 1988). When Porter and Rourke (1985) analyzed profiles on the Personality Inventory for Children, they were able to classify seventy-seven of the one hundred subjects into four behavioral subtypes. About 50 percent of the classified children were rated as well adjusted, and another 10 percent showed normal functioning except for somatic complaints. The remainder showed externalizing or internalizing problems.

Motivation

There is considerable interest in the motivational behavior of children with learning disabilities, since effort is essential for their academic success. Yet, many of the children appear to enter a vicious cycle of academic failure and low motivation that works against them (Licht and Kistner, 1986). Based on academic failure the children come to doubt their intellectual abilities and believe that efforts to achieve are futile. This results in their being frustrated and giving up easily in the face of difficulty. In turn, further failure is experienced, which reinforces the belief in lack of ability. At this point, any achievement is attributed to luck, the ease of the task, help from a teacher, or some other source external to the self (Figure 11–4). Thus, success gives little satisfaction and is unlikely to boost confidence.

There is evidence that this cycle operates. Studies show that children with learning disabilities tend to have lower expectations for success than other children. They are less likely to credit success to their ability, and more likely to attribute failure to inadequate ability. In addition, learning handicapped children tend to believe that their efforts will not improve the situation and that the situation is controlled by external variables (e.g., Allen and Drabman, 1991; Tarnowski and Nay, 1989). Although these beliefs may have some reasonable basis, they also tend to contribute to the difficulties.

Nevertheless, individual differences in response to failure is seen, with some children being more adaptive than others. Licht and Kistner (1986) note several factors that play a role in creating these differences. Unsurprisingly, one factor is the degree of failure experienced: Less failure is associated with more adaptive motivation. For example, one study showed that learning disabled children who were doing somewhat better academically than the others were more likely to attribute failure to insufficient effort on their part.

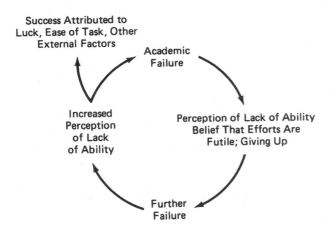

FIGURE 11–4 Learning disabled children may experience a vicious cycle of academic failure and low motivation.

This internal attribution implies that effort could pay off. Even so, some successful youngsters have little confidence in their ability, while some who fail continue to believe that they will succeed sooner or later.

Children's developmental levels may help explain this. In the normal course of events, perceptions of ability change in several ways. Younger children tend to judge their ability independently of others' abilities and believe that the more you try, the more you learn and the greater is your ability. Subsequently, social comparison becomes more important and by age ten most children also view ability as quite stable and less influenced by effort. Older children thus may be more susceptible to negative feedback about their failure (Bjorklund and Green, 1992). Indeed, research shows that children under age seven generally have high opinions of their abilities, and even when they do not, motivational problems may not appear. But this protection gradually disappears for many, although not all, children.

Teacher feedback can also influence children's self-perceptions. Although teacher feedback can be highly critical, teachers may also try to encourage lower-achieving students by giving less criticism and more praise. In fact, praise may be given following quite poor performance. There is some evidence that feedback depends in part on the child's behavior. High criticism and low praise are more likely to be given to defiant children who are hard to manage. Low criticism and high praise are more likely when the child is viewed as low in ability and high in effort. How children interpret these consequences is complex. Younger students and those with learning problems seem to take feedback at face value; that is, praise for effort is taken as simply as that—which might reinforce effort. Nevertheless, praise for performing very easy tasks that require little effort probably does not help children in the long run, when they must persist in the face of difficulty (Licht and Kistner, 1986). To be effective, praise should depend on effortful work and should provide specific information as to how the child might further improve performance.

Parents certainly could be expected to play a role in determining children's self-perceptions and motivation. The belief that their parents accept and love them is related to children's self-esteem (Morvitz and Motta, 1992). Some parents appear to attribute their children's success more to luck and their children's failure more to lack of ability (Pearl et al., 1986). Some also hold low expectations for their children. While parental denial of their children's problems is not helpful, encouragement of internal locus of control and high effort can be supportive. Parents (as well as teachers) are also in the position to build confidence in areas in which the child may already have some confidence, which can contribute to general positive self-regard (cf. Grolnick and Ryan, 1990).

ETIOLOGY

As we have already seen, the assumption that neurological damage or dysfunction underlies learning disabilities has been a dominant hypothesis. This perspective was obvious among early theorists. Orton, Strauss, Werner, Lehtinen, and Kephart, among others, linked brain disorder to children of average intelligence who displayed learning, perceptual, language, and behavioral problems such as hyperactivity (Strauss and Kephart, 1955; Strauss and Lehtinen, 1947).

How has the hypothesis of biological etiology fared? Connections between known brain damage and learning handicaps certainly exist (Bigler, 1987). There are learning disabled children with histories of neurological disorders, such as cerebral palsy, epilepsy, nervous system infections, and head injury (Taylor, 1988). Specific learning disabilities are associated with maternal alcohol use, neurological delays, neurological soft signs, and immune system dysfunction (e.g., Taylor, 1989; Snowling, 1991; Van Dyke and Fox, 1990).

Nevertheless, these findings have often not been compelling. More recently, however, technological advances have revived and strengthened the notion that minimal brain dysfunction underlies specific developmental disorders (Bryan, 1991).

Genetic Influence

Genetic influence on learning disabilities was suspected for some time and has been better established more recently (DeFries and Gillis, 1993; Maughan and Yule, 1994; Snowling, 1991). Although language dysfunctions are known to "run in families" (Bishop, 1992a), reading is the area most extensively examined. Reading disabilities too are familial; that is, parents and siblings of affected persons have a greater chance of reading problems than relatives of control persons. Twin comparisons also indicate inheritance. Given the importance of phonological processing in reading, it is interesting that hereditary influence has been found for this ability.

Some progress is being made in identifying the specific chromosomes and mechanisms that might be responsible for reading disorders. Chromosomes 15 and 6 have been implicated in some cases. Both polygenic and single-gene effects are suspected. In fact, there is considerable evidence that reading disabilities are transmitted through several different genetic mechanisms. Since the disabilities themselves may be heterogeneous, it is tempting to speculate that different genetic mechanisms may underlie different reading disabilities. However, it is too early to draw this conclusion (Smith et al., 1990).

Brain Abnormalities

Some of the most exciting investigations of etiology concern brain abnormalities. While interest exists in both verbal and nonverbal (e.g., spatial) disabilities, efforts are more advanced with regard to verbal and particularly reading dysfunctions (e.g., Semrud-Clikeman and Hynd, 1990).

When studying dyslexia in the late 1930s, Orton proposed that visual information was processed by both hemispheres of the brain but that the right hemisphere held visual stimuli in reversed form and order (Vellutino, 1979). For most children this was not a problem because the left hemisphere became dominant over the right. In dyslexia, left hemisphere dominance was considered flawed so that the right hemisphere gained some control and its reversed patterns were expressed in a variety of ways. Since Orton's time, interest in the hemispheres has continued, based largely on evidence that the left hemisphere is specialized for processing language and the right for processing spatial information. Current hypotheses include the possibilities that the left hemisphere develops more slowly than it should, or that the hemispheres do not properly communicate with each other (Maughan and Yule, 1994).

The most interesting findings, which come from brain scans and postmortem brain studies, implicate the planum temporale (Hynd, Marshall, and Gonzalez, 1991; Hynd and Semrud-Clikeman, 1989a,b; Peterson, 1995). This is a triangular-shaped region on the upper surface of the temporal lobe which extends to the lower surface of the parietal lobe. In normal brains, the left side of the planum temporale is usually larger than the right side. In individuals with dyslexia, this asymmetry is absent. In addition, abnormal cell structure and abnormal activation and metabolism have been found. Importantly, the planum temporale is thought to be involved in phonological processing. A limited number of studies show that functioning of the planum temporale is different in individuals with or without dyslexia when they are engaged in phonological and other reading processing tasks. It is speculated that abnormalities of the planum temporale may be present during the first six months of prenatal development, possibly due to genetic factors. (It is noteworthy that the size of parts of the brain have also been found to differ in persons with and without language disabilities, e.g., Jernigan et al., 1991).

These findings need to be placed in larger context. The research samples are small. Almost all of the brains examined appeared normal, and only refined measures indicated differences. The measurements are not easily accomplished, and replication is important. In addition, the findings are not always consistent and there are individuals with symmetrical temporal lobes who show no reading problems. Nevertheless, the research is fascinating and promising.

Environmental Factors

Although biological variables may be critical causes of LD, environmental influences also operate. In fact, the importance of psychosocial and motivational effects on learning is well recognized by professionals and parents. It is reasonable to speculate that some children with a disposition to a learning disability may escape problems due to advantaged social environments. Several variables known to influence learning might well influence the learning handicapped child: SES, cultural values, family interactions, parental attitudes toward learning, child management practices, child characteristics such as motivation and temperament, and the matching of expectations for the child to the child's ability (Taylor, 1988a). Stevenson and Fredman (1990) found that large family size and certain aspects of mother-child interaction were linked to reading problems, and they noted that family involvement in the child's learning may be especially influential in early reading acquisition. Whitehurst and Fischel (1994) believe that family verbal interaction is not the root of specific language disorders, but once verbal interactions become abnormal—probably due to the child's deficits—they can play a role in maintaining the deficits.

Although most conceptualizations of learning disabilities assign environmental causation a secondary role, not everyone agrees with this emphasis. In 1987, Gerald Coles wrote, *The Learning Mystique: A Critical Look at "Learning Disabilities,"* in which he argued that only a very small percentage of the children identified as LD have neurological dysfunction that may interfere with learning and academic achievement (Coles, 1989). Coles recognized individual differences (not disorders) in biological functioning. However, it was assumed that social, cultural, political, and economic influences are fundamental in creating or preventing LD. Thus, for instance, when a child fails to learn in school, the cause of failure must be explored by examining child-teacher interaction, and also by looking at broader factors, such as how the school's structure and attitudes might be causing failure. It is therefore important to identify social, economic, and political variables that affect the child, teacher, and school.

Coles's position was greeted with strong reactions, perhaps partly because of his challenging style, but also for other reasons. Among other things, Coles was criticized for ignoring the fact that some children display learning problems even when provided good opportunity to learn, ignoring evidence for a brain-LD link, and broadening the definition of learning disabilities to include poor achievers not ordinarily labeled as LD (Galaburda, 1989; Rourke, 1989; Stanovich, 1989). At the same time, some researchers welcomed Coles's challenge as a chance for broad discussion (e.g., Miller, 1990). Others agreed with Coles that some learning handicaps can best be viewed as originating from both neurological and environmental variables (e.g., Adelman, 1989). This interactional approach emphasizes the importance of knowing more about environmental factors, including instructional methods, that might influence whether and how learning handicaps might occur or be maintained. As such, it can be beneficial in furthering knowledge about specific learning problems and in helping to ameliorate them.

DEVELOPMENTAL COURSE AND OUTCOME

Much is yet to be learned about the developmental course and outcome of specific language and learning disabilities. Nevertheless, a range of outcomes is apparent.

Whitehurst and Fischel (1994) recently reviewed the research with regard to specific language problems that are identified during the early preschool years. They concluded that:

Specific language delay in the preschool period is better characterized as a risk factor than a disorder: While some children with specific language delay go on to have learning or language impairments in the school years, the vast majority with specific language delay recover to the normal range by five years of age. Children whose language skills are in the normal range by age 5 have low risk of later language or reading disorder. However, they may continue to be weaker in language and reading than in other areas of their development (p. 631).

Nevertheless, risk increases with the severity of the language deficits and the age of the child. In general, risk for later problems increases from articulation problems to expressive problems to receptive-expressive problems. This hierarchy of risk has been noted by others (e.g., Baker and Cantwell, 1989; Rutter, Mayhood, and Howlin, 1992). In fact, many children with receptive difficulties may eventually acquire language comprehension only after traveling a long and difficult path, and some may never develop completely normal comprehension of language. It is noteworthy that the most language impaired children are also at risk for later social problems.

In reviewing the prognosis for reading disorders, Maughan (1995) points to the shortcomings of the data such as inappropriate comparison groups. Given this, well-designed studies do indicate that reading problems tend to persist during the school years into adolescence and adulthood. However, much individual variation is seen. General intelligence and initial severity of reading problems are the best predictors of outcome. Also, continued practice and experience with literacy materials play a role when reading comprehension and word recognition improve. Interestingly, phonological processing does not improve much in dyslexic children or adults. Since reading failure is so prevalent among those with learning disabilities, it appears that at least for some, LD is a chronic condition (Silver, 1989; Spreen, 1988).

How pervasive are the effects of reading problems? In general, academic progress is impeded, but educational outcome is related to social status and intelligence. College is not out of the question. However, early school dropout is a risk, especially for those less socially advantaged. In turn, occupational outcome is predicted by educational attainment. We still know little about adult outcome, however, as most studies followed participants only into their twenties.

We may ask about the effects of reading difficulties in another way: Are early reading problems related to later social adjustment? Research findings are mixed with regard to this question. Depression and anxiety are sometimes reported; however, poor adjustment is not inevitable. Perhaps the most argued issue has been whether LD is associated with later antisocial behavior. Such an association has been noted, but has more recently been questioned. Perhaps the link is attributable to the co-occurrence of LD and ADHD. Also, the research has focused on general school underachievement rather than LD or reading itself. It now appears that there is little evidence that specific reading disabilities is associated with undue rates of antisocial behavior beyond adolescence.

Finally, it should be noted that, in general, outcome data on reading problems appear to be based on samples of general reading problems as well as specific reading disability. Thus, we do not know which of the findings apply to specific disabilities.

IDENTIFYING LANGUAGE AND LEARNING DISABILITIES

When language disorders are suspected in preschoolers, parents seek assessment from a variety of professionals. Later-occurring or more subtle language problems and learning handicaps are most often evaluated in the educational system, following procedures set for compliance with P.L. 94-142. Teachers typically have the critical role of seeking consultation for the child, most likely having already spoken to the parents about the child's problems. School psychologists do much of the actual assessment; they gather information from the teacher and often are the persons who observe the child in the classroom (Bryan and Bryan, 1986). In some cases, the child may be evaluated in mental health settings, and the school subsequently will do an assessment and then arrange a meeting among school professionals, parents, and other relevant individuals to discuss the evaluation and plan for intervention.

Adequate assessment demands an interview with the parents and seeks information about the child's prenatal, developmental, and medical history; the child's behavioral and social functioning; family background; and family functioning and concerns. Parents have complained that they were not always adequately considered by the educational system. At the same time, all parents are not equally concerned or willing to participate in assessments, which they may even believe are unnecessary. Clearly, it is to everyone's advantage to see themselves as working in a team.

Of obvious importance in identifying disabilities are batteries of tests that help establish the child's academic achievement, general intelligence, and specific language, cognitive, perceptual, or motor skills. A large number of tests are available for this purpose (Bryan and Bryan, 1986; Whitehurst and Fischel, 1994). Selection of tests should, of course, take into consideration reliability and validity, as well as cultural bias.

The focus of academic assessment is usually on reading, spelling, and arithmetic skills, although tests are available to examine other areas, such as social studies knowledge. Among the many tests employed are the Wide Range Achievement Test (Jastak and Wilkinson, 1984), the Peabody Individual Achievement Test (Dunn and Markwardt, 1970), and the Woodcock-Johnson PsychoEducational Battery (Woodcock and Johnson, 1978). In addition to a standardized general test of intelligence, such as the Wechsler test, the child may be given cognitive tests that evaluate specific visual, auditory, motor, language, and thinking skills. It is important that the child's difficulties be described in detail, as they can take several forms and involve several cognitive components (Taylor, 1988a). Strengths also need to be assessed.

When relevant, the evaluator should also discuss the child's study habits, motivations, self-esteem, and concerns. Because learning disabilities are essentially defined in terms of achievement and cognition, there is probably a tendency to inadequately assess the behavioral, social, and motivational contexts in which the child is operating. Figure 11–5 presents Taylor's scheme for all of the areas that a complete evaluation for LD would encompass. Psychosocial and environmental factors, including the match between the child's abilities and expectations, are important aspects of assessment.

It is also the case that identification and assessment should be done at an appropriately early time (Satz and Fletcher, 1988). Most children are not referred for learning problems until after they have experienced several years of academic failure.

TREATMENT APPROACHES

Our discussion of treatment focuses on the amelioration of academic and learning problems, although we recognize that children and families can often profit from more general therapeutic support. Speech therapists appropriately play a dominant role in therapy for the young child with language deficits. Older children's language difficulties, especially less severe ones, are often dealt with as part of the larger effort to ameliorate learning problems. Although learning problems have primarily been viewed as educational problems, they have been addressed by professionals from several disciplines, including physicians, optometrists, and psychologists. There has been considerable controversy over what is considered the best treatment approach, and dialogue about this issue continues.

Medical Treatments

Despite the assumption that biological abnormality causes learning handicaps, direct medical intervention plays only a small role in treating most specific learning disabilities. The medical condition of the child should be especially considered when there is a history of neurological dysfunction or damage (Taylor, 1989).

Medical treatment may also be appropriate in the presence of Attention-Deficit Hyperactivity Disorder. Stimulant medications may be considered. As discussed in Chapter 9, stimulants appear helpful in that they can decrease problems of inattention, impulsivity, and disruptive noncompliant behaviors, and improve classroom productivity and short-term academic performance. When stimulants have been employed with learning disabilities without ADHD, the results are similar. That is, more classroom work may be produced but there is little sustained improvement on achievement tests (Gadow and Pomeroy, 1991). Moreover, still of concern are the adverse medical side effects of stimulants, as well as possible negative attributions. For example, one study found that learning disabled boys taking medication attributed failure more to external causes than those not taking medication (Allen and Drabman, 1991). As we have already recognized, such external attribution can be

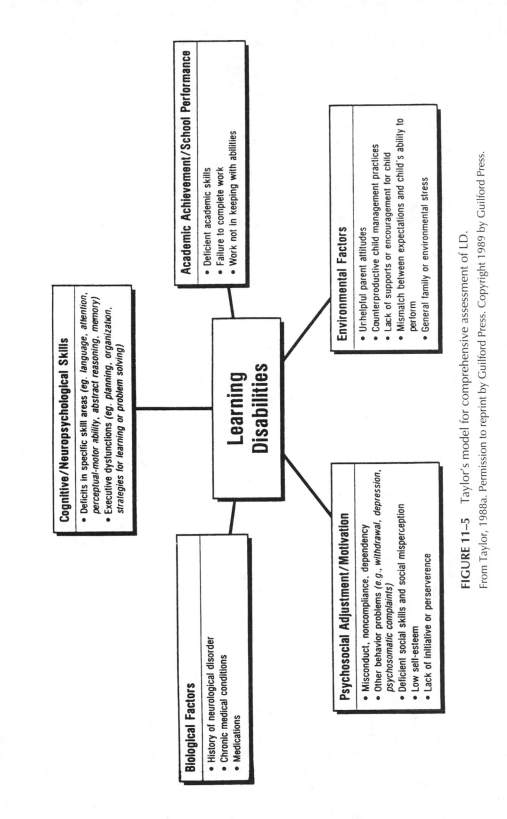

FIGURE 11-5 Taylor's model for comprehensive assessment of LD.
From Taylor, 1988a. Permission to reprint by Guilford Press. Copyright 1989 by Guilford Press.

detrimental because it leads to less motivation to work hard to succeed.

Other biological treatments are viewed with more skepticism by researchers and clinicians. For example, recommendations have been made about antihistamines and the diets of learning disabled children, including the need for massive doses of vitamins and specific elements such as copper and zinc, reduced refined sugar, and the Feingold diet that reduces food additives and preservatives (Silver, 1987; Wilsher, 1991). Some of these proposals go hand in hand with recommendations for decreasing ADHD. Overall, there is little or no evidence that these treatments are effective.

Early Process Approaches

In the late 1960s and 1970s, many different approaches were employed in treating learning disabilities (Hammill, 1993). Most were based on the general belief that treatment must relieve deficits in psychoneurological processes thought to underlie learning. These approaches varied in the processes they targeted for improvement.

Perceptual-motor training was central to several of these treatments. One example is the work of Kephart (1960, 1971), who proposed that children develop through stages, from the motor, through the perceptual, to the conceptual-perceptual. This progression was assumed to have broken down, and treatment aimed at producing normal developmental outcomes. Kephart advocated individual assessment and emphasized early motor-perceptual abilities. Various activities were suggested to establish a "perceptual-motor match," in which children received information from their own movements that allowed them to monitor the correctness of their perceptions and motor actions (Kirk, 1972). These activities included the use of walking boards, trampolines, and games to teach movement; chalkboard exercises to develop the matching of movement and vi-

sual perception; and form perception exercises such as pegboards and puzzles. Another example of perceptual training is Frostig's visual-perception method that trained children in eye-hand coordination, shape constancy, spatial relationships, and the like (Frostig and Horne, 1964). Perceptual training programs offered by some of the best educational specialists, among them Kephart and Frostig, were widely respected for several decades.

Less popular was Doman and Delacato's (1968) method, which attributed learning problems to failure in the early developmental sequence of movement, language, and sensory functions. The approach called for motor and sensory experiences that were extremely demanding of the time and resources of the family. In 1983 the American Academy of Pediatrics concluded that the method had not proven effective (Silver, 1987). Another approach not widely supported was visual or visual-motor training directed by optometrists who believed visual problems to be a central cause of learning handicaps, perhaps especially of reading difficulties.

Still other methods targeted language and how it is received and expressed through the senses (Bryan and Bryan, 1986). Fernald's multisensory method, for example, presented academic material by way of sight, touch, hearing, and kinesthetic (muscle) cues; it assumed that learning is facilitated by multisensory experiences. Other programs identified the modality strengths and weaknesses of the learning handicapped child and worked with the modality strengths. Thus, a child who learns more effectively with visually presented material is encouraged to learn by seeing; the child who processes auditory information better than written information is given oral tests. Several of the modality approaches have been well received by learning disabilities professionals, although their treatment effectiveness is often not established.

Although visual motor activities like working with blocks and puzzles had once been emphasized in treating learning disabilities, they are now given less importance.

Many of the early process approaches fell by the wayside in the 1970s, primarily because they had not been proven successful in either remediating academic performance or in reducing the proposed underlying deficits (Hammill, 1993; Taylor, 1989).

Current Approaches

Current approaches can be viewed as roughly falling into four overlapping models: direct instruction, behavioral, cognitive, and cognitive-behavioral (Lloyd et al., 1991).

Direct instruction methods directly pinpoint academic problems and teach to them. That is, if the child has a disability in read-ing, exercises and practice are provided with letters, words, and other literary materials (Hammill, 1993). Some direct instruction programs are highly organized with regard to content and teacher behavior. Unsurprisingly, educators readily rely on direct instruction.

The *behavioral approach* aims at identifying academic and social skill deficits and modifying them through contingency management, feedback, and modeling. Thus, for example, the goal may be to increase the number of correct arithmetic problems or words read, comprehension of written material, or legibility of handwriting. Or it may be to increase on-task behavior or cooperation. Reinforcement has included verbal praise and desirable activities available during free time; tokens, usually points, are commonly employed. Although the behavioral model is most interested in how environmental variables shape behavior, in practice, behavioral methods often are combined with direct instruction and cognitive models.

Cognitive and cognitive-behavioral models as applied to learning disabilities tend to emphasize the remediation of metacognition and the executive functions in information processing. That is, students are taught to better understand their own cognitive processes and to regulate cognitive activity (Palincsar and Brown, 1986). They are encouraged to be active problem solvers. Instruction emphasizes increasing awareness of task demands, using appropriate strategies, monitoring the success of the strategies, and switching to another strategy when necessary. The approach has been applied to reading comprehension, mathematics, written expression, memory skills, and study skills (Lyon and Moats, 1988).

As an example, we take the work of Schumaker and Deshler and their colleagues, which aimed at improving reading comprehension in junior and high school learning disabled students (Palincsar and Brown, 1987; Schumaker et al., 1984). The students were initially evaluated as to how they were dealing with a reading task. Then failure to use strategies to comprehend the material was discussed. Specific strategies were next proposed and used by the teacher. They consisted of surveying the material for the main ideas, examining the questions at the end of the readings, and re-reading the material while constructing questions about the main points. Students then practiced using these strategies and were able to successfully apply them to school work. In another study Ellis, Deshler, and Schumaker (1989) successfully trained adolescents to more independently generate strategies for novel problems and use them in the classroom.

This and other research indicate that the executive functions of youth with learning disabilities can be enhanced. Of course, successful training no doubt depends on several variables, for example, the teacher's knowledge of the subject matter and the student's past learning experiences and motivation. So far the evidence suggests that such training is indeed worthwhile and that further research will be helpful.

EDUCATIONAL EFFORTS AND POLICY

Educational policy regarding learning disabilities falls under federal government mandates for handicapping conditions (See pp. 266–267 for a review of this topic). Of all children receiving special education in the United States in 1992–1993, fifty-one percent was identified as having specific learning disabilities (U.S. Dept. of Educ., 1994). Consistent with the mandate for the least restrictive placement, however, several school options are available for learning disabled students. Most of these youths are in regular classrooms, the combination of the regular classroom and the resource room, and self-contained special classrooms (Lerner, 1989).

If the regular classroom teacher has no training in learning disabilities, a special education teacher may act as a consultant, provide materials, or actually teach the child in the regular classroom. In the resource room, the teacher typically has special education training and teaching is conducted in small groups. It is important that experiences in the resource room be integrated with those of the regular classroom. Self-contained special classrooms usually serve the most severely handicapped students. Teachers typically have special training and class size is small so that instruction can be better individualized. Some portion of students do not do well even in small groups, but can profit from one-to-one instruction.

Which placement is best for an individual child is debatable and undoubtedly depends on teacher, student, instructional, and other situational factors. Not enough is known about the effectiveness of different placements and approaches. Nevertheless, there is evidence for the general efficacy of several principles of instruction, including the following (Taylor, 1989):

1. Academic competence is related to the amount of time devoted to students' being actively engaged in academic work. As commonsensical as this may seem, research shows that much class time is not spent on academics.
2. Academic competence also is related to the teacher's actively instructing, modeling, directing, and guiding learning. Learning handicapped children do not usually benefit from discovery learning; they require structure and feedback.
3. Some degree of individualized instruction is helpful. This principle is related to the idea of mastery learning: that a fixed minimum level of achievement be set and the child provided with instruction and practice to reach that level.
4. Generalization of learning across tasks and time usually must be deliberately built into instruction. For example, after a child learns a particular arithmetic technique, practice in using the technique on slightly different problems can be given.
5. Incentives are usually helpful and they should be tied to specific goals (e.g., number of words spelled correctly).
6. Training is best aimed at remediating all deficiencies rather than focusing on a single one, because improvement in one skill often is not related to improvement in another (e.g., accuracy in reading and comprehension in reading). In addition, mastery of lower-order skills and knowledge is necessary for higher-order abilities.

These principles are likely to enhance learning in a variety of settings and with various academic difficulties, but the degree to which they can remediate learning disabilities is unclear.

The issue has taken on greater importance since the Regular Education Initiative (REI) was initiated by government representatives and a group of professionals. REI advances the idea that learning handicapped children can be best served in the regular classroom setting (Carnine and Kameenui, 1990). It is part of the broad movement to include people with handicaps in regular education and in society in general (Hammill, 1993). Hammill notes that should REI be successful, changes will occur in the learning disabilities movement. First, increasing numbers of students will be placed in regular classrooms, requiring greater consultation and teamwork between teachers and resource personnel. Second, REI could lead to students not having to be diagnosed and labeled. This, in turn, could lead to reduced funding, reduced training of special education teachers, and fewer organizations devoted to concerns about learning disabilities.

However, REI is controversial (e.g., Kauffman, Gerber, and Semmel, 1988; Keogh, 1988). Concern is expressed, for example, that teachers in regular classrooms are not adequately trained, will not receive the support required, and do not desire to teach students who vary so widely in performance. Moreover, as the Learning Disabilities Association of America notes, placement of all children with LD into regular classrooms can violate federal mandates and children's rights as much as placement of all children into separate classrooms (The Link, 1995).

Meanwhile, students with learning disabilities are increasingly enrolled in postsecondary education programs (Hughes and Smith, 1990). Limited research suggests that they are of average or above average in intellectual ability, but many display special needs. As a group these students are heterogeneous with regard to specific skills and needs. Colleges provide various support services including remediation, tutorials, instruction in study and learning strategies, and classroom accommodations. However, there is so far very little investigation into the effectiveness of these services.

SUMMARY

Concern for learning handicapped children culminated in 1963 in the creation of the category *learning disabilities* (LD) and a new field. The definition of LD used by the Office of Education is now widely employed. Specific learning disabilities refers to deficits in psychological processes involved in language that are manifested in reading, writing, listening, thinking, and the like. Learning disabilities are not primarily due to sensory or motor handicaps, mental retardation, emotional disturbance, or environmental disadvantage. Children are usually identified on the basis of academic achievement being lower than expected based on age, grade, or general intelligence. Several dissatisfactions are expressed with this definition, but it remains influential.

Specific language disabilities fall into three categories: phonological, expressive, and receptive-expressive. These are defined respectively in terms of articulation of sounds, expression of a full range of language forms, and comprehension of language. The prevalence of language disorders is estimated at 2 to 5 percent in the general population and much higher in clinical samples. Many psychological correlates have been discussed as possible underlying causes of language disorders. Of particular interest is the finding of a deficit in rapid processing of auditory signals.

Children and adolescents with learning disabilities show an array of academic problems, especially in reading. Deficits may be isolated but often exist simultaneously in several areas of functioning. Prevalence is estimated as between 5 to 15 percent of school-age children, with higher prevalence

in boys than in girls. Deficiencies in numerous cognitive processes are implicated in learning disabilities, including attention, perception, memory, and metacogntion. In the recent past, much importance was given to perceptual-motor deficits but greater emphasis is currently given to language processing deficits. This shift in thinking parallels research findings on specific reading disability, or dyslexia, which is displayed by many youth with learning disabilities. The research suggests that dyslexia is less a disorder of visual sensory defects, as previously held, and more a disorder of higher-order language skills. Nevertheless, a comprehensive view recognizes that several kinds of deficits might underlie the different learning disabilities.

Research indicates that peers, teachers, and parents have negative attitudes and expectations for at least some learning disabled youth. The degree to which the youngsters display emotional and behavioral problems is not clearly established, but some difficulties exist, particularly with regard to social competence. Youth with learning disabilities may also enter a negative motivational cycle that includes academic failure, perceived lack of ability, attribution of success to external factors, and giving up.

Neurological dysfunction has long been the dominant etiological hypothesis for learning disabilities. Evidence is growing for several kinds of genetic transmission of reading disability; there is also some evidence of brain abnormalities in dyslexia. Overall, the evidence for biological factors is increasing but is still not entirely convincing. Environmental variables undoubtedly also play some causal role in learning disabilities, for example, social class and parental attitudes. An interactionist position would argue that most learning problems can best be explained by the interaction of individual predisposition and social influence.

Many preschoolers with language articulation problems are doing well by school age; those who are not, appear to have later difficulties in language and perhaps in reading. Overall, children with receptive language deficits are at greater risk for later academic difficulties than children with expressive language deficits. Reading disabilities seem to often persist into adolescence and adulthood. Severity of early problems and intelligence predict continuity of reading problems. Early reading deficiencies are related to later educational and occupational status and to psychological adjustment. A range of outcomes is noted, however.

Identification and assessment of learning disabilities most often occurs in the educational system, as part of P.L. 94-142's mandate. The teacher and school psychologist play critical roles. Tests of academic achievement, intelligence, and cognitive processes are central in identifying learning disabilities. Broad assessment is ideal, however, as is early identification.

Treatment of learning disabilities has included several disciplines. Medical care is appropriate in some cases, including when ADHD is present. The older process treatments were based on the assumption that optimal treatment had to remediate underlying cognitive deficits. Many of these approaches focused on perceptual-motor training. Even the best of them failed to remediate learning difficulties, and many are no longer popular. Today's treatments emphasize direct instruction in academic skills, the training of metacognition and learning strategies, and the use of behavioral methods to enhance academic skills and behavior.

In the schools, most children with learning disabilities are served by a combination of the regular classroom and the resource room. Not enough is known about the effectiveness of one placement over another, and several factors can influence effectiveness. General principles of good instruction can be applied in various settings. An important transition is occurring in the schools, due to the Regular Education Initiative and the broad movement to include most students with learning problems in the regular classroom. Learning disabled students are increasingly attending colleges, and these institutions are offering some needed support services.

12

AUTISM AND SCHIZOPHRENIA

This chapter focuses on youth who are given the diagnoses of autism and schizophrenia. These disorders have been linked historically, although not without controversy. Problems are evident in social, emotional, cognitive, and perceptual motor functioning, and are usually pervasive. Development may lag, and may be qualitatively different than normal development. Moreover, although individuals are affected to varying degrees, difficulties often continue into later life.

THE PROBLEM OF DEFINITION

Despite long recognition of the disorders we are about to discuss, description and classification have been confusing and controversial (Newsom, Hovanitz, and Rincover, 1988). To begin with, these disorders have been associated with adult psychoses, that is, to severely disruptive adult disturbances implying "insanity" and the need for supervision and protection (Prior and Werry, 1986).

Adult psychotic disturbances were noted in the early twentieth-century classifications of mental disorders (Goldfarb, 1970). Kraepelin, who set the basis for modern classification, used the term *dementia praecox* and attributed psychoses to biological factors. *Dementia* reflected his belief that progressive deterioration occurred; *praecox* indicated that the disorders began early, usually in young adulthood or adolesence. Bleuler later applied the term *schizophrenias* to the disorders. He argued that deterioration was not inevitable, that psychological factors might play some role, and that time of origin was more varied. In fact, both Kraepelin and Bleuler noted a small number of cases that had begun in childhood (Cantor, 1988).

Ideas about adult disturbance were soon extended to children. Different diagnostic terms were applied, including *dementia infantilis, disintegrative psychoses, childhood schizophrenia,* and *childhood psychosis.* Beginning around 1930 and for several years afterward, childhood schizophrenia served as a general label, while a confusing number of subcategories were employed (Volkmar, 1987; Rutter and Schopler, 1987). Then in 1943 Leo Kanner described what he called *early infantile autism,* arguing that it was different from other cases of severe disturbance, which often had later onset. Kanner's work reflected the broad effort to better understand childhood "psychosis" and whether it was actually one disorder or several.

After Kanner's initial work, this effort was influenced by data showing that severe disturbances were age related. Data from several different countries indicated a large number of cases before age three, remarkably low prevalence in childhood, and increased prevalence in adolescence (Kolvin, 1971; Rutter, 1978). This pattern suggested that different syndromes might underlie the earlier-occurring and later-occurring disturbances. It was argued by some that children whose problems appeared early were different from those whose problems came later, not only in behavior but also in social class, family history, and other factors (Dawson and Castelloe, 1992). Kanner's proposal for a distinct syndrome of early infantile autism was supported by this argument.

Over the years subsequent investigations led to different conceptualizations of what once was considered psychoses of youth. Today autism and schizophrenia are widely recognized as separate disorders. As we shall see, however, knotty classification issues still exist.

AUTISM

Kanner's initial descriptions of eleven of the severely affected children he examined were comprehensive and informative, and with some notable exceptions have stood the test of time (Mesibov and Van Bourgondien, 1992). For example, five-year-old Paul, who had been referred for suspected intellectual deficiency was described as an attractive child who was not retarded in the usual sense but who sometimes displayed atypical speech patterns, strange and repetitious behaviors, and a striking unresponsiveness to other people (Kanner, 1943, reprinted in Kanner, 1973). From the eleven cases, Kanner concluded that of particular importance were communication deficits, good but atyp-

Leo Kanner offered the first description of infantile autism and is considered a pioneer in the study of childhood psychoses.

(The John Hopkins Medical Institutions)

ical cognitive potential, and behavioral problems such as obsessiveness, repetitious actions, and unimaginative play.

He emphasized, however, that the fundamental disturbance was an inability to relate to people and situations from the beginning of life. He quoted parents as referring to their disturbed children as "self-sufficient," "like in a shell," "happiest when left alone," and "acting as if people weren't there" (1973, p. 33). To this extreme disturbance in emotional contact with others Kanner applied the term *autistic,* which means an absoption in the self or subjective mental activity.

Classification

Most of the characteristics originally described by Kanner were subsequently observed by others. Autism was eventually recognized by the major classifications systems as a distinct syndrome accounting for many cases of severe disturbance in infancy or very early life. In 1980, DSM-III first recognized the condition as Infantile Autism, under the general category of pervasive developmental disorders, which indicates lifelong problems. The criteria entailed serious problems in social interaction, communication, and reactions to the environment.

The category was revised in DSM-III-R (1987), and again in DSM-IV (1994). Autistic Disorder, as it is now called, is still classified as a pervasive developmental disorder, and the fundamental behavioral criteria remain. However, subtle modifications have broadened the criteria, for example, making it more likely that higher functioning persons will receive the diagnosis of autistic disorder instead of other diagnoses (Mesibov and Van Bourgondien, 1992). Table 12–1 summarizes the DSM-IV criteria.

Autism can be diagnosed by other than DSM criteria, and the various classification systems now agree quite well on the criteria. ICD-10 calls the disorder Childhood Autism. Both DSM-IV and ICD-10 recognize several other pervasive developmental disorders that have historically been difficult to distinguish from autism and from each other, such as Asperger's syndrome, Rett's syndrome, and Childhood Disintegrative Disorder. The reliabilty and validity of these syndromes demand further investigation, and controversy still surrounds them (e.g., Gillberg, 1994; Rutter, 1994). The long history of confusion and changes in classifica-

---

TABLE 12–1   DSM-IV Diagnostic Criteria for Autistic Disorder

A. At least six items from 1, 2, and 3, with at least two from 1 and one each from 2 and 3.

    1. Qualitative impairment in social interaction manifested by:
       (a) marked impairment in nonverbal behaviors such as eye-to-eye gaze, body posture, gestures
       (b) failure to develop peer relationships appropriate to developmental level
       (c) lack of spontaneous sharing of enjoyment, interests, etc.
       (d) lack of social or emotional reciprocity

    2. Qualitative impairments in communication manifested by:
       (a) delay in or lack of spoken language
       (b) in individuals with adequate speech, marked impairment in initiating or sustaining conversation
       (c) stereotyped, repetitive, or idiosyncratic language
       (d) lack of varied, spontaneous make-believe play or imitative play appropriate to developmental level

    3. Restrictive, repetitive, stereotyped patterns of behavior, interests, and activities manifested by:
       (a) preoccupation with stereotyped restrictive interests, abnormal in intensity or focus
       (b) inflexible adherence to nonfunctional routines or ritual
       (c) stereotyped repetitive motor mannerisms
       (d) persistent preoccupation with parts of objects

B. Delays or abnormal functioning in at least one of the following, with onset prior to age three: (1) social interaction, (2) language as used in social communication, or (3) symbolic or imaginative play.

Adapted and reprinted with permission from the *Diagnostic and Statistical Manual of Mental Disorders, Fourth Edition.* Copyright 1994, American Psychiatric Association.

tion, and especially the many years in which autism was not recognized as a syndrome, creates difficulty in reading the clinical and research literature on autism. We have tried to rely on cases recognized by the terms early infantile autism, infantile autism, early childhood autism, autism, and autism disorder.

Prevalence

Lotter's (1966) pioneering population study showed the frequency of autism to be 4.5 per 10,000 children. Several investigators in different countries subsequently agreed that autism is very rare; they reported less than 5 cases per 10,000 (Gillberg, 1992; Volkmar and Cohen, 1988).

Nevertheless, higher rates have also been reported, going well into double digits (Bryson, Clark, and Smith, 1988; Cialdella and Mamelle, 1989). Should we interpret this as an actual increase in the occurrence of autism? Not necessarily. In some instances, higher rates may reflect better detection of autism. The higher rates may also be due to the broadening of the definition of autism, which has increased the number of children receiving the diagnosis (Gillberg, 1992). When criteria similar to those used by Kanner are employed, the lower rates hold.

Boys quite consistently display autism more than girls, with the ratio of three to five boys to one girl (American Psychiatric Association, 1994; Dawson and Castelloe, 1992). There is some evidence that autism in females is associated with lower IQ scores and less favorable course.

Kanner's (1943) early descriptions noted that autism typically occurs in the upper social classes. However, several large population studies now indicate no social class difference (Gillberg, 1992). If any small disproportion occurs toward the upper classes, it probably involves less severe autism.

Psychological and Behavioral Functioning

Relative to its frequency, autism is of enormous interest to both professionals and the general public. Indeed, it is among the most systematically researched childhood disorders. One reason undoubtedly is the severity and unusualness, even bizarreness, of the behaviors displayed. In this section, behavioral and psychological functioning will be detailed. As these descriptions are being examined, it is important to remember that despite commonalities, autistic children show great individual variation.

Social interaction. Disturbed social interaction is a criterion for autism in all major classification systems (Baron-Cohen, 1988). The level of social skills displayed by children with autism is below what is expected on the basis of their intelligence (Volkmar et al., 1993). Social deficits may change in form with development but they remain into adulthood (Rumsey, Rapoport, and Sceery, 1985; Rutter, 1985).

Most descriptions of very early autism rely on retrospective reports of parents, but researchers have examined home movies recorded by families before autism was recognized in their children. Both kinds of studies indicate that problems of social interaction can begin in infancy (Adrien et al., 1993; Borden and Ollendick, 1992; Gillberg et al., 1990). The young children described in these studies were socially unresponsive, failed to visually track people, avoided parents' gazes or exhibited an "empty" gaze themselves, lacked emotional expression, resisted being held or failed to adjust their bodies when held, and exhibited poor body tone and distractibility.

Such behaviors might well interfere with the establishment of normal social bonds. In fact, early parental attachment may be disturbed. Compared to control children, those with autism show more insecure attachment behaviors and may express attachment in atypical ways (Rogers, Ozonoff, and Maslin-Cole, 1993). Toddlers may fail to follow their parents around, to greet them when they return, or seek comfort and affection from them (Rutter, 1985). At school age or so, the more blatant social impairments may lessen, and interest in social interaction may increase (American Psychiatric Association, 1994). However, aloofness and disinterest in people, inappropriate social actions, lack of understanding of social cues, and disturbed peer interaction are still evident. As people with autism move through their lives, they often have difficulty in forming friendships and they rarely marry.

It is important to recognize, however, that some autistic children have greater social skills than others; for example, some show attachment behaviors that approximate normal (Sigman and Ungerer, 1984; Sigman and Mundy, 1989). Furthermore, all social skills are not equally impaired.

Communication. Disturbed communication is pervasive in autism. Both nonverbal and verbal communication are affected.

Humans "speak" to each other nonverbally by gesture, bodily posture, and facial expression. Even before speech develops normal children use gestures to communicate, and nonverbal communication correlates with language development (Mundy et al., 1987). Overall, autistic children use fewer nonverbal signals and may project an expressionless "woodenness" (Attwood, Frith, and Hermelin, 1988). Disturbed eye contact and the lack of the social smile and facial expression are widely noted. Autistic children also show deficiencies in *joint attention* interactions, compared to children with language disorders, mental retardation, or with no handicaps. Joint attention interactions involve gestures such as pointing, showing, and eye contact that focus the child's and caretaker's attention on an object, presumably for sharing an experience.

Such behavior usually begins to emerge by nine to twelve months in normal children, and is well developed by twenty-four months (McEvoy, Rogers, and Pennington, 1993). Children with autism not only show fewer of these interactions, but may also display less positive affect toward caretakers when they do engage in joint attention interactions (Mundy, Sigman, and Kasari, 1993). Moreover, even when simple instrumental gestures that point to something or communicate "come here" or "be quiet" are used, more complex gestures that express feelings may be lacking, even into the adolescent years (Figure 12–1).

The comprehension of nonverbal communication also is atypical and slow to develop. Currently there is much interest in determining children's perception of the human face. Deficits have been found in autism. For example, in one study control group children attended to and sorted photographs of people on the basis of facial expression such as happy and sad, but children with autism sorted according to the types of hats the people wore (Hobson, 1993). In another study, Hobson (1986) asked participants with autism to select faces showing different emotions that "went with" certain bodily postures/gestures, sounds (such as a moan), and situations (such as receiving a birthday cake). Compared to control groups, participants had difficulties with this task, although they could match nonhuman stimuli (as a car or bird) with appropriate stimuli. In fact, a substantial body of research now suggests that children with autism have special difficulty in understanding nonverbal socioemotional stimuli. Not all the findings are consistent, but they are persuasive enough to suggest the hypothesis that a fundamental deficit of affect underlies autism. We shall return to this hypothesis later.

As with nonverbal communication, both expression and comprehension of spoken language is problematic (Rutter, 1985;

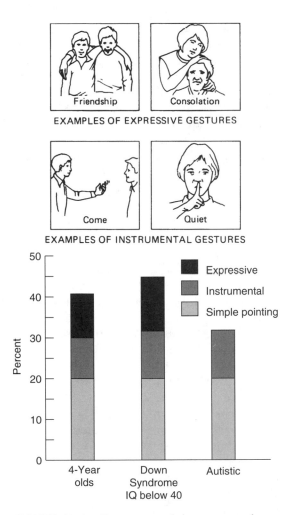

EXAMPLES OF EXPRESSIVE GESTURES

EXAMPLES OF INSTRUMENTAL GESTURES

FIGURE 12–1 Percentage of three types of gestures showed by normal 4-year-olds and adolescents with Down's syndrome or autism.

Adapted from Attwood, A., Frith, U., and Hermelin, B., 1988. The understanding and use of interpersonal gestures by autistic and Down's Syndrome children. Journal of Autism and Developmental Disorders, vol. 180, 241–257. Reprinted by permission of Plenum Publishing Corporation.

Schopler and Mesibov, 1985). Some children remain mute or rarely verbalize spontaneously, or never say more than words or simple phrases. About half do not develop useful speech. Babbling and verbalizations often are abnormal in tone, pitch, and

rhythm, and such deficits may persist into adolescence and adulthood (Tager-Flüsberg, 1993). The development of sounds, grammar, and comprehension may lag or otherwise fall short of normal. And echolalia and pronoun reversal are common.

In *echolalia* the person echoes back what another has said, immediately or at a future time, sometimes with modification (Roberts, 1989). Echolalia is seen in other disorders (e.g., language disorders, schizophrenia), and it is probably a passing feature of normal development. Why echolalia occurs in autism is not known, but it occurs more frequently when settings and tasks are unfamiliar, aversive, or fearful (Charlop, Schriebman, and Kurtz, 1991).

Errors in *pronoun reversal* are quite common. The child may refer to others as *I* or *me,* and to the self as *he, she, them* or *you.* And so the child may request a toy for herself by saying, "She wants the ball." Pronoun reversals may stem from echolalia, failure to attend to how pronouns are used, or failure to understand the roles of speaker-listener (Oshima-Takane and Benaroya, 1989; Tager-Flüsberg, 1993).

Perhaps the most remarkable impairment of language in autism involves pragmatics and social usage (King and Noshpitz, 1991). Pragmatic language skills—abilities to adapt communication to listeners and situations—typically begin early in life, and normal preschoolers have reasonably good skills. In contrast, autistic children show a variety of pragmatic difficulties (Baron-Cohen, 1988; Tager-Flüsberg, 1985, 1993). For example, they ask embarrassing questions, fail to use greetings such as "hello," interrupt, perseverate on a topic, and fail to develop conversation. For many, language rarely goes beyond simple statements or requests. Even when the children advance in the number of words they utter to another person, they fail to advance in the give-and-take of communication and in the amount of new information they add to the conversation (Tager-Flüsberg, 1993). Simply put, their language lacks the rich social and interactive functions observed in normal children or those with other handicapping conditions.

In summary, children with autism show delays and deviances, which can be severe, in nonverbal and verbal communication. Some of these deficits appear unique to autism in comparison with nonautistic children of similar mental age and nonautistic language disorders. The deficits appear especially notable with regard to how children with autism use language as a social tool.

Obssession and stereotypy. Many atypical and bizarre behaviors of autism are described as obsessive fascinations, stereotypies, and resistance to change. These behaviors can be seen as falling into four categories (Charlop, Schriebman, and Kurtz, 1991). First, the child may appear obsessed with specific objects such as spinning tops, vacuum cleaners, or letters of the alphabet. Scraps of paper or bits of string may be hoarded, as if there were an attachment to them. The child may talk incessantly about an object and be upset if it is lost or removed. Such obsessions may change abruptly or last for years. Second, play may be rigid and lacking in imitation and imagination. Indeed, children with autism appear to lack pretend play (Baron-Cohen, 1993), and may simply repeat behaviors over and over, such as lining up items. Third, the child may have a preoccupation with concepts, such as colors, numbers, or scheduling of buses. Fourth, the child may adopt rigid routines that must be followed. Changes in the environment, such as rearrangement of furniture or schedules, may be reacted to with considerable upset.

Perception and movement. Neither perceptional deficits nor abnormal movement is an explicit criterion for autism. However, both are widely observed. Children with autism often flap their hands, whirl their bodies, and rock back and forth. Sensation is intact; that is, the children can see, hear, and the like. But they have dysfunctions in the processing of visual, auditory, touch, smell, and pain stimulation (Ornitz, 1985; Prior, 1986). Auditory processing seems especially impaired so that parents often believe that their child is deaf. Ornitz and Ritvo (1968; Ornitz, 1985) proposed that a defect in the regulation and integration of sensory input is central to autism. They suggested that the child is unable to construct a stable representation of the world, which prevents normal development. Although this hypothesis is not as popular as others, perceptual deficits are a part of the clinical picture of autism. In fact, they may be an early sign that something is wrong (Gillberg, 1990).

Both oversensitivity and undersensitivity to stimulation are reported. In the case of oversensitivity, the child is disturbed by moderate stimulation, for example, moderate noise. Thus, the child may dislike and avoid sensory input. Undersensitivity, perhaps more common, is reflected in many ways. Children may fail to show the startle response or otherwise not respond to verbal communications and sounds, not react to the sight of others, walk into objects, or let objects fall from their hands. Undersensitivity may lead them to seek stimulation by, for example, scratching surfaces or engaging in abnormal movements (Adrien et al., 1987).

Intelligence, learning, and cognition. Kanner originally described autistic children as of average or better intelligence, perhaps with special abilities. Some autistic people do fall into this ability range and some display quite remarkable, so-called savant abilities. However, at least 70 percent of all cases show mental retardation (Marcus and Schopler, 1993; Rutter and Schopler, 1987). Nevertheless, the test performance of people with autism reveals more peaks and valleys compared to the fairly uniform deficits displayed by those diagnosed as mentally retarded (Newsom et al., 1988). There are greater deficits in abstract and sequential thinking, language, and social development. Certain motor-perceptual skills, especially making designs with blocks, appear least deficient (Happe, 1994b; Shah and Frith, 1993).

Intelligence test scores can provide useful information about individuals with autism (Rutter, 1985; Lord and Schopler, 1989). That is, the scores are moderately stable over time and predict academic achievement, occupation, and social status. However, to better understand intellectual functioning in autism, researchers also examine specific learning and cognitive processes.

Deficits appear in basic learning skills. Overselectivity is often apparent; that is, the child selectively attends to a particular stimulus while ignoring other relevant ones (Charlop, Schreibman, and Kurtz, 1991). Learning can obviously be impeded by this. Children with autism do have difficulty responding to complex stimuli. They also show deficits in generalizing what they have learned in one setting to another setting. Thus, although many learn, they often require special environments to learn what most children accomplish in average environments (Lovaas and Smith, 1988). It is worth noting, however, that many of these learning problems also exist in mental retardation, and so they do not uniquely define autism.

The picture regarding memory ability is unclear. Youngsters with autism are well known for recalling phrases and songs, and memory in savants can be extraordinary. But research results are inconsistent, and continued investigation is needed (e.g., Boucher and Lewis, 1989; Ozonoff, Pennington, and Rogers, 1991).

There is evidence for deficits in a variety of information processing mechanisms: coding, categorization, abstracting, sequencing, and using concepts, rules, and meaning (Fine et al., 1986; Hermelin and O'Connor, 1970; Ohta, 1987; Rutter, 1985). Some executive functions also show impairment (McEvoy et al., 1993). Tests of executive functions require the person to plan ahead, inhibit a response, delay responses, switch strategies, and especially to be flexible in problem solving. Again, it should be noted that similar deficits are found in children with disorders other than autism.

A cognitive function that has been of particular interest with regard to autism is *theory of mind*—the ability to infer mental states in one's own self and in others (Perner et al., 1989). Having a theory of mind assumes that mental states (knowledge, beliefs, intentions, desires, feelings) exist, and are connected to action. For example, if we observe another person being exposed to a situation, we assume that the person's mind has knowledge of the situation, holds certain beliefs about the situation, and perhaps has certain emotions about the situation, all of which may help determine how the person behaves. Theory of mind guides our understanding of people and interaction with others. For instance, if we think someone is sad, we may be especially kind.

Researchers evaluate the development of theory of mind by presenting the person with different tasks and questions. Consider, for example, a procedure to test the understanding that another person can hold a false belief. In the Sally Ann test, the child is told that Sally places a marble in a basket and exits the room. Ann then transfers the marble to a box, and Sally returns to the room. The child is asked where Sally will look for the marble. To answer correctly, the child must understand that Sally falsely believes that the marble is still in the basket where she had placed it, and that this belief will guide her action.

Theory of mind develops gradually in normal children, and by three to four years is fairly well underway (Wellman, 1993). Table 12–2 shows some aspects of theory of

TABLE 12–2 Some Aspects of Theory of Mind Understood Early in Life

	Example
Mental states exist apart from the physical world	Bill's mental image of a cookie is different from an actual cookie
People's mental states are private	Linda "sees" a cat in her mind, but Claire cannot directly experience this imaged cat
People have knowledge of something when they have observed it	Nicky saw Nancy drive off in a van, so he knows Nancy is gone
People can hold false beliefs	Lise believes it is raining, even though it is not
People's beliefs, accurate or false, are linked to behavior	Alia put on her heavy coat because she believed it was cold outside
People have desires, which can be linked to behavior	Jamie wants the auto to be neat, so he cleans it
People have emotions, which can be linked to behavior	Mary is smiling and jumping up and down, so she is feeling happy
People have intentions, which can be linked to future behavior	Rick says he will go shopping; he has this planned action in mind

Based on Wellman, 1993

mind that are acquired at least partly by age four. Further growth occurs: for example, being able to think about another person's thinking about a third person's thoughts comes later (Baron-Cohen, 1989). Nevertheless, even very young children use their understanding of mental events to relate to the social world. In autism, theory of mind is severely delayed or fails to develop (Baron-Cohen, 1989, 1993). This deficit is not accounted for by mental retardation or specific language problems. We shall see in later discussion that this finding has become central in attempts to conceptualize the basic nature of autism.

Other characteristics. Other behaviors appear with moderate frequency in autism and some are especially dramatic or troublesome.

Savant abilities appear in about 6 to 10 percent of autistic or autistic-like cases (O'Connor and Hermelin, 1988), more than in the nonautistic mentally retarded population. Amidst even severe mental handicaps, spectacular memory, mathematics and calendar calculations, word knowledge, and music and artistic talents are displayed (e.g., O'Conner and Hermelin, 1990; Pring and Hermelin, 1993). Some savant abilities are indeed spectacular (Treffert, 1988). One savant needed only 1.5 minutes to calculate the number of seconds in seventy years, seventeen days, and twelve hours, considering the effects of leap years. And one five-year-old, despite limited language and retarded daily living skills, had perfect music pitch, a classical piano repertoire, and the ability to improvise music. Such special abilites often emerge early, without training, and without obvious inheritance. What mechanisms might underlie savant abilites? Although rote "unconscious" memory, extraordinary visual imagery, excessively concrete thinking, unusual brain function, genetics, and social reinforcement have all been suggested, savant abilities largely remain a mystery.

Another compelling behavior observed in autism is self-injurious behavior (SIB), such as head banging, biting, scratching, eye gouging, and hair pulling (Charlop, Schreibman, and Kurtz, 1991). SIB tends to be chronic and repetitious, occurring from a few times a day to several times a second. Damage can range from minor to major and even be life threatening.

Children with autism display other behavior problems, including aggressive outbursts, temper tantrums, hyperactivity, and inappropriate or excessive fears. Although not specific to autism, such behaviors are a challenge to good management (King and Noshpitz, 1991).

Is There a Basic Psychological Deficit in Autism?

It is clear that as a group persons with autism display many deficits and problems in many areas of functioning. Equally clear, there is much variation across individuals. Some of the impairments of autism appear specific to the condition, wheras some are also seen in syndromes such as mental retardation and language disorders. Moreover, other pervasive developmental disorders are similar to autism and often difficult to distinguish from autism. A continuing task for researchers has thus been to idenfity the impairments that are unique to autism and to search for what might be the primary, or core, psychological dysfunction. Any primary deficit would, of course, have to explain the varied aberrations displayed in autism. It would also have to be present in all cases of the disorder and be specific to autism (Ozonoff, Pennington, and Rogers, 1991).

Historically, researchers and clinicians have emphasized that the primary deficit of autism is either affective or cognitive (Marcus and Schopler, 1993). Kanner's original work proposed a fundamental affective-social failure that resulted in disturbed relationships with others. Other workers later proposed that cognitive deficits are primary to autism and that they lead to social disturbance.

We have seen that persons with autism display deficits in theory of mind. Based on an extensive review of this research, Baron-Cohen (1993) found that the development of theory of mind is uniquely delayed and proceeds in a different order from what it does in nonautistic children. Baron-Cohen believes this impairment is central in autism, especially with regard to its social and language deficits. He also speculates that theory of mind deficits may first show up as a failure to understand that attention and goal-directedness are part of people's minds. Failing this, children with autism fail to engage in joint attention behaviors that direct their own and another's attention to objects for mutual sharing. Baron-Cohen believes that it is such deficits—*cognitive* in nature—that underlie autism.

Hobson (1993) agrees that children with autism do not fully develop the concept of persons with minds. But he suggests this deficit is due to a more basic innate disturbance in interpersonal relations that is present in infancy. Hobson argues that before infants can understand others' minds they must first understand that persons exist, and that they themselves are both like and different from other persons. Such knowledge arises from relationships with others in which *affect* plays a critical role. Hobson believes that affect is an essential foundation for interpersonal understanding. He points out, for example, that basic emotions and their expression are universally understood. Hobson believes that affect is more basic than cognition and thus is more basic to autistic deficits. And he notes his own and others' research showing that children with autism have difficulties in understanding socioemotional stimuli, such as facial expressions of emotion. However, Hobson also prefers to view affect and cognition as linked together in the child's understanding of persons and the mental and physical worlds.

There are other hypotheses about what might be fundamentally impaired in autism, with a recent emphasis on executive functions and the need to explain the uneven intellectual ability in autism (e.g., Happe, 1994a, 1994b). Moreover, some researchers stress that the search for a single psychological deficit may be misleading, that perhaps several primary deficits underlie autism. Some investigators are attacking the problem by relating deficits to underlying brain dysfunction. They suggest that several core deficits may stem from abnormalities of one or more parts of the brain (Goodman, 1989; Ozonoff et al., 1991; McEvoy et al., 1993). Such an idea raises the issue of the underlying etiology of autism, the topic to which we now turn.

The Causes of Autism: Psychological Theories

The etiology of autism is unknown, but is being vigorously pursued. One striking development in this pursuit has been a shift of emphasis from psychological to biological factors.

Psychological theories of autism have emphasized the role of deviant parental personality or deviant parent-child interaction. Kanner originally described the families of autistic children as highly intelligent and professionally accomplished. He also noted that the parents were preoccupied with scientific, literary, and artistic concerns, and treated their offspring in a coldly mechanical way. Although Kanner did not consistently argue that "refrigerator" parenting completely explained autism (1943, Kanner and Eisenberg, 1956), inadequate parenting was implicated and became a causal hypothesis. In part, this was due to the *zeitgeist*, which from about 1945 to 1965 emphasized the psychoanalytical view that childhood problems might be rooted in parental behavior (Schopler, 1978).

Bettelheim's (1967a, b) theory was the most influential of the psychoanalytic explanations of autism (Mesibov and Van Bourgondien, 1992). He hypothesized that autism is caused by early unsatisfactory and threatening experiences from which the child withdraws. Normal personality depends on the child's acting successfully on the environment to fulfill needs and communicate with others. When healthy interaction develops, parents respond appropriately and contingently to the infant's cries, smiles, and other signals. The child becomes attached to the parent, continues to act on the world, and a sense of self grows. However, when the early environment is not appropriately responsive—when parents react inadequately or pathologically to the child—the child may perceive the world as threatening and destructive and may withdraw. The will to act and to learn is abandoned and the child retreats to an autistic "empty fortress." Some behaviors, such as echolalia and insistence on sameness in the environment, may indicate hostility toward the parents or attempts to control the environment (Charlop, Schreibman, and Kurtz, 1991).

A psychogenic explanation that focused on operant learning also emphasized parenting. Ferster (1961, 1966) proposed that the parents of autistic children failed to properly shape the behavior of their offspring through reinforcement and punishment. The children thus lacked support for a normal behavioral repertoire. Further, self-stimulation and other primitive actions were strengthened by the reinforcements they received. Such failed parenting was thought to be related to parental depression, preoccupation with other activities, rejection of the child, and the like. Thus, despite very different theoretical stances, Ferster and Bettelheim shared the view that early parenting plays a central role in causing autism.

Today, neither theory is given much weight. Bettelheim's ideas suffered from the dwindling influence of psychoanalytic theories. In addition, empirical studies give little support for parental deviancy (Mesibov and Van Bourgondien, 1992; Koegel et al., 1983). Parents of autistic children do not, for the most part, appear different in personality and adaptive behaviors from parents of normal children or children with other behavioral problems. Moreover, parent-child interaction hardly seems adequate to explain the severity and bizarreness of some autistic behaviors, especially when aberrations begin so early in life. At the very least, children and their parents mutually affect one another. And it may be that disturbed interactions between autistic children and their parents are substantially related to the child's characteristics (Borden and Ollendick, 1992). Finally, evidence for biological etiology has been growing. For all these reasons, placing the burden of autism on parents is now viewed as blaming them for something that is largely out of their control.

The Causes of Autism: Biological Dysfunction

Evidence for biological causation of autism comes from various kinds of research.

Medical conditions.   Autism has been associated with several known medical conditions. For example, it has been linked to genetic disorders such as the fragile X chromosome, tuberose sclerosis (a dominant gene disorder), and PKU (a recessive gene disorder). It also is associated with epilepsy and a variety of known infections. However, the strength of such connections is argued. Based on population studies in Sweden, Gillberg (1992) concluded that 37 percent of cases were linked to identifiable medical conditions. From a review of the research, Rutter et al. (1994) estimated a much lower 10 percent. Gillberg suggested that the higher rate might be due to more extensive

medical screening, or perhaps to the specific geographic area from which the cases were drawn. Rutter and his colleagues proposed several other reasons for the discrepancy including the tendency to report the presence but not the absence of medical findings. Interestingly, Rutter et al. point out that cases of autism in which profound mental retardation exists are more strongly linked to medical conditions.

Nervous system functioning.   Other evidence more directly implicates the nervous system. Perhaps 30 to 75 percent of cases of autism show neurologic signs such as motor clumsiness, tremor, and abnormalities of gait, posture, and reflexes (Tsai and Ghaziuddin, 1991). Brain imaging shows tissue abnormalities in a minority of cases (Gillberg, 1992; Tsai and Ghaziuddin, 1991). Some of these findings suggest that malformations may occur during prenatal development (Peterson, 1995). Brain dysfunction is suggested by abnormal findings from EEG and other scans, and by the specific behavioral deficits shown in autism. Many parts of the brain are implicated, including the brainstem, cerebellum, frontal lobe and its connections to the limbic system, and the temporal lobe.

Extensive biochemical analyses are being conducted. A quite consistent finding is that about one-third of mentally retarded autistic cases have higher than normal blood levels of serotonin (Geller et al., 1988; Kuperman et al., 1987). However, elevated serotonin is found in about half of nonautistic mentally retarded persons as well (Lord and Rutter, 1994). Some evidence also exists for high levels of noradrenalin and dopamine and other biochemicals, but further substantiation is necessary (e.g., Garner et al., 1986).

All of these neurobiological findings would seem quite impressive, except that they are often inconsistent and complex.

Inheritance. We have already seen that specific chromosome abnormalities and genetic disorders are linked to autism. Beyond this, twin and family studies shed light on the question of inheritance.

In the first systematic twin study of autism, Folstein and Rutter (1978) examined identical and same-sex fraternal twin pairs who met stringent criteria for autism. They ranged in age from five to twenty-three, one-half were retarded, and almost one-third had average IQs on nonverbal tests of intelligence. Information about the twins came from interviews with them and their parents, direct examinations of the twins, and detailed descriptions that had been collected earlier. The results showed that 36 percent of the identical and none of the fraternal pairs were concordant for autism. Subsequent studies have confirmed and strengthen these findings by showing much higher concordance in identical over fraternal twins (Rutter et al., 1993; Steffenburg et al., 1989).

The twin investigations suggest that what may actually be inherited is a general cognitive/linguistic disability. In the Folstein and Rutter (1978) research, 82 percent of identical and only 10 percent of fraternal twins were concordant for cognitive/linguistic problems. This pattern is indicated in other investigations (Rutter et al., 1993), and suggests that autism could be a severe manifestation of a more general (cognitive/linguistic) inherited dysfunction.

Family studies of autism tell us about the degree to which autism "runs in families." The rate of autism in siblings of autistic children is about 2 to 3 percent. While this rate is low, it is fifty to one hundred times what would be expected by chance based on the frequency of autism in the general population (Rutter et al., 1993). Furthermore, family studies also indicate that the siblings of children with autism have cognitive, language, and social disorders (Rutter et al., 1993; Tsai and Ghaziuddin, 1991). Again,

this suggests that a broad genetic predisposition for cognitive/social deficits might underlie autism and interact with other hazards to produce the condition. Nevertheless, not all studies have shown a family connection, and further research is needed (Lombroso, Pauls, and Leckman, 1994; Szatmari et al., 1993).

Attempt are being made to determine possible genetic mechanisms. Specific known chromosome abnormalities do not account for most cases of autism. At this time several other hypotheses exist, including polygenic, autosomal recessive, and X-linked recessive inheritance (Rutter et al., 1993; Szatmari and Jones, 1991). It is possible, perhaps even likely, that more than one mode of genetic transmission causes varieties of autism.

Prenatal, perinatal, and postnatal factors. Prenatal and birth insults to the brain have also been suggested as causing autism, especially when autism is manifested very early in life (Tsai and Ghaziuddin, 1991). Many pregnancy and birth complications have been identified, including prenatal rubella and influenza, low birth weight and prematurity, older age of mothers, breech delivery, respiratory distress, and maternal bleeding (e.g., Bryson, Smith, and Eastwood, 1988; Levy, Zoltak, and Saelens, 1988). However, autism is not always associated with such a factor. Researchers have used composite scales to measure prenatal and birth complications; that is, a score is assigned that reflects several complications or adverse conditions. The association of autism with composite scores is then examined. This method has not, however, clarified the significance of prenatal and birth complications (Piven et al., 1993).

In addition, Rutter and his colleagues (1993) suggest that prenatal/birth factors cannot be strongly held as causes of autism. For one thing, evidence for inheritance has grown and secondly, birth complications are associated with genetic factors. This suggests that birth complications may result from a genetically abnormal fetus.

Postnatal brain infections and injuries have been suggested as causes of some later-arising autism. These include meningitis and severe brain hemorrhage. We have seen that epilepsy is also commonly associated with autism (Gillberg, 1992). The beginning of seizures most often occurs either in early childhood or at adolescence.

Summary. Despite informative research, no one biological factor or process has been identified as responsible for autism. Perhaps different factors play a role in different cases or varieties of autism. These factors may work alone or in combination to adversely affect the nervous system, thereby causing one or more basic psychological dysfunctions. What parts of the brain are involved, and how brain functioning is disturbed are not established. However, it is now believed that early neurodevelopmental problems underlie most if not all cases of autism.

Developmental Course and Prognosis

Autism is viewed as a chronic disorder that is usually reported by the time the child is age three. Variations in developmental course have been described. Slow stable growth is found, but so is an erratic course with spurts and lags, as well as loss of skills (Burack and Volkmar, 1992; Snow, Hertzig, and Shapiro, 1987). The typical order of behavioral development has been reported, but so has atypical order.

In many but not all cases, childhood brings a lessening of disturbance. Adolescence can be relatively uneventful, show improvement that can persist into adulthood, or be marked by a variety of behavior problems such as increased anxiety and sexual curiosity that can lead to socially inappropriate behavior (Hertzig and Shapiro, 1991; Tsai and Ghaziuddin, 1991). In a minority of cases, adolescence brings serious deterioration from which the individual may never recover (Gillberg, 1992). In young adulthood, some cases of autism show behavioral and social improvements (Lord and Rutter, 1994).

Nevertheless, eventual outcome usually is not favorable (King and Noshpitz, 1991; Mesibov et al., 1989). Kanner (1973) revealed that only eleven of ninety-six children he examined were maintaining themselves in the second and third decades of life. These eleven were doing moderately well (several had achieved a college education and good jobs), although most were living alone with few friends or romantic involvements. Lotter's (1974) review of three independent studies concluded that 61 to 74 percent of cases were judged as having poor or very poor status by adolescence. More recent studies confirm that the majority of children with autism continue to have difficulties into adolescence and adulthood in communication, social relationships, and independent living skills and continue with ritualistic behavior. (Cantwell et al., 1989; Rumsey et al., 1985; Tager-Flüsberg, 1993). Still, quite a bit of variability is found and higher intelligence and language ability predict better outcome (e.g., Venter, Lord, and Schopler, 1992). Degree of behavioral disturbance may also help in prognosis (Lord and Rutter, 1994).

Assessment

Assessment needs to be comprehensive and multidisciplinary, and include a history and both medical and psychological evaluation. Medical assessment is valuable in identifying autism, investigating its causes, and treating associated conditions such as seizures. Professionals do not always agree on what the optimal physical examination should consist of, but brain scans, EEGs, visual and hearing examinations, a neurological exam, and other tests are considered. Interviews with parents and other significant adults, standardized tests, and behavioral observations all play a role in psychological assessment.

Diagnostic checklists. The several checklists that have been developed to evaluate autism focus on the child's behavior, and some also inquire into prenatal, family, and other variables. Ratings are based on actual observation of the child, impressions of the child's past or present behavior, or records. Diagnostic checklists vary in the degree to which reliability and validity have been established, and further research is needed in this area (Newsom et al., 1988; Parks, 1983). Here, we only describe two widely known instruments.

The Childhood Autism Rating Scale (CARS) consists of fifteen scales on which the child is rated during or immediately after observation, usually by professionals. The scales cover many areas of functioning including emotional response, imitation, social relations, communication, perception, and intelligence (Schopler et al., 1980; Schopler, Reichler, and Renner, 1988). Items are rated from normal to severely abnormal, taking into consideration frequency, intensity, and peculiarity of behavior (Parks, 1983). Based on the total score, children are considered severely autistic, mildly to moderately autistic, or nonautistic. Although the validity of CARS to distinguish autism has been questioned on the basis that some of the scales are not central to the present concept of autism (Newsom et al., 1988), this instrument seems useful in screening children and older persons with autism (Mesibov et al., 1989).

The Autism Behavior Checklist (ABC) has fifty-seven items placed in five categories: sensory, relating, body and object use, language, social and self-help skills (Krug, Arick, and Almond, 1978). It was constructed to identify severely handicapped persons who display high levels of autistic behaviors, and is part of a larger assessment instrument aimed at educational planning (Newsom et al., 1988; Volkmar et al., 1988). Each yes/no item is assigned a weight from one to four according to how well it predicts autism. For example, "has no social smile" is rated at two; "has pronoun reversal" is rated at three. Children are rated on the basis of how well each item describes them. Profiles for different age groups are provided, as well as comparisons with other handicapping conditions. The ABC appears most useful in screening individuals for whom the diagnosis of autism is unclear.

Standardized intelligence and adaptive behavior tests. The use of intelligence tests in autism can be problematic since they emphasize language and require cooperation and motivation. But they are worthwhile, for example, in helping to determine classroom placement for higher functioning children and the potential effects of treatments (Newsom et al., 1988). In addition to the Stanford-Binet and the Wechsler scales, several other tests rely less on verbal and more on performance tasks.

AAMR's Adaptive Behavior Scales and the Vineland Adaptive Behavior Scales (p. 244) are widely used to examine adaptive functioning. Research with the Vineland indicates greater social deficits with autism than with other developmental disabilities (Freeman et al., 1991; Volkmar et al., 1987). The deficits are greater than would be expected from IQ scores. They are especially noticeable in social relations, coping skills, and communication. Thus, the scale can help differentiate autism and also provide information critical to treatment planning.

Behavioral and skill analysis. Behavioral and skill analysis focuses on assessment of the individual's behavior in particular environmental settings. It seeks to understand how individuals do or do not meet specific environmental demands. Behavioral observations, analysis of specific tasks, and check-lists are major techniques.

Table 12–3 provides a general guideline for evaluating environmental expectations and further examining the skills required for each specific activity. A critical component of behavioral analysis is the evaluation of the stimuli that are guiding a behavior and the consequences that are reinforcing or weakening it. In addition, it is often necessary to assess behaviors that interfere with the child's being production, such as self-stimulation, self-injury, and high activity level.

Behavioral and skill analysis is commonly used by those working daily with developmentally disabled persons and it is especially valued by behaviorally oriented professionals. The approach is time consuming and requires meticulous observation and implementation. However, it can be enormously useful in all settings for selecting and monitoring treatment.

Family assessment. Now that families are no longer blamed for causing autism, assessment emphasizes understanding family interaction and stress (Newsom et al., 1988).

One aim of assessment is to help relieve stress for the sake of family members themselves. Another aim is to enhance family participation in the management and treatment of autism. Child management practices and parental ability to follow through in home interventions can be evaluated. Warnings of potential difficulties include marital conflict, financial or work-related burdens, and the desire for only medical approaches that require little of parents.

Family assessment depends mostly on interviews and questionnaires. However, observational assessment has been done in treatment programs involving parents as therapists. Here, parental teaching and management skills have been assessed prior and after parent training (e.g., Harris, 1986; Schreibman et al., 1984). Such assessment reflects the importance now given to families as therapeutic agents.

Traditional Psychotherapeutic Treatment

Traditional psychotherapies have been employed with children variously labeled autistic and psychotic, but they are not popular

---

TABLE 12–3   Guidelines to Assessment in Natural Environments

Steps to Evaluate the Environment

1. Determine the important environments in which the child functions (e.g., home, restaurant, supermarket)
2. Divide these environments into subenvironments (e.g., home into kitchen, bedroom, etc.)
3. Identify the most important activities in each subenvironment (e.g., cooking, washing dishes)
4. Identify specific skills needed for child's partial or full participation in the activities (e.g., cutting potatoes, stacking dishes)

Steps to Evaluate Specific Skills Needed by an Activity

1. Analyze skills used by normal persons in the activity
2. Determine the skills the child can perform by observing the child in the environment or a simulated environment
3. Compare the child's performance with that of normal person's to identify missing skills
4. Consider possible adaptations of skills, materials, rules, etc. (e.g., teach a mute child to order restaurant foods with pictures)

Adapted from Newsom, Hovanitz, and Rincover, 1988.

today. Bettelheim's residential program at the Orthogenic School in Chicago is a well-known example of psychoanalytic treatment (Bettelheim, 1967a; Ekstein, Friedman, and Caruth, 1972). As we already saw, Bettelheim attributed autism to failed parenting that involves outright rejection of the child or little mutual interaction. He thus recommended placing the child in an environment away from the parents in which the child can develop as an autonomous person. The environment must permit the child to freely and safely explore, to reach out to the world, to experiment with letting go of autistic withdrawal. The therapist or parent surrogate must be accepting and loving. It is assumed that the child will eventually gain trust, give up autistic withdrawal, and enjoy more normal relationships (Charlop, Schreibman, and Kurtz, 1991).

Bettelheim (1967a) claimed that treated children often never reached normal developmental levels, but that 79 percent of cases showed good or fair progress. This unusually high rate, based on case studies, raised questions about how progress was defined (Werry, 1979b). In addition, research contrasting psychoanalytical therapy with control groups casts serious doubt on its efficacy, and the approach is largely discounted today (Charlop, Schreibman, and Kurtz, 1991).

Medication Treatment

Many kinds of medications have been explored, including antipsychotics (neuroleptics), stimulants, antidepressants, anticonvulsants, and vitamins.

The antipsychotic medications are the medications of first choice today. Among them, haloperidol (Haldol) is considered one of the most effective (Campbell, 1988; Gadow and Pomeroy, 1991). This drug is potent in reducing dopamine. In general, antipsychotic medications can reduce agitation, aggressiveness, stereotypies, emotional instability, and self-injurious behavior (Dawson and Castelloe, 1992). However, negative side effects occur over time in a minority of patients. Of particular concern is dyskinesia and other motor problems (involuntary repetitive movements of the tongue, mouth, limbs, etc.). Side effects can be minimized by initially giving low dosages and gradually increasing them, and by discontinuing the drug from time to time.

The treatment of autism's behavioral and learning problems with stimulants (amphetamines and cylert) is controversial at best (Gadow and Pomeroy, 1991). While some studies show improvements, others do not or even indicate a worsening of hyperactivity, stereotypies, social withdrawal, and other behaviors.

Interest and controversy surrounds fenfluramine, a drug that is similar to amphetamines and reduces brain serotonin. Since about one-third of autistic children show high blood serotonin levels—and those with the higher levels show greater intellectual and stereotypic disturbance—it is reasonable that reduction of serotonin could be beneficial. Some studies report decreased hyperactivity and improvement in social relatedness and attention (Dawson and Castelloe, 1992). Others report no improvements at all or only inconsistent benefits (e.g., Aman and Kern, 1989; Campbell, 1988). The data on side effects are also mixed, but there is concern about at least mild anorexia, weight loss, sedation, impaired learning ability, and irritability in treated individuals, as well as toxic effects as observed on the brain of rats, monkeys, and other animals.

The study of naltrexone began more recently (Campbell et al., 1989; Gadow and Pomeroy, 1991). This medication is antagonistic to the opiates (endorphins), and high levels of opiates in some autistic children could be related to withdrawal, insensitivity to pain, self-mutilation, attention deficits, and other behavioral problems (e.g., Sahley and Panksepp, 1987). Naltrexone may reduce hyperactivity and self-injurious behaviors with only mild adverse side effects, but its effectiveness is not established and requires further research (Campbell et al., 1993).

Lest this discussion be misleadingly simple, we should point out that drug evaluations have improved but are still inadequate for many medications. The pharmacological actions of the medications are not well understood. Moreover, results often indicate little benefit and even a worsening of behavior (Campbell, 1988; Connors and Werry, 1979; Jakab, 1993). Dosage level makes a difference, of course, as do the behavioral problems and the age of the child. And it is particularly difficult to prescribe and monitor medications for young children. In short, some medications can alleviate behavioral disturbances in autism, but they are best seen as adjuncts to other kinds of interventions.

Comprehensive Educational Treatment: TEACCH

TEACCH, which stands for *T*reatment and *E*ducation of *A*utistic and related *C*ommunication handicapped *Ch*ildren, is the only statewide program mandated to provide services, research, and training for autism and related disorders (Schopler, 1994). It operates six regional centers and affiliates with over 160 public classrooms across North Carolina. At the regional centers children are individually assessed for treatment. Classroom activities are tailored to meet each child's needs and parents both conduct a home teaching program and serve as cotherapists for their children. Efforts are made to strengthen and support families and to encourage community involvement. TEACCH is university based, conducts ongoing research, and feeds research results back into the program.

Over the years and thousands of students, TEACCH has been evaluated in various ways. For example, the effectiveness of specific techniques was examined by comparing highly structured operant learning sessions with nondirective and psychoanalytic play therapy. The structured approach more effectively produced change in attention, affect, language, and bizarre behavior. Parental teaching skills were evaluated by rating mother-child interaction before training and two months later. Improvement occurred on all measures, including organization of materials, teaching pace, language use, behavior management, and atmosphere of enjoyment. Seven general outcome studies showed that only 8 percent of the TEACCH students required institutionalization in adulthood compared to 40 to 78 percent of the general autistic population (Schopler, 1987). Another outcome measure, parental perception of the program a few years after participation, indicated extremely positive attitudes. In fact, the program also is well received by children, staff, student trainees, the general public, and the research community.

Behavioral Intervention

As always, this approach focuses on changing specific behaviors rather than on a global condition. The approach has been successful in teaching desirable behaviors related to language, social interaction, and self-care. Undesirable behaviors have also been reduced, such as aggression, self-stimulation, and self-injury. Reinforcement, punishment, extinction, shaping, fading, and generalization techniques are primary tools in this effort. There is a strong thrust to train parents and teachers in behavioral techniques. Over time behavioral intervention has become more effective, particularly with regard to (1) finding the most effective reinforcers and (2) promoting adaptive behaviors in the natural environment. The following discussion provides important examples of this work.

Desirable behavior: language and communication. Lovaas and his colleagues at the University of California at Los Angeles were among the first to teach speech to autistic children, and their techniques are still relevant. Language acquisition was conceptualized as the learning of two basic events (Lovaas, Young, and Newsom, 1978). First, children must acquire verbal responses of increasing complexity: basic speech sounds (phonics), words and parts of words (morphemes), and the arrangement of words into phrases and sentences (syntax). Second, they must acquire skills to use language meaningfully and in a social way.

It is often necessary to prepare children for language learning, especially to suppress behaviors that may interfere with learning and to establish generalized imitation. Autistic children show deficits in observational learning, but can be taught imitation skills. For example, the therapist may at first clap hands and reinforce the child for copying this action. When consistent imitation is established, the therapist can then switch to another motor behavior—perhaps opening the mouth—and eventually to uttering a sound. The child is reinforced in turn for each of these imitations and gradually comes to copy the therapist's novel actions. Imitation of language is then possible.

The acquisition of verbal responses can be seen as a four-step process (Lovaas and Newsom, 1976). First, the child is rewarded with food for any verbalizations. In Step 2 reward is given only when the response immediately follows the therapist's prompt. In Step 3, reward is given for closer and closer approximations to the verbalization of the therapist, until the child matches the verbalization. In Step 4, the therapist introduces other, dissimilar sounds and reinforces only correct responses. Speech sounds, words, and phrases are painstakingly programmed so that the child gradually acquires a repertoire of language through modeling and reinforcement.

But there is, of course, much more to using language in a meaningful way. For example, the child must learn to describe or name an object (such as a cup) when it is presented, and to respond to directives from the teacher (such as "touch the cup"). As such discriminations are acquired, new ones are presented that are based on the already learned ones. With progress, language itself becomes reinforcing, and external rewards and prompts are faded. More abstract terms (pronouns, adjectives, verb tenses) are gradually added. Some children can learn to generate sentences and respond to an array of verbalizations, although immense time and effort are required. Others do less well, but can profit from learning a combination of speech and sign language, or sign language alone.

One weakness of this approach is that learners often do not use acquired speech when they leave the training setting. This generalization problem can be reduced when training is done in different settings, and different situations, and by different teachers (Durand and Carr, 1988). Another difficulty is that children may respond to someone's comment but fail to initiate communication. There is some evidence that this can be overcome when teaching is done in everyday environments, where the child's spontaneous speech is more likely to be followed by reinforcers most relevant to the child.

Reducing maladaptive behavior. Self-stimulation, bizarre speech, tantrums, aggression, and self-injury are among the behaviors that interfere with social relationships, learning, and educational placement, and even directly harm individuals with autism. A variety of techniques have been employed to reduce these behaviors, and success has been documented with single-subject research designs. Nevertheless, success is not inevitable. We will discuss self-injurious behavior to show the complex issues that can surround treatment.

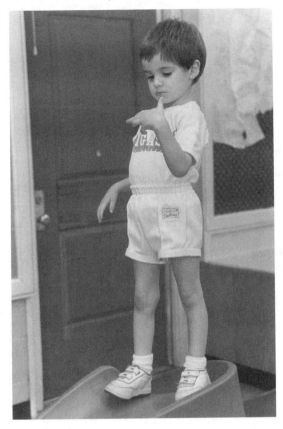

Stereotyped hand movements or pose are among the behaviors often targeted for change in autism.

(Carl Glassman)

Self-injurious behavior (SIB), which usually disappears in normal children by school age, is observed in perhaps 15 percent of developmentally disabled youngsters (Durand and Carr, 1985). Several hypotheses have been put forth to explain self-injury. Organic etiology is possible. Indeed, SIB is associated with the genetic Lesch-Nyhan syndrome and with middle ear infection. Or perhaps an atypical need for sensory stimulation, possibly due to organic factors, underlies self-injury. The injurious behavior, such as scratching or biting, might provide needed or desired sensory stimulation. Better understanding of organic factors could lead to more effective medical treatment.

Even so, SIB can be viewed as an operant behavior that responds to environmental consequences. One of these consequences is attention from others. It is only natural for caretakers to comfort, distract, or verbally persuade a child engaging in self-injury. But such attention can actually increase SIB, whereas withholding attention can reduce it (Lovaas and Simmons, 1969; Russo, Carr, and Lovaas, 1980). Tangibles such as food, toys, and activities can also reinforce self-injury. In addition to such positive reinforcement, SIB can be negatively reinforced. For example, when demands are made on a child, self-injury is sometimes observed to increase. It is easy to understand that when confronted by such a situation, caretakers might readily cease to make demands, thereby negatively reinforcing SIB.

Analysis of SIB as an operant suggests many ways in which reinforcement contingencies might be rearranged to reduce the behavior. Attention, sensory feedback, and escape from unwanted demands can be removed when they are serving as reinforcers. There are also procedures to decrease the chance that SIB will occur at all. One involves the reinforcement of other behaviors that are incompatible with SIB or that distract the child from self-injury. Since environmental conditions (e.g., space, heat, noise) can affect SIB, targeting such factors might also be ameliorative.

Nevertheless, these treatments have not always been effective, and physical and other punishments have been used to manage SIB. For example, The Self-Injurious Behavior Inhibiting System delivers mild shock to the leg or arm in response to head banging. Although such aversive procedures are sometimes effective, they raise serious ethical questions, which have been widely debated for some time. Advocacy groups, government representatives, parents, and professionals have lined up on both sides of the argument (Public Interest, 1989).

Those who oppose aversive treatment see it as inhumane, painful, and potentially the cause of physical side effects, stress, and death. They have worked in groups to gain support for their position, such as the Association for Persons with Severe Handicaps and the American Association on Mental Retardation (Durand, 1990). Supporters of aversive treatment argue that it is an acceptable last resort for persons who engage in extreme self-abuse. They view such treatment as brief and effective, no worse than commonly used aversive medical treatments that bring about long-term gain. They too have organized. In response to the controversy, the National Institutes of Health sponsored a study of SIB, and a preliminary report recommended that aversives be employed only in brief interventions and only after review and consent.

Professional take various positions on the issue. Schopler (1994), for example, suggests that the influence of advocacy groups has unfortunately been more powerful than empirical research, which should be given first consideration. Durand (1990, 1993b) represents those who believe that reasonable and more effective alternatives exist to aversive treatments. We will examine his work in more detail.

Durand and his colleagues view SIB and other maladaptive behavior as intentional communication that functions for the individual. Their approach involves analyzing how SIB is functioning, and then training more adaptive communication that can substitute for the SIB. The approach is called Functional Communication Training.

One way to asses how SIB is functioning is to do a functional analysis—to expose the client to different conditions and observe whether SIB increases or decreases. Durand and Crimmins (1988) also have developed the Motivation Assessment Scale, a teacher rating scale to determine the influence of attention, tangibles, escape, and sensory feedback on SIB.

Functional Communication Training is exemplified in the case of Tim, a twelve-year-old boy who had the diagnosis of autism and moderate mental retardation (Durand and Carr, 1991). Tim easily became frustrated and hit himself several times a day, which periodically required medical attention due to tissue damage. A functional evaluation suggested that self-injury was being reinforced by escape from certain situations. Next, a baseline observation was conducted (during which the teacher was to either ignore the SIB or block the more severe behaviors that might cause injury). Tim was then taught, with modeling and prompting, to request assistance with tasks he might desire to escape by simply saying "Help me." Training took place in the classroom, and several different trainers were deliberately used with two different tasks. Classroom teachers received no instruction in these procedures. The recording of Tim's SIB and unprompted verbal requests showed his progress (Figure 12–2). Further observation also revealed that the behaviors endured when Tim returned to school in two subsequent years.

Based on such demonstrations, as well as other research, Durand and Carr (1991, 1992) believe that Functional Communication Training not only is effective but that it generalizes to other situations and endures over time. For students whose language ability limits the training of verbal responses, communication devices can be utilized (Durand, 1993a). For example, the student can simply touch a pad that generates a voice stating the appropriate verbalization. Functional Communication Training has been successful in schools, residential settings, and the like. Durand and Carr are interested in determining whether students can be taught to use it in other settings, such as buses and stores, with any persons they might encounter.

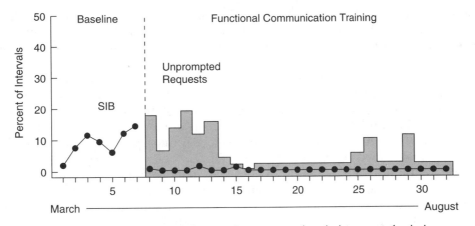

FIGURE 12–2 The occurrence of SIB and unprompted verbal requests for help as a function of intervention. Each point on the graph represents data from each observation day across several months.

Adapted from Durand, V. M., & Carr, E. G. (1991). Functional communications training to reduce challenging behavior: Maintenance and application in new settings. *J. of Applied Behavior Analysis, 24,* 251–264. By permission.

Intensive behavioral treatment: The Young Autism Project. In 1970 Lovaas and his colleagues began a comprehensive program to maximize the benefits of behavior modification by providing full-time treatment (Lovaas, 1987; Lovaas and Smith, 1988). Very young children were chosen because it was assumed that their learning of new behaviors would quite easily generalize to other environments. It was also believed that school mainstreaming, which was considered desirable, would be more easily accomplished in preschools than with older children in elementary schools.

To be accepted into the study children had to (1) have been independently diagnosed as autistic, (2) be less than forty-six months of age, and (3) have a specified mental age. Nineteen subjects were assigned to intensive training (Group I) and nineteen to a minimal training control condition (Group II). Group I had a mean IQ of fifty-three and Group II of forty-six. Comparison was also made with Group III, an outside group of autistic children that received no

training in the project. All three groups were very similar.

Treatment lasted for two or more years. Children in Group I worked one-to-one with student therapists and their parents for more than forty hours each week. Operant techniques were the basis of training. During the first year, treatment focused on reducing maladaptive behaviors, compliance to simple verbal commands, imitation, appropriate play, and extending training in the family. The second year emphasized language growth, interactive play, and teaching children to function in the preschool. The third year emphasized emotional expression, preacademic skills, and learning by observation of other children. Effort was made to place children in normal preschools where teachers would help in training. Children in Group II received almost the same treatment but with less than ten hours of interaction per week.

At initial follow-up the experimental children averaged seven years of age. They had significantly higher educational placement and IQ than the control groups, which did not differ from each other. Table 12–4 shows specific results. Prior to the study only two Group I children had scored in the normal range of IQ while eleven had scored in the severely retarded range; seven had been echolalic and eleven mute.

A second follow-up when Group I children averaged thirteen years of age showed that they had maintained improvements over Group II (McEachin, Smith, and Lovaas, 1993). School placement, with little exception, remained the same. Group I children achieved significantly higher average IQ scores (85 vs. 55) and Vineland adaptive behavior scores (72 vs. 46). Personality test scores were borderline for both groups. Overall, eight of nine Group I children who had done well at the first follow-up continued to function essentially as normal and were holding their own in regular classrooms.

The Young Autism Project has its critics, nevertheless (e.g., Schopler, Short, and Mesibov, 1989; Mundy, 1993). Concerns are expressed, for example, about how participants were assigned to groups and how they were assessed. Also, around-the-clock treatment did not benefit some children. While not agreeing with all the criticisms, Lovaas and his colleagues are interested in methodological improvements and in advances that might help a larger number of children (Smith, McEachin, and Lovaas, 1993). Indeed, improved replication is underway at several sites. Meanwhile, the project raises hope that intensive behavioral programs may make a difference in at least some cases of autism.

In concluding our discussion of specific treatments of autism, we again call attention to the necessity of empirical research on the efficacy of treatment. Too often new approaches have been touted as almost miraculous breakthroughs, resulting in false hope for parents, wasted resources, and worst of all, inappropriate interventions. A recent example concerns a treatment called facilitated communication; Accent 12–1 describes this technique and the unfortunate events surrounding it.

Placement

Lord and Rutter (1994) are among those who have discussed placements for persons with autism. As with other developmental disorders, the environments into which children with autism are placed vary, and depend largely on the needs of the child, family circumstances, and the availability of placements.

The general commitment to least restrictive alternatives and school inclusion has had the expected impact of less institutionalization. Although research on the effects of inclusion is lacking, complete mainstreaming without additional support is not likely to be successful. It is more reasonable to assume that a structured educational en-

TABLE 12–4 Educational Placement and Mean IQ Score at Initial Follow-up in the Young Autism Project

	Percent of children completing regular first grade		Percent of children in language handicapped and LD Class		Percent of children in first grade for autistic-retarded	
Group I	47	IQ: 107	42	IQ: 70	11	IQ: 30
Group II	0		42	IQ: 74	58	IQ: 36
Group III	5	IQ: 99	48	IQ: 67	48	IQ: 44

Adapted from Lovaas, 1987.

ACCENT 12–1 Who Communicates in Facilitated Communication?

Working with disabled patients in Australia, Rosemary Crossley developed the technique of facilitated communication (FC), in which the client types messages on a keyboard with the help of a facilitator-therapist. Although the technique became controversial in Australia, it was brought to the United States by Douglas Biklen and received much attention from Biklen's article in the *Harvard Educational Review* (Mulick, 1994; Schopler, 1994). Media attention became widespread and included programming on television's popular "Primetime" as well as on a soap opera that portrayed a fictional autistic person benefitting from the treatment.

Claims of success appeared quite remarkable. People with autism and other severe disabilites who previously had little or no ability to communicate were reported as sending complex and poetic messages. In some cases intelligence test scores were said to have dramatically risen. Biklen estimated that FC might be the treatment of choice in most cases of autism (Schopler, 1994).

But not everyone was comfortable with these claims of success. FC had not been adequately evaluated. In addition, a number of the communications reportedly sent by clients implicated family and professionals in physical and sexual abuse. Were these reports of abuse credible? Discomfort led to systematic research of FC (e.g., Simon, Toll, and Whitehair, 1994). It now seems quite clear that the messages in facilitated communications originate with the facilitators. For example, when facilitators but not the handicapped clients have access to information, communications are appropriate; this does not hold when only the handicapped clients have the information. No one believes that most facilitators are deliberately deceptive; rather, they seem unaware that their help has gone beyond guidance. Meanwhile the allegations of abuse reported in facilitated messages have been dismissed by the courts.

Still, allegiance to FC continues among some therapists and parents, who claim the technique has been effective for their clients/children. Perhaps their position is supported by certain underlying beliefs (Mundy and Adreon, 1994; Routh, 1994a). It is easy to view a person with autism as a bright individual who, if given the correct key, could escape from an isolated fortress. Although this view oversimplifies autism, FC training might be seen as the key. In addition, FC does assume respect for autistic persons and a belief in their competence. This humanistic philosophy is understandably appealing to those who work with autism. One hopes that it would not, however, lead to mistaken conclusions about FC's efficacy.

---

vironment suited to the individual will have benefits.

Educational opportunity has increased and brought notable improvement in the functioning of autistic youth. For example, a recent study reported that higher-functioning autistic adolescents attained higher levels of reading and math skills compared to a similar sample studied several years ago (Venter et al., 1992). The samples were of comparable intelligence, so it appears that the recent sample had benefitted from participation in a continuous educational program. Still, the academic skills of these adolescents did not match their mental age. Moreover, the picture is not favorable when severe or profound mental retardation exists with autism.

Environments that train the individual for future employment hold promise. Educational experiences that emphasize such things as task completion, self-management, and specific vocational training can be helpful. Work environments that provide job training and support are likely to increase independent living and the quality of life for autistic adults. So too is the increase in alternative living arrangements, such as supervised group homes.

SCHIZOPHRENIA

As noted early in this chapter, both Kraepelin and Bleuler identified a small percentage of cases of schizophrenia in which onset occurred in childhood. By the 1930s, the first descriptive, high-risk, and epidemiological studies of childhood schizophrenia had appeared (Cantor, 1988). Among the early important workers were Potter (1933), Bender (1947), Despert (1940), and Bradley (1947). During subsequent decades, many efforts were made to conceptualize the nature of the condition. This quest was complicated by arguments about how child and adult schizophrenia were related, and whether adult schizophrenia itself was best viewed as a broad category including various behavioral expressions or as a narrow category (Volkmar, 1991). It was on this landscape that Kanner argued for a distinct syndrome of autism, and autism and the various developmental disorders became

diffentiated from schizophrenia and schizophrenia-like disorders. Still, not all workers accept this distinction; they tend to view the disorders as a broad category that manifests itself differently at different ages. Moreover, even among those who agree with the distinction, questions remain about the classification and nature of schizophrenia in young people. Thus, the struggle for understanding goes on, with many old issues still being examined.

DSM-IV Criteria

Although the major classification systems had once recognized the category of childhood schizophrenia, they no longer do so. Underlying this change is the argument that schizophrenia and schizophrenia-like conditions are essentially the same among all age groups. Thus, children and adolescents are classified with schizophrenia if they meet the criteria for the adult disorder.

DSM-IV criteria are summarized in Table 12–5, with section A showing the manifestations of the disorder. *Delusions,* or erroneous beliefs, and *hallucinations,* or erro-

---

TABLE 12–5 DSM-IV Diagnostic Criteria for Schizophrenia

A. Two or more of the following, significantly present for 1 month.

    (1) delusions
    (2) hallucinations
    (3) disorganized speech
    (4) disorganized or catatonic behavior
    (5) negative symptoms, i.e., diminished affect, speech content, goal-directed activities

B. Marked impairment in one or more areas of functioning such as work, interpersonal relations, self-care. In children, failure to reach expected level in school, occupation, interpersonal relations.

C. Continuous disturbance for at least 6 months. At least 1 month of symptoms from Criterion A. May include prior (prodromal) or residual periods, with fewer symptoms.

D. Not due to related conditions: schizoaffective and mood disorder with psychotic features.

E. Not due to drugs, medications, or general medical condition.

F. If there is a history of pervasive developmental disorder, including autistic disorder, diagnosis is made only if prominent delusions and hallucinations are present for at least a month.

Adapted and reprinted with permission from the *Diagnostic and Statistical Manual of Mental Disorders, Fourth Edition.* Copyright 1994, American Psychiatric Association.

neous perceptions, are often considered the hallmarks of schizophrenia. But *disorganized speech*, which reflects disordered thinking, is often noted as the most important feature. *Disorganized behavior* is manifested in many ways: inappropriate silliness, unexpected agitation and aggression, lack of self-care, and the like. *Catatonic behaviors* are motor disturbances, such as decreased or excessive motor reactivity, and rigid and strange bodily postures. All the behaviors so far described are referred to as positive symptoms. However, people with schizophrenia also display negative symptoms, that is, a lack of normally occurring behaviors. Thus they may exhibit little emotion, their speech may consist of brief replies that do not seem to convey much information (alogia), or they may neither initiate nor maintain goal-directed actions (avolition). Not surprisingly, schizophenic behaviors disrupt normal adaptation and relationships. Thus, young people so diagnosed must have shown a higher level of achievement or fail to reach normal levels of achievement.

DSM-IV and other classification systems include subcategories for schizophrenia, such as paranoid and disorganized schizophrenia. However, reliability of the subcategories and their usefulness for youth are not established. Beyond this, other issues arise about the diagnosis of young people. For example, it is unlikely that very young children would be diagnosed as schizophrenic, since their developmental level limits their displaying the psychotic symptoms noted in Criteria A. Researchers who believe that the schizophrenic process can begin very early, perhaps in the second or third year, argue that the early manifestations of schizophrenia are not taken into account (eg., Cantor, 1988).

Prevalence

Data on prevalence and epidemiology are still limited and lacking in quality, due to low frequency of the disorder in youth and the many problems of classification and diagnosis. Prevalence is age related however. It is thought to be extremely low before ages five to six (lower than for autism), to increase somewhat during childhood, and then to rapidly rise into adolescence to reach the adult rate of about 1 percent (McClellan and Werry, 1994). To put this into perspective, it has been estimated that fewer than 20 percent of cases are found before the age of ten years (McKenna, Gordon et al., 1994). At early ages, the condition is more frequent in males than females but this sex difference seems to disappear at puberty (Green et al., 1992; McClellan and Werry, 1994).

Schizophrenia in children may occur at higher rates in less educated and professionally successful families (Volkmar, 1991), and a social class difference has been cited as one way in which it differs from autism. However, the data on social class are mixed and may be biased by a strong reliance on hospital samples (Werry, 1992).

Psychological and Behavioral Functioning

Youth diagnosed with schizophrenia display many problem behaviors, and much variation exists from person to person. In recent years research has documented that the criteria for adult schizophrenia can apply to children, but more easily to adolescents. We will first focus on the primary psychotic features and then on associated characteristics shown by clinic cases. (For a case description, see p. 72.)

Hallucinations. Hallucinations are false perceptions that occur in the absence of identifiable stimuli. Table 12–6, which shows some of the characteristics of four samples of children diagnosed with schizophrenia, indicates that the occurrence of hallucinations is high and remarkably consistent across these investigations. Auditory hallucinations were by far the most common. Visual hallucinations were reported

TABLE 12–6 Some Characteristics of Schizophrenic Children in Four Studies

	Mean Age	Male: Female	Mean IQ	Percent Showing Symptoms			
				Auditory Hallucin- ations	Visual Hallucin- ations	Delusions	Thought Disorder
Kolvin et al., 1971 N = 33	11.1 (est.)	2.66:1	86	82	30	58	60
Green et al., 1992 N = 38	9.58	2.17:1	86	84	47	55	100
Russell et al., 1989 N = 35	9.54	2.2:1	94	80	37	63	40
Volkmar et al., 1988 N = 14	7.86 (est.)	2.5:1	82	79	28	86	93

Adapted from Green et al., 1992, Russell et al., 1989, and Volkmar et al., 1991.

fairly often, while those involving touch and smell were quite rare. These findings are consistent with other studies of children and adults with schizophrenia (Kemph, 1987; Davison and Neale, 1996).

Table 12–7 shows the variety of halluci- nations reported in the Russell, Bott, and Sammons (1989) study and the percentage of subjects who experienced each type. It was not uncommon for a single child to re- port several kinds, but nonauditory halluci- nations never occurred in this sample with- out auditory hallucinations. The following gives a few examples of the children's re- ports of their experiences.

> *Auditory:* The kitchen light said to do things and "shut up."
> *Command:* A man's voice said "murder your stepfather" and "go play outside."
> *Visual:* A ghost with a red, burned, and scarred face was seen several times in differ- ent places.
> *Religious:* God said, "Sorry D., but I can't help you now, I'm helping someone else."
> *Persecutory:* Monsters said child is "stupid" and that they will hurt him.

Delusions. Delusions, false beliefs that are maintained even in the face of realistic

TABLE 12–7 Percentage of Children with Hallucinations and Delusions

Types of Hallucinations	Percent
Nonaffective auditory	80
Command	69
Visual	37
Conversing voices	34
Religious	34
Persecutory	26
Commenting voices	23
Tactile	17
Olfactory	6
Somatic	6

Types of Delusions	Percent
Persecutory	20
Somatic	20
Bizarre	17
Reference	14
Grandiose	11
Thought insertion	11
Control/influence	9
Mind reading	9
Thought broadcasting	6
Thought control	3
Religious	3

From A. T. Russell, L. Bott, and C. Sammons, The phenomenology of schizophrenia occurring in child- hood, Journal of the American Academy of Child and Adolescent Psychiatry, 28(3), 399–407, 1989. © by the Am. Acad. Of Child and Adolescent Psychiatry.

contradiction, occurred relatively frequently and with consistency across the samples summarized in Table 12–6. There were many kinds of delusions, as shown in Table 12–7, and some children reported several types. The following are examples.

> *Persecutory:* A child believed his father had escaped jail and was coming to kill him.
> *Somatic:* One child believed that a boy and a girl spirit lived inside his head.
> *Bizarre:* A boy was convinced he was a dog and growing fur. One time he refused to leave the veterinarian's office unless he got a shot.
> *Grandiose:* A boy had the firm belief that he was different and able to kill people. He felt that when God "zoomed" through him he became very strong.

Thought disorder. Delusions are a disturbance in the content of thought, but the form of thinking is also disordered in schizophrenia. Formal thought disorder is reflected in disorganized speech. The child may display loose associations; that is, the child jumps from topic to topic with no obvious connection between topics and without awareness of the problem. Speech may lack logic and be quite incoherent and incomprehensible to others. It may also be impoverished, conveying little information because it is vague, too abstract or concrete, or repetitive. Loose associations and incoherence are demonstrated by this excerpt from an interview with a seven-year-old boy:

I used to have a Mexican dream. I was watching TV in the family room. I disappeared outside of this world and then I was in a closet. Sounds like a vacuum dream. It's a Mexican dream. When I was close to that dream earth I was turning upside down. I don't like to turn upside down. Sometimes I have Mexican dreams and vacuum dreams. It's real hard to scream in dreams. (Russell et al., 1989, p. 404)

Table 12–6 shows high percentages of thought disorder in the four studies reported, but also large variation across the samples. Although these differences may indeed be real, they may also be due to difficulty in identifying thought disorder and to differences in how it is defined (McKenna, Gordon et al., 1994).

Intellectual/language functioning. Intellectual functioning as evaluated on intelligence tests is somewhat deficient in childhood schizophrenia but scores in the mentally retarded range are nowhere as evident as in autism. Perhaps 10 to 20 percent of cases show low IQ scores (McClellan and Werry, 1994). Many of the children score at borderline to average levels. There are few studies of IQ subtest performance, but relative deficits may exist on verbal tasks and tasks requiring short-term information processing (Asarnow, R.F. et al., 1987; Green et al., 1992).

Laboratory studies also suggest disturbance of information processing, especially in attention. For example, children with schizophrenia responded to auditory stimuli with abnormal brain waves, which were similar to those found in adult schizophrenia (Erwin et al., 1986). From a series of laboratory studies with children, Asarnow, Sherman, and Strandburg (1986) concluded that certain attentional mechanisms fail to develop, mechanisms that are also deficient in adult schizophrenia. These researchers reason that such attention deficits could show up in vague, digressive speech because the child is unable to keep up with the short-term processing demanded by normal conversation. Similarly, inability to attend to various cues at any one moment in social interaction could cause the social ineptness that is seen in children with schizophrenia.

Impaired language development has been reported (Cantor, 1988; Watkins, Asarnow, and Tanguay, 1988), and might be expected in cases with low IQ or very early onset that interferes with general development. Speech obviously can reflect thought disorder, and atypical features occur, such as echolalia and neologisms (made-up and meaningless words). Nevertheless, basic language skills do not seem as deficient as in autism (Prior and Werry, 1986).

Other deficits. Children with schizophrenia often show little emotion or they laugh, cry, or show anger when the situation does not warrant such a response. Other emotional disturbances have been reported such as coldness, moodiness, anxiety, and depression (Eggers, 1978; Prior and Werry, 1986).

Although there is little systematic study of social behavior, a variety of difficulties has been reported (Bettes and Walker, 1987; Kydd and Werry, 1982; Watkins et al., 1988). These include social withdrawal and isolation, inability to initiate social interactions, ineptness, and social anxiety.

Finally, motor abnormalities often are observed. They include awkwardness, delayed milestones, poor coordination, and peculiar posture (Bender, 1972; Cantor, 1988; Eggers, 1978; Watkins et al., 1988).

Developmental Course and Prognosis

Schizophrenia can occur suddenly, after brief episodes leading to a full-blown episode, or gradually (McClellan and Werry, 1994; Prior and Werry, 1986). When it occurs suddenly, it may be associated with stress. Onset before age thirteen tends to be insidious, with nonpsychotic symptoms occurring before psychotic symptoms. These premorbid nonpsychotic disturbances include delays and aberrations in language, motor, sensory, and cognitive functions, as well as social withdrawal, school problems, and "odd" personality (e.g., Watkins et al., 1988).

Hallucinations and delusions show a developmental trend (Eggers, 1978; Russell et al., 1989). The themes of childhood, such as animals and monsters, make their way into reports of children's psychotic experiences. When delusions first appear, they are quite simple (e.g., a monster wants to kill me), but they gradually become more elaborate, complex, abstract, and systematized. These changes are in keeping with cognitive and socioemotional development.

The way in which schizophrenia begins in adolescence is less clear. Perhaps it is not as insidious, appearing more commonly with a sudden outbreak of disturbance (King and Noshpitz, 1991). Stress associated with this time of life arguable plays a role. This picture seems more in keeping with adult schizophrenia. Nevertheless, many adolescents with schizophrenia do have histories of attention, motor-perceptual, and other neurodevelopmental problems as well as excessive worry, shyness, moodiness, and aggression.

What eventual happens to youth who are diagnosed with schizophrenia? The answer to this question is not firmly established. In general, it appears that, as in adult schizophrenia, some individuals have a chronic condition, others experience episodes of difficulties that come and go, and still others recover. For example, Eggers (1978) studied children, ages seven to thirteen, following them for sixteen years on average. About 20 percent appeared recovered, 33 percent showed very poor status, and the remainder fair to poor status. A review of adolescent schizophrenia suggested that about 50 percent of cases had a chronic course, and 20% had full remission of symptoms (Krausz and Muller-Thomsen, 1993). But another study found that 78 percent of the adolescents had been hospitalized at least twice by age thirty and were not otherwise doing well (Gillberg, Hellgren, and Gillberg, 1993). It is very difficult to interpret the different findings from different studies because of discrepancies in diagnostic criteria and length of follow-up.

What we can count on is that outcome is often unfavorable but nevertheless variable. Good premorbid adjustment, sudden onset, and identifiable precipitants appear related to better outcome. In other words, the child or adolescent who seems to be getting along reasonable well and then is taken with acute symptoms associated with specific events has a better chance of recovery. Early age of onset has been reported as predicting poor outcome, but the evidence is mixed. Since younger children tend to show insidious onset, perhaps it is this factor rather than age itself that is associated with poorer prognosis (Werry, 1992). We must wait for future investigations to tell us more about the course and outcome of schizophrenia in youth.

The Causes of Schizophrenia

It is highly likely that the conditions diagnosed as schizophrenia have multiple causes and some biological basis. Again, we acknowledge the relative lack of research on child and adolescent samples, and our discussion necessarily draws on what is known about the causes of adult schizophrenia, with the data coming from several sources including studies of persons at high risk for the disorder (p. 85).

Nervous system factors.　Biological disorder is inferred from many different kinds of data. Some of the clinical characteristics of children with schizophrenia point to nervous system dysfunction, such as motor delay and coordination problems, perceptual deviations, and soft neurological signs (Cantor, 1988; Fish, 1984; Goldfarb, 1970). Bender (1947) described uneven and slow development in every area of nervous system functioning (including sleeping, eating, timing of puberty) and argued for a core biological deficit. Bender is among those who argued that schizophrenia can begin very early in life and that the behavioral manifestations differ with developmental level.

Performance on neuropsychological tests, laboratory tasks, and neurophysiological measures also implicate biological disorder, in both early-onset and adult schizophrenia. For instance, deficits have been found for attention, reaction time, eye tracking, a variety of cognitive tasks, and brain activity. Again, more is known about adult schizophrenia, but some findings hold for children as well. It seems clear that some deficits exist in attention and information processing mechanisms (Asarnow, 1994).

Considerable interest exists in finding possible structural abnormalities of the brain, with most studies involving adult schizophrenia. Autopsy of brains of deceased patients was initially the method used to examine the brain, but brain imaging now more clearly identifies structural abnormalities. Enlargement of the ventricles is a relatively common finding, which suggests underdevelopment or less tissue (Peterson, 1995). Abnormalities in several other areas, such as the prefrontal and limbic areas, have also been revealed (Davison and Neale, 1994; Heinrichs, 1993). Such abnormalities frequently are associated with deficits on neuropsychological tests and with poor premorbid adjustment. Still, perhaps less than half of those evaluated with brain imaging show structural anomalies. Moreover, the limited studies of children with schizophrenia indicate diversity from child to child (Asarnow, 1994).

Brain activity has also been examined. EEG abnormalities have been found. Scans of blood flow and glucose use indicate that the prefrontal area might be underactive. For many years now excess dopamine has been implicated in schizophrenia. For example, medications that can relieve hallucinations, delusions, and disordered thinking appear to lower dopamine. Nevertheless, deficient dopamine is not implicated in the so-called negative symptoms of schizophrenia (Fowles, 1992). The many findings about the brain—some of which fit together well—are promising and are being vigorously pursued. But many pieces of the puzzles are a poor fit and many are no doubt still missing.

Genetic factors. Considerable evidence exists for genetic vulnerability to schizophrenia. The parents of children with schizophrenia have a higher rate of schizophrenia than the general population rate, about 10 percent compared to 1 percent (Volkmar, 1991). Preliminary results from an ongoing study also indicate high occurrence of schizophrenia in the relatives of children with the condition (Asarnow, 1994). These finding are consistent with research on adult schizophrenia done in several countries that indicates increased risk for schizophrenia as genetic relationship to a schizophrenic person increases. Adoption studies also support the hypothesis of genetic transmission in adult schizophrenia (Tienari et al., 1990).

Researchers are examining the genetic data to try to determine the mode of genetic transmission. Single-gene effects may operate in a small number of cases (Gottesman, 1993), but no specific genes have been identified. Moreover, most cases of schizophrenia are thought to involve polygenes, which may often interact with social or other environmental variables. In fact, although the genetic data are impressive, they do not tell the entire story. For example, identical twins of adults with schizophrenia are about as likely not to have schizophrenia as to have it. Thus, the challenge is to explain what and when genetic influence might operate, what other factors might be involved, and how several variables might work together to cause schizophrenia.

Pregnancy and birth complications. Prenatal and birth complications appear linked to some, although not all, cases of child and adult schizophrenia (Cannon et al., 1993; Rieder, Broman, and Rosenthal, 1977). For example, schizophrenia was associated with an influenza epidemic in Denmark, especially when exposure to the virus occurred during the second trimester of pregnancy. Such complications might act alone or might best be seen as precipitating schizophrenia in vulnerable persons (Neuchterlein, 1986). Indeed, a study by Cannon (1993) and his colleagues indicates that etiology can be complex. Their results come from the Danish prospective high-risk research in which children with schizophrenic parents were followed over several years. The findings indicate that pregnancy/birth complications and genetic risk each independently contributed to the occurrence of schizophrenia but in addition these variables acted together to cause the condition.

Social, psychological factors. The research on the social and psychological etiology of schizophrenia recognizes subtle chronic disadvantages of poor education, low intelligence, and lack of social support, but has focused on life events and family characteristics (Fowles, 1992).

Life events are viewed as adverse happenings or demands for change that are stressful. Such events increase in the weeks prior to the onset of schizophrenic symptoms (Fowles, 1992). Perhaps they are the sole cause of symptoms in some cases. More likely, they combine with other factors and contribute to the etiology of schizophrenia in a secondary way (Gottesman, 1991).

It was early hypothesized that childhood schizophrenia was caused by family factors such as immature mothering and passive fathering, inability of the child to separate from the mother, and reactions to pathological family dynamics (Alanen, 1960; Goldfarb, 1970; Mahler, 1952). Families with an adult schizophrenic were described as having deviant interactions (e.g., Bateson et al., 1956; Mishler and Waxler, 1965). However, there were difficulties with this early research: replications failed, no one deviant interaction was consistently found, and deviant interaction could be the result of having a dysfunctioning family member rather than being causal.

Today there is renewed interest in the family, with an emphasis on the interactional model of development. One series of studies has examined communication deviance (CD), defined as vague, unfocused, and distorted communication (Asarnow, 1994). Among the findings is that CD was higher in families of children with schizophrenia (or a related condition) than in families of children showing depression or a related condition (Asarnow, Goldstein, and Ben-Meir, 1988). Children in the high CD families also were the most impaired and showed the poorest attentional functioning. The researchers suggested that vulnerability to attention deficits together with exposure to CD might bring about attentional dysfunction and psychosocial impairment.

High parental expression of hostility, criticism, and emotional overinvolvement (high EE) also has been associated with schizophrenia. In one investigation, parents of children with schizophrenia were more likely to be critical towards their offspring compared to control parents (Asarnow, 1994). Other research shows that EE is linked to the eventual diagnosis of schizophrenia (or related disorders) in high-risk adolescents (Valone, Goldstein, and Norton, 1984). A study involving high EE parents and their nonschizophrenic offspring considered at risk because of behavior problems suggests that both the parents and their offspring were susceptible to high physiologically arousal.

The possible influence of family climate is shown in the Finnish Adoption Study, in which most adopted children who eventually became schizophrenic had schizophrenic biological mothers. In all cases, however, these adoptees had been reared in families rated as having disturbed relationships. Moreover, the adopted offspring of schizophrenics who had healthy rearing environments had rates of schizophrenia at about the general population rates (Goldstein, 1988).

Taken together, family research suggests that vulnerable children who experience certain family interactions are especially stressed (aroused), and that this combination of variables puts them at risk for schizophrenia or related disturbances. The research has weaknesses, however, and is not entirely consistent. Thus, we must be cautious in how much weight we give it.

Diathesis-stress model. Both biological and environmental factors appear to be involved in the etiology of schizophrenia, and neither set of factors well explains the condition. For this reason, the diathesis-stress model is widely endorsed. This multifactor model assumes that schizophrenia results from organismic vulnerability, probably genetic, interacting with stress that originates in the social psychological environment. Possible stressors include subtle disadvantages, adverse life events, and family dynamics, and their effects may accumulate. The degree to which genetic vulnerability and environmental input are involved may vary and produce somewhat different outcomes. In fact, schizophrenia may be several related disorders, which have diverse and often complex etiological pathways.

Assessment

Broad assessment of a child or adolescent suspected of schizophrenia is important, because behavioral manifestations can vary greatly from person to person and optimal treatment demands optimal assessment. The following categories serve as a guide for comprehensive assessment (McClellan and Werry, 1994; Volkmar, 1991):

1. Historical information including pregnancy complications, early development, premorbid personality, medical, and family history
2. Psychological assessment including intelligence, communication, and adaptive skills testing
3. Assessment for the positive and negative symptoms of schizophrenia, and other associated features

4. Medical evaluation, including a neurological exam and possible EEG and brain scans
5. Consultation with the school and social services as necessary

Special concern has been expressed about evaluating the psychological manifestations of childhood schizophrenia. Of help are standarized semistructured interviews, such as the Schedule for Affective Disorders and Schizophrenia for School-aged Children (Kiddie-SADS), but more needs to be done to simplify and adapt standardized instruments to developmental level (McKenna, Gordon, and Rapoport, 1994). Indeed, assessment would benefit by better understanding of how developmental change might impact the clinical picture. For one thing, much emphasis is now placed on psychotic symptoms in diagnosing schizophrenia but, as we have seen, these tend to appear only after nonpsychotic symptoms in children. Moreover, hallucinations and delusions themselves show developmental change.

In addition, it is sometimes difficult to identify true hallucinations and delusions in young children (King and Noshpitz, 1991; McKenna, Gordon et al., 1994). For example, hallucinations may be very brief, and transient hallucinations do not necessarily signal schizophrenia. Children may also report distorted perceptions, and even the vivid imaginations of young children are not always easy to distinguish from true hallucinations. Similarly, it may be especially difficult to tell whether bizarre ideas, obsessions, and preoccupations reported by the young should be considered delusions that indicate schizophrenia.

The identification of thought disorder also can be difficult, especially when language is not well developed. Again, developmental level must be considered. For example, in normal children past age seven, loose associations are not found and illogical thinking decreases. In studying thought dis-

order, Caplan (1994) employed a standardized scale and an interview technique that illicited children's responses to stories. Among the interesting findings is that loose associations may be a particularly strong indicator of childhood schizophrenia.

Assessment of adolescents, especially older adolescents, seems less problematic than that of children. Psychotic symptoms appear more similar to those observed in adult-onset schizophrenia, and assessment scales and procedures for adults are probably more useful. Of course, assessment always requires sensitivity to individual development and functioning. Furthermore, psychotic symptoms in adolescents may not indicate full-blown schizophrenia, and comprehensive assessment is always required (e.g., Mundy et al., 1990).

Treatment

As with other aspects of child and adolescent schizophrenia, there is a lack of systematic research, and to some extent we must generalize from what is known about treatment of adults. Treatment depends on the severity of the case, the phase the case is in, opportunity for treatment, community/family support, and the perspective of the therapist. Some severely disturbed persons remain at home and attend special schools; others are placed in hospitals and other residential settings for periods of time. The best treatment strategy employs multiple methods and approaches to alleviate the multiple problems frequently encountered. Today there is heavy emphasis on facilitating and maintaining the client in natural environments, and thus on efforts to work with families and community agents.

Medical treatment. Electroconvulsive therapy was once used and claimed to be effective for youth with schizophrenia (Bender, 1947). It is not widely accepted today. The medical treatment of choice is antipsychotic medications that reduce dopamine. In adults, such medications can alleviate hallucinations, delusions, thought disturbance, and other symptoms, but do less to relieve negative symptoms. There has been little systematic, controlled research of medication with children and adolescents (Campbell and Spencer, 1988; McClellan and Werry, 1994). The antipsychotics are said to be less effective in child than adult cases, perhaps because the condition has a more pervasive effect on functions that are still developing in the young. Nevertheless, some data do show modest improvement for both children and adolescents (McKenna, Gordon, and Rapoport, 1994). These medications have various side effects, including dyskinesia, rigid posture, and motor restlessness, and they require careful monitoring.

Recent research indicates that a new, atypical antipsychotic medication, clozapine, may also be effective, and especially helpful when people do not respond well to the typical antipsychotics or suffer side effects (Asarnow, 1994; Biederman, 1991). This medication is antagonistic to serotonin and does not have the side effects of the conventional antipsychotics. It may relieve both positive and negative symptoms. On the other hand, it is expensive and has its own side effects (seizures, impairment of the immune system). Preliminary research indicates successful use of clozapine with children and adolescents, and thus it is cautiously regarded as a possible alternative medication (Mozes et al., 1994).

Traditional psychotherapy. Psychoanalytic therapy has focused on the young person's being dominated by id impulses, having poor ego function, and being unable to separate from the mother. A firm distinction often is not made between autism and childhood schizophrenia. Thus, for example, Bettelheim's approach was likely used with both syndromes (p. 314).

The role of the therapist, depending somewhat on the client's age, is to help the child establish a separate self, interpret the world, distinguish reality from fantasy, develop a sense of mastery, and find more adaptive defenses (Cantor and Kestenbaum, 1986; Ekstein et al., 1972). For adolescents, there is a focus on the developmental tasks of this time of life, for example, on identity formation and physical maturation. Regardless of age, an intense, warm, and trusting relationship is critical, and the usual psychoanalytic tools of transference and interpretation are employed. This approach has its advocates, but has been deemphasized in recent years (King and Noshpitz, 1991).

Behavioral and family treatments. Behavioral treatment, regardless of where it is conducted, targets maladaptive, bizarre behaviors that interfere with functioning and also teaches adaptive behaviors. Thus, psychotic behavior may be ignored while social interaction skills are modeled and reinforced. Operant treatment has been employed for some time in hospitals, especially to encourage self-care and other daily living habits. The underlying aim of this approach is not to cure schizophrenia, but to help maintain clients as active agents in their own lives and to facilitate their leaving hospitals for less restrictive environments. Such interventions often meet these goals.

Family approaches recognize that appropriate family involvement and support is critical to clients, and that family members themselves can benefit from counseling and training. The approach of Falloon and his colleagues is particularly interesting. Their aim was to reduce levels of expressed emotion—of hostile emotional involvement—because high EE has been correlated with high rates of relapse (Falloon et al., 1985, cited in Davison and Neale, 1994). Families were assured of the biological nature of schizophrenia and the importance of compliance with medication treatment. They were provided behavioral and cognitive training in the home on how best to express feelings and in problem solving. Comparison with a control group receiving individual psychotherapy indicated that this family intervention was beneficial.

It is clear that a comprehensive approach and a generally supportive environment are needed in treating schizophrenia. Medication, behavioral intervention, family therapy, individual therapy, and the teaching of specific academic or developmental skills are all important. Support is crucial across different phases of schizophrenia, not just during the acute phase, although treatment components may certainly vary with the specific phase. It is also crucial that research on the treatment of youth, especially of children, goes forward.

SUMMARY

Severe childhood disorders similar to adult psychoses have long been recognized, but have been difficult to conceptualize and classify. Age-related frequency and other features argue for a distinction between early-onset and later-onset syndromes. Autism and schizophrenia are recognized by the major classification systems.

Autism is recognize as a pervasive developmental disorder characterized primarily by impaired social interaction, impaired communication, and restricted preoccupations and stereotypies. Additional deficits are also found, including ones in perception. About 70 percent of children with autism show mental retardation, with deficits in abstraction, information processing, and theory of mind. Both cognitive and affective problems have been viewed as the primary deficits in autism, but it is possible that several deficits are primary.

Etiological theories of autism which focused on family factors, such as Bettelheim's and Ferster's, are not supported by research. There is much evidence for biological causation. Nevertheless, no process has been definitively identified as causal and it is likely that various factors or their combination can give rise to autism.

Autism is rare, and occurs more in boys than girls. It typically begins during the first few years of life and shows a varied developmental course. Perhaps two-thirds to three-quarters of all cases have poor outcome. Intelligence level and language ability predict outcome.

Comprehensive assessment methods are useful in autism, including medical, social, behavioral, and intellectual evaluations. Traditional psychotherapeutic treatment is not considered effective. Medications give mixed results and are best considered adjuncts to educational/behavioral approaches. TEACCH and the Young Autism Project report some of the best outcomes. Operant methods can facilitate language and other skills and reduce undesirable behaviors. The use of aversive treatments of SIB has raised ethical concerns; Functional Communication Training appears to be one alternative to aversive methods.

Schizophrenia in childhood and adolescence is diagnosed with the same criteria as for adults. The hallmarks are hallucinations, delusions, and thought disorder. These are referred to as positive symptoms, along with disorganized behavior and catatonia. The negative symptoms are a lack of typical behaviors, such as minimal emotional response and speech. Other abnormalities have been noted in motor behavior, attention, language, and social behavior.

The prevalence of schizophrenia is extremely small in young children, increases some in middle childhood, and increases notably in adolescence, whereupon a sex difference favoring males disappears. Onset can be sudden or gradual; it appears more insidious in childhood, with nonpsychotic symptoms occurring before psychotic symptoms. Hallucinations and delusions show developmental change. The course of schizophrenia varies, but outcome is often unfavorable. Good premorbid adjustment and acute onset predict better outcome.

Biological etiology of schizophrenia is inferred from various investigative methods, but much of the evidence is from studies of adult schizophrenia. The findings suggest that biological vulnerability may interact with psychosocial factors to cause schizophrenia. The vulnerability-stress model is thus popular. Schizophrenia may actually be several related disorders due to multifactor, complex etiology.

As with autism, comprehensive assessment is ideal. It is not always easy to identify psychotic symptoms in childhood; this task is easier in adolescence. Medical treatment of schizophrenia consists of antipsychotic drugs, which appear helpful but further research on their effectiveness and drawbacks is required. Traditional psychoanalytic therapy has its advocates but is now deemphasized in favor of behavioral, family, and educational approaches.

13

DISORDERS OF BASIC PHYSICAL FUNCTIONS

Problems of physical functioning and health are discussed in this chapter and the next. In many ways these problems represent the interface between psychology and pediatrics. The term *pediatric psychology* is often applied to this field of research and practice. For many of the problems discussed, parents first turn to their pediatrician for help (Roberts and Lyman, 1990). For example, early problems with feeding of infants and toddlers, starting and managing toilet training, and difficulties in getting children to sleep are among the problems brought to pediatricians (Gross and Drabman, 1990). Also, the problems discussed here involve issues of physical functioning that require collaboration between psychologists and physicians. The life-threatening starvation of anorexic adolescents and the problem of enlarged colons in encopretic children are two examples.

It is common for children to exhibit some difficulty in acquiring appropriate habits of eating, elimination, and sleep. The child's ability to master these relevant tasks, and the parents' ability to train the child, are important to the immediate well-being of both. How these tasks are handled can also set the foundation for later difficulties. Problems may occur in the same area (for example, the later eating disorder of anorexia ner-

vosa) or in more general ways (for example, problems with authority figures). While parents solve many early difficulties themselves, professional assistance is also frequently sought (Schroeder and Gordon, 1991). In this chapter attention is given to some commonly encountered difficulties that are part of normal development. The principal focus, however, is on problems that are serious enough to make them of clinical concern.

DISORDERS OF EATING

A wide range of problems having to do with eating and feeding are commonly reported (Hertzler, 1983a,b). These include undereating, selective eating, overeating, problems in chewing and swallowing, bizarre eating habits, annoying mealtime behaviors, and delays in self-feeding. Many of these problems can cause considerable concern for parents and appreciable disruption of family life. For example, children's refusing to eat certain foods or vary their diets is a common complaint made by parents. Adequate nutrition and growth are clearly a concern, but restricted eating is also often accompanied by other behavioral problems such as tantrums, spitting, and gagging.

Young children often exhibit feeding and eating problems. This may result in disruption and cause their parents considerable distress.

(Jean-Claude Lejeune/Stock, Boston)

Severe cases of food refusal may be associated with even more difficult social and psychological problems and result in medical complaints and malnourishment. Indeed, some cases of failure to thrive (life-threatening weight loss or failure to gain) can be conceptualized as a special case of food refusal (Kelly and Heffer, 1990). Thus, some eating problems may actually endanger the physical health of the child. The clinical disorders discussed below are some that have attracted attention from researchers and clinicians.

Rumination

Rumination (or mercyism), first described in 1687, is a syndrome with a long history (Kanner, 1972). It is characterized by the voluntary and repeated regurgitation of food or liquid in the absence of an organic cause. When infants ruminate, they appear to deliberately initiate regurgitation. The child's head is thrown back and chewing and swallowing movements are made until food is brought up. In many instances the child initiates rumination by placing his or her fingers down the throat or by chewing on objects. The child exhibits little distress; rather, pleasure appears to result from the activity. If rumination continues, serious medical complications can result, with death being the outcome in extreme cases (American Psychiatric Association, 1994; Halmi, 1985).

Rumination is most often observed in two groups, infants and individuals diagnosed as mentally retarded. Among children who are developmentally normal, rumination usually appears during the first year of life. In mentally retarded individuals a later onset is often observed, and the incidence of the disorder seems to increase with greater degrees of mental retardation. In both groups rumination appears to be more prevalent in males (Mayes, 1992).

Etiology and treatment. Rumination in infants is often attributed to a disturbance in the mother-infant relationship (Mayes, 1992). The mother is either described as having psychological difficulties of her own which prevent her from providing the infant with a nurturant relationship or as experiencing significant life stress that interferes with her ability to attend to the infant.

Rumination is sometimes seen as the infant's attempt to provide this missing gratification. Alternatively, others view the act as habitual in nature. The pattern may start, for example, with the normal occurrence of spitting up by the infant. The behaviors may then be reinforced by a combination of pleasurable self-stimulation and the increased attention from adults that follows (e.g., Kanner, 1972; Linscheid, 1978). It is possible to integrate these various explanations by hypothesizing that the learning of rumination may be more likely in circumstances where the mother does not provide adequate stimulation and attention. Rumination among individuals diagnosed as mentally retarded is commonly viewed as a learned habit.

A wide variety of treatments has been suggested for rumination (Mayes, 1992). Satiation and aversive procedures have been employed with mentally retarded individuals. In *satiation procedures* the individual is fed large quantities of food, often three to six times normal meal portions. *Aversive procedures* most often involve the administration of unpleasant tasting substances or a mild shock contingent on the child's initiating the behaviors that lead to rumination. Both professionals and parents are particularly reluctant to apply aversive procedures to infants and prefer to find nonaversive alternatives. Treatments emphasizing contingent use of social attention have been successful, and there is some suggestion that with infant ruminators noncontingent stimulation and attention are also effective (Mayes, 1992). These procedures have the advantage of being easily implemented by the parents in the home and of being acceptable to them. However, sufficiently controlled evaluations of interventions, particularly with infants, are lacking.

Pica

Pica is the Latin term for magpie, a bird known for the diversity of objects it eats.

This disorder is characterized by the habitual eating of substances usually considered inedible, such as paint, dirt, papers, fabric, hair, and bugs.

During the first year of life, most infants put a variety of objects into their mouths, partly as a way of exploring the environment. Within the next year they typically learn to explore in other ways and come to discriminate between edible and inedible materials. The diagnosis of pica is therefore usually made when there is a persistent eating of inedibles beyond this age, and pica is most common in two- and three-year-olds.

Information regarding the prevalence of pica is limited, but is reported to be particularly high among mentally retarded individuals (e.g., McAlpine and Singh, 1986). Pica can lead to a variety of damage, including parasitic infection and intestinal obstruction due to the accumulation of hair and other materials. It also appears related to accidental poisoning (American Psychiatric Association, 1994; Halmi, 1985).

Etiology and treatment. A number of causes for pica have been postulated. Because youngsters have been observed eating strange substances when food is unavailable, it has been suggested that pica is an attempt to satisfy nutritional deficits. Parental inattention, lack of supervision, and lack of adequate stimulation have also been suggested. Several findings suggest cultural influences (Fultz and Rojahn, 1988; Halmi, 1985; Kanner, 1972; Millican and Lourie, 1970).

Millican and Lourie (1970) found, for the black children they studied, that most of the families had migrated from the southeastern United States, where eating of earth containing clay and laundry starch is a frequent custom among pregnant women (Hálmi, 1985). Certain superstitions are reported to govern this behavior. Eating clay and other nonfood substances is believed to prevent a curse on the fetus, reduce the side effects of pregnancy, produce good blood in the unborn child, and eliminate the possibility of syphilis. Interestingly, the mothers of children with pica were found to have a higher frequency of the behavior than mothers of children without pica. And young black children, who might be strongly affected by cultural acceptance of pica, exhibited a lower rate of psychological difficulties than did older and white children displaying pica.

Educational approaches aimed at informing mothers of the dangers of pica and encouraging them to discourage the behavior may be somewhat successful. However, even reports of successful programs indicate a need to supplement the interventions with more intensive therapeutic endeavors in some cases. Behavioral interventions have been suggested. For example, aversive procedures to stop inappropriate eating along with reinforcement programs to increase appropriate behavior and increase the attention given to the child can be employed (Finney, Russo, and Cataldo, 1982; Halmi, 1985; Millican and Lourie, 1970).

Obesity

Obesity is a common and important health problem with an estimated prevalence of about 20 percent in children and adolescents. Several aspects of the prevalence data point to obesity as a significant health problem. Prevalence increases with age (Aristimuno et al., 1984; Garn and Clark, 1976; Huse et al., 1982) and with age there is also an increase in the percentage of obese children who will become obese adults (Garn et al., 1986; Rolland-Cachera et al., 1987). What is perhaps most striking are reports that indicate that the prevalence of childhood obesity is increasing (Campaigne et al., 1994; Gortmaker et al., 1987). Dietz (1988), comparing national health survey data over a fifteen-year period beginning in the mid-1960s, found that the prevalence of obesity increased 54 percent among six- to eleven-

year-old children and 39 percent among twelve- to seventeen-year-old adolescents.

Obesity in childhood is associated with numerous physical health problems, particularly those related to risk of heart disease (Aristimuno et al., 1984; Johnson and Hinkle, 1993). In addition, there are associations with social and psychological difficulties (e.g., Melbin and Vuille, 1989; Pierce and Wardle, 1993). Indeed, a National Institutes of Health panel concluded that "Obesity creates an enormous psychological burden. In fact, in terms of suffering, this burden may be the greatest adverse effect of obesity" (NIH, 1985, p. 4).

An example of research illustrating the psychological problems associated with obesity is a study by Israel and Shapiro (1985). Parents of overweight children enrolled in a weight-loss program completed Achenbach's Child Behavior Checklist prior to treatment. The behavior problem scores of children in this study were significantly higher than the norms for the general population. However, they were significantly lower than the norms reported for children referred to clinics for psychological services. These findings are illustrated in Figure 13–1. Thus, it would appear that overweight children attending a weight-loss program experience psychological difficulties to a greater extent than do members of the general population, but that their problems are not as severe in most areas as those exhibited by children receiving psychological assistance for other behavioral problems. Clearly, it cannot be determined from this study whether these problems contribute to or result from being overweight.

The obese child's social interactions may be adversely affected by negative evaluations. Children hold negative views of obesity, and children perceived as overweight are ranked as less liked (e.g., Counts et al., 1986; Strauss et al., 1985). While findings of such stigmatization are methodologically controversial, they clearly deserve clinical

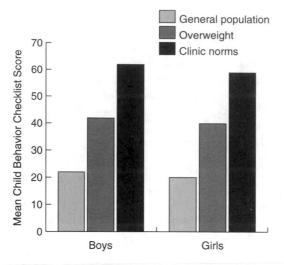

FIGURE 13–1 Mean total behavior problem scores for overweight children, clinic norms and general population norms.

Adapted from Israel and Shapiro, 1985.

and research attention (Jarvie et al., 1983; Woody, 1986). Furthermore, the reduction of activity and dexterity that often accompanies obesity makes social isolation and rejection even more likely.

The etiology of obesity. The causes of obesity are certainly multiple and complex. Any explanation must include biological, psychological, and social/cultural influences (Krasnegor, Grave, and Kretchmer, 1988).

Biological influences include genetic factors (cf. Siervogel, 1988; Zhang et al., 1994) and the metabolic effects of dieting (e.g., Dietz, 1988). One prominent biological theory is known as set point theory. There is some evidence that humans have a point at which body weight is set. Changes away from this set point result in psychological and metabolic changes intended to defend this "ideal" body weight. It is presumed that obese individuals have a high set point. Of course, biological influences are not independent of environmental influences; rather these influences interact.

The influence of psychosocial factors on the development of obesity is acknowledged by most major workers in the field. Both logic and research suggest that obese children have food intake and activity behaviors that are in need of change (cf. Klesges and Hanson, 1988; Schlicker, Borra, and Regan, 1994). Problematic food intake and inactivity are presumed to be affected by environmental influences and learned in the same manner as any other behavior. Children, for example, observe and imitate the eating behavior of their parents and others around them and are reinforced for engaging in that style of eating (e.g., Klesges and Hanson, 1988). Eating and inactivity may also become strongly associated with physical and social stimuli, so that they become almost automatic in some circumstances. Moreover, some people learn to use food to overcome negative mood states such as boredom and anxiety. The treatment of obesity developed from a social learning perspective seeks to break these learned patterns and develop more adaptive ones.

Society's view of obesity is an important cultural influence. Television provides a striking example of how the larger society might contribute to the development of weight problems in children. American children watch a great deal of television, on average about two to three hours each day (Scarr, Weinberg, and Levine, 1986). In addition to the negative effects of inactivity associated with television watching, children's diets are probably adversely influenced (Jeffrey et al., 1979). Indeed, a significant association between time spent watching television and the prevalence of obesity has been reported (Dietz and Gortmaker, 1985).

Behavioral treatment. Multifaceted programs that emphasize behavioral interventions and education have been the most effective treatments for childhood obesity (Epstein and Wing, 1987). The work of Israel and his colleagues (Israel and Solotar, 1988; Israel et al., 1994) illustrates the general approach. Children and parents attend meetings during which four areas are regularly addressed: *Intake,* which includes nutritional information, caloric restriction, and changes in actual eating and food preparation behaviors; *Activity,* which includes both specific exercise programs and increasing the energy expended in daily activities, for example, walking to a friend's house rather than being driven; *Cues,* which identifies the external and internal stimuli associated with excessive eating or inactivity; and *Rewards,* which provides positive consequences for progress by both the child and parent. Homework assignments are employed to encourage the families to change their environments and to practice more appropriate behavior.

Research supports the effectiveness of the behavioral approach to children's weight reduction (Epstein and Wing, 1987; Israel, 1990; Israel and Zimand, 1989). However, there is still a need for improved interventions that produce greater, more consistent, and more long-lasting weight loss. The importance of certain treatment components, including parental involvement, have been emphasized (Foreyt and Goodrick, 1993). Israel, Stolmaker, and Andrian (1985), for example, investigated the contribution of training in general parenting skills. Parents were given a three-week course in the general principles of child management. They then participated with their children in a behavioral weight-reduction program. Throughout these sessions the application of the general parenting skills to weight reduction was emphasized. Another group of parents and children received only the behavioral weight-reduction program. At the end of treatment both groups achieved a significantly greater weight loss than control children not receiving treatment. A measure of eating habits also indicated changes for treated children but not for controls. Par-

ents who received child-management training scored higher on a test of knowledge of behavior change principles than did parents who participated in the behavioral weight-reduction-only group. Importantly, one year following treatment, children whose parents had received separate child-management training had maintained their weight losses better than other treated children.

These results and others suggest the importance of changing family life styles and providing parents with the skills necessary to maintain appropriate behavior once the treatment program has ended (Graves, Meyers, and Clark, 1988; Israel, 1988). This is a particularly important issue in light of repeated evidence that individuals frequently regain the weight they have lost. In addition to parental involvement, the importance of increased activity, particularly when it is part of the family's life style, and various other family factors have been shown to be related to treatment outcome (Foreyt and Goodrick, 1993; Israel, Silverman, and Solotar, 1986).

Parallel to the need to improve parental involvement, the value of enhancing the child's self-regulatory skills has also been suggested (Israel et al., 1994). Children receiving a multidimensional treatment program, comparable to the four area one described above, were compared to children receiving a similar intervention plus enhanced training in comprehensive self-management skills. The results of this study are presented in Figure 13–2. In the three years prior to treatment, children in the two conditions had shown comparable patterns of increasing percent overweight. Both treatment conditions resulted in comparable reductions in percent overweight during treatment. However, while children in the standard condition appeared to return to pretreatment trends in the three years following treatment, children in the enhanced self-regulation condition did not.

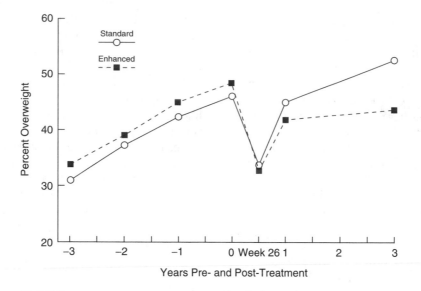

FIGURE 13–2 Mean percentage overweight from 3 years prior to treatment through 3 years following treatment.

From Israel, A. C., Guile, C. A., Baker, J. E., & Silverman, W. K. (1994). An evaluation of enhanced self-regulation training in the treatment of childhood obesity. *Journal of Pediatric Psychology, 19*, 737–749. Reprinted by permission from Plenum Publishing Corporation.

Anorexia Nervosa and Bulimia

Until recently anorexia and bulimia were considered quite rare. The number of cases reported as well as "subclinical" levels of these problems have increased (Lucas et al., 1991; Phelps et al., 1993) and this may be due to actual increases in eating disorders or to greater awareness and reporting of these problems. Revelations of anorexic and bulimic behavior among celebrities such as Karen Carpenter, Jane Fonda, and Princess Diana have also increased popular interest.

There has been considerable debate regarding how to best define eating disorders, and the degree to which disorders overlap. Several dimensions are usually considered in trying to make distinctions between eating disorders or subcategorize a particular disorder. An individual's weight status is one such consideration. A person with an eating disorder may be underweight, within the normal weight range, or overweight.

A second consideration is whether the individual engages in binge-eating. A binge is usually defined by: (1) the person eats a larger amount of food during a discrete period of time (e.g., one hour) than most people would be expected to eat during that time and (2) the person feels that he or she lacks control of eating during this episode (Fairburn and Wilson, 1993).

A third consideration often employed in distinguishing eating disorders is the method used to control one's weight. A distinction is often made between restricting and purging strategies. The first term refers to severely restricting food intake and/or engaging in highly vigorous exercise. The second strategy involves purging oneself of unwanted calories through methods such as vomiting or the use of laxatives.

We turn now to how these dimensions are involved in describing eating disorders. Those individuals with eating disorders whose body weight is well below expected

Grammy award singer Karen Carpenter, who died at age 32 of heart failure, had suffered from the effects of anorexia nervosa for many years.

(Schiffmann/Gamma-Liaison)

levels are likely to be given the diagnosis of Anorexia Nervosa.

It is generally agreed that a drive for extreme thinness and a fear of gaining weight are characteristics of individuals with this diagnosis. The extremeness of weight loss in anorexia is indicated by the significant medical complications that may occur (e.g., anemia, cardiovascular problems, dental problems) and by the life threatening nature of the disorder. It has been reported that over 10 percent of cases end in death (American Psychiatric Association, 1994). The seriousness of this extreme weight loss is also illus-

trated by Bruch's (1979) description of one of her clients:

. . . she looked like a walking skeleton, with her legs sticking out like broomsticks, every rib showing, and her shoulder blades standing up like little wings. Her mother mentioned, "When I put my arms around her I feel nothing but bones, like a frightened little bird." Alma's arms and legs were covered with soft hair, her complexion had a yellowish tint, and her dry hair hung down in strings. Most striking was the face—hollow like that of a shriveled-up old woman with a wasting disease, . . . Alma insisted that she looked fine and that there was nothing wrong with her being so skinny. "I enjoy having this disease and I want it." (pp. 2–3).

The DSM-IV criteria for the diagnosis of Anorexia Nervosa are presented in Table 13–1. In addition to low body weight, fear of weight gain, and disturbance in body perception, other definitions have stressed that psychological variables such as a sense of personal inadequacy are central to defining the disorder (e.g., Bruch, 1973, 1986; Yates, 1989).

A number of considerations support the distinction adopted in DSM-IV between two subtypes of anorexics. This distinction is based upon whether or not the person binges. *Binge-eating/purging* anorexics exhibit a persistent pattern of binge eating and purging. In contrast, *restricting* anorexics achieve their weight loss by fasting and/or exercise and do not binge eat. These subgroups have been found in large clinical samples, and the two groups are reported to differ on a number of individual and family characteristics (DaCosta and Halmi, 1992; Humphrey, 1989; Strober and Humphrey, 1987). This distinction among anorexics is also supported by findings of the importance of binge-eating and purging behavior in understanding eating disorders. For example, binge-eating anorexics were found to be more similar to bulimics who had never met the weight loss criteria for anorexia than to restricting anorexics (Gar-

TABLE 13–1   DSM-IV Criteria for Anorexia Nervosa

A. Refusal to maintain body weight at or above a minimally normal weight for age and height (e.g., weight loss leading to maintenance of body weight less than 85% of that expected; or failure to make expected weight gain during period of growth, leading to body weight less than 85% of that expected).
B. Intense fear of gaining weight or becoming fat, even though underweight.
C. Disturbance in the way in which one's body weight or shape is experienced, undue influence of body weight or shape on self-evaluation, or denial of the seriousness of the current low body weight.
D. In postmenarcheal females, amenorrhea, i.e., the absence of at least three consecutive menstrual cycles. (A woman is considered to have amenorrhea if her periods occur only following hormone, e.g., estrogen, administration.)

Specify type:
   Restricting Type: during the current episode of Anorexia Nervosa, the person has not regularly engaged in binge-eating or purging behavior (i.e., self-induced vomiting or the misuse of laxatives, diuretics, or enemas)
   Binge-Eating/Purging Type: during the current episode of Anorexia Nervosa, the person has regularly engaged in binge-eating or purging behavior (i.e., self-induced vomiting or the misuse of laxatives, diuretics, or enemas)

Adapted and reprinted with permission from the *Diagnostic and Statistical Manual of Mental Disorders, Fourth Edition.* Copyright 1994, American Psychiatric Association.

ner, Garfinkel, and O'Shaughnessy 1985). Also, in all three weight categories (under, normal, and overweight), bulimic women have been reported to differ from nonbulimic women in the same weight category on a number of psychological characteristics such as self-esteem, perceived control, and psychopathology (Shisslak, Pazda, and Crago, 1990). Thus, distinguishing between binge-eating and restricting anorexics is likely to be useful.

In contrast to anorexia nervosa, those individuals with eating disorders whose body weight is not below expected levels are likely to be given the diagnosis of Bulimia Nervosa. Bulimia is in general characterized by recurrent binge eating in the presence of a persistent overconcern with body shape and weight. This of course means that the bulimic individual needs to employ some method of compensating for eating binges. The most frequently cited method is purging by vomiting or the use of laxatives. The DSM-IV criteria for the diagnosis of Bulimia Nervosa are presented in Table 13–2. One

of the issues faced in diagnosing bulimia as a disorder is the high frequency of bulimic behavior reported in the general population of late adolescents and young adults and the high prevalence of concern about body shape and weight among females. These statistics and the newness of bulimia as a diagnosable disorder make it difficult to estimate the real incidence of the disorder (Mitchell and Eckert, 1987).

The issue of subtyping has also arisen in diagnosing bulimia. The principle consideration is whether or not purging is employed to compensate for binge eating. The popular notion of bulimia is of a binge-purge syndrome and, indeed, the vast majority of research on the disorder is based on this population. Whether to limit the diagnosis of bulimia to binge eaters who also purge, or to have purging and nonpurging (those who employ dieting and fasting) subtypes, is at issue (Mitchell, 1992; Wilson and Walsh, 1991). DSM-IV has, however, adopted these subtypes. There has also been consideration of subgrouping bulimics based on whether

TABLE 13–2   DSM-IV Criteria for Bulimia Nervosa

A. Recurrent episodes of binge eating. An episode of binge eating is characterized by both of the following:

   (1) eating, in a discrete period of time (e.g., within any 2-hour period), an amount of food that is definitely larger than most people would eat during a similar period of time and under similar circumstances

   (2) a sense of lack of control over eating during the episode (e.g., a feeling that one cannot stop eating or control what or how much one is eating)

B. Recurrent inappropriate compensatory behavior in order to prevent weight gain, such as self-induced vomiting, misuse of laxatives, diuretics, enemas, or other medications; fasting; or excessive exercise.

C. The binge eating and inappropriate compensatory behaviors both occur, on average, at least twice a week for 3 months.

D. Self-evaluation is unduly influenced by body shape and weight.

E. The disturbance does not occur exclusively during episodes of Anorexia Nervosa.

Specify type:

   Purging Type: during the current episode of Bulimia Nervosa, the person has regularly engaged in self-induced vomiting or the misuse of laxatives, diuretics, or enemas

   Nonpurging Type: during the current episode of Bulimia Nervosa, the person has used other inappropriate compensatory behaviors, such as fasting or excessive exercise, but has not regularly engaged in self-induced vomiting or the misuse of laxatives, diuretics, or enemas

Adapted and reprinted with permission from the *Diagnostic and Statistical Manual of Mental Disorders, Fourth Edition.* Copyright 1994, American Psychiatric Association.

there was a previous history of anorexia or obesity and of subgrouping based on the person's current weight status (normal versus overweight). Evidence regarding these subgrouping dimensions is limited (Mitchell, 1992).

Prevalence and etiology. Eating disorders typically begin in late adolescence or early adulthood, and thus prevalence estimates, ranging from approximately 1 to 4 percent, are largely based on such samples (American Psychiatric Association, 1993; 1994). Females represent over 90 percent of all cases. Anorexia nervosa is reported to occur in 0.5 to 1.0 percent of females in this age group. While the average age of onset is late adolescence, there may be peaks at ages fourteen and eighteen. Cases of earlier onset are rare, but do exist (Gowers et al., 1991; Lask and Bryant-Waugh, 1992). Bu-

limia nervosa is more commonly diagnosed, occurring in 1 to 3 percent of adolescent and young adult females. Lewinsohn et al. (1993) reported a lifetime prevalence rate of approximately 1 to 1.5 percent in a random sample of high school females. The rate of occurrence in males is about one-tenth that in females.

Deliberate self-starvation is clearly a puzzling and bizarre phenomenon, and binging and purging have become alarmingly common. A variety of causal mechanisms have been proposed to explain the development of eating disorders (Yates, 1989). However, no definitive explanation exists. Indeed, it is not necessary to presume that there is a single causal explanation. It may be that the behaviors may result from a variety of different patterns of causal factors. Further, it is most likely that both anorexia and bulimia are multiply determined disorders—that is, no single cause is sufficient to explain their development (Bryant-Waugh and Lask, 1995; Garner and Parker, 1993).

Clinical reports mention early feeding difficulties and there is some support for this position. For example, Marchi and Cohen (1990) longitudinally traced maladaptive eating patterns in a group of children ages one to ten, over a ten-year span. Their findings suggested that early childhood pica was a risk factor and picky eating a protective factor of bulimic symptoms in adolescence. On the other hand, picky eating and digestive problems in early childhood were risk factors for elevated symptoms of anorexia nervosa in adolescence. Certainly, more research is needed to clarify the relationship between early eating/feeding difficulties and later eating disorders. It is not clear that early eating problems are more frequent in children who later develop eating disorders.

Much debated is the idea that self-starvation begins as an attempt to control genuine obesity. For the anorexic, for example, comments that the young girl is "getting plump" may stimulate normal dieting, which evolves into anorexic refusal to eat. The frequency of dieting among adolescent girls, however, raises the question of why some girls who begin this common social ritual persist well beyond the point of socially desired slimness. Greater dissatisfaction with one's weight and body shape and low interoceptive awareness (an inability to accurately read emotional arousal and internal hunger cues) are two factors commonly implicated (e.g., Faust, 1987; Killen et al., 1994; Leon et al., 1993).

Similar considerations have been discussed regarding bulimia. For example, bulimia has been viewed in several ways within a cognitive-behavioral perspective. These explanations, rather than being conflicting, stress different aspects of the multifaceted cognitive-behavioral approach (Wilson and Fairburn, 1993). One explanation hypothe-

sized is that bulimic behavior develops as a faulty weight-control method among individuals who have had poor self-control patterns modeled for them (Orleans and Barnett, 1984). Another view describes individuals who have abnormal attitudes and beliefs about weight regulation, who evaluate their self-worth in terms of their body shape, and who thus become preoccupied with weight control (Fairburn, 1985).

Dissatisfaction with weight and body shape has, indeed, come to be viewed as part of the defining characteristics of eating disorders and one of the early aspects of the development of such problems. Pictorial instruments to graphically assess body dissatisfaction in young children have been developed as part of a comprehensive assessment of eating disorders (Childress et al., 1993; Collins, 1991). Use of such instruments (see Figure 13–3) has contributed to the view that body dissatisfaction and other problematic beliefs and behaviors are common and are present even in very young children. (See Accent 13–1)

The notion that eating disorders evolve out of a response to levels of stress for which existing skills seem inadequate is also common (Bruch, 1973; Foreyt and McGavin, 1989). Since eating disorders generally begin during the adolescent years, stresses associated with this period, such as the onset of puberty, expectations of greater autonomy and responsibility, and increased social demands are implicated (Levine et al., 1994).

Many workers from a cognitive-behavioral perspective, for example, view anorexia as an avoidance response. Stringent dieting prevents the appearance of a mature body and also results in menstruation being avoided or reversed. This is consistent with the view that the anorexic's fear of weight gain is related to concerns about psychosexual maturity (Crisp, 1984). Thus, the anorexic girl's behavior is negatively reinforced since it allows her to avoid negative thoughts, feelings, and fears. The behavior

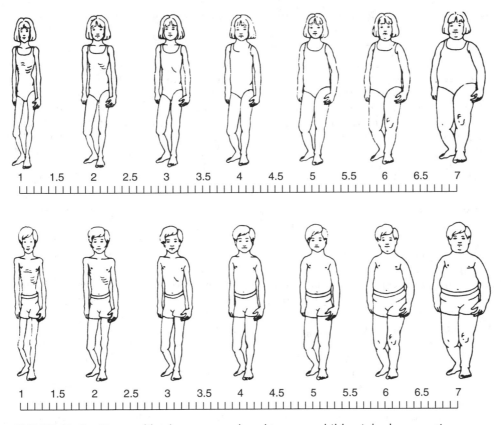

FIGURE 13–3   Pictures like these are employed to assess children's body perception.

Adapted from Collins, E. Body figure perceptions and preferences among preadolescent children. *International Journal of Eating Disorders.* Copyright 1991. Reprinted by permission of John Wiley & Sons, Inc.

is also positively reinforced. The young woman may feel a sense of mastery, self-control, or virtue (Garner and Bemis, 1985).

Explanations involving response to developing sexuality have also been part of the psychodynamic tradition. The psychodynamic perspective of anorexia nervosa has its origins in the early psychoanalytic proposition that equated eating behavior with sexual instinct (S. Freud, 1918/1959).

Bruch and many other clinicians working within the psychodynamic tradition found that this view did not fit their patients, and that classical psychoanalysis was not effective in treating them. They, therefore, shifted their focus from oral/sexual drives to disorders of the mother-child relationship (Bruch, 1973, 1986). This is consistent with other views (discussed below) that have come to emphasize family influences. Anorexia is viewed by Bruch as a deficit in ego development that arises out of disturbances in mother-child interactions. The resulting ego deficiencies are manifested in disturbances in body image, a failure to accurately recognize hunger and appetite, and a severe and pervasive sense of personal ineffectiveness (Bruch, 1986). From this perspective, the anorexic is viewed as poorly prepared to face adulthood and as rejecting

ACCENT 13–1 Are Eating Disorder Problems Occurring Earlier and Becoming More Common?

Although the diagnosis of eating disorders typically occurs in late adolescence, disordered eating behaviors and attitudes are appearing in younger children and at an increasing rate. These problems may be possible precursors of more serious eating disorders.

There is some suggestion that by fourth grade girls are worried about being or becoming overweight and desire to become thinner. Mellin, Irwin, and Scully (1992), for example, found that approximately 31 percent of nine-year-old girls reported a fear of fatness and approximately 46 percent reported restrained eating/dieting. In ten-year-olds, approximately 55 percent reported fear of fatness and 81 percent reported restrained eating/dieting. In this sample of girls aged nine to eighteen, distortion of body image peaked (38 percent) at age eleven. Fifty-eight percent perceived themselves to be overweight, whereas only 15 percent were overweight by objective standards. Such concerns seem more prevalent in girls even at this young age. Thelen et al. (1992), for example, report no gender differences for second graders, but while there was no increase in concerns for boys, fourth- and sixth-grade girls were more concerned than second graders with becoming overweight and were dissatisfied with their body image. Evidence also suggests that extreme weight concern in these young girls is predictive of the emergence of eating disorder symptoms and diagnoses (e.g., Killen et al., 1994).

Among middle school children these problems remain prevalent, and more extreme weight control behaviors seem to be employed by an appreciable number of children. Gender differences also remain. The information in the adjacent table (adapted from Childress et al., 1993) is based on a survey of the responses of over three thousand children in grades five to eight to the Kids' Eating Disorders Survey (KEDS). The percentage of selected items endorsed by these youngsters illustrates the prevalence of these problems as well as gender differences.

The prevalence of these problems seems to have increased over time. In 1984, 1989, and 1992 Phelps and colleagues (1993) surveyed, all female students enrolled in middle school and high school in a suburban school district. The rates of specific weight-control procedures employed by high school girls did not exhibit significant change over time or even decreased (e.g., use of diet pills). However, the percentage of middle school girls using diet pills increased over time (0.8 percent, 1.7 percent, and 6.1 percent, respectively). There was a similar pattern over time for the percentage of middle school girls deliberately vomiting in an effort to lose weight (3.8 percent, 3.3 percent, and 11.4 percent, respectively).

The presence and perhaps increase of problematic eating behaviors and attitudes in young girls poses a risk for the development of diagnosable eating disorders. In addition, these behaviors and attitudes appear to be associated with greater depression, lowered self-esteem, and feelings of inadequacy and personal worthlessness (e.g., Killen et al., 1994; Lewinsohn et al., 1993). Indeed, such feelings may lead to increased concern with weight and shape among girls who already place great personal value on these physical attributes (Cohen-Tovee, 1993).

KEDS Items	Percent Endorsing	
	Girls	Boys
Felt looked fat*	54.4	27.8
Afraid of weight gain*	32.5	13.0
Dieted*	42.6	19.7
Fasted*	11.2	6.0
Vomited to lose weight	5.6	3.9
Used diet pills*	3.6	1.1
Used diuretics	2.2	0.8
Binged*	6.5	26.3

(* indicates a significant gender difference.)

food (the maternal substitute) and the feminine role. Some suggest that it is not rejection of the feminine role, but rather low self-esteem in the face of a desire to accomplish many roles (Yates, 1989).

Bruch (1979) also described the anorexic girl as the object of much family attention and control who is trapped by a need to please. Anorexia is seen as a desperate attempt by the child to express an individual identity.

She enjoyed being home but missed the fuss they had made about her in the past, when everybody was acutely concerned about her. . . . Even as a child Ida had considered herself not worthy of all the privileges and benefits that her family offered her, because she felt she was not brilliant enough. An image came to her, that she was like a sparrow in a golden cage, too plain and simple for the luxuries of her home, but also deprived of the freedom of doing what she truly wanted to do. (pp. 23–24)

Other explanations regarding the etiology of eating disorders have also emphasized family variables. It is difficult, however, to determine whether any pattern observed in a family subsequent to the onset of a disturbance is a cause or effect. This is especially the case in anorexia, in which family observations have frequently followed the offspring's life-threatening refusal to eat. Reviews of research on family characteristics do suggest that family patterns are associated with eating disorders; however, there is no single pathway of influence. Such families tended to have a higher incidence of weight problems, physical illness, affective disorder, and alcoholism. In addition, such families could be described as exhibiting controlling interdependent family relationships together with parental discord (Kog and Vandereycken, 1985; Strober and Humphrey, 1987). How and when family variables come into play is complex and difficult to determine (cf. Dare et al., 1994; Thienemann and Steiner, 1993).

In investigating family variables, mother-daughter relationships have been a particular focus. Pike and Rodin (1991), for example, compared mothers whose adolescent daughters reported clinical levels of disordered eating to mothers of daughters with low levels of eating disturbances. Mothers of daughters with disordered eating viewed their daughters as less attractive and were more likely to think their daughters should lose more weight. These mothers were also more dissatisfied with the functioning of their family system. In addition, these mothers were themselves more eating disordered and had different dieting histories than other mothers. Mothers with eating disorders may in fact adversely influence their child's eating behaviors from early in the child's life. Stein et al. (1994) observed the interactions of two groups of mothers with their twelve- to fourteen-month-old infants. Compared to control mothers who had no eating disorder, mothers who had experienced an eating disorder during the year since their child's birth were more intrusive with their infants during both mealtime and play. These mothers also expressed more negative emotion toward their infants during mealtimes. The infants of eating disordered mothers tended to weigh less than controls and infant weight was inversely related to both amount of mealtime conflict and extent of mother's concern about her own body shape.

Several types of biological influences have also been suggested as contributing to the development of eating disorders. Faulty hormonal regulation is suggested by the nature of some of the symptoms associated with anorexia (e.g., amenorrhea) and the fact that onset is frequently around puberty (cf. Russell, 1985). However, many of the physical abnormalities that have been found in anorexics seem to result from starvation rather than cause it (American Psychiatric Association, 1994). For example, the abnormalities are also found in nonanorexic individuals who have reached starvation weight, and hormonal indicators return to normal when adequate weight is gained (Barbosa-Saldivar and Van Italie, 1979; Kaplan and Woodside, 1987).

A genetic contribution to eating disorders has also been suggested (Rutter et al., 1990b). Some genetic explanations of both anorexia and bulimia link them to family patterns of depression. Episodes of depression have been reported in individuals diagnosed as anorexic and bulimic. Also, unusually high incidences of major mood disorders are reported in relatives. Positive response by bulimics to medications employed for mood disorders is also seen as supportive of such a view (e.g., Hudson et al., 1983; Pope et al., 1983). Nevertheless, not all professionals view the data on family patterns of depression in eating disorder patients as indicating a shared genetic etiology (Rutter et al., 1990b; Strober and Katz, 1987).

Treatment. Case reports have suggested that a number of different pharmacological treatments can be successful with eating-disordered patients. Antidepressant medication is reported in controlled studies to be effective for normal-weight bulimic patients. The reason for the effectiveness of antidepressants is less clear, however, since they do not appear to work via their antidepressant properties (Weltzin and Kaye, 1993; Wilson, 1993). Controlled trials of the use of pharmacological approaches with anorexia nervosa are limited and have, in general, yielded negative or equivocal results. With the use of any medication, caution regarding side effects with individuals who are already physiologically at risk is indicated (Yates, 1990).

With respect to psychotherapeutic approaches, Bruch (1973) presented information on the long-term outcome of a number of cases she treated. However, it is difficult to attribute various outcomes to specific therapeutic procedures. Length of contact varied from brief consultation to long-term psychotherapy, and the mode and length of treatment in each case are not sufficiently detailed.

Treatment of anorexia from a cognitive-behavioral perspective has often been conceptualized as consisting of two phases: intervention to restore body weight and save the patient's life, and subsequent extended interventions to ameliorate long-standing adjustment and family difficulties and to maintain normal weight (Fremouw, Seime, and Dainer, 1993). Behavioral interventions have tended to focus on the first phase and to rely almost exclusively on operant learning principles. One of the strengths of this approach has been relatively precise experimental control. These interventions have successfully employed positive and negative consequences contingent on weight change to produce weight gain in a relatively brief period of time (Agras and Kraemer, 1984; Bemis, 1987). Most interventions focused on treating hospitalized patients at a fairly critical point in their illness, and their effectiveness at this life-threatening point is an obvious contribution. However, there was less success regarding long-term maintenance of weight gain, and the social-emotional adjustment of patients after they left the hospital was not addressed. Behavioral investigators themselves (e.g., Foreyt and Kondo, 1985; Garner, 1988; O'Leary and Wilson, 1987) called for the development of more broadly based cognitive-behavioral strategies that addressed both phases of treatment and introduced multimodal treatments (e.g., Fundudis, 1986; Garner, 1988).

Treatment of bulimia nervosa from a cognitive-behavioral perspective involves a multifaceted treatment program (Fairburn and Cooper, 1989). The patient is educated regarding bulimia nervosa and the cognitive view of the disorder is made clear. The emphasis during this early stage is on behavioral techniques employed to reduce binging and compensatory behaviors (e.g., vomiting) and to establish control over eating patterns. These are supplemented with cognitive restructuring techniques, and as treatment progresses there is an increasingly cognitive focus on targeting inappropriate weight-gain concerns and training self-control strategies. Further cognitively oriented interventions then address inappropriate beliefs concerning food, eating, weight, and body image. Finally, a maintenance strategy to sustain improvements and to prevent relapses is also included.

Bulimia has also been viewed within a behavioral perspective as similar to an obsessive-compulsive disorder (Leitenberg et al., 1984). A typical pattern might be as follows: A young person binges. The overeating is due largely to feeling quite anxious or depressed. The immediate effect is that the negative emotion is reduced. However, the person starts feeling distressed about the binge and fears weight gain. Vomiting reduces this fear and the physical discomfort of feeling full. The vomiting can thus be viewed as a negative reinforcement situation. Like the situation of the compulsive handwasher who relieves the fear of contamination and thereby maintains the compulsive behavior. From this perspective, treatments shown to be successful with anxiety disorders (e.g., obsessive-compulsive behaviors) such as exposure and response prevention are suggested. Thus, treatments would be recommended that require the bulimic individual to eat the foods they binge on (exposure) without allowing vomiting afterward (response prevention). Including such an active exposure/prevention component in a cognitive-behavioral treatment program has been reported to do little to enhance outcome (Agras et al., 1989; Leitenberg et al., 1988; Wilson et al., 1991). However, inclusion of this component may be recommended in some cases. Any success of interventions involving exposure and prevention of vomiting does not, of course, mean that the two-factor anxiety reduction explanation, described above, is correct. In-

deed, success might rest on cognitive factors, such as enhanced self-efficacy regarding coping with triggers for vomiting (Wilson and Fairburn, 1993).

Family therapy for eating disorders derives from the observation by clinicians of varying persuasions that the families are intimately involved in the *maintenance* of this behavior. The family systems approach, represented by Minuchin and his colleagues, views the family context as central to many disorders involving somatic symptoms, including anorexia nervosa (Minuchin, Rosman, and Baker, 1978). These investigators criticize other perspectives for continuing to view the locus of pathology as within the individual and for emphasizing the past. Minuchin does employ behavioral procedures to produce weight gain during brief hospitalization or on an outpatient basis.

The families of anorexics, according to Minuchin, can be described as enmeshed. The members of the family do not have distinct identities. Rather, there are diffuse boundaries among family members—they are highly involved in each others' lives. These families are also overprotective and exhibit a high degree of communication of concern. In this kind of family the child learns to subordinate the self (individuality) to family loyalty. In turn, the child is protected by the family, and this further weakens the child's autonomy. This highly enmeshed family is a tightly woven system in which questioning of the system is not permitted. These kinds of families are described as rigid. Even the usual kind of individual life change threatens the family's equilibrium. Adolescence may produce a particularly difficult crisis in such a family. The child's overinvolvement with the family prevents the individualization that is necessary at this time of life, the view of one's self as independent of the family is blurred at best, and peer experience is lacking.

The anorexic's family also has always had a special concern with eating, diet, and rituals pertaining to food. The anorexic adolescent begins to challenge the family system, and rebellion is exhibited through refusal to eat. The family comes to the "protection" of the child—and maintains its stability—by making the child a sick, incompetent person who requires care. The sick role is reinforced, and the child is both protected and scapegoated.

It follows from this conceptualization that the entire family system must be treated. The specific techniques employed vary with the age of the identified patient and the structural characteristics of the family. Although controlled research is lacking, Minuchin and his colleagues (1978) report that 86 percent of the fifty-three cases they treated recovered from both the anorexia and its psychosocial components. Although empirical support for the existence of hypothesized differences in anorexic families is mixed (Dare et al., 1994; Humphrey, 1989; Leon et al., 1985; Thienemann and Steiner, 1993), the logic of family systems therapy seems compelling, and incorporation of family issues into treatment has become part of many approaches to intervention.

Anorexia and bulimia have proven to be complex and difficult to treat. It is generally agreed that they derive from and are maintained by a variety of influences (Garner and Parker, 1993; Strober and Humphrey, 1987; Yates, 1989). Indeed, there is probably considerable heterogeneity among individuals exhibiting these eating disorders. There are not, at present, treatments that are effective for all individuals, nor can we predict which treatments will work for particular individuals. Treatments that address multiple influences thus seem most likely to be effective (Foreyt and McGavin, 1989; Wilson, 1993; Yates, 1990).

Cultural influences. Any discussion of the development and treatment of eating disorders would be incomplete without a clear acknowledgement of potential cultural influences. Our society's emphasis and valu-ing of slim and young bodies, particularly for women, likely contributes to the development and prevalence of such disorders (Mirkin, 1990). These cultural messages are probably carried by family, peers, and the media (Striegel-Moore and Kearney-Cooke, 1994; Stice, 1994). Guillen and Barr (1994), for example, examined the messages contained in articles, advertisements, and other materials in *Seventeen* magazine between the years 1970 and 1990. In this magazine for adolescent women, the primary reasons presented for following a nutrition or fitness plan were to lose weight and become more attractive. Body shapes of models were less curvaceous than those in adult women's magazines and the hip:waist ratio of models decreased over the years studied.

Some authors remind us, however, that these eating styles are not recent phenomena. An appreciation of history may cause us to carefully examine our conceptualization of these eating disorders. There were, for example, a group of women living in the High Middle Ages (thirteenth through sixteenth centuries) who exhibited extreme restrictions of eating and what might be viewed as bizarre and pervasive behaviors and images regarding eating and food (Bell, 1985; Brumberg, 1986). Descriptions of these women bear a remarkable similarity to contemporary eating disorders. The most interesting "twist" to this tale, however, is that these women were later canonized as saints. Bell (1985) chose the term "holy anorexia" to describe these women and call attention to the cultural dimension that is often lost in current diagnostic efforts. Questions such as why a set of behaviors at one time is viewed as pious and at another as a disease force us to address important issues. To say that anorexia merely went undiagnosed in the past fails to appreciate that behaviors that appear similar may have very different origins and meanings? For example, Habermas (1992) has suggested that if fear of becoming overweight is considered as essential in defining eating disorders, then both anorexia and bulimia should be considered historically new syndromes (late nineteenth and early twentieth centuries). This is just one of the many complexities presented when one includes a cultural perspective into thinking about eating or other disorders.

DISORDERS OF ELIMINATION

Toilet training is an important concern for parents of preschool children (Mesibov, Schroeder, and Wesson, 1977; Schroeder and Gordon, 1991). Parents may view control of elimination as a developmental milestone for the child. Furthermore, entry into daycare or another program may depend on achievement of appropriate toileting. For the child, pleasing the parent, a sense of mastery, and no longer being a "baby" may all contribute to the importance of achieving toileting control.

The usual sequence of acquisition of control over elimination is nighttime bowel control, daytime bowel control, daytime bladder control, and finally, nighttime bladder control. While there is considerable variation in children's developmental readiness, bowel and daytime bladder training usually is completed between the ages of eighteen and thirty-six months.

Parents vary as to the age at which they feel it is appropriate to begin daytime training. Much of this decision is related to cultural values, attitudes, and the real-life pressures on the parent (e.g., daycare requirements, other siblings). An example of how day-to-day considerations probably affect this decision is illustrated by the disposable diaper. Ready availability of disposable diapers changed many parents' attitudes toward the desirability of starting training early and perhaps facing difficulty.

There are probably several factors that contribute to successful training. Judging that the child is developmentally ready to begin training is certainly of importance. Also correctly judging when the child has to go to the toilet can lead to important early success experiences. Adequate preparation, such as using training pants rather than a diaper, having the child in clothes that are easy to remove, and having a child-size potty seat available are also helpful. Finally, the common practice of providing praise and positive reinforcement (e.g., stickers, raisins) for appropriate toileting behavior, and doing so in a relaxed manner, has been demonstrated to be effective (O'Leary and Wilson, 1987; Schroeder and Gordon, 1991).

Enuresis

About 50 percent of two-year-olds in the United States display daytime bladder control; this figure rises to 90 percent for four-year-olds. Nighttime bladder control is achieved more slowly. It is achieved by approximately 70 percent of three-year-olds and 90 percent of eight-year-olds (Erickson, 1987). The comparison between daytime and nighttime control is shown in Figure 13–4.

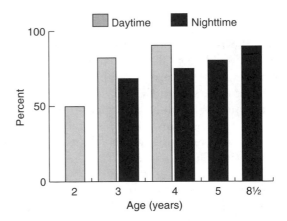

FIGURE 13–4 Percentage of children of various ages achieving daytime and nighttime bladder control.

From Robert M. Liebert, Rita Wicks-Nelson, *Developmental Psychology*: 3rd ed., © 1981, p. 481. Reprinted by permission of Prentice-Hall, Englewood Cliffs, NJ.

The term enuresis comes from the Greek word meaning "I make water." It refers to the repeated voiding of urine during the day or night into the bed or clothes when such voiding is not due to a physical disorder (e.g., diabetes, urinary tract infection). The lack of urinary control is not usually diagnosed as enuresis prior to the age of five. (Doleys, 1989). The frequency of lack of control necessary for diagnosis varies with the age of the child. Often at least two such events per month is the criterion for children five to six years of age, with less frequent wetting required for the diagnosis of enuresis in older children.

A distinction is often made between the more common nocturnal enuresis (nighttime bed wetting) and diurnal (daytime) enuresis. Enuresis is also referred to as "primary" if the child has never demonstrated bladder control, and secondary when the problem is preceded by a period of urinary continence. About 85 percent of all cases of enuresis are of the primary type (Walker, Kenning, and Faust-Campanile, 1989).

The causes of enuresis. A number of factors have been proposed as causes of enuresis, but no definitive cause has been established. At one time the view that enuresis was the result of emotional disturbance was widely held (e.g., Gerard, 1939). More recent evidence does not support this view (Christophersen and Edwards, 1992). When emotional difficulties are also present in a child with enuresis, they may be a consequence of enuresis rather than a cause. Enuretic children, especially as they become older, are very likely to experience difficulties with peers and other family members. It would not be surprising if the child's self-image suffered (Wagner, Smith and Norris, 1988). It may also be the case that enuresis and emotional problems occur in the same children because similar factors contribute to the development of both. For example, a chaotic home environment may contribute to both inadequate toilet training and behavior problems.

It is frequently suggested that sleep abnormalities contribute to the development of enuresis. Many adults, for example, assume that nocturnal enuresis occurs because the child is an unusually deep sleeper. Indeed, parents often spontaneously report difficulty in arousing their enuretic children during the night. However, research regarding the role of sleep and arousal is inconsistent (Doleys, 1989). It appears that wetting can occur in any of the stages of sleep, not just in "deep sleep." This and other evidence raises doubts about viewing enuresis as a disorder of sleep arousal (King and Noshpitz, 1991; Walker et al., 1989).

Family histories of enuretics frequently reveal a number of relatives with the same problem (Christophersen and Edwards, 1992). In a study of Israeli kibbutz children there was a markedly greater incidence of bed wetting among the siblings of enuretic children than among siblings of dry children. This association existed even though each sibling had been toilet trained by a separate caretaker in a different communal house (Kaffman and Elizur, 1977). Also higher rates of concordance for enuresis among monozygotic than dizygotic twins have been reported (e.g., Bakwin, 1971). These results strongly suggest that at least some portion of enuretic children may have an organic predisposition toward enuresis. This, as yet unspecified, risk factor may or may not result in the development of enuresis, depending upon various experiential factors, such as parental attitude and training procedures.

The central tenet of behavioral theories of enuresis is that wetting results from a failure to learn control over reflexive wetting. This failure can result from either faulty training or other environmental influences that interfere with learning (e.g., a chaotic or stressful home environment). Many behavioral theories incorporate some maturational/physical difficulty such as bladder capacity or arousal deficit into their explanation.

Treatment approaches.   Prior to beginning any treatment, the child should be evaluated by a physician to rule out any medical cause for the urinary difficulties. Also, if a parent seeks treatment for a very young child, a discussion of developmental norms may be helpful. Finally, if treatment for enuresis is to be initiated, careful preparation and ensuring of parental cooperation are necessary.

A variety of drugs have been used in the treatment of enuresis. Imipramine hydrochloride (Tofranil), a tricyclic antidepressant, is probably the most commonly employed. The specific mechanisms responsible for imipramine's action are not well understood; however, improvement does not seem to be due to the drug's antidepressant properties or its effect on sleep (Doleys, 1989; King and Noshpitz, 1991). Although a number of studies have demonstrated that imipramine is superior to placebos (e.g., Fritz, Rockney, and Yeung, 1994), the effect seems to rely on the child continuing to take the drug, and it appears that it is not as successful as the urine-alarm procedure, which is described below. Moreover, there is reason for concern regarding possible side effects (Christophersen and Edwards, 1992; Walker et al., 1989).

Another medication, desmopressin, has been suggested as a treatment based on its ability to control high urine output during sleep. Results comparable to those with imipramine have been reported. However, relapse occurs if the drug is discontinued, and cost and potential side effects are also of concern (Warady, Alon, and Hellerstein, 1991).

Behavioral treatments for nocturnal enuresis have received considerable research attention (Doleys, 1989; Houts, Berman, and Abramson, 1994; Walker et al., 1989). The most well known of these

methods is the urine-alarm or bell-and-pad system. This procedure was originally introduced by the German pediatrician Pflaunder in 1904 and was adapted and systematically applied by Mowrer and Mowrer (1938). Since then the device and the procedures have been refined by a number of investigators. The basic device consists of an absorbent bed sheet between two foil pads. When urine is absorbed by the sheet, an electric circuit is completed that activates an alarm that sounds until manually turned off. Newer models use a system that is attached to the child's underpants and to the nightclothes or a small wristwatch-type alarm (see Figure 13–5). The parents are instructed to awaken the child when the alarm sounds. The child is taught to turn off the alarm and go to the bathroom to finish voiding. The bedding is then changed, and the child returns to sleep. Usually records of dry and wet nights are kept, and after four-

FIGURE 13–5 A urine alarm for treatment of enuresis. The child wears a urine sensor in the underclothes attached to an alarm worn on the nightclothes or wrist.

teen consecutive nights of dryness, the device is removed.

According to the Mowrers, the procedure is based upon classical conditioning. Tension of the full bladder (the conditioned stimulus) is paired with the alarm (unconditioned stimulus) to produce awakening (the conditioned response) and inhibition of urination. Eventually the child wakens in response to a full bladder prior to wetting and setting off the alarm. Lovibond (1964) proposed an alternative theoretical explanation—avoidance learning. He suggested that the child learns to inhibit urination in order to avoid the aversive consequences of being awakened by the alarm.

Research conducted on the urine-alarm system indicates that it is successful in 70 to 90 percent of the cases, with treatment durations of between five and twelve weeks. The urine-alarm system also proved to be superior to placebo, no-treatment, and verbal psychotherapy groups, and to achieve success rates greater than those reported for imipramine (Doleys, 1989; Houts et al., 1994). However, relapse has been reported to occur in about 46 percent of cases. Reinstituting training often results in a complete cure, however (Christophersen and Edwards, 1992).

Two modifications of the standard urine-alarm procedures have been found to reduce relapses (Walker et al., 1989). In the *intermittent alarm procedure* the alarm sounds subsequent to some percentage of wettings rather than to each wetting (continuous alarm procedure). With *overlearning*, once the initial criterion for dryness is met, the child's intake of liquids prior to bedtime is increased, and the urine-alarm procedure is continued for some period of time.

A multifaceted and low-cost treatment developed by Houts, Liebert, and Padawar (1983) illustrates the way in which behavioral interventions have been combined in the treatment of nocturnal enuresis. Full Spectrum Home Training was designed to build upon the success of behavioral treatments such as the urine-alarm in achieving initial treatment success. It was also designed to reduce relapse and decrease the rate at which families dropped out of treatment. The procedure is also cost effective. It is a treatment manual-guided package that includes bell-and-pad, cleanliness training (having the child change his or her bed and night clothes), a procedure to increase bladder capacity known as retention control training, and overlearning. The training program is delivered in a single one-hour group session and a contract is completed by parents and children to complete the training at home with regular calls from the treatment staff as the only additional contact.

A study by Houts, Peterson, and Whelan (1986) illustrates the program's success and examines the contribution of the components to reducing relapse. Participating families received one of three treatment combinations: Group 1 received bell-and-pad plus cleanliness training (BP), Group 2 these two components plus retention control training (BP-RCT), and Group 3 these three components plus overlearning (BP–RCT–OL)—the full package. A control group of children was followed over an eight-week period. No spontaneous remission of wetting occurred in control children, and they were then randomly assigned to one of the three treatment conditions.

The findings of this study are illustrated in Table 13–3. While the proportion of success versus failure plus dropouts was slightly greater in the BP–RCT condition, these differences were not statistically significant. The three conditions were also equivalent in terms of the number of dry nights during training. At three-month follow-up, relapse was significantly less in the BP–RCT–OL group than in the other two groups. These results suggest the importance of overlearning in preventing initial relapse.

TABLE 13–3   Results of Treating Enuresis with Components of Full Spectrum Home Training

Group/Assessment time	Success Percent	Failure Percent	Dropout Percent	Relapse Percent
Group 1				
End of treatment	60	20	20	
Three-month follow-up				44
Group 2				
End of treatment	87	0	13	
Three-month follow-up				62
Group 3				
End of treatment	60	27	13	
Three-month follow-up				11

Adapted from Houts, Peterson, and Whelan, 1986. Copyright (1986) by the Association for Advancement of Behavior Therapy. Reprinted by permission of the publisher and the author.

Encopresis

Functional encopresis refers to the passage of feces into the clothing or other unacceptable area when this is not due to physical disorder. The diagnosis is given when this event occurs at least once a month in a child of at least four years of age (American Psychiatric Association, 1994). A primary-secondary encopresis distinction, similar to the distinction made for enuresis, refers to whether the child exhibited a previous period of bowel control.

Less writing and research have been done concerning encopresis than concerning enuresis. Estimates of the incidence of encopresis range from 0.3 to 8 percent of children. Percentages appear to decrease with age, being very rare by adolescence, and the problem occurs more frequently in males (Doleys, 1989). Pediatricians, who are likely to see unselected populations of children, argue that the majority of encopretics have no associated psychopathology, a position supported by other workers (Christophersen and Edwards, 1992; King and Noshpitz, 1991). To the extent that associated psychological difficulties do exist, they may be a consequence rather than an antecedent of the encopresis or both may be related to common environmental factors (e.g., stressful family circumstances).

The causes of encopresis. Most theories acknowledge encopresis may result from a variety of causative mechanisms. Initial constipation/soiling may be influenced by factors such as diet, fluid intake, medications, environmental stresses, or inappropriate toilet training. The rectum and colon may become distended by the hard feces. The bowel then becomes incapable of responding with a normal defecation reflex to normal amounts of fecal matter.

Medical perspectives on the problem tend to stress a neurodevelopmental approach (Doleys, 1989). Encopresis is viewed as more likely to occur in the presence of developmental inadequacies in the structure and functioning of the physiological and anatomical mechanisms required for bowel control. These organic inadequacies are viewed as temporary.

As is the case in enuresis, psychodynamically oriented theorists tend to view encopresis as a sign of some deeper conflict. Recent psychodynamic explanations tend to place more emphasis on family and social context, particularly disruptions in the mother-child relationship (Bemporad, 1978; Pierce, 1985).

The behavioral perspective on encopresis stresses faulty toilet training procedures. Primary encopresis is largely explained by a failure to apply appropriate training methods consistently. Secondary encopresis is accounted for by avoidance conditioning principles. Pain or fear avoidance reinforces retention. Positive consequences may also maintain soiling, and inadequate reinforcement may be given for appropriate toileting (Doleys, 1989). These various learning explanations are not incompatible with physiological explanations. For example, insufficient physiological-neurological mechanisms may be compounded by poor child training.

Treatment approaches. Most treatments for encopresis combine medical and behavioral management (Doleys, 1988; Houts, Mellon, and Whelan, 1988; Walker, Milling, and Bonner, 1988). After educating the parent and child about encopresis, the first step usually consists of the use of enemas to eliminate fecal impactions. Next parents are asked to schedule regular toilet times and to use suppositories if defecation does not occur. Modifications in diet, laxatives, and stool softeners are employed to facilitate defecation. Positive consequences, such as a shared activity chosen by the child, are used to reward unassisted (no suppository) bowel movements in the toilet and clean pants. If soiling occurs children may be instructed to clean themselves and their clothes. Use of laxatives and suppositories are withdrawn. Research suggests that such treatment is highly effective, with success rates up to 100 percent and low relapse rates. As we might expect, program success and duration are related to parental consistency in carrying out the program (Walker et al., 1989).

SLEEP DISORDERS

It is common for parents to complain that their children are having sleep problems. To understand children's sleep disorders and to help parents judge whether and how their child's sleep is problematic, it is necessary to understand the variations in what is normal sleep for children.

At all ages there are wide individual variations in what would be considered normal sleep patterns. Furthermore, patterns of sleep change with development (Horne, 1992). For example, the average newborn infant sleeps about sixteen hours per day. However, variations of four hours more or less are not uncommon. By the time children are one year old, the average amount of sleep has fallen to twelve hours. The typical ten- or eleven-year-old sleeps about eight hours each day. In addition to the number of hours of sleep, other aspects change as well. Newborns distribute their sleeping equally between day and night. Fortunately for parents, by about eight weeks infants begin to develop signs of the day-night pattern typical in adults and by eighteen months sleep patterns are usually more stable. The time spent in different stages of sleep also varies and changes with development. In the first year of life, for example, active or rapid eye movement (REM) sleep changes from about eight hours to about half this amount, thus also reducing the proportion of time spent in REM relative to other phases of sleep. The sequencing or patterns in which the various stages of sleep occur also changes. The phases of sleep are intermixed in irregular patterns in infants. However as the child develops, regular patterns of light, deep, or slow wave sleep, and REM sleep are gradually established.

In this context then, what are the most common complaints regarding children's sleep and how are disorders of sleep defined? During the first year of life, the parents' most frequent complaint is that the child does not sleep through the night. A reluctance to go to sleep and nightmares often occur during the second year, and the three- to five-year-old presents a variety of problems, including difficulty in going to sleep, nighttime awakenings, and nightmares. Surveys suggest that approximately 25 percent of one- to five-year-olds experience some form of sleep disturbance (Mindell, 1993). Even in adolescence complaints regarding sleep are common, particularly the need for more sleep and difficulty in falling asleep. Indeed, while many might think of sleep problems as being associated with young children, about one-third of adolescents in a general population sample reported at least one sleep problem that occurred at least four times per week (Morrison, McGee, and Stanton, 1992). Sleep problems seem to persist as well. Across age groups, follow-ups of one to three years suggest that the child's sleep problems continue to occur (Kataria, Swanson, and Trevathan, 1987; Morrison et al., 1992; Pollock, 1994).

Sleep difficulties are experienced by many children and are not necessarily associated with other psychological or behavioral difficulties. Indeed, if a sleep problem does not cause the child significant distress or result in impairment in social, educational, or other important areas of functioning, then it would not be considered a diagnosable mental disorder (DSM-IV). However, in some instances sleep difficulties may be associated with or predictors of other behavioral problems (e.g., Pollock, 1994).

One reason that sleep difficulties and other childhood problems may occur together is that they may be two manifestations of a common set of etiological mechanisms. Garland and Smith's (1991) description of the case of a nine-year nine-month-old boy illustrates this possibility. The boy was well until he began experiencing partial awakenings approximately two hours after sleep onset. These were accompanied by a fearful appearance, a "racing heart," sweating, crying out, motor agitation, and mumbled fragments of sleep talking. The boy eventually returned to sleep without full awakening and had no memory of the event or its content. This sleep difficulty is often referred to as night (or sleep) terrors and is described below. Within a couple of weeks of the onset of these nightly

attacks, the boy began experiencing spontaneous daytime panic attacks. Within four months these panic attacks were occurring several times per day and led to the boy being repeatedly sent home from school. As the frequency of the attacks increased, anticipatory anxiety and overanxious symptoms also developed involving worries about school performance despite "A" grades, and fears about the safety of family members, earthquakes, or accidents.

The child's pediatrician found no physical cause for the episodes, but the persistence and severity of the problems resulted in a psychiatric consultation being sought. Interviews indicated a family history of anxiety difficulties. In addition, over time, several precipitants of the child's problems were revealed. Severe marital problems, including extramarital affairs on the part of the child's father and an in-home separation of the parents, not discussed with the children, were revealed. The boy had also experienced a hockey accident that damaged his teeth, and intense competition among several friends for school grades was reported.

A combination of imipramine, education regarding the nature of the disorders, relaxation techniques, and parent counseling regarding the potential role of marital stressors are reported to have been highly effective. The sleep problem, panic attacks, and other anxiety problems ceased, the boy returned to school and all activities, and his self-confidence was restored. The authors hypothesized that both night terrors and panic attacks involve a similar constitutional vulnerability related to dysregulation of the brainstem alerting systems.

Sleep disorders are usually classified into two major categories: *dyssomnias* or difficulties in initiating and maintaining sleep or of excessive sleepiness; and *parasomnias* or disorders of arousal, partial arousal, or sleep-stage transitions (American Sleep Disorders Association, 1990; American Psychiatric Association, 1994).

Establishing a predictable bedtime routine is helpful in reducing children's sleep problems.

(Ken Karp)

Dyssomnias

The problems that parents commonly report of difficulty in getting children to sleep and having them sleep through the night, if severe and chronic enough, fall into this category. These sleep and waking problems are indeed common and often occur together. They frequently are viewed as manifestations of the child's neurophysiological development and therefore expected to eventually clear up. However, child, parental, and environmental factors do seem to play a role in a substantial number of cases. For example, a comparison of poor sleepers and good sleepers, between twelve and thirty-six months of age, revealed some surprising findings (Minde et al., 1993). Mothers' sleep diaries indicated more night wakings for the poor sleepers. However, filmed recordings indicated no differences in the actual number of wakings for the two groups. The poor sleepers were unable or unwilling to go back

to sleep and woke their parent. In contrast, good sleepers were able to return to sleep on their own by either looking around and falling asleep or quieting themselves by, for example, hugging a toy animal or sucking their thumbs. Whatever the cause, these problems may persist over many years and they can result in considerable distress to the families involved (Richman et al., 1985; Scott and Richards, 1990).

It is often difficult to discriminate between "true" cases of insomnia and attention seeking. Does the child call to the parent "I can't sleep" or "I woke up" to get parental attention or is he or she experiencing genuine sleep difficulties? Perhaps some genuine sleep problems go unreported because they are dealt with as "attention needs," or, in contrast, perhaps what are viewed as sleep problems are not really that. Before working with a family it is important for the parents to feel secure that the sleep problem is not due to some "genuine" cause such as colic, sleep apnea (obstruction of the airways causing breathing difficulties), or real fears on the child's part. Also, infants' and young children's difficulties may be associated with feeding practices. Sleep difficulties may be caused by the child's being accustomed to nighttime feedings or large nighttime feedings leading to wetting or discomfort. Milk intolerance may also account for some sleep difficulties. In such cases, removal of milk products from the diet should result in normalization of sleep after a relatively short period of time (Horne, 1992).

The child's level of cognitive development is also a factor. In order for children to recognize a sleep problem they must be able to conceptualize difficulties in initiating and maintaining sleep as such (Wilson and Haynes, 1985). In older children sleep problems may also be associated with reports of worrisome cognitions—concerns about school or peers, ruminatious about past or anticipated experiences, or fears. In addition, adolescents may have difficulty in establishing good sleep habits in the context of their changing life style.

Pharmacological agents have been among the most widely used treatments; however, there is not good support for their effectiveness and there is concern regarding negative side effects (e.g., Richman, 1985). Behavioral approaches to the problems of initiating and maintaining children's sleep have included the use of relaxation, but, especially for young children, have focused on the consequences applied to the child's behaviors and techniques of stimulus control (Wilson and Haynes, 1985; Bootzin and Chambers, 1990). So, for example, attention given to the child after saying goodnight can be withdrawn, praise and/or star charts for desired behavior can be given, and a distinct bedtime routine that makes the signs for going to sleep clear can be developed (Durand and Mindell, 1990; Minde, Faucon, and Faulkner, 1994; Richman et al., 1985).

Parasomnias

Several of the childhood sleep disorders that cause concern for parents fall in the second category of parasomnias. These include sleepwalking, sleep terrors, and nightmares.

Sleepwalking. Sleepwalking (somnambulism) begins with the child sitting upright in bed. The eyes are open but appear "unseeing." Usually the child leaves the bed and walks around, but the episode may end before the walking stage is reached. An episode may last for a few seconds or thirty minutes or longer. There is usually no later memory of the episode. It was once believed that the sleepwalking child was exceptionally well coordinated and safe. This has proven to be a myth and although physical injury is rare, it is one danger of the disorder.

Approximately 15 percent of children between the ages of five and twelve have isolated experiences of walking in their sleep. Sleepwalking disorder, that is, persistent sleepwalking, is estimated to occur in 1 to 6 percent of the population. Somnambulism usually persists for a number of years but then disappears by adolescence (American Psychiatric Association, 1994).

The vast majority of sleepwalking episodes occur in the first one to three hours following sleep onset. Sleepwalking occurs during stages of non-REM sleep (deep sleep). This appears to invalidate the idea that sleepwalking is the acting out of a dream, since dreams occur in REM sleep. A characteristic EEG pattern has been found to precede each episode. This EEG pattern exists in 85 percent of all children during the first year of life but is present in only 3 percent of seven to nine-year-olds. Thus it has been suggested that central nervous system immaturity is of significance in sleepwalking disorder, and knowledge that the disorder is usually outgrown is consistent with that conceptualization. This does not, however, rule out psychological or environmental factors. Frequency of sleepwalking has been reported to be influenced by the specific setting, stress, fatigue, and physical illness (American Psychiatric Association, 1994; Mindell, 1993). Greater concordance rates for sleepwalking among monozygotic twins than among dizygotic twins and family patterns of sleepwalking have also been reported, leading some to propose a genetic component to the disorder. Unlike adults, the presence of sleepwalking in children has not been found to be associated with any psychological disturbance (Dollinger, 1986).

Sleep terrors and nightmares. Both sleep terrors and nightmares are fright reactions that occur during sleep. Sleep terrors, also known as night terrors or pavor nocturnus, are experienced by from 1 to 6 percent of children and are more common in males. Sleep terrors typically occur between the ages of four and twelve. Nightmares and sleep terrors are often confused, but they differ in a number of ways (see Table 13–4).

Sleep terrors occur during deep, slow-wave sleep and at a fairly constant time, usually about two hours into sleep. The sleep terror is quite striking in that the still-sleeping child suddenly sits upright in bed and screams. The face shows obvious distress, and there are signs of autonomic arousal, such as rapid breathing and dilated pupils. In addition, repetitive motor movements may occur, and the child appears disoriented and confused. Attempts to comfort the child are largely unsuccessful. The child most often returns to sleep without full awakening and has little or no memory of this event the next morning. The conceptualization of the causes of sleep terrors is similar to that described above for sleepwalking (cf. Wilson and Haynes, 1985) and, indeed, they occur in the same part of the sleep cycle.

In many cases of sleep terrors and sleep walking treatment may not be indicated since the episodes usually disappear spontaneously. However, a number of treatments have been suggested. These include response interruption, contingency management, instructional procedures, and anxiety reduction procedures (Dollinger, 1986; Wilson and Haynes, 1985). Since the literature consists of case studies, one cannot say whether these treatments were responsible for reported changes. Drug treatments of both disorders have also been reported; however, these medications may actually produce effects that set the stage for recurrences of these disorders (Wilson and Haynes, 1985).

TABLE 13–4 Characteristics Differentiating Nightmares and Sleep Terrors

Nightmares	*Sleep Terrors*
Occur during REM sleep	Occur during Non-REM sleep
During middle and latter portions of the night	During first third of night
Verbalizations, if any, are subdued	Child wakes with cry or scream and verbalizations usually present
Only moderate physiological arousal	Intense physiological arousal (increased heart rate, profuse sweating, pupils dilated)
Slight or no movements	Motor activity, agitation
Easy to arouse and responsive to environment	Difficult to arouse and unresponsive to environment
Episodes frequently remembered	Very limited or no memory of the episode
Quite common	Somewhat rare (1 to 4 percent)

Adapted from Wilson and Haynes, 1985.

Nightmares are the other fright reaction that occurs during sleep and are common in children between the ages of three and six years (American Sleep Disorders Association, 1990). These dreams occur during REM sleep. It is frequently thought that the dreams are a direct manifestation of anxieties that the child faces. It has been suggested that children typically extinguish their fears by gradually exposing themselves during daytime hours to the feared stimulus (Kellerman, 1980). Some events, such as parental protectiveness, however, might restrict the child's ability to engage in such exposure, and thus the anxieties and the associated nightmares continue or are exacerbated.

No single theoretical framework has proven successful in explaining the development of nightmares, and explanations allowing for multiple causality (e.g., developmental, physiological, and environmental factors) are most likely to have the greatest utility (Wilson and Haynes, 1985). Consistent with anxiety being viewed as the basis for nightmares, the majority of treatments have involved anxiety reduction techniques. However, no treatment strategy can be stated as most effective, nor are the active components of the various treatments known.

SUMMARY

A number of eating disorders have received attention from researchers and clinicians. Of these, obesity and anorexia/bulimia have probably generated the most interest. Behavioral and biological explanations of the etiology of obesity have probably received the greatest support. The learning of adaptive eating and activity patterns are the basis of behavioral treatment programs. This approach to treatment is probably the most successful; however, greater weight loss and better maintenance results still need to be achieved.

The appropriate way to classify and conceptualize the eating disorders of anorexia and bulimia has received considerable attention. Anorexia nervosa is a serious, life-threatening disorder characterized by extreme weight loss. A number of other physical and psychological problems are present as well. The distinction between restricting and bulimic anorexics has received support. Biological, psychodynamic, cognitive-behavioral, and family systems theorists have all offered explanations for this puzzling phenomenon. An explanation that incorporates multiple influences is most likely, but no particular explanation is clearly supported. The treatment of anorexia has been conceptualized as a two-phase process—resumption of eating with associated weight gain and maintenance of improvement and treatment of associated problems. Anorexia has proven difficult to treat.

Bulimia refers to a repeated pattern of binge eating followed by some compensatory mechanism. Purging and nonpurging subtypes are distinguished in DSM-IV. Cognitive-behavioral treatments are presently considered the most effective intervention.

Increasing prevalence of eating-disordered behavior and attitudes among younger girls has been noted. The importance of cultural influences must be considered in any explanations of eating disorders.

Enuresis and encopresis are disorders of elimination that seem best explained by a combination of biological predisposition and failure to train and/or learn bodily control. The use of imipramine is the most popular and best-supported medically oriented procedure for treating enuresis. Behavioral interventions based on classical conditioning and operant learning theories have reported high success rates and low rates of remission and seem to be the treatments of choice at present. Encopresis, which has received considerably less attention, is probably best dealt with through a combination of medical (for example, enemas) and behavioral (for example, reinforcement) procedures.

Difficulties in initiating and maintaining sleep are most effectively dealt with by establishing bedtime routines and the appropriate cues for sleep. Sleep disorders such as sleepwalking and sleep terrors are probably best conceptualized as resulting from a combination of nervous system immaturity and environmental factors. At present the effectiveness of various treatments remains unclear.

14

PSYCHOLOGICAL FACTORS AFFECTING MEDICAL CONDITION

This chapter continues the discussion of the problems of physical conditions and health. The topics discussed here would in the past have come under the heading of psychosomatic disorders. The main focus of interest was on actual physical conditions such as asthma, headaches, ulcers, and nausea. These were known or presumed to be affected by psychological factors. The terminology for describing these disorders has undergone a number of changes in the last few decades. The term Psychosomatic Disorders was replaced in DSM-II by Psychophysiological Disorders, and in DSM-III and III-R with the term Psychological Factors Affecting Physical Condition. Most recently the term has been modified in DSM-IV to Psychological Factors Affecting Medical Condition.

A CHANGING PERSPECTIVE

The uncertainty over terminology reflects a longstanding controversy over the nature of the relationship between mind and body, the psyche and the soma. One of the most influential statements concerning the mind-body problem is found in the writing of René Descartes, the early seventeenth-century French philosopher. Descartes, influenced by strong religious beliefs, viewed human beings as part divine and as possessing a soul (mind) that somehow must affect the mechanics of the body. The point of contact between the two systems was presumed to be the pineal gland, located in the midbrain. This version of mind-body dualism was part of a long history of shifting opinion about whether or how spiritual or psychological factors affected bodily conditions.

During the twentieth century interest in the impact of psychological processes on the body resulted in the development of the field of psychosomatic medicine. Early workers began to accumulate evidence and develop theories of how psychological factors played a causative role in specific physical disorders (e.g., Alexander, 1950; Grace and Graham, 1952; Selye, 1956). As this field developed, several trends emerged. An increasing number of physical disorders were seen to be related to psychological factors. Even the common cold was thought to be affected by emotional factors. The question therefore arose as to whether it was fruitful to identify a specific group of psychosomatic disorders or whether psychological factors were operating in all physical conditions. In addition, the focus began to shift from psychogenesis, that is psychological cause, to multicausality, the idea that social and psychological (as well as biological) factors all contribute to both health and illness at multiple points. The latter view is holistic, assuming a continuous transaction among influences. This broad scope and interactive perspective has continued to develop (cf. Eiser, 1994; Maier, Watkins, and Fleshner, 1994; Wood, 1994).

With this shift in thinking, the field began to expand considerably. The ongoing role of social and psychological factors in medical conditions; the social, psychological and developmental consequences of medical conditions; the role of psychological treatments for physical disorders; social and psychological aspects of medical treatments; and the role of social and psychological variables in prevention and health maintenance all began to receive increased attention (cf. Drotar, 1981; Routh, Schroeder, and Koocher, 1983; Winett, 1995). Indeed, the concept of psychosomatic disorders as physical conditions caused by emotional factors became inadequate to encompass this expanded perspective (Tuma, 1982). Writers began to suggest other definitions (cf. Wright, 1977), and various other terms came into existence, such as *behavioral medicine, health psychology,* and the term most commonly used in reference to children, *pediatric psychology.*

This chapter is in keeping with these changes. However, it is clearly not possible to survey this rapidly expanding field completely. Whole volumes have been dedicated to the topic or segments of it (e.g., Friedman, Fisher, and Schonberg, 1992; LaGreca et al., 1992) and several scientific journals have emerged to deal exclusively with research in this area (e.g., *Journal of Pediatric Psychology, Behavioral Medicine, Health Psychology*). In this chapter we will examine some of the specific medical problems of children that have received the attention of psychologists and some selected other topics of interest. This will allow us to illustrate the changes that have occurred and the current status and diversity of this field.

AN EXAMPLE OF A CHANGING FOCUS: ASTHMA

In this section we will look at information on asthma in young people. We will see how thinking about the role of psychological variables in physical illness has changed and expanded. Asthma is an example of a disorder for which the early focus was on psychological causation. One particular interest was and continues to be the role of the family in asthma. Thus, this section will also introduce one of the interests of contemporary pediatric psychology, the role of the family in the youngster's illness.

Before beginning our discussion it would also be wise to remember that interest is not limited to a particular issue and a single disorder. For example, the involvement of family in the youngster's illness is clearly relevant to disorders other than asthma. Relatedly, in thinking about any disorder it is likely that many issues will be relevant. Thus, other issues that are dealt with elsewhere in the chapter, for example compliance with treatment recommendations, are relevant to asthma as well. It is important to keep this overlap and complexity in mind and to understand that a simple one-to-one matching of disorders and issues is not a reality. Rather the grouping of issues and disorders is a convenience we have employed to organize information.

Description of Asthma

Asthma is a disorder of the respiratory system. Hyperresponsiveness of the trachea, bronchi, and bronchioles to various stimuli occur with the result that the air passages are narrowed and air exchange is impaired, particularly during expiration. This produces intermittent episodes of wheezing and shortness of breath (dyspnea). Within the same individual as well as across individuals attacks may vary in severity. Thus asthma is an illness that is quite unpredictable, a problem for both research and management of the disorder. Severe attacks, known as *status asthmaticus,* which are life threatening and require emergency medical treatment, are another challenge in treating asthmatic children. The fear of not being able to breathe and the danger of severe attacks are likely to create appreciable anxiety in the young person and family members.

Prevalence and prognosis. Asthma is the most common chronic disease in young people (Newacheck and Taylor, 1992). Based on information from the National Center for Health Statistics, 6.7 percent of youngsters between the ages of three and seventeen are asthmatic (Gergen, Mullally, and Evans, 1988). The impact of the disease on the youngster is considerable. In addition to the psychological difficulties experienced by some young people, many school days are lost due to asthma.

Clearly, the greatest threat is loss of life, and all measures used to treat the physical symptoms of asthma—daily medication to prevent wheezing, environmental control of potential irritants, desensitization to allergens, avoidance of infection, and emergency treatment to stop wheezing—are geared to prevent death. Although much has been done to improve the treatment of asthma, reports of increasing prevalence as well as increases in hospitalization and mortality rates are reasons for continuing concern (Wilson et al., 1993).

Causation. The causes of asthma are complex, and there is a considerable history of controversy concerning etiology. However, it is broadly acknowledged that genetic or other factors place some youngsters at risk for developing asthma. Figure 14–1 presents a simplified schematic description of the asthmatic process. Some cause or variety of causes produces a hypersensitivity of the air passages. Once established, this hypersensitivity results in the youngster responding to a variety of irritants more easily

than would a nonasthmatic individual. The resulting wheezing and shortness of breath may have additional psychological consequences. Anxiety and fear may occur in anticipation of attacks or during them. This in itself may be a contributing irritant that increases the probability or intensity of attacks. A second class of possible psychological consequences is dependency, isolation from peers, and other behavior problems that may result from the management of the asthmatic youngster's physical symptoms.

Whatever its etiology, individuals with highly sensitive and labile respiratory tracts are potentially exposed to a second set of factors that influence whether or not asthmatic attacks occur. This second set of influences has come to be thought of as trigger mechanisms or irritants rather than as causes of asthma. It is widely held that a variety of agents can trigger wheezing in different individuals or on different occasions for the same individual (Creer and Reynolds, 1990).

Repeated respiratory infection may play a role in the development of asthma, and respiratory viral infections can set off or worsen the severity of an attack. It has been recognized that viral infections are transmitted through some type of close contact, for example, from the nasal mucosa to the hand and then to the hand of another. The fact that such infections are likely transmitted to individuals via modifiable behaviors has led some investigators to develop behavioral interventions designed to directly modify such behaviors (e.g., Corley et al., 1987).

Allergies may also be related to the development and occurrence of asthmatic attacks. Allergies may exist to inhaled substances such as dust, the dander of a pet, pollen, or to ingested substances such as milk, wheat, or chocolate. Physical factors such as cold temperatures, tobacco smoke, pungent odors, and exercise and rapid breathing may also contribute to wheezing. Further, psychological stimuli and emotional upset are often considered important

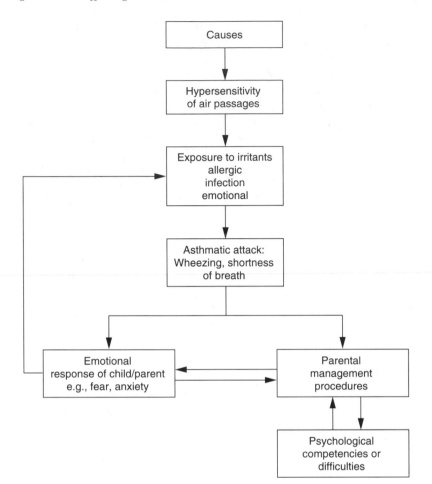

FIGURE 14–1   Schematic diagram of a general model for the development of asthma and its concomitant psychosocial effects.

triggers of asthma attacks (Creer and Reynolds, 1990; Miller and Wood, 1994).

Indeed, it is virtually impossible to assess and analyze asthma without recognizing the multiple psychological factors involved (Williamson, Head, and Baker, 1993). This is powerfully illustrated in an early description by Alexander of the young asthmatic patient.

The early-onset asthma patient and his or her family face some very severe hardships. . . . They face both peers and adults who are variously overindulgent, or lacking in understanding of their difficulties. . . . At home their asthma may

become the sole focus around which all family activities and concerns come to revolve. Their parents may feel responsible, guilty, and helpless; and at other times resentful and angry. Certainly, an asthma sufferer can learn to manipulate others with the disorder, or use it to avoid unpleasant activities or situations. It is also often difficult for the patient to sort out clearly what he or she can really do, from what is accomplished in the face of asthma. Many maladaptive and inappropriate behavior patterns can develop, as patient and family struggle with the ravages of this disorder. Such patterns can severely cripple family life and retard the social and psychological development of the child. Often, the undesirable behavior patterns affect the course of the disorder substantially. Asthma is, of course, potentially life-threatening, and many patients have experienced bouts of status asthmaticus, which on occasion may have brought them close to death. Such experiences often generate enduring anxiety responses which can manifest themselves in fears of death, hospitals, and treatment. Some patients develop conditioned fear responses, which can begin at even the first signs of wheezing. The frantic, worried behavior of parents and those treating the patient can exacerbate the young patient's fears. Moods, too, vary with the severity of symptoms and also in relation to medication taken. . . (Alexander, 1980, p. 274).

Although we have come to view the causes of asthma differently, in much of the early literature asthma was viewed primarily as a disease with psychological causes. Such

disturbances were often attributed to the family.

Role of the Family

Probably the earliest and most widely known psychosomatic explanation of asthma was the psychoanalytic explanation originally offered by French and Alexander (1941). Asthma was hypothesized to arise from an excessive, unresolved dependence on the mother and a resultant fear of separation. The symptoms of wheezing and shortness of breath were viewed as "a suppressed cry for the mother," brought on because crying, and the desire for the mother it represents, become intolerable to the par-

Parental concern over precipitating a symptomatic attack may often lead children with chronic illnesses, such as asthma, to spend appreciable time isolated from their peers.

By permission of U.S. Department of Health and Human Services—Public Health Service (ADM, 77–497).

ent. French and Alexander were clearly influenced by their psychoanalytic training and much of the support for this theory came from other psychoanalysts and from individual case studies. Research studies designed to evaluate the hypothesis often suffered from serious methodological flaws (Freeman et al., 1964) or failed to demonstrate the hypothesized relationships (e.g., McLean and Ching, 1973). It is probably important to examine the specifics of this hypothesis and its validity, however, since as Creer (1982) has pointed out, French and Alexander's ideas about psychological factors and asthma had as much impact as anything written. Moreover, these ideas were applied to other disorders.

Renne and Creer (1985) have summarized the basic aspects of the explanation and the information concerning its validity. The four major conclusions offered by French and Alexander are (1) that a universal conflict exists in asthmatic patients between an infantile dependent attachment to their mothers and other emotions (particularly sexual wishes) that are incompatible with this dependent attitude; (2) asthma attacks are related to an inhibited suppressed cry for the mother; (3) there is a unique personality pattern characteristic of asthmatic patients; (4) psychoanalysis will alleviate the asthmatic symptoms. Recent reviews of research conducted since the publication of the original monograph by French and Alexander suggest that there is little if any support for their conclusions (e.g., Renne and Creer, 1985). No unique relationship appears to exist between asthmatic children and their mothers. To the extent that asthmatic children cry less, this is more likely due to the realization that crying may trigger an attack. Furthermore, there is no evidence for a personality pattern unique to asthma, and asthmatic patients would seem to be as psychologically healthy as other people. Finally, psychotherapy has not been effective in alleviating the disorder.

All in all, there is little, if any, convincing evidence that psychological factors play a significant role in the genesis of the reduced respiratory capacity characteristic of asthma. However, there is evidence that psychological factors may play an important role in *precipitating* asthmatic attacks in at-risk youngsters. Family variables are among those that receive the most frequent attention.

Like many investigators, Purcell and his colleagues—working at the Children's Asthma Research Institute and Hospital (CARIH) in Denver—observed that some children became symptom free fairly soon after being sent away from their parents for treatment. Indeed, in the 1950s "parentectomy" was suggested as the treatment of choice for some children (Peshkin, 1959). Were these effects due to changes in the emotional environment or physical environment? What other variables accounted for this reaction?

An interesting study on separation suggested some answers to these questions, (Purcell et al., 1969). Prior to the beginning of the study, parents of asthmatic children were interviewed and asked about the degree to which emotions precipitated asthmatic attacks. Children for whom emotions were important precipitants were expected to respond positively to separation from their parents (predicted positive), while children for whom emotions played less of a role were not expected to show improvement. Twenty-five asthmatic children participated in four two-week periods labeled (1) qualification, (2) preseparation, (3) separation, and (4) reunion. During the qualification period the families were aware that the project involved a careful evaluation of asthma in children but were unaware of possible separation. During the second phase, preseparation, the idea of separation was introduced. In the third phase the children had no contact with their families but continued their normal daily routines at home under the care of substitute parents.

In the fourth phase the children were reunited with their families. A post-reunion evaluation was also conducted.

For the predicted positive group all measures of asthma improved during the separation period. Figure 14–2 illustrates this finding for the peak expiratory flow rate (PEFR) measure. This is a measure of the maximum expiration of air possible. The children who were not predicted to respond to separation exhibited no differences across phases on any measure.

The findings of this research study, and others like it, led investigators to view changes in the psychological atmosphere as the basis for improvement in asthmatic symptoms. However, over time the investigators at CARIH and others came to view such findings somewhat differently. It was recognized that the magnitude of changes reported might be statistically significant, but were not clinically significant. Obtained changes might have been due to increased compliance with prescribed medical regimens when the surrogate parents moved in and the children's parents lived in a hotel. While high percentages of children treated at CARIH in the early years exhibited rapid remission of their symptoms, this percentage decreased rapidly over the years. This is probably due to several factors. With increasing information and improved medications available, milder cases of asthma came to be treated by the home physician

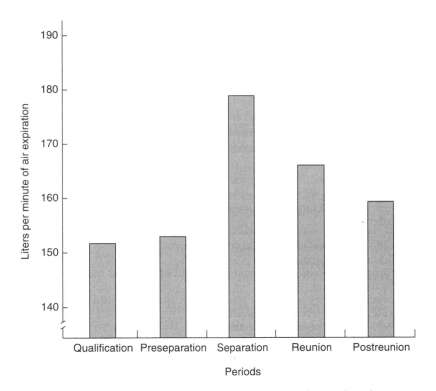

FIGURE 14–2 Mean daily peak expiratory flow rate for predicted positive group during each period of study.

Reprinted by permission of the publisher from article by K. Purcell et al., *Psychosomatic Medicine, 31,* 144–164. Copyright © 1969 by the American Psychosomatic Society, Inc.

cial problems (Kalnins, Churchill, and Terry, 1980). The stress placed on some families may affect the adjustment of both the patient and other children.

Thus, while some youngsters with chronic illness and their families experience adjustment difficulties, not all do. How might we best understand such variation in reactions among young people and their families? Research has examined variables such as the particular disease and its status and dimensions of family functioning. Increasingly, pediatric psychology has conducted research guided by theories that suggest variables that influence psychological outcomes (cf. Drotar, 1994; Wallander, 1992).

Several models are available to guide research. They focus on factors such as the bidirectional influence of risk and resistance factors (cf. Wallander et al., 1989b), and chronic illness as a stressor to which the youngster and family must adapt and develop coping methods (cf. Thompson et al., 1994). Models also differ in the emphasis given to factors idiosyncratic to specific illness versus general dimensions that represent common life experiences of all children with serious medical problems (cf. Ireys et al., 1994).

Adjustment to chronic illness is best thought of as a complex function of a number of variables each of which requires continued investigation. Characteristics of the young person would seem likely to contribute to the adjustment of both the youngster and the family. So, for example, the types and variety of coping skills that the youngster possesses is likely to be important in this process. A second category of variables are disease factors such as severity and degrees of impairment. In addition, the youngster' environment (e.g., family, school, health care) are likely to be a factor in variations in adaptation. An appreciation of the complexity of the problem is illustrated by the transactional model of Thompson and colleagues (1994) (see Figure 14–3). Guided

by the stress and coping model of Lazarus and Folkman (1984) the model suggests a number of processes that are thought to contribute to the adjustment of youngsters with chronic illness and their families (in the example illustrated, particular emphasis is given to their mothers).

Below we examine two of the categories of influences on adjustment to chronic illness that have received considerable research attention: illness parameters and family functioning.

Illness Parameters and Adjustment

The type of disease, the severity of the illness, and the degree of impairment of functioning produced by the illness are among the variables that have been examined as linking medical conditions to psychological adjustment. Of course, it is not always possible to analyze these dimensions separately. For example, certain illnesses are more severe than others, and severity is likely related to greater restrictions in normal functioning. However, each of these variables seems important.

In a review of studies of depression among young people with chronic medical problems, Bennett (1994) found that youngsters with asthma, recurrent abdominal pain, and sickle cell anemia appeared to be more at risk for increased depressive symptoms than did those with cancer, cystic fibrosis, and diabetes. However, as Bennett indicates, the relatively small number of studies and methodological concerns suggest that these patterns be interpreted with caution. In addition, research findings are not consistent with regard to adjustment differences among illness. Steinhausen (1988), for example, found poorer adjustment in youngsters with cystic fibrosis than those with asthma, both diseases affecting the lungs.

What then might be the impact of severity of the medical problem? In addition to the cystic fibrosis and asthma finding de-

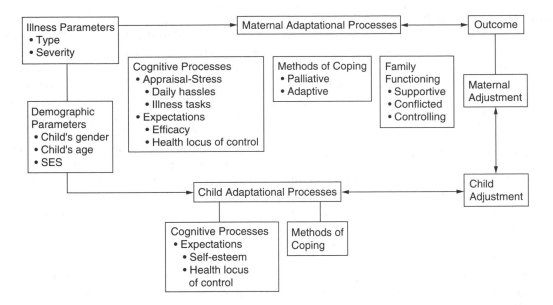

FIGURE 14–3   A transactional stress and coping model for chronic childhood illness.

From Thompson, R. J., Gustafson, K. E., George, L. K., and Spock, A. (1994). Change over a 12-month period in the psychological adjustment of children and adolescents with cystic fibrosis. *Journal of Pediatric Psychology, 19,* 189–203. Reprinted by permission from Plenum Publishing Corporation.

scribed above, Steinhausen (1988) also reported that poorer adjustment was associated with more severe illness in both of these groups, as well as in Crohn's disease and ulcerative colitis (both affecting the colon). Similarly, youngsters suffering from severe forms of arthritis had more behavior problems than healthy children, but children with milder or inactive forms of the disease did not (Billings, Moos, Miller, and Gotlieb, 1987). However, more severe forms of a disorder are not always associated with poorer adjustment (e.g., Wallander, Feldman, and Varni, 1989a).

Other investigators found that adjustment was associated with the degree of functional limitation caused by the condition, for example the number of absences from school or limitations in relationships with friends (Eiser et al., 1992; Ireys et al., 1994). The degree to which the illness is controlled also appears to be important. For example, more emotional and behavioral problems

are found when diabetes is poorly controlled (e.g., Mazze, Lucido, and Shannon, 1984). While these results suggest that anxiety, depression, and the like are outcomes of poor control, investigators acknowledge that the direction of causation is not clearly established. It is possible that anxiety, depression, and the like may contribute to poor metabolic control (e.g., Wiebe et al., 1994).

Ethically, we cannot manipulate emotional conditions or illness severity, nor can we randomly assign children to diseases. Thus, interpreting the impact of the dimensions of illness is inevitably difficult. Furthermore, while illness factors may help predict adjustment, their predictive ability does not appear to be that strong. Integrating illness factors into a more normative approach, one that combines these factors with the stress, risk, and resilience factors included in etiological models for youngsters without chronic medical disorder seems suggested (Timko et al., 1992). Such an approach would also allow for identification of factors relatively unique to chronic illness, as well as those common to other youngsters and families. Among the variables that might be the focus of such a normative approach, family functioning is one that has received some attention.

Family Functioning and Adjustment

As we have seen in previous chapters, family functioning has frequently been linked to young people's adjustment. It is, therefore, not surprising that family functioning is related to the psychological adjustment of chronically ill youngsters as well.

In fact, an early study suggested that poor functioning in families might be especially detrimental to a chronically ill youngster. Comparison of large samples of chronically ill youngsters and healthy controls indicated that both family dysfunction and chronic illness were associated with more adjustment problems. However, youngsters with chronic illness who lived in poorly functioning families had the highest incidence of psychological problems (Pless, Roghmann, and Haggerty, 1972).

Without denying the particular risks and stressors associated with chronic conditions, it is reasonable as a starting point to assume that some of the family influences that are related to adjustment of other children and adolescents, such as parental depression and marital conflict, will also be related to the adjustment of young people with chronic illness. Indeed, this seems to be the case (Lavigne and Faier-Routman, 1993). Timko and her colleagues (Timko et al., 1993), working with youngsters with juvenile rheumatic disease examined how parental risk and resilience factors predicted disease-related functional disabilities (e.g., gripping things, doing routine household chores), pain, and psychosocial adjustments four years following initial contact

with a hospital-based clinic. After age of the youngster and initial levels of the youngster's functioning were controlled for, mothers' and fathers' personal strain and depressed mood and fathers' drinking were associated with poorer adjustment in the youngsters four years later. Better parental social functioning, the mothers' involvement in social activities and the fathers' number of close relationships, on the other hand, seemed to facilitate the child's adjustment. Given that attention has concentrated on the contribution of maternal risk and resilience factors, it is interesting to note that the fathers' risk and resilience factors contributed to the childrens' functioning and adjustment beyond what was already accounted for by maternal factors and other influences.

Wertlieb, Hauser, and Jacobson (1986) in their comparison of diabetic youngsters and matched controls with acute illness found that while overt expression of family conflict was related to greater problem behavior in both groups, other factors differentiated the groups. One particularly interesting finding involved differences in attempts to control and maintain the family system. Among the acutely ill youngsters, a greater control orientation in the family was strongly related to a greater probability of behavior problems. In contrast, low levels of family organization were associated with high levels of behavior problems among the diabetic youth. Families with a diabetic child have appreciable demands placed on them to organize daily routines involved in the management of the illness. Successful management of the diabetes probably requires appreciable organization as well as overtly dealing with issues of control. These data suggest that families with a diabetic child who do not emphasize organization are families more likely to have a child who exhibits behavior problems. Structured and controlling family environments have also been found to be associated with better metabolic control of the diabetic condition (Weist et al., 1993). Family emphasis on rules and control may contribute to greater behavior problems in nondiabetic youngsters, but a different relationship may be optimal in families with a diabetic child or adolescent.

Wysocki (1993) extended some of the previous research on family conflict and diabetes. The families of 115 adolescents with insulin-dependent diabetes mellitus completed the Parent-Adolescent Relationship Questionnaire (PARQ; Robin, Koepke, and Moye, 1990). Consistent with the findings of Wertlieb et al., described above, and others, the families of diabetic adolescents and a normative group of families were not different regarding conflicts or other dimensions. However, scores on a PARQ scale measuring family communication and conflict resolution skills showed a clear relationship to the teens' adjustment to diabetes. These results suggest that at least some families with a diabetic adolescent might benefit from interventions aimed at reduced conflict through improved adolescent-parent communication skills.

Cohesion is another family variable that seems to be important. It is often reported that a life-threatening illness frequently draws family members closer together. Increased cohesion, although not a universal reaction to illness, has been observed in families coping with a variety of illness (Ross et al., 1993; Wood et al., 1989). It is frequently associated with the adjustment of the child or adolescent patient (Brown, Doepke, and Kaslow, 1993; Lavigne and Faier-Routman, 1993). A study of adolescent cancer survivors illustrates the importance of cohesion, but also suggests, again, that relationships are likely to be complex (Rait et al., 1992).

Eighty-eight adolescents who had previously been treated for leukemia, Hodgkin's disease, or non-Hodgkin's lymphoma and were currently in remission participated in the study. The participants were twelve to nineteen years old at the time of the assessment with an average age of 15.6 years. Given the literature on chronic illness and family functioning, the authors hypothesized that the experience of cancer would result in greater family cohesion, and that cohesion would be associated with the psychosocial adjustment of these cancer survivors.

The adolescents completed a standard measure of family adaptability and cohesion. Their scores were compared to a set of normative values on this measure that had been derived from a large community sample. The cancer survivors did differ from the normative group, but not in the predicted direction. The adolescents who had survived cancer described their families as *less* cohesive than the community sample. There was, however, the expected relationship between cohesion and adjustment. Greater cohesion was associated with better post-treatment psychological adjustment. However, an interesting complexity was suggested. Among "recent" survivors (treatment completed a year or less ago) and "long-term" survivors (treatment completed more than five years ago) there was the described strong relationship between family environment and adjustment. For "intermediate" survivors (treatment completed between one and five years ago), however, the association between family environment and adjustment was dramatically decreased. Since childhood cancer patients have a greater chance of survival than ever before, this somewhat surprising finding suggests the need for further exploration concerning how time since treatment, current age, age at time of diagnosis, and other such variables may be related to the association of family environment and the surviving youngster's psychological adjustment.

ACCENT 14–1 From "Dying from" to "Living with" Cancer

The title above describes a shifting emphasis regarding childhood cancer (cf. Eiser, 1994). Cancer has long been viewed as a fatal and little understood disease. While this frightening image still remains, it is not as accurate as was once the case. With increasing survival rates it may now be more appropriate to view cancer as a chronic condition rather than a fatal disease. For example, in 1960 acute lymphocytic leukemia, the most common form of childhood cancer, had a survival rate of 1% five years after diagnosis. Rapid innovations in treatment, have brought dramatic increases in the length of survival and the number of youngsters considered cured.

However, treatments are often lengthy, highly invasive, stressful, and accompanied by considerable pain. Also, the long-term concerns of these youngsters and their families are appreciable. Working with this population presents multiple and complex challenges. In addition to the initial task of helping the youngster and family understand and come to accept the illness, it is important to assist them in coping with a long and stressful treatment regimen and the additional stressors that the illness and its treatment places on them. For example, advice regarding the youngster's school, teacher, and peer group is likely to be important during treatment and afterward. Also, concerns regarding the longer-term impact of the disease are considerable and are probably related to developmental period. For adolescents the disease *may* interfere with the development of autonomy as a result of increased dependence on family and medical staff and may impose restrictions on social life and the development of close interpersonal relationships. Such outcomes are not, however, inevitable. The provision of ongoing and intensive psychosocial services to families throughout this process may buffer the impact of this experience and allow these youngsters to develop and function much like their peers (Noll et al., 1993).

One must also be aware that the very treatments that have resulted in longer survival may contribute to the long-term challenges. Central nervous system prophylactic treatment, for example, is one of the principle factors responsible for the increased life expectancy of youngsters with leukemia. Injection of methotrexate directly into the spinal column and irradiation of the spinal column and cranium reduce the probability of relapse, but may have their own costs. While the immediate and long-term impact of these treatments on cognitive and neurobehavioral functioning are not clear, it appears that impairment does occur in areas such as attention, learning, and academic achievement. This is particularly true for younger children (Butler and Copeland, 1993; Madan-Swain and Brown, 1991).

The shift to coping, adjusting, and adapting to cancer is clearly a more optimistic view. However, while we continue to attempt to understand this process and assist young people and families, it is also necessary to monitor these youngsters for long-term side effects of treatment. In addition, relapse remains possible, and there is an increased risk for secondary cancers. Maintaining such vigilance without creating additional and undue anxiety, and at the same time promoting an optimistic and adaptive attitude presents a considerable challenge.

PSYCHOLOGICAL INFLUENCES ON MEDICAL TREATMENT

Attempts to provide psychological treatment that would improve a patient's medical condition have long been one of the aspects of the interface between psychology/psychiatry and medicine. The vast majority of early attempts sought to provide the patient with psychotherapy as a means of reducing physical symptoms or curing illness. Such direct assaults on illness through psychotherapy proved to be largely ineffective (Werry, 1986). More recent efforts have taken a somewhat different approach to integrating a psychological perspective into the treatment of medical problems. While a comprehensive review of these efforts is beyond the scope of the present chapter, a few important illustrations follow.

Adherence to Medical Regimens

The terms "adherence" and "compliance" are most commonly used to describe how well a youngster or family follows recommended medical treatments. Diabetes provides an excellent opportunity to illustrate the way psychologists have increasingly attempted to understand the complex tasks encountered by families facing chronic childhood disorders (cf. Krasnegor et al., 1993).

The example of diabetes mellitus. Diabetes is the most common endocrine disorder in youngsters, affecting approximately 1.8 youth per 1,000 (Gortmaker and Sappenfield, 1984). It is a chronic, lifelong disorder that results from the pancreas producing insufficient insulin. Type I, also known as insulin-dependent diabetes mellitus (IDDM), requires daily replacement of insulin by injection due to the failure of the pancreas to produce insulin. As the onset of IDDM typically occurs in childhood, this form of diabetes is often referred to as a childhood or juvenile diabetes. In Type II, non-insulin-dependent diabetes mellitus (NIDDM), some insulin is produced by the pancreas. NIDDM is an adult onset disorder; patients may or may not have to take insulin, and weight reduction and careful diet can often help to control this form of diabetes.

Diagnosis of IDDM most often occurs during two age periods, five to six and eleven to thirteen years of age. However, the onset of the disease can occur at any time from infancy to early adulthood. A combination of genetic, immunologic, and viral factors appears to be involved in the etiology of juvenile diabetes. Diabetes is thought to be an autoimmune disease in which the body attacks its own pancreatic cells (Johnson, 1988a,c).

Diabetes is characterized by free fatty acids (ketones) in the blood as well as increased sugar in the blood (hyperglycemia) and urine (glycosuria). Overt symptoms include excessive thirst, increased urination, weight loss, and fatigue. If the disorder is not controlled, a condition known as ketosis or ketoacidosis may occur. This is a very serious condition and can lead to coma and death (Johnson, 1988b).

The youngster and family face a complex treatment regimen (See Table 14–2). This includes dietary restrictions, daily injections of insulin, monitoring of urine, and testing of blood glucose levels using small samples of blood obtained from a finger stick. On the basis of the daily tests for level of sugar and

TABLE 14–2 Some Activities Required of Diabetic Children and Families

Inject insulin regularly
Test blood regularly
Exercise regularly
Avoid sugar
Check for symptoms—low
Check for symptoms—high
Careful when sick
Shower regularly
Wear diabetes ID
Watch weight
Eat meals regularly
Adjust diet to exercise
Carry sugar
Test blood as shown
Change injection site
Inject insulin as shown
Watch dietary fat
Take care of injuries
Eat regular snacks
Control emotions
Inspect feet

Adapted from Karoly and Bay, 1990.

consideration of factors such as timing of meals, diet, exercise, physical health, and emotional state, the daily dosages of insulin must be adjusted. This is a complex therapeutic regimen, and under the best of circumstances "insulin reactions" occur often. Thus, the youngster must be sensitive to the signs and symptoms of both hyperglycemia (excessively high levels of blood glucose) and hypoglycemia (excessively low blood glucose). These reactions involve irritability, headache, shaking, and—if not detected early enough—unconsciousness and seizures. The task of identifying these states is made more complicated by the fact that symptoms are different for different youngsters and are subjectively experienced. Thus, it is possible for families to be misinformed about such reactions. Parents and youngster are, therefore, faced with a difficult, often unpredictable, and emotion-laden therapeutic program. Management of the regimen and its integration into daily life presents a considerable challenge (Delamater, 1986; Johnson, 1988b).

Management of the diabetic condition. The first task in treatment is for the team of professionals to gain and maintain control of the diabetic condition. As this is achieved, insulin requirements often decrease and the initial fears and concerns of the youngster and family are often reduced. This has come to be known as the "honeymoon period." This period of partial remission may terminate gradually and often ends about one to two years after initial diagnosis. A self-management program with families during the first few months after diagnosis may avoid this deterioration in metabolic function (Delamater et al., 1990). This is but one example of the fact that diabetes is not a static disease. Adolescence is another time period during which management of diabetes often deteriorates (Johnson, 1989; LaGreca, 1987). Transferring control for management of the disease from the profes-

sional to the family and adolescent, and requiring maintenance of such control over long periods of time, is one of the challenges of working with chronic illness.

Adherence to the diabetic regimen. The concept of adherence is multifaceted (Johnson, 1993). Probably the initial step addressed in most programs is to educate the youngster and family about the disease. While such efforts are regularly made, it is also a common observation that adequate knowledge can not be assumed (Delamater, 1986). Therefore, efforts have been made toward developing methods to assess knowledge. Behavioral observational methods have been employed to assess whether the youngster knows how to execute necessary skills such as urine and blood glucose testing (e.g., Harkavy et al., 1983). Questionnaires are frequently used to measure knowledge of the disease and the application of that knowledge to different situations (e.g., the role of insulin, and adjusting diet based on blood sugar readings). An example of such an instrument is the Test of Diabetes Knowledge: General Information and Problem Solving (Johnson, 1984). Some of the items included in this test are presented in Table 14–3. Even these few examples illustrate the difficulty and complexity of the information required of youngsters and families. However, adherence is not just a matter of accurate information and knowledge. The young person and family must actually carry out the prescribed tasks accurately and consistently.

There are a number of reasons why it is important to know whether adherence to prescribed regimens occurs. For the clinician working with a particular youngster, effective treatment relies on the patient actually completing the necessary tasks. In a larger sense, it is impossible to assess the effectiveness of treatments without such information. Interventions conducted outside the hospital or doctor's office cannot be

TABLE 14–3   Sample Items from Test of Diabetes Knowledge and Problem Solving

General Information

When giving insulin injections, you should:
  (a) Inject into the same area.
  (b) Inject into different areas every time.
  (c) Inject only in the leg.
  (d) I don't know.
Ketones in the urine of a person with diabetes are:
  (a) A warning sign of an insulin reaction.
  (b) A warning sign of acidosis.
  (c) A warning sign of hypoglycemia.
  (d) I don't know.

Problem Solving

You are trying out for your school's swimming team and practice is midafternoon. Your blood sugar is usually 80–180. You should:
  (a) Not take your insulin the days you practice.
  (b) Eat a big lunch that day and keep a snack handy.
  (c) Increase your insulin to give you more energy that day.
  (d) I don't know.
You take 30 units of NPH insulin each morning. One day your blood sugar at 10:00 A.M. is 300. Your urine has large ketones. In this situation you should:
  (a) Eat less today.
  (b) East more to counteract the ketones.
  (c) Drink extra fluids and check your blood and urine before lunch and again in one hour or two.
  (d) I don't know.

Adapted from Suzanne Bennett Johnson (1984) Test of Diabetes Knowledge, Revised-3. Gainesville: University of Florida, Health Sciences Center.

evaluated unless we know if patients are adhering to recommendations. Is a treatment ineffective in controlling diabetes or was that treatment not followed adequately?

A study by Johnson et al. (1986) provides a way of looking at the daily management faced by the youth and family. This study also provides interesting information about adherence to these management tasks. Interviews were conducted with 168 diabetic children and adolescents and their parents concerning their diabetes-relevant behavior during the previous twenty-four hours. These interviews were conducted on three occasions for each family. A factor analysis of the thirteen behaviors indicated that they grouped into five categories. Table 14–4 presents these categories and behaviors

Adherence in one diabetes management area did not predict the adherence of that same child or adolescent in other areas. Thus adherence can not be viewed as a global concept. Each aspect of the youngster's and family's compliance may need to be separately evaluated and addressed if programming is to be effective.

It was possible to look at the relationship between the reports of the youngsters and their mothers. In general correlations were statistically significant and moderate to strong (.42 to .78). However, the age of the youth seemed to affect mother-child agreement. On measures involving time (e.g., injection-meal timing, exercise duration) correlations were poorer for younger children. The young child's lesser sophistication regarding time is probably responsible. Youngsters in the nine to twelve and thirteen to fifteen age groups had the most consistent parent-child agreement across the thirteen behaviors. Older adolescents (sixteen to nineteen years) had highly variable correlations across behaviors. For example, the correlation for injection interval was quite high (.91), whereas agreement on injection regularity was extremely low (−.04). Older patients are likely to be less frequently monitored by parents, and this also suggests different treatment challenges. These findings and others point to the importance of considering level of development in treatment planning (cf. Band, 1990).

It is not possible to examine all aspects of adherence in this chapter. However, several important variables can be highlighted. As suggested above, developmental level is an

TABLE 14–4 Categories of Thirteen Diabetic Adherences Behaviors

Category I	Exercise
	    Time spent exercising
	    Strenuousness of the exercise
	    Exercise frequency

Category II	Injection
	    Injection regularity
	    Injection-meal timing
	    Regularity of injection-meal
	       timing

Category III	Diet (type)
	    Percent calories: Fat
	    Percent calories: Carbohydrates

Category IV	Testing/Eating Frequency
	    Number of meals and snacks
	       eaten each day
	    Number of glucose or ketone
	       tests per day

Category V	Diet (amount)
	    Calories consumed
	    Quantity of concentrated
	       sweets ingested

Adapted from Johnson et al., 1986.

important variable affecting adherence (Iannotti and Bush, 1993; Johnson, 1993). In general, knowledge and skills seem to increase with age. For example, children under nine years may have difficulty accurately measuring and injecting insulin. Also, it is probably best to avoid giving primary responsibility for glucose testing to children under twelve (Johnson, 1988c).

Adolescence appears to be a period of adherence difficulties. Social and emotional issues such as acceptance and greater participation in peer activities, as well as conflicts over independence with parents. are present. These most likely combine with actual physical changes, like those associated with puberty, and increase management and compliance difficulties (Brooks-Gunn, 1993; LaGreca, 1987).

Another major concern is the accuracy of adherence efforts. For example, it has often been observed that youngsters may be inac-

curate in reading their glucose level tests (Gross, 1990). The majority of such errors are likely errors of knowledge or skill, but actual faking of results, so as to avoid restrictions or the need for additional treatment, must also be considered. Interventions need to be planned that address both forms of inaccuracy.

Attention to the role of the primary health care provider (pediatrician, nurse) has also been examined as an important aspect of the adherence process (Dunbar-Jacob, 1993). There is a considerable discrepancy between what primary providers have recommended and what is recalled by patients and their families (e.g., Page et al., 1981). It also seems that health care providers may not be aware enough of the child's level of cognitive development, treating youngsters of varying ages as essentially the same. Thus, younger children's understanding is likely to be overestimated while the cognitive abilities of older children is underestimated (Perrin and Perrin, 1983).

Doctors and patients also may not share the same goals for treatment. This is illustrated by a comparison of the goals of physicians treating youngsters with diabetes and those of the children's parents. Significant differences were found. Parents' goals were more focused on the short-term consequences of diabetes (e.g., hypoglycemia) and physicians' on more long-term threats (complications). Youngster's diabetic control was more related to the parents' goals (Marteau et al., 1987).

Also, from the perspective of the physician, adherence may be defined as 100 percent compliance with medical recommendations. However, this view may fail to appreciate the ability of parent and child to reasonably adjust treatment regimens— to engage in "adaptive noncompliance" (Deaton and Olbrisch, 1987). Not all interventions may be highly effective for all individuals, and families and patients may respond to these variations. Families may also adjust regimens based on the psychological and social impact of treatment. Taken together, these factors suggest that an important focus of adherence efforts needs to be on the behavior of the health care provider.

It is clear that many other problems regarding adherence are worthy of continued attention. For example, it is important to anticipate environmental obstacles to compliance. Creating interventions that help adolescents deal with peers concerning their diabetes, for instance, may greatly facilitate compliance with recommendations (e.g., Gross et al., 1983). Realization that the immediate consequences of diabetes management are often negative and, therefore, more consistent with nonadherence than with adherence, may also help to anticipate difficulties. For example, the immediate consequence of injections is discomfort and the effects of skipping injections is not immediate. Thus, interventions that reduce the immediate effects of compliance are likely to be of value (e.g., Schafer, Glasgow, and McCaul, 1982).

Psychological Modification of Physical Functions

The Eastern mystic who walks on hot coals, voluntarily slows the heart, and by the power of the mind closes a wound has always fascinated inhabitants of the Western world. Fascinating too are the shaman's cures by removal of evil spirits, the miracles of faith healers, and cures of medical ailments by inert placebos (cf. Ullmann and Krasner, 1975). These phenomena highlight in a dramatic fashion the possible role of psychological interventions in the treatment of medical disorders. Each suggests that psychological procedures can directly affect physical functioning. The systematic and scientific study of how psychology can be used to treat physical symptoms directly has become part of the shifting emphasis in understanding mind-body relationships.

Experimental research demonstrated that responses of the central nervous system could be modified by classical and operant conditioning (e.g., Kotses et al., 1976; Miller, 1969). This suggested that procedures such as relaxation and biofeedback could be employed to train a person to control body systems that are involved in a particular physical disorder. Indeed, a variety of psychological interventions have been applied to children's physical disorders. The research is promising but also limited, and strong conclusions regarding effectiveness cannot be drawn (Andrasik and Attanasio, 1985; Williamson, Baker, and Cubic, 1993).

The use of relaxation and biofeedback to treat children's headaches is one example of attempts to directly modify physical functioning through psychological interventions. Headaches are usually classified as migraine, tension, or a combination of the two. Migraine headaches are presumed to be a vascular disorder—vasoconstriction and vasodilation (narrowing and expansion) of the blood vessels in the head produces pounding and throbbing. Tension headaches, as the name implies, are presumed to result from muscular tension and reduced blood flow to the muscles (Williamson et al., 1993). Although migraines are less common, their treatment has received more research attention (Andrasik, Blake, and McCarran, 1986; Williamson et al., 1993). These headaches produce very intense pain and often are accompanied by nausea and vomiting. This suffering and the desire to avoid potential negative aspects of drug treatment have led to the exploration of nonpharmacological approaches (Andrasik et al., 1986; Masek and Hoag, 1990).

Biofeedback refers to a procedure in which some device provides immediate feedback to the person about a particular biological function. Feedback is usually provided by a signal such as a light or tone or by some graphic display. Such feedback to teach children to warm the temperature of their hands (skin temperature biofeedback), relaxation training, or a combination of the two (autogenic training) have been employed to treat children's migraines. The mechanism whereby controlling hand temperature effects vasodilation is not clear. However, a number of these procedures seem promising in producing clinically meaningful levels of improvement in children's headaches. (Andrasik et al., 1986; Williamson et al., 1993).

Osterhaus and her colleagues (1993), for example, treated a group of school-aged youngsters (twelve to nineteen) with migraine headaches using a combination of relaxation training, temperature biofeedback, and cognitive training (to challenge irrational thoughts and replace them with more rational thoughts that might produce more pleasant feelings and less stress). The treatment was a school-based, after-school program of four group and four individual sessions. Regular home practice was also required. Youngsters in the experimental group were compared to a waiting list control group who received the same treatment after the experimental group had completed treatment. By the end of treatment, the experimental group had improved more than the control group on measures of headache frequency and duration as well as on a weekly headache index of the duration and intensity of every single headache attack. However, groups did not differ significantly regarding headache intensity. At a seven-month follow-up evaluation, the experimental group experienced significant further post-treatment reductions in the duration and intensity of headaches as well as in the headache index. The control group was no longer available for comparison since, because of ethical considerations, they now were receiving treatment for their headaches. The results are illustrated in Figure 14–4. Employing a 50 percent reduction in headache activity as a criterion for clinically significant improvement, 45 percent of the experimental group, as compared to 11 percent of the control group, achieved clinically meaningful reductions in the headache index.

Although procedures such as biofeedback and relaxation have been employed to directly modify physical functioning, findings suggest cautious expectations. Some early

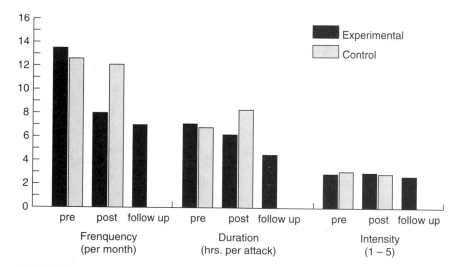

FIGURE 14–4 Mean frequency, duration, and intensity of headache attacks.
Adapted from Osterhaus et al., 1993.

success as well as more recent efforts indicate that the levels and persistence of change may not always be sufficient enough to be viewed as clinically meaningful (e.g., Osterhaus et al., 1993). Thus, rather than always relying on these interventions, psychological interventions might be considered as adjuncts to medical treatment.

Facilitating Medical Treatment

Psychological factors also influence the effective delivery of medical treatments for physical disorders. Developing psychologically based procedures for enhancing the effectiveness of medical treatment is another important and growing area of interest. Procedures for dealing with pain and discomfort and for preparing for hospitalization illustrate this potentially important contribution.

Pain and distress. Despite its seeming simplicity pain is a complex phenomenon that is difficult to assess. It is difficult, for example, to separate the pain or discomfort the person is suffering from the anxiety the person is experiencing while undergoing a painful medical procedure. This has led some to use the term distress to encompass pain, anxiety, and other negative affect (Jay, 1988; Varni, Katz, and Waldron, 1993). Whatever term is employed, three different response systems need to be assessed: behavioral, physiological, and cognitive-affective. Self-report measures of the cognitive-affective component of pain are the most frequently employed measures. This is probably an intentional choice. Pain is a subjective experience, and thus assessing the youth's experience of pain is important. In addition, the greater accessibility of this component and the relative ease of measurement are certainly factors as well. However, measurement of this component is not without its difficulties. For example, the youngster's developmental level will play a large role in selecting a self-report measure.

Older children may be able to describe pain in semantic terms, but younger children need to rely on concrete and visual methods. The use of a pain thermometer that visually represents degrees of pain in numerical terms is one procedure that has been employed (see Figure 14–5). In very young children who may not have the number concepts and discriminations required by this method, different measures can be employed. Thus, faces with expressions from broad smiles to severe frowns and colors to indicate intensity of pain may be useful (Dolgin and Jay, 1989b).

The behavioral component of children's distress (for example, behaviors that require the child to be physically restrained) can often interfere with effective medical treatment. Observational methods are often used to assess children's distress behaviors. Structured behavioral observations employing a system of defined behaviors and trained observers have been employed in a variety of

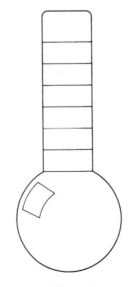

FIGURE 14–5 A child's subjective pain experience must be assessed in a developmentally appropriate manner. A pain thermometer like the one pictured is one way of concretizing differences in pain experience for young children.

contexts (e.g., Elliot, Jay, and Woody, 1987). Because such procedures can be expensive and time consuming, global ratings of distress by parents or nurses are often used to assess the behavioral component.

Assessment of the physiological aspect of pain is far less common. Melamed and Siegel's (1975) measurement of palmer sweat before and after youngsters underwent elective surgery is one of the earliest reports using physiological measures along with self-report and behavioral observation. However, the sophisticated equipment necessary and the difficulty involved in reliably obtaining measures such as heart rate, blood pressure, and skin conductance, result in such measures typically not being employed.

Measurement difficulty is but one aspect of the complexity of evaluating pain. The three response systems are far from perfectly correlated. It is also the case that different measures within a single response system often show less than desirable levels of correlation. To further complicate the issue, developmental level may affect the relationship between the different response systems (Jay, 1988). Developmental issues may also interact with aspects of the pain situation. It has been suggested, for example, that younger, more conceptually concrete children may exhibit greater distress when experiencing a more obvious but relatively minor injury (e.g., a small cut) than when they are subject to internal pain related to a more serious condition such as arthritic joint pain (Johnson, 1988a).

As a means of organizing work on pediatric pain, Varni, Katz, and Dash (1982) delineated four categories: (1) pain associated with a disease state; (2) pain associated with an observable injury; (3) pain not associated with a well-defined or specific disease or injury (e.g., recurrent abdominal pain, headache); (4) pain associated with medical or dental procedures. We will examine some of the research related to this fourth category to illustrate how procedures derived from a psychological perspective have been employed to assist children experiencing medically related pain.

Helping the child cope. Many of the medical treatment procedures used to assess and treat children with chronic disorders are aversive. It is commonly agreed that preparation of the youngster for an aversive procedure is the first step in helping the youngster cope and in reducing distress (cf. Peterson and Mori, 1988). The basic rationale for preparation is that unexpected stress is worse than predictable stress. From the simple statement that preparation is good follows the complex question of how this is best achieved for each young person. Research provides some guidelines and suggests certain procedures. However, it is also clear that more information is still needed, and that different types and timing of procedures will need to be matched to individual youth (Dahlquist, 1992). Some general recommendations have been made, in part based on suggestions made by youngsters themselves (Ross, 1988). Many of these suggestions cluster around the perception of being in control (Carpenter, 1992) and many involve the youngster controlling the environment during the aversive treatment procedure. The following comment by a ten-year-old boy undergoing emergency room burn treatment illustrates this well.

I said, "How about a hurting break?" and he (intern) said, "Hey, man, are you serious?" And I said, "Sure. Even when ladies are having babies they get a little rest between the bad pains." And they (the pediatric emergency room personnel) all laughed and he said, "OK, you get a 60-second break whenever you need it," and then it was *much, much better*, like you wouldn't believe it. (Ross, 1988, p. 5)

While children may be capable of generating their own strategies for coping with pain and distress, procedures for teaching effective stress management/coping skills are also needed (Manne et al., 1993) and have received considerable attention (cf. Jay, 1988; Varni, Walco, and Wilcox, 1990). Most current interventions consist of a variety of coping strategies derived from behavioral and cognitive-behavioral perspectives. Table 14–5 lists some of the skills included in such programs.

The work of Jay and her colleagues on reducing the stress of youngsters undergoing bone marrow aspirations is a good example of such efforts (e.g., Jay et al., 1987; 1991). Bone marrow aspirations (BMA) need to be routinely conducted for youngsters with leukemia in order to examine the marrow for evidence of cancer cells. A large needle is inserted into the hip bone and the marrow is suctioned out. This is a very painful procedure. An injection of lidocaine is given to anesthetize the skin surface and bone, but does not lessen the excruciating pain that is experienced with the suctioning of the marrow. The use of general anesthesia is avoided due to medical risks and expense. Intramuscular injections of sedatives are relatively unpopular, since they are painful and there is concern regarding substantial side effects.

The intervention package developed by Jay and her colleagues consists of five major components: filmed modeling, positive incentive, breathing exercises, emotive imagery/distraction, and behavioral rehearsal. The intervention package is administered on the day of the scheduled BMA, about thirty to forty-five minutes prior to the procedure.

In the first step youngsters are shown an eleven-minute film of a same-age model. While undergoing the BMA, the model, on a voice overlay, narrates the steps involved in the procedure as well as his or her thoughts and feelings at crucial points. The model also exhibits positive coping behaviors and self-statements. The film is based on a coping rather than mastery model. The child in the film exhibits a realistic amount of anxiety, but copes with it rather than having exhibited no anxiety and distress at all.

Next, the youngsters are taught simple breathing exercises. These are intended as active attention distracters, but may also promote some relaxation.

The youngsters are then taught imagery/distraction techniques. Emotive imagery (Lazarus and Abramavitz, 1962) is a technique in which images are used to inhibit anxiety. A child's hero images are ascertained in a discussion with the child. They are then woven into a story that elicits positive affect that is presumed to be incompatible with anxiety, that transforms the meaning of the pain, and encourages mastery rather than avoidance of pain. One girl's emotive imagery resembled the following story.

TABLE 14–5 Some Skills Taught to Assist Children in Coping with Medical Procedures

Deep breathing exercises (deep inhalation and slow exhalation)
Distraction (e.g., counting ceiling tiles)
Emotive imagery (reconceptualizing the setting or pain)
Relaxing imagery
Behavioral or imaginal rehearsal (of the medical procedures)
Progressive muscle relaxation (relaxing muscle groups)
Rewards for using coping strategies

Adapted from Dahlquist, 1992.

She pretended that Wonderwoman had come to her house and asked her to be the newest member of her Superpower Team. Wonderwoman had given her special powers. These special powers made her very strong and tough so that she could stand almost anything. Wonderwoman asked her to take some tests to try out these superpowers. The tests were called bone marrow aspirations and spinal taps. These tests hurt, but with her new superpowers, she could take deep breaths and lie very still. Wonderwoman was very proud when she found out that her superpowers worked, and she made the Superpower team. (Jay et al., 1985, p. 516).

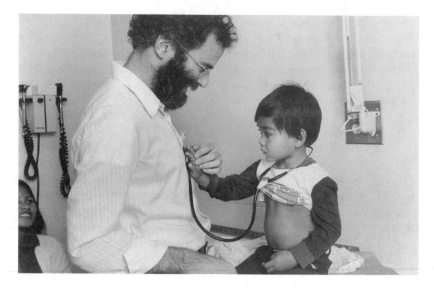

Fears of medical procedures are common among children, particularly for children who must undergo frequent treatment. Techniques that reduce fearful behavior can facilitate good medical care.

(Nita Winter, The Image Works)

Another imagery distraction technique involves teaching the youngster to form a pleasant image that is incompatible with the experience of pain (e.g., a day at the beach). The youngster chooses either the emotive or incompatible strategy and is given guidance during the bone marrow procedure to help in forming the images.

The positive incentive component of the intervention consists of a trophy presented as a symbol of mastery and courage. The youngster is told she can win the trophy if she does "the best that she can possibly do." The situation is structured so that every youngster can be successful in getting the trophy.

During the behavioral rehearsal phase younger children "play doctor" with a doll, while older children are guided in conducting a "demonstration." The youngsters are instructed step-by-step in the administration of the BMA. As the youngster goes through the procedure the doll is instructed to lie still and do the breathing exercises and imagery.

Jay et al. (1987) compared this cognitive behavioral package to a low-risk pharmacological intervention (oral Valium) and a minimal treatment-attention control condition. Each youngster experienced each of these interventions during three different BMAs. Which of the six possible orders of these interventions a youngster received was randomly determined. When in the cognitive-behavioral intervention condition, youngsters had significantly lower behavioral distress, lower pain ratings, and lower pulse rates than when they were in the control condition. When youngsters were in the Valium condition they showed no significant differences from the control condition except that they had lower blood pressure scores.

The findings of this study represent one example of developing interventions that will help youngsters and families cope with the distress associated with certain medical procedures. Incorporation of parents to assist in promoting coping skills is a direction that will likely improve the maintenance of child coping and improve the cost-effectiveness of interventions that otherwise may require a great deal of professional time (Manne et al., 1993; Powers et al., 1993). Such interventions hold the promise of making delivery of effective medical treatment more likely.

Hospitalization. Youngsters suffering from chronic illness often require periodic hospitalization to stabilize their functioning. Normal youngsters, too, often need to enter the hospital for minor surgery. In the mid-1950s the importance of the child's psychological reaction to early hospitalization and surgery began to be recognized. Researchers noted that a majority of children experienced mild to extreme stress reactions during and following hospitalization and that many demonstrated behavioral problems following surgery (e.g., Prugh et al., 1953). A particularly impactful finding was Douglas's (1975) examination of the long-term effects of early hospitalization. Follow-ups were conducted on a sample consisting of one out of every four children born in Great Britain during a particular week. Approximately 20 percent of the children who were later hospitalized before the age of five seemed to experience some immediate adverse effect. Adolescent conduct disorders and reading difficulties seemed to occur more frequently among some small proportion of those children who had experienced early hospitalization. Early research thus seemed to indicate that at least some aspects of hospitalization could be damaging to children.

Improvements have occurred since the 1950s and 1960s when much of this research was conducted. For example, in 1954 most New York hospitals allowed parental contact only during two visiting hours per week. In contrast, Roberts and Wallander (1992), describing a 1988 survey of 286 hospitals in the United States and Canada, found that 98 percent of the hospitals had unrestricted visiting for parents and 94 percent allowed parent rooming in.

Most hospitals now also offer prehospital preparation for both the child and parents (Roberts and Wallander, 1992). Nevertheless, procedures used are not always those best supported by research (Peterson and Mori, 1988). One well supported method of preparation involves the use of models who, although apprehensive, cope with the hospitalization stresses. Melamed and Siegel's (1975) film, "Ethan Has an Operation," showed a seven-year-old boy prior to, during, and after surgery. It has been shown to be an effective means of preparation for hospitalization and surgery (e.g., Melamed and Siegel, 1980; Peterson et al., 1984). This is but one example of the use of modeling. Other films and the use of puppets have been shown to be effective as well (e.g., Peterson et al., 1984). Current efforts are directed at preparation procedures that are cost-effective and, therefore, likely to be used and that are matched to individual characteristics of the child, parent and family (Peterson and Mori, 1988; Peterson et al., 1990)

Despite the improvements in hospitalization, children are still faced with stressors related to their hospitalization. Spirito, Stark, and Tyc (1994), for example, found that 50 percent of the *chronically* ill youngsters they asked to name a stressor since they were in the hospital, described a specific aspect of hospitalization (e.g., noises preventing sleep, rude staff, slow service). By way of comparison, only 33 percent and 17 percent, respectively, indicated pain-related concerns or an illness-related problem (e.g., side effects of treatment, problems or limitations caused by their illness). In contrast, the percentages of youngsters hospitalized for *acute* illness or injuries who indicated hospital, pain, or illness-related stressors were 39 percent, 51 percent, and 10 percent, respectively. Hospital stressors require attention, since improvements in these areas are likely to enhance the mood state and adjustment of youngsters, particularly those who are chronically ill and may require frequent hospitalizations.

THE DYING CHILD

Clearly, one of the most distressing aspects of working with severely ill youngsters is the prospect of death. Several important questions are raised. What is the child's understanding of death? How can we best prepare the youngster and the family? How do we prepare people for death while sustaining their motivation for treatment? Can we help the family begin to accept the child's impending death but yet prevent it from premature distancing from the child? What do we do after the youngster dies? How is the helper affected by working with the dying child? These are difficult questions.

It does appear that children's conceptions of death are influenced by their parents' views and change during development (e.g., Candy-Gibbs, Sharp, and Petrun, 1984, 1985). Young children may think of death as being less alive and assume it to be reversible. At about five years of age, an appreciation of the finality of death may be present, but death still does not seem inevitable. An understanding of death as final and inevitable and of personal mortality emerges at about age nine or ten. Cognitive development plays a role in the evolving conceptualization of death (Ferrari, 1990). Koocher (1973), employing a Piagetian framework, evaluated seventy-five healthy youth ranging in age from six to fifteen years to determine their level of cognitive functioning. In addition, they were asked four questions: "What makes things die? How can you make dead things come back to life? When will you die? What will happen then?" The youngster's understanding became more realistic and reflected higher levels of cognitive organization as their levels of cognitive functioning progressed from preoperational, to concrete-operational, to formal operational. Fatally ill youngster's concepts of death do not appear to be more advanced than physically well youth (Jay et al., 1987).

While developmental differences in cognitive understanding exist, it must also be appreciated that children may be aware of death and worried about their fatal illness even if they do not have a fully developed concept of death.

What of family members? Certainly, they too must be made aware of the seriousness of the youngster's illness. However, an appropriate balance between acceptance of death and hope for life is probably adaptive. It is a genuine challenge to prepare parents for the death of their child yet enable them to help the child emotionally and assist with the treatment regimen. It requires mental health staff who are knowledgeable and sensitive. As our ability to lengthen survival—and perhaps raise hopes of some future cure—increases, the problem will become even more difficult. Integration of support services into the total treatment program and immediate availability and access are important in delivering needed help. Moreover, the family should not be abandoned after the young person's death (Rando, 1983). Continued assistance and support should be a part of the total treatment.

Caregivers, too, are not immune to the effects of observing a youngster dying. Koocher (1980) suggests that efforts must be made to reduce the high cost of helping: the inevitable stress, feelings of helplessness, and the likelihood of burnout. These are not trivial matters. The helpers' adjustment and efficiency are not the only concern. The potential impact of their behavior on the family and youngster is also significant. In "Who's Afraid of Death on a Leukemia Ward?" Vernick and Karon (1965) offer poignant anecdotes to this effect. One describes the impact of helpers' behavior on a nine-year-old patient who, after taking a turn for the worse, received some medical treatment and began to show improvement.

One day while she was having breakfast I commented that she seemed to have gotten her old appetite back. She smiled and agreed. . . . I mentioned that it looked as if she had been through the worst of this particular siege. She nodded in agreement. I went on to say that it must have been very discouraging to feel so sick that all she could do was worry—worry about dying. She nodded affirmatively. I recognized that the whole episode must have been very frightening and that I knew it was a load off her mind to be feeling better. She let out a loud, "Whew," and went on to say that except for me, nobody really talked with her. "It was like they were getting ready for me to die." (p.395)

Certainly, one of the most difficult decisions is what to tell the dying youngster. A protective approach or "benign lying" was once advocated. The youngster was not to be burdened, and a sense of normalcy and optimism was to be maintained. Many workers now feel that this approach is not helpful and probably is doomed to failure anyway. The stress on the family of maintaining this deception is great, and the likelihood that the youngster will believe the deception is questionable. Some balance must be struck that takes into consideration the child's developmental level, past experiences, timing and an understanding of the family's belief system (Dolgin and Jay, 1989a). An example of such a balance is illustrated in the following excerpt:

A child with a life-threatening illness should be told the name of the condition, given an accurate explanation of the nature of the illness (up to the limit of his ability to comprehend), and told that it is a serious illness of which people sometimes die. At the same time, however, the child and family can be told about treatment options and enlisted as allies to fight the disease. An atmosphere must be established in which all concerned have the opportunity to ask questions, relate fantasies, and express concerns, no matter how scary or far fetched they may seem.

When the patient is feeling sick, weak, and dying, there is no need to [be reminded] of the prognosis. If a family and patient know a prognosis is poor but persist in clinging to hope, one has no right to wrest that from them. The truth, humanely tempered, is important, but we must be mindful of the patient and how [the patient's] needs are served. To tell the "whole truth" or a "white lie" for the benefit of the teller serves no one in the end. (Koocher and Sallan, 1978, p. 300)

SUMMARY

Attempting to determine the role of psychological factors in physical disorders is part of a long tradition of trying to understand the relationship between mind and body. The current view that psychological factors are relevant to physical disorders in a number of different ways represents a shift from the earlier more limited view of psychosomatic diseases caused by emotional factors.

Current conceptualizations of the role of psychological factors in asthma illustrate many of the changes that have occurred regarding causation. For example, a distinction is made between the causes of the asthmatic disorder and the mechanisms which trigger an asthmatic attack. Psychological influences are one of a variety of possible trigger mechanisms that can bring on an asthmatic episode. There is, however, little support for the idea that psychological factors play a role in causing reduced respiratory capacity. For asthma, as well as for other disorders, there has been a shift from exploring the role of emotional factors in the genesis of physical conditions to examining the multiple ways that psychological factors affect youth with these conditions. One principle focus of such efforts has been on the role of the family.

The appreciable social and emotional consequences of chronic illness have received increasing attention. For juvenile diabetes and other chronic illness, there is likely to be considerable individual variability in how youngsters and families cope. The first task for the professional is to achieve and maintain control of the medical condition. The youngster and family's acceptance of the disorder and attitude toward its control are crucial in successful treatment. At the same time, the impact on the youngster's overall development and the family's functioning is likely to be substantial. Researchers have sought to determine the impact of parameters of the illness such as severity, and aspects of family functioning such as conflict, on the chronically ill child or adolescent's adjustment.

Psychology can contribute to effective treatment of medical conditions in a number of ways. Medical treatment is often rendered ineffective due to failure of the patient and family to adhere to prescribed treatment regimens. Adherence is a complex process and attempts to improve adherence require attention to multiple dimensions such as developmental status, family patterns, and the role of the health-care professional.

Psychological treatments (for example, relaxation and biofeedback) may be able to modify physical functioning directly. Initial successes with disorders such as children's headaches suggest a cautious optimism regarding their potential.

Psychology may also facilitate the delivery of medical interventions. By reducing the anxiety felt by youngsters undergoing medical procedures, not only do psychologists make the youngster more comfortable, but they also make the task of medical personnel easier.

The prospect of death is one of the most distressing aspects of working with some chronically ill youth. Psychological contributions to understanding the child's conception of death and the mechanisms of coping with this possibility can aid effective and caring treatment. The impact of death on the professional working with these youngsters is important for that person as well as for the influence it will have on the ability to help.

15

EVOLVING CONCERNS FOR YOUTH

This final chapter focuses on concerns for the well-being of young people. It is a truism that the future of every society depends on its youth. The welfare of the young is tied to not only economic conditions but also to social and political attitudes, so that care varies enormously around the world. Unsurprisingly, basic care and opportunity are especially problematic in poor, developing countries. In the United States, concern for youth has always been expressed (Kopp and Kaler, 1989), but policy and actual practice has not consistently reflected this concern. Although much is being done for youth today, much more needs to be done.

Some of today's concerns for children and adolescents living in the United States hark back to the 1960s and 1970s, when emphasis was placed on the rights of individuals deemed disadvantaged and powerless in society. In addition, the economic and sociopolitical changes of the more recent years have brought new concerns. The lives of youth are impacted by what is happening in the personal lives of their parents, the value assigned to the young, the priorities given to health care and education, the economy, and a host of other factors. Sensitive and caring adults are looking at these influences with an eye toward better care for youth.

Progress in understanding human development has also stimulated efforts toward optimizing the potential of the young. Although no one would deny that knowledge about development is incomplete, we have come far from simply viewing the young as little adults. Their unique needs are better known; the general course of physical, intellectual, and social growth is well on the way to being mapped; and developmental influences, including risk and protective factors, are increasingly understood. Child specialists and others are enthusiastic about using this knowledge to enhance development and enrich lives.

Thus, both broad cultural and professional factors shape concerns for youth and the ways in which these concerns are manifested in programs and policies. Our discussion is necessarily selective. Focusing on behavioral and psychological issues, we recognize many interacting influences, as is consistent with our general view of development. We also focus on the United States, but we conclude the chapter by acknowledging concerns for youth growing up in circumstances that can be very different from those in the United States. We seek not only to discuss developmental risk but also to point to the future with some optimism.

One of the themes of this chapter is the need for prevention and we begin there.

PREVENTION

Few would dispute the proposition that, at least in the abstract, prevention is superior to treating conditions that already exist. From a humanitarian point of view, prevention clearly is more desirable: it averts discomfort and suffering. Practical considerations also argue for prevention. With regard to psychological disturbance, we have seen that population surveys often identify about 20 percent of children and adolescents as having clinic-level problems. The severity of disorders identified by this method is arguable, but even a conservative estimate of 10 percent would indicate enormous need for mental health care (Rae Grant, 1991). Treatment is often costly and sometimes unavailable for groups of needy people. It is also difficult to undo certain kinds of damage once they set in. Moreover, resources have long been recognized as inadequate in face of the substantial need for treatment. Perhaps 5 percent of youth with diagnosable conditions receive any kind of mental health care (Costello et al., 1993). Thus, for three decades influential mental health workers have taken a stand for a greater emphasis on prevention.

Conceptualizing Prevention

In the United States, interest in prevention can be traced to the early twentieth-century writings of Clifford Beers, the mental hygiene movement, and the creation of the child guidance clinics (Hightower and Braden, 1991). Caplan's work, *Principles of Preventive Psychiatry* (1964), provided a framework for conceptualizing prevention of behavioral or psychological disorder. A three-prong attack was suggested, consisting of primary, secondary, and tertiary prevention.

Figure 15–1 depicts the continuum of preventive efforts, which range from the promotion of health to rehabilitation (Rae Grant, 1991). *Primary* prevention attempts to stave off disorders in the first place. It involves both general health enhancement and prevention of specific dysfunction. *Secondary* prevention is usually defined as the effort to shorten the duration of existing cases through early referral, diagnosis, and treatment. It is a "nipping in the bud" strategy. *Tertiary* prevention aims to reduce problems that are residual to disorders. Thus, it might seek to minimize the negative impact of labeling a child as learning disabled or to rehabilitate a person who has suffered a severe mental disorder. Although primary, secondary, and tertiary efforts can

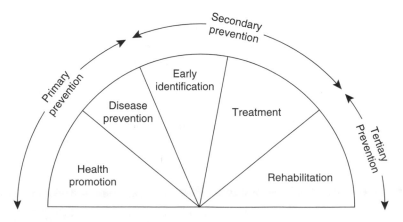

FIGURE 15–1 The continuum of prevention.

Rae Grant, 1991. In M. Lewis (Ed.), *Child and adolescent psychiatry. A comprehensive textbook.* William & Wilkins. By permission.

all reduce disorder and suffering in some way, it is primary prevention that most comes to mind when the term prevention is employed. Landsman (1994) suggests that primary prevention is akin to the work done by architects, who attempt to build healthy and aesthetic surroundings by working with large populations of people and how they interact with their environments. Primary prevention similarly attempts to build societies that optimize health. Secondary and tertiary efforts only come into play when primary prevention fails or is insufficient.

The difference between treatment and prevention is clear in the case of primary prevention. Unlike treatment, primary prevention focuses on an unreferred population rather than a referred individual and aims to protect or promote health. Disorders with known etiology that lead to brain dysfunction are largely preventable, for example, disorders caused by infections and poisons. However, the etiology of most psychological disorder is multifactorial and unknown. Even so, prevention is still possible. The general model calls for the study of people identified as showing the disorder so that correlates can be identified and hypotheses can be constructed about its path of development. The study of risk and protective factors is especially fruitful, as it points to what is best avoided and what is best provided or strengthened (Coie et al., 1993). As we have seen throughout this text, research has established correlations between behavioral disorders and many biological and psychosocial variables, including specific early stressors, family dysfunction, and poverty. Thus, there is a base for preventive efforts.

Examples of Prevention Programs

Prevention programs for youth vary tremendously in focus and setting. They include, for example, genetic screening, which aims to decrease the number of infants born with hereditary disorders. Infant high-risk interventions provide specific inputs to parents to help overcome the adverse affects associated with infant low birth weight or difficult temperament and with parenting by single adolescents. Early screening of general intelligence, reading deficits, attention deficits, school maladjustment, and other problems is seen as crucial for an array of secondary prevention programs. Still another approach is the alleviation of stress and potential crisis, such as when the child enters school or experiences parental divorce. Efforts also are made to develop child competence on the assumption that competence goes hand-in-hand with good decision making, social support, and coping with stress. Still other efforts encourage positive life styles, as in fostering an unfavorable attitude toward drug use.

Many prevention programs target young people affected by poverty. Even in a country as wealthy as the United States, between 20 to 25 percent of children live below the federal guidelines for poverty (Routh, 1994b). Moreover, poverty rates for children have been higher than for other age groups since 1975. Poverty is disproportionately high among minority groups and mother-headed households. Although a complex of factors has created increasing poverty among children, it is nevertheless appalling that child poverty is higher in the United States than in similar countries (Dubow and Ippolito, 1994; Pollitt, 1994). Of course, it is well known that poverty puts children at risk with regard to diet, health, teenage pregnancy, exposure to drugs, family stress, educational achievement, and occupational opportunity.

Although it has taken many years to mount prevention programs, a considerable number of well-designed and well-evaluated programs currently exist. We will now detail a few of these efforts, two that are family or community based and two that are school based.

Mother-infant programs. These programs target the development of low birth weight or premature infants. Six to seven percent of all births in the U.S. are of low birth weight (Kopp and Kaler, 1989). The association of low birth weight with a variety of adverse outcomes was reported many years ago, but it took several years of research to clearly demonstrate that infant outcome depended in part on the care that infants received (p. 33). Except for cases of extreme physical damage, adverse effects can be reduced or overcome by a high quality of care, which appears related to parents' attitudes and skills, family resources, and social support (e.g., Greenberg and Crnic, 1988; Sameroff, 1990). The transactional model of development frequently has been used to explain this finding. Complex, ongoing interactions among the child, parents, and larger social environment produce various developmental paths which differentially affect infant growth. Extraordinary medical intervention is often critical to favorable outcome, but so too is parental care.

There are many examples of successful infant-mother programs. The Mother-Infant Transactional Program (MITP) is one. Its purpose was to assist mothers in adjusting to the care of their low birth weight infants and enhance infant development (Achenbach et al., 1990; Rauh et al., 1988). A fundamental assumption was that confident, knowledgeable, and effective parenting would reduce the probability of infant developmental problems. Each mother worked with a supportive, specially trained nurse for three months in order to (1) better appreciate her infant's unique characteristics, (2) recognize the infant's communications, and (3) appropriately respond to these signals. The eleven interactional sessions included the infants, and fathers when possible. Techniques entailed direct instruction, demonstration, modeling, and practical experience in handling the infant. The nurse encouraged parental feelings of comfort and confidence.

Infants in the MITP intervention were compared to low birth weight infants randomly assigned to no-treatment and to normal birth infants. It was demonstrated that for the most part mothers in the intervention group expressed more self confidence and satisfaction with the mothering role, and perceived their infants as less difficult temperamentally. Infant cognitive status was measured at several times. As Figure 15–2 shows, treated infants became different from the low birth weight controls and more similar to the full-term controls. Future follow-up will evaluate school achievement and behavior problems as well as cognitive growth.

Other research indicates the efficacy of intervention for low birth weight or premature infants (Olds and Kitzman, 1993). The Infant Health and Development Program consisted of a three-year pediatric follow-up, family education and support, and educational day care (Bradley et al., 1994). It was conducted at several sites. Evaluations showed positive effects on infant health and development that went beyond the effects of pediatric care.

Mother-infant programs often entail several components, delivered in the home, at centers, or in both settings. They often target families with multiple stressors due, for instance, to poverty or single-parenting. Intervention can be successful in spite of multiple stressors, although multiple stressors and minimal protection take their toll. More research is needed as to the long-term effectiveness of infant-mother intervention. Nevertheless, these programs clearly show that preventive efforts are feasible and worthwhile. Early intervention can help create a more positive pathway for future development.

Head Start. Head Start was federally funded in 1964 by the Economic Opportunity Act, as part of the general War on Poverty. From the beginning, it was conceptualized as a comprehensive developmental

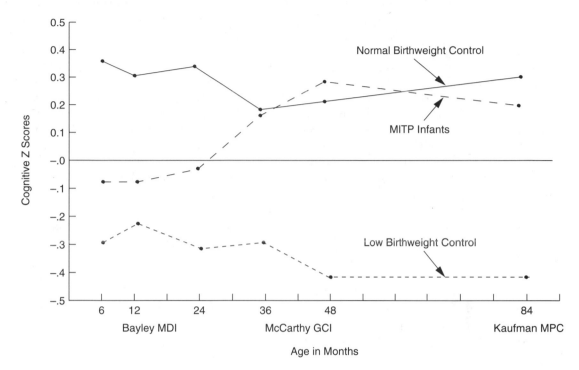

FIGURE 15–2 Cognitive test scores at different ages for the MITP infants, low birth weight controls, and normal birth weight controls.

From Achenbach et al., 1990.

program to enhance mental processes, social and emotional growth, health, and family and community relationships (Zigler and Styfco, 1993). A central assumption was that poor youngsters are at risk for low academic achievement which, in turn, works against their attaining decent jobs, self-worth, and healthy, fulfilling lives. It was also assumed that early experience is especially important for later growth and thus that intervention during the preschool years would put the children on the road to achievement. Head Start thus encompassed several major components.

1. *Education.* The educational component places children into classes with a high teacher-student ratio that try to meet each child's needs. The ethnic and cultural characteristics of the community are considered

in structuring the educational experience. For example, when a majority of the children are bilingual, there is a mandate for some of the staff to speak the children's native language.

2. *Health.* Physical and mental health are emphasized. Meals are served that must meet specific nutritional standards, and parents are offered education in nutrition. Medical examinations include hearing, vision, and dental check-ups; follow-up medical treatment is provided when appropriate. A mental health professional is available to evaluate special needs and to provide training in child development for staff and parents.

3. *Parent Involvement.* Community involvement is fundamental to Head Start. Parents participate in decisions about daily activities and planning and managing the program. Many serve as volunteers or employees. Many also participate in workshops related to the welfare of their children or the family.

4. *Social Services.* Head Start families often have needs for other services; it is the task of the Head Start social service coordinator to help obtain these services. The object is to strengthen the family unit so that it may do the best job possible in rearing children and supporting its adult members.

In addition to the components just described, Head Start has had several special projects to evaluate other ways of helping children and families. For example, Home Start focused on training mothers in their homes, on the premise that the mother-child relationship should not be disrupted by removing the child from the home and that maternal training would generalize to other children at home. Nevertheless, out-of-home intervention has remained the cornerstone of Head Start, which has served over thirteen million preschoolers. Evaluations of the program have been extensive and have played a role in support for Head Start.

Evaluations of Head Start have not always been favorable. In fact, the program barely got off the ground when it was concluded that it did not result in intellectual advancement for preschoolers (e.g., Jensen, 1969; Cronbach, 1975). However, the test of time favors the conclusion that Head Start can be beneficial. The evidence comes from data on actual Head Start programs or similar preschool interventions.

For example, the Consortium of Longitudinal Studies published data from eleven independent well-planned and well-researched programs for the disadvantaged, two of them Head Start programs (Haskins, 1989; U.S. Department of Health and Human Services, 1979). Taken as a whole, the evaluations showed that preschool participants did better academically as they proceeded through school than did control children. They were less likely to have been retained at grade level and less likely to have been assigned to special education. Fif-

A critical component of Head Start is preschool experience that offers multiple activities and a high teacher-child ratio.

(Elizabeth Crews/Stock, Boston)

teen percent more completed high school. Interestingly, early gains on tests of intelligence held for only a few years, and much concern has been expressed about this "fade-out".

Several other studies of specific Head Start programs also indicate initial enhancement of cognitive skills and school readiness, better immunization rates and nutrition, enhanced socioemotional functioning, and strengthening of family life (Zigler and Styfco, 1993).

To the extent that educational benefits accrue, the intriguing question is, Why? There is little evidence that any permanent change in intellectual functioning accounts for the finding that participants more successfully make their way through the school system (Woodhead, 1988). Initial gains in tested intelligence are not maintained. Rather, benefits appear to occur by indirect paths. First, upon entering the public schools, the children had been more able to do the work, had more positive attitudes, and had adapted more easily to school. There is evidence that teachers viewed them as competent and treated them as such. Positive attitudes and motivation for school were thus reinforced, and this chain of success continued. This analysis is similar to Sylva's (1994) conclusion that the positive effects of early education derive from the child's aspirations for education, which are shaped by schools with a learning orientation. Second, indirect effects likely operated through the home. Head Start parents themselves have overwhelmingly considered the program a success (e.g., Zigler, 1978). Among other things they have noted improved understanding of children, increased opportunity for education and employment, increased aspirations, and increased commitment to the community. In the words of one mother: "Parents are invited to be in the classroom as volunteers. I feel this is good for us because a lot of times we can see a more positive way to handle our children" (O'Keefe, 1979, p. 22).

In examining the process underlying the long-term effectiveness of Head Start, Woodhead (1988) suggests that it is like a relay race: the burst of cognitive and school readiness fades, but not before the baton has been given to other runners on the team—teacher expectations, self-confidence, school promotions, avoidance of special education, parental aspirations, and so forth.

Whatever the mechanisms for success, a favorable attitude toward Head Start has resulted in continuous federal funding, despite the threatened curtailment of many government programs. In addition, however, it is recognized that *quality* is essential, and a portion of the funding is mandated for program improvement. Presently, Head Start staff is underpaid and undertrained; too many programs have not met standards for medical examinations; mental health consultation and training does not meet the preschoolers' needs, and family support is inadequate (Piotrkowski et al., 1994; Zigler and Styfco, 1993). The demand has increased for performance standards and better monitoring of the programs (Kassebaum, 1994).

In addition, Head Start is being viewed more realistically than it was at its inception. It is now better understood that brief intervention, even when comprehensive and of high quality, cannot indefinitely ameliorate continuing poverty and adversity. Thus, there is renewed interest in programs that continue to support children as they move into elementary schools. The initial Follow Through program did not receive adequate funding, but the Head Start Transition Project currently attempts to extend Head Start into the schools (Zigler, 1994). At the same time, there is also interest in creating Head Start for children from birth to three years of age.

Finally, it is recognized that as Head Start moves into the twenty-first century it must confront changing social conditions. The economic and social conditions that necessitated Head Start have worsened. Not only are more children living in poverty; many are also experiencing unsurpassed violence, fear, and despair in their communities (Takanishi and DeLeon, 1994). The excess number of guns, substance abuse, and HIV in our society especially impacts poor children. In short, poverty is worse than what it once was. The burdens of Head Start have thus become weightier. Fortunately, much has been learned about meeting the needs of disadvantaged youth, and these lessons can make the task easier. In addition, it is understood that Head Start cannot solely "fix" poverty, but it must be linked to welfare reform, community development, and training adults for a global economy.

The Rochester Primary Mental Health Project (PMHP). This project, initiated in 1957 by Cowen, Zax, and their colleagues, took the school as its focus for preventive efforts (Cowen et al, 1975; Zax and Cowen, 1967). The school was selected not only because it is the setting for much socialization and learning but also because children were experiencing school maladjustment. Teachers complained that several children were demanding a disproportionate amount of time and energy. These students were not being well served, the rest of the class was being disrupted, and teacher morale was suffering. Mental health services for these children were either unavailable or it was assumed that troubles would disappear with time. They did not (e.g., Cowen et al., 1966).

Although PMHP has evolved over the years, its continuing thrust has been systematic early identification and prompt preventive intervention for school maladjustment. The project's focus is secondary prevention (the term "primary" in the title refers to the primary grades). What follows is a brief description of the principal aspects of the program. More extensive descriptions are available elsewhere (e.g., Cowen and Hightower, 1989a, 1990).

One of the innovative aspects of PMHP is mass screening of youngsters soon after they begin school. Screening methods have consisted of parental interviews, psychological testing, teacher reports, and direct observations. Diverse kinds of data are collected concerning developmental and health history, school problem behaviors and competencies, and factors in the children's life situations that may relate to school adjustment. Information is obtained from multiple informants.

Children identified in PMHP as already manifesting maladjustment, or as likely to do so in the future, become the recipients of special treatment by nonprofessional child aides. Conversation, books, games, and media provide a framework for interaction with the child. The child is encouraged to access problem areas and feelings, and enhancement of self-esteem is considered important. Specific activities depend on the needs of the individual child. The utilization of minimally paid nonprofessionals as "therapists" is a noteworthy dimension of PMHP. Many of the child aides are mothers with relatively modest formal education. They receive some training at the project, but personal qualities are also considered a potent treatment resource. Although the use of nonprofessional child aides was initially justified on the basis of professional shortages and financial austerity, the child aides are now seen as an asset of the program rather than a compromise (Cowen and Hightower, 1989b; Hightower and Braden, 1991).

The general model of the PMHP has thus, been characterized by: (1) its focus on young children; (2) use of active, systematic screening for early school maladjustment; (3) expansion of services through the use of nonprofessional aides; and (4) the use of professionals in activities such as training, supervision, consultation, and research/program evaluation. The program has been flexibly applied so as to meet the demands of particular situations.

Research has been an essential component of the PMHP; from the start it was designed to improve the program and to demonstrate possible benefit. Research has been conducted, for example, on assessment instruments to initially screen children and to evaluate their progress (e.g., Gesten, 1976; Hightower et al., 1987). Evaluation of the program's effectiveness has been extensive. Examination of several hundred children who participated in PMHP at some time during 1974–1981 suggested reductions in acting-out, shyness, and learning problems, as well as gains in sociability, assertiveness, and tolerance of frustration (Weissberg et al., 1983). However, the raters knew that the children were PMHP participants, and the study had no control group.

While the realistic constraints of doing research in schools has often limited the rigor of research designs, the large number of evaluations over the years do suggest that the program has been effective. And importantly, research findings have been fed back into the program to structure improvements (Cowen and Hightower, 1989b; Hightower and Braden, 1991). For example, not all the findings over the years have been positive; some data indicated that those most helped were the shy-anxious children, and greater efforts then were made to facilitate the aides' effectiveness with acting-out and learning-disabled students (Cowen, Gersten, and Wilson, 1979; Lorion, Cowen, and Caldwell, 1974).

PMHP began as a single demonstration project and by 1983 twenty PMHP projects were operating in the Rochester, New York, area. Through active dissemination efforts, the program has also been adopted elsewhere and the project staff estimates that there are 350 implementing school districts around the world (Cowen and Hightower, 1989b).

Based on their experiences in PMHP, Cowen and his colleagues have more recently developed the Rochester Child Resilience Project (RCRP). This project is conceptually and empirically rooted in understanding the impact of chronic life stress on children and the resilience of some children experiencing monumental adverse circumstances. In this context the project was designed to investigate the correlates and antecedents of resilient outcomes among highly stressed fourth-to-sixth-grade urban children (Cowen et al., 1990). Early results from RCRP have begun to identify variables that differentiate stress-affected and stress-resilient children and their parents (Cowen et al., 1990; Cowen et al., 1994). Some of these are child variables, such as an internal and realistic sense of control, problem-solving skills, coping strategies, and self-esteem. Other variables involve the parent-child relationship and the caregiver's sense of being an effective parent. This research is an example of how investigations of resiliency can be useful to those concerned with enhancing the wellness of children and families at risk due to highly stressful environments (Cowen, 1994).

The School Transitional Environment Project (STEP).   STEP is designed to avert future difficulties for students who are functioning adaptively in their schools (Felner and Adan, 1988; Felner et al., 1993; Hightower and Braden, 1991). The focus is on a regularly occurring life event—the transition into middle, junior, or high school. School transition can be a risky time for youngsters; it is associated with diminished academic performance, substance abuse, delinquency, and school drop-out. Transition is considered riskier in schools that provide little social support and have complex organization (e.g., students feeding in from many other schools, many new social demands). Thus, STEP targets such schools.

Central to STEP is the creation of units in which a group of students is assigned to a homeroom and to academic classes as well. STEP homerooms are placed in physical proximity, so that cohesion is increased and complexity of the large school decreased. In addition, homeroom teachers take on new tasks in guidance and monitoring. For example, they assist students in selecting classes, provide brief counseling, and oversee attendance and truancy. Teachers receive training in these areas. Coordination is structured through regular teacher meetings to discuss student functioning, needs for referral, and problems. Thus, STEP units simulate small schools by creating small units in which groups of people are in close contact and responsible to each other.

Over the years STEP has serviced students from working, semiskilled, and blue-collar families in both urban and rural settings. Evaluations show its effectiveness. For example, in the beginning program the 21 percent school drop-out rate for STEP students compared favorably to the 43 percent drop-out rate for control students. The STEP students attended school at higher rates, and had higher grades. This favorable outcome has generally held in subsequent programs, indicating STEP's contribution to primary prevention.

Issues In Prevention

Despite the logic of arguments for prevention, the approach has a relatively small constituency, is still underfunded, and is underresearched (Peterson, Zink, and Farmer, 1992). Prevention has been resisted and criticized on a number of grounds. For one, society's focus on treatment has a long history and remains strong. Professionals are trained for treatment (Goldston, 1986) and are financially rewarded for treatment. Second, it is difficult to deflect funding from the obvious needs of those already displaying problems, a need that is never completely met. Third, questions have been raised about the effectiveness of prevention. It is fair to say that recent evaluations have weakened this concern. Nevertheless, the

issue is not completely laid to rest. In fact, by its very nature the impact of prevention can be difficult to demonstrate (Peterson et al., 1992). Large numbers of subjects are often required, making the research expensive and demanding.

In addition, ethical concerns have been voiced about prevention. These concerns are especially compelling when large segments of the population are involved— which is the intent of the preventive ideology (Seidman, 1987). A major concern is the relationship of professionals and clients, and the question of who is to have the power to select goals. For example, the goals of Head Start seem simple enough: to provide educational input, health services, and community support to disadvantaged families. But initially these programs were often based on the *deficit* model, which suggested that poor, frequently minority, children were disadvantaged by inferior genetic endowment, subculture, or both (Ginsburg, 1972; Rappaport, 1977). According to this model, intervention required an injection of middle-class culture, the earlier the better. This model raises the fundamental question about differential value being placed on the behaviors of one social class or some ethnic groups over the behaviors of others. In fact, there is an alternative approach, the *difference* model, that assumes that poor children are not deficient: they learn, think, and operate successfully in their home environments. Professionals who endorse the difference model argue that programs must build on what children already possess. These workers recognize the richness of the environments of the poor and culturally different. The difference model may suggest, for example, the valuing and use of nonstandard language, with middle-class language and customs gradually being presented as a necessary alternative. Only in this way, it is argued, can the young develop self-respect and motivation. This controversy, often heard in the earlier days of Head Start, is akin to concerns about "top-down" approaches in which the "experts" fail to acknowledge the unique strengths and diversities of the communities they seek to help (Gesten and Jason, 1987). In so doing, they fail to enhance people's sense of control and to understand what approach might be most effective. Some of the pitfalls of the top-down approach may have been avoided in Head Start by placing some control in the hands of the community. In addition, the input of professionals whose cultural backgrounds are other than "mainstream" has increasingly helped avoid the deficit model (Rogoff and Morelli, 1989).

All of the above and other factors have hindered preventive interventions. At the same time, influential people have argued for primary prevention that is so broadly defined that it might be viewed as social engineering. As Figure 15–1 indicates, primary prevention includes the promotion of physical and psychological health, a very broad domain. Albee (1986), for example, argues that the causal connection between emotional disturbance and poverty, sexism, and racism is clear. He thus desires broad social change and competence building, noting that his position is threatening to those who hold that certain groups (e.g., blacks, women, southern Europeans) are defective due to organic factors.

Cowen (1991, 1995) has analyzed what he calls "wellness" and he suggests specific areas that might prove critical in its enhancement. Wellness is defined as going beyond the absence of malfunction to having a sense of such things as belongingness, purpose, control, and satisfaction with oneself and one's life. Cowen (1995) cites five main, mutually helpful elements as central to wellness: forming wholesome early attachments, acquiring age-appropriate competencies, experiencing life in environments that favor healthy development, having a sense of control over one's fate, and coping positively with stress. These elements are viewed as similar to inoculations, as protection against possible later adverse outcomes. Moreover, Cowen argues that all people can benefit from this approach. Intervention would take many pathways—working with individuals, settings, communities, society's structures, and social policy to promote the well-being of the many. It would require input from diverse fields: mental health, human development, community planning, social policy, and the like.

Such primary prevention programs aimed at mental health promotion do exist. However, most current prevention programs target at-risk populations and specific "disease" prevention. The degree to which we will commit future resources to prevention is unclear, and depends not only on available resources but also on many other variables including better understanding of development, demonstration of the effectiveness of prevention, values, and commitment to the welfare of youth. Prevention is clearly linked to broad social and political issues. We shall see more of this connection as we proceed.

FAMILIES IN TRANSITION

The importance of family influences on children's development has been evident throughout this book. In this section we will highlight three family topics that are not necessarily related to any particular childhood disorder. Rather, they illustrate how contemporary change in the family is part of evolving concerns for the child.

The current state of the family and its future is a common topic in the media and of conversations at social events, over the dinner table, in shopping malls, and, indeed, wherever people meet. It is also a politically salient topic (e.g., Bennett, 1987; Schroeder, 1989). While it is often assumed that the issue is the decline of the traditional family, it need not, and indeed should not, be articulated in this way. Scholars who have studied the history of the American family have argued that we are suffering from the "mystique of the traditional family." Bahr (1988), for example, challenges the idea that the family has decayed from some past idyllic form: well ordered, agreeably run, psychologically supportive of its members, and superior to today's families. Undoubtedly stable, warm, and supportive families with "traditional" structures did, and do, exist. But they have probably been atypical in all times and places. In fact, Bahr suggests that the family is as strong as ever, and perhaps our notions of family are more adaptable than before

Several factors have caused us to rethink our definitions of family. Among these is the increasing number of children raised in single-parent homes and the new family relationships created by remarriages (U.S. Bureau of the Census, 1994; Hetherington, 1989; Schroeder, 1989). The number of women working outside of the home also influences contemporary conceptualizations of family.

Maternal Employment and Child Care

Social and economic influences have resulted in the majority of mothers being employed outside the home. Among two-parent families with school-aged children the rate of maternal employment is approximately 68 percent (U.S. Bureau of Census, 1994). In their examination of women's changing work roles, Matthews and Rodin (1989) examined the increase in maternal employment over time. Table 15–1 illustrates this pattern in the years between 1975 and 1993. Increases occurred for mothers with children of all ages, and it is notable that by 1985 the majority of mothers of children below school age were working outside of the home.

Considerable attention has been given to the impact of maternal employment on the

TABLE 15–1 Percent of Mothers in Two-Parent Families in the Labor Force by Age of Own Youngest Child

Age of Child	1975	1985	1993
Under 3	32.7	50.5	57.3
3 to 5	42.2	58.4	63.1
6 to 13	51.8	68.2	74.7
14 to 17	53.5	67.0	75.6
Total	44.9	60.8	67.5

Adapted from U.S. Bureau of the Census, *Statistical Abstract of the United States: 1994* (114th edition). Washington, DC, 1994.

women themselves, marital relations, and of course on the development of their children (Hoffman, 1989; Scarr, Phillips, and McCartney, 1989). In general, there are few differences among two-parent families in which the mothers do or do not work (Muller, 1995; Silverstein, 1991). The impact of maternal employment depends on a host of factors, including the child's age, the amount of time parents spend at work, how remaining time is used by the family, the quality of child-care arrangements, parental attitudes toward work and their various roles, family structure, and other psychological, social, and economic variables (Gottfried and Gottfried, 1988; Hoffman, 1989; Scarr et al., 1989). Indeed, the question of maternal employment could be framed in terms of what variables affect families in general and what conditions should be provided to maximize the functioning of all families (Scarr, Phillips, and McCartney, 1990; Silverstein, 1991).

Child care. Increased maternal employment has focused attention on the need for a variety of child-care arrangements (e.g., Clarke-Stewart, 1992; Schroeder, 1989; Stipek and McCroskey, 1989). Children of employed mothers are most commonly cared for by family members or nonrelatives in either the child's own home or another's home. However, a substantial proportion attend some type of day care facility.

The impact of early care arrangements has been the topic of much debate among professionals (Belsky, 1986; Clarke-Stewart, 1989; Scarr et al., 1990). Parents are often concerned about finding arrangements that can provide the kinds of care they desire and that help shape their children's development in a manner consistent with their own values. In general, it would appear that the effects of day care on the child depend on both the quality of the care and the involvement of the child's parents. The development of children in high quality care can be as good as that of their peers raised at home by their parents, and in some cases development may even be accelerated.

There is concern as well for children of school age. Some older children have no formal provisions for care. These are the so-called "latchkey" children, who must use a key to let themselves into their empty homes after school. Less value-laden terms, such as "children in self care" have increasingly been advocated to describe this situation. Although an accurate estimate is hard to come by, estimates of the number of children in self-care range from 7.2 percent to 15 to 20 percent of early elementary and 45 percent of late elementary school-age children (Peterson and Magrab, 1989).

Attention to self-care is relatively recent, and the developmental implications for children are uncertain (Peterson and Magrab, 1989). Of course, the impact will not be the same for all children. The amount of time in self-care, parental attitudes, the child's developmental level, other family influences, and available social supports are likely to influence an individual child's reaction.

One question regarding self-care focuses on its potential impact on cognitive and academic functioning. Does self-care preclude after-school interactions with an adult that enhance cognitive development and assure the completion of school assignments? Per-

Many children return to empty homes after school. The impact of such "self-care" requires further study.

haps these needs are met later in the evening, as working parents appear to participate in child-centered activities by attending less to homemaking chores (Scarr et al., 1989). Much has also been written about the possibility that self-care has negative emotional effects on children. However, there is little carefully conducted research to support the hypothesis of adjustment difficulties among latchkey children (Lovko and Ullman, 1989).

It may be that self-care, even if not ideal, is an alternative arrangement for some children. When self-care is employed, it is necessary to ensure that the child is adequately prepared. Peterson (1989) suggests that three major areas need to be considered in preparation: injury risk, emotional difficulties, and selection of activities. Preparation has several components, including discussion with the child and arranging for a contact person if the child feels help is needed. It is also essential that the child have a safe and secure environment.

Single Parenting

Many of the issues raised about the impact of maternal employment in two-parent families apply to children being reared in single-parent homes. Parenting is a difficult task even when undertaken by two parents, and a single parent takes on the responsibilities on her or his own.

The growing number of children being reared in single-parent homes in the United States and elsewhere has made the issue an important one (Hernandez, 1994). Figure 15–3 illustrates the increasing percentage of homes headed by a single parent. Thirty percent of all U.S. families and over sixty percent of all African American families with children were headed by a single parent in 1993. Single-parent households include many children born to unmarried teenage mothers. These children, in particular, have been reported to encounter developmental problems in preschool (e.g., Furstenberg, Brooks-Gunn, and Chase-Lansdale, 1989).

Many young single mothers live in poverty and this likely contributes to the findings.

Not all single-parent homes are headed by never-married mothers, however. Many are created by divorce. Professionals have also been concerned with the impact of divorce on children and adolescents.

The Impact of Divorce

That many marriages end in divorce is well documented. The divorce rate in the U.S. more than doubled between 1970 and 1981 (Guidubaldi and Perry, 1985). Although this has leveled off and perhaps declined in recent years, large numbers of children will experience their parents' divorce (U.S. Bureau of the Census, 1994; Hernandez, 1994). However compelling, statistics do not completely capture the impact of the problem. Many children experience more than one divorce. Some experience periodic separation and discord in families where divorce petitions are filed and withdrawn. Thus divorce and remarriage are not static events, but a series of family transitions that modify the lives of children (Hetherington, Stanley-Hagan, and Anderson, 1989; Wallerstein, 1991).

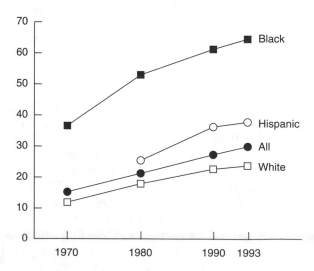

FIGURE 15–3   Percent of single-parent families by race and Hispanic origin, from 1970 to 1993.

Adapted from U.S. Bureau of the Census, *Statistical Abstract of the United States: 1994* (114th edition). Washington, DC, 1994.

The divorce process can be conceptualized as an ongoing highly stressful life event calling for a variety of competencies and coping strategies. Research repeatedly shows that in the first few years following divorce, children experience more behavior problems than children from intact families (Emery, 1982; Guidubaldi and Perry, 1985; Hetherington and Camara, 1984; Kurdek, 1981; Wallerstein, 1991). However, behavioral reactions may have begun several years earlier in response to the long-standing conflicts and disruptions that lead to many divorces. The behavior characteristics of children and adolescents in the postdivorce years is probably continuous with their behavior over the several previous years (Block, Block, and Gjerde, 1986, 1988).

Youngsters frequently react to divorce with aggressive, antisocial, impulsive, and noncompliant behaviors. Boys appear to suffer greater reactions than girls (Guidubaldi and Perry, 1985; Hetherington, Cox, and Cox, 1982). Age also appears to be a factor. For example, Stolberg and Bush (1985) found that externalizing problems related to two background variables, a history of marital hostility and children's age. Younger children had more externalizing problems, which were related to greater life changes.

Research on the immediate impact of divorce has been helpful in guiding clinicians who work with separating or divorcing families. However, the challenge faced by these youngsters and their families is one of a series of transitions over a longer period. Several major longitudinal studies have reported on some longer term findings (Allison and Furstenberg, 1989; Guidubaldi and Perry, 1985; Hetherington, 1989; Johnston, Kline, and Tschann, 1989; Wallerstein, 1991).

Long term results are available from Wallerstein's (1991) California Children of Divorce Study. The original project that began in 1971 was designed to explore the divorce experience in a nonclinical population of families with children between the ages of two and eighteen at the time of the marital separation (Wallerstein and Kelly, 1980). The primary method of assessment was in-depth clinical interviews with parents and children. It is important to keep in mind that generalizations based on this work are limited by the restricted sample of middle-class families from California. Moreover, all of the children had reached appropriate developmental milestones, were performing at appropriate levels of school, and had never been referred for treatment of psychological problems. As Wallerstein (1985) suggests, these children were "probably skewed in the direction of psychological health."

Wallerstein reported on two age groups of children, the younger being two-and-a-half to six years at the time of divorce (Wallerstein, 1984). Follow-up interviews were conducted when the children were in their teens. While this age group was more affected by the divorce crisis, few memories of the intact family or the marital rupture remained at follow-up. These children had spent a great portion of their lives in divorced or remarried households and most were performing well in school. Many did express sorrow at the emotional and economic deprivations they felt they had suffered. They spoke wistfully of the better life that they imagined in intact families and half had fantasies of parental reconciliation. While relationships with the custodial mother reflected closeness and concern for her difficulties, a need to establish relationships with absent fathers was heightened as the children approached adolescence. This seemed to be especially true for girls. Interestingly, these children looked forward to marriage and family and expected to avoid the unhappiness they associated with their parents' divorce.

Wallerstein's other sample was of children nine years or older at the time of their parent's separation, and nineteen to twenty-nine years at follow-up (Wallerstein, 1985). They appeared more adversely affected than the offspring who had experienced divorce earlier in life. A significant number was burdened by memories of marital strife and break-up. Most were committed to marriage and a conservative morality, but were concerned about repeating their parents' unhappy marriage. About one-third of the young women seemed to have problems about commitment and seemed caught in a series of short-term sexual relationships. While the majority of these young people were law-abiding students or self-supporting citizens, a significant number, especially women, seemed to be troubled and drifting. Sixty-eight percent of the sample had engaged in mild to serious illegal activity, with the young men far more likely than the women to have been involved in the serious violations.

Overall, Wallerstein's (1991) findings indicate that over half of the youngsters she studied have become compassionate and competent people. Apart from their individual resources, a supportive relationship with another adult, usually the mother, seems to have been most helpful. This is consistent with other findings that the quality of the mother-child relationship is an important factor in the ongoing adjustment of children experiencing divorce (e.g., Wolchik et al., 1993). Although boys had a harder time over the years than girls, this difference was no longer evident at young adulthood. The project does provide a longitudinal sample of rich clinical information. The lack of an appropriate comparison group and objective measures, however, suggests caution in interpreting the results.

Guidubaldi and Perry (1985) have reported on a follow-up of the National Association of School Psychologists study. This research employed a more random and nationwide sample than previous studies. A national sample of school psychologists collected a variety of assessments from randomly selected children from single-parent divorced families and intact families. At the second assessment, data were available for the forty children from divorced families, and the average time since divorce was 6.41 years. Consistent with the original findings, children from divorced families performed more poorly than those from intact families on several measures, and boys exhibited more adverse effects than girls. One particularly interesting finding was that socioeconomic stress produced by the divorce seems to have been a major influence on the child's adjustment. Other researchers have also commented on how family economics can both contribute to divorce and be changed by divorce, and can impact family adjustment. The relationship between economics and divorce has implications for social policy regarding predivorce and postdivorce families (Duncan, 1994; Hernandez, 1994).

Hetherington and her colleagues have also conducted longitudinal research on the impact of divorce (Hetherington, 1989; Hetherington, Cox, and Cox, 1985). As in the Wallerstein study, the research relied on a restricted sample: well-educated, middle-class, white families. In this research, however, comparisons were made among nondivorced families and divorced families in which remarriage had or had not occurred. In addition, multiple methods of assessment (interviews, rating scales, and observations) from multiple sources (parent, child, teachers, peers) and settings (school and home) were employed. Data were collected during the first two years following divorce and in a six year follow-up, when the children averaged ten years of age.

One of the findings addressed the stability of behavior problems and social competence. Externalizing problems were more stable for boys and internalizing problems were more stable for girls. However, the importance of earlier levels of externalizing behavior was clear for both sexes: Early externalizing problems were significantly correlated with later internalizing problems for both sexes. In addition, early aggression also predicted later problems in social competence, and this relationship was stronger for girls than for boys.

Another result, found in other research as well, was the impact of perceived stress in families that had experienced divorce. Reports of negative life events since divorce were correlated with both internalizing and externalizing behavior problems in children at the six-year follow-up. The relationships were greater with externalizing problems for boys and internalizing problems for girls.

The follow-up data also suggest that divorce has more long-term adverse effects on boys and that remarriage is more disruptive for girls, at least when they are living with remarried mothers and step-fathers. In divorced families where the mother had not remarried, daughters were similar in their adjustment to those from nondivorced families while sons still exhibited more externalizing and other problems. However, in families in which remarriage had occurred the findings were quite different. In general, when the remarriage had occurred less than two years earlier, both boys and girls exhibited more problems than youngsters from nondivorced families, perhaps because they were adapting to another life transition. In families where the remarriage had occurred more than two years earlier, daughters but not sons exhibited more problems. These girls, however, did appear to adapt to the remarriage over time.

In sum, the long-term results of research indicate that while many children do indeed suffer negative outcomes related to divorce and remarriage, many also do quite well. Indeed, for some, coping with these life transitions can have developmental benefits. Increased understanding of the protective variables and resiliencies of these children can contribute to interventions to reduce or eliminate the potential negative impact of divorce.

Several kinds of divorce intervention programs have been attempted and some seem promising (Grych and Fincham, 1992; Stolberg, 1988). Many of the programs attempt to enhance adjustment by working directly with the child. Although such programs are widespread there is not a great deal of evidence to support their effectiveness. One program that has proven successful is the Children of Divorce Project (cf. Alpert-Gillis, Pedro-Carroll, and Cowen, 1989). Children experiencing separation or divorce meet in groups that provide support, skill building, exploration of feelings, and examination of perceptions of divorce. School-based intervention programs, such as this one, have the advantage of working with children in a natural setting with similar peers.

Much of what we have learned about the impact of divorce on children suggests working with the parents. Divorce mediation programs involve bringing together divorcing adults to discuss with an impartial party the resolution of disputes. With respect to children, the intent is to develop cooperative coparenting and to lay the groundwork for resolving future conflicts. Other prevention programs intervene with single parents. By improving parenting skills and parent-child interactions, they can enhance child adjustment (e.g., Stolberg and Garrison, 1985). The Program for Prevention Research (Wolchik et al., 1993) is a good example of an intervention based on the empirical literature. This program targeted five variables thought to be related to adjustment: quality of the custodial parent-child relationship, contact with the noncustodial parent, negative divorce-related events including interparental conflict, contact with and support from nonparental adults, and discipline strategies. Divorced mothers attended ten weekly group sessions and two individual sessions. Each session included a short lecture, skill demonstrations, skill practice, and assignment and review of homework. Compared to wait list controls, program participants showed higher quality mother-child relationships and discipline, fewer negative divorce events, and better adjustment outcomes.

MALTREATMENT OF YOUTH

Although the problem of child maltreatment has probably existed since the beginning of civilization, recent concern is usually dated to the early 1960s (Cicchetti and Olsen, 1990). Especially influential was an article by pediatrician C. Henry Kempe and his colleagues, in which the term "battered child syndrome" was coined (Kempe et al., 1962). Their efforts were stimulated by alarm at the large number of children at pediatric clinics with nonaccidental injuries. Subsequent efforts resulted in all fifty states adopting mandated child abuse reporting laws by the year 1970.

Since the late 1970s the problem has become a major public concern. For example, in 1976 only 10 percent of the population thought abuse was a serious problem compared to over 90 percent in 1983 (Magnuson, 1983). In fact, reported cases of child maltreatment continue to increase. Between 1982 and 1991, the number of cases of alleged maltreatment doubled (National Center for Child Abuse and Neglect, 1993). According to the U.S. Bureau of the Census (1994), the number of victims increased between 1990 and 1992 from about 801,000 to 918,000. Such reports raise the question of whether we are uncovering a larger proportion of existing cases or whether actual maltreatment is increasing.

Nonetheless, there is agreement that child abuse and neglect is a serious and prevalent problem. What is not as clear is an agreed upon definition of what constitutes abuse or neglect and therefore what the real prevalence of the problem is. This obviously creates difficulties for research, interventions, and legal practice (Cicchetti, 1994).

When most people hear the widely used term "child abuse," they assume that it refers to physical assault and serious injury. However, the general legal definition that has evolved over several decades includes both the commission of injuries and acts of omission, that is, failure to care for and protect (National Institute of Mental Health, 1977). Thus, neglect needs to be addressed along with physical assault.

Figure 15–4 illustrates the relative rates of various forms of maltreatment reported in 1992 in the United States (U.S. Bureau of the Census, 1994). Approximately 52 percent of the cases involved neglect and 25 percent physical abuse. Based on previous reports (American Humane Association, 1984), it is likely that most physical abuse involved minor injuries (e.g., small cuts, welts, bruises) rather than major injuries (e.g., skull or bone fracture, internal injuries, burns). Thus, the majority of the total maltreated population experiences neglect, and the majority of physical injuries are minor. This profile contrasts with the public's image of maltreatment as mainly involving severe physical injury (Wolfe and St. Pierre, 1989).

In addition to physical abuse and neglect, two other aspects of maltreatment have received increasing attention—sexual and psychological abuse. In general, sexual abuse refers to sexual experiences that occur between youth and older persons, or the sexual exploitation of the young such as in pornographic film. The extent of the problem is difficult to estimate, but most experts agree that it is underreported. This is suggested by adults' retrospective reports of their childhood experiences and by the increase in the reporting of sexual abuse in both the United States and Canada (Green, 1993; Wolfe and Wolfe, 1988). Recent statistics suggest that sexual abuse occurs in

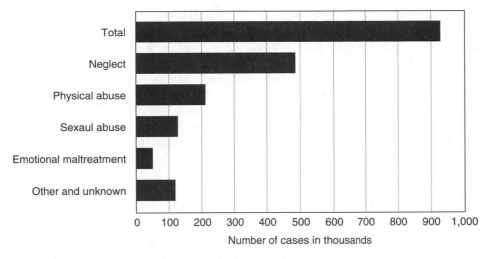

FIGURE 15–4   Child abuse and neglect cases: 1992.

Note: More than one type of maltreatment may be substantiated per child. Therefore, items add up to more than the total shown. Source: Chart prepared by U.S. Bureau of the Census, 1994.

about 14 percent of substantiated child maltreatment (U.S. Bureau of the Census, 1994). Abuse of girls is more common than of boys (e.g., Finkelhor, 1994; Trickett, McBride-Chang, and Putman, 1994). This may, in part, be due to the fact that the data are based on cases in which the perpetrator is a caregiver, but boys are more likely to be sexually abused by nonfamily members. Of considerable concern is the possibility that sexual abuse occurs in day-care settings. While reports of such occurrences are frightening, it is important to remember that young children are more likely to be sexually abused at home (Kelly, Brant, and Waterman, 1993; Schroeder and Gordon, 1991).

The definition of psychological (or emotional) maltreatment is probably most difficult and controversial (cf. Cicchetti, 1991; McGee and Wolfe, 1991). Nevertheless, psychological maltreatment is increasingly seen as part of all abuse and neglect (Garbarino, 1991; Hart and Brassard, 1991). Thus, thinking in terms of physical/sexual abuse alone does not capture the broad nature of

the problem. Nevertheless, societal and community standards always come into play in judging "abusive" behaviors and "harmful" outcomes (Barnett, Manly, and Cicchetti, 1991; Belsky, 1991; Sternberg and Lamb, 1991). Different standards for both appropriate parenting and valued outcomes are particularly at issue when psychological maltreatment is considered.

The study of child abuse and neglect has focused on the factors that cause maltreatment and the consequences for the child. The majority of research on etiology has focused on physical abuse (Emery, 1989; Wolfe and St. Pierre, 1989).

The causes of abuse encompass characteristics of the abusing parent and the child, parenting or parent-child interactional processes, and social-cultural influences. This later category includes both the immediate social environment (employment, extended family, social network) and larger societal-cultural context (e.g., societal tolerance for violence). It is impossible to even enumerate all of the influences that have been examined. However, contemporary efforts to understand child abuse recognize complex, multiple, and interrelated determinants of the problem (Azar and Wolfe, 1989; Belsky, 1993; Cicchetti and Olsen, 1990; Okun, Parker, and Levendosky, 1994). Further research is needed to better understand the factors leading to different forms of maltreatment, and the multiple pathways to any specific form (Cicchetti and Olsen, 1990; Wolfe and St. Pierre, 1989). Here we highlight only some of the key findings (cf. Emery, 1989; Wolfe, 1988).

A strong relationship has consistently emerged between socioeconomic disadvantage and abuse and neglect. While it is hard to isolate the specific causal factors, reduced resources, stress, and other problems that are associated with socioeconomic disadvantage put the child at increased risk. It has been suggested that neglect, in particular, is related to low SES (Wolock and Horowitz, 1984). However, it is important to recognize that the majority of families who experience chronic deprivation do not maltreat their offspring.

A particular child in the family is often the target for maltreatment. Research suggests that children and adolescents at highest risk for abuse are those who display behavioral and physical problems or interactional styles that adversely interact with parental characteristics and family stress (e.g., Bonner et al., 1992). Age of the child plays a role as well, although maltreatment occurs at all ages. For example, in 1992 in the United States 13 percent of cases occurred with children of age two and under, 26 percent with age two to five, 23 percent with age six to nine, 20 percent with age ten to thirteen, and 15 percent with age fourteen to seventeen (U.S. Bureau of the Census, 1994).

For the most part, parents or parent surrogates are the perpetrators of abuse. Parents who began their families at a younger age, many in their teens, are the most typical perpetrators (Connelly and Straus,

1992). In general, more female than male caregivers are reported for maltreatment. However, more males are reported for physical injury, and females for neglect. It is likely that these patterns reflect differential social, cultural, and economic influences on men and women.

Several other characteristics of abusive parents have been noted including social isolation from family and friends, more emotional symptoms and mood changes, more physical health problems, inadequate parenting skills, limited childrearing knowledge, inappropriate expectations regarding developmentally suitable behavior, lower tolerance for common demanding behavior such as infant crying, and misattributions of the child's motivation for misbehaving. These factors are part of the complex influences that contribute to the development of abuse and neglectful interactions.

Finally, in looking at the development of abuse and neglect it is important to address intergenerational patterns of maltreatment. In a review of the literature, Kaufman and Zigler (1987) found that abuse is more common in the backgrounds of abusing parents. However, they also found that many parents who had not been abused became abusive and some who had been abused did not. They estimate that based on all forms of maltreatment approximately 30 percent of maltreated children repeat the cycle as adults. It is generally agreed that the majority of maltreated children do not perpetuate the intergenerational cycle. A number of positive influences, including the development of supportive intimate relationships, help break the cycle (Egeland, Jacobvitz, and Sroufe, 1988; Wolfe and St. Pierre, 1989).

With regard to the consequences of maltreatment for the child, no single pattern of emotional or behavioral difficulties has been found. Rather, youngsters manifest appreciable impairments in all early developmental domains and in a variety of areas of later adjustment (Cicchetti and Olsen, 1990; Wolfe and St. Pierre, 1989). Difficulties include increased aggression, poor peer relationships, insecure attachments, impaired social-cognitive abilities, anxiety, depression, speech and language deficiencies, and poor grades and achievement test scores (e.g., Cummings et al., 1994; Dodge, Pettit, and Bates, 1994; Shields, Cicchetti, and Ryan, 1994; Wolfe and Birt, 1995). Thus, the impact of abuse is best viewed as undermining a variety of normal developmental processes (cf. Beeghly and Cicchetti, 1994; Sroufe and Fleeson, 1987).

Interventions for maltreatment have been parent and family centered rather than child centered. The problem of neglect has been given lower priority than abuse, perhaps because neglect is associated with poverty and also because there is less consensus about society's right to intervene when parental behavior is less overtly offensive (Melton and Davidson, 1987). Given the combination of factors that contributes to the development of maltreatment, effective intervention needs to address many domains (individual, familial, community and societal) and thus include multiple components (Belsky, 1993; Krugman, 1993). As we gain more precise understanding about the different types of maltreatment, we will be better able to shape treatments to fit specific needs (cf. Crittenden, Claussen, and Sugarman, 1994; Manly, Cicchetti, and Barnett, 1994).

Educational efforts are part of the preventive approach to the problem of maltreatment. In addition to promoting public awareness, these efforts seek to decrease the rates of child maltreatment. Earlier we noted that the incidence of reported maltreatment has risen and the question was raised as to whether this represented an actual increase in maltreatment or a greater sensitivity to the problem. It would be encouraging if the latter were the case. Perhaps educational efforts have increased public awareness and rejection of abusive behavior. Cultural values, such as tolerance for violence and neglect as well as rigid reluctance to intrude on family autonomy, are part of the context in which abusive and neglectful relationships develop. To the extent that families are being harmed by these values, change is appropriate.

YOUTH SERVICES

So far in this chapter we have discussed prevention and examined the changing family and maltreatment of youth. We now more broadly examine the delivery of services to young people. We will comment on the delivery of medical, mental health, and foster care. As we have seen, services are delivered in a variety of settings: clinics, hospitals, schools, home, and other institutions. Accent 15–1 details home visiting programs. To various degrees services depend on federal and state governments, "third-party" (insurance) companies, and clients themselves. At the present time, there is a perceived shortage of funds for government programs and skyrocketing of health care costs, which adversely impact both middle and lower class families.

The medical needs of youth, especially poor youth, are not being adequately met. Federal and state health programs do provide relief for low-income families. For example, the Early and Periodic Screening, Diagnosis, and Treatment Program (EPSDT) was originated as part of the Social Security Act of 1967 (Meisels, 1984). It calls for prevention and treatment as early in life as possible and periodical follow-ups. Early screening (for example, for PKU, deafness, early symptoms of contagious disease, and developmental problems) is designed as prevention. Individuals with positive or suspicious findings can be further examined, diagnosed, and treated. The EPSDT program is helpful, but overall needs are not being met. For example, in 1990 over 20%

ACCENT 15–1 Home Visiting As a Strategy for Delivering Services

Sending visitors into the homes of needy families is an old strategy for delivering services, and one that is more popular today than ever before (Gomby et al., 1993). In the United States, programs are funded by private sources and also by public agencies such as the Departments of Education and Health and Human Services. Many programs are aimed at prevention and they vary in many ways, including the focus of their efforts. Some focus on a single goal, such as preventing low birth weight or enhancing cognitive development. Others have multiple goals, for example, promotion of physical and cognitive development and prevention of child abuse. The content of the programs also vary. Some deliver a curriculum during home visits or assess the physical health of participants while others provide information, evaluate needs, and make referrals. Programs also vary not only in the kinds of professional staff employed but also in the use of paraprofessional staff.

Moreover, there is diversity in the families serviced by the programs. Current programs serve all social classes and racial/ethnic groups at all levels of need. Such diversity imposes substantial demands on program designers and those who implement services. Programs need to fit and accommodate cul-

tural characteristics. For example, the role of the extended family in African-American families should be considered in planning and delivering services. The strengths and needs of individual families are also important considerations. Families with multiple needs are a special challenge, of course, since it is unlikely that any specific goal will be met without addressing several problem areas.

Gomby and her colleagues (1993) have reviewed research on the outcome of preventative home visiting programs. The findings show mixed outcome. Although the findings probably reflect inadequacies of the research, some poor results no doubt are due to failure of the programs themselves. For example, the goal of preventing low birth weight simply by providing social support may not be achieved without the provision of help to change lifestyles. Gomby et al. have also proposed several guidelines for future programs including multiple goals, flexibility in intensity and duration, sensitivity to the unique characteristics of the families, and realistic expectations. They also warn that little can be accomplished without ongoing comprehensive support for youth. There is no quick inexpensive inoculation or pill that can do the job.

---

of children from families with annual incomes below $20,000 had no contact with a physician (Pollitt, 1994). And measles, which can be controlled by immunization, has dangerously increased in recent years, particularly among certain minority groups.

Over the years, many studies of mental health services have been conducted. It is widely agreed that children and adolescents are underserved (Kazdin, 1993a,b). This is particularly so for specific groups such as those of minority background and those with physical handicaps. State governments carry a relatively heavy burden for financing services. Services are delivered in vari-

ous settings including mental health clinics, hospitals and residential centers, private professional practices, child welfare and juvenile agencies, and the schools. Analyses of mental health needs recognize both lack of funding and a fragmentation of services.

In addition, mental health services are sometimes seen as not taking advantage of what is known about behavior problems and their treatment. In fact, there is ample documentation of the overall efficacy of psychological, behavioral, and educational treatments (Lipsey and Wilson, 1993). Furthermore, it is clear that treatment for young people is effective for a variety of disorders in a variety of settings, including hospitals (Kazdin 1993a; Saxe, Cross, and Silverman, 1988). Benefits can accrue from prevention programs as well. Nevertheless, there seems little doubt that more funding is needed to effectively apply present knowledge.

Calls have gone out for comprehensive, integrated, community-based services (e.g., Illback, 1994). Because behavior dysfunctions are multifactorial, services often must have several components. To take a relatively uncomplicated hypothetical case, a child displaying Attention-Deficit Hyperactivity Disorder may require a psychologist to plan and monitor a behavior modification program, school personnel to coordinate an academic program, and a psychiatrist for medication evaluation. In more complex cases, still other services are needed. For the most part, though, mental health services are not well coordinated. In recognition of this problem, the federal government has instituted the Child and Adolescent Service System Program (CASSP). By providing leadership and funding to the states, CASSP has encouraged a comprehensive model of care, interagency collaboration, parental advocacy, and sensitivity to the needs of minority groups (Lourie et al., 1990). It appears that some progress is being made.

Concern is also expressed about the social service system that administers out-of-home or foster care when the family is unable to provide adequate care. Almost half a million youth are now in out-of-home care in the United States (Shealy, 1995). Much control of this system belongs to the states, although the federal government has a role. It is certainly preferable for children and adolescents to remain with their families, but substitute care is not always avoidable. Substitute placement occurs voluntarily when families are unable to care for their offspring or when children are involuntarily removed from their homes due to neglect, abuse, abandonment, or some emergency.

What alternatives exist for these children? One study showed that 73 percent of displaced youth lived in foster homes, 17 percent in group homes or shelters, 3 percent in nonfinalized adoptive homes, and the remaining 7 percent in a variety of other placements (Lewit, 1993).

The number of children in substitute care rose by an alarming 69 percent between 1982 and 1992. With this increase came an increase in formal placement of children with relatives. Although there are probably many reasons for the rise in substitute care, parental drug abuse, especially crack cocaine use by mothers, appears to be an important factor.

Many concerns are expressed about foster care (Lewit, 1993; Tuma, 1989). A fundamental question, of course, is whether it might be reduced by better support of families. There is also a need for more complete data about substitute care and for stronger monitoring of the quality of care. In addition, too often youth are moved from placement to placement, and too many remain in care for long periods of time. Foster care is intended as temporary, but more than two-thirds of youth have been found to remain until they reach the legal age to be on their own (Tuma, 1989). Such "foster care drift" can be alleviated by prompt, decisive action to either support children in their family homes or locate permanent placement for them, a policy encouraged by the federal government. Overall, more resources, innovative problem solving, and a greater commitment to improving substitute care are required.

YOUTH IN THE GLOBAL SOCIETY

As we turn our attention to the international scene, one striking fact is that mass transportation and communication are making the functional world smaller day by day. The lives of youth are already being strongly influenced by this phenomenon and the impact will become even more pervasive in the twenty-first century.

An obvious implication of the shrinking world is the increased need to deal well with others of different color, facial appearance, dress, and custom. The challenge of adapting to ethnic and racial differences is an age-old one, of course. In the United States, which is enormously heterogeneous, the issue has long been of concern. Prejudice and fears too often have had adverse effects on peoples of various groups—Native Americans, African Americans, Irish, Poles, Jews, and Catholics, to name a few. Being of "minority" status is a risk factor in that it is linked to stress and reduced quality of life and opportunity (e.g., Albee, 1986). We continue today to grapple with this issue, as exemplified in controversy about immigration and bilingualism in schools and other institutions. Although change undoubtedly must be gradual, a reasonable goal is to not only increase tolerance for those who are different from us but also to recognize that heterogeneity can be enormously enriching.

While poverty in the United States is rightly of concern, the effects of being poor are dramatically worse in the developing countries with regard to death rates, disease, and lack of opportunity. The link between poverty and bodily and psychological development is observed in various measures. For example, in developing countries the prevalence of iron-deficiency anemia for children up to four years of age is about 51 percent (Pollitt, 1994). These children consistently score lower on a variety of developmental and cognitive tests. Research from several countries also indicates the effects of poor diet and that early supplements of high calorie, high protein foods can enhance mental and motor development in high-risk populations.

Exposure to armed conflict influences the development of a significant minority of young people (Jensen and Shaw, 1993; Ziv-

cic, 1993). The character of war varies and brings different kinds of impacts. In recent limited conflicts more civilians have been killed than military personnel (e.g., in Croatia). In addition to bodily threats to the self and loved ones, however, are uncertainty, separation from family and community, inadequate nutrition, lack of shelter, control by the "enemy," and the like. One way to view armed conflict is as a trauma that can result in post-traumatic stress disorder. However, wars that are low-to-moderate in intensity and that are long-lasting may not well fit this view because people can generate cognitive defenses over time. In fact, although anxiety and depression are reported in youth experiencing armed conflict, many children and adolescents show remarkable adaptation. Outcome depends on specific experiences, as well as on individual, family, and community variables. For example, negative outcome is lower when armed conflict is viewed as necessary by the community and when other social support is present. The more we understand about such mediators, the better we will be in the position to avoid emotional adversity. Efforts to alleviate the impact of war and violence through psychological intervention are ongoing (Bloch and Cvitkovic, 1995). Nevertheless, few would dispute the opinion that war "must be regarded with abhorrence in terms of its terrible human toll in human suffering, especially on its most innocent bystanders—children and adolescents" (Jensen and Shaw, 1993, p. 697).

An important outgrowth of closer communication among the peoples of the world is increased cooperation in solving problems and optimizing conditions. Over the last decades world attention has been drawn to promoting the healthy development of youth. This is exemplified in the activities of the United Nations. Several U.N. agencies focus on children's welfare, and special summits on youth are convened. The United Nations declared 1979 the International

Year of The Child, and subsequently has written official statements on the rights of children. In 1990 the World Summit for Children was convened to promote universal rights for survival, protection, and optimal development (UNICEF, 1991). The girl child has been singled out as especially needy. Data collected around the world, and particularly in developing countries, point to many inequalities suffered by females. In developing countries girls have less food, less adequate health care, and fewer educational opportunities. Early maternity has adverse effects on nutrition, health, and educational and occupational status. Gender bias is reflected by a disproportionate preference for sons and selective abortion of females fetuses.

Overall, concerned professionals and other citizens are increasingly addressing global issues such as poverty, high birth rates, infant mortality, environmental pollution and destruction, and the lack of medical and mental health services. All of these can have dramatic influence on the development of children and adolescents.

SUMMARY

The care received by children and adolescents reflects what is known about development but also the social, political, and economic conditions in which they are living. Present day concerns for the young recognize that they are shaped by a broad spectrum of influences.

Prevention of disordered development is widely conceptualized according to Caplan's model of primary, secondary, and tertiary prevention. The continuum of prevention ranges from promotion of health to rehabilitation with primary prevention being clearly different from treatment. Although prevention is an easier task when etiology is known, preventive efforts can succeed in the face of complex, less understood etiology. Known risk and protective factors provide a basis for prevention.

Many effective prevention programs now exist. They vary in their goals, methods, and settings. The Mother-Infant Interaction Program has enhanced the welfare of mothers and their low birth weight infants. Head Start has shown benefits in the children's health, short-term cognitive gains, higher success in school for some of the children, and family support. The Rochester Primary Mental Health Project can benefit elementary school children who are screened for school maladjustment, and is now investigating resilience to stress. The School Transitional Environmental Project has had success in restructuring complex junior and senior high schools in ways that protect well functioning students from potential adverse effects of school transitions.

Despite the need for and the success of prevention programs, hindrances exist. The training and economic well-being of professionals are geared to treatment, treatment appears more urgent than prevention, and the benefits of prevention can be difficult to establish. In addition, ethical concerns are debated, as well as the wisdom of broadly conceived primary prevention that attempts to promote wellness.

Concerns about transitions in the family are uppermost in the minds of many people. Much attention is given to the huge increase in maternal employment and how it may affect children. Many factors influence child outcome, including the alternative ways in which they receive care. Greater recognition is also being given to the difficulties that may be experienced by increasing numbers of single-parent families. Studies of the impact of divorce so far indicate, among other things, that adverse short-term effects occur, age of the child may make a difference, boys tend to externalize while girls internalize, and divorce may be harder on boys and remarriage on girls.

Research on abuse of children and adolescents shows that it occurs in diverse forms and is linked with characteristics of the abused and abuser, as well as social and cultural variables. Abuse can lead to many kinds of behavioral disturbances. Intervention is usually parent and family centered and can be effective.

Concern is also expressed about unmet needs regarding the physical and mental health of youth and the systems that provide services. Funding for services come from both governmental and private sectors, and services are delivered in many settings. There is a consensus that youth is underserved, that increased funding is essential, and that integrated, comprehensive systems are required. Some progress is being made in improving mental health services.

As we look to the global society of the twenty-first century, several challenges to the development of young people are evident. Among these are failure to adapt to and welcome differences among people, failure to reduce poverty, and failure to avoid armed conflict. International cooperation to improve the lives of youth is reflected in the work of the United Nations, which has taken the position that all young people have the right to survive, to be protected, and to develop optimally.

GLOSSARY

ABA′ (reversal) research design Single-subject quasi-experimental design in which the relevant behavior is measured during a baseline period (A), manipulation (B), and a period in which the manipulation is removed (A′). The reintroduction of the manipulation (B′) is added when treatment is the goal.

Accommodation In Piagetian theory, the process of adapting one's mental schemas of the world to fit with new experiences.

Acute onset The sudden (rather than gradual) onset of a disorder.

Adaptive behavior scales Psychological instruments that measure an individual's ability to perform in the everyday environment, for example, to wash one's hair, interact socially, and communicate. Used mostly for evaluation of retarded or severely disturbed persons.

Adoption studies In genetic research, the comparison of adopted children with their biological and their adoptive families to determine hereditary and environmental influences on characteristics.

Affect The conscious, subjective aspect of an emotion.

Anaclitic depression A period of withdrawal and sadness in very young children in reaction to prolonged separation from their parents.

Anoxia Lack of oxygen.

Antisocial behavior A pattern of behavior that violates widely held social norms and brings harm to others (e.g., stealing, lying).

Aphasia A general term referring to language disturbances not caused by general intellectual deficiency. *Developmental aphasia* refers to receptive and expressive language disorders in childhood.

Assimilation In Piagetian theory, the process of taking in or interpreting new information according to existing mental schemas of the world.

Attachment A strong socioemotional bond between individuals. Usually discussed in terms of the child-parent or child-caretaker relationship, attachment is generally viewed as having a strong influence on a child's development.

Attribution (attributional style) The way an individual thinks about or explains actions and outcomes; for example, a child's attributing his or her school failure to lack of innate intelligence.

Autoimmune disorder A condition in which the body's immune system attacks it's own healthy tissue.

Autonomic nervous system A part of the nervous system that consists of ganglia along the spinal cord and nerves to peripheral organs (e.g., glands and blood vessels). It regulates functions usually considered involuntary, such as the operation of smooth muscles and glands. The system controls physiological changes associated with the expression of emotion.

Baseline The measured rate of a behavior before an intervention is introduced. Baseline rates of the behavior can then be compared to rates during and following the intervention.

Behavior modification An approach to the treatment of behavior disorders that is based primarily on learning principles. Also referred to as *behavior therapy*.

Binge A relatively brief episode of excessive consumption (e.g., of food) over which the individual feels no control.

Biofeedback Procedures by which the individual is provided immediate information (feedback) about some aspect of physiological functioning (e.g., muscle tension, skin temperature). It is assumed that the individual can come to control bodily functioning through such feedback.

Case study Descriptive method of research in which an individual case is described. The case study can be informative but cannot be generalized to other persons or situations with confidence.

Central nervous system In humans, the brain and spinal cord. (*See* autonomic nervous system)

Child guidance movement An early to mid-20th century effort in the U.S. to treat and prevent childhood mental disorders. Importance was given to influences of family and wider social systems on the child.

Chromosome   A threadlike structure in the cell nucleus that contains the genetic code. With the exception of the ova and sperm, human cells possess 23 pairs, 22 pairs of autosomes and 1 pair of sex chromosomes. The ova and sperm possess 23 single chromosomes.

Chromosome abnormalities   Abnormalities in the number and/or structure of the chromosome complement that often lead to fetal death or anomalies in development.

Classical conditioning   A form of learning, also referred to as Pavlovian conditioning. An individual comes to respond to a stimulus (conditioned stimulus or CS) that did not previously elicit a response. Classical conditioning occurs when a CS is paired with another stimulus (the unconditioned stimulus, or UCS) that does elicit the desired response (unconditioned response, or UCR). When this response is elicited by the conditioned stimulus alone it is called a conditioned response (CR).

Classificatory variable   In research methodology, attributes of subjects (e.g., age, sex, diagnosis) that are investigated in some way. Classificatory variables are sometimes erroneously taken for independent variables. (*See* mixed research design)

Clinical significance   The degree to which research findings are meaningful regarding real-life applications.

Clinical utility   A criterion for judging the adequacy of a classification system, diagnosis, or assessment instrument. Judgments are based on how fully the observed phenomena are described and on how useful the descriptions are.

Cognitive strategies   Information processing and memory strategies; for example, rehearsing and categorizing information.

Cohort   A particular age group of participants in a cross-sectional or longitudinal research study. A cohort may differ in life experiences and values from an age group born and raised during a different era.

Comorbidity   The term used when individuals simultaneously meet the criteria for more than one disorder (e.g., depression and anxiety).

Compulsions   Behaviors the individual feels compelled to repeat over and over again, even though they appear to have no rational basis.

Computerized tomography (CT scan)   An x-ray procedure to directly assess abnormalities of the brain such as blood clots or tumors. Also sometimes referred to as computerized axial tomography or CAT scan.

Concordant   In genetic research, refers to individuals who are similar in particular attributes, for example, concordant for hair color or activity level.

Conditioned stimulus (CS)   A neutral stimulus, which through repeated pairings with a stimulus (unconditioned stimulus) that already elicits a particular response, comes to elicit a similar response (conditioned response).

Contingency management   Procedures that seek to modify behavior by altering the causal relationship between stimulus and response events, for example, between a behavior and its reinforcer.

Control group   In an experiment, a group of subjects treated differently than subjects who receive the experimental manipulation and later compared with them. The purpose of control groups is to insure that the results of the experiment can be attributed to the manipulation rather than to other variables.

Correlation coefficient   A number obtained through statistical analysis that reflects the presence or absence of a correlation, the strength of a correlation, and the direction (positive or negative) of a correlation. Person r is a commonly used coefficient. (*See* positive and negative correlation)

Correlational research   A research strategy aimed at establishing whether two or more variables covary, or are associated. (*See* positive correlation and negative correlation.) The establishment of a correlation permits prediction of one variable from the other, but does not establish a causal relationship.

Covert behaviors   Behaviors that are not readily observeable. When describing antisocial behaviors this term refers to behaviors that are concealed, such as lying, stealing, and truancy. (*See* overt behaviors)

Critical period   A relatively limited period of development during which an organism may be particularly sensitive to specific influences.

Cross-sectional research   A research strategy that observes and compares different groups of subjects at one point in time. It is a highly practical way to gather certain kinds of information.

Defense mechanisms   In psychoanalytic theory, psychological processes that distort or deny reality so as to control anxiety. Examples are repression, projection, reaction formation.

Deficit vs. difference model   Antagonistic models to explain atypical functioning of poor or minority children. The deficit model suggests that these children are deficient due to inheritance and/or inferior subculture. The difference model argues that the children merely learn different content and styles that disadvantage them on intelligence tests and in institutions that stress middle-class values.

Deinstitutionalization   The movement to place/treat people with disorders in various community settings rather than in large institutions.

Delinquency   A legal term that refers to an illegal act by a person under 18. Such behavior may be illegal for an adult as well, such as theft, or may only be illegal when committed by a juvenile, for example, truancy.

Delusion   An idea or belief that appears contrary to reality and is not widely accepted in the culture (e.g., delusions of grandeur or persecution).

Dependent variable   In the experimental method of research, the measure of behavior that may be influenced by the manipulation (independent variable).

Development   Change in structure and function that occurs over time in living organisms. Typically viewed as change from the simple to the complex, development is the result of transactions among several variables.

Developmental level   The level at which an individual is functioning with regard to physical, intellectual, or socioemotional characteristics. Individuals can be assigned to a developmental level based on age-norms or theoretical constructions.

Developmental psychopathology   The study of behavioral disorders within the context of developmental influences.

Developmental quotient (DQ)   A measure of performance on infant tests of intelligence, paralleling the intelligence quotient (IQ) derived from intelligence tests for older children.

Developmental vs. difference controversy   Theoretical dispute about atypical functioning, especially about mental retardation. The developmental view argues that retarded persons function intellectually in the same ways as do the nonretarded, but that they develop more slowly and perhaps reach a ceiling. The difference view maintains that the intellective processes of retarded persons are qualitatively different than normal processes.

Diathesis   A predisposition toward a disease or disorder.

Differential reinforcement of other behaviors (DRO)   In behavior modification, refers to applying relatively more reinforcement to desirable behaviors that are incompatible with specific undesirable behaviors.

Discordant   In genetic research, refers to individuals who are dissimilar in particular attributes, for example, discordant in hair color or activity level.

Discrimination   The process by which an individual comes to learn that a particular stimulus, but not others, signals that a certain response is likely to be followed by a particular consequence.

Diversion programs   An approach to delinquency that attempts to intervene by providing services (e.g., education, vocational training) that will *divert* delinquent youth away from the juvenile justice system.

Dizygotic twins   Twins resulting from two independent unions of ova and sperm that occur at approximately the same time. Dizygotic twins are genetically no more alike than are nontwin siblings.

DNA   Deoxyribonucleic acid. The chemical carrier of the genetic code that is found in the chromosomes. The spiral-shaped DNA molecule is composed of sugar, phosphates, and nucleotides. The nucleotides carry the hereditary information that directs protein synthesis.

Dyslexia   General term referring to the inability to read.

Echolalia   The repetition of the speech of others, either immediately or delayed in time. A pathological speech pattern commonly found in autism and psychoses.

Ego   According to psychoanalytic theory, this is the structure of the mind that operates predominantly at the conscious level. It mediates between instinctual urges and reality and is responsible for decision making.

Electroencephalograph (EEG)   A recording of the electrical activity of the brain.

Empirical   The process of verification or proof by accumulating information or data through observation or experiment (in contrast to reliance on impression or theory).

Epidemiology   The study of the occurrence and distribution of a disorder within a specific population. Seeks to understand risk and etiology.

Etiology   The cause or origin of a disease or behavior disorder.

Eugenics   Efforts to improve human characteristics through systematic control of reproduction and thus genetics.

Executive functions   A term that refers to the ability to select, monitor, evaluate and revise strategies employed in information processing and memory.

Experimental research   A research strategy that can establish causal relationships between variables. Subjects are treated by the independent variable to determine possible effects on the dependent variable. Comparison groups are included to control for extraneous influences and the procedures are carefully controlled by the researchers.

External validity   In research, refers to the degree to which findings of an investigation can be generalized to other populations and situations.

Externalizing disorders   Behavioral disorders in which the problems exhibited seem directed at others; for example, aggression and lying.

Extinction   A weakening of a learned response that is produced when reinforcement that followed the response no longer occurs.

Factor analysis   A statistical procedure that correlates each item with every other item, and then groups correlated items into factors.

Fraternal twins   *See* dizygotic twins.

Gene   The smallest unit of the chromosome that transmits genetic information.

Generalization   The process by which a response is made to a new stimulus that is different but similar to the stimulus present during learning.

Generalized imitation   The tendency to imitate across persons, situations, and time.

Genotype   The complement of genes that a person inherits; the genetic endowment.

Hallucination   A false perception (e.g., hearing a noise, seeing an object) that occurs in the absence of any apparent environmental stimulation.

Heritability   The degree to which genetic influences account for variations in an attribute among individuals.

Heterotypic continuity   The continuity of a disorder over time in which the form of the behaviors change over time with development. (Contrasts with homotypic continuity.)

Hypothesis   In science, a proposition or "educated guess" put forth for evaluation by some scientific method.

Id   According to psychoanalytic theory this is developmentally the earliest of the structures of the mind—it is present at birth. The source of all psychic energy, the Id operates entirely at the unconscious level, seeking immediate gratification of all instinctual urges (the pleasure principle).

Impulsivity   The tendency to act quickly without reflection. Hyperactive children are viewed as impulsive.

Incidence   In studying the occurrence of a behavior disorder, incidence refers to the number of new cases in a given population in a given time period. (*See* prevalence)

Identical twins *See* monozygotic twins.

Independent variable In the experimental method of research, the variable manipulated by the researcher.

Individual Education Plan (IEP) Detailed educational plan mandated by P.L. 94–142 for each person being served by special education.

Information processing Complex mental processes by which the organism attends to, perceives, interprets, and stores information. (*See* memory, executive functions, metamemory, cognitive strategies)

Informed consent In research, the ethical and legal guideline that potential subjects be reasonably informed about the research as a basis for their volunteering to participate.

Intelligence quotient (IQ), deviation A standard score derived from statistical procedures that reflects the direction and degree to which an individual's performance on an intelligence test deviates from the average score of the individual's age group.

Intelligence quotient (IQ), ratio The ratio of mental age (MA), derived from performance on tests of intelligence, to chronological age (CA), multiplied by 100. IQ = MA/CA × 100.

Interactional model of development The view that development is the result of the interplay of organismic and environmental variables. (*See* transactional model of development)

Internalizing disorders The large category of disorders—many of which were traditionally referred to as neuroses—in which the problems exhibited seem directed more at the self than at others; for example, fears, depression, and withdrawal.

Internal validity In research, refers to the degree to which findings can be attributed to certain factors. Frequently concerns the degree to which a result of an *experiment* can be attributed to the experimental manipulation (the independent variable), rather than to extraneous factors.

Interrater reliability The extent to which different raters agree on a particular diagnosis or measurement.

In vivo A term referring to the natural context in which behavior occurs. For example, in vivo treatment is delivered in the setting in which the behavior problem occurs (e.g., the home rather than the clinic).

Joint attention interactions Behaviors, such as pointing and eye contact, that simultaneously focus the attention of two or more people on the same object or situation, presumably for sharing an experience.

Learned helplessness Passivity and a sense of lack of control over one's environment that is learned through experiences where one's behavior was ineffective in controlling events.

Least restrictive environment A term that refers to the idea that handicapped individuals have a right to be educated with and to live with the nonhandicapped to the extent that is maximally feasible. (*See* Public Law 94–142)

Longitudinal research A research strategy that observes the same subjects over a relatively long period of time, measuring behavior at certain points. It is particularly helpful in tracing developmental change.

Magnetic resonance imaging (MRI) A procedure that allows one to directly assess abnormalities in the brain.

Mainstreaming The placing of handicapped individuals into the least restrictive environments in which they are capable of functioning. More specifically, the placement of handicapped children in regular, rather than special classes. (*See* Public Law 94–142)

Masked depression This term refers to cases in which a child's depression is "masked" by other problems such as hyperactivity or delinquency. These "depressive equivalents" are thought to be manifestations of the underlying depression.

Maturation Changes that occur in individuals of a species relatively independent of the environment provided that basic conditions are satisfied. For example, most humans will walk, given normal physical capacity, nourishment, and opportunity for movement.

Maturational lag A slowness or falling behind in development; often implies a lag in brain or nervous system development.

Mediational processes Strategies by which stimuli are connected so that learning and thinking are facilitated. Examples are the use of imagery, words, clustering, and rehearsal.

Meiosis The specialized maturational process that results in the ova and sperm containing half (23) of the number of chromosomes found in other cells.

Memory Complex process by which perceived information can be recalled in some way. According to a widely-held model, information is first taken in by a sensory register, is passed to short-term storage, and then to long-term storage.

Mental age (MA) The score corresponding to the chronological age (CA) of children whose intellectual test performance the examinee equals. For the average child, MA = CA.

Mental hygiene movement An effort organized in the United States early in the 20th century to bring effective, humane treatment to the mentally ill and to prevent mental disorders. Closely associated with the child guidance movement.

Metacognition The understanding of one's own information processing system. (*See* executive functions)

Metamemory The understanding of the working of one's memory or the strategies used to facilitate memory. (*See* Executive functions)

Migraine headache A severe form of headache caused by sustained dilation of the extracranial arteries.

Minimal brain dysfunction (MBD) The assumption that the central nervous system or brain is functioning in a pathological way to a degree that is not clearly detectable. MBD is hypothesized as a cause of hyperactivity and learning disabilities, as well as other behavior disorders.

Mixed research design A research design in which subjects are assigned into groups on the basis of some attribute (i.e., a classificatory variable such as age), and then an experimental manipulation is applied. In interpretation of results, care must be taken not to view the classificatory variable as an independent variable.

Monozygotic twins   Twins resulting from one union of an ovum and sperm. The single zygote divides early into two, with the new zygotes having identical genes (and thus being of the same sex).

Morphology   In language, the study of word formation.

Multiple baseline research design   Single subject experimental designs in which a manipulation is made and multiple behaviors or subjects are measured over time.

Mutation   Spontaneous change in the genes that can be transmitted to the next generation. One of the genetic mechanisms that accounts for variation in species and individuals.

Nature vs. nurture controversy   The continuing debate about the relative influence of innate and experiential factors on the shaping of the individual. Also known as the maturation vs. learning and heredity vs. environment controversy.

Negative corrrelation   When two (or more) variables are negatively correlated they co-vary such that high scores on one variable are associated with low scores on the other, and vice versa.

Negative reinforcement   The process whereby the probability of a response increases because the response was followed by the removal of an aversive stimulus.

Neuropsychological assessment   The use of psychological tests and behavioral measures to *indirectly* evaluate the functioning of the nervous system. Performance on these measures is known or presumed to reflect specific aspects of the functioning of the brain.

Neurosis   A traditional term employed to describe any of a group of nonpsychotic disorders that are characterized by unusual levels of anxiety and associated problems. Phobias, obsessions, and compulsions are examples of disorders in this category.

Neurotransmitter   A chemical that carries the nerve impulse from one neuron across the synaptic space to another neuron. Examples are serotonin, dopamine, and norepinephrine.

Nonshared environment   A term derived from genetic research which describes that portion of environmental influences on an attribute that is experienced by one family member but not other members.

Normal distribution (curve)   The bell-shaped theoretical distribution or probability curve that describes the way in which many attributes (e.g., height, intelligence) are assumed to occur in the population. Extreme values of the attribute occur with less frequency than middle values of the attribute.

Normalization   Assumption that the goal of treatment of behavior disorders should be behaviors that are as normal as possible, and that this goal should be reached by methods as culturally normal as possible. (*See* mainstreaming and least restrictive environment)

Norms   Data based on information gathered from a segment of the population that represents the entire population. Norms serve as standards to evaluate individual development or functioning.

Nuclear family   A family unit consisting of the father, mother, and children.

Observational learning   The learning that occurs through viewing the behavior of others. Modeled behavior can be presented in live or symbolic form.

Obsessions   Recurring and intrusive irrational thoughts over which the individual feels no control.

Operant conditioning   Learning processes by which responses are acquired, maintained, or eliminated as a function of consequences (e.g., reinforcement, punishment).

Operational criteria (definition)   A specified set of observable operations that are measurable and allow one to define some concept. For example, maternal deprivation might be defined by measuring the amount of time the child is separated from its mother.

Overlearning   The procedure whereby learning trials are continued beyond the point at which the child has completed the stated criteria. This is intended to increase the likelihood that the new behavior will be maintained.

Overt behaviors   Behaviors that are readily observable. When describing antisocial behaviors this term refers to behaviors that are confrontational such as physical aggression, temper tantrums, and defiance. (*See* covert behaviors)

Paradigm   The set of assumptions and conceptions shared by a group of scientists that is used in collecting data and interpreting the phenomena of interest.

Paradoxical drug effect   An effect of a drug that contradicts the expected effect. An example is the quieting of hyperactivity by stimulant medications.

Partial correlation statistical procedure   A statistical procedure that aids in the interpretation of a demonstrated correlation by removing the effects of one or more specific variables.

Participant modeling   A treatment method in which observation of a model is followed by the observer joining the model in gradual approximations of the desired behavior.

Pedigree analysis   A research method that examines the pattern of distribution of a disorder, as well as the genetic makeup, in an extended family in order to assist in making inferences regarding the contribution of genetics to that disorder.

Perceptual-motor training   Approach to rectify learning disabilities that is based on the assumption that perceptual and motor functioning have gone awry or have developed abnormally. Training emphasizes exercises in sensory reception and motor responses, such as practicing right/left orientation, balancing, and learning simple forms and shapes.

Perinatal   The period of development at or around the time of birth.

Perspective   *See* paradigm.

Phenotype   The observable attributes of an individual that result from genetic endowment, developmental processes, and the transactions of these.

Phobia   Anxiety about, and avoidance of, some object or situation that is judged to be an excessive, overly persistent, unadaptive, or inappropriate fear.

Phonology   The study of speech sounds.

Pica   The habitual eating of substances usually considered inedible such as dirt, paper, and hair.

Placebo   A treatment—psychological or chemical—that alters a person's behavior because he or she expects that change will occur. Placebos are often employed as control treatments to evaluate whether a treatment being tested is effective for reasons other than the person's belief in it.

Polygenetic inheritance   Inheritance of a characteristic that is influenced by many genes rather than a single one.

Positive correlation   When two (or more) variables are positively correlated they co-vary with each other such that high scores on one variable are associated with high scores on the other variable, and low scores on the one variable are associated with low scores on the other.

Positive reinforcement   The process whereby the probability of a response increases because the response is followed by a positive stimulus.

Positron emission tomography (PET scan)   A procedure to directly assess activity in different parts of the brain.

Pragmatics (of language)   The use of speech and gesture in a communicative way, considering the social context. Pragmatic skills include using appropriate gestures and language style and not interrupting others.

Predictive validity   The extent to which predictions about future behavior can be made by knowing an individual's diagnosis or performance on some test.

Premorbid adjustment   The psychological, social, and academic/vocational adjustment of a person prior to onset of the symptoms of a disorder or its diagnosis.

Prenatal   The period of development that occurs during pregnancy.

Prevalence   In studying the occurrence of a behavior disorder, prevalence refers to the number of cases in the population at a given time. It may be expressed by number of cases or percent of the population. (*See* incidence)

Primary prevention   The prevention of disorders in the population by methods that preclude their occurrence. Examples are parent education in child management and prevention of poverty.

Proband   The designated individual whose relatives are assessed to determine if an attribute occurs in other members of that family.

Projection   A defense mechanism whereby the ego protects against unacceptable thoughts or impulses by attributing them to another person or some object.

Projective tests   Psychological tests which present ambiguous stimuli to the person. The subject's response is presumed to reflect unconscious thoughts and feelings that are unacceptable to the ego and therefore cannot be expressed directly.

Pronoun reversal   Deviant speech pattern in which speakers refer to themselves as "you" or "she" or "he" and refer to others as "I" or "me." Often found in autism.

Prospective research designs   Designs that identify subjects and then follow them over time. (*See* retrospective research designs)

Protective factors   Variables that lessen the effects of risk; sometimes referred to as resiliencies.

Psychoactive drugs   Chemical substances that influence psychological processes (e.g., behavior, thinking, emotions) by their influence on nervous system functioning. Examples are stimulants and tranquilizers.

Psychogenesis   The view that development of a particular disorder is due to psychological influence.

Psychosis   A general term for severe mental disorder that affects thinking, the emotions, and other psychological systems. The hallmark of a psychosis is disturbed contact with reality.

Public Law 94–142   The federal *Education for all Handicapped Children Act of 1975*, that sets guidelines for the rights of handicapped children to appropriate education. Now entitled *The Individuals with Disabilities Education Act*, it assures public education and services in the least restrictive environment, parental decision making, and assistance to the states.

Public Law 99–457   An amendment to the federal Public Law 94–142 that mandates the evaluation and special care of children from birth to three years of age.

Punishment   A process whereby a response is followed by either an unpleasant stimulus or the removal of a pleasant stimulus, thereby decreasing the frequency of that response.

Random assignment   In research, the assignment of individuals to different groups in such a way that each individual has an equal chance of being assigned to any group. Such chance assignment helps make the groups comparable on factors that might influence the findings.

Recidivism   The return to a previous undesirable pattern. The juvenile delinquent who again commits a crime after completing a treatment program illustrates recidivism.

Reflexes   Automatic, unlearned responses to specific stimulation. Examples are the sucking and coughing reflexes. Reflexes are considered relatively simple acts, some of which give way to voluntary, learned responses.

Regular Education Initiative (REI)   Controversial proposal that learning handicapped children be educated in regular classrooms rather than special education classrooms.

Reinforcement   A process whereby a stimulus that occurs contingent on a particular behavior results in an increase in the likelihood of that behavior. (*See* positive reinforcement and negative reinforcement)

Relapse   The reoccurrence of a problem after it has been successfully treated.

Reliability   The degree to which an observation is consistently made. The term can be applied to a test or other measurement or to a system of classification. (*See* test-retest and interrater reliability)

Repression   According to psychoanalytic theory, the most basic defense mechanism. Thoughts or impulses unacceptable to the ego are forced back into the unconscious.

Resilience The ability to overcome risk factors, to function adaptively despite negative circumstances.

Respite care Brief alternative care provided to disabled persons in order to lighten the burdens of care carried by the primary caretakers.

Response prevention A behavioral treatment procedure in which the person is not allowed to, or discouraged from, engaging in a compulsive ritual or avoidant behavior.

Retrospective research designs Designs that utilize information about past events; follow-back designs. (*See* prospective research designs)

Risk The degree to which variables (risk factors) operate to increase the chance of behavior problems. (*See* protective factors)

Rumination The voluntary regurgitation of food by infants.

Savant abilities Specific and remarkable cognitive abilities (e.g., memory, arithmetical) observed in individuals who are otherwise intellectually handicapped.

Schema Mental concepts or constructions of the world. The development of complex schemas is central to Piaget's theory of cognitive growth.

School phobia An extreme reluctance to go to school which is frequently accompanied by somatic complaints. The term *school refusal* is preferred by some clinicians, since an actual fear of school may not be present.

Scientific method An empirical approach to understanding phenomena. The scientific approach involves systematic observation, measurement and testing of relationships, and explanations of phenomena.

Secondary prevention The prevention of disorders in the population by shortening the duration of existing cases through early diagnosis and treatment, especially of at-risk populations.

Self-injurious behavior Repetitious action that damages the self physically, such as head banging, scratching the self, and pulling one's own hair. Often observed in psychotic and mentally retarded persons, but occurs in a small percentage of young, normal children.

Self-monitoring A procedure in which the individual observes and records his or her own behaviors or thoughts and the circumstances under which they occur.

Self-stimulatory behavior Sensory-motor behavior that serves as stimulation for the person. Often refers to a pathological process, for example, as when an autistic child repetitiously flaps his or her hands.

Semantics The study of the meanings in language.

Separation anxiety Childhood anxiety regarding separation from the mother or other major attachment figures.

Sequential research designs Various designs that combine the longitudinal and cross-sectional research strategies to maximize the strengths of these methods.

Shared environment A term derived from genetic research which describes that portion of environmental influences on an attribute that is experienced by two or more family members. (*See* nonshared environment)

Single-subject experiments Various experimental research designs employed with a single (or a few) subject(s), in which a manipulation is made and measurements are taken across time periods. (*See* ABA' and multiple baseline designs)

Socioeconomic status (SES) Classification of people according to social class. Indices of SES include monetary level, amount of education, and occupational level. Many factors vary with SES, such as medical care and child-rearing practices.

Somatogenesis The view that development of a particular disorder is due to biological—rather than psychological—causes.

Stage theories of development Explanations of development that postulate that growth occurs in a recognizable order of noncontinuous stages or steps, which are qualitatively different from each other. Examples: Piaget's cognitive theory and Freud's psychosexual theory.

Statistical significance In research, refers to a low probability that the findings are merely chance occurrences. By tradition a finding is statistically significant when there is a 5 percent or less probability that it occurred by chance ($p \leq .05$).

Stereotypy A repetitive action or movement, such as hand flapping or incessantly lining up objects in rows.

Stress A situation or event that brings strain to the individual. Considered a risk factor for behavioral and physical health.

Superego The third of Freud's three structures of the mind. It is the conscience or self-critical part of the individual that reflects society's morals and standards as they have been learned from parents and others.

Sympathetic nervous system A part of the autonomic nervous system which, among other things, accelerates heart rate, increases blood glucose, inhibits intestinal activity, and in general seems to prepare the organism for stress or activity.

Syndrome A group of behaviors or symptoms which are known or thought to be likely to occur together in a particular disorder.

Syntax The aspect of grammar that deals with the way words are put together to form phrases, clauses, and sentences.

Systematic desensitization A behavioral treatment of anxiety. The client visualizes a hierarchy of scenes, each of which elicits more anxiety than the previous scene. These visualizations are paired with relaxation until they no longer produce anxiety.

Systematic direct observation Observation of specific behaviors of an individual or group of individuals in a particular setting, with the use of a specific observational code or instrument.

Temperament A variety of socioemotional behaviors viewed as relatively stable attributes of individuals, such as activity level, and social responsiveness.

Teratogens Conditions or agents that tend to cause developmental malformations, defects, or death of the fetus.

Tertiary prevention   The prevention of disorders in the population by reducing problems residual to disorders. An example is support groups for persons who are returning to the community after hospitalization for mental disorders.

Test-retest reliability   The degree to which a test or diagnostic system yields the same result when applied to an individual at different times.

Theory   An integrated set of propositions that explains phenomena and guides research.

Theory of mind   The ability to infer mental states (e.g., beliefs, knowledge) in others or the self. Autistic children appear to show deficits in this ability.

Time-out   Behavior modification technique in which an individual displaying an undesirable behavior is removed from the immediate environment, usually by placement into an isolated room. Conceptually time-out is viewed as elimination of positive reinforcement or as punishment.

Token economy   A behavioral treatment procedure developed from operant conditioning principles. A set of behaviors that earn or cost reward points, given in the form of some scrip, such as poker chips, is set up. These tokens can then be exchanged for prizes, activities, or privileges.

Transactional model of development   The view that development is the result of the continuous interplay of organismic and environmental variables. It is conceptually similar to the interactional model of development but it emphasizes the ongoing, mutual influences of factors.

Twin study   A type of research investigation frequently employed to examine the effects of hereditary and environmental variables. Pairs of genetically-identical monozygotic twins and dizygotic twins, which share on average half their genes, are examined to determine whether the former are more alike than the latter.

Unconditioned stimulus   A stimulus which elicits a particular response prior to any conditioning trails. The loud noise that causes an infant to startle is an example of an unconditioned stimulus.

Validity   A term used in several different ways, all of which address issues of correctness, meaningfulness, and relevancy. (*See* internal validity, external validity, predictive validity)

Zeitgeist   A german word for the general viewpoint and attitudes of a given society at a particular time. A literal translation is *zeit* (time) *geist* (spirit).

Zygote   The cell mass formed by the joining of an ovum and sperm; the fertilized egg.

REFERENCES

Abramson, L. Y., Metalsky, G. I., & Alloy, L. B. (1989). Hopelessness depression: A theory-based subtype of depression. *Psychological Bulletin, 96,* 358–372.

Abramson, L. Y., Seligman, M. E. P., & Teasdale, J. D. (1978). Learned helplessness in humans: Critique and reformulation. *Journal of Abnormal Psychology, 87,* 49–74.

Achenbach, T. M. (1974, 1982). *Developmental psychopathology.* New York: Wiley.

Achenbach, T. M. (1978). *Research in developmental psychology: Concepts, strategies, methods.* New York: Free Press.

Achenbach, T. M. (1985). *Assessment and taxonomy of child and adolescent psychopathology.* Beverly Hills: Sage.

Achenbach, T. M. (1990). Conceptualizations of developmental psychopathology. In M. Lewis & S. M. Miller (Eds.), *Handbook of developmental psychopathology.* New York: Plenum.

Achenbach, T. M. (1991a). *Integrative guide for the 1991 CBCL/4-18, YSR and TRF profiles.* Burlington, VT: University of Vermont Department of Psychiatry.

Achenbach, T. M. (1991b). *Manual for the Child Behavior Checklist/4-18 and 1991 profile.* Burlington, VT: University of Vermont Department of Psychiatry.

Achenbach, T. M. (1991c). *Manual for the Teachers Report Form and 1991 profile.* Burlington, VT: University of Vermont Department of Psychiatry.

Achenbach, T. M. (1991d). *Manual for the Youth Self-Report and 1991 profile.* Burlington, VT: University of Vermont Department of Psychiatry.

Achenbach, T. M. (1993). *Empirically based taxonomy: How to use syndromes and profile types derived from the CBCL/4-18, TRF, and YSR.* Burlington, VT: University of Vermont Department of Psychiatry.

Achenbach, T. M., Connors, C. K., Quay, H. C., Verhults, F. C., & Howell, C. T. (1989). Replication of empirically derived syndromes as a basis for taxonomy of child/adolescent psychopathology. *Journal of Abnormal Child Psychology, 17,* 299–323.

Achenbach, T. M., & Edelbrock, C. S. (1989). Diagnostic, taxonomic, and assessment issues. In T. H. Ollendick & M. Hersen (Eds.), *Handbook of child psychopathology* (2nd ed.). New York: Plenum.

Achenbach, T. M., & Howell, C. T. (1993). Are American children's problems getting worse? A 13-year comparison. *Journal of the American Academy of Child and Adolescent Psychiatry, 32,* 1145–1154.

Achenbach, T. M., Howell, C. T., McConaughy, S. H., & Stanger, C. (1995a). Six-year predictors of problems in a national sample of children and youth: I. Cross-informant syndromes. *Journal of the American Academy of Child and Adolescent Psychiatry, 34,* 336–347.

Achenbach, T. M., Howell, C. T., McConaughy, S. H., & Stanger, C. (1995b). Six-year predictors of problems in a national sample of children and youth: II. Signs of disturbance. *Journal of the American Academy of Child and Adolescent Psychiatry, 34,* 488–498.

Achenbach, T. M., Howell, C. T., Quay, H. C., & Conners, C. K. (1991). National survey of problems and competencies among four- to sixteen-year-olds. *Monographs of the Society for Research in Child Development, 56* (3, Serial No. 225).

Achenbach, T. M., McConaughy, S. H., & Howell, C. T. (1987). Child/adolescent behavioral and emotional problems: Implications of cross-informant correlations for situational specificity. *Psychological Bulletin, 101,* 213–232.

Achenbach, T. M., Phares, V., Howell, C. T., Ruah, V. A., & Nurcombe, B. (1990). Seven-year outcome of the Vermont Intervention Program for low-birthweight infants. *Child Development, 61,* 1672–1681.

Ackerman, P. T., Anhalt, J. M., Dykman, R. A., & Holcomb P. J. (1986). Effortful processing deficits in children with learning and attention disorders. *Brain and Cognition, 5,* 22–40.

Adams, J. A. (1984). Learning of movement sequences. *Psychological Bulletin, 96,* 3–28.

Adelman, H. S. (1989). Beyond the learning mystique: An interactional perspective on learning disabilities. *Journal of Learning Disabilities, 22,* 301–304; 328.

Adrien, J. L., Lenoir, P., Martineau, J., Perrot, A., Hameury, L., Larmande, C., & Sauvage, D. (1993). Blind ratings of early symptoms of autism based upon home movies. *Journal of the American Academy of Child and Adolescent Psychiatry, 32,* 617–626.

Adrien, J. L., Ornitz, E., Barthelemy, C., Sauvage, D., & Lelord, G. (1987). The presence or absense of certain behaviors associated with infantile autism in severely retarded autistic and nonaustistic retarded childen and very young normal children. *Journal of Autism and Developmental Disorders, 17,* 407–416.

Agras, W. S., Chapin, H. N., & Oliveau, D. C. (1972). The natural history of phobia. *Archives of General Psychiatry, 26,* 315–317.

Agras, W. S., & Kraemer, H. (1984). The treatment of anorexia nervosa: Do different treatments have different outcomes. In A. J. Stunkard & E. Stellar (Eds.), *Eating and its disorders.* New York: Raven Press.

Agras, W. S., Schneider, J. A., Arnow, B., Raeburn, S. D., & Telch, C. F. (1989). Cognitive-behavioral and response-prevention treatments for bulimia nervosa. *Journal of Consulting and Clinical Psychology, 57,* 215–221.

Ainsworth, M., Behar, M., Waters, E., & Wall, S. (1978). *Patterns of attachment.* Hillsdale, NJ: Erlbaum.

Alanen, Y. (1960). Some thoughts on schizophrenia and ego development in the light of family investigations. *Archives of General Psychiatry, 3,* 650–656.

Albano, A. M., & Barlow, D. H. (1996). Cognitive behavioral group treatment for adolescent social phobia. In E. D. Hibbs & P. S. Jensen (Eds.), *Psychosocial treatment research of child and adolescent disorders.* Washington, DC: American Psychological Association Press.

Albee, G. W. (1986). Toward a just soceity. Lessons from observations on the primary prevention of psychopathology. *American Psychologist, 41,* 891–898.

Alessi, N. E., & Magen, J. (1988). Comorbidity of other psychiatric disturbances in depressed psychiatrically hospitalized children. *American Journal of Psychiatry, 145,* 1582–1584.

Alessi, N. E., Robbins, D. R., & Dilsaver, S. C. (1987). Panic and depressive disorders among psychiatrically hospitalized adolescents. *Psychiatry Research, 20,* 275–283.

Alexander, A. B. (1980). The treatment of psychosomatic disorders. In B. B. Lahey & A. E. Kazdin (Eds.), *Advances in clinical child psychology,* Vol. 3. New York: Plenum.

Alexander, F. (1950). *Psychosomatic medicine.* New York: W. W. Norton and Co.

Alexander, J. F. (1973). Defensive and supportive communications in normal and deviant families. *Journal of Consulting and Clinical Psychology, 40,* 223–231.

Alexander, J. F., Barton, C., Schiavo, R. S., & Parsons, B. V. (1976). Systems-behavioral intervention with families of delinquents: Therapist characteristics, family behavior, and outcome. *Journal of Consulting and Clinical Psychology, 44,* 656–664.

Alexander, J. F., Haas, L. J., Klein, N. C., & Warburton, J. R. (1980, May). *Functional family therapy.* Paper presented at meeting of Western Psychological Association. Honolulu, Hawaii.

Alexander, J. F., & Parsons, B. V. (1973). Short-term behavioral intervention with delinquent families: Impact on family process and recidivism. *Journal of Abnormal Psychology, 81,* 219–225.

Alexander, J. F., & Parsons, B. V. (1982). *Functional family therapy: Principles and procedures.* Carmel, CA: Brooks/Cole.

Alexander, J. F., Waldron, H. B., Barton, C., & Mas, C. H. (1989). The minimizing of blaming attributions and behaviors in delinquent families. *Journal of Consulting and Clinical Psychology, 57,* 19–24.

Algozzine, B. (1977). The emotionally disturbed child: Disturbed or disturbing? *Journal of Abnormal Child Psychology, 5,* 205–211.

Allen, A. J., Leonard, H. L., & Swedo, S. E. (1995a). A new infection-triggered, autoimmune subtype of pediatric OCD and Tourette's syndrome. *Journal of the American Academy of Child and Adolescent Psychiatry, 34,* 307–311.

Allen, A. J., Leonard, H. L., & Swedo, S. E. (1995b). Current knowledge of medications for the treatment of childhood anxiety disorders. *Journal of the American Academy of Child and Adolescent Psychiatry, 34,* 976–986.

Allen, J. S., & Drabman, R. S. (1991). Attributions of children with learning disabilities who are treated with psychostimulants. *Learning Disability Quarterly, 14,* 75–79.

Allen, K., Hart, B., Buell, J., Harris, F., & Wolf, M. (1964). Effects of social reinforcement on isolated behavior of a nursery school child. *Child Development, 35,* 511–518.

Allison, P. D., & Furstenberg, F. F., Jr. (1989). How marital dissolution affects children. *Developmental Psychology, 25,* 540–549.

Alloy, L. B., Lipman, A. J., & Abramson, L. Y. (1992). Attributional style as a vulnerability factor for depression. *Cognitive Therapy and Research, 16,* 391–407.

Alpert-Gillis, L. J., Pedro-Carroll, J. L., & Cowen, E. L. (1989). The Children of Divorce Intervention Program: Development, implementation, and evaluation of a program for young urban children. *Journal of Consulting and Clinical Psychology, 57,* 583–589.

Aman, M. G., Hammer, D., & Rojahn, J. (1993). Mental retardation. In T. H. Ollendick & M. Hersen (Eds.), *Handbook of child and adolescent assessment.* Boston: Allyn and Bacon.

Aman, M. G., & Kern, R. A. (1989). Review of fenfluamine in the treatment of the developmental disabilities. *Journal of the American Academy of Child and Adolescent Psychiatry, 28,* 549–565.

Aman, M. G., Van Bourgondien, M. E., Wolford, P. L., & Sarphare, G. (1995). Psychotropic and anticonvulsant drugs in subjects with autism: Prevalence and patterns of use. *Journal of the American Academy of Child and Adolescent Psychiatry, 34,* 1672–1681.

Amato, P. R., & Keith, B. (1991). Parental divorce and the well-being of children: A metaanalysis. *Psychological Bulletin, 110,* 26–46.

American Association on Mental Retardation (1992). *Mental retardation. Definition, classification, and systems of support.* Washington, DC: American Association on Mental Retardation.

American Humane Association. (1984). *Trends in child abuse and neglect: A national perspective.* Denver: Author.

American Psychiatric Association (1952, 1968, 1980, 1987, 1994). *Diagnostic and statistical manual of mental disorders.* Washington, DC: American Psychiatric Association.

American Psychiatric Association (1993). Practice guidelines for eating disorders. *American Journal of Psychiatry, 150,* 207–228.

American Sleep Disorders Association, Diagnostic Classification Steering Committee. (1990). *The international classification of sleep disorders: Diagnostic and coding manual.* Rochester, MN: American Sleep Disorders Association.

Anastasi, A. (1982, 1988). *Psychological testing.* New York: Macmillan.

Anastopoulos, A. D., & Barkley, R. A. (1988). Biological factors in attention deficit-hyperactivity disorder. *Behavior Therapist, 11,* 47–53.

Anastopoulos, A. D., & Barkley, R. A. (1992). Attention-deficit hyperactivity disorder. In C. E. Walker & M. C. Roberts (Eds.), *Handbook of clinical child psychology.* NY: John Wiley.

Anderson, J. C., & McGee, R. (1994). Comorbidity of depression in children and adolescents. In W. M. Reynolds & H. F. Johnston (Eds.), *Handbook of depression in children and adolescents.* New York: Plenum Press.

Anderson, J. C., Williams, S., McGee, R., & Silva, P. A. (1987). DSM-III disorders in preadolescent children: Prevalence in a large sample from the general population. *Archives of General Psychiatry, 44,* 69–76.

Anderson, K. E., Lytton, H., & Romney, D. M. (1986). Mothers interactions with normal and conduct-disordered boys: Who affects whom? *Developmental Psychology, 22,* 604–609.

Andrasik, F., & Attansio, V. (1985). Biofeedback in pediatrics: Current status and appraisal. In M. L. Wolraich & D. K. Routh (Eds.), *Advances in developmental and behavioral pediatrics,* Vol. 6, Greenwich, CT: JAI.

Andrasik, F., Blake, D. D., & McCarran, M. S. (1986). A biobehavioral analysis of pediatric headache. In N. A. Krasnegor, J. D. Arasteh, & M. F. Cataldo (Eds.), *Child health behavior: A behavioral pediatrics perspective.* New York: Wiley.

Angold, A., & Rutter, M. (1992). Effects of age and pubertal stratus on depression in a large clinical sample. *Development and Psychopathology, 4,* 5–28.

Anthony, E. J. (1970). Behavior disorders. In P. H. Mussen (Ed.), *Carmichael's manual of child psychology,* Vol. II. New York: John Wiley.

Anthony, E. J. (1981). The psychiatric evaluation of the anxious child: Case record summarized from the clinic records. In E. J. Anthony & D. C. Gilpin (Eds.), *Three further clinical faces of childhood.* New York: S P Medical & Scientific Books.

Aoki, C., & Siekevitz, P. (1988). Plasticity in brain development. *Scientific American, 259,* 56–64.

Arbuthnot, J., & Gordon, D. A. (1986). Behavioral and cognitive effects of a moral reasoning development intervention for high-risk behavior-disordered adolescents. *Journal of Consulting and Clinical Psychology, 54,* 208–216.

Aristimuno, G. G., Foster, T. A., Voors, A. W., Srinivasan, S. R., & Berenson, G. S. (1984). Influence of persistent obesity in children on cardiovascular risk factors: The Bogalusa Heart Study. *Circulation, 69,* 895–904.

Armbruster, P., & Kazdin, A. E. (1994). Attrition in child psychotherapy. In T. H. Ollendick & R. J. Prinz (Eds.), *Advances in clinical child psychology. Vol 16.* NY: Plenum.

Arnold, L. E. and colleagues (1995). Ethical issues in biological psychiatric research with children and adolescents. *Journal of the American Academy of Child and Adolescent Psychiatry, 34,* 929–939.

Asarnow, J. R. (1994). Childhood-onset schizophrenia. *Journal of Child Psychology and Psychiatry, 35,* 1345–1371.

Asarnow, J. R., Goldstein, M. J., & Ben-Meir, S. (1988). Parental communication deviance in childhood onset schizophrenia spectrum and depressive disorders. *Journal of Child Psychology and Psychiatry, 29,* 825–838.

Asarnow, R., Sherman, T., & Strandburg, R. (1986) The search for the psychobiological substrate of childhood onset schizophrenia. *Journal of the American Academy of Child and Adolescent Psychiatry, 25,* 601–604.

Asarnow, R. F., Tanguay, P.E., Bott, L., & Freeman, B. J. (1987). Patterns of intellectual functioning in non-retarded autistic and schizophrenic children. *Journal of Child Psychology and Psychiatry, 28,* 273–280.

Asendorpf, J. B. (1993). Abnormal shyness in children. *Journal of Child Psychology and Psychiatry, 34,* 1069–1081.

Atkinson, L., Scott, B., Chrisholm, V., Blackwell, J., Dickens, S., Tam, F., & Goldberg, S. (1995). Cognitive coping, affective distress, and maternal sensitivity: Mothers of children with Down syndrome. *Developmental Psychology, 31,* 668–676.

Attwood, A., Frith, U., & Hermelin, B. (1988). The understanding and use of interpersonal gestures by autistic and Down's Syndrome children. *Journal of Autism and Developmental Disorders, 18,* 241–257.

August, G. J., & Garfinkel, B. D. (1989). Behavioral and cognitive subtypes of ADHD. *Journal of the American Academy of Child and Adolescent Psychiatry, 28,* 739–748.

August, G. J., & Garfinkel, B. D. (1993). The nosology of attention-deficit hyperactivity disorder. *Journal of the*

American Academy of Child and Adolescent Psychiatry, 32, 155–165.

Axline, V. M. (1947). *Play therapy.* Boston: Houghton Mifflin.

Azar, B. (1995, Sept.). The bond between mother and child. *The APA Monitor, 26,* 28.

Azar, S. T., & Wolfe, D. A. (1989). Child abuse and neglect. In E. J. Mash & R. A. Barkley (Eds.), *Treatment of childhood disorders.* New York: Guilford.

Bahr, H. M. (1988). Family change and the mystique of the traditional family. In L. A. Bond & B. M. Wagner (Eds.), *Families in transition: Primary prevention programs that work.* Newbury Park, CA: Sage.

Bailey, G. W. (1989). Current perspectives on substance abuse in youth. *Journal of the American Academy of Child and Adolescent Psychiatry, 28,* 151–162.

Baker, L., & Cantwell, D. P. (1989). Specific language and learning disorders. In T. H. Ollendick & M. Hersen (Eds.). *Handbook of child psychopathology.* New York: Plenum.

Baker, L., & Cantwell, D. P. (1991a). Disorders of language, speech, and communication. In M. Lewis (Ed.), *Child and adolescent psychiatry: A comprehensive textbook.* Baltimore: Williams & Wilkins.

Baker, L., & Cantwell, D. P. (1991b). The development of speech and language. In M. Lewis (Ed.), *Child and adolescent psychiatry: A comprehensive textbook.* Baltimore: Williams & Wilkins.

Bakwin, H. (1971). Enuresis in twins. *American Journal of Diseases in Childhood, 121,* 222–225.

Band, E. B. (1990). Children's coping with diabetes: Understanding the role of cognitive development. *Journal of Pediatric Psychology, 15,* 27–41.

Bandura, A. (1965). Influence of models' reinforcement contingencies on the acquisition of imitative responses. *Journal of Personality and Social Psychology, 1,* 589–595.

Bandura, A. (1977a). Self-efficacy: Towards a unifying theory of behavior change. *Psychological Review, 84,* 191–215.

Bandura, A. (1977b). *Social learning theory.* Englewood Cliffs, NJ: Prentice Hall.

Bandura, A. (1982). Self-efficacy mechanisms in human agency. *American Psychologist, 37,* 122–147.

Bandura, A. (1986). *Social foundations of thought and action.* Englewood Cliffs, NJ: Prentice Hall.

Bandura, A., & Menlove, F. L. (1968). Factors determining vicarious extinction of avoidance behavior through symbolic modeling. *Journal of Personality and Social Psychology, 8,* 99–108.

Barbarin, O. A. (1990). Adjustment to serious childhood illness. In B. B. Lahey & A. E. Kazdin (Eds.), *Advances in clinical child psychology,* Vol. 13. New York: Plenum Press.

Barbosa-Saldivar, J. L., & Van Italie, T. B. (1979). Semistarvation: An overview of an old problem. *Bulletin of the New York Academy of Medicine, 55,* 774–797.

Barkley, R. A. (1981). Hyperactivity. In E. J. Mash & L. G. Terdal (Eds.), *Behavioral assessment of childhood disorders.* New York: Guilford Press.

Barkley, R. A. (1988a). Attention deficit disorder with hyperactivity. In E. J. Mash and L. G. Terdal (Eds.). *Behavioral assessment of childhood disorders. Selected core problems.* New York: Guilford.

Barkley, R. A. (1988b). Child behavior rating scales and checklists. In M. Rutter, A. H. Tuma, & I. S. Lann (Eds.), *Assessment and diganosis in child psychopathology.* New York: Guilford.

Barkley, R. A. (1989). Attention deficit-hyperactivity disorder. In E. J. Mash and R. A. Barkley (Eds.), *Treatment of childhood disorders.* New York, Guilford.

Barkley, R. A. (1990). *Attention-deficit hyperactivity disorder.* New York: Guilford.

Barkley, R. A., Anastopoulos, A. D., Guevremont, D. C., & Fletcher, K. E. (1992). Adolescents with attention deficit hyperactivity disorder: Mother-adolescent interactions, family beliefs and conflicts, and maternal psychopathology. *Journal of Abnormal Child Psychology, 20,* 263–287.

Barkley, R. A., & Edelbrock, C. S. (1987). Assessing situational variation in children's behavior problems: The Home and School Situations Questionnaire. In R. Prinz (Ed.), *Advances in behavioral assessment of children and families,* Vol. 3. Greenwich, CT: JAI.

Barkley, R. A., Grodzinsky, G., & DuPaul, G. J. (1992). Frontal lobe functions in attention deficit disorder with and without hyperactivity: A review and research report. *Journal of Abnormal Child Psychology, 20,* 163–188.

Barlow, D. H., & Hersen, M. (1984). *Single case experimental designs: Strategies for studying behavior change.* Elmsford, NY: Pergamon.

Barnes, G. G. (1994). Family therapy. In M. Rutter, E. Taylor, & L. Hersov (Eds.), *Child and adolescent psychiatry. Modern approaches.* Cambridge, MA: Blackwell Scientific.

Barnett, D., Manly, J. T., & Cicchetti, D. (1991). Continuing toward an operational definition of psychological maltreatment. *Development and Psychopathology, 3,* 19–30.

Barnett, W., & Spitzer, M. (1994). Pathological fire-setting 1951–1991: A review. *Medicine Science and the Law, 34,* 4–20.

Baron–Cohen, S. (1988). Social and pragmatic deficits in autism: Cognitive or affective? *Journal of Autism and Developmental Disorders, 18,* 379–397.

Baron–Cohen, S. (1989). The autistic child's theory of mind: A case of specific developmental delay. *Journal of Child Psychology and Psychiatry, 30,* 285–297.

Baron–Cohen, S. (1993). From attention-goal psychology to belief-desire psychology: the development of a theory of mind, and its dysfunction. In S. Baron-Cohen, H. Tager-Flusberg, & D. J. Cohen (Eds.), *Understanding other minds.* New York: Oxford Press.

Barrios, B. A., & Hartmann, D. P. (1988). Fears and anxieties. In E. J. Mash & L. G. Terdal (Eds.), *Behavioral assessment of childhood disorders,* 2nd ed. New York: Guilford.

Barrios, B. A., & O'Dell, S. L. (1989). Fears and anxieties. In E. J. Mash & R. A. Barkley (Eds.). *Treatment of childhood disorders.* New York: Guilford.

Barton, C., Alexander, J. F., Waldron, H., Turner, C. W., & Warburton, J. (1985). Generalizing treatment effects of functional family therapy: Three replications. *The American Journal of Family Therapy, 13,* 16–26.

Bashir, A. S., & Scavuzzo, A. (1992). Children with language disorders: Natural history and academic success. *Journal of Learning Disabilities, 25,* 53–65.

Bates, J. E. (1987). Temperament in infancy. In J. D. Osofsky (Ed.), *Handbook of infant development.* New York: Wiley.

Bateson, G., Jackson, D. D., Haley, J., & Weakland, J. (1956). Toward a theory of schizophrenia. *Behavioral Science, 1,* 251–264.

Bauer, D. H. (1976). An exploratory study of developmental changes in children's fears. *Journal of Child Psychology and Psychiatry, 17,* 69–74.

Bauer, R. H. (1987). Control processes as a way of understanding, diagnosing, and remediating learning disabilities. In H. L. Swanson (Ed.), *Memory and learning disabilities: Suppl. 2. Advances in learning and behavioral disabilities.* Greenwich, CT: JAI Press.

Bauer, R. H., & Newman, D. R. (1991). Allocation of study time and recall by learning disabled and nondisabled children of different ages. *Journal of Experimental Child Psychology, 52,* 11–21.

Baum, C. G. (1989). Conduct disorders. In T. H .Ollendick & M. Hersen (Eds.), *Handbook of child psychopathology,* 2nd ed. New York: Plenum.

Baumeister, A. A. (1987). Mental retardation: Some conceptions and dilemmas. *American Psychologist, 42,* 796–800.

Bauermeister, J. J., Bird, H. R., Canino, G., Rubio-Stipec, M., Bravo, M., & Alegria, M. (1995). Dimensions of attention deficit hyperactivity disorder: Findings from teacher and parent reports in a community sample. *Journal of Clinical Child Psychology, 24,* 264–271.

Baumrind, D. (1964). Some thoughts on ethics of research—after reading Milgram's "Behavioral study of obedience." *American Psychologist, 19,* 421–423.

Baumrind, D. (1986). Sex differences in moral reasoning: Response to Walker's (1984) conclusion that there are none. *Child Development, 57,* 511–521.

Bayley, N. (1969, 1993). *Bayley Scales of Infant Development: Birth to two years.* San Antonio, TX: Psychological Corporation.

Beardslee, W. R., & Podorefsky, D. (1988). Resilient adolescents whose parents have serious affective and other psychiatric disorders: Importance of self-understanding and relationships. *American Journal of Psychiatry, 145,* 63–69.

Beck, A. T. (1967). *Depression: Clinical, experimental, and theoretical aspects.* New York: Harper & Row.

Beck, A. T. (1976). *Cognitive theory and emotional disorders.* New York: International Universities Press.

Beck, A. T. (1993). Cognitive therapy: Past, present, and future. *Journal of Consulting and Clinical Psychology, 61,* 194–198.

Beck, A. T., Ward, C. H., Mendelson, M., Mock, J. E., & Erbaugh, J. K. (1962). Reliability of psychiatric diagnosis: II. A study of consistency of clinical judgements and ratings. *American Journal of Psychiatry, 119,* 351–357.

Beeghly, M., & Cicchetti, D. (1994). Child maltreatment, attachment, and the self system: Emergence of an internal state lexicon in toddlers at high social risk. *Development and Psychopathology, 6,* 5–30.

Beelmann, A., Pfingsten, U., & Losel, F. (1994). Effects of training social competence in children: A meta-analysis of recent evaluation studies. *Journal of Clinical Child Psychology, 23,* 260–271.

Beidel, D. C., & Randall, J. (1994). Social phobia. In T. H. Ollendick, N. J. King, & W. Yule (Eds.), *International handbook of phobic and anxiety disorders in children and adolescents* (pp. 111–130). New York: Plenum Press.

Beilen, H. (1992). Piaget's enduring contribution to developmental psychology. *Developmental Psychology, 28,* 191–204.

Bell, R. (1985). *Holy anorexia.* Chicago: University of Chicago Press.

Bell-Dolan, D. J. (1995). Social cue interpretation of anxious children. *Journal of Clinical Child Psychology, 24,* 2–10.

Bell-Dolan, D. J., Reaven, N. M., & Peterson, L. (1993). Depression and social functioning: A multidimensional study of the linkages. *Journal of Clinical Child Psychology, 22,* 306–315.

Bellak, L. (1993). *The T.A.T., C.A.T., and S.A.T. in clinical use* (5th ed.). Boston: Allyn & Bacon.

Bellak, L., & Bellak, S. (1949). *The Children's Apperception Test.* New York: C.P.S. Company.

Belsky, J. (1986). Infant day care: A cause for concern. *Zero to Three, 6(5),* 1–9.

Belsky, J. (1991). Psychological maltreatment: Definitional limitations and unstated assumptions. *Development and Psychopathology, 3,* 31–36.

Belsky, J. (1993). Etiology of child maltreatment: A developmental-ecological analysis. *Psychological Bulletin, 114,* 413–434.

Bem, S. L. (1985). Androgyny and gender schema theory: A conceptual and empirical integration. In T. B. Sonderegger (Ed.), *Nebraska symposium on motivation, 1984: Psychology and gender.* Lincoln, NE: University of Nebraska Press.

Bemis, K. (1987). The present status of operant conditioning for treatment of anorexia nervosa. *Behavior Modification, 11,* 432–464.

Bemporad, J. (1991). Psychoanalysis and psychodynamic therapy. In J. M. Weiner (Ed.), *Textbook of child and adolescent psychiatry.* Washington, DC: American Psychiatric Press.

Bemporad, J. R. (1978). Encopresis. In B. B. Wolman, J. Egan, & A. O. Ross (Eds.), Handbook of treatments in childhood and adolescence. Englewood Cliffs, NJ: Prentice Hall.

Bender L. (1947). One hundred cases of childhood schizophrenia treated with electric shock. *Trans. American Neurological Association, 72,* 165–169.

Bender, L. (1972). Childhood schizophrenia. In S. I. Harrison & J. F. McDermott (Eds.), *Childhood psychopathology.* New York: International Universities Press.

Bendersky, M., & Lewis, M. (1994). Environmental risk, biological risk, and developmental outcome. *Developmental Psychology, 30,* 484–494.

Benedict, R. (1934a). Anthropology and the abnormal. *Journal of General Psychology, 10,* 59–82.

Benedict, R. (1934b). *Patterns of culture.* Boston: Houghton-Mifflin.

Bennett, D. S. (1994). Depression among children with chronic medical problems: A meta-analysis. *Journal of Pediatric Psychology, 19,* 149–169.

Bennett, W. J. (1987). The role of the family in the nurture and protection of the young. *American Psychologist, 42,* 246–250.

Berecz, J. M. (1968). Phobias of childhood: Etiology and treatment. *Psychological Bulletin, 70,* 694–720.

Berg, I., & Jackson, A. (1985). Teenage school refusers grow up: A follow-up study of 168 subjects ten years on average after inpatient treatment. *British Journal of Psychiatry, 147,* 366–370.

Bergen, D. J., & Williams, J. E. (1991). Sex stereotypes in the United States revisited: 1972–1988. *Sex Roles, 24,* 413–424.

Berger, J. (1990). Interactions between parents and their infants with Down syndrome. In D. Cicchetti & M. Beeghly (Eds.), *Children with Down syndrome.* New York: Cambridge University Press.

Berger, M., & Yule, W. (1985). IQ tests and assessment. In A. M. Clarke, A. D. B. Clarke, & J. M. Berg (Eds.), *Mental deficiency. The changing outlook.* New York: The Free Press.

Bernstein, G. A. (1994). Psychopharmacological interventions. In T. H. Ollendick, N. J. King, & W. Yule (Eds.), *International handbook of phobic and anxiety disorders in children and adolescents* (pp. 439–452). New York: Plenum Press.

Bertenthal, B. J., & Campos, J. J. (1987). New directions in the study of early experience. *Child Development, 58,* 560–567.

Bettelheim, B. (1967a). *The empty fortress.* New York: Free Press.

Bettelheim, B. (1967b, Feb. 12). Where self begins. *New York Times.*

Bettes, B. A., & Walker, E. (1987). Positive and negative symptoms in psychotic and other psychiatrically disturbed children. *Journal of Child Psychology and Psychiatry, 28,* 555–568.

Biederman, J. (1991). Psychopharmacology. In J. Wiener (Ed.), *Textbook of child and adolescent psychiatry.* Washington, DC: American Psychiatric Association.

Biederman, J., Rosenbaum, J. F., Bolduc-Murphy, E. A., Faraone, S. V., Chaloff, J., Hirshfeld, D. R., & Kagan, J. (1993). A 3-year follow-up of children with and without behavioral inhibition. *Journal of the American Academy of Child and Adolescent Psychiatry, 32,* 814–821.

Bierman, K. L. (1989). Improving the peer relationships of rejected children. In B. B. Lahey & A. E. Kazdin (Eds.), *Advances in clinical child psychology.* Vol. 12. New York: Plenum Press.

Bierman, K., & Furman, W. (1984). The effects of social skills training and peer involvement on the social adjustment of preadolescents. *Child Development, 55,* 151–162.

Bierman, K. L., & Schwartz, L. A. (1986). Clinical child interviews: Approaches and developmental considerations. *Journal of Child and Adolescent Psychotherapy, 3,* 267–278.

Bifulco, A., Harris, T., & Brown, G. (1992). Mourning or early inadequate care? Reexamining the relationship of maternal loss in childhood with adult depression and anxiety. *Development and Psychopathology, 4,* 433–449.

Bigler, E. D. (1987). Acquired cerebral trauma. *Journal of Learning Disabilities, 20,* 455–457.

Bijou, S. W., Peterson, R. F., Harris, F. R., Allen, K. E., & Johnston, M. S. (1969). Methodology for experimental studies of young children in natural settings. *The Psychological Record, 19,* 177–210.

Biller, H. B. (1993). *Fathers and families. Paternal factors in child development.* Westport, CT: Auburn House.

Billings, A. G., & Moos, R. H. (1983). Comparisons of children of depressed and nondepressed parents: A social-environmental perspective. *Journal of Abnormal Child Psychology, 11,* 463–485.

Billings, A. G., & Moos, R. H. (1986). Children of parents with unipolar depression: A controlled 1-year follow-up. *Journal of Abnormal Child Psychology, 14,* 149–166.

Billings, A. G., Moos, R. H., Miller, J. J., & Gotlieb, J. E. (1987). Psychosocial adaptation in juvenile rheumatic disease: A controlled evauation. *Health Psychology, 6,* 343–359.

Bishop, D. V. M. (1992a). The biological basis of specific language impairment. In P. Fletcher & D. Hall (Eds.), *Specific speech and language disorders in children: Correlates, characteristics and outcome.* San Diego, CA: Singular Publishing Group.

Bishop, D. V. M. (1992b). The underlying nature of specific language impairment. *Journal of Child Psychology and Psychiatry. 33,* 3–66.

Bjorklund, D. F., & Green, B. L. (1992). The adaptive nature of cognitive immaturity. *American Psychologist, 47,* 46–54.

Blacher, J. (1984). Sequential stages of parental adjustment to the birth of a child with handicaps: Fact or artifact? *Mental Retardation, 22,* 55–68.

Blagg, N., & Yule, W. (1994). School refusal. In T. H. Ollendick, N. J. King, & W. Yule (Eds.), *International handbook of phobic and anxiety disorders in children and adolescents* (pp. 169–186). New York: Plenum Press.

Blasi, A. (1980). Bridging moral congition and moral action: A critical review of the literature. *Psychological Bulletin, 88,* 1–45.

Bloch, E. L., & Cvitkovic, J. (1994, Jan.). Trauma intervention project. *Advancing the public interest, Vol. VI.* Washington, DC: American Psychological Association.

Block, J. H., Block, J., & Gjerde, P. F. (1986). The personality of children prior to divorce. *Child Development, 57,* 827–840.

Block, J., Block, J. H., & Gjerde, P. F. (1988). Parental functioning and the home environment in families of divorce. *Journal of the American Academy of Child and Adolescent Psychiatry, 27,* 207–213.

Boivin, M., & Begin, G. (1989). Peer status and self-perception among early elementary school children: The case of the rejected children. *Child Development, 60,* 591–596.

Bonner, B. L., Kaufman, K. L., Harbeck, C., & Brassard, M. R. (1992). Child maltreatment. In C. E. Walker & M. C. Roberts (Eds.), *Handbook of clinical child psychology.* New York: Wiley.

Bootzin, R. R., & Chambers, M. J. (1990). Childhood sleep disorders. In A. M. Gross & R. S. Drabman (Eds.), *Handbook of clinical behavioral pediatrics.* New York: Plenum.

Borden, M. C., & Ollendick, T. H. (1992). The development and differentiation of social subtypes in autism. In B. B. Lahey & A. E. Kazdin (Ed.), *Advances in clinical child psychology.* New York: Plenum.

Borduin, C. M. (1994). Innovative models of treatment and service delivery in the juvenile justice system. *Journal of Clinical Child Psychology, 23 (Suppl.),* 19–25.

Borkovec, T. D. (1970). Autonomic reactivity to sensory stimulation in psychopathic, neurotic and normal delinquents. *Journal of Consulting and Clinical Psychology, 35,* 217–222.

Borkowski, J. G., & Cavanaugh, J. C. (1979). Maintenance and generalization of skills and strategies by the retarded. In N. R. Ellis (Ed.), *Handbook of mental deficiency.* Hillsdale, NJ: Erlbaum.

Borkowski, J. G., Johnston, M. B., & Reid, M. K. (1987). Metacognition, motivation, and controlled performance. In S. J. Ceci (Ed.), *Handbook of cognitive, social, and neuropsychologial aspects of learning disabilities.* Hillsdale, NJ: Erlbaum.

Bornstein, M., Bellack, A., & Hersen, M. (1977). Social skills training for unassertive children: A multiple baseline analysis. *Journal of Applied Behavior Analysis, 10,* 183–195.

Botuck, S., & Winsberg, B. G. (1991). Effects of respite on mothers of school-age and adult children with severe disabilities. *Mental Retardation, 29,* 43–47.

Boucher, J., & Lewis, V. (1980). Memory impairments and communication in relatively able autistic children. *Journal of Child Psychology and Psychiatry, 30,* 99–122.

Bowen, M. (1980). Introduction: Family systems theory. In S. I. Harrison & J. F. McDermott, Jr. (Eds.), *New directions in child psychopathology,* Vol. 1. New York: International Universities Press.

Bowers, D. W., Clement, P. W., Fantuzzo, J. W., Sorenson, D. A. (1985). Effects of teacher-administered and self-administered reinforcers on learning disabled children. *Behavior Therapy, 16,* 357–369.

Bowlby, J. (1960). Grief and mourning in infancy and early childhood. *Psychoanalytic Study of the Child, 15,* 9–52.

Bowlby, J. (1977). The making and breaking of affectional bonds. *British Journal of Psychiatry, 130,* 201–210.

Boyce, G. C., & Barnett, W. S. (1993). Siblings of persons with mental retardation. In Z. Stoneman & P. W. Berman (Eds.), *The effects of mental retardation, disability, and illness on sibling relationships. Research issues and challenges.* Baltimore: Paul H. Brookes Pub.

Braddock, D., & Heller, T. (1985a). The closure of mental retardation institutions I: Trends in the United States. *Mental Retardation, 23,* 168–176.

Braddock, D., & Heller, T. (1985b). The closure of mental retardation institutions II: Implications. *Mental Retardation, 23,* 222–229.

Bradley, C. (1947). Early evidence of psychoses in children, with special reference to schizophrenia. *Journal of Pediatrics, 30,* 529–540.

Bradley, L. J., & Meredith, R. C. (1991). Interpersonal development: A study with children classified as educable mentally retarded. *Education and Training in Mental Retardation, 26,* 130–141.

Bradley, R. H., Whiteside, L., Mundfrom, D. J., Casey, P. H., Kelleher, K. J., & Pope, S. K. (1994). Contributions of early interventions and early caregiving experiences to resilience in low-birthweight, premature children living in poverty. *Journal of Clinical Child Psychology, 23,* 425–434.

Bradley, S. J., & Hood, J. (1993). Psychiatrically referred adolescents with panic attacks: Presenting symptoms, stressors, and comorbidity. *Journal of the American Academy of Child and Adolescent Psychiatry, 32,* 826–829.

Brady, E. U., & Kendall, P. C. (1992). Comorbidity of anxiety and depression in children and adolescents. *Psychological Bulletin, 111,* 244–255.

Braungart-Rieker, J., Rende, R. D., Plomin, R., DeFries, J. C., & Fulker, D. W. (1995). Genetic mediation of longitudinal associations between family environment and childhood behavior problems. *Development and Psychopathology, 7,* 233–245.

Bregman, J. D. (1991). Current developments in the understanding of mental retardation: Part II. Psychopathology. *Journal of the American Academy of Child and Adolescent Psychiatry, 30,* 861–872.

Bregman, J. D., & Hodapp, R. M. (1991). Current developments in the understanding of mental retardation: Part I. Biological and phenomenological perspectives. *Journal of the American Academy of Child and Adolescent Psychiatry, 30,* 707–719.

Brier, N. (1989). The relationship between learning disability and delinquency: A review and reappraisal. *Journal of Learning Disabilities, 22,* 546–553.

Broman, S., Nichols P. L., Shaughnessy P., & Kennedy, W. (1987). *Retardation in young children: A developmental study of cognitive deficit.* Hillsdale, NJ: Erlbaum.

Bromley, B. E., & Blacher, J. (1991). Parental reasons for out-of-home placement of children with severe handicaps. *Mental Retardation, 29,* 275–280.

Bronfenbrenner, U. (1986). Ecology of the family as a context for human development: Research perspectives. *Developmental Psychology, 22,* 723–742.

Brooks-Gunn, J. (1993). Why do adolescents have difficulty adhering to health regimes? In N. A. Krasnegor, L. Epstein, S. B. Johnson, & S. Yaffe (Eds.), *Developmental aspects of health compliance behavior.* Hillsdale, NJ: Lawrence Earlbaum Associates.

Brown, R. T., Doepke, K. J., & Kaslow, N. J. (1993). *Clinical Psychology Review, 13,* 119–132.

Brownell, C. A. (1986). Convergent developments: Cognitive-developmental correlates of growth in infant/toddler peer skills. *Child Development, 57,* 275–286.

Bruch, H. (1973). *Eating disorders: Obesity, anorexia nervosa, and the person within.* New York: Basic Books.

Bruch, H. (1979). *The golden cage: The enigma of anorexia nervosa.* New York: Vintage Books.

Bruch, H. (1986). Anorexia nervosa: The therapeutic task. In K. D. Brownell & J. P. Foreyt (Eds.), *Handbook of eating disorders: Physiology, psychology, and treatment of obesity, anorexia, and bulimia.* New York: Basic Books.

Bruininks, R. H., Hauber, F. A., & Kudla, M. J. (1980). National survey of community residential facilities: A profile of facilities and residents in 1977. *American Journal of Mental Deficiency, 84,* 470–478.

Brumberg, J. J. (1986). "Fasting girls": Reflections on writing the history of anorexia nervosa. In A. B. Smuts & J. W. Hagen (Eds.), History and research in child development. *Monographs of the Society for Research in Child Development, 50*(4–5, Serial No. 211).

Bryan, T. (1991). Selection of subjects in research on learning disabilities: A view from the social side. *Learning Disability Quarterly, 14,* 297–302.

Bryan, T., & Bryan, J. (1990). Social factors in learning disabilities: An overview. In H. L. Swanson & B. Keogh (Eds.), *Learning disabilities. Theoretical and research issues.* Hillsdale, NJ: Erlbaum.

Bryan, T. H., & Bryan, J. H. (1975, 1986). *Understanding learning disabilities.* Palo Alto, CA: Mayfield.

Bryant-Waugh, R., & Lask, B. (1995). Eating disorders in children. *Journal of Child Psychology and Psychiatry, 36,* 191–202.

Bryson, S. E., Clark, B. S., & Smith, I. M. (1988). First report of a Canadian epidemiological study of autistic syndromes. *Journal of Child Psychology and Psychiatry, 29,* 433–445.

Bryson, S. E., Smith, I. M., & Eastwood, D. (1988). Obstetrical suboptimality in autistic children. *Journal of the American Academy of Child and Adolescent Psychiatry, 27,* 418–422.

Buckstein, O. G. (1993). Overview of pharmacological treatment. In V. B. Van Hasselt & M. Hersen (Eds.), *Handbook of behavior therapy and pharmacotherapy for children: A comparative analysis.* Boston: Allyn and Bacon.

Buhrmester, D., Whalen, C., Henker, B., MacDonald, V., & Hinshaw, S. (1992). Prosocial behavior in hyperactive boys: Effects of stimulant medication and comparison with normal boys. *Journal of Abnormal Child Psychology, 20,* 103–119.

Bullock, M., & Russell, J. A. (1986). Concepts of emotion in developmental psychology. In C. E. Izard & P. B. Read (Eds.), *Measuring emotions in infants and children,* Vol. 2. New York: Cambridge University Press.

Burack, J. A. (1990). Differentiating mental retardation: The two-group approach and beyond. In R. M. Hodapp, J. A. Burack, & E. Zigler (Eds.), *Issues in the developmental approach to mental retardation.* New York: Cambridge University Press.

Burack, J. A., & Volkmar, F. R. (1992). Development of low- and high-functioning autistic children. *Journal of Child Psychology and Psychiatry, 33,* 607–616.

Burchard, J., & Clark, R. (1990). The role of individualized care in a service delivery system for children and adolescents with severely maladjusted behavior. *Journal of Mental Health Administration, 17,* 48–60.

Burke, A. E., & Silverman, W. K. (1987). The prescriptive treatment of school refusal. *Clinical Psychology Review, 7,* 353–362.

Busch-Rossnagel, N. A., & Vance, A. K. (1982). The impact of the schools on social and emotional development. In B. B. Wolman (Ed.), *Handbook of developmental psychology.* Englewood Cliffs, NJ: Prentice Hall.

Buss, A. H., & Plomin, R. (1986). The EAS approach to temperament. In R. Plomin and J. Dunn (Eds.), *The study of temperament: Changes, continuities, and challenges.* Hillsdale, NJ: Erlbaum.

Butler, L., Miezitis, S., Friedman, R., & Cole, E. (1980). The effect of two school-based intervention programs on depressive symptoms in preadolescents. *American Educational Research Journal, 17,* 111–119.

Butler, R. W., & Copeland, D. R. (1993). Neuropsychological effects of central nervous system prophylactic treatment in childhood leukemia. *Journal of Pediatric Psychology, 18,* 319–338.

Butterfield, E. C., & Belmont, J. M. (1977). Assessing and improving the executive cognitive functions of mentally retarded people. In I. Bialer & M. Sternlicht (Eds.), *Psychological issues in mental retardation.* New York: Psychological Dimensions.

Camp, B. W., Blom, G. E., Herbert, R., & Van Doornick, W. J. (1977). "Think aloud": A program for developing self-control in young aggressive boys. *Journal of Abnormal Child Psychology, 5,* 157–169.

Campaigne, B. N., Morrison, J. A., Schumann, B. C., Faulkner, F., Lakatos, E. Sprecher, D., & Schreiber, G. B. (1994). Indexes of obesity and comparisons with previous national survey data in 9- and 10-year-old black and white girls: The National Heart, Lung, and Blood Institute Growth and Health Survey. *Journal of Pediatrics, 124,* 675–680.

Campbell, D. T., & Stanley, J. C. (1963). *Experimental and quasi-experimental designs for research.* Chicago: Rand McNally.

Campbell, M. (1988). Annotation. Fenfluramine treatment of autism. *Journal of Child Psychology and Psychiatry, 29,* 1–10.

Campbell, M., Anderson, L. T., Small, A. M., Adams, P., Gonzalez, N. M., & Ernst, M. (1993). Naltrexone in autistic children: Behavioral symptoms and attentional learning. *Journal of the American Academy of Child and Adolescent Psychiatry, 32,* 1283–1291.

Campbell, M., & Cueva, J. E. (1995). Psychopharmacology in child and adolescent psychiatry: A review of the past seven years. Part I. *Journal of the American Academy of Child and Adolescent Psychiatry, 34,* 1124–1132.

Campbell, M., Overall, J. E., Small, A. M., Sokol, M. S., Spencer, E. K., Adams, P., Foltz, R. L., Monti, K. M., Perry, R., Nobler, M., & Roberts, E. (1989). Naltrexone in autistic children: An acute open dose range tolerance trial. *Journal of the American Academy of Child and Adolescent Psychiatry, 28,* 200–206.

Campbell, M., & Spencer, E. K. (1988). Psychopharmacology in child and adolescent psychiatry: A review of the past five years. *Journal of the American Academy of Child and Adolescent Psychiatry, 27,* 269–279.

Campbell, S. B. (1986). Developmental issues in childhood anxiety. In R. Gittleman (Ed.), *Anxiety disorders of childhood.* New York: Guilford.

Campbell, S. B. (1987). Parent-referred problem three-year- olds: Developmetnal changes in symptoms. *Journal of Child Psychology and Psychiatry, 28,* 835–845.

Campbell, S. B. (1990). The socialization and social development of hyperactive children. In M. Lewis & S. M. Miller (Eds.). *Handbook of developmental psychopathology.* NY: Plenum.

Campbell, S. B. (1995). Behavior problems in preschool children: A review of recent research. *Journal of Child Psychology and Psychiatry, 36,* 113–149.

Campbell, S. B., Cohn, J. F., & Meyers, T. (1995). Depression in first-time mothers: Mother-infant interaction and depression chronicity. *Developmental Psychology, 31,* 349–357.

Candy-Gibbs, S. E., Sharp, K. C., & Petrun, C. J. (1985). The effects of age, object, and cultural/religious background on children's concepts of death. *Omega Journal of Death and Dying, 15,* 329–346.

Cannon, T. D., Mednick, S. A., Parnas, J., Schulsinger, F., Praestholm, J., & Vestergaard, A. (1993). Developmental brain abnormalities in the offspring of schizophrenic mothers. *Archives of General Psychiatry, 50,* 551–564.

Cantor, S. (1988). *Childhood schizophrenia.* New York: Guilford.

Cantor, S., & Kestenbaum, C. (1986). Psychotherapy with schizophrenic children. *Journal of the American Academy of Child Psychiatry, 25,* 623–630.

Cantwell, D. P. (1980). The diagnostic process and diagnostic classification in child psychiatry: DSM-III. *Journal of the American Academy of Child Psychiatry, 19,* 345–355.

Cantwell, D. P. (1986). Attention deficit and associated childhood disorders. In T. Mellon & G. L. Klerman (Eds.), *Contemporary directions in psychopathology: Toward DSM- IV.* New York: Guilford.

Cantwell, D. P., Baker, L., Rutter, M., & Mawhood, L. (1989). Infantile autism and developmental receptive aphasia. *Journal of Autism and Developmental Disorders, 19,* 19–31.

Cantwell, D. P., & Rutter, M. (1994). Classification: Conceptual issues and substantive findings. In M. Rutter, E. Taylor, & L. Hersov (Eds.), *Child and adolescent psychiatry. Modern approaches.* Boston: Blackwell Scientific.

Capaldi, D. M., & Patterson, G. R. (1991). The relation of parental transition to boys' adjustment problems: I. A. linear hypothesis, and II. Mothers at risk for transitions and unskilled parenting. *Developmental Psychology, 27,* 489–504.

Caplan, G. (1964). *The principles of preventive psychiatry.* New York: Basic Books.

Caplan, M., & Douglas, V. (1969). Incidence of parental loss in children with depressed mood. *Journal of Child Psychology and Psychiatry, 10,* 225–232.

Caplan, R. (1994). Thought disorder in childhood. *Journal of the American Academy of Child and Adolescent Psychiatry, 33,* 605–615.

Carlson, E. A., Jacobvitz, D., & Sroufe, L. A. (1995). A developmental investigation of inattentiveness and hyperactivity. *Child Development, 66,* 37–54.

Carlson, G. A. (1994). Adolescent bipolar disorder: Phenomenology and treatment implications. In W. M. Reynolds and H. F. Johnston (Eds.), *Handbook of depression in children and adolescents.* New York: Plenum Press.

Carlson, G. A., & Cantwell, D. P. (1980). Unmasking masked depression in children and adolescents. *American Journal of Psychiatry, 137,* 445–449.

Carlson, G. A., & Kashani, J. H. (1988). Phenomenology of major depression from childhood through adulthood: Analysis of three studies. *American Journal of Psychiatry, 1245,* 1222–1225.

Carnine, D. W., & Kameenui, E. J. (1990). The general education intitiative and children with special needs: A false dilemma in the face of true problems. *Journal of Learning Disabilities, 23,* 141–144, 148.

Carpenter, P. J. (1992). Perceived control as a predictor of distress in children undergoing invasive medical procedures. *Journal of Pediatric Psychology, 17,* 757–773.

Carr, J. (1994). Long term outcome for people with Down's syndrome. *Journal of Child Psychology and Psychiatry, 35,* 425–439.

Carron, A. V., & Bailey, D. A. (1974). Strength development in boys from 10 through 16 years. *Monographs of the Society for Research in Child Development, 39 (4),* No. 157, 1–37.

Carson, C., & Rutter, M. (1991). Comorbidity in child psychopathology: Concepts, issues and research strategies. *Journal of Child Psychology and Psychiatry, 32,* 1063–1080.

Casaer, P. (1993). Old and new facts about perinatal brain development. *Journal of Child Psychology and Psychiatry, 34,* 101–109.

Caspi, A., Elder, G. H. Jr., & Bem, D. J. (1987). Moving against the world: Life-course paterns of explosive children. *Developmental Psychology, 23,* 308–313.

Caspi, A., Elder, G. H., Jr., & Bem, D. J. (1988). Moving away from the world: Life-course patterns of shy children. *Developmental Psychology, 24,* 824–831.

Caspi, A., Henry, B., McGee, R., Moffitt, T. E., & Silva, P. A. (1995). Temperamental origins of child and adolescent behavior problems: From age three to fifteen. *Child Development, 65,* 55–68.

Centers for Disease Control (1995). Suicide among children, adolescents, and young adults—United States, 1980–1992. *Morbidity and Mortality Weekly Report, 44(15),* 289–291.

Chalfant, J. C. (1989). Learning disabilities: Policy issues and promising approaches. *American Psychologist, 44,* 392–398.

Chandler, M. J. (1973). Egocentrism and antisocial behavior: The assessment and training of social perspective-taking skills. *Developmental Psychology, 9,* 326–332.

Chandola, C. A., Robling, M. R., Peters, T. J., Melville-Thomas, G., & McGuffin, P. (1992). Pre- and perinatal factors and the risk of subsequent referral for hyperactivity. *Journal of Child Psychology and Psychiatry, 33,* 1077–1090.

Charlop, M. H., Schreibman, L., Kurtz, P. F. (1991). Childhood autism. In T. R. Kratochwill & R. J. Morris (Eds.), *The practice of child therapy.* Boston: Allyn and Bacon.

Chatoor, I., Conley, C., & Dickson, L. (1988). Food refusal after an incident of choking: A posttraumatic eating disorder. *Journal of the American Academy of Child and Adolescent Psychiatry, 27,* 105–110.

Chess, S. (1988). Child and adolescent psychiatry come of age: A fifty year perspective. *Journal of the Amercan Academy of Child and Adolescent Psychiatry, 27,* 1–7.

Chess, S., & Thomas, A. (1972). Differences in outcome with early intervention in children with behavior disorders. In M. Roff, L. Robins, & M. Pollack (Eds.), *Life history research in psychopathology,* Vol. 2. Minneapolis: University of Minnesota Press.

Chess, S., & Thomas, A. (1977). Temperamental individuality from childhood to adolescence. *Journal of American Academy of Child Psychiatry, 16,* 218–226.

Childress, A. C., Brewerton, T. D., Hodges, E. L., & Jarrell, M. P. (1993). The Kids' Eating Disorders Survey (KEDS): A study of middle school students. *Journal of the American Academy of Child and Adolescent Psychiatry, 32,* 843–850.

Chinn, P. C., & Hughes, S. (1987). Representation of minority students in special education classes. *Remedial and Special Education, 8,* 41–46.

Christophersen, E. R., & Edwards, K. J. (1992). Treatment of elimination disorders: State of the art 1991. *Applied and Preventive Psychology, 1,* 15–22.

Cialdella, Ph., & Mamelle, N. (1989). An epidemiological study of infantile autism in a French Department (Rhone): A research note. *Journal of Child Psychology and Psychiatry, 30,* 165–175.

Cicchetti, D. (1984). The emergence of developmental psychopathology. *Child Development, 55,* 1–7.

Cicchetti, D. (1989). Developmental psychology: Some thoughts on its evolution. *Development and Psychopathology, 1,* 1–3.

Cicchetti, D. (1991). Defining psychological maltreatment: Reflections and future directions. *Development and Psychopathology, 3,* 1–2.

Cicchetti, D. (1994). Advances and challenges in the study of the sequelae of child maltreatment. *Development and Psychopathology, 6,* 1–4.

Cicchetti, D., & Olsen, K. (1990). The developmental psychopathology of child maltreatment. In M. Lewis & S. M. Miller (Eds.), *Handbook of developmental psychopathology*. New York: Plenum Press.

Cicchetti, D., Rogosch, F. A., & Toth, S. L. (1994). A developmental psychopathology perspective on depression in children and adolescents. In W. M. Reynolds and H. F. Johnston (Eds.), *Handbook of depression in children and adolescents*. New York: Plenum Press.

Cicchetti, D., & Schneider-Rosen, K. (1986). An organizational approach to childhood depression. In M. Rutter, C. Izard, & P. Read (Eds.), *Depression in young people: Clinical and developmental perspectives*. New York: Guilford.

Cicchetti, D., Toth, S., & Bush, M. (1988). Developmental psychopathology and incompetence in childhood: Suggestions for intervention. In B. B. Lahey & A. E. Kazdin (Eds.), *Advances in clinical child psychology*, Vol. 11. New York: Plenum.

Clarizio, H. F. (1994). Assessment of depression in children and adolescents by parents, teachers, and peers. In W. M. Reynolds and H. F. Johnston (Eds.), *Handbook of depression in children and adolescents*. New York: Plenum Press.

Clark, D. B., Smith, M. G., Neighbors, B. D., Skerlec, L. M., & Randall, J. (1994). Anxiety disorders in adolescence: Characteristics, prevalence, and comorbidities. *Clinical Psychology Review, 14*, 113–137.

Clark, L. A., & Watson, D. (1991). Tripartite model of anxiety and depression: Psychometric evidence and taxonomic implications. *Journal of Abnormal Psychology, 100*, 316–336.

Clarke, A. D. B., & Clarke, A. M. (1984). Constancy and change in the growth of human characteristics. *Journal of Child Psychology and Psychiatry, 25*, 191–210.

Clarke, A. M., & Clarke, A. D. B. (1985) Criteria and classification. In A. M. Clarke, A. D. B. Clarke & J. M. Berg (Eds.), Mental deficiency. The changing outlook. New York: The Free Press.

Clarke-Stewart, A. (1989). Infant day care: Maligned or malignant? *American Psychologist, 44*, 266–273.

Clarke-Stewart, A. (1992). *Daycare* (2nd ed.), Cambridge, MA: Harvard University Press.

Cohen, N. J., Davine, M., Hododezky, N., Lipsett, L., & Isaacson, L. (1993). Unsuspected language impairment in psychiatrically disturbed children: Prevalence and language and behavioral characteristics. *Journal of the American Academy of Child and Adolescent Psychiatry, 32*, 595–601.

Cohen, P., Cohen, J., & Brook, J. (1993). An epidemiological study of disorders in late childhood and adolescence -II. Persistence of disorders. *Journal of Child Psychology and Psychiatry, 34*, 869–877.

Cohen, P., Cohen, J., Kasen, S., Velez, C. N., Hartmark, C., Johnson, J., Rojas, M., Brook, J., & Streuning, E. L. (1993). An epidemiological study of disorders in late childhood and adolescence-I. Age- and gender-specific prevalence. *Journal of Child Psychology and Psychiatry, 34*, 851–867.

Cohen-Tovee, E. M. (1993). Depressed mood and concern with weight and shape in normal young women. *International Journal of Eating Disorders, 14*, 223–227.

Coie, J. D., Belding, M., & Underwood, M. (1988). Aggression and peer rejection in childhood. In B. B. Lahey & A. E. Kazdin (Eds.), *Advances in clinical child psychology*, Vol. 11. *New York: Plenum.*

Coie, J. D., Watt, N. F., West, S. G., Hawkins, J. D., Asarnow, J. R., Markman, H. J., Ramey, S. L., Shure, M. B., & Long. B. (1993). The science of prevention: A conceptual framework and some directions for a national research program. *American Psychologist, 48*, 1013–1022.

Coles, G. S. (1987). *The learning mystique*. New York: Pantheon.

Coles, G. S. (1989). Excerpts from The Learning Mystique: A Critical Look at "Learning Disabilities." *Journal of Learning Disabilities, 22*, 267–273, 277.

Collins, E. (1991). Body figure perceptions and preferences among preadolescent children. *International Journal of Eating Disorders, 10*, 199–208.

Collins, W. A., & Russell, G. (1991). Mother-child and father-child relationships in middle childhood and adolescence: A developmental analysis. *Development Review, 11*, 99–136.

Combrinck-Graham, L. (1990). Developments in family systems theory and research. *Journal of the American Academy of Child and Adolescent Psychiatry, 29*, 501–512.

Compas, B. E., Ey, S., & Grant, K. E. (1993). Taxonomy, assessment, and diagnosis of depression during adolescence. *Psychological Bulletin, 14*, 323–344.

Compas, B. E., Hinden, B. R., & Gerhardt, C. (1995). Adolescent development: Pathways and processes of risk and resilience. *Annual Review of Psychology, 46*, 265–293.

Conduct Problems Prevention Research Group (1992). A developmental and clinical model for the prevention of conduct disorder: The FAST Track Program. *Development and Psychopathology, 4*, 509–527.

Conger, J., & Keane, S. (1981). Social skills intervention in the treatment of isolated or withdrawn children. *Psychological Bulletin, 90*, 478–495.

Connell, J. P. (1985). A new multidimensional measure of children's perceptions of control. *Child Development, 56*, 1018–1041.

Connelly, C. D., & Straus, M. A. (1992). Mother's age and risk for physical abuse. *Child Abuse & Neglect, 16*, 709–718.

Conners, C. K. (1969). A teacher rating scale for use with drug studies with children. *American Journal of Psychiatry, 126*, 884–888.

Conners, C. K. (1980). Artificial colors in the diet and disruptive behavior. In R. M. Knights & D. J. Bakker (Eds.). *Treatment of hyperactive and learning disabled children*. Baltimore: University Park Press.

Conners, C. K. (1990). *Conner's Rating Scales manual*. North Tonawanda, NY: Multi-Health Systems.

Conners, C. K., & Werry, J. S. (1979). Pharmacotherapy. In H. C. Quay & J. S. Werry (Eds.), *Psychopathological disorders of childhood*. New York: Wiley.

Coplan, R. J., Rubin, K. H., Fox, N. A., Calkins, S. D., & Stewart, S. L. (1994). Being alone, playing alone, and acting alone: Distinguishing among reticence and passive and active solitude in young children. *Child Development, 65*, 129–137.

Corbett, J. A. (1985). Mental retardation: Psychiatric aspects. In M. Rutter & L. Hersov (Eds.), *Child and adolescent psychiatry*. Boston: Blackwell Scientific Publications.

Corkum, P. V., & Siegel, L. S. (1993). Is the continuous performance task a valuable research tool for use with children with attention-deficit-hyperactivity disorder? *Journal of Child Psychology and Psychiatry, 34*, 1217–1239.

Corley, D. L., Gevirtz, R., Nideffer, R., & Cummins, L. (1987). Prevention of post-infectious asthma in children by reducing self-inoculatory behavior. *Journal of Pediatric Psychology, 12*, 519–531.

Corsaro, W. A., & Eder, D. (1980). Children's peer cultures. *Annual Review of Sociology, 16*, 197–220.

Costello, E. J. (1989). Developments in child psychiatric epidemiology. *Journal of the American Academy of Child and Adolescent Psychiatry, 28*, 836–841.

Costello, E. J. (1990). Child psychiatric epidemiology. In B. B. Lahey & A. E. Kazdin (Eds.), *Advances in clinical child psychology.* Vol. 14. New York: Plenum.

Costello, E. J., Burns, B. J., Angold, A., & Leaf, P. J. (1983). How can epidemiology improve mental health services of children and adolescents? *Journal of the American Academy of Child and Adolescent Psychiatry, 32,* 1106–1117.

Cotler, S. (1986). Epidemiology and outcome. In J. M. Reisman (Ed.), *Behavior disorders in infants, children, and adolescents.* New York: Random House.

Counts, C. R., Jones, C., Frame, C. L. Jarvie, G. J., & Strauss, C. C. (1986). The perception of obesity by normal-weight versus obese school-age children. *Child Psychiatry and Human Development, 17,* 113–120.

Cowen, E. L. (1991). In pursuit of wellness. *American Psychologist, 46,* 404–408.

Cowen, E. L. (1994). The enhancement of psychological wellness: Challenges and opportunities. *American Journal of Community Psychology, 22,* 149–179.

Cowen, E. L. (1995). The enhancement of psychological wellness: Challenges and opportunity. *American Journal of Community Psychology, 22,* 149–179.

Cowen, E. L., Gesten, E. L., & Wilson, A. B. (1979). The Primary Mental Health Project (PMHP): Evaluation of current program effectiveness. *American Journal of Community Psychology, 3,* 293–303.

Cowen, E. L., & Hightower, A. D. (1989a). The Primary Mental Health Project: Alternatives in school based preventive interventions. In T. B. Gutkin & C. R. Reynolds (Eds.), *Handbook of school psychology,* 2nd ed. New York: Wiley.

Cowen, E. L., & Hightower, A. D. (1989b). The Primary Mental Health Projects: Thirty years after. In R. E. Hess, & J. DeLeon (Eds.), *Prevention in human services,* Vol. 6, No. 2, New York: Haworth.

Cowen, E. L., & Hightower, A. D. (1990). The Primary Mental Health Project: Alternative approaches in school-based prevention interventions. In R. E. Hess (Ed.), *Prevention in human services.* New York: Haworth Press.

Cowen, E. L., Trost, M. A., Lorion, R. P., Dorr, D., Izzo, L. D., & Issacson, R. V. (1975). *New ways in school mental health: Early detection and prevention of school maladaptation.* New York: Human Sciences Press.

Cowen, E. L., Work, W. C., Wyman, P. A., & Jarrell, D. D. (1994). Relationship between retrospective parent reports of developmental milestones and school adjustment at ages 10 to 12 years. *Journal of the American Academy of Child and Adolescent Psychiatry, 33,* 400–406.

Cowen, E. L., Wyman, P. A., Work, W. C., & Parker, G. R. (1990). The Rochester Child Resilience Project: Overview and summary of first year findings. *Development and Psychopathology, 2,* 193–212.

Cowen, E. L., Zax, M., Izzo, L. D., & Trost, M. A. (1966). Prevention of emotional disorders in the school setting: A further investigation. *Journal of Consulting Psychology, 30,* 381–387.

Cowen, E., Pederson, A., Babigian, H. Izo, L., & Trost, N. (1973). Long term follow-up of early detected vulnerable children. *Journal of Consulting and Clinical Psychology, 41,* 438–446.

Cox, A., & Rutter, M. (1985). Diagnostic appraisal and interviewing. In M. Rutter & L. Hersov (Eds.), *Child and adolescent psychiatry: Modern approaches.* Oxford: Blackwell Scientific Publications.

Cozby, P. C., Worden, P. E., & Kee, D. W. (1989). *Research methods in human development.* Mountain View, CA: Mayfield.

Craig, E. M., & McCarver, R. B. (1984). Community placement and adjustment of deinstitutionalized clients: Issues and findings. In N. R. Ellis & N. W. Bray (Eds.), *International review of research in mental retardation.* New York: Academic Press.

Cravens, H. (1992). A scientific project locked in time: The Terman genetic studies of genius, 1920s–1950s. *American Psychologist, 47,* 183–189.

Creer, T. L. (1982). Asthma. *Journal of Consulting and Clinical Psychology, 50,* 912–921.

Creer, T. L. (1991). The application of behavioral procedures to childhood asthma: Current and future perspectives. *Patient Education and Counseling, 17,* 9–22.

Creer, T. L., & Reynolds, R. V. C. (1990). Asthma. In A. M. Gross & R. S. Drabman (Eds.), *Handbook of clinical behavioral pediatrics.* New York: Plenum.

Crick, N. R. (1995). Relational aggression: The role of intent attributions, feelings of distress, and provocation type. *Development and Psychopathology, 7,* 313–322.

Crick, N. R. & Dodge, K. A. (1994). A review and reformulation of social information-processing mechanisms in children's social adjustment. *Psychological Bulletin, 115,* 74–101.

Crisp, A. H. (1984). The psychopathology of anorexia nervosa: Getting the 'heat' out of the system. In A. J. Stunkard & E. Stellar (Eds.), *Eating and its disorders.* New York: Raven Press.

Crittenden, P. M., Claussen, A. H., & Sugarman, D. B. (1994). Dimensions of child maltreatment and their relationship to adolescent adjustment. *Development and Psychopathology, 6,* 145–164.

Crnic, K. A. (1988). Mental retardation. In E. J. Mash & L. G. Terdal (Eds.), *Behavioral assessment of childhood disorders. Selected core problems.* New York: Guilford.

Crockenberg, S. B. (1988). Infant irritability, mother responsiveness, and social support influences on the security of infant-mother attachment. In E. M. Hetherington & R. G. Parke (Eds.), *Contemporary readings in child psychology.* New York: McGrawHill.

Cronbach, L. J. (1975). Five decades of public controversy over mental testing. *American Psychologist, 30,* 1–14.

Cummings, E. M., & Cicchetti, D. (1990). Towards a transactional model of relations between attachment and depression. In M. Greenberg, D. Cicchetti, & E. M. Cummings (Eds.), *Attachment in the preschool years: Theory, research, and intervention* (pp. 339–372). Chicago: The University of Chicago Press.

Cummings, E. M., & Davies, P. T. (1994). Maternal depression and child development. *Journal of Child Psychology and Psychiatry, 35,* 73–112.

Curry, J. F., & Craighead, W. E. (1993). Depression. In T. H. Ollendick & M. Hersen (Eds.), *Handbook of child and adolescent assessment.* Boston: Allyn and Bacon.

Cushna, B. (1980). The psychological definition of mental retardation: A historical review. In L. S. Szymanski & P. E. Tanguay (Eds.), *Emotional disorders of mentally retarded persons.* Baltimore: University Park Press.

Cuskelly, M., & Dadds, M. (1992). Behavioural problems in children with Down's syndrome and their siblings. *Journal of Child Psychology and Psychiatry, 33,* 749–761.

Cytryn, L., & Lourie, R. S. (1980). Mental retardation. In H. I. Kaplan, A. M. Freedman, & B. J. Sadock (Eds.), *Comprehensive textbook of psychiatry/III,* Vol. 3. Baltimore: Williams & Wilkins.

Cytryn, L., & McKnew, D. (1974). Factors influencing the changing clinical expression of the depressive process in children. *American Journal of Psychiatry, 131,* 879–881.

Cytryn, L., McKnew, D. H., & Bunney, W. E. (1980). Diagnosis of depression in children. A reassessment. *American Journal of Psychiatry, 137,* 22–25.

DaCosta, M., & Halmi, K. A. (1992). Classifications of anorexia nervosa: Question of subtypes. *International Journal of Eating Disorders, 11,* 305–313.

Dadds, M. R., Rapee, R. M., Barrett, P. M. (1994). Behavioral observation. In T. H. Ollendick, N. J. King, & W. Yule (Eds.), *International handbook of phobic and anxiety disorders in children and adolescents* (pp. 349–364). New York: Plenum Press.

Dadds, M. R., Sanders, M. R., Morrison, M., & Rebgetz, M. (1992). Childhood depression and conduct disorder: II. An analysis of family interaction patterns in the home. *Journal of Abnormal Psychology, 101,* 505–513.

Dadds, M. R., Schwartz, S., & Sanders, M. R. (1987). Marital discord and treatment outcome in behavioral treatment of child conduct disorders. *Journal of Consulting and Clinical Psychology, 55,* 396–403.

Dahlquist, L. M. (1992). Coping with aversive medical treatments. In A. M. La Greca, L. J. Siegel, J. L. Wallander, & C. E. Walker (Eds.). *Stress and coping in child health.* New York: Guilford.

Danforth, J. S., & Drabman, R. S. (1990). Community living skills. In J. L. Matson (Ed.), *Handbook of behavior modification with the mentally retarded.* New York: Plenum.

Dangel, R. F., & Polster, R. A. (1984). *Parent training: Foundations of research and practice.* New York: Guilford.

Daniels, D., Moos, R. H., Billings, A. G., & Miller, J. J. (1987). Psychosocial risk and resistance factors among children with chronic illness, healthy siblings, and healthy controls. *Journal of Abnormal Child Psychology, 15,* 295–308.

Dare, C. (1985). Psychoanalytic theories of development. In M. Rutter & L. Hersov (Eds.), *Child and adolescent psychiatry: Modern approaches.* Oxford: Blackwell Scientific Publications.

Dare, C., Le Grange, D. L., Eisler, I., & Rutherford, J. (1994). Redefining the psychosomatic family: Family process of 26 eating disorder families. *International Journal of Eating Disorders, 16,* 211–226.

Daugherty, T. K., & Shapiro, S. K. (1994). Behavior checklists and rating forms. In T. H. Ollendick, N. J. King, & W. Yule (Eds.), *International handbook of phobic and anxiety disorders in children and adolescents* (pp. 331–348). New York: Plenum Press.

Davidson, W. S., & Basta, J. (1989). Diversion from the juvenile justice system: Research evidence and a discussion of issues. In B. B. Lahey & A. E. Kazdin (Eds.), *Advances in clinical child psychology,* Vol. 12, New York: Plenum.

Davies, R. R., & Rogers, E. S. (1985). Social skills training with persons who are mentally retarded. *Mental Retardation, 23,* 186–196.

Davison, G. C. & Neale, J. M. (1978, 1982, 1990, 1994, 1996). *Abnormal psychology.* New York: Wiley.

Dawson, G., & Castelloe, P. (1992). Autism. In C. E. Walker & M. C. Roberts (Eds.), *Handbook of clinical child psychology.* New York: Wiley.

Deaton, A. V. (1985). Adaptive noncompliance in pediatric asthma: The parent as expert. *Journal of Pediatric Psychology, 10,* 1–14.

Deaton, A. V., & Olbrisch, M. E. (1987). Adaptive noncompliance: Parents as experts and decision makers in the treatment of pediatric asthma patients. In M. Wolraich & D. K. Routh (Eds.), *Advances in developmental and behavioral pediatrics.* Greenwich, CT: JAI.

DeFries, J. C., & Gillis, J. J. (1993). Genetics of reading disability. In R. Plomin & G. E. McClearn (Eds.), *Nature, nurture & psychology.* Washington, DC: American Psychological Association.

Dekovic, M., & Janssens, A. M. (1992). Parents' child-rearing style and child's sociometric status. *Developmental Psychology, 28,* 925–932.

DeKraai, M. B., & Sales, B. (1991). Legal issues in the conduct of child therapy. In T. R. Kratochwill & R. J. Morris (Eds.), *The practice of child therapy.* Boston: Allyn and Bacon.

Delamater, A. M. (1986). Psychological aspects of diabetes mellitus in children. In B. B. Lahey & A. E. Kazdin (Eds.), *Advances in clinical child psychology,* Vol. 9, New York: Plenum.

Delamater, A. M., Bubb, J., Davis, S. G., Smith, J. A., Schmidt, L., White, N. H., & Santiago, J. V. (1990). Randomized prospective study of self-management training with newly diagnosed diabetic children. *Diabetes Care, 13,* 492–498.

Delamater, A. M., & Lahey, B. B. (1983). Physiological correlates of conduct problems and anxiety in hyperactive and learning-disabled children. *Journal of Abnormal Child Psychology, 11,* 85–100.

Delfini, L. F. Bernal, M. E., & Rosen, P. M. (1976). Comparison of deviant and normal boys in home settings. In E. J. Mash, L. A. Hammerlynck, & L. C. Handy (Eds.), *Behavior modification and families.* New York: Brunner/Mazel.

DeMyer-Gapin, S., & Scott, T. J. (1977). Effects of stimulus novelty on stimulation-seeking in anti-social and neurotic children. *Journal of Abnormal Psychology, 86,* 96–98.

Despert, J. L. (1940). A comparative study of thinking in schizophrenic children and in children of preschool age. *American Journal of Psychiatry, 97,* 189–213.

DeStefano, L., & Thompson, D. S. (1990). Adaptive behavior: The construct and its measurement. In C. R. Reynolds & R. W. Kamphaus (Eds.), *Handbook of psychological & educational assessment of children. Personality, behavior, and context.* New York: Guilford.

Deutsch, C. K., & Kinsbourne, M. (1990). Genetics and biochemistry in attention deficit disorder. In M. Lewis & S. M. Miller (Eds.), *Handbook of developmental psychopathology.* New York: Plenum.

Deutsch, C. K., Matthysse, S., Swanson, J. M., & Farkas, L. G. (1990). Genetic latent structure analysis of dysmorphology in attention deficit disorder. *Journal of the American Academy of Child and Adolescent Psychiatry, 29,* 189–194.

Deveaugh-Geiss, J., Moroz, G., Biederman, J., Cantwell, D., Fontaine, R., Greist, J. H., Reichler, R., Katz, R. & Landau, P. (1992). Clomipramine hydrochloride in childhood and adolescent obsessive-compulsive disorder—A multicenter trial. *Journal of the American Academy of Child and Adolescent Psychiatry, 31,* 45–49.

Dietz, W. H. (1988). Metabolic aspects of dieting. In N. A. Krasnegor, G. D. Grave, & N. Kretchmer (Eds.), *Childhood obesity: A biobehavioral perspective.* Caldwell, NJ: The Telford Press.

Dietz, W. H., Jr., & Gortmaker, S. L. (1985). Do we fatten our children at the television set? Obesity and television viewing in children and adolescents. *Pediatrics, 75,* 807–812.

Dodge, K. A. (1989). Problems in social relationships. In E. J. Mash & R. A. Bakley (Eds.), *Treatment of childhood disorders.* New York: Guilford.

Dodge, K. A. (1990). Developmental psychopathology in children of depressed mothers. *Developmental Psychology, 26,* 3–6.

Dodge, K. A. (1993). Social-cognitive mechanisms in the development of conduct disorder and depression. *Annual Review of Psychology, 44,* 559–584.

Dodge, K. A., Pettit, G. S., & Bates, J. E. (1994). Effects of physical maltreatment on the development of peer relations. *Development and Psychopathology, 6,* 43–56.

Dodge, K. A., & Somberg, D. R. (1987). Hostile attributional biases among aggressive boys are exacerbated under conditions of threats to self. *Child Development, 58,* 213–224.

Doleys, D. M. (1988). Encopresis. In M. Hersen & C. G. Last (Eds.), *Child behavior therapy casebook.* New York: Plenum.

Doleys, D. M. (1989). Enuresis and encopresis. In T. H. Ollendick & M. Hersen (Eds.), *Handbook of child psychopathology,* 2nd ed. New York: Plenum.

Dolgin, M. J., & Jay, S. M. (1989a). Childhood cancer. In T. H. Ollendick & M. Hersen (Eds.), *Handbook of child psychopathology,* 2nd ed. New York: Plenum.

Dolgin, M. J., & Jay, S. M. (1989b). Pain management in children. In E. J. Mash & R. A. Barkley (Eds.), *Treatment of childhood disorders.* New York: Guilford.

Doll, E. A. (1965). *Vineland Social Maturity Scale.* 1965 Edition. Circle Pines, MN: American Guidance Service.

Dollinger, S. J. (1986). Childhood sleep disturbances. In B. B. Lahey & A. E. Kazdin (Eds.), *Advances in clinical child psychology,* Vol. 9. New York: Plenum.

Doman, G., & Delacato, C. (1968). Doman-Delacato philosophy. *Human Potential, 1,* 112–116.

Douglas, J. (1975). Early hospital admissions and later disturbances of behaviour and learning. *Developmental Medicine and Child Neurology, 17,* 456–480.

Douglas, V. I. (1983). Attentional and cognitive problems. In M. Rutter (Ed.), *Developmental neuropsychiatry.* New York: Guilford.

Downey, G. & Coyne, J. C. (1990). Children of depressed parents: An integrative review. *Psychological Bulletin, 108,* 50–76.

Drotar, D. (1981). Psychological perspectives in chronic childhood illness. *Journal of Pediatric Psychology, 6,* 211–228.

Drotar, D. (1994). Psychological research with pediatric conditions: If we specialize can we generalize? *Journal of Pediatric Psychology, 19,* 403–414.

Dubas, J. S., Graber, J. A., & Petersen, A. C. (1991). The effects of pubertal development on achievement during adolescence. *American Journal of Education, 99,* 444–460.

Dubow. E. F. Huesmann, L. R., & Eron, R. D. (1987). Childhood correlates of adult ego development. *Child Developement, 58,* 859–869.

Dubow, E. F., & Ippolito, M. F. (1994). Effects of poverty and quality of the home environment on changes in the academic and behavioral adjustment of elementary school-age children. *Journal of Clinical Child Psychology, 23,* 401–412.

Dulcan, M. K. (1989). Attention deficit disorders. In C. G. Last & M. Hersen (Eds.), *Handbook of child psychiatric diagnosis.* New York: Wiley.

Dumas, J. E. (1989). Treating antisocial behavior in children: Child and family approaches. *Clinical Psychology Review, 9,* 197–222.

Dummitt, E. S. III & Klein, R. G. (1994). Panic disorder. In T. H. Ollendick, N. J. King, & Yule, W. (Eds.), *International handbook of anxiety disorders in children and adolescents.* New York: Plenum.

Dunbar-Jacob, J. (1993). Contributions to patient adherence: Is it time to share the blame? *Health Psychology, 12,* 91–92.

Duncan, S. W. (1994). Economic impact of divorce on children's development: Current findings and policy implications. *Journal of Clinical Child Psychology, 23,* 444–457.

Dunn, J. (1988). Annotation. Sibling influences on childhood development. *Journal of Child Psychology and Psychiatry, 29,* 119–127.

Dunn, J., & McGuire, S. (1992). Sibling and peer relationships in childhood. *Journal of Child Psychology and Psychiatry, 33,* 67–105.

Dunn, L. M. (1968). Special education for the mildly retarded—is much of it justifiable? *Exceptional Children, 35,* 5–22.

Dunn, L. M., & Markwardt, F. C. (1970). *The Peabody Individual Achievement Test.* Circle Pines, MN: American Guidance Service.

DuPaul, G. J., & Barkley, R. A. (1993). Behavioral contributions to pharmacotherapy: The utility of behavioral methodology in medical treatment of children with attention deficit hyperactivity disorder. *Behavior Therapy, 24,* 47–65.

DuPaul, G. J., Guevremont, D. C., & Barkley, R. A. (1991). Attention-deficit hyperactivity disorder. In T. R. Kratochwill & R. J. Morris (Eds.), *The practice of child therapy.* Boston: Allyn and Bacon.

DuPaul, G. J., & Rapport, M. D. (1993). Does methylphenidate normalize the classroom performance of children with attention deficit disorder? *Journal of the American Academy of Child and Adolescent Psychiatry, 32,* 190–198.

Durand, V. M. (1990). *Severe behavior problems. A functional communication training approach.* New York: Guilford.

Durand, V. M. (1993a). Functional communication training using assistive devices: Effects on challenging behavior and affect. *Augmentative Alternative Communication, 9,* 168–176.

Durand, V. M. (1993b). Problem behavior as communication. *Behaviour Change, 10,* 197–207.

Durand, V. M., & Carr, E. G. (1985). Self-injurious behavior: Motivating conditions and guidelines for treatment. *School Psychology Review, 14,* 171–176.

Durand, V. M. & Carr, E. G. (1988). Autism. In V. B. Van Hasselt, P. S. Strain, & M. Hersen (Eds.), *Handbook of developmental and physical disabilities.* New York: Pergammon Press.

Durand, V. M., & Carr, E. G. (1991). Functional communication training to reduce challenging behavior: Maintenance and application in new settings. *Journal of Applied Behavior Analysis, 24,* 251–264.

Durand, V. M., & Carr, E. G. (1992). An analysis of maintenance following functional communication training. *Journal of Applied Behavior Analysis, 25,* 777–794.

Durand, V. M., & Crimmins, D. B. (1988). Identifying the variables maintaining self-injurious behavior. *Journal of Autism and Developmental Disorders, 18,* 99–117.

Durand, V. M., & Mindell, J. A. (1990). Behavioral treatment of multiple childhood sleep disorders: Effects on child and family. *Behavior Modification, 14,* 37–49.

Dush, D. M., Hirt, M. L., & Schroeder, H. E. (1989). Self-statement modification in the treatment of child behavior disorders. *Psychological Bulletin, 106,* 97–106.

Earls, F. (1994). Oppositional-defiant and conduct disorders. In M. Rutter, E. Taylor, & L. Hersov (Eds.). *Child and adolescent psychiatry: Modern approaches.* 3rd ed. London: Blackwell Scientific Publications.

Earls, F., & Jung, K. G. (1987). Temperament and home environment characteristics as causal factors in the early development of childhood psychopathology. *Journal of the American Academy of Child and Adolescent Psychiatry, 26,* 491–498.

Eccles, J. S., Midgley, C., Wigfield, A., Buchanan, C. M., Reuman, D., Flanagan, C., & MacIver, D. (1993). Development during adolescence: The impact of stage-environment fit on young adolescents' experiences in schools and in families. *American Psychologist, 48,* 90–101.

Edelbrock, C., & Costello, A. J. (1988a). Convergence between statistically derived behavior problem syndromes and child psychiatric diagnoses. *Journal of Abnormal Child Psychology, 16,* 219–231.

Edelbrock, C., & Costello, A. J. (1988b). Structured psychiatric interviews for children. In M. Rutter, A. H. Tuma, & I. S. Lann (Eds.), *Assessment and diagnosis in child psychopathology.* New York: Guilford.

Edelbrock, C., & Costello, A. J., Dulcan, M. K., Kalas, R., & Conover, N.C. (1985). Age differences in the realiability of the psychiatric interview of the child. *Child Development, 56,* 265–275.

Edelbrock, C., & Rancurello, M. D. (1985). Childhood hyperactivity: An overview of rating scales and their applications. *Clinical Psychology Review, 5,* 429–445.

Edelbrock, C., Rende, R., Plomin, R., & Thompson, L. A. (1995). A twin study of competence and problem behavior in childhood and early adolescence. *Journal of Child Psychology and Psychiatry, 36,* 775–785.

Egeland, B., Jacobvitz, D., & Sroufe, L. A. (1988). Breaking the cycle of abuse. *Child Development, 59,* 1080–1088.

Eggers, C. (1978). Course and prognosis of childhood schizophrenia. *Journal of Autism and Childhood Schizophrenia, 8,* 21–36.

Eiser, C. (1994). The eleventh Jack Tizard Memorial Lecture. Making sense of chronic disease. *Journal of Child Psychology and Psychiatry, 35,* 1373–1389.

Eiser, C., Havermans, T., Pancer, M., & Eiser, J. R. (1992). Adjustment to chronic disease in relation to age and gender: Mother's and father's reports of their children's behavior. *Journal of Pediatric Psychology, 17,* 261–275.

Ekstein, R., Friedman, S., & Carruth, E. (1972). The psychoanalytic treatment of childhood schizophrenia. In B. B. Wolman (Ed.), *Manual of child psychology.* New York: McGraw Hill.

Elia, J., Welsh, P. A., Gullotta, C. S., & Rapport, J. L. (1993). Classroom academic performance: Improvement with both methylphenidate and dextroamphetamine in ADHD boys. *Journal of Child Psychology and Psychiatry, 34,* 785–804.

Elias, G., Hayes, A., & Broerse, J. (1988). Aspects of structure and content of maternal talk with infants. *Journal of Child Psychology and Psychiatry, 29,* 523–531.

Elliot, C. H., Jay, S. M., & Woody, P. (1987). An observational scale for measuring children's distress during painful medical procedures. *Journal of Pediatric Psychology, 12,* 543–551.

Ellis, E. F. (1988). Asthma: Current therapeutic approach. *Pediatric Clinics of North America, 35,* 1041–1052.

Ellis, E. S., Deshler, D. D., & Schumaker, J. B. (1989). Teaching adolescents with learning disabilities to generate and use task-specific strategies. *Journal of Learning Disabilities, 22,* 108–119.

Ellis, P. L. (1982). Empathy: A factor in social behavior. *Journal of Abnormal Child Psychology, 10,* 123–134.

Emerson, E. B. (1985). Evaluating the impact of deinstitutionalization on the lives of mentally retarded people. *American Journal of Mental Deficiency, 90,* 277–288.

Emery, R. E. (1982). Interparental conflict and the children of discord and divorce. *Psychological Bulletin, 92,* 310–330.

Emery, R. E. (1989). Family violence. *American Psychologist, 44,* 321–328.

Emery, R. E., Hetherington, E. M., & DiLalla, L. F. (1984). Divorce, children, and social policy. In H. W. Stevenson & A. E. Siegel (Eds.), *Child development research and social policy.* Chicago: Univ. of Chicago Press.

Empey, L. T. (1978). *American delinquency.* Homewood, IL: Dorsey.

Emslie, G. J., Rush, A. J., Weinberg, W. A., Rintelmann, J. W., & Roffwarg, H. P. (1990). Children with major depression show reduced rapid eye movement latencies. *Archives of General Psychiatry, 47,* 119–124.

Emslie, G. J., Weinberg, W. A., Kennard, B. D., & Kowatch, R. A. (1994). Neurobiological aspects of depression in children and adolescents. In W. M. Reynolds & H. F. Johnston (Eds.), *Handbook of depression in children and adolescents.* New York: Plenum.

Epple, W. A., Jacobson, J. W., & Janicki, M. P. (1985). Staffing ratios in public institutions for persons with mental retardation in the United States. *Mental Retardation, 23,* 115–124.

Epstein, L. H., & Wing, R. R. (1987). Behaviorial treatment of childhood obesity. *Psychological Bulletin, 101,* 331–342.

Erickson, M. T. (1987). *Behavior disorders of children and adolescents.* Englewood Cliffs, NJ: Prentice Hall.

Erlenmeyer-Kimling, L., Cornblatt, B. A., Bassett, A. S., Moldin, S. O., Hilldorf-Adamo, U., & Roberts. S. (1990). High-risk children in adolescence and young adulthood: Course of global adjustment. In L. N. Robins & M. Rutter (Eds.), *Straight and devious pathways from childhood to adulthood.* New York: Cambridge University Press.

Erwin, R. J., Edwards, R., Tanguay, P. E., Buchwald, J., & Letai, D. (1986). Abnormal P300 responses in schizophrenic children. *Journal of the American Academy of Child Psychiatry, 25,* 615–622.

Evans, J. A., & Hammerton, J. L. (1985). Chromosomal anomalies. In A. M. Clarke, A. D. B. Clarke, & J. M. Berg (Eds.), *Mental deficiency. The changing outlook.* New York: The Free Press.

Evans, R. B., & Koelsch, W. A. (1985). Psychoanalysis arrives in America. *American Psychologist, 40,* 942–948.

Eysenck, H. J. (1986). A critique of contemporary classifications and diagnosis. In T. Millon & G. L. Klerman (Eds.), *Contemporary directions in psychopathology: Toward DSM-IV.* New York: Guilford.

Fagan, T. K. (1992). Compulsory schooling, child study, clinical psychology, and special education: Origins of school psychology. *American Psychologist, 47,* 236–243.

Fairburn, C. G. (1985). Cognitive-behavioral treatment for bulimia. In D. M. Garner & P. E. Garfinkel (Eds.), *Handbook of psychotherapy for anorexia nervosa and bulimia.* New York: Guilford.

Fairburn, C. G. & Cooper, P. J. (1989). Eating disorders. In K. Hawton, P. M. Salkovskis, J. Kirk, & D. M. Clark (Eds.), *Cognitive behaviour therapy for psychiatric problems.* New York: Oxford University Press.

Fairburn, C. G. & Wilson, G. T. (1993). Binge eating: Definition and classification. In C. G. Fairburn & G. T. Wilson (Eds.), *Binge eating: Nature, assessment, and treatment.* New York: Guilford.

Farrington, D. P. (1986). Stepping stones to adult criminal careers. In D. Olweus, J. Block, & M. R. Yarrow (Eds.), *Development of antisocial behavior and prosocial behavior.* New York: Academic Press.

Farrington, D. P. (1987). Early precursors of frequent offending. In J. Q. Wilson & G. C. Loury (Eds.), *From children to citizens: Vol. III. Families, schools, and delinquency prevention.* New York: Springer-Verlag.

Farrington, D. P. (1991). Longitudinal research strategies: Advantages, problems, and prospects. *Journal of the American Academy of Child and Adolescent Psychiatry, 30,* 369–374.

Faust, J. (1987). Correlates of the drive for thinness in young adolescent females. *Journal of Clinical Child Psychology, 16,* 313–319.

Feingold, B. F. (1975). *Why your child is hyperactive.* New York: Random House.

Feinstein, C., & Aldershof, A. (1991). Developmental disorders of language and learning. In J. M. Weiner (Ed.), *Textbook of child & adolescent psychiatry*. Washington, DC: American Psychiatric Press.

Felner, R. D., & Adan, A. M. (1988). The School Transition Environment Project: An ecological intervention and evaluation. In R. H. Price, E. L. Cowen, R. P. Lorion, & J. Ramos-McKay (Eds.), *Fourteen ounces of prevention: A casebook for practioners*. Washington, DC: American Psychological Association.

Felner, R., Brand, S., Adam, A. A., Mulhall, P. F., Flowers, N., Sartain, B., & DuBois, B. L. (1993). Restructuring the ecology of the school as an approach to prevention during school transitions: Longitudinal follow-up and extensions of the School Transition Environment Project (STEP). *Prevention and Human Services, 10*, 103–136.

Felton, R. H., & Wood, F. B. (1989). Cognitive deficits in reading disability and attention deficit disorder. *Journal of Learning Disabilities, 22*, 3–13.

Ferguson, H. B., & Pappas, B. A. (1979). Evaluation of psychophysiological, neurochemical, and animal models of hyperactivity. In R. L. Trites (Ed.), *Hyperactivity in children*. Baltimore: University Park Press.

Ferguson, L. R. (1978). The competence and freedom of children to make choices regarding participation in research: A statement. *Journal of Social Issues, 34*, 114–121.

Fergusson, D. M., Horwood, L. J., & Lloyd, M. (1991). Confirmatory factor models of attention deficit and conduct disorder. *Journal of Child Psychology and Psychiatry, 32*, 257–274.

Fergusson, D. M., Horwood, L. J., & Lynskey, M. T. (1993). Early dentine lead levels and subsequent cognitive and behavioural development. *Journal of Child Psychology and Psychiatry, 34*, 215–227.

Fergusson, D. M., Horwood, L. J., & Lynskey, M. T. (1995). The stability of disruptive childhood behaviors. Journal of Abnormal Child Psychology, 23, 379–396.

Ferrari, M. (1990). Developmental issues in behavioral pediatrics. In A. M. Gross & R. S. Drabman (Eds.), *Handbook of clinical behavioral pediatrics*. New York: Plenum.

Ferster, C. B. (1961). Positive reinforcement and behavorial deficits of autistic children. *Child Development, 32*, 437–456.

Ferster, C. B. (1966). The repertoire of the autistic child in relation to principles of reinforcement. In L. Gottschalk & A. H. Averback (Eds.), *Methods of research of psychotherapy*. New York: Appleton-Century-Crofts.

Ferster, C. B. (1974). Behavioral approaches to depression. In R. J. Friedman & M. M. Katz (Eds.), *The psychology of depression: Contemporary theory and research*. Washington, DC: Winston.

Field, T. (1992). Infants of depressed mothers. *Development and Psychopathology, 4*, 49–66.

Fine, D., Pennington, B., Markowitz, P., Braverman, M., & Waterhouse, L. (1986). Toward a neuropsychlogical model if infantile autism: Are the social deficits primary? *Journal of the American Academy of Child Psychiatry, 25*, 198–212.

Fine, R. (1985). Anna Freud. *American Psychologist, 40*, 230–232.

Finkelhor, D. (1994). The international epidemiology of child sexual abuse. *Child Abuse & Neglect, 18*, 409–417.

Finkelstein, H. (1988). The long term effects of early parent death: A review. *Journal of Clinical Psychology, 44*, 3–9.

Finney, J. W., Russo, D. C., & Cataldo, M. F. (1982). Reduction of pica in young children with lead poisoning. *Journal of Pediatric Psychology, 7*, 197–207.

Fischer, M., Barkley, R. A., Fletcher, K. E., & Smallish, L. (1993). The adolescent outcome of hyperactive children: Predictors of psychiatric, academic, social, and emotional adjustment. *Journal of the American Academy of Child and Adolescent Psychiatry, 32*, 324–332.

Fish, B. (1984). Characteristics and sequelae of the neurointegrative disorder in infants at risk for schizophrenia: 1952–1982. In N. F. Watt, E. J. Anthony, L. C. Wynne, & J. E. Rolf (Eds.), *Children at risk for schizophrenia: A longitudinal perspective*. New York: Cambridge University Press.

Fixsen, D. L., Wolf, M. M., & Phillips, E. L. (1973). Achievement place: a teaching-family model of community-based group homes for youth in trouble. In L. Hammerlynck, L. Handy, and E. Mash (Eds.), *Behavior change: Methodology, concepts and practice*. Champaign, IL: Research Press.

Flament, M. F., Whitaker, A., Rapoport, J. L., Davies, M., Berg, C. Z., Kalikow, K., Sceery, W., & Shafer, D. (1988). Obsessive compulsive disorder in adolescence: An epidemiological study. *Journal of the American Academy of Child and Adolescent Psychiatry, 27*, 764–771.

Flavell, J. H. (1963). *The developmental psychology of Jean Piaget*. New York: Van Nostrand.

Fleming, J. E., Offord, D. R., & Boyle, M. H. (1989). Prevalence of childhood and adolescent depression in the community: Ontario Child Health Study. *British Journal of Psychiatry, 155*, 647–654.

Fletcher, J. M. (1988). Brain-injured children. In E. J. Mash & L. G. Terdal (Eds.), *Behavioral assessment of childhood disorders*, 2nd ed. New York: Guilford.

Flicek, M. (1992). Social status of boys with both academic problems and attention-deficit hyperactivity disorder. *Journal of Abnormal Child Psychology, 20*, 353–366.

Flynt, S. W., Wood, T. A., & Scott, R. L. (1992). Social support of mothers of children with mental retardation. *Mental Retardation, 30*, 233–236.

Folstein, S., & Rutter, M. (1978). A twin study of individuals with infantile autism. In M. Rutter & E. Schopler (Eds.), *Autism: A reappraisal of concepts and treatment*. New York: Plenum.

Forehand, R., Brody, G., & Smith, K. (1986). Contributions of child behavior and marital dissatisfaction to maternal perceptions of child maladjustment. *Behavior Research and Therapy, 24*, 43–48.

Forehand, R., Furey, W. M., & McMahon, R. J. (1984). The role of maternal distress in a parent training program to modify child non-compliance. *Behavioral Psychotherapy, 12*, 93–108.

Forehand, R., King, H. E., Peed, S., & Yoder, P. (1975). Mother-child interactions: Comparisons of a noncompliant clinic group and a non-clinic group. *Behaviour Research and Therapy, 13*, 79–84.

Forehand, R., & McMahon, R. J. (1981). *Helping the noncompliant child: A clinician's guide to parent training*. New York: Guilford.

Forehand, R., Wells, K. C., & Griest, D. L. (1980). An examination of the social validity of a parent training program. *Behavior Therapy, 11*, 488–502.

Forehand, R., Wierson, M., Frame, C. L., Kemptom, T., & Armistead, L. (1991). Juvenile firesetting: A unique syndrome or an advanced level of antisocial behavior? *Behaviour Research and Therapy, 29*, 125–128.

Foreyt, J. P. & Goodrick, G. K. (1993). Obesity in children. In R. T. Ammerman & M. Hersen (Eds.), *Handbook of behavior therapy with children and adults: A developmental and longitudinal perspective*. Boston: Allyn & Bacon.

Foreyt, J. P. & Kondo, A. T. (1985) Eating disorders. In P. H. Bornstein & A. E. Kazdin (Eds.), *Handbook of clinical behavior therapy with children*. Homewood, IL: Dorsey.

Foreyt, J. P., & McGavin, J. K. (1989). Anorexia nervosa and bulimia nervosa. In E. J. Mash & R. A. Barkley

(Eds.), *Treatment of childhood behavior disorders.* New York: Guilford.

Foster, G. G., & Salvia, J. (1977). Teacher response to the label of learning disabled as a function of demand characterists. *Exceptional Children, 43,* 533–534.

Fowles, D. C. (1992). Schizophrenia: Diathesis-stress revisited. *Annual Review of Psychology, 43,* 303–336.

Frankel, M. S. (1978). Social, legal, and political responses to ethical issues in the use of children as experimental subjects. *Journal of Social Issues, 34,* 101–113.

Fredericksen, N. (1986). Toward a broader conception of human intelligence. *American Psychologist, 41,* 445–452.

Freeman, B. J., Rahbar, B., Ritvo, E. R., Bice, T. L., Yokota, A., & Ritvo, R. (1991). The stability of cognitive and behavioral parameters in autism: A twelve-year prospective study. *Journal of the American Academy of Child and Adolescent Psychiatry, 30,* 479–482.

Freeman, E. H., Feingold, B. F., Schlesinger, K., & Gorman, F. J. (1964). Psychological variables in allergic disorders: A review. *Psychosomatic Medicine, 26,* 543–575.

Fremouw, W., Seime, R., & Damer, D. (1993). Behavioral treatment. In V. B. Van Haselt & M. Hersen (Eds.), *Handbook of behavior therapy and pharmacotherapy for children: A comparative analysis.* Boston: Allyn & Bacon.

French, D. C. (1988). Heterogeneity of peer-rejected boys: Aggressive and nonaggressive subtypes. *Child Development, 59,* 976–985.

French, D. C. (1990). Heterogeneity of peer-rejected girls. *Child Development, 59,* 976–985.

French, T. M., & Alexander, F. (1941). Psychogenic factors in bronchial asthma. *Psychosomatic Medicine Monograph, 4,* 2–94.

Freud, A. (1946). *The psycho-analytical treatment of children.* London: Imago.

Freud, S. (1949). *An outline of psycho-analysis.* Translated and newly edited by J. Strachey. New York: W. W. Norton and Co.

Freud, S. (1953). Analysis of a phobia in a five-year-old boy (1909). *Standard Edition.* Vol. 10. Ed. and trans. James Strachey, London: The Hogarth Press.

Freud, S. (1959). From the history of an infantile neurosis. In *Collected papers.* Vol. 3. New York: Basic Books. Originally published in 1918.

Frick, P. J. (1994). Family dysfunction and the disruptive disorders: A review of recent empirical findings. In T. H. Ollendick & Prinz, R. J. (Eds.), *Advances in clinical child psychology.* Vol. 16. New York: Plenum Press.

Frick, P. J., Van Horn, Y., Lahey, B. B., Christ, M. A. G., Loeber, R., Hart, E. A., Tannenbaum, L. & Hanson, K. (1993). Oppositional defiant disorder and conduct disorder: A metal-analytic review of factor analyses and cross-validation in a clinic sample. *Clinical Psychology Review, 13,* 319–340.

Friedman, A. G., & Mulhern, R. K. (1992). Psychological aspects of childhood cancer. In B. B. Lahey & A. E. Kazdin (Eds.), *Advances in clinical child psychology,* Vol. 14. New York: Plenum Press.

Friedman, S. B., Fisher, M., & Schonberg, S. K. (Eds.). (1992). *Comprehensive adolescent health care.* St. Louis: Quality Medical Publishing.

Fritz, G. K., Rockney, R. M., & Yeung, A. S. (1994). Plasma levels and efficacy of imipramine treatment for enuresis. *Journal of the American Academy of Child and Adolescent Psychiatry, 33,* 60–64.

Frostig, M., & Horne, D. (1964). The Frostig Program for the Development of Visual Perception. Chicago: Follett Corp.

Fultz, S. A., & Rojahn, J. (1988). Pica. In M. Hersen & C. G. Last (Eds.), *Child behavior therapy casebook.* New York: Plenum.

Fundudis, T. (1986). Anorexia nervosa in a pre-adolescent girl: A multimodal behavior therapy approach. *Journal of Child Psychology and Psychiatry, 27,* 261–273.

Furman, W., Rahe, D., & Hartup, W. (1979). Rehabilitation of socially withdrawn peschool children through mixed-age and same-age socialization. *Child Development, 50,* 915–922.

Furstenberg, F. F., Jr., Brooks-Gunn, J., & Chase-Lansdale, L. (1989). Teenage pregnancy and childbearing. *American Psychologist, 44,* 313–320.

Gadow, K. D. (1985). Relative efficacy of pharmacological, behavioral, and combination treatments for enhancing academic performance. *Clinical Psychology Review, 5,* 513–533.

Gadow, K. D. (1992). Pediatric psychopharmacology: A review of recent research. *Journal of Child Psychology and Psychiatry, 33,* 153–195.

Gadow, K. D., & Pomeroy, J. C. (1991). An overview of psychopharmacotherapy for children and adolescents. In T. R. Kratochwill & R. J. Morris (Eds.), *The practice of child therapy.* Boston: Allyn and Bacon.

Galaburda, A. M. (1989). Learning disability: Biological, societal, or both? A response to Gerald Coles, *Journal of Learning Disabilities, 22,* 278–282: 286.

Garbarino, J. (1991). Not all bad developmental outcomes are the result of child abuse. *Development and Psychopathology, 3,* 45–50.

Garcia, J. (1981). The logic and limits of mental aptitude testing. *American Psychologist, 36,* 1172–1180.

Gardner, E. F., Rudman, H. C., Kurlsen, B. & Merwin, J. C. (1982). *Stanford Achievement Test.* San Antonio, TX: The Psychological Corporation.

Garland, E. J., & Smith, D. H. (1991). Simultaneous prepubertal onset of panic disorder, night terrors, and somnambulism. *Journal of the American Academy of Child and Adolescent Psychiatry, 30,* 553–555.

Garmezy, N. (1975). The experimental study of children vulnerable to psychopathology. In A. Davids (Ed.), *Child personality and psychopathology,* Vol. 2. New York: Wiley-Interscience.

Garmezy, N. (1994). Foreword. In C. A. Nelson, (Ed.), *Threats to optimal development: Integrating biological, psychological, and social risk factors. The Minnesota symposium on child psychology.* Vol. 27. Hillsdale, NJ: Erlbaum.

Garmezy, N., & Masten, A. S. (1994). Chronic adversities. In M. Rutter, E. Taylor, & L. Hersov (Eds.), *Child and adolescent psychiatry. Modern approaches.* Cambridge, MA: Blackwell Scientific.

Garn, S. M., & Clark, D. C. (1976). Trends in fatness and the origins of obesity: Ad hoc committee to review the ten-state nutrition survey. *Pediatrics, 57,* 443–456.

Garn, S. M., LaVelle, M., Rosenberg, K. R., & Hawthorne, V. M. (1986). Maturational timing as a factor in female fatness and obesity. *The American Journal of Clinical Nutrition, 43,* 879–883.

Garner, C., Comoy, E., Barthelemy, C., Leddet, I., Garreau, B, Muh, J. P., & Lelord, G. (1986). Dopamine beta hydroxylase (DBH) and homovanillic acid (HVA) in autistic children. *Journal of Autism and Developmental Disorders, 16,* 23–28.

Garner, D. M. (1988). Anorexia nervosa. In M. Hersen & C. G. Last (Eds.), *Child behavior therapy casebook.* New York: Plenum.

Garner, D. M., & Bemis, K. M. (1985). Cognitive therapy for anorexia nervosa. In D. M. Garner & P. E. Garfinkel (Eds.), *Handbook of psychotherapy for anorexia and bulimia.* New York: Guilford.

Garner, D. M., Garfinkel, P. E., & O'Shaughnessy, M. (1985). The validity of the distinction between bulimia with and without anorexia nervosa. *American Journal of Psychiatry, 142,* 581–587.

Garner, D. M. & Parker, P. (1993). Eating disorders. In T. H. Ollendick & M. Hersen (Eds.), *Handbook of child and adolescent assessment.* Boston: Allyn & Bacon.

Gath, A. (1985). Chromosomal abnormalities. In M. Rutter & L. Hersov (Eds.), *Child and adolescent psychiatry: Modern approaches,* 2nd ed. Oxford: Blackwell Scientific Publications.

Gaylin, W. (1982). The "competence" of children: No longer all or none. *Journal of the American Academy of Child Psychiatry, 21,* 153–162.

Ge, X., Conger, R. D., Lorenz, F. O., Shanahan, M., & Elder, G. H. (1995). Mutual influences in parent and adolescent psychological distress. *Developmental Psychology, 31,* 406–419.

Geller, B., Cooper, T. B., Graham, D. L., Fetner, H. H., & Marsteller, R. A. (1992). Pharmacokinetically diagnosed double-blind placebo-controlled study of nortriptyline in 6- to 12-year olds with major depressive disorder. *Journal of the American Academy of Child and Adolescent Psychiatry, 31,* 34–44.

Geller, D. A., Biederman, J., Reed, E. D., Spencer, T., & Wilens, T. E. (1995). Similarities in response to fluoxetine in the treatment of children and adolescents with obsessive-compulsive disorder. *Journal of the American Academy of Child and Adolescent Psychiatry, 34,* 36–44.

Geller, E., Yuwiler, A., Freeman, B. J., & Ritvo, E. (1988). Platelet size, number, and serotonin content in blood of autistic, childhood schizophrenic, and normal children. *Journal of Autism and Developmental Disorders, 18,* 119–126.

Gerard, M. W. (1939). Enuresis: A study in etiology. *American Journal of Orthopsychiatry, 9,* 48–58.

Gergen, P. J., Mullally, D. I. & Evans, R. (1988). National survey of prevalence of asthma among children in the United States, 1976 to 1980. *Behavioral Medicine, 81,* 1–7.

Gerrity, K. M., Jones, F. A., & Self, P. A. (1983). Developmental psychology for the clinical child psychologist. In C. E. Walker and M. C. Roberts (Eds.), *Handbook of clinical child psychology.* New York: Wiley.

Gesten, E. L. (1976). A Health Resources Inventory: The development of a measure of the personal and social competence of primary grade children. *Journal of Consulting and Clinical Psychology, 44,* 775–786.

Gesten, E. L., & Jason, L. A. (1987). Social and community interventions. In M. R. Rosenzweig and L. W. Porter (Eds.), *Annual reivew of psychology,* Vol. 38. Palo Alto, CA: Annual Reviews Inc.

Giaconia, R. M., Reinherz, H. Z., Silverman, A. B., Pakiz, B., Frost, A. K., & Cohen, E. (1994). Ages of onset of psychiatric disorders in a community population of older adolescents. *Journal of the American Academy of Child and Adolescent Psychiatry, 33,* 706–717.

Gillberg, C. (1990). Autism and pervasive developmental disorders. *Journal of Child Psychology and Psychiatry, 31,* 99–119.

Gillberg, C. (1994). Having Rett syndrome in the ICD-10 PDD category does not make much sense. *Journal of Child Psychology and Psychiatry, 35,* 377–378.

Gillberg, C. L. (1992). The Emmanuel Miller Memorial Lecture 1991. Autism and autistic-like conditions: Subclasses among disorders of empathy. *Journal of Child Psychology and Psychiatry, 33,* 813–842.

Gillberg, C., Ehlers, S., Schaumann, H., Jakobsson, G., Dahlgren, S. O., Lindblom, R., Bagenholm, A., Tjuus, T., & Blidner, E. (1990). Autism under age 3 years: A clinical study of 28 cases referred for autistic symptoms in infancy. *Journal of Child Psychology and Psychiatry, 31,* 921–934.

Gillberg, I. C., Hellgren, L., & Gillberg, C. (1993). Psychotic disorders diagnosed in adolescence. Outcome at age 30 years. *Journal of Child Psychology and Psychiatry, 34,* 1173–1185.

Gilligan, C. (1982). *In a different voice.* Cambridge, MA: Harvard University Press.

Gillin, J. C., Duncan, W., Pettigrew, K. D., Frankel, B., & Synder, F. (1979). Successful separation of depressed, normal and insomniac subjects by EEG sleep data. *Archives of General Psychiatry, 36,* 85–90.

Gillis, J. J., Gilger, J. W., Pennington, B.F., & DeFries, J. C. (1992). Attention deficit disorder in reading-disabled twins: Evidence for genetic etiology. *Journal of Abnormal Child Psychology 20,* 303–315.

Ginsburg, H. (1972). *The myth of the deprived child: Poor children's intellect and education.* Englewood Cliffs, NJ: Prentice Hall.

Gislason, I. L, & Neri, C. L. (1993). Pharmacological treatment. In V. B. Van Hasselt & M. Hersen (Eds.), *Handbook of behavior therapy and pharmacotherapy for children: A comparative analysis.* Boston: Allyn and Bacon.

Glidden, L. M. (1985). Semantic processing, semantic memory, and recall. In N. R. Ellis & N. W. Bray (Eds.), *International Review of Research in Mental Retardation,* Vol. 13. New York: Academic Press.

Glueck, S., & Glueck, E. T. (1968). *Delinquents and nondelinquents in perspective.* Cambridge, MA: Harvard University Press.

Goddard, H. H. (1912). *The Kallikak family.* New York: Macmillan.

Goldberg, J. O., & Konstantareas, M. M. (1981). Vigilance in hyperactive and normal children on a self-paced task. *Journal of Child Psychiatry and Psychology, 22,* 55–63.

Goldfarb, W. (1970). Childhood psychosis. In P. H. Mussen (Ed.), *Carmichael's manual of child psychology, Vol. 2.* New York: Wiley.

Goldfield, E. C. (1989). Transition from rocking to crawling: Postural constraints on infant movement. *Developmental Psychology, 25,* 913–919.

Goldsmith, H. H., Bradshaw, D. L., & Reiser-Danner, L. A. (1986). Temperament as a potential developmental influence on attachment. In J. V. Lerner & R. M. Lerner (Eds.), *Temperament and social interaction during infancy and childhood.* New Directions for Child Development, No. 31, San Francisco: Jossey-Bass.

Goldstein, M. J. (1988). The family and psychopathology, *Annual Review of Psychology.* Palo Alto, CA: Annual Reviews Inc.

Goldston, S. E. (1986). Primary prevention. Historical perspectives and a blueprint for action. *American Psychologist, 41,* 453–460.

Gomby, D. S., Larson, C. S., Lewit, E. M., & Behrman, R. E. (1993). Home visiting: Analysis and recommendations. *The Future of Children. Home Visiting, 3,* 6–21.

Gonzalez, N. M. & Campbell, M. (1994). Cocaine babies: Does parental exposure to cocaine affect development? *Journal of the American Academy of Child and Adolescent Psychiatry, 33,* 16–19.

Goodman, R. (1989). Infantile autism: A syndrome of multiple primary deficits? *Journal of Autism and Developmental Disorders, 19,* 409–424.

Goodman, R., & Stevenson, J. (1989). A twin study of hyperactivity-II. The aetiological role of genes, family relationships and perinatal adversity. *Journal of Child Psychology and Psychiatry, 30,* 691–709.

Gortmaker, S. L., Dietz, W. H., Jr., Sobol, A. M., & Wehler, C. A. (1987). Increasing pediatric obesity in the United States. *American Journal of Diseases in Children, 141,* 535–540.

Gortmaker, S. L., & Sappenfield, W. (1984). Chronic childhood disorders: Prevalence and impact. *Pediatric Clinics of North America, 31,* 3–18.

Gottesman, I. I. (1991). *Schizophrenia genesis. The origins of madness.* New York: W. H. Freeman and Company.

Gottesman, I. I. (1993). Origins of schizophrenia: Past as prologue. In R. Plomin & G. E. McClearn (Eds.), *Nature and nurture & psychology.* Washington, DC: American Psychological Association.

Gottfried, A. E., & Gottfried, A. W. (1988). Maternal employment and children's development. An integration of longitudinal findings with implications for social policy. In A. E. Gottfried and A. W. Gottfried (Eds.), *Maternal employment and children's development.* New York: Plenum.

Gottman, J., Gonso, J., & Rasmussen, B. (1975). Social interaction, social competence and friendship in children. *Child Development, 46,* 709–718.

Gottman, J., Gonso, J., & Schuler, P. (1976). Teaching social skills to isolated children. *Journal of Abnormal Child Psychology, 4,* 170–185.

Gould, J. S. (1981). *The mismeasure of man.* New York: W. W. Norton.

Gould, M. S., Shaffer, D., & Kaplan, D. (1985). The characteristics of dropouts from a child psychiatric clinic. *Journal of the American Academy of Child Psychiatry, 24,* 316–328.

Gowers, S. G., Crisp, A. H., Joughin, N., & Bhat, A. (1991). Premenarcheal anorexia nervosa. *Journal of Child Psychology and Psychiatry, 32,* 515–524.

Goyette, C. H., Conners, C. K., & Ulrich, R. F. (1978). Normative data on revised Conners parent and teacher rating scales. *Journal of Abnormal Child Psychology, 6,* 221–236.

Grace, W. J., & Graham, D. T. (1952). Relationship of specific attitudes and emotions to certain bodily diseases. *Psychosomatic Medicine, 14,* 243–251.

Grannel de Aldaz, E., Vivas, E., Gelfand, D. M., & Feldman, L. (1984). Estimating the prevalence of school refusal and school-realted fears: A Venezuelan sample. *Journal of Nervous and Mental Disease, 172,* 722–729.

Graves, T., Meyers, A. W., & Clark, L. (1988). An evaluation of parental problem-solving training in the behavioral treatment of childhood obesity. *Journal of Consulting and Clinical Psychology, 56,* 246–250.

Gray, J. A. (1985). Issues in the neuropsychology of anxiety. In A. H. Tuma & J. D. Maser (Eds.), *Anxiety and the anxiety disorders.* Hillsdale, NJ: Lawrence Earlbaum.

Gray, J. A. (1987). *The psychology of fear and stress.* New York: Cambridge University Press.

Gray, J. W., Dean, R. S., & Lowrie, R. A. (1988). Relationship between socioeconomic status and perinatal complications, *Journal of Clinical Child Psychology, 17,* 352–358.

Graziano, A. M., & Mooney, K. C. (1982). Behavioral treatment of "nightfears" in children: Maintenance of improvement at $2\frac{1}{2}$ to 3-year follow-up. *Journal of Consulting and Clinical Psychology, 50,* 598–599.

Graziano, A. M., DeGiovanni, I. S., & Garcia, K. A. (1979). Behaviorial treatment of children's fears: A review. *Psychological Bulletin, 86,* 804–830.

Green, A. H. (1993). Child sexual abuse: Immediate and long-term effects and intervention. *Journal of the American Academy of Child and Adolescent Psychiatry, 32,* 890–902.

Green, W. H., Padron-Gayol, M., Hardesty, A. S., & Bassiri, M. (1992). Schizophrenia with childhood onset: A phenomenological study of 38 cases. *Journal of American Academy of Child and Adolescent Psychiatry, 31,* 968–976.

Greenberg, M. T., & Crnic, K. A. (1988). Longitudinal predictors of developmental status and social interaction in premature and full-term infants at age two. *Child Development, 59,* 554–570.

Greenberger, E., & Goldberg, W. A. (1989). Work, parenting, and the socialization of children. *Developmental Psychology, 25,* 22–35.

Greenberger, E., O'Neil, R., & Nagel, S. K. (1994). Linking workplace and homeplace: Relations between the nature of adults' work and their parenting behavior. *Developmental Psychology, 30,* 990–1002.

Greene, R. W. (1995). Students with ADHD in school classrooms: Teacher factors related to compatibility, assessment, and intervention. *School Psychology Review, 24,* 81–93.

Greenhill, L. L. (1991). Attention-deficit hyperactivity disorder. In J. M. Wiener (Ed.), *Textbook of child & adolescent psychiatry.* Washington, DC: American Psychiatric Press.

Greenough, W. T., Black, J. E., & Wallace, C. S. (1987). Experience and brain development. *Child Development, 58,* 539–559.

Gresham, F. M., & Elliott, S. N. (1989). Social skills deficits as a primary learning disability. *Journal of Learning Disabilities, 22,* 120–124.

Griest, D. L., Forehand, R., Rogers, T., Breiner, J., Furey, W. & Williams, C. A. (1982). Effects of parent enhancement therapy on the treatment outcome and generalization of a parent training program. *Behaviour Research and Therapy, 20,* 429–436.

Griest, D. L., Forehand, R., Wells, K. C., & McMahon, R. J. (1980). An examination of differences between nonclinic and behavior-problem clinic-referred children and their mothers. *Journal of Abnormal Psychology, 89,* 497–500.

Griffin, B. S., & Griffin, C. T. (1978). *Juvenile delinquency in perspective.* New York: Harper & Row.

Grinder, R. E. (1967). *A history of genetic psychology.* New York: John Wiley.

Grolnick, W. S., & Ryan, R. M. (1990). Self-perceptions motivation and adjustment in children with learning disabilities: A multiple group comparison study. *Journal of Learning Disabilities, 23,* 177–183.

Gross, A. M. (1990). Behavioral management of the child with diabetes. In A. M. Gross & R. S. Drabman (Eds.), *Handbook of clinical behavioral pediatrics.* New York: Plenum.

Gross, A. M., & Drabman, R. S. (1990). Clinical behavioral pediatrics: An introduction. In A. M. Gross & R. S. Drabman (Eds.), *Handbook of clinical behavioral pediatrics.* New York: Plenum.

Gross, A. M., Heimann, L., Shapiro, R., & Schultz, R. (1983). Social skills training and hemoglobin A_{ic} levels in children with diabetes. *Behavior Modification, 7,* 151–184.

Gross, M. D., Tofanelli, R. A., Butzirus, S. M., & Snodgrass E. W. (1987). The effects of diets rich in and free from additives on the behavior of children with hyperkinetic and learning disorders. *Journal of the American Academy of Child and Adolescent Psychiatry, 26,* 53–55.

Grusec, J. E. (1992). Social learning theory and developmental psychology: The legacies of Robert Sears and Albert Bandura. *Developmental Psychology, 28,* 776–786.

Grych, J. H., & Fincham, F. D. (1992). Interventions for children of divorce: Toward greater integration of research and action. *Psychological Bulletin, 111,* 434–454.

Guidubaldi, J., & Perry, J. D. (1985). Divorce and mental health sequelae for children: A two-year follow-up of a nationwide sample. *Journal of the American Academy of Child Psychiatry, 24,* 531–537.

Guillen, E. O., & Barr, S. I. (1994). Nutrition, dieting, and fitness messages in a magazine for adolescent women, 1970–1990. *Journal of Adolescent Health, 15,* 464–472.

Gunn, P., & Berry, P. (1990). Financial costs for home-reared children with Down syndrome: An Australian perspective. In W. I. Fraser (Ed.), *Key issues in mental retardation.* New York: Routledge.

Gutterman, E. M., O'Brien, J. D., & Young, J. G. (1987). Structured diagnostic interviews for children and adolescents: Current status and future directions. *Journal of the American Academy of Child and Adolescent Psychiatry, 26,* 621–630.

Habermas, T. (1992). Further evidence on early case descriptions of anorexia nervosa and bulimia nervosa. *International Journal of Eating Disorders, 11,* 351–359.

Hafner, A. J., Quast, W., & Shea, M. J. (1975). The adult adjustment of one thousand psychiatric patients: Initial findings from a twenty-five year follow-up. In R. O. Wirt, G. Winokur, & M. Roff (Eds.), *Life history in psychopathology,* Vol. 4, Minneapolis: University of Minnesota Press.

Hagamen, M. B. (1980). Family adaptation to the diagnosis of mental retardation in a child and strategies of intervention. In L. S. Szymanski & P. E. Tanguay (Eds.), *Emotional disorders of mentally retarded persons.* Baltimore: University Park Press.

Hagerman, R. J. (1992). Fragile X syndrome: Advances and controversy. *Journal of Child Psychology and Psychiatry, 33,* 1127–1139.

Hallahan, D. P., & Kauffman, J. M. (1978). *Exceptional children: Introduction to special education.* Englewood Cliffs, NJ: Prentice Hall.

Halmi, K. A. (1985). Eating disorders. In H. I. Kaplan & B. J. Sadock (Eds.), *Comprehensive textbook of psychiatry,* 4th ed. Baltimore: Williams & Wilkins.

Hamlett, K. W., Pellegrini, D. S., & Katz, K. S. (1992). Childhood chronic illness is a family stressor. *Journal of Pediatric Psychology, 17,* 33–47.

Hammen, C. (1990). Cognitive approaches to depression in children: Current findings and new directions. In B. Lahey, and A. Kazdin (Eds.), *Advances in clinical child psychology* (Vol. 13). New York: Plenum.

Hammen, C. (1992). Cognitive, life stress, and interpersonal approaches to a developmental psychopathology model of depression. *Development and Psychopathology, 4,* 189–206.

Hammill, D. D. (1993). A brief look at the learning disabilities movement in the United States. *Journal of Learning Disabilities, 26,* 295–310.

Hamsher, K. deS. (1990). Specialized neuropsychological assessment methods. In G. Goldstein & M. Hersen (Eds.), *Handbook of psychological assessment.* 2nd ed. New York: Pergamon.

Hanna, G. L. (1995). Demographic and clinical features of obsessive-compulsive disorder in children and adolescents. *Journal of the American Academy of Child and Adolescent Psychiatry, 34,* 19–27.

Happe, F. G. E. (1994a). Annotation: Current psychological theories of autism: The "theory of mind" account and rival theories. *Journal of Child Psychology and Psychiatry, 35,* 215–229.

Happe, F. G. E. (1994b). Wechsler IQ profile and theory of mind in autism: a research note. *Journal of Child Psychology and Psychiatry, 35,* 1461–1471.

Harkavy, J., Johnson, S. B., Silverstein, J., Spillar, R., McCallum, M., & Rosenbloom, A. (1983). Who learns what at a diabetes summer camp. *Journal of Pediatric Psychology, 8,* 143–153.

Harley, J. P., & Matthews, C. G. (1980). Food additives and hyperactivity in children: Experimental investiga-tions. In R. M. Knights and D. J. Bakker (Eds.), *Treatment of hyperactive and learning disordered children.* Baltimore: University Park Press.

Harper, L. V., & Huie, K. S. (1987). Relations among preschool children's adult and peer contacts and later academic achievement. *Child Development, 58,* 1051–1065.

Harris, P. L. (1994). The child's understanding of emotion: Developmental change and the family environment. *Journal of Child Psychology and Psychiatry, 35,* 3–28.

Harris, S. L. (1979). DSM-III—Its implications for children. *Child Behavior Therapy, 1,* 37–46.

Harris, S. L. (1986). Families of children with autism: Issues for the behavior therapist. *The Behavior Therapist, 9,* 175–177.

Harrison, N. S. (1979). *Understanding behavioral research.* Belmont, CA: Wadsworth.

Harrison, S. I., & McDermott, J. K. (1972). *Childhood psychopathology.* New York: International Univ. Press.

Hart, B., & Risley, T. R. (1992). American parenting of language-learning children: Persisting differences in family-child interactions observed in natural home environment. *Developmental Psychology, 28,* 1096–1105.

Hart, S. N., & Brassard, M. R. (1991). Psychological maltreatment: Progress achieved. *Development and Psychopathology, 3,* 61–70.

Harter, S. (1985). *Manual for the Self-Perception Profile for Children.* Denver, CO: University of Denver.

Hartmann, D. P., & Wood, D. D. (1990). Observational methods. In A. S. Bellack, M. Hersen, & A. E. Kazdin (Eds.), *International handbook of behavior modification and therapy,* 2nd ed. New York: Plenum.

Hartup, W. W. (1970). Peer interaction and social organization. In P. H. Mussen (Ed.), *Carmicheal's manual of child psychology.* New York: Wiley.

Hartup, W. W. (1983). Peer relations. In P. H. Mussen (Ed.), *Handbook of child psychology,* Vol. IV, New York: Wiley.

Hartup, W. W. (1989). Social relationships and their developmental significance. *American Psychologist, 44,* 120–126.

Haskins, R. (1989). Beyond metaphor: The efficacy of early childhood education. *American Psychologist, 44,* 274–282.

Haywood, H. C., Meyers, C. E., & Switzky, H. N. (1982). Mental retardation. In M. R. Rosenzweig & L. W. Porter (Eds.), *Annual review of psychology.* Palto Alto, CA: Annual Reviews Inc.

Heavey, C. L., Adelman, H. S., Nelson, P., & Smith, D. C. (1989). Learning problems, anger, perceived control, and misbehavior. *Journal of Learning Disabilities, 22,* 47–50.

Hechtman, L. (1991). Developmental, neurobiological, and psychosocial aspects of hyperactivity, impulsivity, and inattention. In M. Lewis (Ed.), *Child and adolescent psychiatry. A comprehensive textbook.* Baltimore: Williams & Wilkins.

Heinrichs, R. W. (1993). Schizophrenia and the brain. *American Psychologist, 48,* 221–233.

Helms, J. E. (1992). Why is there no study of cultural equivalence in standardized cognitive ability testing? *American Psychologist, 47,* 1083–1101.

Henggeler, S. W. (1994). A consensus: Conclusions of the APA Task Force Report on Innovative Models of Mental Health Services for children, Adolescents, and Their Families. *Journal of Clinical Child Psychology, 23 (Suppl.),* 3–6.

Henggeler, S. W., & Borduin, C. M. (1990). *Family therapy and beyond: A multisystemic approach to treating the behavior* *problems of children and adolescents.* Pacific Grove, CA: Brooks/Cole.

Henggeler, S. W., Melton, G. B., & Smith, L. A. (1992). Family preservation using multisystemic therapy: An effective alternative to incarcerating serious juvenile offenders. *Journal of Consulting and Clinical Psychology, 60,* 953–961.

Henker, B., & Whalen, C. K. (1980). The changing faces of hyperactivity: Retrospect and prospect. In C. K. Whalen & B. Henker (Eds.), *Hyperactive children.* New York: Academic Press.

Hermelin, B., & O'Connor, N. (1970). *Psychological experiments with autistic children.* London: Pergamon.

Hernandez, D. J. (1994). Children's changing access to resources: A historical perspective. *Social Policy Report: Society for Research in Child Development, 8(1),* 1–23.

Hersov, L. A. (1960). Persistent non-atendance at school. *Journal of Child Psychology and Psychiatry, 1,* 130–136.

Hertzig, M. E., & Shapiro, T. (1990). Autism and pervasive developmental disorders. In M. Lewis & S. M. Miller (Eds.), *Handbook of developmental psychopathology.* New York: Plenum.

Hertzler, A. A. (1983a). Children's food patterns—A review. I. Food preferences and feeding problems. *Journal of the American Dietetic Association, 83,* 551–554.

Hertzler, A. A. (1983b). Children's food patterns—A review. II. Family and group behavior. *Journal of the American Dietetic Association,* 555–560.

Hetherington, E. M. (1989). Coping with family transitions: Winners, losers, and survivors. *Child Development, 60,* 1–14.

Hetherington, E. M., & Camara, K. A. (1984). Families in transition: The process of dissolution and reconstitution. In R. D. Parke (Ed.), *Review of child development research: The family,* Vol. 7. Chicago: University of Chicago Press.

Hetherington, E. M., Cox, M., & Cox, R. (1982). Effects of divorce on parents and children. In M. E. Lamb (Ed.), *Nontraditional families: Parenting and child development.* Hillsdale, NJ: Erlbaum.

Hetherington, E. M., Cox, M., & Cox, R. (1985). Long-term effects of divorce and remarriage on the adjustment of children. *Journal of the American Academy of Child Psychiatry, 24,* 518–530.

Hetherington, E. M., & Martin, B. (1986). Family factors and psychopathology in children. In H. C. Quay & J. S. Werry (Eds.), *Psychopathological disorders of childhood,* 3rd ed. New York: Wiley.

Hetherington, E. M., Reiss, D., & Plomin, R. (Eds.) (1994). *Separate social worlds of siblings: The impact of nonshared environment on development.* Hillsdale, NJ: Erlbaum.

Hetherington, E. M., Stanley-Hagan, M., & Anderson, E. R. (1989). Marital transitions: A child's perspective. *American Psychologist, 44,* 303–312.

Hieronymous, A. N., & Hoover, H. D. (1985). *Iowa Tests of Basic Skills, Forms G and H.* Chicago: Riverside.

Hightower, A. D., & Braden, J. (1991). Prevention. In T. R. Kratochwill & R. J. Morris (Eds.), *The practice of child therapy* (2nd ed.). New York: Pergamon Press.

Hightower, A. D., Cowen, E. L., Spinell, A. P., Lotyczewski, B. S., Guare, J. C., Rohrbeck, C. A., & Brown, L. P. (1987). The Child Rating Scale: The development and psychometric refinement of a socioemotional self-rating scale for young children. *School Psychology Review, 16,* 239–255.

Hinshaw, S. P., & Erhardt, D. (1993). Behavioral treatment. In V. B. Van Hasselt & M. Hersen (Eds.), *Handbook of behavior therapy and pharmacotherapy for children: A comparative analysis.* Boston: Allyn and Bacon.

Hinshaw, S. P., Hanker, B., Whalen, C. K., Erhardt, D., & Dunnington, R. E. (1989). Aggressive, prosocial, and nonsocial behavior in hyperactive boys: Dose effects of methylphenidate in naturalistic settings. *Journal of Consulting and Clinical Psychology, 57,* 636–643.

Hinshaw, S. P., Lahey, B. B., & Hart, E. L. (1993). Issues of taxonomy and comorbidity in the development of conduct disorder. *Development and Psychopathology, 5,* 31–49.

Hirshfeld, D. R., Rosenbaum, J. F., Biederman, J., Bloduc, E. A., Farone, S. V., Snidman, N., Reznick, J. S., & Kagan, J. (1992). Stable behavioral inhibition and its association with anxiety disorder. *Journal of the American Academy of Child and Adolescent Psychiatry, 31,* 103–111.

Hobbs, N. (1975). *The futures of children.* San Francisco: Jossey-Bass.

Hobson, P. (1993). Understanding persons: The role of affect. In S. Baron-Cohen, H. Tager-Flusberg, & D. J. Cohen (Eds.), *Understanding other minds.* New York: Oxford Press.

Hobson, R. P. (1986). The autistic child's appraisal of expressions of emotions. *Journal of Child Psychology and Psychiatry, 27,* 321–342.

Hodapp, R. M., Burack, J. A., & Zigler, E. (1990). Summing up and going forward: New directions in the developmental approach to mental retardation. In R. M. Hodapp, J. A. Burack, & E. Zigler (Eds.), *Issues in the developmental approach to mental retardation.* New York: Cambridge University Press.

Hodapp, R. M., & Zigler, E. (1990). Applying the developmental perspective to individuals with Down syndrome. In D. Cicchetti & M. Beeghly (Ed.), *Children with Down syndrome.* New York: Cambridge University Press.

Hodges, K. (1994). Evaluation of depression in children and adolescents using diagnostic clinical interviews. In W. M. Reynolds and H. F. Johnston (Eds.), *Handbook of depression in children and adolescents.* New York: Plenum Press.

Hodges, K. McKnew, D., Cytryn, L., Stern, L., & Kline, J. (1982). The Child Assessment Schedule (CAS) diagnostic interview: A report on reliability and validity. *Journal of the American Academy of Child Psyciatry, 21,* 468–473.

Hodges, K., & Zeman, J. (1993). Interviewing. In T. H. Ollendick & M. Hersen (Eds.), *Handbook of child and adolescent assessment.* Boston: Allyn & Bacon.

Hoffman, L. W. (1989). Effects of maternal employment in the two-parent family. *American Psychologist, 44,* 283–292.

Hoffman, M. L. (1979). Development of moral thought, feeling, and behavior. *Amercan Psychologist, 34,* 958–966.

Holden, G. W., Moncher, M. S., & Schinke, S. P. (1990). Substance abuse. In A. S. Bellack, M. Hersen, & A. E. Kazdin (Eds.), *International handbook of behavior modification and therapy,* 2nd ed. New York: Plenum.

Hollingsworth, C. E., Tanguay, P. E., Grossman, L., & Pabst, P. (1980). Long-term outcome of obsessive-compulsive disorder in childhood. *Journal of the American Academy of Child Psychiatry, 19,* 134–144.

Holmes, L. B. (1978). Genetic counseling for the older pregnant woman: New data and questions. *New England Journal of Medicine, 298,* 1419–1421.

Hooper, S. R., & Hynd, G. W., (1993). The neuropsychological basis of disorders affecting children and adolescents: An Introduction. *Journal of Clinical Child Psychology, 22,* 138–140.

Hops, H. (1995). Age- and gender-specific effects of parental depression: A commentary. *Developmental Psychology, 31,* 428–431.

Hops, H., Biglan, A., Sherman, L., Arthur, J., Friedman, L., & Osteen, V. (1987). Home observations of family interactions of depressed women. *Journal of Consulting and Clinical Psychology, 55,* 341–346.

Hops, H., Davis, B., & Longoria, N. (1995). Methodological issues in direct observation: Illustrations with the Living in Familial Environments (LIFE) coding system. *Journal of Clinical Child Psychology, 24,* 193–203.

Hops, H., & Greenwood, C. R. (1988). Social skill deficits. In E. J. Mash & L. C. Terdal (Eds.), *Behavioral assessment of childhood disorders,* 2nd ed. New York: Guilford.

Horne, J. (1992). Sleep and its disorders in children. *Journal of Child Psychology and Psychiatry, 33,* 473–487.

Horowitz, F. D. (1992). John B. Watson's legacy: Learning and environment. *Developmental Psychology, 28,* 360–367.

Houts, A. C., Berman, J. S., & Abramson, H. (1994). Effectiveness of psychological and pharmacological treatments for nocturnal enuresis. *Journal of Consulting and Clinical Psychology, 62,* 737–745.

Houts, A. C., Liebert, R. M., & Padawar, W. (1983). A delivery system for the treatment of primary enuresis. *Journal of Abnormal Child Psychology, 11,* 513–520.

Houts, A. C., Mellon, M. W., & Whelan, J. P. (1988). Use of dietary fiber and stimulus control to treat retentive encopresis: A multiple baseline investigation. *Journal of Pediatric Psychology, 13,* 435–445.

Houts, A. C., Peterson, J. K., & Whelan, J. P. (1986). Prevention of relapse in full-spectrum home training for primary enuresis: A component analysis. *Behavior Therapy, 17,* 462–469.

Howlin, P. (1994). Special education treatment. In M. Rutter, E. Taylor, & L. Hersov (Eds.), *Child and adolescent psychiatry. Modern approaches.* Cambridge MA: Blackwell Scientific.

Hudson, J. I., Pope, H. G., Jonal, J. M., & Yurgelun-Todd, D. (1983). Family history of anorexia nervosa and bulimia. *British Journal of Psychiatry, 142,* 133–138.

Huesmann, L. R., Eron, L. D., Lefkowitz, M. M., & Walder, L. O. (1984). Stability of aggression over time and generations. *Developmental Psychology, 20,* 1120–1134.

Hughes, C. A., & Smith, J. O. (1990). Cognitive and academic performance of college students with learning disabilities: A synthesis of the literature. *Learning Disability Quarterly, 13,* 66–79.

Huizinga, D., Loeber, R., & Thornberry, T. P. (1993). *Public Health Reports, 108 (Supp. 1),* 90–96.

Hulme, C., & Roodenrys, S. (1995). Verbal working memory development and its disorders. *Journal of Child Psychology and Psychiatry, 36,* 373–398.

Humphrey, L. L. (1989). Observed family interaction among subtypes of eating disorders using structured analysis of social behavior. *Journal of Consulting and Clinical Psychology, 57,* 206–214.

Humphreys, J., Kopet, T., & Lajoy, R. (1994). Clinical considerations in the treatment of juvenile firesetters. *Clinical Child Psychology Newsletter, 9 (3),* 2–3.

Humphreys, L., Forehand, R., McMahon, R., & Roberts, M. (1978). Parent behavioral training to modify child noncompliance: Effects on untreated siblings. *Journal of Behavior Therapy and Experimental Psychiatry, 9,* 235–238.

Huntington's Disease Collaborative Research Group (1993). A novel gene containing a trinucleotide repeat that is expanded and unstable on Huntington's disease chromosomes. *Cell, 72,* 971–983.

Huse, D. M., Branes, L. A., Colligan, R. C., Nelson, R. A., & Palumbo, P. J. (1982). The challenge of obesity in childhood: I. Incidence, prevalence, and staging. *Mayo Clinic Proceedings, 57,* 279–284.

Huston, A. C. (1983). Sex-typing. In P. Mussen (Ed.), *Handbook of child psychology.* Vol. IV. New York: Wiley.

Huttenlocher, P. R. (1994). Synaptogenesis, synapse elimination, and neural plasticity in human cerebral cortex. In C. A. Nelson (Ed.), *Threats to optimal development: Integrating biological, psychological, and social risk factors.* Hillsdale, NJ: Lawrence Erlbaum Associates.

Hynd, G. W., & Semrud-Clikeman, M. (1989a). Dyslexia and brain morphology. *Psychological Bulletin, 106,* 447–482.

Hynd, G. W., & Semrud-Clikeman, M. (1989b). Dyslexia and neurodevelopmental pathology: Relationships to cognition, intelligence, and reading skill acquisition. *Journal of Learning Disabilities, 22,* 205–218.

Hynd, G. W., Marshall, R., & Gonzalez, J. (1991). Learning disabilities and presumed central nervous system dysfunction. *Learning Disability Quarterly, 14,* 283–296.

Hynd, G. W., Snow, J., & Becker, M. G. (1986). Neuropsychological assessment in clinical child psychology. In B. B. Lahey & A. E. Kazdin (Eds.), *Advances in a Clinical Child Psychology,* Vol. 9. New York: Plenum.

Ialongo, N. S., Horn, W. F., Pascoe, J. M., Greenberg, G., Packard, T., Lopez, M., Wagner, A., & Puttler, L. (1993). The effects of a multimodal intervention with attention-deficit hyperactivity disorder children: A 9-month follow-up. *Journal of the American Academy of Child and Adolescent Psychiatry, 32,* 182–189.

Iannotti, R. J. & Bush, P. J. (1993). Toward a developmental theory of compliance. In N. A. Krasnegor, L. Epstein, S. B. Johnson, & S. Yaffe (Eds.), *Developmental aspects of health compliance behavior.* Hillsdale, NJ: Lawrence Earlbaum Associates.

Illback, R. J. (1994). Poverty and crisis in children's services: The need for services integration. *Journal of Clinical Child Psychology, 23,* 413–424.

Inderbitzen, H. M. (1994). Adolescent peer social competence: A critical review of assessment methodologies and instruments. In T. H. Ollendick & R. J. Prinz, *Advances in Clinical Child Psychology, 16.* New York: Plenum.

Ireys, H. T., Werthamer-Larsson, L. A., Kolodner, K. B., & Gross, S. S. (1994). Mental health of young adults with chronic illness: The mediating effect of perceived impact. *Journal of Pediatric Psychology, 19,* 205–222.

Israel, A. C. (1988). Parental and family influences in the etiology and treatment of childhood obesity. In N. A. Krasnegor, G. D. Grave, & N. Kretchmer (Eds.), *Childhood obesity: A biobehavioral perspective.* Caldwell, NJ: The Telford Press.

Israel, A. C. (1990). Childhood obesity. In A. S. Bellack, M. Hersen, & A. E. Kazdin (Eds.), *International handbook of bheavoir modification and therapy.* New York: Plenum.

Israel, A. C., & Shapiro, L. S. (1985). Behavior problems of obese children enrolling in a weight reduction program. *Journal of Pediatric Psychology, 10,* 449–460.

Israel, A. C., & Solotar, L. C. (1988). Obesity. In M. Hersen, & C. G. Last (eds.), *Child behavior therapy casebook.* New York: Plenum.

Israel, A. C., & Zimand, E. (1989). Obestiy. In M. Hersen (Ed.), *Innovations in child behavior therapy.* New York: Springer.

Israel, A. C., Guile, C. A., Baker, J. E., & Silverman, W. K. (1994). An evaluation of enhanced self-regulation training in the treatment of childhood obesity. *Journal of Pediatric Psychology, 19,* 737–749.

Israel, A. C., Pravder, M. D., & Knights, S. (1980). A peer-administered program for changing the classroom behavior of disruptive children. *Behavioural Analysis and Modification, 4,* 224–238.

Israel, A. C., Silverman, W. K., & Solotar, L. C. (1986). An investigation of family influences on initial weight status, attrition, and treatment outcome in a childhood obesity program. *Behavior Therapy, 17,* 131–143.

Israel, A. C., Stolmaker, L., & Andrian, C. A. G. (1985). The effects of training parents in general child management skills in a behavioral weight loss program for children. *Behavior Therapy, 16,* 169–180.

Izard, C. E. (1986). Introduction. In C. E. Izard & P. B. Read (Eds.), *Measuring emotion in infants and children,* Vol. 2. New York: Cambridge Univ. Press.

Jacob, R. G., O'Leary, K. D., & Rosenblad, C. (1978). Formal and informal classroom settings: Effects on hyperactivity, *Journal of Abnormal Child Psychology, 6,* 47–59.

Jacobson, S. W., Jacobson, J. J., & Fein, G. G. (1986). Environmental toxins and infant development. In H. E. Fitzgerald, B. M. Lester, and M. W. Yogman (Eds.), *Theory and research in behavioral pediatrics,* Vol. 3. New York: Plenum.

Jacobvitz, D., Sroufe, L. A., Stewart, M., & Leffert, N. (1990). Treatment of attentional and hyperactivity problems in children with sympathomimetic drugs: A comprehensive review. *Journal of the American Academy of Child and Adolescent Psychiatry, 29,* 677–688.

Jakab, I. (1993). Pharmacological treatment. In V. B. Van Hasselt & M. Hersen (Eds.), *Handbook of behavior therapy and pharmacotherapy for children: A comparative analysis.* Boston: Allyn and Bacon.

James, A., & Talor, E. (1990). Sex differences in the hyperkinetic syndrome of childhood. *Journal of Child Psychology and Psychiatry, 31,* 437–446.

James, E. M., Reynolds, C. R. & Dunbar, J. (1994). Self-report instruments. In T. H. Ollendick, N. J. King, & W. Yule (Eds.), *International handbook of phobic and anxiety disorders in children and adolescents* (pp. 317–330). New York: Plenum Press.

Jarvie, G. J., Lahey, B., Graziano, W., & Framer, E. (1983). Childhood obesity and social stigma: What we know and what we don't know. *Developmental Review, 3,* 237–273.

Jastak, S., & Wilkinson, G. S. (1984). *Wide Range Achievement Test—Revised.* Wilmington, DE: Jastak Associates.

Jay, S. M. (1988). Invasive medical procedures: Psychological intervention and assessment. In D. K. Routh (Ed.), *Handbook of pediatric psychology,* New York: Guilford.

Jay, S. M., Elliot, C. H., Katz, E., & Siegel, S. E. (1987). Cognitive behavioral and pharmacologic intervention for children's distress during painful medical procedures. *Journal of Consulting and Clinical Psychology, 55,* 860–865.

Jay, S. M., Elliot, C. H., Ozolins, M., Olson, R., & Pruitt, S. (1985). Behavoiral management of children's distress during painful medical procedures. *Behavior Research and Therapy, 23,* 513–520.

Jay, S. M., Elliot, C. H., Woody, P. D., & Siegel, S. (1991). An investigation of cognitive-behavioral therapy combined with oral valium for children undergoing painful medical procedures. *Health Psychology, 10,* 317–322.

Jeffrey, D. B., Lemnitzer, N. B., Hess, J. M., Hickey, J. S., McLellarn, R. W., & Stroud, J. (1979). *Children's responses to television food advertising: Experimental evidence of actual food consumption.* Paper presented at a meeting of the American Psychological Association, New York City, September.

Jennings, K. D., Connors, R. E., & Stegman, E. E. (1988). Does a physical handicap alter the development of mastery motivation during the preschool years? *Journal of Child and Adolescent Psychiatry, 27,* 312–317.

Jensen, A. R. (1969). How much can we boost IQ and scholastic achievement? *Harvard Educational Review, 39,* 1–123.

Jensen, P. S., Bloedau, L., Degroot, J., Ussery, T., & Davis, H. (1990). Children at risk I: Risk factors and child symptomatology. *Journal of the American Academy of Child and Adolescent Psychiatry, 29,* 51–59.

Jensen, P.S. & Shaw, J. (1993). Children as victims of war: Current knowledge and future research needs. *Journal of the American Academy of Child and Adolescent Psychiatry, 32,* 697–708.

Jernigan, T. L., Hesselink, J. R., Sowell, E., & Tallal, P. A. (1991). Cerebral structure on magnetic resonance imaging in language- and learning-impaired children. *Archives of Neurology, 48,* 539–545.

Jersild, A. T., & Holmes, F. B. (1935). Children's fears. *Child Development Monograph,* No. 20.

Jessor, R. (1993). Successful adolescent development among youth in high-risk settings. *American Psychologist, 48,* 117–126.

Jessor, R., & Jessor, S. L. (1977). *Problem behavior and psychosocial development.* New York: Academic Press.

Johnson, J. H., Rasbury, W. C., & Siegel, L. J. (1986). *Approaches to child treatment: Introduction to theory, research, and practice.* New York: Pergamon.

Johnson, S. B. (1984). *Test of Diabetes Knowledge Revised—2.* Gainsville: University of Florida, Department of Psychiatry.

Johnson, S. B. (1988a). Chronic illness and pain. In E. J. Mash & L. G. Terdal (Eds.), *Behaviorial assessment of childhood disorders,* 2nd ed. New York: Guilford.

Johnson, S. B. (1988b). Diabetes mellitus in childhood. In D. K. Routh (Ed.), *Handbook of pediatric psychology.* New York: Guilford.

Johnson, S. B. (1988c). Psychological aspects of childhood diabetes. *Journal of Child Psychology and Psychiatry, 29,* 729–738.

Johnson, S. B. (1989). Juvenile diabetes. In T. H. Ollendick & M. Hersen (Eds.), *Hnadbook of child psychopathology,* 2nd ed. New York: Plenum.

Johnson, S. B. (1993). Chronic diseases of childhood: Assessing compliance with complex medical regimens. In N. A. Krasnegor, L. Epstein, S. B. Johnson, & S. Yaffe (Eds.), *Developmental aspects of health compliance behavior.* Hillsdale, NJ: Lawrence Earlbaum Associates.

Johnson, S. B., Silverstein, J., Rosenbloom, A., Carter, R., & Cunningham, W. (1986). Assessing daily management in childhood diabetes. *Health Psychology, 5,* 545–564.

Johnson, S. B., Wahl, G., Martin, S., & Johansson, S. (1973). How deviant is the normal child? A behavioral analysis of the preschool child and his family. In R. D. Rubin, J. P. Brady, & J. D. Henderson (Eds.), *Advances in behavior therapy,* Vol. 4. New York: Academic Press.

Johnson, W. G. & Hinkle, L. K. (1993). Obesity. In T. H. Ollendick & M. Hersen (Eds.), *Handbook of child and adolescent assessment.* Boston: Allyn & Bacon.

Johnston, H. F., & Fruehling, J. J. (1994). Pharmacotherapy for depression in children and adolescents. In W. M. Reynolds and H. F. Johnston (Eds.), *Handbook of depression in children and adolescents.* New York: Plenum Press.

Johnston, J. R. (1992). Cognitive abilities of language-impaired children. In P. Fletcher & D. Hall (Eds.), *Specific speech and language disorders in children: Correlates, characteristics and outcomes.* San Diego, CA: Singular Publishing Group.

Johnston, J. R., Kline, M., & Tschann, J. M. (1989). Ongoing post-divorce conflict. *American Journal of Orthopsychiatry, 59,* 576–592.

Jones, F. R., Garrison, K. C., & Morgan, R. F. (1985). *The psychology of human development.* New York: Harper & Row.

Jones, M. C. (1924). A laboratory study of fear: The case of Peter, *Pedagogical Seminary, 31,* 308–315.

Jouriles, E. N., Murphy, C. M., & O'Leary, K. D. (1989). Interspousal aggression, marital discord, and child problems. *Journal of Consulting and Clinical Psychology, 57,* 453–455.

Joyce, K., Singer, M., & Isralowitz, R. (1983). Impact of respite care on parents' perceptions of quality of life. *Mental Retardation, 21,* 153–156.

Judd, L. J. (1965). Obsessive-compulsive neurosis in children. *Archives of General Psychiatry, 12,* 136–143.

Jurkovic, G. J. (1980). The juvenile delinquent as a moral philosopher: A structural-developmental perspective. *Psychological Bulletin, 88,* 709–727.

Jurkovic, G. J., & Prentice, N. M. (1977). Relation of moral and cognitive development to dimensions of juvenile delinquency. *Journal of Abnormal Psychology, 86,* 414–420.

Kaffman, K., & Elizur, E. (1977). Infants who become enuretics: A longitudinal study of 161 Kibbutz children. *Monographs of the Society for Research in Child Development, 42,* (4,Serial No. 170).

Kagan, J. (1984). *The nature of the child.* New York: Basic Books.

Kagan, J., Arcus, D., & Snidman, N. (1993). The idea of temperament: Where do we go from here? In R. Plomin & G. E. McClearn (Eds.), *Nature, nurture & psychology.* Washington, DC: American Psychological Association.

Kagan, J., Reznick, J. S., & Snidman, N. (1990). The temperamental qualities of inhibition and lack of inhibition. In M. Lewis & S. M. Miller (Eds.), *Handbook of developmental psychopathology.* New York: Plenum Press.

Kagan, J., Snidman, N., & Arcus, D. (1993). On the temperamental categories of inhibited and uninhibited children. In K. H. Rubin & J. B. Asendorpf (Eds.), *Social withdrawal, inhibition, and shyness in childhood.* Hillsdale, NJ: Lawrence Erlbaum Associates.

Kahn, E., & Cohen, L. H. (1934). Organic driveness: A brain syndrome and an experience—with case reports. *New England Journal of Medicine, 210,* 748–756.

Kalnins, I. V., Churchill, M. P., & Terry, G. E. (1980). Concurrent stresses in families with a leukemic child. *Journal of Pediatric Psychology, 5,* 81–92.

Kamin, L. J. (1974). *The science and politics of IQ.* Potomac, MD: Erlbaum

Kamphaus, R. W. (1993). *Clinical assessment of children's intelligence.* Boston: Allyn & Bacon.

Kandel, D. B. (1982). Epidemiological and psychosocial perspectives on adolescent drug use. *Journal of the American Academy of Child Psychiatry, 21,* 328–347.

Kandel, D., & Yamaguchi, K. (1993). From beer to crack: Developmental patterns of drug involvement. *American Journal of Public Health, 83,* 851–855.

Kanfer, F. H., Karoly, P., & Newman, A. (1975). Reduction of children's fear of the dark by competence-related and situational threat-related verbal cues. *Journal of Consulting and Clinical Psychology, 43,* 251–258.

Kanner, L. (1943). Autistic disturbances of affective contact, *Nervous Child, 2,* 217–250.

Kanner, L. (1972). *Child psychiatry,* 4th ed. Springfield, IL: Chas. C. Thomas.

Kanner, L. (1973). *Childhood psychoses: Initial studies and new insights.* Washington, DC: V. H. Winston & Sons.

Kanner, L., & Eisenberg, L. (1956). Early infantile autism, 1943–1955. *American Journal of Orthopsychiatry, 26,* 55–65.

Kaplan, A. S., & Woodside, D. B. (1987). Biological aspects of anorexia nervosa and bulimia nervosa. *Journal of Consulting and Clinical Psychology, 55,* 645–653.

Kaplan, B. J., McNicol, J., Conte, R. A., & Moghadam, H. K. (1989). Overall nutrient intake of preschool hyperactive and normal boys. *Journal of Abnormal Child Psychology, 17,* 127–132.

Kaplan, R. M. (1985). The controversy related to the use of psychological tests. In B. Wolman (Ed.), *Handbook of intelligence.* New York: Wiley.

Kashani, J. H., & Orvaschel, H. (1990). A community study of anxiety in children and adolescents. *American Journal of Psychiatry, 147,* 313–318.

Kashani, J. H., Carlson, G. A., Beck, N. C., Hoeper, E. W., Corcoran, C. M., McAllister, J. A., Fallahi, C., Rosenberg, T. K., & Reid, J. C. (1987). Depression, depressive symptoms, and depressed mood among a community sample of adolescents. *American Journal of Psychiatry, 144,* 931–934.

Kashani, J. H., Daniel, A. E., Dandoy, A. C., & Holcomb, W. R. (1992). Family violence: Impact on children. *Journal of the American Academy of Child and Adolescent Psychiatry, 31,* 181–189.

Kashani, J. H., Orvaschel, H., Rosenberg, T. K., & Reid, J. C. (1989). Psychopathology in a community sample of children and adolescents: A developmental perspective. *Journal of the American Academy of Child and Adolescent Psychiatry, 28,* 701–706.

Kaslow, N. J., Brown, R. T., & Mee, L. (1994). Cognitive and behavioral correlates of childhood depression: A developmental perspective. In W. M. Reynolds and H. F. Johnston (Eds.), *Handbook of depression in children and adolescents.* New York: Plenum Press.

Kaslow, N. J., Deering, C. G., & Racusin, G. R. (1994). Depressed children and their families. *Clinical Psychology Review, 14,* 39–59.

Kaslow, N. J., & Racusin, G. R. (1990). Childhood depression: Current status and future directions. In A. S. Bellack, M. Hersen, & A. E. Kazdin (Eds.), *International handbook of behavior modification and therapy,* 2nd ed. New York: Plenum.

Kaslow, N. J., & Racusin, G. R. (1994). Pharmacotherapy for depression in children and adolescents. In W. M. Reynolds and H. F. Johnston (Eds.), *Handbook of depression in children and adolescents.* New York: Plenum Press.

Kaslow, N. J., Rehm, L. P., & Siegel, A. W. (1984). Social-cognitive and cognitive correlates of depression in children. *Journal of Abnormal Child Psychology, 12,* 605–620.

Kaslow, N. J., Rehm, L. P., Pollack, S. L., & Siegel, A. W., (1988). Attributional style and self-control behavior in depressed and nondepressed children and their parents. *Journal of Abnormal Child Psychology, 16,* 163–175.

Kassebaum, N. L. (1994). Head Start: Only the best for America's childrens. *American Psychologist, 49,* 123–126.

Kataria, S., Swanson, M. S., & Trevathon, G. E. (1987). Persistence of sleep disturbances in preschool children. *Behavioral Pediatrics, 110,* 642–646.

Katz, L. J., & Slomka, G. T. (1990). Achievement Testing. In G. Goldstein & M. Hersen (Eds.), *Handbook of psychological assessment.* 2nd ed. New York: Pergamon.

Kauffman, J. M., Gerber, M. M., & Semmel, M. I. (1988). Arguable assumptions underlying the regular education initiative. *Journal of Learning Disabilities, 21,* 6–11.

Kaufman, A. S., & Kaufman, N. L. (1983). *Administration and scoring manual for the Kaufman Assessment Battery for Children.* Circle Pines, MN: American Guidance Service.

Kaufman, J., & Zigler, E. (1987). Do abused children become abusive parents? *American Journal of Orthopsychiatry, 57,* 186–192.

Kazdin, A. E. (1981). Drawing valid inferences from case studies. *Journal of Consulting and Clinical Psychology, 49,* 183–192.

Kazdin, A. E. (1985). *Treatment of antisocial behavior in children and adolescents.* Homewood, IL: Dorsey.

Kazdin, A. E. (1987). Treatment of antisocial behavior in children: Current status and future directions. *Psychological Bulletin, 102,* 187–203.

Kazdin, A. E. (1988). Childhood depression. In E. J. Mash & L. G. Terdal (Eds.), *Behavioral assessment of childhood disorders,* 2nd ed. New York: Guilford.

Kazdin, A. E. (1989a). Conduct and oppositional disorders. In C. G. Last & M. Hersen (Eds.), *Handbook of psychiatric diagnosis.* New York: Wiley.

Kazdin, A. E. (1989b). Identifying depression in children: A comparison of alternative selection criteria. *Journal of Abnormal Child Psychology, 17,* 437–454.

Kazdin, A. E. (1990). Conduct disorders. In A. S. Bellack, M. Hersen, & A. E. Kazdin (Eds.), *International handbook of behavior modification and therapy,* 2nd ed. New York: Plenum.

Kazdin, A. E. (1993a). Adolescent mental health. Prevention and treatment programs. *American Psychologist, 48,* 127–141.

Kazdin, A. E. (1993b). Psychotherapy for children and adolescents. Current progress and future research directions. *American Psychologist, 48,* 644–657.

Kazdin, A. E. (1993c). Treatment of conduct disorder: Progress and directions in psychotherapy research. *Development and Psychopathology, 5,* 277–310.

Kazdin, A. E. (1994). Informant variability in the assessment of childhood depression. In W. M. Reynolds and H. F. Johnston (Eds.), *Handbook of depression in children and adolescents.* New York: Plenum Press.

Kazdin, A. E. (1995). Child, parent, and family dysfunction as predictors of outcome in cognitive-behavioral treatment of antisocial children. *Behaviour Research and Therapy, 33,* 271–281.

Kazdin, A. E., Esveldt-Dawson, K., Sherick, R. B., & Colbus, D. (1985). Assessment of overt behavior and childhood depression among psychiatrically disturbed children. *Journal of Consulting and Clinical Psychology, 53,* 201–210.

Kazdin, A. E., Kolko, D. J. (1986). Parent psychopathology and family functioning among childhood firesetters. *Journal of Abnormal Child Psychology, 14,* 315–329.

Kazdin, A. E., Rodgers, A., & Colbus, D. (1986). The Hopelessnes Scale for Children: Psychometric characteristics and concurrent validity. *Journal of Consulting and Clinical Psychology, 54,* 241–245.

Kazdin, A. E., Siegel, T. C., & Bass, D. (1992). Cognitive problem-solving skills training and parent management training in the treatment of antisocial behavior in children. *Journal of Consulting and Clinical Psychology, 60,* 733–747.

Kearney, C. A., & Silverman, W. K. (1990). A preliminary analysis of a functional model of assessment and treatment for school refusal behavior. *Behavior Modification, 14,* 340–366.

Kearney, C. A., & Silverman, W. K. (1992). Let's not push the "panic button": A critical analysis of panic and panic disorder in adolescents. *Clinical Psychology Review, 12,* 293–305.

Kearney, C. A., Eisen, A., & Silverman, W. K. (1995). The legend and myth of school phobia. *School Psychology Quarterly, 10,* 65–85.

Keller, M. B., Lavori, P. W., Wunder, J., Beardslee, W. R., Schwartz, C. E., & Roth, J. (1992). Chronic course of anxiety disorders in children and adolescents. Journal of the *American Academy of Child and Adolescent Psychiatry, 31,* 595–599.

Kellerman, J. (1980). Rapid treatment of nocturnal anxiety in children. *Journal of Behavior Therapy and Experimental Psychiatry, 11,* 9–11.

Kelly, M. L., & Heffer, R. W. (1990). Eating disorders: Food refusal and failure to thrive. In A. M. Gross & R. S. Drabman (Eds.), *Handbook of clinical behavioral pediatrics.* New York: Plenum.

Kelly, S. J., Brant, R., & Waterman, J. (1993). Sexual abuse of children in day care centers. *Child Abuse & Neglect, 17,* 71–89.

Kelty, M. (1981). Protection of persons who participate in applied research. In G. T. Hannah, W. P. Christian, & H. B. Clark (Eds.), *Preservation of client rights.* New York: Free Press.

Kempe, C. H., Silverman, F. N., Steele, B. B., Droegemueller, W., & Silver, H. K. (1962). The battered child syndrome. *Journal of the American Medical Association, 181,* 17–24.

Kemph, J. P. (1987). Hallucinations in psychotic children. *Journal of the American Academy of Child and Adolescent Psychiatry, 26,* 556–559.

Kendall, P. C. (1987). Ahead to basics: Assessment with children and families. *Behavioral Assessment, 9,* 321–332.

Kendall, P. C. (1991). Guiding theory for therapy with children and adolescents. In P. C. Kendall (Ed.), *Child and adolescent therapy: Cognitive-behavioral procedures.* New York: Guilford.

Kendall, P. C. (1993). Cognitive-behavioral therapies with youth: Guiding theory, current status, and emerging developments. *Journal of Consulting and Clinical Psychology, 61,* 235–247.

Kendall, P. C., & Panichelli-Mindel, S. M. (1995). Cognitive-behavioral treatments. *Journal of Abnormal Child Psychology, 23,* 107–124.

Kendall, P. C., Stark, K. D., & Adams, T. (1990). Cognitive deficit or cognitive distortion in childhood depression. *Journal of Abnormal Child Psychology, 18,* 255–270.

Kendler, K. S., Neale, M. C., Kessler, R. C., Heath, A. C., & Eaves, L. J. (1992a). A population-based twin study of major depression in women: The impact of varying definitions of illness. *Archives of General Psychiatry, 49,* 257–266.

Kendler, K. S., Neale, M. C., Kessler, R. C., Heath, A. C., & Eaves, L. J. (1992b). The genetic epidemiology of phobias in women: The interrelationship of agoraphobia, social phobia, situational phobia, and simple phobia. *Archives of General Psychiatry, 49,* 273–281.

Kennedy, W. A. (1965). School phobia: Rapid treatment of 50 cases. *Journal of Abnormal Psychology, 70,* 285–289.

Keogh, B. (1988). Improving services for problem learners: Rethinking and restructuring. *Journal of Learning Disabilities, 21,* 19–22.

Kephart, N. C. (1960, 1971). *The slow learner in the classroom.* Columbus, OH: Chas. E. Merrill.

Kerr, M., Lambert, W. W., Stattin, H., & Klackenberg-Larsson, I. (1994). Stability of inhibition in a Swedish longitudinal sample. *Child Development, 65,* 138–146.

Kessler, J. W. (1966, 1988). *Psychopathology of childhood.* Englewood Cliffs, NJ: Prentice Hall.

Kessler, J. W. (1980). History of minimal brain dysfunctions. In H. E. Rie & E. D. Rie (Eds.), *Handbook of minimal brain dysfunctions.* New York: John Wiley.

Kiernan, C. (1985). Behaviour modification. In A. M. Clarke, A. D. B. Clarke, & J. M. Berg (Eds.), *Mental deficiency. The changing outlook.* New York: The Free Press.

Killen, J. D., Hayward, C., Wilson, D. M., Taylor, C. B., Hammer, L. D., Litt, I., Simmonds, B., & Haydel, F. (1994a). Factors associated with eating disorder symptoms in a community sample of 6th and 7th grade girls. *International Journal of Eating Disorders, 15,* 357–367.

Killen, J. D., Taylor, C. B., Hayward, C., Wilson, D. M., Haydel, K. F., Hammer, L. D., Simmonds, B., Robinson, T. N., Litt, I., Varady, A., & Kraemer, H. (1994b). Pursuit of thinness and onset of eating disorder symptoms in a community sample of adolescent girls: A three-year prospective analysis. *International Journal of Eating Disorders, 16,* 227–238.

King, N. (1994). Physiological assessment. In T. H. Ollendick, N. J. King, & W. Yule (Eds.), *International handbook of phobic and anxiety disorders in children and adolescents* (pp. 365–396). New York: Plenum Press.

King, N. J. (1993). Simple and social phobias. In T. H. Ollendick & R. J. Prinz (Eds.), *Advances in clinical child psychology,* Vol. 15. (pp. 305–341). New York: Plenum Press.

King, N. J., Mietz, L. T., & Ollendick, T. H. (1995). Psychopathology and cognition in adolescents experiencing severe test anxiety. *Journal of Clinical Child Psychology, 24,* 49–54.

King N. J., Ollendick, T. H., & Gullone, E. (1990). School-related fears of children and adolescents. *Australian Journal of Education, 34,* 99–112.

King, N. J., Ollier, K., Iacuone, R., Schuster, S., Bays, K., Gullone, E., & Ollendick, T. H. (1989). Fears of children and adolescents: A cross-sectional Australian study using the Revised-Fear Survey Schedule for Children. *Journal of Child Psychology and Psychiatry, 30,* 775–784.

King, R. A., & Noshpitz, J. D. (1991). *Pathways of growth: Essentials of child psychiatry,* Vol. 2. New York: John Wiley & Sons.

King, R. A., Pfeffer, C., Gammon, G. D., & Cohen, D. J. (1992). Suicidality of childhood and adolescence: Review of the literature and proposal for establishment of a DSM-IV category. In B. B. Lahey & A. E. Kazdin (Eds.), *Advances in clinical child psychology,* Vol. 14, New York: Plenum.

Kirby, F. D., & Toler, H. C. (1970). Modification of preschool isolate behavior: A case study. *Journal of Applied Behavior Analysis, 3,* 309–314.

Kirigin, K. A., Braukmann, C. J., Atwater, J. D., & Wolf, M. M. (1982). An evaluation of Teaching-Family (Achievement Place) group homes for juvenile offenders. *Journal of Applied Behavior Analysis, 15,* 1–16.

Kirk, S. A. (1963). *Behavioral diagnosis and remediation of learning disabilities.* Proceedings of the First Annual Meeting of the ACLD Conference on Exploration into the Problems of the Perceptually Handicapped Child. Chicago, IL.

Kirk, S. A. (1972). *Educating exceptional children.* Boston: Houghton Mifflin.

Kirk, S. A., & Gallagher, J. J. (1989). *Educating exceptional children.* Boston: Houghton Mifflin.

Kirkpatrick, D. R. (1984). Age, gender, and patterns of common intense fears among adults. *Behaviour Research and Therapy, 22,* 141–150.

Klein, D. F., Mannuzza, S., Chapman, T., & Fyer, A. (1992). Child panic revised. *Journal of the American Academy of Child and Adolescent Psychiatry, 31,* 112–113.

Klein, M. (1932). *The psycho-analysis of children.* London: Hogarth Press.

Klein, N. C., Alexander, J. F., & Parsons, B. V. (1977). Impact of family systems intervention on recidivism and sibling delinquency: A model of primary prevention and program evaluation. *Journal of Consulting and Clinical Psychology, 45,* 469–474.

Klesges, R. C., & Hanson, C. L. (1988). Determining the environmental causes and correlates of childhood obesity: methodological issues and future research directions. In N. A. Krasnegor, G. D. Grave, & N. Kretchmer (Eds.), *Childhood obesity: A biobehavioral perspective.* Caldwell, NJ: The Telford Press.

Klinnert, M. D., Mrazek, P. J., & Mrazek, D. A. (1994). Early asthma onset: The interaction between family

stressors and adaptive parenting. *Psychiatry: Interpersonal and Biological Processes, 57,* 51–61.

Klorman, R., Brumaghim, J. T., Fitzpartrick, P. A., & Borgstedt, A. D. (1990). Clinical effects of a controlled trial of methylphenidate on adolescents with attention deficit disorder. *Journal of the American Academy of Child and Adolescent Psychiatry, 29,* 702–709.

Knobloch, H., & Pasamanick, B. (1974). *Gesell and Amatruda's developmental diagnosis.* New York: Harper & Row Pub.

Koegel, R. L., O'Dell, M. C., & Koegel, L. K. (1987). A natural language teaching paradigm for nonverbal autistic children. *Journal of Autism and Developmental Disorders, 17,* 187–200.

Koegel, R., Schreibman, L., O'Neill, R. E., & Burke, J. C. (1983). The personality and family-interaction characteristics of parents of autistic children. *Journal of Consulting and Clinical Psychology, 51,* 683–692.

Kog, E., & Vandereycken, W. (1985). Family charcteristics of anorexia nervosa and bulimia: A review of the research literature. *Clinical Psychology Review, 5,* 159–180.

Kohlberg, L. (1964). Development of moral character and moral ideology. In M. Hoffman & L. Hoffman (Eds.), *Review of child development research,* Vol 1. New York: Russell Sage Foundation.

Kohlberg, L. (1976). Moral stages and moralization: The cognitive-developmental approach. In T. Lickona (Ed.), *Moral development and behavior: Theory, research and social issues.* New York: Holt, Rinehart and Winston.

Kolko, D. (1987). Simplified inpatient treatment of nocturnal enuresis in psychiatrically disturbed children. *Behavior Therapy, 18,* 99–112.

Kolko, D. J. (1985). Juvenile firesetting: A review and methodological critique. *Clinical Psychology Review, 5,* 345–376.

Kolko, D. J. (1989). Fire setting and pyromania. In C. Last & M. Hersen (Eds.), *Handbook of child psychiatric diagnosis.* New York: Wiley.

Kolko, D. J., & Kazdin, A. E. (1986). A conceptualization of firesetting in children and adolescents. *Journal of Abnormal Child Psychology, 14,* 49–61.

Kolko, D. J., & Kazdin, A. E. (1989). Assessment of dimensions of childhood firesetting among patients and nonpatients: The Firesetting Risk Interview. *Journal of Abnormal Child Psychology, 17,* 157–176.

Kolko, D. J., Kazdin, A. E., & Meyer, E. C. (1985). Aggression and psychopathology in childhood firesetters: Parent and child reports. *Journal of Consulting and Clinical Psychology, 53,* 377–385.

Kolvin, I. (1971). Psychoses in childhood—a comparative study. In M. Rutter (Ed.), *Infantile autism: Concepts, characteristics, and treatments.* London: Churchill-Livingstone.

Koocher, G. P. (1973). Childhood, death, and cognitive development. *Developmental Psychology, 9,* 369–375.

Koocher, G. P. (1980). Pediatric cancer: Psychosocial problems and the high costs of helping. *Journal of Clinical Child Psychology, 9,* 2–5.

Koocher, G. P., & Sallan, S. E. (1978). Pediatric oncology. In P. R. Magrab (Ed.), *Psychological management of pediatric problems,* Vol. 1. Baltimore: University Park Press.

Kopp, C. B. (1983). Risk factors in development. In P. H. Mussen (Ed.), *Handbook of child psychology,* Vol. II. New York: Wiley

Kopp, C. B. (1994). Trends and directions in studies of developmental risk. In C. A. Nelson (Ed.), *Threats to optimal development: Integrating biological, psychological, and social risk factors. The Minnesota symposium on child psychology. Vol. 27.* Hillsdale, NJ: Erlbaum.

Kopp, C. B., & Kaler, S. R. (1989). Risk in infancy: Origins and implications. *American Psychologist, 44,* 224–230.

Korn, S. J., & Gannon, S. (1983). Temperament, cultural variation, and behavior disorder in preschool children. *Child Psychiatry and Human Development, 13,* 203–212.

Kotses, H., Glaus, K. D., Crawford, P. L., Edwards, J. E., & Scherr, M. S. (1976). Operant reduction of frontalis EMG activity in the treatment of asthma in children. *Journal of Psychosomatic Research, 10,* 453–459.

Kovacs, M. (1985). The interview schedule for children. (ISC). *Psychopharmacology Bulletin, 21,* 991–994.

Kovacs, M. (1989). Affective disorder in children and adolescents. *American Psychologist, 44,* 209–215.

Kovacs, M. (1992). *Children's Depression Inventory.* North Tonawanda, NY: Multi-Health Systems.

Kovacs, M., Feinberg, T. L., Crouse-Novak, M. A., Paulauskas, S. L., & Finkelstein, R. (1984). Depressive disorders in childhood: I. A longitudinal prospective study of characteristics and recovery. *Archives of General Psychiatry, 41,* 229–237.

Kovacs, M., Goldston, D., & Gatsonis, C. (1993). Suicidal behaviors and childhood-onset depressive disorders: A longitudinal investigation. *Journal of the American Academy of Child and Adolescent Psychiatry, 32,* 8–20.

Kraemer, S. (1987). Working with parents: Casework or psychotherapy? *Journal of Child Psychology and Psychiatry, 28,* 207–213.

Krahn, G. L., Hohn, M. F., & Kime, C. (1995). Incorporating qualitative approaches into clinical child psychology research. *Journal of Clinical Child Psychology, 24,* 204–213.

Krasnegor, N. A., Epstein, L., Johnson, S. B., & Yaffe, S. J. (1993). (Eds.) *Developmental aspects of health compliance behavior.* Hillsdale, NJ: Lawrence Earlbaum Associates.

Krasnegor, N. A., Grave, G. D., & Kretchmer, N. (Eds.) (1988). *Childhood obesity: A biobehavioral perspective.* Caldwell, NJ: The Telford Press.

Kratochwill, T. R., & Levin, J. R. (1992). *Single-case research design and analysis.* Hillsdale, NJ: Lawrence Erlbaum.

Krausz, M., & Muller-Thomsen, T. (1993). Schizophrenia with onset in adolescence: An 11-year followup. *Schizophrenia Bulletin, 19,* 831–841.

Krug, D. A., Arick, J., & Almond, P. (1978). *Autism Screening Instrument For Educational Planning.* Portland, OR: ASIEP Education.

Krugman, R. D. (1993). Universal home visiting: A recommendation from the U.S. Advisory Board on Child Abuse and Neglect. *The Future of Children, 3 (3),* 184–191.

Krupski, A. (1986). Attention problems in youngsters with learning handicaps. In J. K. Torgesen & B. Y. L. Wong (Eds.), *Psychological and educational perspectives on learning disabilities.* New York: Academic Press.

Kuhn, T. S. (1962). *The structure of scientific revolutions.* Chicago: University of Chicago Press.

Kuhnley, E. J., Hendren, R. L., & Quinlan, D. M. (1982). Firesetting by children. *Journal of the American Academy of Child Psychiatry, 21,* 560–563.

Kuperman, S., Beeghly, J., Burns, T., & Tsai, L. (1987). Association of serotonin concentration to behavior and IQ in autistic children. *Journal of Autism and Developmental Disorders, 17,* 133–140.

Kuperman, S., Gaffney, G. R., Hamdan-Allen, G., Preston, D. F., & Venkatesh, L. (1990). Neuroimaging in child and adolescent psychiatry. *Journal of the American Academy of Child and Adolescent Psychiatry, 19,* 159–172.

Kupersmidt, J. B., & Patterson, C. J. (1991). Childhood peer rejection, aggression, withdrawal, and perceived competence as predictors of self-reported behavior problems in preadolescence. *Journal of Abnormal Child Psychology, 19,* 427–449.

Kupfer, D. J., & Reynolds, C. F. (1992). Sleep and affective disorders. In E. S. Paykel (Ed.), *Handbook of affective disorders* (2nd ed.). New York: Guilford Press.

Kutcher, S. Bulos, M. J., Ward, B., Marton, P., Simeon, J., Ferguson, H. B., Szlai, J., Katic, M., Roberets, N., Dubois, C., & Reed, K. (1994). Response to desipramine treatment in adolescent depression: A fixed-dose, placebo-controlled, trial. *Journal of the American Academy of Child and Adolescent Psychiatry, 33,* 686–694.

Kutcher, S., Malkin, D., Silverberg, J., Marton, P., Williamson, P., Malkin, A., Szalai, J., & Katic, M. (1991). Nocturnal cortisol, thyroid stimulating hormone, and growth hormone secretory profiles in depressed adolescents. *Journal of the American Academy of Child and Adolescent Psychiatry, 30,* 407–414.

Kydd, R. R., & Werry, J. S. (1982). Schizophrenia in children under 16 years. *Journal of Autism and Developmental Disorders, 12,* 343–357.

Ladd, G. (1981). Social skills and peer acceptance: Effects of a social learning method for training verbal social skills. *Child Development, 52,* 171–178.

LaGreca, A. M. (1987). Diabetes in adolescence: Issues in coping and management. *Newsletter of the Society of Pediatric Psychology, 11,* 13–18.

LaGreca, A. M. (1993). Social skills training with children: Where do we go from here. *Journal of Clinical Child Psychology, 22,* 288–298.

LaGreca, A., & Santogrossi, D. (1980). Social skills training with elementary school students: A behavioral group approach. *Journal of Consulting and Clinical Psychology, 48,* 220–228.

LaGreca, A. M., Siegel, L. J., Wallander, J. L., & Walker, C. E. (Eds.). (1992). *Stress and coping in child health.* New York: Guilford.

LaGreca, A. M., & Stone, W. L. (1993). Social anxiety scale for children-revised: Factor structure and concurrent validity. *Journal of Clinical Child Psychology, 22,* 17–27.

Lahey, B. B., Applegate, B., McBurnett, K., Biederman, J., Greenhill, L., Hynd, G. W., Barkley, R. A., Newcorn, J., Jensen, P., Richters, J., Garfinkel, B., Kerdyk, L., Frick, P. J., Ollendick, T., Perez, D., Hart, E. L., Waldman, I., & Shaffer, D. (1994). DSM-IV field trials for attention deficit hyperactivity disorder in children and adolescents. *American Journal of Psychiatry, 151,* 1673–1685.

Lahey, B. B., & Carlson, C. L. (1991). Validity of the diagnostic category of attention deficit disorder without hyperactivity: A review of the literature. *Journal of Learning Disabilities, 24,* 110–120.

Lahey, B. B., Hartdagen, S. E., Frick, P. J., McBurnett, K., Conner, R., & Hynd, G. W. (1988). Psychopathology and antisocial behavior in the parents of children with conduct disorder and hyperactivity. *Journal of the American Academy of Child and Adolescent Psychiatry, 29,* 620–626.

Lambert, N. M. (1988). Adolescent outcomes for hyperactive children: Perspectives on general and specific patterns of childhood risk for adolescent educational, social, and mental health problems. *American Psychologist, 43,* 786–799.

Landesman, S. (1990). Institutionalization revisited: Expanding views on early and cumulative life experiences. In M. Lewis & S. M. Miller (Eds.), *Handbook of developmental psychopathology.* New York: Plenum.

Landsman, M. S. (1994). Comment. Needed: Metaphors for the prevention model of mental health. *American Psychologist, 49,* 1086–1087.

Landry, S. H., & Chapieski, M. L. (1989). Joint attention and infant toy exploration: Effects of Down Syndrome and prematurity. *Child Development, 60,* 103–118.

Landry, S. H., & Loveland, K. A. (1988). Communication behaviors in autism and developmental language delay. *Journal of Child Psychology and Psychiatry, 29,* 621–634.

Lang, P. J. (1984). Cognition in emotion: Concept and action. In C. E. Izard, J. Kagan, R. B. Zajonc (Eds.), *Emotions, cognition, and behavior.* New York. Cambridge University Press.

Langer, D. H. (1985). Children's legal rights as research subjects. *Journal of the American Academy of Child Psychiatry, 24,* 653–662.

Lapouse, R., & Monk, M. (1958). An epidemiologic study of behavior characteristics in children. *American Journal of Public Health, 48,* 1134–1144.

Lapouse, R., & Monk, M. A. (1959). Fears and worries in a representative sample of children. *American Journal of Orthopsychiatry, 29,* 803–818.

Lask, B. & Bryant-Waugh, R. (1992). Early-onset anorexia nervosa and related eating disorders. *Journal of Child Psychology and Psychiatry, 33,* 281–300.

Last, C. G., Hersen, M., Kazdin, A. E., Orvaschel, H., & Perrin, S. (1991). Anxiety disorders in children and their families. *Archives of General Psychiatry, 48,* 928–934.

Last, C. G., Perrin, S., Hersen, M., & Kazdin, A. E. (1992). DSM-III-R anxiety disorders in children: Sociodemographic and clinical characteristics. *Journal of the American Academy of Child and Adolescent Psychiatry, 31,* 1070–1076.

Last, C. G., & Strauss, C. C. (1989). Panic disorder in children and adolescents. *Journal of Anxiety Disorders, 3,* 87–95.

Last, C. G., & Strauss, C. C. (1990). School refusal in anxiety-disordered children and adolescents. *Journal of the American Academy of Child and Adolescent Psychiatry, 29,* 31–35.

Laucht, M., Esser, G., & Schmidt, M. H. (1994). Contrasting infant predictors of later cognitive functioning. *Journal of Child Psychology and Psychiatry, 35,* 649–662.

Lavigne, J. V. & Faier-Routman, J. (1993). Correlates of psychological adjustment to pediatric physical disorders: A meta-analytic review and comparison with existing models. *Developmental and Behavioral Pediatrics, 14,* 117–123.

Lazarus, A., & Abramavitz, A. (1962). The use of emotive imagery in the treatment of children's phobia. *Journal of Mental Science, 108,* 191–192.

Lazarus, R. S. & Folkman, S. (1984). *Stress, appraisal, and coping.* New York: Springer.

Lee, M., & Prentice, N. M. (1988). Interrelations of empathy, cognition, and moral reasoning with dimensions of juvenile delinquency. *Journal of Abnormal Child Psychology, 16,* 127–139.

Lefkowitz, M. (1977). Discussion of Dr. Gittelman-Klein's chapter. In J. G. Schulterbrandt & A. Raskin (Eds.), *Depression in childhood: Diagnosis, treatment, and conceptual models.* New York: Raven Press, 1977.

Lefkowitz, M., & Burton, N. (1978). Childhood depression: A critique of the concept. *Psychological Bulletin, 85* (4), 716–726.

Lefkowitz, M., & Tesiny, E. (1980). Assessment of childhood depression. *Journal of Consulting and Clinical Psychology, 48,* 43–50.

Leitenberg, H., Gross, J., Peterson, J., & Rosen, J. C. (1984). Analysis of an anxiety model and the process of change during exposure plus response prevention treatment of bulimia nervosa. *Behavior Therapy, 15,* 3–20.

Leitenberg, H., Rosen, J. C., Gross, J., Nudelman, S., & Vara, L. S. (1988). Exposure plus response-prevention treatment of bulimia nervosa. *Journal of Consulting and Clinical Psychology, 56,* 535–541.

Leitenberg, H., Yost, L. W., & Carroll-Wilson, M. (1986). Negative cognitive errors in children: Questionnaire development, normative data, and comparisons between children with and without self-reported symptoms of depression, low self-esteem, and evaluation anxiety. *Journal of Consulting and Clinical Psychology, 54,* 528–536.

Lemanek, K. L. (1994). Research on pediatric chronic illness: New directions and recurrent confounds. *Journal of Pediatric Psychology, 19,* 143–148.

Lemert, E. M. (1971). *Instead of court: Diversion in juvenile justice.* Rockville, MD: National Institute of Mental Health.

Lenane, M. C., Swedo, S. E., Leonard, H. L., Pauls, D. L., Sceery, W., & Rapoport, J. L. (1990). Psychiatric disorders in first degree relatives of children and adolescents with obsessive compulsive disorder. *Journal of the American Academy of Child and Adolescent Psychiatry, 29,* 407–412.

Leon, G. R., Fulkerson, J. A., Perry, C. L., & Cudeck, R. (1993). Personality and behavioral vulnerabilities associated with risk status for eating disorders in adolescent girls. *Journal of Abnormal Psychology, 102,* 438–444.

Leon, G. R., Lucas, A. R., Colligan, R. C., Ferdinande, R. J., & Kamp, J. (1985). Sexual, body-image, and personality attitudes in anorexia nervosa. *Journal of Abnormal Child Psychology, 13,* 245–257.

Leonard, H. L., Goldberger, E. L., Rapoport, J. L., Cheslow, D. L., & Swedo, S. E. (1990). Childhood rituals: Normal development or obsessive-compulsive symptoms? *Journal of the American Academy of Child and Adolescent Psychiatry, 29,* 17–23.

Leonard, H. L., Swedo, S. E., Allen, A. J., & Rapoport, J. L. (1994). Obsessive-compulsive disorder. In T. H. Ollendick, N. J. King, & Yule, W. (Eds.), *International handbook of anxiety disorders in children and adolescents.* New York: Plenum.

Leonard, H. L., Swedo, S. E., Lenane, M. C., Rettew, D. C., Hamburger, S. D., Bartko, J. J., & Rapoport, J. L. (1993). A two to seven year follow-up study of 54 obsessive compulsive children and adolescents. *Archives of General Psychiatry, 50,* 429–439.

Leonard, H. L., Swedo, S. E., Rapoport, J. L., Koby, E. V., Lenane, M. C., Cheslow, D. L., & Hamburger, S. D. (1989). Treatment of childhood obsessive compulsive disorder with clomipramine and desipramine: A double-blind crossover comparison. *Archives of General Psychiatry, 46,* 1088–1092.

Lerner, J. W. (1989). Educational interventions in learning disabilities. *Journal of the American Academy of Child and Adolescent Psychiatry, 28,* 326–331.

Lerner, J. W., & Galambos, N. L. (1986). Child development and family change: The influences of maternal employment on infants and toddlers. In L. P. Lipsitt and C. Rovee-Collier (Eds.), *Advances in infancy research,* Vol. 4. Norwood, NJ: Ablex.

Lerner, R. M. (1987). The concept of plasticity in development. In J. J. Gallagher and C. T. Ramey (Eds.), *The malleability of children.* Baltimore: Brookes Publishing.

Leung, P. W. L., & Connolly, K. J. (1994). Attentional difficulties in hyperactive and conduct-disorder children: A processing deficit. *Journal of Child Psychology and Psychiatry, 35,* 1229–1245.

Levine, M. P., Smolak, L., Moodey, A. F., Shuman, M. D., & Hessen L. D. (1994). Normative developmental challenges and dieting and eating disturbances in middle school girls. *International Journal of Eating Disorders, 15,* 11–20.

Levine, R. J. (1991). Respect for children as research subjects. In M. Lewis (Ed.), *Child and adolescent psychiatry. A comprehensive textbook.* Baltimore: Williams & Wilkins.

Levitt, M. J., Guacci-Franco, N., & Levitt, J. L. (1993). Convoys of social support in childhood and early adolescence: Structure and function. *Developmental Psychology, 29,* 811–818.

Levy, S. R., Jurkovic, G. L., & Spiro, A. (1995). A multisystems analysis of adolescent suicide attempters. *Journal of Abnormal Child Psychology, 23,* 221–234.

Levy, S., Zoltak, B., & Saelens, T. (1988). A comparison of obstetrical records of autistic and nonautistic referrals for psychoeducational evaluations. *Journal of Autism and Developmental Disorders, 18,* 573–581.

Lewinsohn, P. (1974). A behavioral approach to depression. In R. J. Friedman & M. M. Katz (Eds.), *The psychology of depression: Contemporary theory and research.* Washington, DC: Winston.

Lewinsohn, P. M., Clarke, G. N., Hops, H., & Andrews, J. (1990). Cognitive behavioral treatment for depressed adolescents. *Behavior Therapy, 21,* 385–402.

Lewinsohn, P. M., Clarke, G. N., & Rohde, P. (1994). Psychological approaches to the treatment of depression in adolescents. In W. M. Reynolds and H. F. Johnston (Eds.), *Handbook of depression in children and adolescents.* New York: Plenum Press.

Lewinsohn, P. M., Hops, H., Roberts, R. E., Seeley, J. R., & Andrews, J. A. (1993). Adolescent psychopathology: I. Prevalence and incidence of depression and other DSM-III-R disorders in high school students. *Journal of Abnormal Psychology, 102,* 133–144.

Lewis, S. (1974). A comparison of behavior therapy techniques in the reductio of fearful avoidance behavior. *Behavior Therapy, 5,* 648–655.

Lewit, E. M. (1993). Children in foster care. *The Future of Children. Home Visiting, 3,* 192–200.

Liaw, F. & Brooks-Gunn, J. (1994). Cumulative familial risk and low-birthweight children's cognitive and behavioral development. *Journal of Clinical Child Psychology, 23,* 360–372.

Licht, B. G., & Kistner, J. A. (1986). Motivational problems of learning-disabled children: Individual differences and their implications for treatment. In J. K. Torgesen & B. Y. L. Wong (Eds.), *Psychological and educational perspectives on learning disabilities.* New York: Academic Press.

Lillienfeld, S. O., Waldman, I. D., & Israel, A. C. (1994). A critical examination of the use of the term and concept of comorbidity in psychopathology research. *Clinical Psychology: Science and Practice, 1,* 71–83.

Lilly, M. S. (Ed.). (1979a). *Children with exceptional needs: A survey of special education.* New York: Holt, Rinehart and Winston.

Lilly, M. S. (1979b). Special education. Emerging issues. In M. S. Lilly (Ed.), *Children with exceptional needs.* New York: Holt, Rinehart and Winston.

Lilly, M. S. (1979c). Special education. Historical and traditional perspectives. In M. S. Lilly (Ed.), *Children with exceptional needs.* New York: Holt, Rinehart and Winston.

Link, The (Spring–Summer 1995). Policies and position statements on inclusive schools. Charleston, WV: Appalachia Education Laboratory.

Linscheid, T. R. (1978). Disturbances of eating and feeding. In P. R. Magrab (Ed.), *Psychological management of pediatric problems, Vol. 1: Early life conditions and chronic diseases.* Baltimore: University Park Press.

Lipsey, M. W., & Wilson, D. B. (1993). The efficacy of psychological, educational, and behavioral treatment. *American Psychologist, 48,* 1181–1209.

Lloyd, J. W., Hallahan, D. P., Kauffman, J. M., & Keller, C. E. (1991). Academic problems. In T. R. Kratochwill & R. J. Morris (Eds.)., *The practice of child therapy.* Boston: Allyn and Bacon.

Lobitz, G. K., & Johnson, S. M. (1975). Deviant and normal children. *Journal of Abnormal Child Psychology, 3,* 353–374.

Loeber, R. (1988). Natural histories of conduct problems, delinquency, and associated substance use: Evidence for developmental progressions. In B. B. Lahey & A. E. Kazdin (Eds.), *Advances in clinical child psychology,* Vol. 11. New York: Plenum.

Loeber, R. (1991). Antisocial behavior: more enduring than changeable? *Journal of the American Academy of Child and Adolescent Psychiatry, 30,* 383–397.

Loeber, R., Green, S. M., Keenan, K., & Lahey, B. (1995). Which boys will fare worse? Early predictors of the onset of conduct disorder in a six-year longitudinal study. *Journal of the American Academy of Child and Adolescent Psychiatry, 34,* 499–509.

Loeber, R., & Schmaling, K. B. (1985) Empirical evidence for overt and covert patterns of antisocial conduct problems: A meta-analysis. *Journal of Abnormal Child Psychology, 13,* 337–354.

Loeber, R., Wung, P., Keenan, K., Giroux, B., Stouthamer-Loeber, M., Van Kammen, W. B., & Maughan, B. (1993). Developmental pathways in disruptive child behavior. *Development and Psychopathology, 5,* 103–133.

Lombroso, P. J., Pauls, D. L., & Leckman, J. F. (1994). Genetic mechanisms in childhood psychiatric disorders. *Journal of the American Academy of Child and Adolescent Psychiatry, 33,* 921–938.

Lord, C., & Rutter, M. (1994). Autism and pervasive developmental disorders. In M. Rutter, E. Taylor & L. Hersov (Eds.), *Child and adolescent psychiatry. Modern approaches.* Boston: Blackwell Scientific.

Lord, C., & Schopler, E. (1989). Stability of assessment results of autistic and non-autistic language-impaired children from preschool years to early school age. *Journal of Child Psychology and Psychiatry, 30,* 575–590.

Lord, J., & Pedlar, A. (1991). Life in the community: Four years after the closure of an institution. *Mental Retardation, 29,* 213–221.

Lorion, R. P., Cowen, E. L., & Caldwell, R. A. (1974). Problem types of children referred to a school based mental health program: Identification and outcome. *Journal of Consulting and Clinical Psychology, 42,* 491–496.

Lotter, V. (1966). Epidemiology of autistic conditions in young children. I. Prevalence. *Social Psychiatry, 1,* 124–137.

Lotter, V. (1974). Factors related to outcome in autistic children. *Journal of Autism and Childhood Schizophrenia, 4,* 263–277.

Lourie, I. S., Stroul, B. A., Katz-Leavy, J., Magrab, P. R., Friedman, R. M., & Friesen, B. (1990). Advances in children's mental health. *American Psychologist, 45,* 407–408.

Lovaas, O. I. (1987). Behavioral treatment and normal educational and intellectual functioning in young autistic children. *Journal of Consulting and Clinical Psychology, 55,* 3–9.

Lovaas, O. I., & Newsom, C. D. (1976). Behavior modification with psychotic children. In H. Leitenberg (Ed.), *Handbook of behavior modification and behavior therapy.* Englewood Cliffs, NJ: Prentice Hall.

Lovaas, O. I., & Simmons, J. Q. (1969). Manipulation of self-destruction in three retarded children. *Journal of Applied Behavior Analysis, 2,* 143–157.

Lovaas, O. I., & Smith, T. (1988). Intensive behavioral treatment for young autistic children. In B. B. Lahey & A. E. Kazdin (Eds.), *Advances in clinical child psychology,* Vol. 2. New York: Plenum.

Lovaas, O. I., Young, D. B., & Newsom, C. D. (1978). Childhood psychosis: Behavioral treatment. In B. B. Wolman (Ed.), *Handbook of treatment of mental disorders in childhood and adolescence.* Englewood Cliffs, NJ: Prentice Hall.

Lovibond, S. H. (1964). *Conditioning and enuresis.* Oxford: Pergamon.

Lovko, A. M., & Ullman, D. G. (1989). Research on the adjustment of latchkey children: Role of background/demographic and latchkey situation variables. *Journal of Clinical Child Psychology, 18,* 16–24.

Lucas, A. R., Beard, C. M., O'Fallon, W. M., & Kurlan, L. T. (1991). 50-year trends in the incidence of anorexia nervosa in Rochester, Minn.: A population-based study. *American Journal of Psychiatry, 148,* 917–922.

Luthar, S. S. (1993). Methodological and conceptual issues in research on childhood resilience. *Journal of Child Psychology and Psychiatry, 34,* 441–453.

Luxenberg, J. S., Swedo, S. E., Flament, M. F., Friedland, R., Rapoport, J. L., & Rapoport, S. I. (1988). Neuroanatomical abnormalities in obsessive-compulsive disorder detected with quantitative x-ray computed tomography. *American Journal of Psychiatry, 145,* 1089–1093.

Lynn, D. B. (1974). *The father: His role in child development.* Monterey, CA: Brooks/Cole.

Lynskey, M. T., & Fergusson, D. M. (1995). Childhood conduct problems, attention deficit behaviors, and adolescent alcohol, tobacco, and illicit drug use. *Journal of Abnormal Child Psychology, 23,* 281–302.

Lyon, G. R., & Moats, L. C. (1988). Critical issues in the instruction of the learning disabled. *Journal of Consulting and Clinical Psychology, 56,* 830–835.

Lytton, H., & Romney, D. M. (1991). Parents' differential socialization of boys and girls: A meta-analysis. *Psychological Bulletin, 109,* 267–296.

Maccoby, E. E. (1992). The role of parents in the socialization of children: An historic overview. *Developmental Psychology, 28,* 1006–1017.

Maccoby, E. E., & Martin, J. A. (1983). Socialization in the context of the family: Parent-child interaction. In P. H. Mussen (Ed.), *Handbook of child psychology,* Vol. IV. New York: Wiley

MacFarlane, J. W., Allen, L., & Honzik, M. P. (1954). *A developmental study of the behavior problems of normal children between 21 months and 14 years.* Berkeley: University of California Press.

Machover, K. (1949). *Personality projection in the drawing of the human figure.* Springfield, IL: Chas. C. Thomas.

MacLean, W. E., Perrin, J. M., Gortmaker, S., & Pierre, C. B. (1992). Psychological adjustment of children with asthma: Effects of illness severity and recent stressful life events. *Journal of Pediatric Psychology, 17,* 159–171.

MacMillan, D. L. (1982). *Mental retardation in school and society,* 2nd ed. Boston: Little-Brown.

MacMillan, D. L., & Kavale, K. A. (1986). Educational intervention. In H. C. Quay & J. S. Werry (Eds.), *Psychopathological disorders of childhood,* 3rd ed. New York: Wiley.

MacMillan, D. L., Keogh, B. K., & Jones, R. L. (1986). Special educational research on mildly handicapped learners. In M. C. Wittrock (Ed.), *Handbook of research on teaching.* New York: Macmillan.

Madan-Swain, A. & Brown, R. T. (1991). Cognitive and psychosocial sequelae for children with acute lymphocytic leukemia and their families. *Clinical Psychology Review, 11,* 267–294.

Maerov, S. L., Brummett, B., Patterson, G. R., & Reid, J. B. (1978). Coding family interactions. In J. B. Reid (Ed.), *A social learning approach to family intervention, Vol. 2, Observation in home settings.* Eugene, OR: Castalia.

Magnuson, E. (1983). Child abuse: The ultimate betrayal. *Time* (Sept. 5), pp. 16–18.

Mahler, M. S. (1952). *The psychoanalytic study of the child.* New York: International Universities Press.

Mahoney, M. J. (1993). Introduction to special section: Theoretical developments in the cognitive psychotherapies. *Journal of Consulting and Clinical Psychology, 61,* 187–193.

Maier, S. F., Watkins, L. R., & Fleshner, M. (1994). Psychoneuroimmunology: The interface between behavior, brain, and immunity. *American Psychologist, 49,* 1004–1017.

Maisto, S. A., & Carey, K. B. (1985). Origins of alcohol abuse in children and adolescents. In B. B. Lahey & A. E. Kazdin (Eds.), *Advances in clinical child psychology,* Vol. 8. New York: Plenum.

Malamed, B. G., & Siegel, L. J. (1975). Reduction of anxiety in children facing hospitalization and surgery by use of filmed modeling. *Journal of Consulting and Clinical Psychology, 43,* 511–521.

Malatesta, C. Z., Grigoryev, P., Lamb, K., Albin, M., & Culver, C. (1986). Emotion socialization and expressive development in preterm and full-term infants. *Child Development, 57,* 316–330.

Malcarne, V. L., & Ingram, R. E. (1994). Cognition and negative affectivity. In T. H. Ollendick & R. J. Prinz, (Eds.), *Advances in clinical child psychology,* Vol. 16. New York: Plenum.

Malik, N. M., & Furman, W. (1993). Practitioner review: Problems in children's peer relations: What can the clinician do. *Journal of Child Psychology and Psychiatry, 34,* 1303–1326.

Malmquist, C. P. (1977). Childhood depression: A clinical and behavioral prespective. In J. G. Schulterbrandt & A. Raskin (Eds.), *Depression in childhood: Diagnosis, treatment, and conceptual models.* New York: Raven Press.

Manly, J. T., Cicchetti, D., & Barnett, D. (1994). The impact of subtype, frequency, chronicity, and severity of child maltreatment on social competence and behavior problems. *Development and Psychopathology, 6,* 121–144.

Mann, V. A. (1986). Why some children encounter reading problems: The contribution of difficulties with language processing and phonological sophistication to early reading disability. In J. K. Torgesen & B. Y. L. Wong (Eds.), *Psychological and educational perspectives on learning disabilities.* New York: Academic Press.

Mann, V. A., & Brady, S. (1988). Reading disability: The role of language deficiencies. *Journal of Consulting and Clinical Psychology, 56,* 811–816.

Manne, S. L., Bakeman, R., Jacobsen, P., & Redd, W. H. (1993). Children's coping during invasive medical procedures. *Behavior Therapy, 24,* 143–158.

Mannuzza, S., Klein, R. G., Bessler, A., Malloy, P., & La-Padula, M. (1993). Adult outcome of hyperactive boys. *Archives of General Psychiatry, 50,* 565–576.

Mansheim, P. (1979). Emotional and behavioral data in a case of the 48, XXYY syndrome. *Journal of Pediatric Psychology, 4,* 363–370.

March, J. S. (1995). Cognitive-behavioral psychotherapy for children and adolescents with OCD: A review and recommendations for treatment. *Journal of the American Academy of Child and Adolescent Psychiatry, 34,* 7–18.

Marchetti, A. G., & Campbell, V. A. (1990). Social skills. In J. L. Matson (Ed.), *Handbook of behavior modification with the mentally retarded.* New York: Plenum.

Marchi, M. & Cohen, P. (1990). Early childhood eating behaviors and adolescent eating disorders. *Journal of the American Academy of Child and Adolescent Psychiatry, 29,* 112–117.

Marcus, J., Hans, S. L., Auerbach. J. G., & Auerbach, A. G. (1993). Children at risk for schizophrenia: The Jerusalem Infant Development Study. *Archives of General Psychiatry, 50,* 797–809.

Marcus, L. M., & Schopler, E. (1993). Pervasive developmental disorders. In T. H. Ollendick & M. Hersen (Eds.), *Handbook of child and adolescent assessment.* Boston: Allyn and Bacon.

Margalit, M. (1989). Academic competence and social adjustment of boys with learning disabilities and boys with behavior disorders. *Journal of Learning Disabilities, 22,* 41–45.

Marshall, P. (1989). Attention deficit disorder and allergy: A neurochemical model of the relation between the illnesses. *Psychological Bulletin, 106,* 434–446.

Marteau, T., Johnston, M., Baum, J. D., & Bloch, S. (1987). Goals of treatment in diabetes: A comparison of doctors and parents of children with diabetes. *Journal of Behavioral Medicine, 10,* 33–48.

Masek, B. J., & Hoag, N. L. (1990). Headache, In A. M. Gross & R. S. Drabman (Eds.), *Handbook of clinical behavioral pediatrics.* New York: Plenum.

Mash, E. J., & Lee, C. M. (1993). Behavioral assessment with children. In R. T. Ammerman & M. Hersen (Eds.), *Handbook of behavior therapy with children and adults.* Boston: Allyn & Bacon.

Matarazzo, J. D. (1990). Psychological assessment versus psychological testing: Validation from Binet to the school, clinic, and courtroom. *American Psychologist, 45,* 999–1017.

Matarazzo, J. D. (1992). Psychological testing and assessment in the 21st century. *American Psychologist, 47,* 1007–1018.

Matson, J. L., & Coe, D. A. (1991). Mentally retarded children. In T. R. Kratochwill & R. J. Morris (Eds.), *The practice of child therapy.* Boston: Allyn and Bacon.

Matthews, K. A., & Rodin, J. (1989). Women's changing work roles: Impact on health, family, and public policy. *American Psychologist, 44,* 1389–1393.

Maughan, B. (1995). Long-term outcomes of developmental reading problems. *Journal of Child Psychology and Psychiatry, 36,* 357–371.

Maughan, B. & Yule, W. (1994). Reading and other learning disabilities. In M. Rutter, E. Taylor, & L. Hersov (Eds.), *Child and adolescent psychiatry. Modern approaches.* Cambridge, MA: Blackwell Scientific.

Mayes, S. D. (1992). Rumination disorder: Diagnosis, complications, mediating variables, and treatment. In B. B. Lahey & A. E. Kazdin (Eds.), *Advances in clinical child psychology,* Vol. 14. New York: Plenum.

Mazze, R. S., Lucido, D., & Shannon, H. (1984). Psychological and social correlates of glycemic control. *Diabetes Care, 7,* 360–366.

McAlpine, C., & Singh, N. N. (1986). Pica in institutionalized mentally retarded persons. *Journal of Mental Deficiency Research, 30,* 171–178.

McArdle, P., O'Brien, G., & Kolvin, I. (1995). Hyperactivity: prevalence and relationship with conduct disorder. *Journal of Child Psychology and psychiatry, 36,* 279–303.

McBurnett, K., Hobbs, S. A., & Lahey, B. B. (1989). Behavioral treatment. In T. H. Ollendick & M. Hersen (Eds.), *Handbook of child psychopathology,* 2nd ed. New York: Plenum.

McCall, R. B., Applebaum, M. I., & Hogarty, P. S. (1973). Developmental changes in mental performance. *Monographs of the Society for Research in Child Development, 38* (Whole No. 150).

McCauley, E., Kay, T., Ito, J., & Treder, R. (1987). The Turner Syndrome: Cognitive deficits, affective discrim-ination, and behavior problems. *Child Development, 58,* 464–473.

McCauley, E., Mitchell, J. R., Burke, P., & Moss, S. (1988). Cognitive attributes of depression in children and adolescents. *Journal of Consulting and Clinical Psychology, 56,* 903–908.

McClellan, J., & Werry, J. (1994). Practice parameters for the assessment and treatment of children and adolescents with schizophrenia. *Journal of the American Academy of Child and Adolescent Psychiatry, 33,* 616–635.

McDermott, J. (1991). The effects of ethnicity on child and adolescent development. In M. Lewis (Ed.), *Child and adolescent psychiatry. A comprehensive textbook.* Baltimore: Williams & Wilkins.

McDonnell, J., Hardman, M., Hightower, J., & Kiefer-O'Donnell, R. (1991). Variables associated with in-school and after-school integration of secondary students with severe disabilities. *Education and Training in Mental Retardation, 26,* 243–257.

McEachin, J. J., Smith, T., & Lovaas, O. I. (1993). Long-term outcome for children with autism who received early intensive behavioral treatment. *American Journal on Mental Retardation, 97,* 359–372.

McEvoy, R. E., Rogers, S. J., & Pennington, B. F. (1993). Executive functions and social communication deficits in young autistic children. *Journal of Child Psychology and Psychiatry, 34,* 563–578.

McGee, R., Feehan, M., Williams, S., & Anderson, J. (1992). DSM-III disorders from age 11 to age 15 years. *Journal of the American Academy of Child and Adolescent Psychiatry, 31,* 50–59.

McGee, R., Feehan, M., Williams, S., Partridge, F., Silva, P. A., & Kelly, J. (1990). DSM-III disorders in a large sample of adolescents. *Journal of the American Academy of Child and Adolescent Psychiatry, 29,* 611–619.

McGee, R., Partridge, F., Williams, S., & Silva, P. A. (1991). A twelve-year follow-up of preschool hyperactive children. *Journal of the American Academy of Child and Adolescent Psychiatry, 30,* 224–232.

McGee, R., & Share, D. L. (1988). Attention deficit disorder-hyperactivity and academic failure: Which comes first and what should be treated? *Journal of the American Academy of Child and Adolescent Psychiatry, 27,* 318–325.

McGee, R. A., & Wolfe, D. A. (1991). Psychological maltreatment: Toward an operational definition. *Development and Psychopathology, 3,* 3–18.

McGrew, K. S., Bruininks, R. H., & Thurlow, M. L. (1992). Relationship between measures of adaptive functioning and community adjustment for adults with mental retardation. *Exceptional Children, 58,* 517–529.

McGue, M., Bouchard, T. J., Iacono, W. G., & Lykken, D. T. (1993). Behavioral genetics of cognitive ability: A life-span perspective. In R. Plomin & G. E. McClearn (Eds.), *Nature, nurture & psychology.* Washington, DC: American Psychological Association.

McKenna, K., Gordon, C. T., Lenane, M., Kaysen, D., Fahey, K., & Rapoport, J. L. (1994). Looking for childhood-onset schizophrenia: The first 71 cases screened. *Journal of the American Academy of Child and Adolescent Psychiatry, 33,* 636–644.

McKenna, K., Gordon, C. T., & Rapoport, J. L. (1994). Childhood-onset schizophrenia: Timely neurobiological research. *Journal of the American Academy of Child and Adolescent Psychiatry, 33,* 771–781.

McLean, J., & Ching, A. (1973). Follow-up study of relationships between family situation and bronchial asthma in children. *Journal of the American Academy of Child Psychiatry, 10,* 142–161.

McLoyd, V. C. (1990). The impact of economic hardship on black families and children: Psychological distress, parenting, and socioemotional development. *Child Development, 61*, 311–346.

McMahon, R. J. (1984). Behavioral checklists and rating scales. In T. H. Ollendick & M. Hersen (Eds.), *Child behavioral assessment: Principles and procedures.* New York: Pergamon.

McMahon, R. J., & Forehand, R. (1988). Conduct disorders. In E. J. Mash & L. G. Terdal (Eds.), *Behavioral assessment of childhood disorders,* 2nd ed. New York: Guilford.

McMahon, R. J., & Wells, K. C. (1989). Conduct disorders. In E. J. Mash & R. A. Barkley (Eds.), *Treatment of childhood disorders.* New York: Guilford.

McNabb, W. L., Wilson-Pessano, S. R., & Jacobs, A. M. (1986). Critical self-management competencies for children with asthma. *Journal of Pediatric Psychology, 11,* 103–117.

McReynolds, P. (1987). Lightner Whitmer: Little-known founder of clinical psychology. *American Psychologist, 42,* 849–858.

Mechanic, D., & Rochefort, D. A. (1990). Deinstitutionalization: An appraisal of reform. *Annual review of sociology, 16,* 301–327.

Mednick, S. A., Gabrielli, W. F., & Hutchings, B. (1984). Genetic influences in criminal convictions: Evidence from an adoption cohort. *Science, 224,* 891–894.

Mednick, S. A., & Schulsinger, F. (1968). Some premorbid characteristics related to breakdown in children with schizophrenic mothers. In D. Rosenthal and S. S. Kety (Eds.), *The transmission of schizophrenia.* Elmsford, NY: Pergamon Press.

Meichenbaum, D. (1993). Changing conceptions of cognitive behavior modification: Retrospect and prospect. *Journal of Consulting and Clinical Psychology, 61,* 202–204.

Meichenbaum, D. H., & Goodman, J. (1971). Training impulsive children to talk to themselves: A means of developing self-control. *Journal of Abnormal Psychology, 77,* 115–126.

Meisels, S. J. (1984). Prediction, prevention, and developmental screening in the EPSTD program. In H. W. Stevenson & A. E. Siegel (Eds.), *Child development research and social policy.* Chicago: University of Chicago Press.

Melamed, B. G., & Siegel, L. J. (1975). Reduction of anxiety in children facing hospitalization and surgery by use of filmed modeling. *Journal of Consulting and Clinical Psychology, 43,* 511–521.

Melamed, B. G., & Siegel, L. J. (1980). *Behavioral medicine: Practical applications in health care.* New York: Springer.

Melbin, T. & Vuille, J. C. (1989). Further evidence of an association between psychosocial problems and increase in relative weight between 7 and 10 years of age. *Acta Paediatica Scandinavica, 78,* 576–580.

Mellin, L. M., Irwin, C. E., & Scully, S. (1992), Prevalence of disordered eating in girls: A survey of middle-class children. *Journal of the American Dietetic Association, 92,* 851–853.

Melton, G. B., & Davidson, H. A. (1987). Child protection and society: When should the state intervene? *American Psychologist, 42,* 172–175.

Mercer, C. D., King-Sears, P., & Mercer, A. R. (1990). Learning disabilities definitions and criteria used by state education departments. *Learning Disability Quarterly, 13,* 141–152.

Mesibov, G. B. (1992). Letters to the editors. Response to Thompson and McEvoy. *Journal of Autism and Developmental Disorders, 22,* 672–673.

Mesibov, G. B., Schopler, E., Schaffer, B., & Michal, N. (1989). Use of the Childhood Autism Rating Scale with autistic adolescents and adults. *Journal of the American Academy of Child and Adolescent Psychiatry, 28,* 538–541.

Mesibov, G. B., Schroeder, C. S., & Wesson, L. (1977). Parental concerns about their children. *Journal of Pediatric Psychology, 2,* 13–17.

Mesibov, G., B., & Van Bourgondien, M. E. (1992). Autism. In S. R. Hooper, G. W. Hynd, & R. E. Mattison (Eds.), *Developmental disorders. Diagnostic criteria and clinical assessment.* Hillsdale, NJ: Erlbaum.

Meyer, N. E., Dyck, D. G., & Petrinack, R. J. (1989). Cognitive appraisal and attributional correlates of depressive symptoms in children. *Journal of Abnormal Child Psychology, 17,* 325–336.

Milgram, S. (1963). Behavioral study of obedience. *Journal of Abnormal and Social Psychology, 67,* 371–378.

Milich, R. (1994). The response of children with ADHD to failure: If at first you don't succeed, do you try, try again? *School Psychology Review, 23,* 11–28.

Milich, R., Loney, J., & Roberts, M. (1986). Playroom observations of activity level and sustained attention: Two-year stability. *Journal of Consulting and Clinical Psychology, 54,* 272–274.

Miller, B. D. & Wood, B. L. (1991). Childhood asthma in interaction with family, school, and peer systems: A developmental model for primary care. *Journal of Asthma, 28,* 405–414.

Miller, B. D. & Wood, B. L. (1994). Psychophysiologic reactivity in asthmatic children: A cholinergically mediated confluence of pathways. *Journal of the American Academy of Child and Adolescent Psychiatry, 33,* 1236–1245.

Miller, J. L. (1990). Apocalypse or renaissance or something in between? Toward a realistic appraisal of *The Learning Mystique. Journal of Learning Disabilities, 23,* 86–91.

Miller, L. C., Barrett, C. L., & Hampe, E. (1974). Phobias of childhood in a prescientific era. In A. Davids (Ed.), *Child personality and psychopathology: Current topics,* Vol. 1. New York: John Wiley.

Miller, L. C., Barrett, C. L., Hampe, E., & Noble, H. (1972). Comparison of reciprocal inhibition psychotherapy and waiting list control for phobic children. *Journal of Abnormal Psychology, 79,* 269–279.

Miller, N. E. (1969). Learning of visceral and glandular responses. *Science, 163,* 434–445.

Millican, F. K., & Lourie, R. S. (1970). The child with pica and his family. In E. J. Anthony and C. Koupernik (Eds.), *The child in his family,* Vol. 1. New York: Wiley-Interscience.

Minde, K., Faucon, A., & Faulkner, S. (1994). Sleep problems in toddlers: Effects of treatment on their daytime behavior. *Journal of the American Academy of Child and Adolescent Psychiatry, 33,* 1114–1121.

Minde, K., Popiel, K., Leos, N., Falkner, S., Parker, K., & Handley-Derry, M. (1993). The evaluation and treatment of sleep disturbances in young children. *Journal of Child Psychology and Psychiatry, 34,* 521–533.

Mindell, J. A. (1993). Sleep disorders in children. *Health Psychology, 12,* 151–162.

Minuchin, S., Rosman, B. L., & Baker, L. (1978). *Psychosomatic Families: Anorexia nervosa in context.* Cambridge, MA: Harvard University Press.

Mirkin, M. P. (1990). Eating disorders: A feminist family therapy perspective. In M. P. Mirkin (Ed.), *The social and political contexts of family therapy.* Boston: Allyn & Bacon.

Mishler, E. G., & Waxler, N. E. (1965). Family interactional processes and schizophrenia: A review of current theories. *Merrill-Palmer Quarterly, 11,* 269–315.

Mitchell, J. E. (1992). Subtyping of bulimia nervosa. *International Journal of Eating Disorders, 11,* 327–332.

Mitchell, J. E., & Eckert, E. D. (1987). Scope and significance of eating disorders. *Journal of Consulting and Clinical Psychology, 55*, 628–634.

Moffitt, T. E. (1993a). Adolescence-limited and life-course-persistent antisocial behavior: A developmental taxonomy. *Psychological Review, 100*, 674–701.

Moffitt, T. E. (1993b). The neuropsychology of conduct disorder. *Development and Psychopathology, 5*, 135–152.

Moore, D. R., & Arthur, J. L. (1989). Juvenile delinquency. In T. H. Ollendick & M. Hersen (Eds.), *Handbook of child psychopathology*, 2nd ed. New York: Plenum.

Morris, R. D. (1988). Classification of learning disabilities: Old problems and new approaches. *Journal of Consulting and Clinical Psychology, 56*, 789–794.

Morris, R. J., & Kratochwill, T. R. (1983). *Treating children's fears and phobias: A behavioral approach*. Elsmford, NY: Pergamon Press.

Morris, S., Alexander, J. F., & Waldron, H. (1988). Functional family therapy: Issues in clinical practice. In I. R. H. Falloon (Ed.), *Handbook of behavioral family therapy*. New York: Guilford.

Morrison, D. N., McGee, R., & Stanton, W. R. (1992). Sleep problems in adolescence. *Journal of the American Academy of Child and Adolescent Psychiatry, 31*, 94–99.

Morrison, M. M., & Smith, Q. T. (1987). Psychiatric issues of adolescent chemical dependence. *Pediatric Clinics of North America, 34*, 461–480.

Morrow-Bradley, C., & Elliot, R. (1986). Utilization of psychotherapy research by practicing psychotherapists. *American Psychologist, 41*, 188–197.

Morvitz, E., & Motta, R. W. (1992). Predictors of self-esteem: The roles of parent-child perceptions, achievement, and class placement. *Journal of Learning Disabilities, 25*, 72–80.

Mowrer, O. H., & Mowrer, W. M. (1938). Enuresis: A method for its study and treatment. *American Journal of Orthopsychiatry, 8*, 436–459.

Mozes, T., Toren, P., Chernauzan, N., Mester, R., Yoran-Hegesh, R., Blumensohn, R., & Weizman, A. (1994). Case study: Clozapine treatment in very early onset schizophrenia. *Journal of the American Academy of Child and Adolescent Psychiatry, 33*, 65–70.

Mufson, L., Moreau, D., Weissman, M. M., Wickramaratne, P., Martin, J., & Samoilov, A. (1994). Modification of interpersonal psychotherapy with depressed adolescents (IPT-A): Phase I and II studies. *Journal of the American Academy of Child and Adolescent Psychiatry, 33*, 695–705.

Mulick, J. A. (1994, Nov./Dec.). The non-science of facilitated communication. *Psychological Science Agenda, 7*, 8–9.

Muller, C. (1995). Maternal employment, parent involvement, and mathematics achievement among adolescents. *Journal of Marriage and the Family, 57*, 85–100.

Mulvey, E. P., Arthur, M. W., & Reppucci, N. D. (1993). The prevention and treatment of juvenile delinquency: A review of the research. *Clinical Psychology Review, 13*, 133–167.

Mundy, P. (1993). Normal versus high functioning status in children with autism. *American Journal on Mental Retardation, 97*, 381–384.

Mundy, P., & Adreon, D. (1994). Commentary. Facilitated communication: Attitude, effect, and theory. *Journal of Pediatric Psychology, 19*, 677–680.

Mundy, P., Robertson, M., Robertson, J., & Greenblatt, M. (1990). The prevalence of psychotic symptoms in homeless adolescents. *Journal of the American Academy of Child and Adolescent Psychiatry, 29*, 724–731.

Mundy, P., Sigman, M., & Kasari, C. (1993). The theory of mind and joint-attention deficits in autism. In S. Baron-Cohen, H. Tager-Flusberg, & D. J. Cohen

(Eds.), *Understanding other minds*. New York: Oxford University Press.

Mundy, P., Sigman, M., Ungerer, J., & Sherman, T. (1987). Nonverbal communication and play correlates of language development in autistic children. *Journal of Autism and Developmental Disorders, 17*, 349–364.

Murphy, D. A., Greenstein, J. J., & Pelham, W. E. (1993). Pharmacological treatment. In V. B. VanHasselt & M. Hersen (Eds.), *Handbook of behavior therapy and pharmacotherapy for children: a comparative analysis*. Boston: Allyn and Bacon.

Murray, H. A. (1943). *Thematic Apperception Test*. Cambridge, MA: Harvard University Press.

Murray, L. (1992). The impact of postnatal depression on infant development. *Journal of Child Psychology and Psychiatry, 33*, 543–561.

Murray, T. (1988). Learning to deceive. In J. Rubinstein & B. Slife (Eds.), *Taking sides*. Guilford, CT: Dushkin.

Myers, C. E., Nihira, K., & Zetlin, A. (1979). The measurement of adaptive behavior. In N. R. Ellis (Ed.), *Handbook of mental deficiency*. Hillsdale, NJ: Erlbaum.

Nader, K., Pynoos, R. S., Fairbanks, L. & Frederick, C. (1991). Childhood PTSD reactions one year after a sniper attack. *American Journal of Psychiatry, 147*, 1526–1530.

Nathan, P. E. (1994). DSM-IV: Empirical, accessible, not yet ideal. *Journal of Clinical Psychology, 50*, 103–110.

National Center for Child Abuse and Neglect. (1993). *National child abuse and neglect data system: Working paper 2-1991 Summary data component*. Washington, DC: U.S. Government Printing Office.

National Institute of Drug Abuse (1992). National Household Survey on Drug Abuse. *Statistical Abstract of the United States 1992* (112th ed.), U.S. Department of Commerce, Bureau of the Census.

National Insitute of Mental Health (1977). *Child abuse and neglect programs: Practice and theory*. Washington, DC: U.S. Government Printing Office.

Nelson, J. R., Smith, D. J., & Dodd, J. (1990). The moral reasoning of juvenile delinquents: A meta-analysis. *Journal of Abnormal Child Psychology, 18*, 231–239.

Nelson, K. (1981). Individual difference in language development: Implications for development and language. *Developmental Psychology, 17*, 170–187.

Nettelbeck, T. (1985). Inspection time and mild mental retardation. In N. R. Ellis & N. W. Bray (Eds.), *International review of research in mental retardation. Vol. 13*. New York: Academic Press.

Neuchterlein, K. H. (1986). Childhood precursors of adult schizophrenia. *Journal of Child Psychology and Psychiatry, 27*, 133–144.

Newacheck, P. W. & Taylor, W. R. (1992). Childhood chronic illness: Prevalence, severity and impact. *American Journal of Public Health, 82*, 364–371.

Newcomb, A. F., & Bagwell, C. L. (1995). Children's friendship relations: A meta-analytic review. *Psychological Bulletin, 117*, 306–347.

Newcomb, A. F., Bukowski, W. M., Pattee, L. (1993). Children's peer relations: A meta-analytic review of popular, rejected, neglected, controversial, and average sociometric status. *Psychological Bulletin, 113*, 99–128.

Newcomb, M. D., Maddahian, E., & Bentler, P. M. (1986). Risk factors for drug use among adolescents. *American Journal of Public Health, 76*, 525–531.

Newsom, C., Hovanitz, C., & Rincover, A. (1988). Autism. In E. J. Mash and L. G. Terdal (Eds.), *Behavioral assessment of childhood disorders. Selected core problems*. New York: Guilford.

Niccols, G. A. (1994). Fetal alcohol syndrome: Implications for psychologists. *Clinical Psychology Review, 14*, 91–111.

Nichols, M. P., & Schwartz, R. C. (1991). *Family therapy: Concepts and methods* (2nd ed.). Boston: Allyn & Bacon.

Nihira, K., Leland, H., & Lambert, N. (1993). *AAMR Adaptive Behavior Scales—Residential and Community.* Austin, TX: Pro-ed.

Ninio, A., & Rinott, N. (1988). Fathers' involvement in the care of their infants and their attributions of cognitive competence to infants. *Child Development, 59,* 652–663.

Nolen-Hoeksema, S. N., & Girgus, J. S. (1994). The emergence of gender differences in depression during adolescence. *Psychological Bulletin, 115,* 424–443.

Nolen-Hoeksema, S. N., Mumme, D., Wolfson, A., & Guskin, K. (1995). Helplessness in children of depressed and nondepressed mothers. *Developmental Psychology, 31,* 377–387.

Noll, R. B., Bukowski, W. M., Davies, W. H., Koontz, K., & Kulkarni, R. (1993). Adjustment in the peer system of adolescents with cancer: A two-year study *Journal of Pediatric Psychology, 18,* 351–364.

Nordyke, N. S., Baer, D. M., Etzel, B. C., & Le Blanc, J. M. (1977). Implications of the stereotyping of modification of sex role. *Journal of Applied Behavior Analysis, 10,* 553–557.

Nottelmann, E. D., & Jensen, P. S. (1995). Bipolar affective disorders in children and adolescents: Introduction. *Journal of the American Academy of Child and Adolescent Psychiatry, 34,* 705–708.

Nowakowski, R. S. (1987). Basic concepts of CNS development. *Child Development, 58,* 568–595.

Nurcombe, B. (1994). The validity of the diagnosis of major depression in childhood and adolescence. In W. M. Reynolds and H. F. Johnston (Eds.), *Handbook of depression in children and adolescents.* New York: Plenum Press.

O'Connor, N., & Hermelin, B. (1988). Annotation. Low intelligence and special abilities. *Journal of Child Psychology and Psychiatry, 29,* 391–396.

O'Connor, N., & Hermelin, B. (1990). The recognition failure and graphic success of idot-savant artists. *Journal of Child Psychology and Psychiatry, 31,* 203–215.

O'Connor, R. D. (1969). Modification of social withdrawal through symbolic modeling. *Journal of Applied Behavior Analysis, 2,* 15–22.

O'Connor, R. D. (1972). The relative efficacy of modeling, shaping, and combined procedures. *Journal of Abnormal Psychology, 79,* 327–334.

Oden, S., & Asher, S. (1977). Coaching children in skills for friendship making. *Child Development, 48,* 495–506.

Odom, S. L., & Strain, P. S. (1984). Peer-mediated approaches to promoting children's social interaction: A review. *American Journal of Orthopsychiatry, 54,* 544–557.

Offord, D. R., & Fleming, J. E. (1991). Epidemiology. In M. Lewis (Ed.), *Child and adolescent psychiatry. A comprehensive textbook.* Baltimore: Williams & Wilkins.

Ohta, M. (1987). Cognitive disorders of infantile autism: A study employing the WISC, spatial relationship conceptualization, and gesture imitations. *Journal of Autism and Developmental Disorders, 17,* 45–62.

O'Keefe, A. (Ed.) (1979). *What Head Start means to families.* Washington, DC: U.S. Department of Health and Human Services.

Okun, A., Parker, G., & Levendosky, A. A. (1994). Distinct and interactive contributions of physical abuse, socioeconomic disadvantage, and negative life events to children's social, cognitive and affective adjustment. *Development and Psychopathology, 6,* 77–98.

Olds, D. L., & Kitzman, H. (1993). Review of research on home visiting for pregnant women and parents of young children. *Home Visiting, 3,* 53–92.

O'Leary, K. D., & Emery, R. E. (1985). Marital discord and child behavior problems. In M. D. Levine & P. Satz (Eds.), *Developmental variation and dysfunction.* New York: Academic Press.

O'Leary, K. D., & Wilson, G. T. (1987). *Behavior therapy: Application and outcome,* 2nd ed. Englewood Cliffs, NJ: Prentice Hall.

O'Leary, K. D., Pelham, W. E., Rosenbaum, M. A., & Price, G. H. (1976). Behavioral treatment of hyperkinetic children. *Clinical Pediatrics, 15,* 510–515.

Ollendick, T. H. (1983). Reliability and validity of the Revised Fear Survey Schedule for Children (FSSC-R). *Behaviour Research and Therapy, 21,* 685–692.

Ollendick, T. H., & Cerny, J. A. (1981). *Clinical behavior therapy with children.* New York: Plenum.

Ollendick, T. H., & Greene, R. (1990). Behavioral assessment of children. In G. Goldstein & M. Hersen (Eds.), *Handbook of psychological assessment* (2nd ed.). New York: Pergamon.

Ollendick, T. H., & King, N. J. (1991). Origins of childhood fears: An evaluation of Rachman's theory of fear acquisition. *Behaviour Research and Therapy, 29,* 117–123.

Ollendick, T. H., King, N. J., & Frary, R. B. (1989). Fears in children and adolescents: Reliability and generalizability across gender, age and nationality. *Behaviour Research and Therapy, 27,* 19–26.

Ollendick, T. H., King, N. L., & Hamilton, D. I. (1991). Origins of childhood fears: An evaluation of Rachman's theory of fear acquisition. *Behaviour Research and Therapy, 29,* 117–123.

Ollendick, T. H., Mattis, S. G., & King, N. J. (1994). Panic in children and adolescents: A review. *Journal of Child Psychology and Psychiatry, 35,* 113–134.

Ollendick, T. H., & Mayer, J. A. (1984). School phobia. In S. M. Turner (Ed.), *Behavioral treatment of anxiety disorders.* New York: Plenum.

Ollendick, T. M., & Prinz, R. J. (Eds.), (1995). *Advances in clinical child psychology. Vol. 17.* New York: Plenum Press.

Olweus, D. (1979). Stability of aggressive reaction patterns in males: A review. *Psychological Bulletin, 86,* 852–875.

Olweus, D. (1993). *Bullying at school: What we know and what we can do.* Cambridge, MA: Blackwell.

Olweus, D. (1994). Bullying at school: Basic facts and effects of a school based intervention program. *Journal of Child Psychology and Psychiatry, 35,* 1171–1190.

Orleans, C. T., & Barnett, L. R. (1984). Bulimarexia: Guidelines for behavioral assessment and treatment. In R. C. Hawkins, W. J. Fremouw, & P. F. Clement (Eds.), *The binge-purge syndrome: Diagnosis, treatment, and research.* New York: Springer.

Ornitz, E. M. (1985). Neurophysiology of infantile autism. *Journal of the American Academy of Child Psychiatry, 24,* 251–262.

Ornitz, E. M., & Ritvo, E. R. (1968). Perceptual inconstancy in early infantile autism. *Archives of General Psychiatry, 18,* 76–98.

Orris, J. B. (1969). Visual monitoring performance in three subgroups of male delinquents. *Journal of Abnormal Psychology, 74,* 227–229.

Orton, S. T. (1937). *Reading, writing, and speech problems in children.* New York: W. W. Norton and Co.

Orvaschel, H., Ambrosini, P., & Rabinovich, H. (1993). Diagnostic issues in child assessment. In T. H. Ollendick & M. Hersen (Eds.), *Handbook of child and adolescent assessment.* Boston: Allyn and Bacon.

Orvaschel, H., Walsh-Allis, G., & Ye, W. (1988). Psychopathology in children of parents with recurrent depression. *Journal of Abnormal Child Psychology, 16,* 17–28.

Osborne, A. G. (1992). Legal standards for an appropriate education in the post-Rowley era. *Exceptional Child, 58,* 488–494.

Oshima-Takane, Y., & Benaroya, S. (1989). An alternative view of pronominal errors in autistic children. *Journal of Autism and Developmental Disorders, 19,* 73–85.

Öst, L. (1987). Age of onset in different phobias. *Journal of Abnormal Psychology, 96,* 123–145.

Osterhaus, S. O. L., Passchier, J., vander Helm-Hylkema, H., de Jong, K. T., Orlebeke, J. F., de Grauw, A. J. C., & Dekker, P. H. (1993). Effects of behavioral psychophysiological treatment on school children with migraine in a nonclinical setting: Predictors and process variables. *Journal of Pediatric Psychology, 18,* 697–715.

Ozonoff, S., Pennington, B. F., & Rogers, S. J. (1991). Executive functions deficits in high-functioning autistic individuals: relationship to theory of mind. *Journal of Child Psychology and Psychiatry, 32,* 1081–1105.

Page, P., Verstraete, D. G., Robb, J. R., & Etzwiler, D. D. (1981). Patient recall of self-care recommendations in diabetes. *Diabetes Care, 4,* 95–98.

Palinscar, A. S., & Brown, A. L. (1986). Interactive teaching to promote indepenent learning from text. *The Reading Teacher, 39,* 771–777.

Palinscar, A. S., & Brown, D. A. (1987). Enhancing instructional time through attention to metacognition. *Journal of Learning Disabilities, 20,* 66–75.

Papousek, H., & Papousek, M. (1983). Biological basis of social interactions: Implications of research for an understanding of behavioral deviance. *Journal of Child Psychology and Psychiatry, 24,* 117–129.

Park, K. A., & Waters, E. (1989). Security of attachment and preschool friendships. *Child Development, 60,* 1076–1081.

Parke, R. D., & Ladd, G. W. (1992). *Family-peer relationships: Modes of linkage.* Hillsdale, NJ: Earlbaum.

Parker, J. G., & Asher, S. R. (1987). Peer relations and later personal adjustment: Are low-accepted children at risk? *Psychological Bulletin, 102,* 357–389.

Parks, S. (1983). The assessment of autistic children: A selective review of available instruments. *Journal of Autism and Developmental Disorders, 13,* 255–267.

Parnas, J., Cannon. T. D., Jacobsen, B., Schulsinger, H., Schulsinger, F., & Mednick, S. A. (1993). Lifetime DSM-III-R diagnostic outcomes in the offspring of schizophrenic mothers. *Archives of General Psychiatry, 50,* 707–714.

Parsons, B. V., & Alexander, J. F. (1973). Short-term family intervention: A therapy outcome study. *Journal of Consulting and Clinical Psychology, 41,* 195–201.

Patterson, G. R. (1975). *Families.* Champaign, IL: Research Press.

Patterson, G. R. (1976a). *Living with children: New methods for parents and teachers,* rev. ed. Champaign, IL: Research Press.

Patterson, G. R. (1976b). The aggressive child: Victim and architect of a coercive system. In L. A. Hamerlynck, L. C. Handy, & E. J. Mash (Eds.), *Behavior modification and families.* New York: Brunner/Mazel.

Patterson, G. R. (1977). Naturalistic observation in clinical assessment. *Journal of Abnormal Child Psychology, 5,* 309–322.

Patterson, G. R. (1982). *Coercive family process: A social learning approach,* Vol. 3. Eugene, OR: Castalia.

Patterson, G. R. (1986). Performance models for antisocial boys. *American Psychologist, 41,* 432–444.

Patterson, G. R., Chamberlain, P., & Reid, J. B. (1982). A comparative evaluation of a parent-training program. *Behavior Therapy, 13,* 638–650.

Patterson, G. R., DeBaryshe, B. D., & Ramsey, E. (1989). A developmental perspective on antisocial behavior. *American Psychologist, 44,* 329–335.

Patterson, G. R., Littman, R. A., & Bricker, W. (1967). Assertive behavior in children: A step toward a theory of aggression. *Monographs of the Society for Research in Child Development, 32* (Serial No. 113).

Patterson, G. R., Reid, J. B., & Dishion, T. J. (1992). *Antisocial boys.* Eugene, OR: Castalia Publishing Company.

Patterson, G. R., Reid, J. B., Jones, R. R., & Conger, R. E. (1975). *A social learning approach to family intervention,* Vol. 1. Eugene, OR: Castalia.

Patton, J. R., Beirne-Smith, M., & Payne, J. S. (1990). *Mental retardation.* New York: Macmillan.

Patzer, G. L., & Burke, D. M. (1988). Physical attractiveness and childhood adjustment. In B. B. Lahey & A. E. Kazdin (Eds.), *Advances in clinical child psychology.* New York: Plenum.

Pearl, R., Donahue, M., & Bryan, T. (1986). Social relationships of learning-disabled children. In J. K. Torgesen & B. Y. L. Wong (Eds.), *Psychological and educational perspectives on learning disabilities.* New York: Academic Press.

Pennington, B. F., & Bennetto, L. (1993). Main effects or transactions in the neuropsychology of conduct disorder? Commentary on "The neuropsychology of conduct disorder." *Development and Psychopathology, 5,* 153–164.

Pennington, B. F., Groisser, D., & Welsh, M. C. (1993). Contrasting cognitive deficits in attention deficit hyperactivity disorder versus reading disability. *Developmental Psychology, 29,* 511–523.

Perlman, M. D., & Kaufman, A. S. (1990). Assessment of Child Intelligence. In G. Goldstein & M. Hersen (Eds.), *Handbook of psychological assessment* (2nd ed.). New York: Pergamon.

Perner, J., Frith, U., Leslie, A. M., & Leekam, S. R. (1989). Exploration of the autistic child's theory of mind: Knowledge, belief, and communication. *Child Development, 60,* 689–700.

Perrin, E. C., & Perrin, J. M. (1983). Clinician's assessments of children's understanding of illness. *American Journal of Disease in Children, 137,* 874–878.

Perry, D. G., Perry, L. C., & Rasmussen, P. (1986). Cognitive social learning mediators of aggression. *Child Development, 57,* 700–711.

Perry, D. G., Perry, L. C., & Weiss, R. J. (1989). Sex differences in the consequences that children anticipate for aggression. *Developmental Psychology, 25,* 312–319.

Persson-Blennow, I., & McNeil, T. (1988). Frequencies and stability of temperament types in childhood. *Journal of the American Academy of Child and Adolescent Psychiatry, 27,* 619–622.

Peshkin, M. M. (1959). Intractable asthma of childhood: Rehabilitation at the institutional level with a follow-up of 150 cases. *International Archives of Allergy, 15,* 91–101.

Petersen, G. A. (1982). Cognitive development in infancy. In B. B. Wolman (Ed.), *Handbook of developmental psychology.* Englewood Cliffs, NJ: Prentice Hall.

Peterson, B. S. (1995). Neuroimaging in child and adolescent neuropsychiatric disorders. *Journal of the American Academy of Child and Adolescent Psychiatry, 34,* 1560–1576.

Peterson, L. (1989). Latchkey children's preparation for self-care: Overestimated, underrehearsed, and unsafe. *Journal of Clinical Child Psychology, 18,* 36–43.

Peterson, L. & Bell-Dolan, D. (1995). Treatment outcome research in child psychology: Realistic coping with the "ten commandments of methodology." *Journal of Clinical Child Psychology, 24,* 149–162.

Peterson, L., Farmer, J., Harbeck, C., & Chaney, J. (1990). Preparing children for hospitalization and threatening medical procedures. In A. M. Gross & R. S. Drabman (Eds.), *Handbook of clinical behavioral pediatrics.* New York: Plenum.

Peterson, L., & Magrab, P. (1989). Introduction to the special section: Children on their own. *Journal of Clinical Child Psychology, 18,* 2–7.

Peterson, L. J., & Mori, L. (1988). Preparation for hospitalization. In D. K. Routh (Ed.), *Handbook of pediatric psychology.* New York: Guilford.

Peterson, L., Schultheis, K., Ridley-Johnson, R., Miller, D. J., & Tracy, K. (1984). Comparison of three modeling procedures on the presurgical and postsurgical reactions of children. *Behavior Therapy, 15,* 197–203.

Peterson, L., Zink, M., & Farmer, J. (1993). Prevention of disorders in children. In C. E. Walker & M. C. Roberts (Eds.) *Handbook of clinical child psychology.* New York: Wiley.

Petti, T. A. (1989). Depression. In T. H. Ollendick & M. Hersen (Eds.), *Handbook of child psychopathology,* 2nd ed. New York: Plenum.

Phares, V. (1992). Where's Poppa?: The relative lack of attention to the role of fathers in child and adolescent psychopathology. *American Psychologist, 47,* 656–664.

Phelps, L., Andrea, R., Rizzo, F. G., Johnston, L., & Main, C. M. (1993). Prevalence of self-induced vomiting and laxative-medication abuse among female adolescents: A longitudinal study. *International Journal of Eating Disorders, 14,* 375–378.

Phillips, E. L. (1968). Achievement Place: Token reinforcement procedures in a home-style rehabilitation setting for 'pre-delinquent' boys. *Journal of Applied Behavior Analysis, 1,* 213–223.

Pick, H. L. (1989). Motor development: The control of action. *Developmental Psychology, 25,* 867–870.

Pierce, C. M. (1985). Encopresis. In H. I. Kaplan & B. J. Sadock (Eds.), *Comprehensive textbook of psychiatry/IV.* Baltimore: Williams & Wilkins.

Pierce, J. W. & Wardle, J. (1993). Self-esteem, parental appraisal and body size in children. *Journal of Child Psychology and Psychiatry, 34,* 1125–1136.

Pike, K. M., & Rodin, J. (1991). Mothers, daughters, and disordered eating. *Journal of Abnormal Psychology, 100,* 198–204.

Piotrkowski, C. S., Collins, R. C., Knitzer, J., & Robinson, R. (1994). Strengthening mental health services in Head Start: A challenge for the 1990s. *American Psychologist, 49,* 133–139.

Piven, J., Simon, J., Chase, G., Wzorek, M., Landa, R., Gayle, J., & Folstein, S. (1993). The etiology of autism: Pre-, peri-, and neonatal factors. *Journal of the American Academy of Child and Adolescent Psychiatry, 32,* 1256–1263.

Pless, I. B., Roghmann, K., & Haggerty, R. J. (1972). Chronic illness, family functioning and psychological adjustment: A model for the allocation of preventive mental health services. *International Journal of Epidemiology, 1,* 271–277.

Pliszka, S. R., Maas. J. W., Javors, M. A., Rogeness, G. A., & Baker, J. (1994). Urinary catecholamines in attention-deficit hyperactivity disorder with and without comorbid anxiety. *Journal of the American Academy of Child and Adolescent Psychiatry, 33,* 1165–1173.

Plomin, R. (1994a). *Genetics and experience: The interplay between nature and nurture.* Thousand Oaks, CA: Sage.

Plomin, R. (1994b). Genetic research and identification of environmental influences. *Journal of Child Psychology and Psychiatry, 35,* 817–834.

Plomin, R. (1995). Genetics and children's experiences in the family. *Journal of Child Psychology and Psychiatry, 36,* 33–68.

Plomin, R., Chipuer, H. M., & Neiderhiser, J. M. (1994). Behavioral genetic evidence for the importance of nonshared environment. In E. M. Hetherington, D. Reiss, & R. Plomin, (Eds.) *Separate social worlds of siblings: The impact of nonshared environment on development.* Hillsdale, NJ: Erlbaum.

Plomin, R., DeFries, J. C., & McClearn, G. E. (1990). *Behavioral genetics: A primer,* 2nd ed. New York: W. H. Freeman and Company.

Plomin, R., & Rende, R. (1991). Human behavioral genetics. *Annual review of psychology, 42,* 161–190.

Plomin, R., & Thompson, L. (1988). Life-span developmental behavioral genetics. In P. B. Baltes, D. L. Featherman, & R. M. Lerner (Eds.), *Life-span development and behavior,* Vol. 8, Hillsdale, NJ: Erlbaum.

Poling, A., Gadow, K. D., & Cleary, J. (1991). *Drug therapy for behavior disorders: An introduction.* New York: Pergamon.

Pollitt, E. (1994). Poverty and child development: Relevance of research in developing countries to the U.S. *Child Development, 65,* 283–295.

Pollock, J. I. (1994). Night-waking at five years of age: predictors and prognosis. *Journal of Child Psychology and Psychiatry, 35,* 699–708.

Polloway, E. A., Patten, J. R., Smith, J. D., & Roderique, T. W. (1991). Issues in program design for elementary students with mild retardation: Emphasis on curriculum development. *Education and Training in Mental Retardation, 26,* 144–150.

Pope, A. W., Bierman, K. L., & Mumma, G. H. (1987). Peer relations of hyperactive and aggressive boys. Paper presented at the Annual Meeting of the Society for Behavioral Pediatrics, April 27, Anaheim, CA.

Pope, H. G., Hudson, J. I., Jonas, J. M., & Yurgelun-Todd, D. (1983). Bulimia treated with imipramine: A placebo-controlled double-blind study. *American Journal of Psychiatry, 140,* 554–558.

Porrino, L. J., Rapoport, J. L., Behar, D., Sceery, W., Ismond, D. R., & Bunney, W. E. (1983). A naturalistic assessment of the motor activity of hyperactive boys: I. Comparison with normal controls. *Archives of General Psychiatry, 40,* 681–687.

Porter, J. E., & Rourke, P. B. (1985). Socioemotional functioning of learning-disabled children: A subtype analysis of personality patterns. In P. B. Rouke (Ed.), *Neuropsychology of learning disabilities: Esssentials of subtype analysis.* New York: Guilford.

Potter, H. W. (1933). Schizophrenia in children. *American Journal of Psychiatry, 12,* 1253–1270.

Potter, H. W. (1972). Mental retardation in historical perspective. In S. I. Harrison & J. F. McDermott (Eds.), *Childhood psychopathology.* New York: International Universities Press.

Powers, S. W., Blount, R. L., Bachanas, P. J., Cotter, M. W., & Swan, S. C. (1993). Helping preschool leukemia patients and their parents cope during injections. *Journal of Pediatric Psychology, 18,* 681–695.

Powers, S. W., & Roberts, M. W. (1995). Simulation training with parents of oppositional children: Preliminary findings. *Journal of Clinical Child Psychology, 24,* 89–97.

Poznanski, E. O., & Mokros, H. B. (1994). Phenomenology and epidemiology of mood disorders in children and adolescents. In W. M. Reynolds and H. F. Johnston (Eds.), *Handbook of depression in children and adolescents.* New York: Plenum Press.

Prechtl, H. F. R. (1981). The study of neural development as a perspective of clinical problems. In J. K. Connolly & H. F. R. Prechtl (Eds), *Clinics in developmental medicine No. 77/78. Maturation and development.* Philadelphia: Lippincott.

Pressley, M., & Levin, J. R. (1987). Elaborative learning strategies for the inefficient learner. In S. J. Ceci (Ed.), *Handbook of cognitive, social and neuropsychological aspects of learning disabilities.* Hillsdale, NJ: Erlbaum.

Pring, L., & Hermelin, B. (1993). Bottle, tulip, and wineglass: semantic and structural picture processing by savant artists. *Journal of Child Psychology and Psychiatry, 34,* 1365–1385.

Prinz, R. J., & Riddle, D. B. (1986). Associations between nutrition and behavior in five-year-old children. *Nutrition Reviews, 44*(Suppl.), 151–157.

Prior, M. (1986). Developing concepts of childhood autism: The influence of experimental cognitive research. In S. Chess & A. Thomas (Eds.), *Annual progress in child psychiatry and child development, 1985.* New York: Brunner/Mazel.

Prior, M. (1992). Childhood temperament. *Journal of Child Psychology and Psychiatry, 33,* 249–279.

Prior, M., & Werry, J. S. (1986). Autism, schizophrenia, and allied disorders. In H. C. Quay and J. S. Werry (Eds.), *Psychopathological disorders of childhood.* New York: Wiley.

Prugh, D. G., Staub, E. M., Sands, H. H., Kirschbaum, R. M., & Lenihan, E. A. (1953). A study of the emotional reactions of children and families to hospitalization and illness. *American Journal of Orthopsychiatry, 23,* 70–106.

Public Interest. Self-injury 'consensus' stirs strife, not accord. (1989, June). *APA Monitor.*

Puig-Antich, J. (1983). Neuroendocrine and sleep correlates of prepubertal major depressive disorder: Current status of the evidence. In D. P. Cantwell & G. A. Carlson (Eds.), *Affective disorders in childhood and adolescence: An update.* New York: Spectrum.

Puig-Antich, J. (1986). Psychobiological markers: Effects of age and puberty. In M. Rutter, C. E. Izard, & P. B. Read (Eds.), *Depression in young people: Developmental and clinical perspectives.* New York: Guilford.

Puig-Antich, J., & Chambers, W. (1978). *The Schedule for Affective Disorders and Schizophrenia for School-aged Children.* New York: New York State Psychiatric Institute.

Puig-Antich, J., & Gittelman, R. (1982). Depression in childhood and adolescence. In E. S. Paykel (Ed.), *Handbook of affective disorders.* New York: Guilford.

Puig-Antich, J., Goetz, D., Davies, M., Kaplan, T., Davies, S., Ostrow, L., Asnis, L., Toomey, J., Iyengar, S., & Ryan, N. (1989). A controlled family history study of prepubertal major depressive disorder. *Archives of General Psychiatry, 46,* 406–418.

Puig-Antich, J., Perel, J., Lupatkin, W., Chambers, W. J., Tabrizi, M. A., King, J., Davies, M., Johnson, R., & Stiller, R. (1987). Imipramine in prepubertal major depressive disorders. *Archives of General Psychiatry, 44,* 81–89.

Purcell, K., Brady, K., Chai, H., Muser, J., Molk, L., Gordon, N., & Means, J. (1969). The effect on asthma in children of experimental separation from the family. *Psychosomatic Medicine, 31,* 144–164.

Putallaz, M., & Dunn, S. E. (1990). The importance of peer relations. In M. Lewis & S. M. Miller, *Handbook of developmental psychopathology.* New York: Plenum.

Pynoos, R. S., Frederick, C., Nader, K., Arroyo, W., Steinberg, A., Eth, S., Nunez, F., & Fairbanks, L. (1987). Life threat and posttraumatic stress in school-age children. *Archives of General Psychiatry, 44,* 1057–1063.

Quay, H. C. (1986a). Classification. In H. C. Quay & J. S. Werry (Eds.), *Psychopathological disorders of childhood,* 3rd ed. New York: Wiley.

Quay, H. C. (1986b). Conduct disorders. In H. C. Quay & J. S. Werry (Eds.), *Psychopathological disorders of childhood,* 3rd ed. New York: Wiley.

Quay, H. C. (1993). The psychobiology of undersocialized aggressive conduct disorder: A theoretical perspective. *Development and Psychopathology, 5,* 165–180.

Quay, H. C., LaGreca, A. M. (1986). Disorders of anxiety, withdrawal, and dysphoria. In H. C. Quay & J. S. Werry (Eds.), *Psychopathological disorders of childhood,* 3rd ed. New York: John Wiley & Sons.

Quay, H. C., & Peterson, D. R. (1983). *Interim manual for the Revised Behavior Problem Checklist.* Coral Gables, Fl.: University of Miami.

Quine, L., & Rutter, D. R. (1994). First diagnosis of severe mental and physical disability: A study of doctor-parent communication. *Journal of Child Psychology and Psychiatry, 35,* 1273–1287.

Rachman, S. J. (1977). The conditioning theory of fear-acquisition: A critical examination. *Behaviour Research and Therapy, 15,* 375–387.

Radke-Yarrow, M., & Brown, E. (1993). Resilience and vulnerability in children of multiple-risk families. *Development and Psychopathology, 5,* 581–592.

Rae Grant, N. I. (1991). Primary prevention. In M. Lewis (Ed.). *Child and adolescent psychiatry. A comprehensive textbook.* Baltimore: Williams & Wilkins.

Raine, A., & Venables, P. H. (1984). Tonic heart rate level, social class and antisocial behaviour in adolescents. *Biological Psychology, 18,* 123–132.

Rainer, J. D. (1980). Genetics and psychiatry. In H. I. Kaplan, A. M. Freedman, & B. J. Sadock (Eds.), *Comprehensive textbook of psychiatry/III,* Vol. 3. Baltimore: Williams & Wilkins.

Rait, D. S., Ostroff, J. S., Smith, K., Cella, D. F., Tan, C., & Lesko, L. M. (1992). Lives in a balance—perceived family functioning and the psychosocial adjustment of adolescent cancer survivors. *Family Process, 31,* 383–397.

Ramey, C. T., & Campbell, F. A. (1984). Preventive education for high-risk children: Cognitive consequences of the Carolina Abecedarian Project. *American Journal of Mental Deficiency, 88,* 515–523.

Ramey, C. T., & Campbell, F. A. (1987). The Carolina Abecedarian Project: An educational experiment concerning human malleability. In J. J. Gallagher & C. T. Ramey (Eds.), *The malleability of children.* Baltimore: Paul Brookes.

Rando, T. A. (1983). An investigation of grief and adaptation in parents whose children have died from cancer. *Journal of Pediatric Psychology, 8,* 3–20.

Rapee, R. M., Barrett, P. M., Dadds, M. R., & Evans, L. (1994). Reliability of the DSM-III-R childhood anxiety disorders using structured interview: Interrater and parent-child agreement. *Journal of the American Academy of Child and Adolescent Psychiatry, 33,* 984–992.

Rapoport, J. L. (1989). The biology of obsessions and compulsions. *Scientific American, 260,* 83–89.

Rappaport, J. (1977). *Community psychology: Values, research, and action.* New York: Holt, Rinehart and Winston.

Rapport, M. D. (1993). Attention deficit hyperactivity disorder. In T. H. Ollendick & M. Hersen (Eds.), *Handbook of child and adolescent assessment.* Boston: Allyn and Bacon.

Rauh, V. A., Achenbach, T. M., Nurcombe, B., Howell, C. T., & Teti, D. M. (1988). Minimizing adverse effects of low birthweight: Four-year results of an early intervention program. *Child Development, 59,* 544–553.

Rehm, L. P. (1977). A self-control model of depression. *Behavior Therapy, 8,* 787–804.

Reid, J. B., Kavanagh, K., & Baldwin, D. V. (1987). Abusive parents' perceptions of child problem behaviors: An example of parental bias. *Journal of Abnormal Child Psychology, 15,* 457–466.

Reid, W. J., & Crisafulli, A. (1990). Marital discord and child behavior problems: A meta-analysis. *Journal of Abnormal Child Psychology, 18,* 105–117.

Rekers, G. A., & Lovaas, I. O. (1974). Behavioral treatment of deviant sex role behaviors in a male child. *Journal of Applied Behavior Analysis, 7,* 173–190.

Rende, R. D., Plomin, R., Reiss, D., & Hetherington, E. M. (1993). Genetic and environmental influences on depressive symptomatology in adolescence: Individual differences and extreme scores. *Journal of Child Psychology and Psychiatry, 34,* 1387–1398.

Renne, C. M., & Creer, T. L. (1985). Asthmatic children and their families. In M. Wolraich & D. Routh (Eds.). *Advances in developmental and behavioral pediatrics,* Vol. 6. Greenwich, CT: JAI.

Renouf, A. G., & Kovacs, M. (1994). Concordance between mothers' reports and children's self-reports of depressive symptoms: A longitudinal study. *Journal of the American Academy of Child & Adolescent Psychiatry, 33,* 208–216.

Reschly, D. J. (1992). Mental retardation: Conceptual foundations, definitional criteria, and diagnostic operations. In S. R. Hooper, G. W. Hynd, & R. W. Mattison (Eds.), *Assessment and diagnosis of child and adolescent psychiatric disorders, Vol. II. Developmental disorders.* Hillsdale, NJ: Erlbaum.

Resnick, R. J. (1993). DSM-IV: It is to be but does it help? *Register Report, 19 (2),* 1–6.

Rest, J. (1983). Morality. In J. Flavell & E. Markman (Eds.), *Manual of child psychology: Vol. 3, Cognitive Development.* New York: Wiley.

Rettew, D. C., Swedo, S. E., Leonard, H. L., Lenane, M. C., & Rapoport, J. L. (1992). Obsessions and compulsions across time in 79 children and adolescents with obsessive compulsive disorder. *Journal of the American Academy of Child and Adolescent Psychology, 31,* 1050–1056.

Rey, J. M. (1993). Oppositional defiant disorder. *American Journal of Psychiatry, 150,* 1769–1778.

Reynolds, C. R., & Richmond, B. O. (1978). What I think and feel: A revised measure of children's manifest anxiety. *Journal of Abnormal Child Psychology, 6,* 271–280.

Reynolds, C. R., & Richmond, B. O. (1985). *Revised Children's Manifest Anxiety Scale.* Los Angeles: Western Psychological Service.

Reynolds, W. M. (1987). *Reynolds Adolescent Depression Scale: Professional Manual.* Odessa, FL: Psychological Assessment Resources.

Reynolds, W. M. (1989). *Reynolds Child Depression Scale:* Odessa, FL: Psychological Assessment Resources.

Reynolds, W. M. (1993). Self-report methodology. In T. H. Ollendick & M. Hersen (Eds.), *Handbook of child and adolescent assessment.* Boston: Allyn & Bacon.

Reynolds, W. M. (1994). Assessment of depression in children and adolescents by self-report questionnaires. In W. M. Reynolds and H. F. Johnston (Eds.), *Handbook of depression in children and adolescents.* New York: Plenum Press.

Reynolds, W. M., & Johnston, H. F. (1994). The nature and study of depression in children and adolescents. In W. M. Reynolds and H. F. Johnston (Eds.), *Handbook of depression in children and adolescents.* New York: Plenum Press.

Reynolds, W. M., & Mazza, J. J. (1994). Suicide and suicidal behaviors in children and adolescents. In W. M. Reynolds and H. F. Johnston (Eds.), *Handbook of depression in children and adolescents.* New York: Plenum Press.

Richardson, S. A., Koller, H., & Katz, M. (1985). Relationship of upbringing to later behavior disturbance of mildly mentally retarded young people. *American Journal of Mental Deficiency, 90,* 1 8.

Richman, N. (1985). A double-blind drug trial of treatment in young children with waking problems. *Journal of Child Psychology and Psychiatry, 26,* 591–598.

Richman, N., Douglas, J., Hunt, H., Lansdown, R., & Levere, R. (1985). Behavioural methods in the treatment of sleep disorders—A pilot study. *Journal of Child Psychology and Psychiatry, 26,* 581–590.

Richters, J. E. and colleagues (1995). NIMH collaborative multisite multimodal treatment study of children with ADHD: I. Background and rationale. *Journal of the American Academy of Child and Adolescent Psychiatry, 34,* 987–1000.

Rickard, K. M., Forehand, R., Wells, K. C., Griest, D. L., & McMahon, R. J. (1981). Factors in the referral of children for behavioral treatment: A comparison of mothers of clinic-referred deviant, clinic-referred nondeviant, and nonclinic children. *Behaviour Research and Therapy, 19,* 201–205.

Riddle, M. A., Scahill, L., King, R., Hardin, M. T., Towbin, K. E., Ort, S. I., Leckman, J. F., & Cohen, D. J. (1992). Obsessive compulsive disorder in children and adolescents: Phenomenology and family history. *Journal of the American Academy of Child and Adolescent Psychology, 29,* 766–772.

Rie, H. E. (1971). Historical perspectives of concepts of child psychopathology. In H. E. Rie (Ed.), *Perspectives in child psychopathology.* New York: Aldine-Atherton.

Rieder, R. O., Broman, S. H., & Rosenthal, D. (1977). The offspring of schizophrenics. *Archives of General Psychiatry, 34,* 789–799.

Ritter, D. R. (1989). Social competence and problem behavior of adolescent girls with learning disabilities. *Journal of Learning Disabilities, 22,* 460–461.

Roberts, J. A. M. (1989). Echolalia and comprehension in autistic children. *Journal of Autism and Developmental Disorders, 19,* 271–281.

Roberts, M. C., & Lyman, R. D. (1990). The psychologist as a pediatric consultant: Inpatient and outpatient. In A. M. Gross & R. S. Drabman (Eds.), *Handbook of clinical behavioral pediatrics.* New York: Plenum.

Roberts, M. C. & Wallander, J. L. (1992). Family issues in pediatric psychology: An overview. In M. C. Roberts & J. L. Wallander (Eds.), *Family issues in pediatric psychology.* Hillsdale, NJ: Erlbaum.

Robin, A. L., & Foster, S. L. (1989). *Negotiating parent-adolescent conflict: A behavioral family systems approach.* New York: Guilford.

Robin, A. L., Koepke, T., & Moye, A. (1990). Multidimensional assessment of parent-adolescent relations. *Psychological Assessment, 2,* 451–459.

Robins, L. N. (1978). Sturdy childhood predictors of adult antisocial behavior: Replication from longitudinal studies. *Psychological Medicine, 8,* 611–622.

Robins, L. N., Murphy, G. E., Woodruff, R. A., Jr., & King, L. J. (1971). The adult psychiatric status of black school boys. *Archives of General Psychiatry, 24,* 338–345.

Robins, P. M. (1992). A comparison of behavioral and attentional functioning in children diagnosed as hyperactive or learning disabled. *Journal of Abnormal Child Psychology, 20,* 65–82.

Robinson, E. A. (1985). Coercion theory revisited: Toward a new theoretical perspective on the etiology of conduct disorders. *Clinical Psychology Review, 5,* 597–625.

Robinson, N. M., & Robinson, H. B. (1976). *The mentally retarded child.* New York: McGraw-Hill.

Roff, J. D., & Wirt, R. D. (1984). Childhood aggression and social adjustment as antecedents of delinquency. *Journal of Abnormal Child Psychology, 12,* 111–126.

Roff, M. (1961). Childhood social interactions and young adult bad conduct. *Journal of Abnormal and Social Psychology, 63,* 333–337.

Roff, M., Sells, S., & Golden, M. (1972). *Social adjustment and personality development in children.* Minneapolis: University of Minnesota Press.

Rogers, S. J., Ozonoff, S., & Maslin-Cole, C. (1993). Developmental aspects of attachment behavior in young children with pervasive developmental disorders. *Journal of the American Academy of Child and Adolescent Psychiatry, 32,* 1274–1282.

Rogoff, B., & Morelli, G. (1989). Perspectives on children's development from cultural psychology. *American Psychologist, 44,* 343–348.

Rolf, J., & Read, P. B. (1984). Programs advancing developmental psychopathology. *Child Development, 55,* 8–16.

Rolland-Cachera, M. F., Deheeger, M., Guilloud-Bataille, M., Avons, P., Patois, E., & Sempe, M. (1987). Tracking the development of adiposity from one month of age to adulthood. *Annals of Human Biology, 14,* 219–229.

Rosenthal, D. (1975). Heredity in criminality. *Criminal Justice and Behavior, 2,* 3–21.

Rosenthal, T. L. (1984). Some organizing hints for communicating applied information. In B. Gholson & T. L. Rosenthal (Eds.), *Applications of cognitive-developmental theory.* Orlando, FL: Academic Press.

Roshon, M. S., & Hagen, R. L. (1989). Sugar consumption, locomotion, task orientation, and learning in preschool children. *Journal of Abnormal Child Psychology, 17,* 349–357.

Ross, A. O. (1972). The clinical child psychologist. In B. J. Wolman (Ed.), *Manual of child psychopathology.* New York: McGraw-Hill.

Ross, C. K., Lavigne, J. V., Hayford, J. R., Berry, S. L., Sinacore, J. M., & Pachman, L. M. (1993). Psychological factors affecting reported pain in juvenile rheumatoid arthritis. *Journal of Pediatric Psychology, 18,* 561–573.

Ross, D. M. (1988). Aversive treatment procedures: The school-age child's view. *Newsletter of the Society of Pediatric Psychology, 12,* 3–6.

Rothbart, M. K. (1986). Longitudinal observation of infant temperament. *Developmental Psychology, 22,* 356–365.

Rothblum, E. D., Solomon, L. J., & Albee, G. W. (1986). A sociopolitical perspective of DSM-III. In T. Millon & G. L. Klerman (Eds.), *Contemporary directions in psychopathology: Toward DSM-IV.* New York: Guilford.

Rourke, B. P. (1988). Socioemotional disturbances of learning disabled children. *Journal of Consulting and Clinical Psychology, 56,* 801–810.

Rourke, B. P. (1989). Coles's learning mystique: The good, the bad, and the irrelevant. *Journal of Learning Disabilities, 22,* 275–277.

Rourke, B. P. (1994). Neuropsychological assessment of children with learning disabilities: Measurement issues. In G. R. Lyon (Eds.), *Frames of reference for the assessment of learning disabilities.* Baltimore: Brookes.

Rourke, B. P., Young, G. C., & Leenaars, A. A. (1989). A childhood learning disability that predisposes those afflicted to adolescent and adult depression and suicide risk. *Journal of Learning Disabilities, 22,* 169–175.

Routh, C. P., Hill, J. W., Steele, H., & Dewey, M. E. (1995). Maternal attachment status, psychosocial stressors and problem behaviour: Follow-up after parent training courses for conduct disorder. *Journal of Child Psychology and Psychiatry, 36,* 1179–1198.

Routh, D. K. (1994a). Commentary: Facilitated communication as unwitting ventriloquism. *Journal of Pediatric Psychology, 19,* 673–675.

Routh, D. K. (1994b). Impact of poverty on children, youth, and families: Introduction to the special issue. *Journal of Clinical Child Psychology, 23,* 346–348.

Routh, D. K., Schroeder, C. S., & Koocher, G. P. (1983). Psychology and primary health care for children. *American Psychologist, 38,* 95–98.

Rubin, K. H. (1994). From family to peer group—relations between relationships systems. *Social Development, 3,* iii–viii.

Rubin, K. H., Fein, G. G., & Vandenberg, B. (1983). Play. In P. H. Mussen (Ed.), *Handbook of child psychology: Vol. 4, Socialization, personality, and social behavior.* New York: Wiley.

Rubin, K. H., Stewart, S. L., & Coplan, R. J. (1995). Social withdrawal in childhood. In T. H. Ollendick and R. Prinz (Eds.), *Advances in clinical child psychology,* Vol. 17. New York: Plenum.

Rumsey, J. M., Rapoport, J. L., & Sceery, W. R. (1985). Autistic children as adults: Psychiatric, social, and behavioral outcomes. *Journal of the American Academy of Child Psychiatry, 24,* 465–473.

Russ, S. W. (1995). Play psychotherapy research: State of the science. In T. H. Ollendick & R. J. Prinz (Eds.), *Advances in clinical child psychology. Vol. 17.* New York: Plenum.

Russell, A. T., Bott, L., & Sammons, C. (1989). The phenomenology of schizophrenia occurring in childhood. *Journal of the American Academy of Child and Adolescent Psychiatry, 28,* 399–407.

Russell, G. F. M. (1985). Anorexia and bulimia nervosa. In M. Rutter & L. Hersov (Eds.), *Child and adolescent psychiatry: Modern approaches.* Oxford: Blackwell Scientific Publications.

Russo, D. C., Carr, E. G., & Lovaas, O. I. (1980). Self-injury in pediatric populations. In J. J. Ferguson & C. B. Taylor (Eds.), *The comprehensive handbook of behavioral medicine,* Vol. 3. New York: Spectrum Publications.

Russo, M. F., & Beidel, D. C. (1994). Comorbidity of childhood anxiety and externalizing disorders: Prevalence, associated characteristics, and validation issues. *Clinical Psychology Review, 14,* 199–221.

Russo, M. F., Loeber, R., Lahey, B. B., & Keenan, K. (1994). Oppositional defiant and conduct disorders: Validation of the DSM-III-R and an alternative diagnostic option. *Journal of Clinical Child Psychology, 23,* 56–68.

Rutter, M. (1978). Diagnosis and definition. In M. Rutter and E. Schopler (Eds.), *Autism: A reappraisal of concepts and treatments.* New York: Plenum.

Rutter, M. (1983). School effects on pupils progress: Research findings and policy implications. *Child Development, 54,* 1–29.

Rutter, M. (1985). Infantile autism and other pervasive developmental disorders. In M. Rutter & L. Hersov (Eds.), *Child and adolescent psychiatry.* Boston: Blackwell Scientific Publications.

Rutter, M. (1986a). Child psychiatry: Looking 30 years ahead. *Journal of Child Psychology and Psychiatry, 27,* 803–840.

Rutter, M. (1986b). Depressive feelings, cognitions, and disorders: A research postscript. In M. Rutter, C. E. Izard, & P. B. Read (Eds.), *Depression in young people: Developmental and clinical perspectives.* New York: Guilford.

Rutter, M. (1987). Psychosocial resilience and protective mechanisms. *American Journal of Orthopsychiatry, 57,* 316–331.

Rutter, M. (1989a). Isle of Wight revisited: Twenty-five years of child psychiatric epidemiology. *Journal of the American Academy of Child and Adolescent Psychiatry, 28,* 633–653.

Rutter, M. (1989b). Pathways from childhood to adult life. *Journal of Child Psychology and Psychiatry, 30,* 23–51.

Rutter, M. (1990). Commentary: Some focus and process considerations regarding effects of parental depression on children. *Developmental Psychology, 26,* 60–67.

Rutter, M. (1994). There are connections between brain and mind and it is important that Rett syndrome be classified somewhere. *Journal of Child Psychology and Psychiatry, 35,* 379–381.

Rutter, M., & Cox, A. (1985). Other family influences. In M. Rutter and L. Hersov (Eds.). *Child and adolescent psychiatry*. Boston: Blackwell Scientific Publications.

Rutter, M., Bailey, A., Bolton, P., & Le Couteur, A. (1993). Autism: Syndrome definition and possible genetic mechanisms. In R. Plomin & G. E. McClearn (Eds.), *Nature, nurture & psychology*. Washington DC: American Psychological Association.

Rutter, M., Bailey, A., Bolton, P., & Le Courteur, A. (1994). Autism and known medical conditions: Myth and substance. *Journal of Child Psychology and Psychiatry, 35,* 311–322.

Rutter, M., Bolton, P., Harrington, R., Le Couteur, A., Macdonald, H., & Simonoff, E. (1990a). Genetic factors in child psychiatric disorders—I. A review of research strategies. *Journal of Child Psychology and Psychiatry, 31,* 3–37.

Rutter, M., Garmezy, N. (1983). Developmental psychopathology. In P. H. Mussen (Ed.), *Handbook of child psychology,* Vol. IV. New York: Wiley.

Rutter, M., & Giller, H. (1984). *Juvenile delinquency: Trends and perspectives.* New York: Guilford.

Rutter, M., & Gould, M. (1985). Classification. In M. Rutter & L. Hersov (Eds.), *Child and adolescent psychiatry. Modern approaches.* Oxford: Blackwell Scientific Publications.

Rutter, M., Graham, P., & Yule, W. (1970). *A neuropsychiatric study in childhood.* Clinics in Developmental Medicine, Nos. 35/36. London: Heinemann.

Rutter, M., Izard, C. E., & Read, P. B. (Eds.). (1986). *Depression in young people: Developmental and clinical perspectives.* New York: Guilford.

Rutter, M., Macdonald, H., Le Couteur, A., Harrington, R., Bolton, P., & Baily, A. (1990b). Genetic factors in child psychiatric disorders—II. Empirical Findings. *Journal of Child Psychology and Psychiatry, 31,* 39–83.

Rutter, M., Mayhood, L., & Howlin, P. (1992). Language delay and social development. In P. Fletcher & D. Hall (Eds.), *Specific speech and language disorders in children.* San Diego, CA: Singular Publishing Group.

Rutter, M., and Schopler, E. (1987). Autism and pervasive developmental disorders: Concepts and diagnostic issues. *Journal of Autism and Developmental Disorders, 17,* 159–186.

Rutter, M., Tizard, J., & Whitmore, K. (Eds.). (1970). *Education, health, and behavior.* London: Longmans.

Rutter, M., Tizard J., Yule, W., Graham, P., & Whitmore, K. (1976). Research report: Isle of Wight studies, 1964–74. *Psychological Medicine, 6,* 313–332.

Ryan, N. D., Puig-Antich, J., Ambrosini, P., Ravinovich, H., Robinson, D., Neilson, B., Iyenhar, S., & Toomey, J. (1987). The clinical picture of major depression in children and adolescents. *Archives of General Psychiatry, 44,* 854–861.

Sahley, T. L., & Panksepp, J. (1987). Brain opiods and autism: An updated analysis of possible linkages. *Journal of Autism and Developmental Disorders, 17,* 201–216.

Saler, L., & Skolnick, N. (1992). Childhood parental death and depression in adulthood: Roles of surviving parent and family environment. *American Journal of Orthopsychiatry, 62,* 504–516.

Sameroff, A. J. (1987). Transactional risk factors and prevention. In J. A. Steinberg & M. M. Silverman (Eds.), *Preventing mental disorders.* Washington, DC: Department of Health and Human Services, National Institutes of Mental Health.

Sameroff, A. J. (1990). Neo-environmental perspectives on developmental theory. In R. M. Hodapp, J. A. Burack, & E. Zigler (Eds.), *Issues in the developmental approach to mental retardation.* New York: Cambridge University Press.

Sameroff, A. J., & Chandler, M. J. (1975). Reproductive risk and the continuum of caretaking casualty. In F. D. Horowitz (Ed.), *Review of child development research.* Vol. 4, Chicago: University of Chicago Press.

Sanson, A., Smart, D., Prior, M., & Oberklaid, F. (1993). Precursors of hyperactivity and aggression. *Journal of the American Academy of Child and Adolescent Psychiatry, 32,* 1207–1216.

Santostefano, S. (1978). *A biodevelopmental approach to clinical child psychology.* New York: Wiley-Interscience.

Satterfield, J. H. (1994). Prediction of antisocial behavior in ADHD. Letters to the editor. *Journal of the American Academy of Child and Adolescent Psychiatry, 34,* 398–400.

Satterfield, J. H., Satterfield, B. T., & Schell, A. M. (1987). Therapeutic interventions to prevent delinquency in hyperactive boys. *Journal of the American Academy of Child and Adolescent Psychiatry, 26,* 56–64.

Sattler, J. M. (1988). *Assessment of children,* 3rd ed. San Diego: Jerome M. Sattler, Publisher.

Satz, P., & Fletcher, J. M. (1980). Minimal brain dysfunctions: An appraisal of research concepts and methods. In H. E. Rie and E. D. Rie (Eds.), *Handbook of minimal brain dysfunctions.* New York: John Wiley.

Satz, P., & Fletcher, J. M. (1988). Early identification of learning disabled children: An old problem revisited. *Journal of Consulting and Clinical Psychology, 56,* 824–829.

Saxe, L., Cross, T., & Silverman, N. (1988). Children's mental health. *American Psychologist, 43,* 800–807.

Saylor, C. F., Powell, P., & Swenson, C. (1992). Hurricane Hugo blows down the broccoli: Preschoolers' post-disaster play and adjustment. *Child Psychiatry and Human Development, 22,* 139–149.

Scarr, S. (1982). Testing for children: Assessment and the many determinants of intellectual competence. In S. Chess & A. Thomas (Eds.), *Annual Progress In Child Psychiatry and Child Development 1982.* New York: Brunner/Mazel.

Scarr, S., Phillips, D., & McCartney, K. (1989). Working mothers and their families. *American Psychologist, 44,* 1402–1409.

Scarr, S., Phillips, D., & McCartney, K. (1990). Facts, fantasies, and the future of child care in the United States, *Psychological Science, 1,* 26–35.

Scarr, S., Weinberg, R. A., & Levine, A. (1986). *Understanding development.* San Diego: Harcourt, Brace, Jovanovich.

Schachar, R. (1991). Childhood hyperactivity. *Journal of Child Psychology and Psychiatry, 32, 155–191.*

Schachar, R., & Logan, D. L. (1990). Impulsivity and inhibitory control in normal development and childhood psychopathology. *Developmental Psychology, 26,* 710–720.

Schachar, R., & Tannock, R. (1995). Test of four hypotheses for the comorbidity of attention-deficit hyperactivity disorder and conduct disorder. *Journal of the American Academy of Child and Adolescent Psychiatry, 34,* 639–648.

Schacht, T., & Nathan, P. E. (1977). But is it good for psychologists? Appraisal and status of DSM-III. *American Psychologist, 32,* 1017–1025.

Schafer, L. C., Glasgow, R. E., & McCaul, K. D. (1982). Increasing the adherence of diabetic adolescents. *Journal of Behavioral Medicine, 5,* 353–362.

Schaughency, E., McGee, R., Raja, S. N., Feehan, M., & Silva, P. A. (1994). Self-reported inattention, impulsivity, and hyperactivity at ages 15 and 18 years in the general population. *Journal of the American Academy of Child and Adolescent Psychiatry, 33,* 173–184.

Scheerenberger, R. C. (1982). Public residential services, 1981: Status and trends. *Mental Retardation, 20,* 210–215.

Scheerenberger, R. C. (1983, 1987). *A history of mental retardation.* Baltimore: Brookes Publishing Co.

Schlicker, S. A., Borra, S. T., & Regan, C. (1994). The weight and fitness status of United States children. *Nutrition Reviews, 52,* 11–17.

Schmidt, K., Solanto, M. V., & Bridger, W. H. (1985). Electrodermal activity of undersocialized aggressive children: A pilot study. *Journal of Child Psychology and Psychiatry, 26,* 653–660.

Schneider, B. H. (1992). Didactic methods for enhancing children's peer relations: A quantitative review. *Clinical Psychology Review, 12,* 363–382.

Schneider-Rosen, K., & Rothbaum, F. (1993). Quality of parental caregiving and security of attachment. *Developmental Psychology, 29,* 358–367.

Schopler, E. (1978). Limits of methodological differences in family studies. In M. Rutter & E. Schopler (Eds.), *Autism: A reappraisal of concepts and treatments.* New York: Plenum.

Schopler, E. (1987). Specific and nonspecific factors in the effectiveness of a treatment system. *American Psychologist, 42,* 376–383.

Schopler, E. (1994). Behavioral priorities for autism and related developmental disorders. In E. Schopler & G. B. Mesibov (Eds.), *Behavioral issues in autism.* New York: Plenum.

Schopler, E., & Mesibov, G. B. (Eds.). (1985). *Communication problems in autism.* New York: Plenum.

Schopler, E., Reichler, R. J., DeVellis, R. F., & Daly K. (1980). Toward objective classification of childhood autism: Childhood Autism Rating Scale (CARS). *Journal of Autism and Developmental Disorders, 10,* 91–103.

Schopler, E., Reichler, R. J., & Renner, B. R. (1988). The Childhood Autism Rating Scale (CARS). Los Angeles: Western Psychological Services.

Schopler, E., Short, A., & Mesibov, G. (1989). Relation of behavioral treatment to "normal functioning": Comment on Lovaas. *Journal of Consulting and Clinical Psychology, 57,* 162–164.

Schreibman, L., Koegel, R. L., Mills, D. L., & Burke, J. C. (1984). Training parent-child interactions. In E. Schopler and G. Mesibov (Eds.), *The effects of autism on the family.* New York: Plenum.

Schroeder, C. S. & Gordon, B. N. (1991). *Assessment and treatment of childhood problems: A clinician's guide.* New York: Guilford.

Schroeder, P. (1989). Toward a national family policy. *American Psychologist, 44,* 1410–1413.

Schumaker, J., Deshler, D., Alley, G., Warner, M., & Denton, P. (1984). Multipass: A learning strategy for improving reading comprehension. *Learning Disability Quarterly, 5,* 295–304.

Schumaker, J. B., Deshler, D. D., Ellis, E. S. (1986). Intervention issues related to the education of LD adolescents. In J. K. Torgesen and B. Y. L. Wong (Eds.), *Psychological and educational perspectives on learning disabilities.* New York: Academic Press.

Schwartz, D., Dodge, K. A., & Coie, J. D. (1993). The emergence of chronic peer victimization in boys' play groups. *Child Development, 64,* 1755–1772.

Scott, G. & Richards, M. P. M. (1990). Night waking in infants: Effects of providing advice and support for parents. *Journal of Child Psychology and Psychiatry, 31,* 551–567.

Scott, K. C., & Carran, D. T. (1987). The epidemiology and prevention of mental retardation. *American Psychologist, 42,* 801–804.

Scott, S. (1994). Mental retardation. In M. Rutter, E. Taylor, & L. Hersov (Eds.), *Child and adolescent psychiatry. Modern approaches.* Cambridge, MA: Blackwell.

Sears, R. R. (1975). *Your ancients revisited: A history of child development.* Chicago: University of Chicago Press.

Seidman, E. (1987). Toward a framework for primary prevention research. In J. A. Steinberg & A. A. Silverman (Eds.), *Preventing mental disorders.* Rockville, MD. National Institute of Mental Health.

Seligman, M. P., & Peterson, C. (1986). A learned helplessness perspective on childhood depression: Theory and research. In M. Rutter, C. E. Izard, & P. B. Read (Eds.), *Depression in young people: Developmental and clinical perspectives.* New York: Guilford.

Seligman, R., Gleser, G., Rauh, J., & Harris L. (1974). The effect of earlier parental loss in adolescence. *Archives of General Psychiatry, 31,* 475–479.

Selye, H. (1956). *The stress of life.* New York: McGraw-Hill.

Semrud-Clikeman, M., & Hynd, G. W. (1992). Developmental arithmetic disorder. In S. R. Hooper, G. W. Hynd, & R. E. Mattison (Eds.), *Developmental disorders: Diagnostic criteria and clinical assessment.* Hillsdale, NJ: Erlbaum.

Semrud-Clikeman, M., Filipek, P. A., Biederman, J., Steingard, R., Kennedy, D., Renshaw, P., & Bekken, K. (1994). Attention-deficit hyperactivity disorder: Magnetic resonance imaging morphometric analysis of the corpus callosum. *Journal of the American Academy of Child and Adolescent Psychiatry, 33,* 875–881.

Shaffer, D., Campbell, M., Cantwell, D., Bradley, S., Carlson, G., Cohen, D., Denckla, M., Frances, A., Garfinkel, B., Klein, R., Pincus, H., Spitzer, R. L., Volkmar, F., & Widiger, T. (1989). Child and adolescent psychiatric disorders in DSM-IV: Issues facing the work group. *Journal of the American Academy of Child and Adolescent Psychiatry, 28,* 830–835.

Shaffer, D., Garland, A., Gould, M., Fisher, P., & Trautman, P. (1988). Preventing teenage suicide: A critical review. *Journal of the American Academy of Child and Adolescent Psychiatry, 27,* 675–687.

Shaffer, D., Schwab-Stone, M., Fisher, P., Cohen, P., Piacentini, J., Davies, M., Conners, C. K., & Regier, D. (1993). The Diagnostic Interview for Children—Revised version (DISC-R). I. Preparation, field testing, interrater reliability, and acceptability. *Journal of the American Academy of Child and Adolescent Psychiatry, 32,* 643–650.

Shah, A., & Frith, U. (1993). Why do autistic individuals show superior performance on the block design task? *Journal of Child Psychology and Psychiatry, 34,* 1351–1364.

Shapiro, T., & Esman, A. (1992). Psychoanalysis and child and adolescent psychiatry. *Journal of the American Academy of Child and Adolescent Psychiatry, 31,* 6–13.

Shaw, J. G., Hammer, D., & Leland, H. (1991). Adaptive behavior of preschool children with developmental delays: Parent versus teacher ratings. *Mental Retardation, 29,* 49–53.

Shealy, C. N. (1995). From Boys Town to Oliver Twist: Separating facts from fiction in welfare reform and out-of-home placement of children and youth. *American Psychologist, 50,* 565–580.

Sheldrick, C. (1985). Treatment of delinquents. In M. Rutter & L. Hersov (Eds.), *Child and adolescent psychiatry: Modern approaches,* 2nd ed. Oxford: Blackwell Scientific Publications.

Shields, A. M., Cicchetti, D., & Ryan, R. M. (1994). The development of emotional and behavioral self-regulation and social competence among maltreated school-age children. *Development and Psychopathology, 6,* 57–76.

Shisslak, C. M., Pazda, S. L., & Crago, M. (1990). Body weight and bulimia as discriminators of psychological characteristics among anorexic, bulimic, and obese women. *Journal of Abnormal Psychology, 99,* 380–384.

Shultz, T. R., Wright, K., & Schleifer, M. (1986). Assignment of moral responsibility and punishment. *Child Development, 57,* 177–184.

Siegel, L. S. (1989). IQ is irrelevant to the definition of learning disabilities. *Journal of Learning Disabilities, 22,* 469–478, 486.

Siegel, O. (1982). Personality development in adolescence. In B. B. Wolman (Ed.), *Handbook of developmental psychology.* Englewood Cliffs, NJ: Prentice Hall.

Siegler, R. S. (1992). The other Alfred Binet. *Developmental Psychology, 28,* 179–190.

Siervogel, R. M. (1988). Genetic and familial factors in human obesity. In N. A. Krasnegor, G. D. Grave, & N. Kretchmer (Eds.), *Childhood obesity: A biobehavioral perspective.* Caldwell, NJ: The Telford Press.

Sigman, M., & Mundy, P. (1989). Social attachments in autistic children. *Journal of the American Academy of Child and Adolescent Psychiatry, 28,* 74–81.

Sigman, M., & Ungerer, J. A. (1984). Attachment behaviors in autistic children. *Journal of Autism and Developmental Disorders, 14,* 231–244.

Silva, P. A., Hughes, P., Williams, S., & Faed, J. M. (1988). Blood lead, intelligence, reading attainment, and behaviour in eleven year old children in Dunedin, New Zealand. *Journal of Child Psychology and Psychiatry, 29,* 43–52.

Silver, L. B. (1987). The "magic cure": A review of the current controversial approaches for treating learning disabilities. *Journal of Learning Disabilities, 20,* 498–504.

Silver, L. B. (1989). Learning disabilities. Introduction. *Journal of the American Academy of Child and Adolescent Psychiatry, 28,* 309–313.

Silver, L. B. (1991). Developmental learning disorders. In M. Lewis (Ed.), *Child and adolescent psychiatry: A comprehensive textbook.* Baltimore: Williams & Wilkins.

Silverman, W. K. (1993). DSM and classification of anxiety disorders in children and adults. In C. G. Last (Ed.), *Anxiety across the lifespan: A developmental perspective.* New York: Springer.

Silverman, W. K. (1994). Structured diagnostic interviews. In T. H. Ollendick, N. J. King, & W. Yule (Eds.), *International handbook of phobic and anxiety disorders in children and adolescents* (pp. 293–316). New York: Plenum Press.

Silverman, W. K., & Eisen, A. R. (1992). Age differences in the reliability of parent and child reports of child anxious symptomatology using a structured interview. *Journal of the American Academy of Child and Adolescent Psychiatry, 31,* 117–124.

Silverman, W. K., & Rabian, B. (1994). Specific phobias. In T. H. Ollendick, N. J. King, & W. Yule (Eds.), *International handbook of phobic and anxiety disorders in children and adolescents.* New York: Plenum Press.

Silverstein, A. B. (1982). Note on the constancy of the IQ. *American Journal of Mental Deficiency, 87,* 227–228.

Silverstein, L. B. (1991). Transforming the debate about child care and maternal employment. *American Psychologist, 46,* 1025–1032.

Simon, E. W., Toll, D. M., & Whitehair, P. M. (1994). A naturalistic approach to the validation of facilitated communication. *Journal of Autism and Developmental Disorders, 24,* 647–657.

Siperstein, G. N., & Bak, J. J. (1985). Effects of social behavior on children's attitudes toward their mildly and moderately mentally retarded peers. *American Journal of Mental Deficiency, 90,* 319–327.

Skinner, B. F. (1948). *Walden two.* London: Macmillan.

Skinner, B. F. (1953). *Science and human behavior.* New York: Macmillan.

Skinner, B. F. (1968). *The technology of teaching.* New York: Appleton-Century-Crofts.

Skrzypek, G. J. (1969). Effect of perceptual isolation and arousal on anxiety, complexity preference, and novelty preference in psychopathic and neurotic delinquents. *Journal of Abnormal Psychology, 74,* 321–329.

Slaby, R. G., & Guerra, N. G. (1988). Cognitive mediators of aggression in adolescent offenders: 1. assessment, *Development Psychology, 24,* 580–588.

Slater, A. (1995). Individual differences in infancy and later IQ. *Journal of Child Psychology and Psychiatry, 36,* 69–112.

Slomka, G. T., & Tarter, R. E. (1993). Neuropsychological assessment. In T. H. Ollendick & M. Hersen (Eds.), *Handbook of child and adolescent assessment.* Boston: Allyn & Bacon.

Slomkowski, C., Klein, R., & Mannuzza, S. (1995). Is self-esteem an important outcome in hyperactive children? *Journal of Abnormal Child Psychology, 23,* 303–315.

Sloper, P., Knussen, C., Turner, S., & Cunningham, C. (1991). Factors related to stress and satisfaction with life in families of children with Down's syndrome. *Journal of Child Psychology and Psychiatry, 32,* 655–676.

Smith, G. T., & Goldman, M. S. (1994). Alcohol expectancy theory and the identification of high risk adolescents. *Journal of Research on Adolescence, 4,* 229–248.

Smith, G. T., Goldman, M. S., Greenbaum, P. E., and Christiansen, B. A. (1995). Expectancy for social facilitation from drinking: The divergent paths of high-expectancy and low-expectancy adolescents. *Journal of Abnormal Psychology, 104,* 32–40.

Smith, J. & Prior, M. (1995). Temperament and stress resilience in school-age children: A within-families study. *Journal of the American Academy of Child and Adolescent Psychiatry, 34,* 168–179.

Smith, L., & Hagen, V. (1984). Relationship between the home environment and sensorimotor development of Down Syndrome and nonretarded infants. *American Journal of Mental Deficiency, 89,* 124–132.

Smith, P. K. (1988). Children's play and its role in early development: A re-evaluation of the "play ethos." In A. D. Pellegrini (Ed.), *Psychological bases for early education.* New York: Wiley.

Smith, S. D., Pennington, B. E., Kimberling, W. J., & Ing, P. S. (1990). Familial dyslexia. Use of genetic linkage data to define subtypes. *Journal of the American Academy of Child and Adolescent Psychiatry, 29,* 204–213.

Smith, S. L. (1970). School refusal with anxiety: A review of 60 cases. *Canadian Psychiatric Association Journal, 15,* 257–264.

Smith, T., McEachin, J. J., & Lovaas, O. I. (1993). Comments on replication and evaluation of outcome. *American Journal on Mental Retardation, 96,* 385–391.

Snarey, J. R. (1985). Cross-cultural universality of social-moral development: A critical review of Kohlbergian research. *Psychological Bulletin, 97,* 202–232.

Snow, M. E., Hertzig, M. E., & Shapiro, T. (1987). Rate of development in young autistic children. *Journal of the American Academy of Child and Adolescent Psychiatry, 26,* 834–835.

Snowling, M. J. (1991). Developmental reading disorders. *Journal of Child Psychology and Psychiatry, 32,* 49–77.

Solomon, S. (1985). Neurological evaluation. In H. I. Kaplan & B. J. Sadock (Eds.), *Comprehensive textbook of psychiatry/IV,* 4th ed. Baltimore: Williams & Wilkins.

Sonuga-Barke, E. J. S. (1994). On dysfunction and function in psychological theories of childhood disorder. *Journal of Child Psychology and Psychiatry, 35,* 801–815.

Sonuga-Barke, E. J. S., Houlberg, K., & Hall, M. (1994). When is "impulsiveness" not impulsive? The case of hyperactive children's cognitive style. *Journal of Child Psychology and Psychiatry, 35,* 1247–1253.

Sonuga-Barke, E. J. S., Lamparelli, M., Stevenson, J., Thompson, M, & Henry, A. (1994). Behaviour problems and pre-school intellectual attainment: The associations of hyperactivity and conduct problems. *Journal of Child Psychology and Psychiatry, 35,* 949–960.

Sparrow, S. S., Balla, D., & Cicchetti, D. V. (1984). *Vineland Adaptive Behavior Scales.* Circle Pines, MN: American Guidance Service.

Spence, S. H. (1994). Cognitive therapy with children and adolescents: from theory to practice. *Journal of Child Psychology and Psychiatry, 35,* 1191–1228.

Spirito, A., Stark, L. J., & Tyc, V. L. (1994). Stressors and coping strategies described during hospitalization by chronically ill children. *Journal of Clinical Child Psychology, 23,* 314–322.

Spitz, R. A. (1946). Anaclitic depression. In *The psychoanalytic study of the child,* Vol. 2. New York: International Universities Press.

Spivack, G., & Shure, M. B. (1974). *Social adjustment of young children: A cognitive approach to solving real-life problems.* Washington, DC: Jossey-Bass.

Spock, B. M., & Rothenberg, M. (1992). *Dr. Spock's baby and child care.* New York: Pocket Books.

Spreen, O. (1988). Prognosis of learning disability. *Journal of Consulting and Clinical Psychology, 56,* 836–842.

Sprich-Buckminster, S., Biederman, J., Milberger, S., Faraone. S. V., & Lehman, B. K. (1993). Are perinatal complications relevant to the manifestation of ADD? Issues of comorbidity and familiality. *Journal of the American Academy of Child and Adolescent Psychiatry, 32,* 1032–1037.

Spring, B., Chiodo, J., & Bowen, D. J. (1987). Carbohyrates, tryptophan, and behavior: A methodological review. *Psychological Bulletin, 102,* 234–256.

Sroufe, L. A. (1986). Appraisal: Bowlby's contribution to psychoanalytic theory and developmental psychology; attachment; separation; loss. *Journal of Child Psychology and Psychiatry, 27,* 841–849.

Sroufe, L. A., & Fleeson, J. (1986). Attachment and the construction of relationships. In W. W. Hartup & Z. Rubin (Eds.), *Relationships and development.* Hillsdale, NJ: Erlbaum.

Sroufe, L. A., & Rutter, M. (1980). The domain of developmental psychopathology. *Child Development, 55,* 17–29.

Stahl, A. (1991). Beliefs of Jewish-Oriental mothers regarding children who are mentally retarded. *Education and Training in Mental Retardation, 26,* 361–369.

Stanley, L. (1980). Treatment of ritualistic behavior in an eight-year-old girl by response prevention: A case report. *Journal of Child Psychology and Psychiatry, 21,* 85–90.

Stanovich, K. E. (1986). Cognitive processes and the reading problems of learning-disabled children: Evaluating the assumption of specificity. In J. K. Torgesen and B. Y. L. Wong (Eds.), *Psychological and educational perspectives on learning disabilities.* New York: Academic Press.

Stanovich, K. E. (1989). Learning disabilities in broader context. *Journal of Learning Disabilities, 22,* 287–291, 297.

Stanovich, K. E. (1991). Conceptual and empirical problems with discrepancy definitions of reading disability. *Learning Disability Quarterly, 14,* 269–280.

Stanovich, K. E. (1994). Does dyslexia exist? *Journal of Child Psychology and Psychiatry, 35,* 579–595.

Stark, J. (1992). Presidential Address 1992: A professional and personal perspective on families. *Mental Retardation, 30,* 247–254.

Stark, K. D., Reynolds, W. M., & Kaslow, N. J. (1987). A comparison of the relative efficacy of self-control therapy and a behavioral problem-solving therapy for depression in children. *Journal of Abnormal Child Psychology, 15,* 91–113.

Stark, K. D., Rouse, L. W., & Kurowski, C. (1994). Psychological treatment approaches for depression in children. In W. M. Reynolds & H. F. Johnston (Eds.), *Handbook of depression in children and adolescents.* New York: Plenum Press.

Stattin, H., & Magnusson, D. (1990). *Paths through life: Vol. 2. Pubertal maturation in female development.* Hillsdale, NJ: Erlbaum.

Steffenburg, S., Gillberg, C., Hellgren, L., Andersson, L., Gillberg, I. C., Jakobsson, G., & Bohman, M. (1989). A twin study of autism in Denmark, Finalnd, Iceland, Norway and Sweden. *Journal of Child Psychology and Psychiatry, 30,* 405–416.

Stein, A., Woolley, H., Cooper, S. D., & Fairburn, C. G. (1994). An observational study of mothers with eating disorders and their infants. *Journal of Child Psychology and Psychiatry, 35,* 733–748.

Steinhausen, H. C. (1988). Comparative studies of psychosomatic and chronic diseases among children and adolescents. In E. J. Anthony & C. Chiland (Eds.), *The child in his family,* Vol. 8. New York: Wiley.

Steinhausen, H.-C., Willms, J., & Spohr, H.-L. (1993). Long-term psychopathological and cognitive outcome of children with fetal alcohol syndrome. *Journal of the American Academy of Child and Adolescent Psychiatry, 32,* 990–994.

Stephan, C. W., & Langlois, J. H. (1984). Baby beautiful: Adult attributions of infant competence as a function of infant attractiveness. *Child Development, 55,* 576–585.

Sternberg, K. J., & Lamb, M. E. (1991). Can we ignore context in the definition of child maltreatment? *Development and Psychopathology, 3,* 87–92.

Stevenson, J., & Fredman, G. (1990). The social environmental correlates of reading ability. *Journal of Child Psychology and Psychiatry, 31,* 681–698.

Stevenson, J., Pennington, B. F., Gilger, J. W., DeFries, J. C., & Gillis, J. J. (1993). Hyperactivity and spelling disability: Testing for shared genetic aetiology. *Journal of Child Psychology and Psychiatry, 34,* 1137–1152.

Stewart, R. B., Mobley, L. A., Van Tuyl, S. S., & Salvador, M. A. (1987). The first-born's adjustment to the birth of a sibling: A longitudinal assessment. *Child Development, 58,* 341–355.

Sticc, E. (1994). Review of the evidence for a sociocultural model of bulimia nervosa and an exploration of the mechanisms of action. *Clinical Psychology Review, 14,* 633–661.

Stipek, D., & McCroskey, J. (1989). Investing in children: Government and workplace policies for parents. *American Psychologist, 44,* 416–423.

Stolberg, A. L. (1988). Prevention programs for divorcing families. In L. A. Bond & B. M. Wagner (Eds.), *Families in transition: Primary prevention programs that work. Primary prevention of psychopathology,* Vol. XI. Beverly Hills, CA: Sage.

Stolberg, A. L., & Bush, J. P. (1985). A path analysis of factors predicting children's divorce adjustment. *Journal of Clinical Child Psychology, 14,* 49–54.

Stolberg, A. L., & Garrison, K. M. (1985). Evaluating a primary prevention program for children of divorce: The Divorce Adjustment Project. *American Journal of Community Psychology, 13,* 111–124.

Stone, W. L., & LaGreca, A. M. (1990). The social status of children with learning disabilities. A reexamination. *Journal of Learning Disabilities, 23,* 23–37.

Stormont-Spurgin, M., & Zentall, S. S. (1995). Contributing factors in the manifestation of aggression in preschoolers with hyperactivity. *Journal of Child Psychology and Psychiatry, 36,* 491–509.

Stothard, S. E., & Hulme, C. (1995). A comparison of phonological skills in children with reading comprehension difficulties and children with decoding difficulties. *Journal of Child Psychology and Psychiatry, 36,* 399–408.

Strauss, A., & Corbin, J. (1990). *Basics of qualitative research.* Newbury Park, CA: Sage.

Strauss, A. A., & Kephart, N. C. (1955). *Psychopathology and education of the brain-injured child,* Vol. II. New York: Grune & Stratton.

Strauss, A. A., & Lehtinen, L. (1947). *Psychopathology and education of the brain-injured child.* New York: Grune & Stratton.

Strauss, C. C. (1988). Social deficits of children with internalizing disorders. In B. B. Lahey & A. E. Kazdin (Eds.), *Advances in clinical child psychology,* Vol. 11, New York: Plenum.

Strauss, C. C. (1994). Overanxious disorder. In T. H. Ollendick, N. J. King, & W. Yule (Eds.), *International handbook of phobic and anxiety disorders in children and adolescents.* New York: Plenum Press.

Strauss, C. C., Lease, C. A., Last, C. G., & Francis, G. (1988). Overanxious disorder: An examination of developmental differences. *Journal of Abnormal Child Psychology, 16,* 433–443.

Strauss, C. C., Smith, K., Frame, C., & Forehand, R. (1985). Personal and interpersonal characteristics associated with childhood obesity. *Journal of Pediatric Psychology, 10,* 337–343.

Strean, H. S. (1970). *New approaches in child guidance.* Metuchen, NJ: The Scarecrow Press.

Streissguth, A. P., Barr, H. M., Sampson, P. D., Darby, B. L., & Martin, D. C. (1989). IQ at age 4 in relation to maternal alcohol use and smoking during pregnancy. *Developmental Psychology, 25,* 3–11.

Streissguth, A. P., Martin, D. C., Barr, H. M., Sandman, B. M., Kirchner, G. L., & Darby, D. L. (1984). Intrauterine alcohol and nicotine exposure: Attention and reaction time in 4-year-old children. *Developmental Psychology, 20,* 533–541.

Striegel-Moore, R. H., & Kearney-Cooke, A. (1994). Exploring parents' attitudes and behaviors about their children's physical appearance. *International Journal of Eating Disorders, 15,* 377–385.

Strober, M., & Humphrey, L. (1987). Familial contributions to the etiology and course of anorexia nervosa and bulimia. *Journal of Consulting and Clinical Psychology, 55,* 654–659.

Strober, M., & Katz, J. L. (1987). Do eating disorders and affective disorders share a common etiology? *International Journal of Eating Disorders, 6,* 171–180.

Susman, E. J. (1993). Psychological, contextual, and psychobiological interactions: A developmental perspective on conduct disorder. *Development and Psychopathology, 5,* 181–189.

Swanson, H. L. (1991). Operational definitions and learning disabilities: An overview. *Learning Disability Quarterly, 14,* 242–254.

Swanson, J. M., McBurnett, K., Christian, D. L., & Wigal, T. (1995). Stimulant medications and the treatment of children with ADHD.

Swedo, S. E., Rapoport, J. L., Cheslow, D. L., Leonard, H. L., Ayoub, E. M., Hosier, D. M., & Wald, E. R. (1989b). High prevalence of obsessive-compulsive symptoms in patients with Sydenhams' Chorea. *American Journal of Psychiatry, 146,* 246–249.

Swedo, S. E., Rapoport, J. L., Leonard, H., Lenane, M., & Cheslow, D. (1989c). Obsessive-compulsive disorder in children and adolescents: Clinical phenomenology of 70 consecutive cases. *Archives of General Psychiatry, 46,* 335–341.

Swedo, S. E., Schapiro, M. B., Grady, C. L., Cheslow, D. L., Leonard, H. L., Kumar, A., Friedland, R., Rapoport, S. I., & Rapoport, J. L. (1989a). Cerebral glucose metabolism in childhood-onset obsessive-compulsive disorder. *Archives of General Psychiatry, 46,* 518–523.

Sylva, K. (1994). School influences on children's development. *Journal of Child Psychology and Psychiatry, 35,* 135–170.

Szatmari, P., & Jones, M. B. (1991). IQ and the genetics of autism. *Journal of Child Psychology and Psychiatry, 32,* 897–908.

Szatmari, P., Jones, M. B., Tuff, L., Bartolucci, G., Fisman, S., & Mahoney, W. (1993). Lack of cognitive impairment in first-degree relatives of children with pervasive developmental disorders. *Journal of the American Academy of Child and Adolescent Psychiatry, 32,* 1264–1273.

Szymanski, L. S. (1980). Individual psychotherapy with retarded persons. In L. S. Szymanski & P. E. Tanguay (Eds.), *Emotional disorders of mentally retarded persons.* Baltimore: University Park Press.

Szymanski, L. S., & Crocker, A. C. (1985). Mental retardation. In H. I. Kaplan & B. J. Sadock (Eds.), *Comprehensive textbook of psychiatry/IV.* Baltimore: Williams and Wilkins.

Szymanski, L. S., & Kaplan, L. C. (1991). Mental retardation. In J. M. Wiener (Ed.), *Textbook of child & adolescent psychiatry.* Washington, DC: American Psychiatric Association.

Szymanski, L. S., & Rosefsky, Q. B. (1980). Group psychotherapy with mentally retarded persons. In L. S. Szymanski & P. E. Tanguay (Eds.), *Emotional disorders of mentally retarded persons.* Baltimore: University Park Press.

Tager-Flüsberg, H. (1981). On the nature of linguistic functioning in early infantile autism. *Journal of Autism and Developmental Disorders, 11,* 45–56.

Tager-Flüsberg, H. (1985). Psycholinguistic approaches to language and communication in autism. In E. Schopler and G. B. Mesibov (Eds.), *Communication problems in autism.* New York: Plenum.

Tager-Flüsberg, H. (1993). What language reveals about the understanding of minds in children with autism. In S. Baron-Cohen, H. Tager-Flusberg, & D. J. Cohen (Eds.), *Understanding other minds.* New York: Oxford.

Takanishi, R., & DeLeon, P. H. (1994). A Head Start for the 21st century. *American Psychologist, 49,* 120–122.

Tanner, J. M. (1970). Physical growth. In P. H. Mussen (Ed.), *Carmichael's manual of child development,* Vol. 1. New York: John Wiley.

Tanner, J. M. (1978). *Foetus into man.* Cambridge, MA: Harvard Univ. Press.

Tao, K-T. (1992). Hyperactivity and attention deficit disorder syndrome in China. *Journal of the American Academy of Child and Adolescent Psychiatry, 31,* 1165–1166.

Taras, M. E., & Matese, M. (1990). Acquisition of self-help skills. In J. L. Matson (Ed.), *Handbook of behavior modification with the mentally retarded.* New York: Plenum.

Target, M. and Fonagy, P. (1994). The efficacy of psychoanalysis for children: Prediction of outcome in a developmental context. *Journal of the American Academy of Child and Adolescent Psychiatry, 33,* 1134–1144.

Tarnowski, K. J., & Nay, S. M. (1989). Locus of control in children with learning disabilities and hyperactivity: A subgroup analysis. *Journal of Learning Disabilities, 22,* 381–383.

Tarullo, L. B., DeMulder, E. K., Ronsaville, D. S., Brown, E., & Radke-Yarrow, M. (1995a). Maternal depression and maternal treatment of siblings as predictors of child psychopathology. *Developmental Psychology, 31*, 395–405.

Tarullo, L. B., Richardon, D. T., Radke-Yarrow, M., & Martinez, P. E. (1995b). Multiple sources in child diagnosis: Parent-child concordance in affectively ill and well families. *Journal of Clinical Child Psychology, 24*, 173–183.

Taylor, E. (1994). Syndromes of attention deficit and hyperactivity. In M. Rutter, E. Taylor, & L. Hersov (Eds.), *Child and adolescent psychiatry: Modern approaches.* New York: Blackwell Scientific.

Taylor, H. G. (1988a). Learning disabilities. In E. J. Mash & L. G. Terdal (Eds.), *Behavioral assessment of childhood disorders,* 2nd ed. New York: Guilford.

Taylor, H. G. (1988b). Neuropsychological testing: Relevance for assessing children's learning disabilities. *Journal of Consulting and Clinical Psychology, 56*, 795–800.

Taylor, H. G. (1989). Learning disabilities. In E. J. Mash & R. A. Barkley (Eds.), *Treatment of childhood disorders.* New York: Guilford.

Taylor, H. G., & Fletcher, J. M. (1990). Neuropsychological assessment of children. In G. Goldstein & M. Hersen (Eds.), *Handbook of psychological assessment* (2nd ed.). New York: Pergamon.

Tennant, C. (1988). Parental loss in childhood: Its effects in adult life. *Archives of General Psychiatry, 45*, 1045–1050.

Teodori, J. B. (1993). Neurological assessment. In T. H. Ollendick & M. Hersen (Eds.), *Handbook of child and adolescent assessment.* Boston: Allyn & Bacon.

Terr, L. (1979). Children of Chowchilla. *The Psychoanalytic Study of the Child, 34*, 522–563.

Terr, L. (1983). Chowchilla revisited: The effects of psychic trauma four years after a school-bus kidnapping. *American Journal of Psychiatry, 140*, 1543–1550.

Tesman, J. R., & Hills, A. (1994). Developmental effects of lead exposure in children. *Social Policy Report. Society for Research in Child Development, VIII (3)*, 1–16.

Teti, D. M., Messinger, D. S., Gelfand, D. M., & Isabella, R. (1995). Maternal depression and the quality of early attachment: An examination of infants, preschoolers, and their mothers. *Developmental Psychology, 31*, 364–376.

Thapar, A., Gottesman, I. I., Owen, M. J., O'Donovan, M., & McGuffin, P. (1994). The genetics of mental retardation. *British Journal of Psychiatry, 164*, 747–758.

Thapar, A., & McGuffin, P. (1995). Are anxiety symptoms in childhood heritable? *Journal of Child Psychology and Psychiatry, 36*, 439–447.

Thatcher, R. W. (1994). Psychopathology of early frontal lobe damage: Dependence on cycles of development. *Development and Psychopathology, 6*, 565–596.

Thelen, E. (1986). Treadmill-elicited stepping in seven-month-old infants. *Child Development, 57*, 1498–1506.

Thelen, E., & Adolph, K. E. (1992). Arnold L. Gessell: The paradox of nature and nurture. *Developmental Psychology, 28*, 368–380.

Thelen, E., Skala, K. D., & Kelso, J. A. S. (1987). The dynamic nature of early coordination: Evidence from bilateral leg movements in young infants. *Developmental Psychology, 23*, 179–186.

Thelen, M. H., Powell, A. L., Lawrence, C., & Kuhnert, M. E. (1992). Eating and body image concerns among children. *Journal of Consulting and Clinical Psychology, 21*, 41–46.

Thienemann, M. & Steiner, H. (1993). Family environment of eating disordered and depressed adolescents. *International Journal of Eating Disorders, 14*, 43–48.

Thompson, J. R., & McEvoy, M. A. (1992). Letters to the editor. Normalization—still relevant today. *Journal of Autism and Developmental Disorders, 22*, 666–671.

Thompson, R. A., Connell, J. P., & Bridges, L. J. (1988). Temperament, emotion, and social interactive behavior in the Strage Situation: A component analysis of attachment system functioning. *Child Development, 59*, 1002–1010.

Thompson, R. J. Jr., Gustafson, K. E., George, L. K., & Spock, A. (1994). Change over a 12-month period in the psychological adjustment of children and adolescents with cystic fibrosis. *Journal of Pediatric Psychology, 19*, 189–203.

Thompson, R. J., & Kronenberger, W. (1990). Behavior problems in children with learning problems. In H. L. Swanson & B. Keogh (Eds.), *Learning disabilities. Theoretical and research issues.* Hillsdale, NJ: Erlbaum.

Thomson, G. O. B., Raab, G. M., Hepburn, W. S., Hunter, R., Fulton, M., & Laxen, D. P. H. (1989). Blood-lead levels and children's behaviour—results from the Edinburgh Lead Study. *Journal of Child Psychology and Psychiatry, 30*, 515–528.

Thorndike, E. L. (1905). *The elements of psychology.* New York: Seiler.

Thorndike, R. L., Hagen, E. P., & Sattler, J. M. (1986). *Stanford-Binet Intelligence Scale,* 4th ed. Chicago: Riverside.

Tienari, P., Lahti, I., Sorri, A., Naarala, M., Moring, J., Kaleva, M., Wahlberg, K-E., & Wynne, L. C. (1990). Adopted-away offspring of schizophrenics and controls: The Finnish adoptive family study of schizophrenia. In L. N. Robins & M. Rutter (Eds.), *Straight and devious pathways from childhood to adulthood.* New York: Cambridge University Press.

Timko, C., Baumgartner, M., Moos, R. H., & Miller, J. III (1993). Parental risk and resistance factors among children with juvenile rheumatic disease: A four-year predictive study. *Journal of Behavioral Medicine, 16*, 571–588.

Timko, C., Stovel, K. W., Moos, R. H., & Miller, J. J. (1992). A longitudinal study of risk and resistance factors among children with juvenile rheumatic disease. *Journal of Clinical Child Psychology, 21*, 132–142.

Tolan, P. H. (1987). Implication of age of onset for delinquency risk. *Journal of Abnormal Child Psychology, 15*, 47–65.

Tolan, P. H., & Guerra, N. G. (1994). Prevention of delinquency: Current status and issues. *Applied & Preventive Psychology, 3*, 251–273.

Tolan, P. H., & Thomas, P. (1995). The implications of age of onset for delinquency risk II: Longitudinal data. *Journal of Abnormal Child Psychology, 23*, 157–181.

Tonge, B. (1994). Separation anxiety disorder. In T. H. Ollendick, N. J. King, & W. Yule (Eds.), *International handbook of phobic and anxiety disorders in children and adolescents.* New York: Plenum Press.

Torgersen, S. (1993). Relationship between adult and childhood anxiety disorders: Genetic hypothesis. In C. G. Last (Ed.), *Anxiety across the lifespan: A developmental perspective.* New York: Springer.

Torgesen, J. K. (1986). Learning disabilities theory: Its current state and future prospects. *Journal of Learning Disabilities, 19*, 399–407.

Toro, P. A., Weissberg, R. P., Guare, J., & Liebenstein, N. L. (1990). A comparison of children with and without learning disabilities on social problem-solving skill, school behavior, and family background. *Journal of Learning Disabilities, 23*, 115–120.

Treffert, D. A. (1988). The idiot savant: A review of the syndrome. *American Journal of Psychiatry, 145*, 563–572.

Trickett, P. K., McBride-Chang, C., & Putnam, F. W. (1994). The classroom performance and behavior of sexually abused females. *Development and Psychopathology, 6,* 183–194.

Tryphonas, H. (1979). Factors possibly implicated in hyperactivity. In R. L. Trites (Ed.), *Hyperactivity in children.* Baltimore: University Park Press.

Tsai, L. Y. & Ghaziuddin, M. (1991). Autistic disorder. In J. M. Wiener (Ed.), *Textbook of child & adolescent psychiatry.* Washington, DC: American Psychiatric Press.

Tsuang, M. T. (1993). From DSM-III-R to DSM-IV: Some reflections on process and method. *Harvard Review of Psychiatry, 1,* 126–128.

Tuddenham, R. D. (1962). The nature and measurement of intelligence. In L. Postman (Ed.), *Psychology in the making.* New York: Knopf.

Tuma, J. M. (1982). Pediatric psychology: Conceptualization and definition. In J. M. Tuma (Ed.), *Handbook for the practice of pediatric psychology.* New York: Wiley.

Tuma, J. M. (1989). Mental health services for children: The state of the art. *American Psychologist, 44,* 188–199.

Tuma, J. M., & Pratt, J. M. (1982). Clinical child psychology practice and training: A survey. *Journal of Clinical Child Psychology, 11,* 27–34.

Turkington, C. (1992, Dec.). Ruling opens door—a crack—to IQ-testing some black kids. *The APA Monitor, 23,* 28–29.

Turnure, J. E. (1985). Communication and cues in the functional cognition of the mentally retarded. In N. R. Ellis & N. W. Bray (Eds.), *International Review of Research in Mental Retardation, Vol. 13.* New York: Academic Press.

Twardosz, S., & Nordquist, V. M. (1987). Parent training. In M. Hersen & V. B. Van-Hasselt (Eds.), *Behavior therapy with children and adolescents: A clinical approach.* New York: Wiley.

Tyson, R. L. (1986). The roots of psychopathology and our theories of development. *Journal of the American Academy of Child Psychiatry, 25,* 12–22.

Udwin, O. (1993). Annotation: Children's reactions to traumatic events. *Journal of Child Psychology and Psychiatry, 34,* 115–127.

UNICEF (1991). *The girl child.* NY: United Nations Children's Fund Programme Publications.

Ullmann, C. A. (1957). Teachers, peers, and tests as predictors of adjustment. *Journal of Educational Psychology, 48,* 257–267.

Ullmann, L. P., & Krasner, L. (1975). *A psychological approach to abnormal behavior,* 2nd ed. Englewood Cliffs, NJ: Prentice Hall.

U.S. Bureau of the Census (1994). *Statistical Abstract of the United States: 1994* (114th edition). Washington, DC: U.S. Government Printing Office.

U.S. Department of Education, Office of Special Education Programs, 16th Annual Report to Congress, 1994.

U.S. Department of Health and Human Services (1979). *Lasting effects after preschool.* Washington, D.C.: Superintendent of Documents. U.S. Government Printing Office.

U.S. Office of Education. (1977). Definition and criteria for defining students as learning disabled. Federal Register, 42:250, p. 65083. Washington, DC: U.S. Government Printing Office.

Valla, J. P., Bergeron, L., Gaudet, N., Reydellet, C., & Harris, T. O. (1994). An empirical comparison between the DSM and psychodynamic approaches for assessment of child disorders in children attending outpatient clinics. *Journal of Child Psychology and Psychiatry, 35,* 1409–1418.

Valone, K., Goldstein, M. J., & Norton, J. P. (1984). Parental expressed emotion and psychophysiological reactivity in an adolescent sample at risk for schizophrenia spectrum disorder. *Journal of Abnormal Psychology, 93,* 448–457.

van Balkom, A. J. L. M., van Oppen, P., Vermeulen, A. W. A., van Dyck, R., Nauta, M. C. E., & Vorst, H. C. M. (1994). A metaanalysis on the treatment of obsessive compulsive disorder: A comparison of antidepressants, behavior, and cognitive therapy. *Clinical Psychology Review, 14,* 359–381.

van der Meere, J., & Sergeant, J. (1988). Focused attention in pervasively hyperactive children. *Journal of Abnormal Child Psychology, 16,* 627–639.

van der Meere, J., Wekking, E., & Sergeant, J. (1991). Sustained attention and pervasive hyperactivity. *Journal of Child Psychology and Psychiatry, 32,* 275–284.

Van Dyke, D. C., & Fox, A. A. (1990). Fetal drug exposure and its possible implications for learning in the preschool and school-age population. *Journal of Learning Disabilities, 23,* 161–163.

Varni, J. W., Katz, E., & Dash, J. (1982). Behavioral and neurochemical aspects of pediatric pain. In D. C. Russo & J. W. Varni (Eds.), *Behavioral pediatrics: Research and practice.* New York: Plenum.

Varni, J. W., Katz, E. R., & Waldron, S. A. (1993). Cognitive-behavioral treatment interventions in childhood cancer. *The Clinical Psychologist, 46,* 192–197.

Varni, J. W., Waldo, G. A., & Wilcox, K. T. (1990). Cognitive-behavioral assessment and treatment of pediatric pain. In A. M. Gross & R. S. Drabman (Eds.), *Handbook of clinical behavioral pediatrics.* New York: Plenum.

Vellutino, F. R. (1979). *Dyslexia. Theory and research.* Cambridge MA: MIT Press.

Vellutino, F. R. (1987). Dyslexia, *Scientific American, 256,* 34–41.

Venter, A., Lord, C., & Schopler, E. (1992). A follow-up study of high-functioning autistic children. *Journal of Child Psychology and Psychiatry, 33,* 489–507.

Verhulst, F. C., & Koot, H. M. (1991). Longitudinal research in child and adolescent psychiatry. *Journal of the American Academy of Child and Adolescent Psychiatry, 30,* 361–368.

Verhulst, F. C., & Koot, H. M. (1992). *Child psychiatric epidemiology.* Newbury Park, CA: Sage.

Verhulst, F. C., & van der Ende, J. (1993). "Comorbidity" in an epidemiological sample: A longitudinal perspective. *Journal of Child Psychology and Psychiatry, 34,* 767–783.

Vernberg, E., Beery, S. H., Ewell, K. K., & Absender, D. A. (1993). Parents' use of friendship facilitation strategies and the formation of friendships in early adolescence: A prospective study. *Journal of Family Psychology, 7,* 356–369.

Vernberg, E. M., & Vogel, J. M. (1993). Interventions with children after disasters. *Journal of Clinical Child Psychology, 22,* 485–498.

Vernick, J., & Karon, M. (1965). Who's afraid of death on a leukemia ward? *American Journal of Diseases of Children, 109,* 393–397.

Vogel, J. M., & Vernberg, E. M. (1993). Children's psychological responses to disasters. *Journal of Clinical Child Psychology, 22,* 464–484.

Volkmar, F. R. (1987). Annotation. Diagnostic issues in the pervasive developmental disorders. *Journal of Child Psychology and Psychiatry, 28,* 365–369.

Volkmar, F. R. (1991). Childhood schizophrenia. In M. Lewis (Ed.), *Child and adolescent psychiatry. A comprehensive textbook.* Baltimore: Williams and Wilkins.

Volkmar, F. R., Carter, A., Sparrow, S. S., & Cicchetti, D. V. (1993). Quantifying social development in autism. *Journal of the American Academy of Child and Adolescent Psychiatry, 32,* 627–632.

Volkmar, F. R., Cicchetti, D. V., Dykens, E., Sparrow, S. S., Leckman, J. F., & Cohen, D. J. (1988). An evaluation of the Autism Behavior Checklist. *Journal of Autism and Developmental Disorders, 18,* 81–97.

Volkmar, F. R., & Cohen, D. J. (1988). Diagnosis of pervasive developmental disorders. In B. B. Lahey & A. E. Kazdin (Eds.), *Advances in clinical child psychology,* Vol. 2, New York: Plenum.

Volkmar, F. R., Sparrow, S. S., Goudreau, D., Cicchetti, D. V., Paul, R., & Cohen, D. J. (1987). Social deficits in autism. An operational approach using the Vineland Adaptive Behavior Scales. *Journal of the American Academy of Child and Adolescent Psychiatry, 26,* 156–161.

Wagner, W. G., Smith D., & Norris, W. R. (1988). The psychological adjustment of enuretic children: A comparison of two types. *Journal of Pediatric Psychology, 13,* 33–38.

Wahler, R. G., & Dumas, J. E. (1984). Changing the observational coding styles of insular and noninsular mothers: A step towards maintenance of parent training effects. In R. F. Dangel & R. A. Polster (Eds.), *Parent training: Foundations of research and practice.* New York: Guilford.

Wahler, R. G., & Dumas, J. E. (1989). Attentional problems in dysfunctional mother-child interactions: An interbehavioral model. *Psychological Bulletin, 105,* 116–130.

Wakefield, J. C. (1992). The concept of mental disorder: On the boundary between biological facts and social values. *American Psychologist, 47,* 373–388.

Waldman, I. D., Lillienfeld, S. O., & Lahey, B. B. (1995). Toward construct validity in the childhood disruptive behavior disorders: Classification and diagnosis in DSM-IV and beyond. In T. H. Ollendick & R. J. Prinz, (Eds.), *Advances in clinical child psychology.* Vol. 17. New York: Plenum Press.

Walker, C. E., Kenning, M., & Faust-Companile, J. (1989). Enuresis and encopresis. In E. J. Mash & R. A. Barkley (Eds.), *Treatment of childhood behavior disorders.* New York: Guilford.

Walker, C. E., Milling, L., & Bonner, B. (1988). Incontinence disorders: Enuresis and encopresis. In D. Routh (Ed.), *Handbook of pediatric psychology.* New York: Guilford.

Walker, H., Greenwood, C., Hops, H., & Todd, N. (1979). Differential effects of reinforcing topographic components of social interaction. *Behavior Modification, 3,* 291–321.

Walker, L. J. (1984). Sex differences in the development of moral reasoning: A critical review. *Child Development, 55,* 677–691.

Walker, L. J. (1986). Sex difference in the development of moral reasoning: A rejoinder to Baumrind. *Child Development, 57,* 522–526.

Wallander, J. L. (1992). Theory-driven research in pediatric psychology: A little bit on why and how. *Journal of Pediatric Psychology, 17,* 521–535.

Wallander, J. L., Feldman, W. S., & Varni, J. W. (1989a). Physical status, and psychosocial adjustment in children with spina bifida. *Journal of Pediatric Psychology, 14,* 89–102.

Wallander, J. L., Varni, J. W., Babani, L., De Haan, C. B., Wilcox, K. T., & Banis, H. T. (1989b). The social environment and the adaptation of mothers of physically handicapped children. *Journal of Pediatric Psychology, 14,* 371–387.

Wallerstein, J. S. (1984). Children of divorce: Preliminary report of a ten-year follow-up of young children. *American Journal of Orthopsychiatry, 54,* 444–458.

Wallerstein, J. S. (1985). Children of divorce: Preliminary report of a 10-year follow-up of older children and adolescents. *Journal of the American Academy of Child Psychiatry, 24,* 538–544.

Wallerstein, J. S. (1991). The long-term effects of divorce on children: A review. *Journal of the American Academy of Child and Adolescent Psychiatry, 30,* 349–360.

Wallerstein, J. S., & Corbin, S. B, (1991). The child and the vicissitudes of divorce. In M. Lewis (Ed.), *Child and adolescent psychiatry. A comprehensive textbook.* Baltimore: Williams and Wilkins.

Wallerstein, J., & Kelly, J. (1980). Effects of divorce on the visiting father-child relationship. *American Journal of Psychiatry, 137*(12), 1534–1539.

Warady, B. A., Alon, U., & Hellerstein, S. (1991). *Pediatric Annals, 20,* 246–255.

Ward, C. H., Beck, A. T., Mendelson, M., Mock, J. E., & Erbaugh, J. K. (1962). The psychiatric nomenclature: Reasons for diagnostic disagreement. *Archives of General Psychiatry, 7,* 198–205.

Warm, J. S., & Berch, D. B. (1985). Sustained attention in the mentally retarded: The vigilance paradigm. In N. R. Ellis & N. W. Bray (Eds.), *International review of research in mental retardation, Vol. 13,* New York: Academic Press.

Watkins, J. M., Asarnow, R. F., & Tanguay, P. E. (1988). Symptom development in childhood onset schizophrenia. *Journal of Child Psychology and Psychiatry, 29,* 865–878.

Watson, J. B. (1913). Psychology as the behaviorist views it. *Psychological Review, 20,* 158–177.

Watson, J. B. (1963). *Behaviorism.* Chicago: University of Chicago Press.

Watson, J. B., & Rayner, R. (1920). Conditioned emotional reactions. *Journal of Experimental Psychology, 3,* 1–14.

Weber, D. O. (1992). Getting the lead out. *The Hanover, 2,* 11–14.

Webster-Stratton, C. (1985a). Predictors of treatment outcome in parent training for conduct-disordered children. *Behavior therapy, 16,* 223–243.

Webster-Stratton, C. (1985b). The effects of father involvement in parent training for conduct problem children. *Journal of Child Psychology and Psychiatry, 26,* 801–810.

Webster-Stratton, C. (1994). Advancing videotape parent training: A comparison study, *Journal of Consulting and Clinical Psychology, 62,* 583–593.

Wechsler, D. (1989). *Wechsler Preschool and Primary Scale of Intelligence—Revised (WPPSI-R).* San Antonio, TX: The Psychological Corporation.

Wechsler, D. (1991). *Manual for the Wechsler Intelligence Scale for Children—Third Edition (WISC-III).* San Antonio, TX: The Psychological Corporation.

Weinberg, R. A. (1989). Intelligence and IQ: Landmark issues and great debates. *American Psychologist, 44,* 98–104.

Weinrott, M. R., Jones, R. R., & Howard, J. R. (1982). Cost-effectiveness of teaching family programs for delinquents: Results of a national evauation. *Evaluation review, 6,* 173–201.

Weintraub, S., Winters, K. C., & Neale, J. M. (1986). Competence and vulnerability in children with an affectively disordered parent. In M. Rutter, C. E. Izard, & P. B. Read (Eds.), *Depression in young people: Developmental and clinical perspectives.* New York: Guilford.

Weiss, B. (1982). Food additives and environmental chemicals as sources of childhood behavior disorders. *Journal of Child Psychiatry, 21,* 144–152.

Weiss, G. (1991). Attention deficit hyperactivity disorder. In M. Lewis (Ed.), *Child and adolescent psychiatry. A comprehensive textbook.* Baltimore: Williams & Wilkins.

Weiss, G., & Hechtman, L. T. (1986). *Hyperactive children grown up.* New York: Guilford.

Weissberg, R. P., Cowen, E. L., Lotyczewski, B. S., & Gesten, E. L. (1983). The primary mental health project: Seven consecutive years of program outcome research. *Journal of Consulting and Clinical Psychology, 51,* 100–107.

Weissman, M. M., Kidd, K. K., & Prusoff, B. A. (1982). Variability in rates of affective disorders in relatives of depressed and normal probands. *Archives of General Psychiatry, 39,* 1397–1403.

Weissman, M. M., Leckman, J. F., Merikangas, K. R., Gammon, D., & Prusoff, B. A. (1984). Depression and anxiety disorders in parents and children. Results from the Yale family study. *Archives of General Psychiatry, 43,* 430–434.

Weissman, M. M., Warner, V., Wichramaratne, P., & Prusoff, B. A. (1988). Onset of major depression in adolescence and early adulthood: Findings from a family study of children. *Journal of Affective Disorders, 15,* 269–277.

Weist, M. D., Finney, J. W., Barnard, M. U., Davis, C. D., & Ollendick, T. H. (1993). Empirical selection of psychosocial treatment targets for children and adolescents with diabetes. *Journal of Pediatric Psychology, 18,* 11–28.

Weisz, J. R., Chaiyasit, W., Weiss, B., Eastman, K. L., & Jackson, E. W. (1995). A multimethod study of problem behavior among Thai and American children in school: Teacher reports versus direct observations. *Child Development, 66,* 402–415.

Weisz, J. R., Suwanlet, S., Chaiyasit, W., Weiss, B., Walter, B., R., & Anderson, W. W. (1988). Thai and American perspectives on over- and undercontrolled child behavior problems: Exploring the threshold model among parents, teachers, and psychologists. *Journal of Consulting and Clinical Psychology, 56,* 601–609.

Weithorn, L. A. (1987). Informed consent for prevention research involving children: Legal and ethical issues. In J. A. Steinberg & M. M. Silverman (Eds.), *Preventing mental disorders.* Rockvill, MD: U.S. Department of Health and Human Services.

Wellman, H. M. (1993). Early understanding of mind: The normal case. In S. Baron-Cohen, H. Tager-Flusberg, & D. J. Cohen (Eds.), *Understanding other minds.* New York: Oxford Press.

Wells, K. (1987). Annotation. Scientific issues in the conduct of case studies. *Journal of Child Psychology and Psychiatry, 28,* 783–790.

Wells, K. C., & Forehand, R. (1985). Conduct and oppositional disorders. In P. H. Bornstein & A. E. Kazdin (Eds.), *Handbook of clinical behavior therapy with children.* Homewood, IL: Dorsey.

Wells, K. C., Forehand, R., & Griest, D. L. (1980). Generality of treatment effects from treated to untreated behaviors resulting from a parent training program. *Journal of Clinical Child Psychology, 9,* 217–219.

Welner, Z., Reich, W., Herjanic, B., Jung, K. G., & Amado, H. (1987). Reliability, validity, and parent-child agreement studies of the Diagnostic Interview for Children and Adolescents (DICA). *Journal of the American Academy of Child and Adolescent Psychiatry, 26,* 649–653.

Weltzin, T., & Kaye, W. (1993). Pharmacological treatment. In V. B. Van Hasselt & M. Hersen (1993). *Handbook of behavior therapy and pharmacotherapy for children: A comparative analysis.* Boston: Allyn & Bacon.

Wender, P. H., Kety, S. S., Rosenthal, D., Schulsinger, F., Ortmann, J., & Lunde, I. (1986). Psychiatric disorders in the biological and adoptive families of adopted individuals with affective disorders. *Archives of General Psychiatry, 43,* 923–929.

Werner, E. E., & Smith, R. S. (1982). *Vulnerable but invincible.* New York: McGraw-Hill.

Werry, J. S. (1968). Studies of the hyperactive child: IV. An empirical analysis of the minimal brain dysfunction syndrome. *Archives of General Psychiatry, 19,* 9–16.

Werry, J. S. (1979a). Organic factors: In H. C. Quay & J. S. Werry (Eds.), *Psychopathological disorders of childhood,* 2nd ed. New York: John Wiley.

Werry, J. S. (1979b). The childhood psychoses. In H. C. Quay & J. S. Werry (Eds.), *Psychopathological disorders of childhood,* 2nd ed. New York: John Wiley.

Werry, J. S. (1986). Physical illness, symptoms and allied disorders. In H. C. Quay & J. S. Werry (Eds.), *Psychopathological disorders of childhood,* 3rd ed. New York: Wiley.

Werry, J. S. (1992). Child and adolescent (early onset) schizophrenia: A review in light of DSM-III-R. *Journal of Autism and Developmental Disorders, 22,* 601–624.

Werry, J. S. (1994). Diagnostic and classification issues. In T. H. Ollendick, N. J. King, & W. Yule (Eds.), *International handbook of phobic and anxiety disorders in children and adolescents.* New York: Plenum.

Wertlieb, D., Hauser, S. T., & Jacobson, A. M. (1986). Adaptation to diabetes: Behavior symptoms and family context. *Journal of Pediatric Psychology, 11,* 463–479.

West, D. J. (1982). *Delinquency: Its roots, careers, and prospects.* London: Heinemann.

West, D. J. (1985). Delinquency. In M. Rutter & L. Hersov (Eds.), *Child and adolescent psychiatry: Modern approaches,* 2nd ed. Oxford: Blackwell Scientific Publications.

West, M. O., & Prinz, R. J. (1987). Parental alcoholism and childhood psychopathology. *Psychological Bulletin, 102,* 204–218.

West, S. G., Sandler, I., Pillow, D. R., Baca, L., & Gersten, J. C. (1991). The use of structural equation modeling in generative research: Toward the design of a preventative intervention for bereaved children. *American Journal of Community Psychology, 19,* 459–480.

Whalen, C. K. (1989). Attention deficit and hyperactivity disorders. In T. H. Ollendick & M. Hersen (Eds.), *Handbook of child psychopathology.* New York: Plenum.

Whalen, C. K., & Henker, B. (1985). The social worlds of hyperactive (ADDH) children. *Clinical Psychology Review, 5,* 447–448.

Whalen, C. K., Henker, B., Buhrmester, D., Hinshaw, S. P., Huber A., & Laski, K. (1989). Does stimulant medication improve the peeer status of hyperactive childen? *Journal of Consulting and Clinical Psychology, 57,* 545–549.

Whalen, C. K., Henker, B., & Hinshaw, S. P. (1985). Cognitive-behavioral therapies for hyperactive children: Premises, problems, and prospects. *Journal of Abnormal Child Psychology, 13,* 391–409.

Whitaker, A., Johnson, J., Shaffer, D., Rappoport, J., Kalikow, K., Walsh, B. T., Davies, M., Braiman, S., & Dolinsky, A. (1990). Uncommon troubles in young people: Prevalence estimates of selected psychiatric disorders in a nonreferred adolescent population. *Archives of General Psychiatry, 47,* 487–496.

White, D. M., & Sprague, R. L. (1992). The "attention deficit" in children with attention-deficit hyperactivity disorder. In B. B. Lahey & A. E. Kazdin (Eds.), *Advances in clinical child psychology.* Vol. 14. New York: Plenum.

White, J. L., Moffitt, T. E., & Silva, P. A. (1989). A prospective replication of the protective effects of IQ in subjects at high risk for juvenile delinquency. *Journal of Consulting and Clinical Psychology, 57,* 719–724.

White, K. J., & Kistner, J. (1992). The influence of teacher feedback on young children's peer preferences and perceptions. *Developmental Psychology, 28,* 933–940.

White, S. H. (1992). G. Stanley Hall: From philosophy to developmental psychology. *Developmental Psychology, 28,* 25–34.

Whitehill, M., DeMyer-Gapin, S., & Scott, T. J. (1976). Stimulation-seeking in antisocial pre-adolescent children. *Journal of Abnormal Psychology, 85,* 101–104.

Whitehurst, G. J. (1982). Language development. In B. B. Wolman (Ed.), *Handbook of developmental psychology.* Englewood Cliffs, NJ: Prentice Hall.

Whitehurst, G. J., & Fischel, J. E. (1994). Early developmental language delay: What, if anything, should the clinician do about it? *Journal of Child Psychology and Psychiatry, 35,* 613–648.

Whitehurst, G. J., & Valdez-Menchaca, M. C. (1988). What is the role of reinforcement in early language acquisition? *Child Development, 59,* 430–440.

Whitman, T. L., Hantula, D. A., & Spence, B. H. (1990). Current issues in behavior modification with mentally retarded persons. In J. L. Matson (Ed.), *Handbook of behavior modification with the mentally retarded.* New York: Plenum.

Widiger, T. A., Frances, A. J., Pincus, H. A., Davis, W. W., & First, M. B. (1991). Toward an empirical classification for DSM-IV. *Journal of Abnormal Psychology, 100,* 280–288.

Wiebe, D. J., Alderfer, M. A., Palmer, S. C., Lindsay, R., & Jarrett, L. (1994). Behavioral self-regulation in adolescents with type I diabetes: Negative affectivity and blood glucose symptom perception. *Journal of Consulting and Clinical Psychology, 62,* 1204–1212.

Williams, C. D. (1959). The elimination of tantrum behavior by extinction procedures: Case report. *Journal of Abnormal and Social Psychology, 59,* 269.

Williams, L. (1988, Jan. 15). Parents and doctors fear growing misuse of drug used to treat hyperactive kids. *Wall Street Journal,* 21.

Williamson, D. A., Baker, J. D., & Cubic, B. A. (1993). Advances in pediatric headache research. In T. H. Ollendick & R. J. Prinz (Eds.) *Advances in clinical child psycholog.* Vol. 15. New York: Plenum Press.

Williamson, D. A., Head, S. B., & Baker, J. D. (1993). Behavioral treatment. In V. B. Van Hassel & M. Hersen (Eds.), *Handbook of behavior therapy and pharmacotherapy for children: A comparative analysis.* Boston: Allyn and Bacon.

Willner, A. C., Braukmann, G. J., Kirigin, K. A., & Wolf, M. M. (1978). Achievement Place: A community model for youths in trouble. In D. Marholin (Ed.), *Child behavior therapy.* New York: Gardner.

Wilsher, C. (1991). Is medicinal treatment of dyslexia advisable? In M. Snowling & M. Thomson (Eds.), *Dyslexia: Integrating theory and practice.* London: Whurr Publishers.

Wilson, C. C., & Haynes, S. N. (1985). Sleep disorders. In P. H. Bornstein & A. E. Kazdin (Eds.), *Handbook of clinical behavior therapy with children.* Homewood, IL: Dorsey.

Wilson, G. T. (1993). Psychological and pharmacological treatments of bulimia nervosa: A research update. *Applied and Preventive Psychology, 2,* 35–42.

Wilson, G. T., Eldredge, K. L., Smith, D., & Niles, B. (1991). Cognitive-behavioral treatment with and without response prevention for bulimia. *Behaviour Research and Therapy, 29,* 575–583.

Wilson, G. T., & Fairburn, C. G. (1993). Cognitive treatments for eating disorders. *Journal of Consulting and Clinical Psychology, 61,* 261–269.

Wilson, G. T., & Walsh, B. T. (1991). Eating disorders in the DSM-IV. *Journal of Abnormal Psychology, 100,* 362–365.

Wilson, R. S., & Matheny, A. P. (1986). Behavior-genetics research in infant temperament: The Louisville Twin Study. In R. Plomin & J. Dunn (Eds.), *The study of temperament: Changes, continuities and challenges.* Hillsdale, NJ: Erlbaum.

Wilson, S. R., Mitchell, J. H., Rolnick, S. & Fish, L. (1993). Effective and ineffective management behaviors of parents of infants and young children with asthma. *Journal of Pediatric Psychology, 18,* 63–81.

Windle, M. (1990). A longitudinal study of antisocial behaviors in early adolescence as predictors of late adolescent substance use: Gender and ethnic group differences. *Journal of Abnormal Psychology, 99,* 86–91.

Winett, R. A. (1995). A framework for health promotion and disease prevention programs. *American Psychologist, 50,* 341–350.

Wolchik, S. A., West, S. G., Westover, S., Sandler, I. N., Martin, A., Lustig, J., Tein, J., & Fisher, J. (1993). The children of divorce parenting intervention: Outcome evaluation of an empirically based program. *American Journal of Community Psychology, 21,* 293–331.

Wolf, M. M., Braukmann, C. J., & Ramp, K. A. (1987). Serious delinquent behavior as part of a significantly handicapping condition: Cures and supportive environments. *Journal of Applied Behavior Analysis, 20,* 347–359.

Wolfe, B. E. (1979). Behavioral treatment of childhood gender disorders. *Behavior Modification, 4,* 550–575.

Wolfe, D. A. (1988). Child abuse and neglect. In E. J. Mash & L. G. Terdal (Eds.), *Behavioral assessment of childhood disorders,* 2nd ed. New York: Guilford.

Wolfe, D. A., & St. Pierre, J. (1989). Child abuse and neglect. In T. H. Ollendick & M. Hersen (Eds.), *Handbook of child psychopathology,* 2nd ed. New York: Plenum.

Wolfe, P. H. (1981). Normal variations in human maturation. In K. J. Connolly & H. F. R. Prechtl (Eds.), *Clinics in developmental medicine No. 77/78. Maturation and development.* Philadelphia: Lippincott.

Wolfe, V. V., & Birt, J. (1995). The psychological sequelae of child sexual abuse. In T. H. Ollendick & R. J. Prinz (Eds.), *Advances in clinical child psychology.* Vol. 17. New York: Plenum Press.

Wolfe, V. V., & Wolfe, D. A. (1988). The sexually abused child. In E. J. Mash & L. G. Terdal (Eds.), *Behavioral assessment of childhood disorders,* 2nd ed. New York: Guilford.

Wolfensberger, W. (1980). *The principle of normalization in human services.* Toronto: National Institute on Mental Retardation.

Wolman, B. B. (1972). Psychoanalytic theory of infantile development. In B. B. Wolman (Ed.), *Handbook of child psychoanalysis: Research theory and practice.* New York: Van Nostrand Reinhold.

Wolock, I., & Horowitz, B. (1984). Child maltreatment as a social problem: The neglect of neglect. *American Journal of Orthopsychiatry, 54,* 530–543.

Wolraich, M., Milich, R., Sumbo, P., & Schultz, F. (1985). The effects of sucrose ingestion on the behavior of hyperactive boys. *Journal of Pediatrics, 106,* 675–682.

Wood, B. L. (1994). One articulation of the structural family therapy model: A biobehavioral family model of chronic illness in children. *Journal of Family Therapy, 16,* 53–72.

Wood, B., Watkins, J. B., Boyle, J. T., Noguiera, J., Aimand, E., & Carrol, L. (1989). The "psychosomatic family" model: An empirical analysis. *Family Process, 28,* 399–417.

Woodcock, R. W., & Johnson, M. B. (1978). *Woodcock-Johnson Psycho-Educational Battery.* Allen, TX: DLM/ teaching Resources.

Woodcock, R. W., Mather, N. & Barnes, E. K. (1987). *Woodcock Mastery Tests-Revised: Examiner's Manual, Forms G and H.* Circle Pines, MN: American Guidance Service.

Woodhead, M. (1988). When psychology informs public policy. The case of early childhood intervention. *American Psychologist, 43,* 443–454.

Woodward, W. M. (1979). Piaget's theory and the study of mental retardation. In N. R. Ellis (Ed.), *Handbook of mental deficiency*. Hillsdale, NJ: Erlbaum.

Woody, E. Z. (1986). The obese child as a social being and developing self. *Canadian Psychology, 27,* 286–298.

World Health Organization (1978). *International Classification of Diseases,* 9th revision. Geneva: World Health Organization.

World Health Organization (1992). *International classification of diseases: Tenth revision.* Chapter V. Mental and behavioural disorders. Diagnostic criteria for research. Geneva: Author.

Wright, H. F. (1960). Observational child study. In P. H. Mussen (Ed.), *Handbook of research methods in child development.* New York: John Wiley.

Wright, L. (1977). Conceptualizing and defining psychosomatic disorders. *American Psychologist, 32,* 625–628.

Wysocki, T. (1993). Associations among teen-parent relationships, metabolic control, and adjustment to diabetes in adolescents. *Journal of Pediatric Psychology, 18,* 441–452.

Yates, A. (1989). Curent perspectives on the eating disorders: I. History, psychological and biological aspects. *Journal of the American Academy of Child and Adolescent Psychiatry, 28,* 813–828.

Yates, A. (1990). Current perspectives on the eating disorders: II. Treatment, outcome, and research directions. *Journal of the American Academy of Child and Adolescent Psychiatry, 29,* 1–9.

Youngblade, L. M., & Belsky, J. (1992). Parent-child antecedents of five-year olds' close friendships: A longitudinal analysis. *Developmental Psychology, 28,* 700–714.

Ysseldyke, J. E., Thurlow, M. L., Christenson, S. L., & Muyskens, P. (1991). Classroom and home learning differences between students labeled as educable mentally retarded and their peers. *Education and Training in Mental Retardation, 26,* 3–17.

Yule, W. (1994). Posttraumatic stress disorder. In T. H. Ollendick, N. J. King, & W. Yule (Eds.), *International handbook of phobic and anxiety disorders in children and adolescents* (pp. 223–240). New York: Plenum Press.

Yule, W., Udwin, O., & Murdoch, K. (1990). The "Jupiter" sinking: Effects on children's fears, depression and anxiety. *Journal of Child Psychology and Psychiatry, 31,* 1051–1061.

Zahn-Waxler, C. (1995). Introduction to special section: Parental depression and distress: Implications for development in infancy, childhood, and adolescence. *Developmental Psychology, 31,* 347–348.

Zametkin, A. J., & Rapoport, J. L. (1986). The pathophysiology of attention deficit disorder with hyperactivity: A review. In B. B. Lahey & A. E. Kazdin (Eds.), *Advance in clinical child psychology.* Vol. 9. New York: Plenum.

Zametkin, A. J., & Rapoport, J. L. (1987). Neurobiology of attention deficit disorder with hyperactivity: Where have we come in 50 years? *Journal of the American Academy of Child and Adolescent Psychiatry, 26,* 676–686.

Zaslow, M. J., & Hayes, C. D. (1986). Sex differences in children's response to psychosocial stress: Toward a cross-context analysis. In M. E. Lamb, A. L. Brown, & B. Rogoff (Eds.), *Advances in developmental psychology.* Vol. 4. Hillsdale, NJ: Erlbaum.

Zax, M., & Cowen, E. L. (1967). Early identification and prevention of emotional disturbance in a public school. In E. L. Cowen, E. A. Gardner, & M. Zax (Eds.), *Emergent approaches to mental health problems.* New York: Appleton-Century-Crofts.

Zeaman, D., & House, B. J. (1979). A review of attention theory. In N. R. Ellis (Ed.), *Handbook of mental deficiency.* Hillsdale, NJ: Erlbaum.

Zeanah, C. H., Anders, T. F., Seifer, R., & Stern, D. N. (1989). Implications of research on infant development for psychodynamic theory and practice. *Journal of the American Academy of Child and Adolescent Psychiatry, 28,* 657–668.

Zentall, S. S., & Meyer, M. J. (1987). Self-regulation of stimulation for ADD-H children during reading and vigilance task performance. *Journal of Abnormal Child Psychology, 15,* 519–536.

Zero to Three/National Center for Clinical Infant Programs (1995). *Diagnostic classification: 0–3.* Arlington, VA: Author.

Zhang, Y., Proenca, R., Maffei, M., Barone, M., Leopold, L., & Friedman, J. M. (1994). Positional cloning of the mouse obese gene and its human homologue. *Nature, 373,* 425–432.

Zigler, E. (1978). The effectiveness of Head Start: Another look. *Educational Psychologist, 13,* 71–77.

Zigler, E. (1994). Reshaping early childhood intervention to be a more effective weapon against poverty. *American Journal of Community Psychology, 22,* 37–47.

Zigler, E., Balla, D., & Hodapp, R. (1984). On the definition and classification of mental retardation. *American Journal of Mental Deficiency, 89,* 215–230.

Zigler, E., & Styfco, S. J. (1993). Using research and theory to justify and inform Head Start expansion. *Social Policy Report. Society for Research In Child Development. VII, Number 2.*

Zivcic, I. (1993). Emotional reactions of children to war stress in Croatia. *Journal of the American Academy of Child and Adolescent Psychiatry, 32,* 709–713.

NAME INDEX

SUBJECT INDEX